Silverlight 4 Business Intelligence Software

Bart Czernicki

Apress®

Silverlight 4 Business Intelligence Software

ISBN-13 (pbk): 978-1-4302-3060-1

ISBN-13 (electronic): 978-1-4302-3061-8

Printed and bound in the United States of America 9 8 7 6 5 4 3 2 1

President and Publisher: Paul Manning
Lead Editor: Jonathan Hassell
Technical Reviewer: Ivan Dragoev
Editorial Board: Clay Andres, Steve Anglin, Mark Beckner, Ewan Buckingham, Gary Cornell, Jonathan Gennick, Jonathan Hassell, Michelle Lowman, Matthew Moodie, Duncan Parkes, Jeffrey Pepper, Frank Pohlmann, Douglas Pundick, Ben Renow-Clarke, Dominic Shakeshaft, Matt Wade, Tom Welsh
Coordinating Editor: Tracy Brown-Collins
Copy Editor: Mary Behr
Compositor: Bytheway Publishing Services
Indexer: Julie Grady
Artist: April Milne
Cover Designer: Anna Ishchenko

Distributed to the book trade worldwide by Springer Science+Business Media, LLC, 233 Spring Street, 6th Floor, New York, NY 10013. Phone 1-800-SPRINGER, fax 201-348-4505, e-mail orders-ny@springer-sbm.com, or visit www.springeronline.com.

For information on translations, please e-mail rights@apress.com, or visit www.apress.com.

Apress and friends of ED books may be purchased in bulk for academic, corporate, or promotional use. eBook versions and licenses are also available for most titles. For more information, reference our Special Bulk Sales–eBook Licensing web page at www.apress.com/info/bulksales.

To my family and friends.

Contents at a Glance

Contents

About the Author

 Bart Czernicki is a senior technologist focusing on Rich Interactive Applications and Business Intelligence. Bart is currently employed as a software architect, focusing on bringing business intelligence tools to life using cutting edge technology. Most recently, Bart championed the Silverlight platform across the organization as the foundation for the next-generation set of business intelligence products.

Bart has had a strong online presence for the last several years. He has authored numerous technical articles on www.silverlighthack.com and other sites. He remains active as one of the leading contributors to the Silverlight community on www.silverlight.net. Recently he started a web site that will bring BI 2.0 and Silverlight together www.silverlightbusinessintelligence.com.

Bart lives in Mount Laurel, NJ. Previously he lived in Zawiercie, Poland. He is best described as a tech geek and is on the computer a majority of the day. Bart also loves to read about history, statistics, finance and of course new technologies.

About the Technical Reviewer

 Ivan Dragoev has over 10 years practical experience in the sphere of information technology and in particular, the Microsoft technologies. He participates in the designing of many enterprise applications in different domains—from building to health services. Four years ago Ivan made his own IT company, which aims to be proactive and to offer its clients innovative integral solutions, based on the Microsoft technologies. He is a co-founder of www.silverlightshow.net—a community site entirely dedicated to the Microsoft's RIA technology Silverlight. The site offers daily information, articles on recent threads and events in the sphere of Silverlight and its target are not only developers but also decision makers. Ivan is also co-founder of the first and the only one of its kind Silverlight user group in Bulgaria. At the moment Ivan is occupied with the design of projects based on the Silverlight technology and in the providing of consultant services and trainings.

Introduction

It is a very exciting time to be in the software development industry. The governing concepts of developing software are changing and rapidly evolving before our eyes. Skills and frameworks that you may have used even just two years ago could very well be considered obsolete and replaced with something more efficient. This is why software vendors and the developers of engineering products need to stay on top of emerging technology concepts in order to remain competitive.

Two technologies that are experiencing exponential growth and are quickly becoming in demand are *business intelligence (BI)* and *rich interactive applications (RIAs)*. Knowing how to use and implement either of these technologies will be vital in order to develop modern-looking applications in the near future. More importantly, learning how to use BI concepts and bringing them to life with RIA technology will allow you to deliver superior software that is a cut above the competition.

The first core technology this book focuses on is BI. BI can be simply defined as delivering key insight quickly from large data repositories. This information can be presented in the form of reports, charts, analytical aggregates, data grids, and so on. Until recently, BI deployments have not been cheap and often required expensive hardware and enterprise-scale software to perform complex data calculations. Furthermore, the tools that presented BI information were geared for people with a background in number crunching (statistical analytics). This really limited the scope of BI because in order to use BI tools, you had to have a good understanding of the numbers you were looking at in order to analyze them properly. BI technology's steep learning curve limits its adoption to larger enterprise organizations. Just like any other technology, BI is maturing as a platform and adopting new concepts from emerging software development methodologies.

Business intelligence 2.0 (BI 2.0) is improving the way we design and implement BI applications. BI 2.0 is essentially all about bringing technical wisdom to the average user quickly without having to deploy a monolithic infrastructure and not requiring a deep understanding of analytical tools. Therefore, to accomplish this, the visual implementation needs to be simple and easy to understand. In addition, a BI 2.0 application also needs to be lightweight and easy to deploy. A typical user will simply reject anything that takes serious time to download or is packaged in a complex installation. Simple software design and making the analytical tools not feel like business tools broaden the scope of the BI audience beyond technical users.

The second core technology this book focuses on is the rich interactive application (RIA). RIAs are a class of web applications that bring a desktop-like experience to the end user. RIAs are generally superior web user interfaces (UIs) because they can bring additional animations, transitions, and computational processing on the client workstation at much greater speeds than HTML or Ajax. Furthermore, RIA technologies such as Microsoft Silverlight and Adobe Flash/Flex are lightweight and can be fully tailored for ease of use. This makes RIAs ideal UI solutions for architecting applications that need to present complex analytics in BI 2.0 applications.

This book's goal is to show you how you can deliver key concepts of BI 2.0 with the Microsoft Silverlight RIA platform. These two technologies used together can form very powerful applications that extend the BI 2.0 platform's core tenets: ease of use and delivery to a broader audience. We will start by introducing you in detail to BI 2.0 concepts and how they can be implemented in Microsoft Silverlight RIA technology. The introductory chapters are a great starting point for readers who are not already familiar with BI 2.0 or Silverlight. Next, we will proceed to look at how we can utilize key RIA features like interactivity, animations, visualizations, and client processing in BI 2.0 implementations. The following sections will show you how to bring a Silverlight BI application to life and make it easier for the user to understand. In the latter part of this resource, we will cover emerging technologies like collective intelligence and predictive analytics which are becoming important in BI 2.0 software delivery.

Who Should Read This Book?

Anyone who is interested in applying BI 2.0 concepts using cutting-edge visualization technology like Silverlight should net great value from reading this book. This book is written with an "introduce, then apply concept" philosophy. Chapters 2 through 11 introduce the BI 2.0 concepts and show how they are applied in Silverlight. Coding exercises can be found in a majority of these chapters to further reinforce the introduced topics. Non-technical users will be able to follow along the scenarios and interact with the final coding scenario end product by leveraging the companion web site. The companion web site includes many of the coding scenario applications running live directly on the web not requiring any development environment.

Silverlight Developers or Architects

Developers who are familiar with Silverlight usually need to apply the fundamentals they have learned into a *line-of-business (LOB) application*. This book allows developers to see how Microsoft Silverlight can bring a technology concept to life with its unique RIA features. This is a very important distinction from most Silverlight books out there which tend to concentrate on the Silverlight fundamentals and basic use of the developer tools. This book jumps straight from the concept chapters (Chapters 1 and 2) right into Silverlight BI features in Chapter 3 (i.e., You are out of luck if you want to see a chapter on how to draw a button on a canvas). This book aims to be unique by showing you features in Silverlight used in practical ways to apply BI 2.0 concepts. Silverlight developers will benefit from the C#/Silverlight coding exercises and follow along to learn how to create BI components. Lastly, developers who aren't familiar with BI 2.0 will gain valuable domain knowledge of the business side of BI implementations.

This audience will achieve the following goals by reading this book:

- You'll receive important business domain knowledge about BI.
- You'll be exposed to BI 2.0 fundamentals.
- You'll see how Silverlight can be applied to LOB applications beyond the basics.

BI Professionals

Professionals who have made their career working with BI will uncover valuable information in this book. This may sound contradictory at first, as this book is meant as a technical resource. However, BI professionals who have spent several years writing static reports, creating cubes, analyzing data in Excel, and so on, know the limitations of many analytical tools. Using this book as a guide, you'll be able to see via examples how BI can be applied in Silverlight to deliver key insights more quickly to the end user via richer interfaces. The knowledge you'll gain from the material in this book will benefit you tremendously in your career, as it will broaden the scope of understanding of the implementation of the technology. While the book requires some knowledge of an RIA technology (like Silverlight), each chapter has been written with the broader target in mind and can be understood without a deep understanding of Silverlight or C#.

In sum, this audience will achieve the following goals by reading this book:

- You'll be exposed to the Microsoft Silverlight RIA technology.
- You'll learn how RIA functionality can extend BI by making tools simpler and more interactive.
- You'll see how next-generation BI makes some of the tools you currently use obsolete.

Strategic Decision Makers in Technology

Executive-level professionals who have an interest in BI can net a different perspective from understanding the topics covered in this book. This is a real exciting time when these relatively new technologies are coming together and will leverage each other in reshaping next-generation BI software. This book aims to provide senior management with the key strategic ideas and fundamentals to be able to gauge the use of new BI concepts in their deliverables. Decision makers do not have to be part of a BI software vendor to get a valuable return from this information. For example, you may have an existing product that you want to enhance with next-generation BI. This book is the guide that can provide ideas on how to achieve that. It goes without saying: the content provided in this book aims to include cutting-edge material, and senior managers should be able to utilize it to gain a competitive advantage.

By reading this book, this audience will achieve the following goals:

- You'll learn how to take advantage of Silverlight with BI 2.0 to form a competitive advantage in terms of content, delivery, and adoption.
- You'll amass ideas on possibly extending current applications with lightweight Silverlight BI modules.
- You'll understand how simple, interactive, and easy-to-learn analytical tools can broaden the audience of BI products.

Technical and Nontechnical Audiences

The preceding list may leave you scratching your head, as few technical books can claim that they can effectively target a broader audience beyond a technical reader (i.e., developer or architect). If you fall into the nontechnical audience, you may be rightfully skeptical by my claim that this book is right for you. How do I plan on targeting a nontechnical audience? The key word I want to focus on in the first statement in this paragraph is *effectively*. In a nutshell, this book aims to cover the implementation of business concepts applied with a technical framework. Therefore, at a high level, I plan on striking a balance between the BI 2.0 concepts and the technical Silverlight content.

The following list describes the details of how this book strikes a technical and nontechnical balance:

- Beginning with the Chapter 2, each chapter has an introduction that explains how it implements key BI 2.0 disciplines with examples and includes a graphic that quickly highlights which BI 2.0 concepts will be applied in that chapter.

- For each chapter, takeaway goals will be provided for the three different audiences.
- Working demos of the examples are provided on the companion website (www.silverlightbusinessintelligence.com). For nontechnical readers that cannot build the source code using Visual Studio, they can simply navigate to the link provided and interact with working examples.
- Before jumping blindly into exercises, I explain the approach being taken in the implementation using language you would normally hear during a functional/design meeting.
- Each chapter includes notes, sidebars, and most importantly, visuals that will help guide you in understanding the information as well as relating it to concepts that you may have used many times previously.

■ **Note** The Internet includes numerous open-source resources that will act as additional resources that amplify the core content in this book.

I believe that my having written this book with those features in mind allows its scope to go beyond just a technical audience. Obviously, technical consumers of this book who are familiar with Silverlight fundamentals will be able to take additional advantage of this book, as they will be able to follow along with the technical exercises. However, as you can see, I have taken the business audience into serious consideration when choosing the material to cover. The technical audience that invests in this resource will broaden their business intelligence knowledge. Conversely, the non-technical audience will learn about how Silverlight can be leveraged for business intelligence scenarios.

Why Should You Invest in This Book?

I am the epitome of someone who loves to harvest more and more information about technology. In my opinion, there is not enough time during the day to soak in all the information available! I love to get valuable information from any resource, whether it's a book, a periodical, the Internet, a webcasts, or anything else. Each resource has its benefits and flaws. For example, the Internet is a great resource to get the most up-to-the-minute information and updates to anything. However, much of the information on the Internet tends to be poorly researched, and the Internet has a high rate of providing incorrect information. Furthermore, it is very hard to find complete technical or deep business concepts on the Net. A book, on the other hand, has a well-researched foundation, and the information tends to have fewer errors. However, books that focus on technologies rather than overall concepts tend to be outdated more quickly than information on the Internet. One advantage of this book is that it's not just a book on Silverlight 4 features. This book is a marriage of BI 2.0 and Silverlight that uses a forward-thinking approach to application design. Concepts tend to evolve more slowly than the technologies in which they are implemented. By investing in this resource, you will receive well researched and thought-out information that you will not see outdated in the near future. I hope this resource provides you with an invaluable vision toward creating fantastic-looking BI applications and gives your software a competitive advantage.

Chapter Roadmap

Chapter 1 is an introductory chapter to BI. This chapter will introduce BI and the new wave of BI 2.0. It will show how BI is evolving and embracing new software development advancements. This chapter will contrast classic BI and BI 2.0 by showing numerous examples of current software offerings. Lastly, this chapter will define the core concepts of BI 2.0 that will be implemented throughout this book using Silverlight.

Chapter 2 introduces the Microsoft RIA technology: Silverlight. This chapter is dedicated to analyzing the current Microsoft BI product offering and providing opinions on why Silverlight is a good fit for implementing BI tenets. After reading this chapter, you will understand the key enterprise and business integration features of Silverlight that will be discussed in this book.

Chapter 3 looks at what makes an effective BI client. It goes on to specifically detail Silverlight tools and features that can be used to create a fantastic functioning analytical experience. The chapter goes into specific functionality such as LINQ data queries, business algorithm implementations, and local storage.

In Chapter 4, the information from the previous chapters is used to show how to use Silverlight to bring interactivity to BI applications. This chapter will teach by example on how to add simple interactions that can make a BI client easier to use and feel more fluid. It concludes with how these concepts can be leveraged for future designs with multitouch screens to create the ultimate interactive experience.

Chapter 5 is the first chapter in a series of chapters about visual intelligence. The content in this chapter will show the empirical advantages of creating a visual representation of data (data visualizations) versus classic tabular layouts. This chapter shows how visualizing data has matured and grown over the last several years. The concept of natural visualizations is introduced by defining the different characteristics and Silverlight implementations.

Chapter 6 continues to build on the visual intelligence topic by showing how to enhance data visualizations with features to turn them into analytical tools. This chapter will show you how to create advanced visualizations by extending the default Silverlight data visualization presentation.

Chapter 7 is the last chapter that focuses on creating complex composite data visualizations. You will also see how Silverlight as a professional visual intelligence environment can implement BI 2.0 functionality.

Chapter 8 introduces collective intelligence as a form of social BI. This chapter defines the importance of collective intelligence on the Web today. Furthermore, you will see how Silverlight can be used to gather collective intelligence and surface it to users.

Chapter 9 will describe how to integrate forward-looking data structures into your client logic to perform what-if scenarios. This chapter will also show how statistics used on aggregates can deliver instant insight on future events.

Chapter 10 is an advanced chapter that covers additional enhancements that can be gained by using multiple cores to aid in BI calculations. You will see how you can enhance the performance of BI modules by leveraging Silverlight's advanced CPU and GPU programming features.

Chapter 11 will show you how to apply the concepts that you have learned and integrate them into new solutions or existing BI systems. This chapter covers Silverlight in a SaaS delivery model as well as Silverlight web parts.

Chapter 12 introduces mobile intelligence as a paradigm for delivering business intelligence to mobile and tablet devices. In this chapter, you will apply the knowledge in the previous chapters towards the Windows Phone 7 development environment.

Chapter 13 describes the conventions used to create business solutions for the SharePoint 2010 environment. This part will focus on component based architecture and deploying Silverlight web parts.

Chapter 14 focuses on the Silverlight PivotViewer control. This section will show you a great example of how Microsoft is utilizing a highly interactive and visual PivotViewer control to deliver business intelligence insight.

Appendix A includes a short primer on prototyping data applications in Microsoft Expression Blend 4. This short section provides a quick overview on how to use Blend's dynamic data feature to quickly create and add data to UI functionality without having to spend time architecting databases and services. This is a powerful tool to prototype BI 2.0 analytical modules without needing access to large-scale data repositories.

Appendix B demonstrates how to create a bullet graph user control. This control has several advantages over a traditional business intelligence gauge visualization and you will see how to easily create one in this section.

What Is *Not* Covered in This Book?

This book is intended to be a BI 2.0 concept book applied using Silverlight technology. Obviously, not every possible aspect and feature of BI can be covered. This book strictly focuses on delivering intelligence to the end user. Therefore, middle-tier and back-end BI concepts like data warehousing, master data management, service orientation, ETL, and so on are not covered. While those concepts are very important, they are well beyond the scope of this material. Furthermore, important Silverlight architectural concepts like the MVVM design pattern, Management Extensibility Framework (MEF), PRISM are not covered either. I felt this would overcomplicate even simple scenarios.

This book covers the core information of BI 2.0 and has step-by-step instructions on how to create the examples included. However, this book is not meant to be a substitute for an introduction to either technology (Silverlight or BI). If you are a Silverlight novice, you may need to supplement your knowledge with some of the many resources available to gain a solid foundation of the Silverlight framework.

Why Aren't Data Services Covered in This Book?

As just mentioned, data services are not covered in this book. Data services are an integral part of BI applications, and without them, you cannot deploy a proper Silverlight BI solution. So why isn't the data service layer covered in this book?

Microsoft Silverlight version 4 has several data access methods that allow for consuming data services. Unfortunately, Microsoft is quickly evolving these methodologies in a LOB framework called WCF RIA Services which is based on ADO.NET Data Services. WCF RIA Services is scheduled to be released in the summer of 2010. Furthermore, the Visual Studio 2010/.NET 4.0 development stack improves data access methodologies with enhancements to the OR/M (object/relational mapping), WCF REST–based design, asynchronous programming, and ADO.NET Services. Therefore, I felt it was not correct to write a book showing best practices of BI data access when the technologies were evolving rapidly and would be fundamentally different in a matter of months.

I have decided to alleviate the need for service data sets by using Expression Blend's Dynamic Data feature and creating in-memory data. This allows the coding scenarios and examples to focus on the client BI principles rather than focusing on another unrelated tier. I believe this targets the proper audience for this book, as more content can be presented on surfacing BI data with Silverlight technology.

▓ **Note** If you are familiar with BI and want additional clarification on what BI tier is covered, please see Chapter 1.

Following the Coding Exercises in the Book

This book includes many technical exercises that aim to reinforce key principles of BI.

As aforementioned, you don't need to follow along with all of the exercises to net all the knowledge from this book, as all of the examples are online on the companion web site. This allows non-developers to follow along with the concepts implemented in this book without having knowledge of compiling source code. This amplifies that this book is a resource for more than just developers, as most books only provide source code that requires development knowledge.

▓ **Note** If you would like to see the available demos online, go to
www.silverlightbusinessintelligence.com/demos.aspx

If you are not a developer or do not want to go through manually coding the exercises, you will see links provided before each coding scenario or sample with a direct link to the demonstration.

▓ **Note** Not all of the coding scenarios are available as demos on the companion site to this book. The Windows Phone 7 examples require an active emulator, which cannot be run on the web. Furthermore, the SharePoint 2010 examples would require a SharePoint 2010 Internet site, which I do not host.

Software You Need to Follow the Exercises

If you are a developer and would like to compile and follow the exercises, you will need the following core Silverlight development software:

- Visual Studio 2010 (Any of the Express, Premium, Ultimate, or Team System versions will work.). Visual Studio 2008 cannot be used for Silverlight 4 development.
- Silverlight 4 SDK and Visual Studio 2010 Developer Tools
- Silverlight Control Toolkit (April 2010 release or newer)
- Microsoft Expression Blend 4

Links to this core Silverlight development software are updated constantly. The main page for getting started with Microsoft Silverlight, at http://silverlight.net/getstarted, provides a complete set of links to install all the required components.

In addition to the core Silverlight development software above, the Delivering Mobile Intelligence with Silverlight (Chapter 12) requires the following software:

- Windows Phone 7 Developer Tools (includes Expression Blend for Windows Phone)

Links to this Windows Phone 7 software are updated constantly. The main page for getting started with Windows Phone 7 development, at http://developer.windowsphone.com, provides a complete set of links to install all the required components.

In addition to the core Silverlight development software, the Silverlight Business Intelligence in SharePoint 2010 (Chapter 13) requires the following software:

- SharePoint 2010 development tools for Visual Studio 2010 installed
- SharePoint 2010 Server installed

In addition to the core Silverlight development software, the Working with Pivot Collections (Chapter 14) requires the following software:

- Silverlight PivotViewer control, which can be downloaded at www.getpivot.com/silverlight

---

▧ **Note** While Visual Studio 2010 Express Editions, Silverlight 4 SDK, Silverlight Control Toolkit, and the Silverlight 4 runtime can be attained for no cost, Expression Blend 4 is a rather expensive product. There are a couple of different ways I would recommend acquiring this at minimal cost to you. As of this book's publication, Microsoft offers a 60-day trial of its Expression Blend product. This will probably satisfy the need to access Expression Blend 4 for the duration of reading this book. Expression Blend 4 is also provided with some of the higher-tier MSDN subscriptions. If you are a paying subscriber, please feel free to download the product from the MSDN site.

Also, all of these exercises can be done in other ways without the Expression Blend tool. Furthermore, in Visual Studio 2010, the designer provides a rich design canvas for Silverlight applications. However, I have decided to use Expression Blend for the visual and prototyping exercises in this resource. In addition, Expression Blend is a first-class design tool, and it is necessary for delivering enterprise-level applications.

Companion Web Site

As mentioned in the previous section, this book aims to target both a technical and nontechnical audience. Therefore, some readers might not be able to take advantage of building upon some of the technical guidance in this book. I have created a companion web site that includes all of the examples covered in the chapters with some bonus material. Therefore, even nontechnical users will be able to learn by seeing the implementations of the material with live examples. The companion web site is located at www.silverlightbusinessintelligence.com.

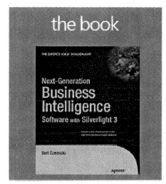

Figure Intro-1. The main page of the companion site for this book

The companion site includes several key important resources:

- A blog that includes updated articles related to the material covered in this book
- A page that contains live demonstrations of coding scenarios and samples of Silverlight business intelligence tools
- Updated source code for the book
- An external resources page, which includes many links to books, articles and samples on the web for business intelligence
- An errata & best practices page that includes any changes, updates and fixes to the content that has been published

Throughout this book, you will see me refer to the companion web site for additional content (links, source code, live examples) that did not fully make it into this resource.

What about Silverlight 3 Support?

Many of the principles, conventions, code and best practices will apply to the Silverlight 3 development environment. Version 1.0 and 2.0 of the source code on the companion site is compatible with Silverlight 3 and Visual Studio 2008. It does not include all of the examples covered in this book. However, almost all of the examples through the first eleven chapters are included in a Silverlight 3 project.

■ **Note** The previous edition of the book explicitly targets Silverlight 3 and Visual Studio 2008 explicitly.

Author on the Internet

I have a pretty unique name. Therefore, you can find me on the Internet by doing a simple search. Chances are, if you search my name and you find something that deals with technical content about .NET, you've probably found me. In addition, the following list provides my e-mail address and the places I am most active currently on the Internet:

- *Name*: Bart Czernicki
- *E-mail address*: bartczernicki@gmail.com
- *Companion web site*: www.silverlightbusinessintelligence.com
- *Blog/web site*: www.silverlighthack.com
- *Follow me on Twitter*: www.twitter.com/bartczernicki
- *Silverlight Business Intelligence on Twitter*: www.twitter.com/silverlightbi
- *Silverlight forums*: www.silverlight.net

■ ■ ■

CHAPTER 1

Business Intelligence 2.0 Defined

What is business intelligence 2.0? This is the question this chapter aims to answer definitively. Before you dive into implementing the different concepts associated with business intelligence (BI), you need to understand it. This chapter is dedicated to demystifying what constitutes BI. As you will soon see, the term *BI* is very loose in that it can be attributed to a series of technologies, data, and practices, which makes its raw definition very ambiguous. Therefore, the sections of this chapter are designed to build on each other, fluidly progressing with details about BI. After you complete this chapter, the components of BI will become clear and you will have enough knowledge to understand what we will be implementing in the following chapters.

This chapter will cover the following:

- How the success and innovation of decision support systems in large enterprise deployments laid the foundation for BI

- Definitions of business intelligence 1.0 (BI 1.0) and business intelligence 2.0 (BI 2.0)

- How the challenges of BI implementations helped evolve into BI 2.0

- How to identify the differences between BI 1.0 and BI 2.0

- How BI 2.0 is transforming the intelligence landscape beyond the enterprise

- A comparison of BI 1.0 and BI 2.0

■ **Note** Additional resources to this chapter can be found on the book's companion site
http://silverlightbusinessintelligence.com/BookResources/ExternalResources/BusinessIntelligence20.aspx.

The Need to Make Better Decisions

If only one term had to be used to describe the competitive business environment, it would be *cutthroat*. No matter what the industry or its size, every company is constantly trying to get a competitive advantage over its adversaries. Companies have been trying to one-up each other for hundreds of years, and this is nothing new, even in current times. One way an organization can attain an edge over its competition is by making decisions that have an increased positive impact and contain less risk.

Making the proper decision on any difficult task can be hard. This is amplified in business when any decision could lead to a great success or a massive failure. Not having nor being able to understand a key piece of information could easily affect the case for selecting one decision path. Not too long ago, tough business decisions were made by long-time industry experts who had intimate knowledge of the business. These decisions were largely made on past historical or financial situations and rarely took into account data models. This led to high levels of failure, and some successful decisions could be attributed more to luck than effective decision-making techniques.

Processes for making decisions started to involve computers in the '60s and '70s. As the computer revolution started making its way from academia and government projects to mainstream businesses, people started leveraging computers to do continuous number crunching. Computers could process more data, and this eliminated some of the human error factors involved with complex statistics. This is where computers have an empirical advantage over humans, as they are tailored for mathematical computations and can be harnessed to run almost 24 hours per day. However, even enterprise-level computers in those days were not even close to the power of what we are used to today. Most of them couldn't do much more than today's programmable scientific calculator. The early horsepower of computer systems had to be specifically tailored for basic mathematical computations on data, as anything complex as artificial intelligence (AI) was completely out of the question.

Organizations quickly saw the benefit of having computer systems aid them in their everyday business processes. Even though the early computers weren't that powerful, they could be used to garner vast amounts of data and perform complex business algorithms on it. The resultant data could then be used in the boardroom to shape corporate strategies via actionable decisions from executive information systems (EISs), group decision support systems (GDSSs), organizational decision support systems (ODSSs), and so on.

Decision Support Systems

The need for company executives to make better decisions and the rapid evolution of computing power led to the birth of *decision support systems (DSSs)*. A DSS is a type of computer information system whose purpose is to support decision-making processes. A well-designed DSS is an interactive software system that helps decision makers aggregate useful information from raw data, documents, and business models to solve problems and make decisions.

While these systems were first implemented in executive circles, they have quickly grown to be used by trained professionals as well. Various remnants of DSS software implementations can be found everywhere from the Internet to your local bank branch. For example, when you go to a bank and apply for a loan, complex DSS software is used to determine the risk to the bank based on your financial history. The result of this information will aid the loan officer as to whether the bank should make the decision to loan you money.

■ **Note** One of the first large-scale implementations of a DSS was the Gate Assignment Display System (GADS). This DSS was implemented at Chicago's O'Hare Airport in 1987 in order to reduce travel delays significantly. Hundreds of computers and servers were used in order to synchronize relevant information from airplane reservations to displaying flight information to travelers.

DSSs gained tremendous popularity in the late '80s and early '90s. The first systems that were deployed targeted large-scale organizations that needed help with large amounts of data which included the government, and the automobile and health care industries. These systems were very successful and delivered tremendous return on investment.

Early DSS projects, while largely successful, did have some challenges however:

- *Customizability*: DSS software did not exist in the way it does today. A vendor couldn't simply download a tool or customize a preexisting system. Usually, these tools had to be designed and programmed from scratch.

- *Multiple vendors*: Implementations of early DSSs were a mix of software, hardware, servers, networking, and back-end services. In the '80s and early '90s, there wasn't a single company that could provide all of the necessary components of complex systems at once. Multiple vendors usually worked on a single project together on a single DSS implementation.

- *Uniqueness*: Early DSS software was unique and often the first of its kind. This usually meant that a great deal of planning had to be done to get concepts moved from theory into a working information system. Architects and programmers in the early days of DSS couldn't rely on how-to guides to implement a unique custom system.

- *Long deployments*: Projects that included custom software and hardware from multiple vendors obviously led to implementations that took a long time to complete.

- *Expensiveness*: DSS systems in the '80s and '90s were very expensive and easily carried budgets of tens of millions of dollars.

DSSs allowed for entire organizations to function more effectively, as the underlying software powering those organizations provided insights from large amounts of data. This aided human decision makers to apply data models into their own decision-making processes.

DSS software at its start was considered a luxury, as only the largest of organizations could afford its power. Since the software was custom and worked with the cooperation of multiple vendors, it was hard to apply these systems as reusable and resalable deployments. Tens of thousands of hours were invested in making these systems come to life. In the process of designing these complex systems, many innovations and great strides were made in the young software industry. These innovations were screaming to be let out into the wild and used in conjunction with other pieces of software.

The demand for DSS software was ripe and the vendors were beginning to taste the huge amounts of potential profits. If only they could make the software a little more generic and resalable, they could start selling smaller DSS implementations to a much larger audience. This idea led to applying the core innovations of complex DSS software into many smaller principles like data mining, data aggregation, enterprise reporting, and dimensional analysis. Enterprise software vendors started delivering pieces of DSS as separate application packages, and the early seeds of BI were sown.

Business Intelligence Is Born

In the early '90s, software vendors were offering many types of decision-making systems to enterprise clients. These applications leveraged a lot of what was learned in building complex monolithic DSS systems over the past decade, but on a smaller scale. Concepts were made more generic, and this allowed these algorithms to be packaged into configurable software packages. In addition, implementations could be customized further with custom programming.

The new "DSS extension" software ranged from mainframe computers that performed analysis on large numerical data sets to software that created visual reports. Even though the software was provided by a variety of vendors implemented on different hardware and provided various functionalities, it still was being used for the single purpose in aiding business processes.

All of these pieces of software that shared the common goal of what they provided did not have a collective name. Each vendor described its software differently, and this added to the confusion. In 1996, the Gartner Group stamped a label on the collective technology that was being used, calling it business intelligence. Here is the exact quote from the report: *"Data analysis, reporting, and query tools can help business users wade through a sea of data to synthesize valuable information from it—today these tools collectively fall into a category called 'Business Intelligence.'"*

■ **Note** As of 2001, the Gartner Group is now known as Gartner, Inc. (`www.gartner.com`). It is a publicly traded company that specializes in research of technology concepts. Its specialty areas lie with large companies as well as the government. Gartner's research services are used by many executives to gain insight on upcoming industry trends and in what technologies those executives should be investing.

Business Intelligence Defined

BI defines a category of applications, practices, and presentations that help users make sense of a mountain of data. In my opinion, Gartner's definition of BI is correct; however, to someone unfamiliar with BI, it still leaves many questions unanswered. BI does not have an explicit definition, and this gives many people a little trouble when trying to comprehend it initially.

In a nutshell, the term *business intelligence* is an umbrella term for not just applications, but also for intangible practices and skills that are constantly evolving. Therefore, it is hard to grasp the term properly unless the whole context can be evaluated. Trouble with comprehending BI fully can also be amplified when business users use the term improperly.

■ **Note** The definition of *Internet* is similar to the term *business intelligence*, as it is not simple to define. If you had to describe to someone what the Internet was, what would you say? You might have been using the Internet for over a decade and still not be able to properly articulate it in layman's terms. For example, in 2006, senator Ted Stevens (Alaska) referred to the Internet as a "series of tubes," and this led many people to label him as someone who did not understand technology. In my opinion, his definition is a pretty good one of what the Internet is at its core. But as you can see with ambiguous or umbrella terms, it is very hard to be correct without the purist community pointing out a flaw.

BI Terms

In the preceding sections, I have provided some background information about BI. We are at a point where I want to define the BI terms that are used in this book. Usually in technical books, you'll find this section in the Introduction. However, since this book is targeting several audiences that may not have a good grasp of what BI is, I wanted to do it after the intro.

- Business intelligence (BI) in this book refers to the industry concept as a whole, similar to the way Gartner defined it. The scope of the term *business intelligence* includes the software, best practices, data algorithms, and so on that can be used in aiding business users in their work.

- Business intelligence 1.0 (BI 1.0) in this book refers to BI applications, practices, and so on that have been implemented using a specific feature set (which I will define later in this chapter). Similarly to the way we define software versions, it applies a version of 1.0 to define the feature scope explicitly. BI 1.0 applications have been around since 1996.

- Business intelligence 2.0 (BI 2.0) in this book refers to BI applications, practices, and so on that have been implemented using a specific feature set (which I will define later in this chapter) leveraging newer software design practices. BI 2.0 is an extension of BI 1.0 and aims to evolve the feature set of BI. Similarly to the way we define software versions, it applies a version of 2.0 to define the feature scope explicitly. Unlike BI 1.0, BI 2.0 applications have just started making their way into the mainstream.

Note Business intelligence 1.0 is also referred to as *classic business intelligence*, as some of its core implementation concepts are becoming obsolete. Furthermore, BI 1.0 is being substituted by BI 2.0, and this is another reason for the "classic" reference.

Note Business intelligence 2.0 is also referred to as *next-generation business intelligence*, as some of its principles and tenets are still being refined. Once formally defined, these concepts will be driving next-generation BI software. This book and the examples and concepts it covers in the chapters ahead will be applying BI 2.0 concepts.

The distinction between the BI terms is very important to understand. Right now, what you should understand is that the term *business intelligence* refers to the technology of aiding business users in their respective organizations. When the term *business intelligence* is used, it encompasses both BI 1.0 and BI 2.0 implementations. BI 1.0 and BI 2.0, on the other hand, are *implementations* of business intelligence ideas using software methodologies. The reason why most people agree to assign these "fake software versions" to them is because BI 1.0 applications share distinct similarities in how they are designed across different vendors. Furthermore, BI 2.0 aims to extend BI 1.0 further, and those applications have evolved different implementations that warrant the "2.0" label. Later on in this chapter, I will break down the distinct differences of whatprovided the two versions of BI encompass.

■ **Note** The term *BI 2.0* has its roots in the popularity of the semantic term *Web 2.0*. Web 2.0 is discussed in the "How BI 2.0 Came to Be" section later in this chapter.

Architecture of a Business Intelligence System

At this point, you should understand the core definition of BI and the theory behind the technology. However, understanding a definition of a technology that you may not be familiar with does not mean much. You can only claim to truly understand a technology concept when you start thinking about implementation scenarios. When you start thinking about how you could use it to aid you in your everyday work or how it can improve a business process, then you have grasped more than just the theory behind it.

A fully implemented BI system has a lot of moving data, modules, processes, and components. BI systems tend to be some of the most complex pieces of software implemented in an organization because of the involvement of many disconnected systems. Therefore, an important concept to understand is that a BI implementation is a lot more than just the software that surfaces the BI data to the user.

In order to make this clearer, we will take a look at a mock BI system a consulting company may use. By laying out the high-level architecture, I will show the pieces that go into a complete BI implementation. Furthermore, you will be able to clearly see how the BI system comes together and why it is fairly complex to implement properly.

Component Overview of a BI Architecture

In this section, we will look at the major components of the BI architecture. The four main tiers of a BI implementation are the data feeds, the extract-transform-load process, the data warehouse, and the presentation layer. The example I decided to use while describing these components is a high-level implementation at some fictitious consulting company.

The consulting industry deals with lots of information on a daily basis. A large consulting company (over 100 consultants) needs to keep track of a great deal of information in order to be efficient and maximize profits. It is hard to attain key insights from different systems with large amounts of data that changes rapidly. This example will show how a consulting company can leverage BI into improving the health of its business.

A typical consulting company deals with projects on an hourly basis or fixed-fee projects. Hourly projects usually require consultants to enter their time into a time entry system so that invoices can be delivered to their respective clients. A fixed-fee project may also require time entry to ensure that the project remains on track and is profitable. Time entry and revenue information are enough to do some interesting analysis on the health and profitability of a business. However, BI is all about bringing information from different systems and making sense of that data. If we add human resources (HR) information into our data feeds, then we can consume interesting information like payroll and costs associated with having the consultant as an employee. Having data sourced from different systems will allow us to create interesting data aggregates that will deliver information from both systems at once on a single screen or UI module.

Data Feeds

A BI system is nothing without a valid data source. When designing a BI system, we first need to determine what data we want to consume for analysis. Most organizations have various information systems that aid them in their day-to-day operations. Internal data from a system that aids in everyday operations of an organization is usually a good candidate for a BI project. Data can also come from external or even public data sources as well. These data sources that provide the information that drives a BI implementation are referred to as *data feeds*.

Data feed sources can be anything that provides the required data in a well-structured format. They can be exposed in a variety of formats, such as databases, XML files, CSV files, and even API (application programming interface) service calls. There is no one-size-fits-all format type for a data feed. For example, XML files are good sources for smaller data that doesn't change much. However, data that changes rapidly and is large might be better sourced from a database. In some cases, the BI architect might not have a choice when consuming external data. For example, if you want to consume public data from a web site that provides guidance on salary information, you may have to use that site's API. A vendor that provides data as a service is unlikely to make available a backup of its entire database nightly; however, it is more likely to provide an external-facing API as a service.

Figure 1-1 shows three separate feeds going into our BI system. Two feeds are internal and are sourced via database repositories. In addition, we are consuming a web service API data feed on salary information for consultants. We don't know how the data is getting there, but we have architecturally defined what data we want to consume.

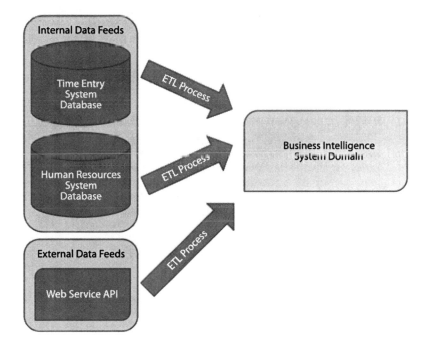

Figure 1-1. Three different data feeds consumed by a BI system

▨ **Note** Time entry and HR systems are highly transactional with multiple updates happening every minute. Using the underlying databases directly as the source for data is not a good idea. The data feed sources need to pull data that is transitionally accurate, and pulling them from a live system does not guarantee that. Furthermore, large-scale data pulls can adversely affect the performance of the underlying system.

Most BI implementations use a snapshot or a backup of the data that happens at a given point in time. The snapshots can be in the form of synchronization that can give an almost real-time feed to the data; alternatively, snapshots of the data can be taken at monthly intervals. This allows the data feed to "bridge" itself from the operations and transactions of the system.

Extract-Transform-Load Process

Now that we have isolated the data we want to expose in our BI system, we need a process to move it into our BI platform. This process can be implemented using a multitude of different methodologies. I will focus on a couple of them. The three data feeds make up our global source in this example. We need a process to transform the data and a destination for that transformed data.

The process of converting the data into something usable by BI software is called an *extract-transform-load (ETL) process*. The ETL process has a source and a destination. The data feeds are the source and the data warehouse (which I'll talk about in detail in the next section) is the destination. The name itself gives away the three main components of an ETL process:

- *Extract*: This refers to the action that performs the extraction of the raw data from the data feed. For example, for a database, this could be a `select` statement on a table. If the data source is an API, this could call a method that extracts all your contractor names.

- *Transform*: This refers to the action of transforming the data into the required layout in the data warehouse or data mart. This is where the heavy lifting of the ETL process takes place and is usually the part that takes the most time to complete. The data source is rarely in the format that we want for making BI operations easy. Therefore, it is advantageous to perform different types of transforms to prepare the structure of the data in such a way that it can be consumed inside a BI visualization without the need for these complex structural manipulations. Typically, the transform portion of ETL focuses on several main tasks: vertical partitioning, horizontal partitioning, aggregations, and other less time-consuming tasks like sorting or splitting up tables.

  Vertical partitioning refers to filtering the data sets and stripping off unwanted rows from the data. For example, if we had information in our data feed that spanned the years 1950 to 2010 and only the last decade were relevant, we could simply avoid processing the older years to the destination.

  Horizontal partitioning is similar to vertical partitioning. However, horizontal partitioning strips off unwanted columns or attributes from the data. For example, if we had address information (city, state, and ZIP) for our consultants in the data feed and this was deemed not relevant to our BI solution, we could simply ignore those columns. The benefit would be that less space would be taken up in our data warehouse.

Aggregation is essentially taking related data for input and returning a single scalar result (e.g., if we wanted to sum up all the hours our consultants worked in a given time period).

- *Load*: This refers to taking the output of the transformation step and placing it into the appropriate location in the data warehouse, which could be a database or an in-memory data structure. The transform step "massages" the data structure so that it will easily fit into the destination tables.

■ **Note** In Figure 1-2, note that the example consultant entity is being horizontally partitioned (by removing the No rows from the IsEmployed column) and vertically partitioned (by removing the City column) before being transferred into the BI data warehouse.

■ **Note** There are many enterprise ETL tools on the market such as SQL Server Integration Services (which is included in SQL Server 2005 and 2008) that provide a visual way of designing, debugging, deploying, and managing data management processes.

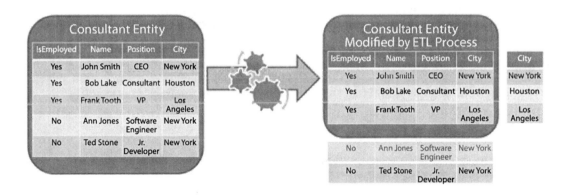

Figure 1-2. Example of an ETL transform

The Data Warehouse

The data warehouse is a storage repository for data that is used in BI software. The end result of the ETL process is a data repository that is highly optimized for analysis and querying.

Data warehouses tend to hold a great deal of historical information and tend to have large storage requirements. Therefore, they are usually stored in enterprise database software (such as Microsoft SQL Server) that allows for optimal use of the server hardware.

The data warehouse can be the primary repository that communicates with BI tools in the presentation layer or it can be used as a staging area for further data transformations. For example, from our data warehouse, we could create a set of Analysis Services cubes for multidimensional analysis or create secondary smaller data marts for reporting or querying.

■ **Note** A *hub-and-spoke* architecture includes a central data hub (usually a data warehouse) that feeds data into separate spokes (usually data marts). The hub is a very large data warehouse that is too cumbersome to satisfy all of the BI needs. It is used as a staging area and further broken down into smaller data marts, or spokes, that better satisfy the query needs of BI operations.

The BI Presentation Layer (Presentation of Knowledge)

The presentation layer is a logical tier in the architecture where BI client software is used by the business users. The responsibility of these visual tools is to surface the data cleanly from a data warehouse or data mart to the user. This tier is sometimes referred to as the *presentation of knowledge*, as it is responsible for presenting not just data but insight in an easy-to-consume format.

In a typical BI implementation, usually there isn't just one type of presentation software used. BI client software includes specific tools for different audiences. For example, a company executive may be interested in a high-level overview of the business and prefer looking at the data in a highly visual format such as a dashboard or a report. Conversely, a financial analyst who is very familiar with the data might prefer the power of a spreadsheet-like format, forgoing some of the simplicity of charts and graphs. This is why most BI software implementations provide a mixed bag of tools that is tailored to not only specific tool functionality but the audience as well.

Presentation tools can take many different forms, including web, desktop, and mobile. Furthermore, they can be homegrown, custom-developed pieces of software or third-party pieces of software that sit on top of data warehouse structures. For example, Microsoft Performance Point Server is a piece of software that exposes multidimensional data that is found in Analysis Services cubes.

Challenges of Bringing the BI Tiers Together

The four core BI components come together and form a complete BI solution. Each tier plays an important role in keeping the system current and running. As you can probably guess, implementing and maintaining a system like this is not easy and is fairly complex.

Very simple errors in the first tiers could have a ripple effect into the entire system, making pieces of the implementation meaningless. Developing on an existing piece of BI software is not trivial. The BI system has a total of four complex tiers that need to communicate with each other effectively. Adding a business requirement to add another piece of data changes the logic in all four tiers of the implementation. Figure 1-3 shows the four different tiers that make up the full BI implementation.

Handling changes and maintaining a clean BI environment are the two main obstacles facing BI architects in creating a successful BI implementation. Not being able to handle these obstacles effectively is one of the main reasons why complex BI implementations fail in the long run. This tends to cause the costs of maintaining the system to rise and in the long run makes the BI project ineffective.

Figure 1-3. *The four main tiers of a BI implementation*

Business Intelligence 1.0 Implementation

Now that you have a general idea of BI, let's look at how it was implemented in BI 1.0. As mentioned earlier, BI 1.0 software implementations developed in the late '90s through the present have shared similar attributes. This has allowed this type of software to be labeled with a 1.0 "version."

The features of BI 1.0 can be broken down into three main perspectives: the intended audience, applications, and system design. Since the mid-'90s, the BI "version 1.0" concepts have matured and are generally thought of as an accepted standard when talking about BI.

BI 1.0's Intended Audience

You already know that BI is software that aids business professionals in their everyday work. However, who are the "business professionals" that specifically use BI tools?

Many of us take the current state of computer technology for granted. Just two decades ago, many organizations still relied on paper rather than providing their data to employees electronically. However, the productivity of computers quickly gave way to many organizations implementing computer systems to aid their workers. Many of the initial computer systems were created years before visual design patterns were popular; thus, they were not intuitive to learn. Finally, you did not start to see GUI (graphical user interface) standardization until the mid-'90s, and many software vendors implemented interfaces differently. For the user, this meant having to relearn similar functions all over each time new software was implemented. What is my point? Business users who were also pretty good with navigating complex software were a hard commodity to find until after the Internet boom. Software was not designed to be intuitive, and different vendors did not help by adding their own implementation of common tasks.

BI 1.0 implementations not only required users to understand software, but also needed someone who understood the data behind it. BI is all about delivering valuable insight from analyzing large amounts of data. If someone can navigate through the data sets but cannot analyze it or—even worse—cannot understand what they are looking at, what good is the system? Effective BI 1.0 users needed to do both of these tasks; thus, the intended audience was limited to tech-savvy business users that had intricate domain knowledge of the company's data.

Two Distinct Users of BI 1.0

In order to fully utilize BI 1.0 software, business professionals had two basic requirements: they had to be good with navigating complex computer software, and they needed specific domain knowledge of their organization's data. BI 1.0 business professionals usually ended up being analysts that had a background in finance, statistics, mathematics, or other analytical fields.

This had the effect of splitting up the BI 1.0 audience into two groups: power users and consumers. Power users of BI were professionals that were able to use all the BI software tools as well as comprehend the knowledge the tools provided. The consumers, on the other hand, just consumed the derived insight from BI and rarely used the BI 1.0 tools.

■ **Note** We have all seen a movie or a TV show where the main character is stressed out and has to deliver a report to his boss on a tight deadline. This is essentially how you can relate to the BI 1.0 power user. They were the ones using the software and performing the detailed analysis. The result from the analytics they performed could have been a report that they delivered to their boss. Their boss would "consume" the BI data at a higher level; however, usually they would be abstracted completely from the process of performing the actual analytics and using BI software.

The essential takeaway is that BI 1.0 software was created such that it limited its full adoption to the power users, who were a select few in the whole organization. Even though BI analytical information was consumed by a larger amount of people, not everyone was tech savvy or had the deep understanding of the data to use it.

BI 1.0 has the drawback of its inherent complexity. It creates a "middle layer" of analysts that are responsible for delivering the insight to a higher level. This summarized data can be used to perform decision-making activities.

YOU AS A BUSINESS INTELLIGENCE CONSUMER

My wife is always trying to get me to eat healthier. She constantly e-mails me articles about what to eat or what not to eat. It seems that I see one type of research that says a certain food is good for you, and then the next week I get an article that contradicts that finding. If you are like me, you are probably more confused as to what is healthy and what isn't. This is a great example that puts you into the role of a BI 1.0 consumer, as you have to rely on the findings.

Let's take a look at a high level how the process of recommending a food as "healthy" goes. On one side of the process, we have researchers who create the experiments to determine if a piece of food can be deemed healthy or unhealthy. The researchers perform the various tests and compile the data from the subjects. This research process is very analogous to the work analysts perform in their organizations. The findings are then presented in an academic journal or in a web article, and then the insight is consumed by the reader.

As you can see, this follows the BI 1.0 consumer audience process very well. The consumer is not really part of the analysis and has to rely on the validity of the research performed. As I mentioned above, you seemingly get contradicting data on what is healthy depending on who does the research. This is exactly the problem that challenges executives in organizations. Executives are not part of the analysis process and are handed just a summary of the wisdom from their analysts. They essentially have to trust their team to give them good analysis.

There are many other examples in everyday life that place you in the role of a BI consumer. Given the differences with research findings on healthy/unhealthy food, I hope you can relate better to the issues that can arise with this kind of model.

Proper Understanding of BI Models

BI software can be very powerful in the right hands. The initial tendency in BI was to allow users an "open realm" where they could model and look at the data in any shape they wanted to. While giving more options to analyze data is powerful, it has several drawbacks. The obvious drawbacks are that the user has to learn the software and be well versed with the data (these are the essential BI 1.0 requirements for the end user). However, software that allows an open analysis of company data could lead to disastrous errors. When using complex software, users might quickly create models that are error prone, or they might not fully understand the model they are implementing. This could actually lead to potentially poor decisions made from the analysis of the data. BI is supposed to make decisions easier and remove a degree of risk. Having a complex BI system that can have a higher degree of errors could actually have the opposite effect and increase decision-making costs.

Applications

BI 1.0 applications were the first generation of applications that were derived from DSS concepts. No standards existed for this type of software, and many software types were clear innovations in their own areas.

The implementation of BI 1.0 applications initially favored a desktop application installed on a workstation. These applications were usually developed in a higher-level language such as C++, Java, or

Visual Basic. The application would receive information from a data store usually via a client-server messaging architecture.

The initial focus of BI was putting the data in front of clients and allowing them the power to create complex data models. One of the most popular tools that allowed this was the spreadsheet.

Spreadsheets like Microsoft Excel are a perfect example of BI 1.0 applications, as complex Excel models required functions/macros. Data models had to be manually created and were error prone. The focus was on the data, not the visuals; the models were not interactive (unless programming was done); and the insight was not centralized, as the analytics were stored locally on a user workstation. Figure 1-4 shows an example of a simple spreadsheet that lists some data. Even the very simple example shown in the figure required the use of an addition function and the manual creation of a chart. Imagine having the task of creating a complex financial model with Excel and assigning a common task to multiple spreadsheet users. Chances are, everyone would do the layout and calculations differently. Perhaps they would even deliver different insight based on their approaches. Having the users routinely manipulate the data using their own perspective on BI is not a good idea. However, this is exactly what happened with decentralized BI systems. This enhanced "power" of analyzing data every which way led to increased costs of running BI software.

In the late 1990s and early 2000s, the explosive growth of the Web drove many software vendors to create BI software implemented on the new web platform to which everyone was congregating. The technology started to mature when improvements on hardware and software allowed increased network bandwidth to transmit more data to the end user.

The initial wave of web-based BI applications were a port from the desktop to the Web. Many of them tried using desktop-like plug-ins (Java, ActiveX, etc.) to deliver the analytical behavior, which was hard to do with JavaScript/HTML technology. Unfortunately, many of these applications just could not provide all of the functionality a BI user was used to in the desktop version. Initially, many of the web-based ports of BI applications were severely limited in functionality. The initial BI software on the web platform was poorly received by a majority of the users. It wasn't all bad though. As the web technology matured, it became easier to add visualizations such as charts, grids, and other visual cues to the users in a much more centralized manner.

	Operational Hours	Hourly Wage	Operational Cost
Smith, Joe	456	$12.50	$5,700.00
Mayer, Colleen	676.4	$17.50	$11,837.00
Fulte, Tom	343.5	$13.24	$4,547.94
Preston, Brian	235	$17.00	$3,995.00
Yo, Ken	560	$10.75	$6,020.00
Hartman, Steve	454	$20.00	$9,080.00
Magro, Phil	300	$17.50	$5,250.00
Maine, Frank	500	$16.75	$8,375.00

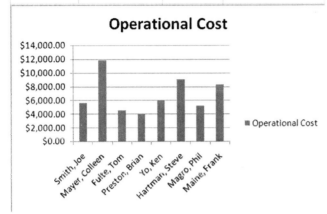

Figure 1-4. Even basic Excel spreadsheets require an understanding of functions.

■ **Note** In order to see examples of bad BI platform ports, do a web search with some of the keywords mentioned previously. There are a lot of great articles out there from several years ago that detail many failures of desktop-to-web ports of BI software. Some people who deem the "initial BI implementations" (BI 1.0) failures point to the inflexibility of the systems to be adopted by other platforms, such as the Internet.

BI software started improving as developers got a better understanding of the web platform. The web platform was used to deliver content to users from a centralized location. This started to mitigate some of the problems with users storing insight locally and delivered the analytical tools in a common shared format.

One example of how this was done is *web-based reporting*. Web-based reporting in the BI 1.0 time frame was usually a static report that was either printed out or distributed electronically to a set of users. These reports were not interactive and were essentially the result of the work done by an author who manually created these reports. Figure 1-5 shows a sample Microsoft Reporting Services report that could be delivered to many consumers. These reports had to be authored manually and provided very little interaction. Basic interactivity could be added via parameter controls like drop-downs; however, the end result was still another view of the same data.

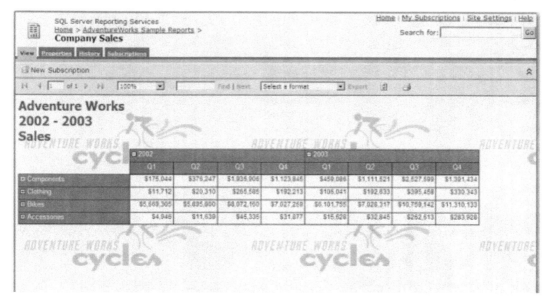

Figure 1-5. Sample AdventureWorks report from Microsoft Reporting Services

Static and Noninteractive Data

Static and noninteractive reports reiterate the drawbacks of BI 1.0, as first the reports need to be created by a business analyst, and then the insight needs to be delivered to some consumer (an executive). The problem with this approach is that the consumer misses out on important information such as how the data got there and the process of deriving the resultant analytics. In this approach, the consumer relies entirely on the competence of the person using the BI tools. What if the consumer of the data has additional information that is necessary for the analysis? What if the consumer is unaware of an inefficient or—even worse—outdated process to attain the data? This approach has its clear disadvantages and incurs additional costs of maintaining better processes so that consumers and analysts are on the same page. It would be much better if the consumer of the BI could also perform the analytics. In order for that to happen, however, the tools had to become simpler and easier to use.

■ **Note** Some of the drawbacks of not having the consumer see where the numbers came from could be mitigated by creating a "drill-down" report. This type of report allowed the consumer to click additional links to navigate to the underlying details of the summarized data. However, these kinds of reports usually had to be manually created and included custom code.

System Design

System design is another big component that BI shares across different software vendors. BI 1.0 systems are much like Figure 1-3 (shown previously), which depicts complex and monolithic systems with dependencies.

As mentioned in the preceding section, initial BI 1.0 concepts came from innovations from DSS. These systems were proprietary, and many software vendors were providing innovations not seen before in business software. The fact that BI companies were creating unique intellectual property usually meant that they were operating under a closed architecture and wary of opening up their system algorithms. However, this did not stop vendors from opening up some of their functionality via APIs. These APIs were unfortunately implemented via custom scripting languages that usually varied across vendors. This underscores one of the disadvantages of BI 1.0 software: lack of standardization.

■ **Note** One example of a proprietary language that is used to retrieve information from multidimensional structures is *MDX*, Microsoft's language to query OLAP cubes. For example, developers who want to consume the data from an Analysis Services cube can write MDX and expose it inside their custom applications. MDX can also be natively used as a query language inside Reporting Services or Excel. This may seem like a standard architecture until you realize this is limited to the Microsoft BI stack only. While MDX support is provided by many tooling vendors that hook into Analysis Services, MDX is not used as a query language beyond the Microsoft domain. Although MDX is a powerful language, it has many drawbacks in distributed BI architecture that truly limit its usefulness.

BI 1.0 software tools were .themselves designed and programmed by a software vendor. During the time of BI 1.0, agile development methodologies weren't yet popular. Most software was written and designed using classic development processes such as the waterfall method. Complex BI implementations truly exposed the limitations of these classic software methodologies. Using these methodologies, the requirements were all gathered first and converted into big specifications. With these inherently complex systems, many things were usually overlooked, and this led to software that was hard to change after programming had started.

BI 1.0 systems are usually very rigid. As shown previously in Figure 1-3, a multiple-tier application tightly coupled to the next tier is not very flexible if you want to make a change. Furthermore, many of the data feeds that were used were also collected in a manner that did not allow for much leeway. This led to BI systems becoming "stale," as they were not able to keep up with the demand of the changes that rapidly happened in business. For example, changes in accounting practices or an acquisition could rapidly change the analytic landscape for an organization.

Some improvements were made in BI 1.0 apps as modular software development techniques and service orientation were used to decouple tight operations between tiers. However, it wasn't until BI 2.0 system architecture design concepts started getting .applied that progress was truly made.

Business Intelligence 2.0 Implementation

At this point, you should understand at a high level how software was implemented following BI 1.0 concepts. In this section, I will cover how BI 2.0 improved and extended BI 1.0 using new technology and software design techniques.

In the BI 2.0 section, I will first describe the shift in technology that led to the migration of BI concepts to BI 2.0. This section will follow along the three main perspectives of BI: the intended audience, applications, and system design introduced in the previous section. Additionally, I will highlight some of the information from the previous section to contrast the different methodologies of BI 1.0 and BI 2.0.

How BI 2.0 Came to Be

How did we get from BI 1.0 to BI 2.0? Developers and BI vendors didn't simply wake up one day and say, "We have been writing software one way for over a decade; let's start designing it in this new-and-improved way."

The shift to BI 2.0 has much to do with the evolution of the software industry, and BI applications are simply following the trends. The BI industry is a component of the software industry which is rapidly evolving and improving engineering concepts. Figure 1-6 illustrates the main trends in technology and the software industry that caused a fundamental change in the way BI software was designed. The technology changes include Web 2.0, agile development methodologies, and service orientation.

Figure 1-6. Three main technology trends that helped shape BI 2.0 software

---

■ **Note** The following sections are not meant to be an in-depth dive into each technology. Each of these topics could easily have its own book dedicated to it! I encourage you to do more research on any topic you want to understand in greater depth.

Web 2.0

Web 2.0 refers to the second generation of principles that govern the design, development, and utilization of the Web by developers and end users. The term *Web 2.0* became a popular buzzword in 2004 and refers to using the Internet as a platform for software. Many social networking sites that started up during that time are considered Web 2.0 sites (e.g., Facebook, MySpace, and Flickr). You can interact with a web site for a few minutes and quickly make the distinction between a classic web site and a Web 2.0 web site. This same distinction applies to a BI application implemented with BI 1.0 or BI 2.0, as each will inherently behave differently.

Web 2.0 techniques advocate the use of things such as open APIs, standard syndication feeds, improved UI responsiveness (e.g., using Ajax and RIAs), and social networking. More Internet sites being created in the mid-2000s started using Web 2.0 principles and leveraged the Internet as a platform. It made sense for BI software to follow suit.

Agile Development Methodologies

Agile development processes are an evolution over the classic waterfall software development processes used in the late 1990s and early 2000s. Agile development concedes the fact that most functional requirements and specs will change after development on the product starts. In order to mitigate this, agile development proposes an iterative process in which frequent surveys are made as the development of the software progresses. This allows teams to quickly adapt to changes and make alterations during the development phase, resulting in higher-quality software. Furthermore, being "agile" not only allows you to reduce the overall risk of development, but also gives you the flexibility to survive in the fast-changing world of BI.

Agile development has led to measurable changes in BI software quality. Large-scale implementations that can take months to plan and even longer to develop can be more flexible. Agile development methodologies mitigate some of the rigidity of BI 1.0, as development sprints can quickly point out faults in design. This leads to improvements that can be made or planned for in the system long before it is scheduled to go live.

Data is gold in a BI system. Another popular agile methodology is *test-driven development (TDD)*. TDD is a style that advocates testing your source code as you add business functionality. TDD proves out the successes or flaws in your code quickly and iteratively. It mitigates software defects by ensuring that your code changes have not added flawed logic. TDD use in BI 2.0 is very important, as it enhances code quality dramatically.

Service Orientation

Figure 1-3 showed how complex and tightly coupled the different tiers in a BI implementation can be. Loose coupling should be promoted across the different tiers in order to create pluggable software components. Wouldn't it also be better if the business logic was exposed in such a way that it could be consumed from other services? This is exactly what service orientation solves.

Service-oriented architecture (SOA) is about using a series of independent services that can communicate business logic with each other. These services can be used independently or together to form *business platforms* that come together and provide value. Investing in services that expose important business functionality allows for a much simpler integration effort. Furthermore, SOA allows for exposing some of the business logic as APIs and creating "mashable" applications (both of which are Web 2.0 concepts). With properly designed SOA, the services become the most important part of the BI implementation, as they end up driving the data.

In the last couple of years, you have probably heard about moving data to "the cloud." The cloud is another abstraction of service orientation where the service architecture is hosted on the Internet. By hosting using the Internet platform, the cloud completely abstracts the technology implementation from the service consumers. Many public services are starting to be hosted on the cloud which allows you to enhance your BI offerings. For example, some government agencies provide large amounts of statistical data that can be freely consumed as a data feed in a BI system.

BI 2.0's Intended Audience

BI 2.0 is sometimes referred to as "BI for the masses." This name should strike a powerful shift in the philosophy for which it was designed. One of the primary goals of designing a product on the next-generation BI platform is to reach an audience beyond tech-savvy business professionals.

This concept of BI for the masses does not mean just delivering BI for more people in enterprise organizations. It also strives to target the tens of millions of users of the Internet.

At its core, BI 2.0 software is designed for the nontechnical user, regardless of whether that person is a boardroom executive or just a casual Internet user. Essentially, the idea is that the applications are easy to understand. This is primarily achieved by using newer user experience–oriented design patterns that users are already familiar with. In addition, data is presented in a cleaner, more visually driven format. This allows the insight to be derived from visual cues and UI interactions rather than statistical number crunching. These designs leverage a lot of patterns that have been popularized during the Internet boom. Since these designs take advantage of standardization, the user has less to learn about the UI interactivity and can focus on other aspects.

In classic BI, users could manipulate data by writing custom macros, scripts, or functions to get answers from the data. BI 2.0 simplifies that by translating these statistical manipulations into UI interactions that users are already familiar with.

Figure 1-7 shows an example of this interaction. In the example, the user has two questions: should the company offer a 5 percent sale on its products, and how will that impact the bottom line? BI 2.0 UIs provide specific interactions to allow the user to quickly gauge if this is a good idea. In the figure, there is a slider that the user can slide to adjust the sale percentage of the products. As it slides from 0 percent to 5 percent, an algorithm processes the information and displays how this will increase sales but lower the margin on the product. The user gains real-time insight by seeing instant visual feedback from the chart. We will be implementing a very similar example in the following chapters.

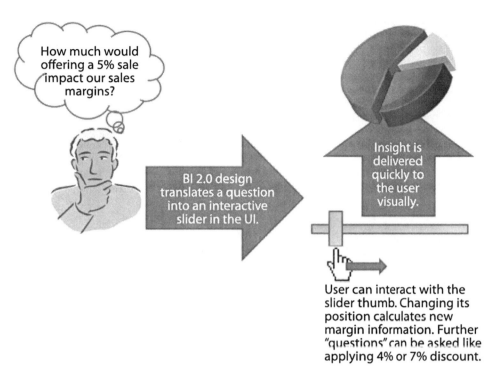

Figure 1-7. A next-generation UI provides answers to questions via simple UI interactions.

These interactions are usually limited to keep the software from being overly complex. For example, you may have a screen that allows users to query some data that you want them to focus on. This allows users to quickly learn the interactions on that screen and not have to worry about other possible functionality. In a BI 1.0 system, such a screen might have allowed the user to manipulate the data with programming scripts or additional functions. However, limiting the possible interactions allows software vendors to target a much larger audience. Very few people can write a programming script and embed it into a data set. Conversely, many people can understand a visual chart, for example. Furthermore, by using predefined UI controls and seeing real-time impact from interactions, users learn very quickly.

Empowering the BI 2.0 User

BI 2.0 empowers users to gain insights themselves and empowers them to make decisions. This is best illustrated by one of the most innovative business consultants of the twentieth century, Peter Drucker, who said, "Most discussions of decision-making assume that only senior executives make decisions or that only senior executives' decisions matter. This is a dangerous mistake."

Peter Drucker was a brilliant management consultant who came up with the term *knowledge worker*. He felt that too many of the decisions being made in an organization were being made by a select few. Therefore, he advocated passionately through his business philosophy that workers need to be empowered and use knowledge in order for a business to be successful. He proved that useful business information in the work environment led to more innovative and progressive organizations.

BI 2.0 is the software implementation of the "empower the users" business management concept. It is not about having analysts crunch numbers and then pass them off to an executive who can understand and derive a decision from them. BI 2.0 puts the information and knowledge right in front of all users in a simple format. Not only can users see the information quickly, but they can interact with it to produce powerful data models that can aid decision-making processes. Effective use of the knowledge in a BI system leads employees to derive strategic decisions on their own.

An important note to take away is that BI 2.0 users are not performing simple routine tasks like data scrubbing or aggregation. This makes the users more invested in the company, as they feel more valuable to the organization. As a business professional, what would you rather deliver to your boss—a new sales strategy concept derived on current market conditions or a routine monthly report? This is exactly what BI 2.0 implementations allow a user to deliver: strategic business decisions.

Applications

BI 2.0 applications extend BI 1.0 design with simpler interfaces, new technology, and SOA. A large part of BI's maturing into BI 2.0 has to do with improvements in software development.

Previously in the chapter, I covered a lot of the enhancements that are being made in BI 2.0 applications. Rather than repeating these again, let's take a look at a couple of examples of BI 2.0 Internet applications.

Wordle (`www.wordle.net`) is a site that provides a tool for creating word clouds (aka tag clouds). The site is simple to use and allows users to do everything themselves inside the tool. The user can paste in some text or provide a URL that has some kind of text. After clicking the Submit button, the user is presented with a colorful visualization that highlights the most popular words in the provided text. The graphic can then be exported or shared with others. Figure 1-8 shows a word cloud made from the text of this chapter using the Wordle tool. Think about how powerful this data visualization is. You can take text that you haven't read and get immediate keywords to give you insight on what the text is all about. As a practical example, you could take a transcript from a president's speech and get the key highlights of it.

This simple tool has many powerful BI 2.0 attributes driving its functionality: its process is simple, it's easy for the average user to use, and it delivers accurate insight from the data provided. One important aspect of Wordle is the "self-service" implementation of the tool. The information is derived entirely from users' actions and the data they provided. Therefore, Wordle is a great example of a simple BI 2.0 tool that any user can use to gain a quick analysis of their data.

Figure 1-8. A word cloud of the text in this chapter

Swivel (`www.swivel.com`) is an interesting example of an Internet site that brings together BI and social aspects of Web 2.0. Swivel can be best described by their motto, which is "Upload and explore data." Essentially, the site allows users to build and upload data and then view it using data visualizations (charts) that can be shared with users on the Web (see Figure 1-9). It implements many BI 2.0 characteristics: it's easy to use, it allows you to get specific insights simply, it's tailored for the masses, and it allows for easy sharing of information. Furthermore, Swivel embraces Web 2.0 concepts by being community driven and leveraging Web 2.0 lightweight UI design. Web 2.0 social networking provides a twist to delivering BI insight, as members of the community are responsible for voting for visualizations that they find the most interesting.

Imagine you are interested in data regarding shark attacks. You can go to `www.swivel.com` and enter this search item, and you'll be presented quickly with several visualizations to choose from. The highest-rated and most popular visualizations are presented first with comments to further describe the data. This is a very powerful implementation of BI 2.0 in that insight is presented not only via the tool, but also by the BI wisdom of the community.

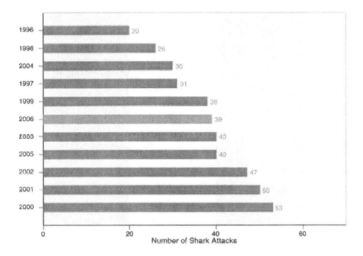

Figure 1-9. Data visualization showing shark attack data

System Design

BI 2.0 system design is actually a lot simpler than BI 1.0 design at a higher level. BI 2.0 systems tend to leverage existing enterprise services for data, business algorithms, or visualizations. Furthermore, BI 2.0 implementations have a higher level of quality, as more mature software engineering concepts are applied to the design of these systems.

Leveraging services allows BI 2.0 software to be highly flexible. Changes in the service algorithms can automatically propagate down through the BI software to the end user. For example, if we have a service that exposes a bar chart and this does not test well with our users, by using a service implementation, we could change the logic to render a line chart which would automatically propagate to the client without requiring massive changes to the system. Using services that already exist allow BI architects to simply consume them in the BI system rather than trying to replicate them from scratch.

The overall system maintenance cost of BI 2.0 is less than BI 1.0. This is due to improved software methodologies such as agile and TDD which allow for the system to adapt more quickly and mitigate bugs on delivery. Iterative and testable techniques applied in system engineering improve the perceived health of the system as users' concerns are handled much more quickly.

Comparison of Business Intelligence 1.0 and 2.0

This chapter has introduced a lot of concepts regarding the history of BI. Table 1-1 summarizes some of these concepts.

Table 1-1. *BI 1.0 vs. BI 2.0*

BI Concept	BI 1.0	BI 2.0
Intended audience	Includes business professionals only	Includes business professionals and casual users
	Requires deep understanding of the data as well as the ability to use complex software	Doesn't necessarily require understanding of the data and complex software (newer-generation applications do not require users to be tech savvy or have deep knowledge of the data)
	Has a limited audience	Attempts to provide BI to the masses
Applications	Is complex and requires training	Is simple to use without much training investment
	Uses a mix of desktop and web platforms	Uses the web platform almost exclusively
	Uses classic UI design patterns	Leverages Web 2.0 and RIA UI design patterns
	Presents data statically and allows only limited interactivity	Presents data dynamically and allows for high interactivity
	Allows for open-world modeling and a provides for near-unlimited data manipulation which is error prone	Provides a focused set of features, limiting the possibility of errors
	Focuses on data and numbers	Focuses on data visualizations for netting quick insight and provides a fallback to raw numbers and data when necessary
System design	Uses classic software development engineering methodologies	Uses newer development methodologies like agile and TDD
	Has inflexible architecture, making changes and enhancements difficult	Is designed to allow for easy changes and enhancements

BI Concept	BI 1.0	BI 2.0
	Is expensive to implement	Isn't necessarily expensive to implement (some newer systems have very quick implementation timelines)
	Uses a decentralized store of data feeds and insight (e.g., on a client workstation)	Uses a centralized store of insight on servers (e.g., users are prevented from doing something on the system that is not sharable or saved for future reuse)
	Doesn't always provide facilities for sharing data	Provides an easy way for users to share BI knowledge with each other
	Usually uses proprietary architecture	Uses service-based architecture in loosely coupled services, allowing for easy creation of mashable applications
	Doesn't always provide an API; sometimes uses closed systems because of proprietary formats	Usually provides open APIs into some of the BI insight to be consumable by other systems

Summary

This chapter introduced high-level business intelligence concepts. While there is much more to BI than could possibly be covered in an introductory chapter, I wanted to focus on the core BI features to give you an idea of what BI software is and help make the distinction between BI 1.0 and BI 2.0.

Your main takeaway from this chapter should be the understanding of BI 2.0 and its features, as this is the focus in this book. You should be able to contrast BI 1.0 and 2.0 and describe how BI 2.0 positively extends BI functionality.

If you understand that BI 2.0 is focused on BI for the masses by making BI software simpler, more visual, and easier to understand, you are in good shape to proceed to Chapter 2 which introduces the Microsoft Silverlight technology. As you proceed further in the book, you will see many of these BI 2.0 concepts implemented using Silverlight technology.

CHAPTER 2

■ ■ ■

Advantages of Applying Business Intelligence 2.0 Using Microsoft Silverlight

This chapter will focus on Microsoft Silverlight technology, which is an RIA (rich interactive application) technology based on the .NET platform. In this chapter, you will learn the fundamental advantages this new technology can bring to BI software.

We will start by looking at the challenges companies face in delivering their content to an ever-increasing audience across multiple platforms. Next, we will explore Silverlight technology as a potential answer to surfacing rich content while keeping development costs down. In addition, we will compare Silverlight to other next-generation RIA technologies and see how Silverlight stacks up. This is followed by the most important section in which we will look at the Silverlight integration with the Microsoft product horizontals and verticals.

After reading this chapter, you will see why Silverlight is a great integration technology to use with your next BI 2.0 project. Hopefully this chapter will get you excited about this new and upcoming technology.

The following table outlines the specific goals that different types of readers will achieve by reading this chapter.

Audience	Goals
Silverlight developers	Take your Silverlight knowledge to the next level by seeing where Silverlight concepts can be applied in business applications.
	Learn why Silverlight RIA technology fits into the client tier of BI distributed architecture.
	Reinforce some of the BI 2.0 concepts introduced in the previous chapter with details of how this applies to Silverlight and the Microsoft business intelligence stack.
Business intelligence professionals	Receive an introduction to Microsoft Silverlight technology.

27

Audience	Goals
	Understand how Silverlight can enhance existing and new development projects.
	Understand the Microsoft BI stack and how it can be enhanced with Silverlight.
Strategic decision makers	Understand Silverlight as a great business RIA technology.
	Receive guidance on how Silverlight can help integrate with existing Microsoft solutions and services.
	Understand if integrating Silverlight will net your products a competitive advantage.

Industry Trends

The way products and services are being offered to users is changing dramatically. Companies want to maximize their product offerings by targeting an ever-increasing audience. Conversely, users are challenging companies to offer engaging experiences.

Over the last decade, you have probably seen your favorite web sites change dramatically and provide much more engaging designs. Web sites are now providing rich media content and interactive visuals that are being integrated into the companies' business offerings. And these engaging experiences aren't just limited to the Web. Next-generation phones like the iPhone are providing further ways to deliver applications while offering a great user experience.

Content providers are looking for innovative technology solutions that help them achieve the largest target audience possible while keeping costs at a minimum.

Delivery to Multiple Platforms

Companies are currently challenged with bringing these next-generation user experiences in such a way that gets the consumers engaged with their offerings and coming back frequently. This challenge is further amplified in that today's audience expects these services to work on their platform of choice, which includes mobile, web, and desktop. Furthermore, upcoming next-generation interaction platforms such as multitouch and full-body recognition complicate the selection of the delivery platform

Using classic technology, an organization can surface its offerings using multiple platforms. The downside of this approach is that this usually involves using different programming frameworks for each individual platform. For example, a technology such as HTML works great on the Web and can even can be tailored to look presentable for mobile devices. However, HTML is probably not the best technology to use for a desktop UI. Currently, an organization will solve this problem by creating a desktop application using a framework that is optimized to be used on a workstation (i.e., WPF or Winforms). This increases the cost of delivering a common functionality across the different platforms, as it requires experienced developers who are well versed in creating solutions using different skill sets.

■ **Note** The desktop, web, mobile and tablet platforms are the "big four" user platforms right now. These four cover the majority of the current UI platforms out there. However, be aware there are many other platforms developers can target and many more to come in the near future. For example, Microsoft Surface is a new platform that users can interact with using multiple hand gestures. It doesn't really fit into any of the four and it provides a unique experience of its own. In addition, there are many older platforms that still have to be accounted for like the mainframe/console platform.

The desktop, web, and mobile platforms are inherently different. Desktop UIs tend to be more interactive and performant. Web UIs are usually navigated in a standard way and they provide a rich multimedia experience. Mobile devices are usually smaller and contain simpler visualizations. Each platform is consumed differently and therefore must be designed differently.

The Desktop Platform

The desktop platform is the oldest platform of the current big four platforms. The desktop platform can be defined as a modern GUI interface displayed locally on the user's workstation. Users of this platform can expect to receive a rich experience that consists of highly interactive features and Responsive user interfaces.

The desktop platform suffers from a couple of main drawbacks; one being that it is mainly developed for the operating system (OS), not the platform itself. For example, developing for the Windows desktop vs. a Mac desktop is completely different. You could bridge the gap by using a cross-OS language such as Java or C++, but differences would still be present. The challenge of developing on an OS is further complicated by the fact that the OSs themselves have different versions. For example, I would expect any major desktop application to support Windows XP, Windows Vista, and Windows 7.

Desktop applications also require some kind of deployment mechanism. This translates to an installation program persisting the configuration and program files to local storage. Because of the different workstation configurations and app requirements, this usually turns into a big headache.

The Web Platform

The web platform is relatively young and still evolving. Arguably, the Web has been around since the late '80s; however, it has not come to be popularized until the late '90s. To access this platform, users use a thin client (web browser).

The user's browser is usually an isolated sandbox that cedes the major processing to the remote servers it is accessing. The browser is mainly used for rendering the content that is being presented. This is done using the HTML markup language. In the mid 2000s, the next generation of web sites became popular. They put a little more of the processing on the browser, and this allowed for more dynamic content. This was done using lightweight frameworks based on JavaScript that could execute tasks and manipulate the user experience without having the server play any role.

The web platform was an improvement in some respects over the desktop, as it could reach a much larger audience. Users with different OSs were presented with the exact same experience using their browsers. However, reaching this broader audience came at the cost of the performance and interactivity of the web interfaces. Web 2.0 designs and Ajax patterns improve the Web and provide a much more desktop-like experience; however, they are not 100 percent there. The web governing body of Internet standards are trying to evolve HTML 5 in order to dramatically improve the user experience by adding video, audio and rich GPU accelerated graphics.

The web platform also caused some issues for the developers. Web browsers could implement the HTML, CSS, and JavaScript engines in a set of different ways. Even though the body of Internet standards (WSC) put out governance on how the web platform technology should be implemented, each browser did things its own way. This caused major pain for development shops that had to support not only different browsers but also the different versions of each browser client.

The Mobile Platform

The mobile platform has been around longer than the Web; however, it is just now maturing as a valid business platform. Mobile has the largest target audience of all the big four platforms and is actually growing much faster than the other two. Mobile UIs are usually consumed via a cell phone or a music device such as an iPod. The user experience on a mobile device is obviously much simpler, as the form factor is much smaller. Until several years ago, UIs on the mobile platform resembled the older web pages of the Internet. However, this is changing rapidly as mobile devices are getting true multimedia features like video, audio, gesture support, accelerometers, and great graphics.

■ **Note** Mobile devices such as the iPhone that provide up to 32GB of storage space are changing the need for mobile devices to be constantly connected to a data service source. Furthermore, some of the newer models include processors up to 1 GigHz, that are capable of doing complex computations on the device in real-time. Features like this make the delivery of interactive business intelligence modules on mobile devices much more attractive.

There are literally hundreds of different cell phone models out there, provided by a wide variety of carriers. It may not be obvious to the phone user, and every phone runs some kind of OS (e.g., iPhone OS, Symbian, Android, or Windows Mobile). Currently, there is no clear winner in the mobile OS domain. A mobile OS that has 10 percent of the market may have hundreds of millions of users. The obvious challenge for organizations is being able to target as many OSs as possible.

Developers have to choose which mobile carrier and which mobile OS they want to target. There are so many mobile device users out there that getting even a small piece of the market can mean millions of potential users. The good news is that as the mobile industry matures, mobile carriers and OSs will start to consolidate into common platforms. Currently, cell phone carriers and even mobile OSs have a lot of control to what they allow on the mobile platform. This is probably the biggest drawback of the mobile platform. For example, a phone carrier may not allow certain applications that compete with their own service offerings (e.g., Skype or Google Voice). Even the widely successful Apple iPhone OS does not include Adobe Flash. Therefore, a mobile developer has to be aware of potential restrictions of a particular mobile platform.

The Tablet Platform

The tablet platform is one of the hottest and emerging platforms in 2010. After Apple launched the iPad earlier this year, many competitors are scrambling to create their own form factor running on a variety of operating systems (i.e., Windows 7, Android, Linux, WebOS etc.).

One of the misconceptions about the tablet platform is that it is new. It has actually been conceptualized since the 1960s, well before the web and mobile paradigms existed. There were several devices in the late 1990s and early 2000s that tried to create a market for this form factor. For example, during the 1990s Apple provided a personal assistant called Newton. Conversely, Microsoft released a version of Windows XP called "Tablet Edition" and several manufacturers like Compaq provided Microsoft-based tablets. However, the technology was not ready for the tablet platform. The devices suffered from stylus-based input, poor battery life, crippled processors that overheated, didn't support multi-touch etc.

In 2010 the technology has finally caught up to deliver a great user experience on the tablet platform. The screens used in tablets support capacitive touch sensing enabling responsive multi-touch. The processors that are used in tablets are specifically geared to balance performance and battery-life. Furthermore, tablet processors include additional instruction sets to be able to play video in 1080p.

The tablet platform is not much different the current generation of the mobile platform. While the form factor is larger, for the most part most of the architectural design patterns remain the same. For example, some cynics have called the iPad just a "large iPhone". One of the biggest drawbacks to the new resurrection of the tablet platform is that the devices and software is going to be highly proprietary until that market matures into consolidation.

Value in Services

Users don't want to have to install large applications to get their content. Businesses started seeing that they could provide their content via a service and have it consumed with generic programs that a client may have already installed. For example, during the Internet boom, there were different video players out there that a user had to install in order to play video. There were also different formats that videos were displayed in that required specific players. For example, Real Player was a popular media player in the early days of the Internet that played media files in the Real media format. Today, many of these media formats are standardized, and both Flash and Silverlight can play a variety of them.

Companies started providing their content via services that could be monetized by licensing. Clients would consume this using software that had a high probability of already being installed on the user's workstation. This allowed content providers to focus on building value in their services rather than spending resources on creating applications to consume them. In order for this concept to be successful, the standard software for consuming these services needs to work with a variety of standardized data formats.

Virtualizing Resources on the Cloud

In order to deliver scalable enterprise products and services, companies need to invest in their computing hardware infrastructure. If these services run poorly or the servers go down often, users will perceive the offerings as inferior and often do business elsewhere. Therefore, companies are challenged with providing content with the highest uptime while trying to mitigate cost.

Virtualization has been a recent trend among enterprises. Companies don't want to spend money on servers that are only utilized a small fraction of the time. Some businesses have started consolidating their server hardware using virtualization software. This has allowed IT data centers to dynamically allocate processing and memory resources as needed. For example, Figure 2-1 shows a chart of an e-mail server's CPU utilization. You can see that during the early morning and evening hours, the processor is not used heavily at all. If the server is a physical machine, then it is underutilized during the off-peak hours.

Virtualizing physical hardware into servers that could share resources from a pool of hardware was an improvement. However, organizations still needed to make the investment in virtualization, which was not cheap.

Figure 2-1. CPU utilization on a sample e-mail server during a 24-hour period

Some companies simply did not have the money or time to invest in moving their content from hardware to virtualized solutions. Enterprise software vendors saw this as an opportunity and started lending their hardware resources to other organizations. This allowed companies to provide their content from third-party data centers. This content then was exposed as services on the Internet. The process of leveraging hardware resources of another party and then providing the services on the Internet is commonly referred to as *cloud computing*. Cloud computing is experiencing tremendous growth, and many companies love the idea of only paying for what you use. This allows them to eliminate a great deal of IT infrastructure costs.

The software and services still need to be designed and deployed in order to run on the cloud however. While some existing software content can be implemented to leverage cloud computing, for a majority of the content, some changes will have to be made. Companies are challenged with finding technology to invest in that will scale not only on their internal hardware, but well beyond using the cloud.

■ **Note** Understanding concepts like virtualization and cloud computing is very important for both BI and Silverlight. In the preceding sections, I covered these concepts very generally in the context of challenges organizations face. If you don't feel familiar enough with these concepts, you can do a simple web search on them to get further insight.

In the next section, I will introduce Microsoft Silverlight: a technology that can help organizations deal with delivering content to a wide audience that spans multiple platforms while keeping delivery costs to a minimum.

What Is Silverlight?

According to Microsoft, "Silverlight is a free runtime that powers rich application experiences and delivers high quality, interactive video across multiple platforms and browsers, using the .NET Framework." This is a great definition that packs a lot of information in one cohesive sentence. However, just like any summarization of any term, we need to break it down to understand what it means. The information in this section aims to show you why a technology like Silverlight is needed to power the next-generation business platforms.

■ **Note** There are currently four major Silverlight releases that the public can use. The focus of this book is Silverlight 4, but many of the concepts will also apply to previous versions of Silverlight including Silverlight 3 and Silverlight 2. Since Microsoft is on a nine- to twelve-month development-to-release cycle for Silverlight, it is worth mentioning that a large majority of these concepts should apply to the next version as well. In fact, at the time of this writing Silverlight 5 is already in private beta.

The Silverlight Solution

Wouldn't it be great to program on a single framework, target multiple platforms, and not have to worry about platform differences? Wouldn't it be great to use a framework that could scale easily into the cloud if necessary? This is exactly the advantage Microsoft Silverlight technology brings to the table.

Silverlight is an RIA framework that allows developers to create performant, desktop-like user experiences. These Silverlight RIA applications can then be consumed by the user's desktop, web browser, Windows 7 Phone or tablet (with a Windows OS) all from one framework. Furthermore, Silverlight hooks into Microsoft Azure which is a cloud OS. This allows users to consume data and services that are displayed from the Internet cloud.

■ **Note** This book refers to RIA as a *rich interactive application*. The term *RIA* also is known by the more popular term *rich Internet application*. I do not like the latter term, as it implies deployment only on the Internet, and Silverlight can be consumed on the desktop, the Web, tablet and mobile devices that don't necessarily need a dedicated Internet connection.

Less Plumbing, More Designing

Microsoft Silverlight allows you to focus more on the software itself than the secondary requirements that make the software work—that is, it allows you to focus on the design, not the plumbing. Plumbing is secondary code that is necessary to make a piece of software work under different environments. Furthermore, plumbing code does not add any perceived business value to the user. Writing large amounts of plumbing code forces many software vendors on fixed timetables to have to scale back on adding new functionality.

■ **Note** If you have been a web developer for a while, then you are quite familiar with writing plumbing code. Trying to get all of the HTML, CSS, JavaScript to work on all of the major browsers can be a major pain.

Microsoft Silverlight technology supports multiple platforms and deals with a great deal of plumbing code for you automatically. Silverlight supports the desktop, web and mobile platforms. Furthermore, the Silverlight technology implementation deals with all the platform intricacies. For example, if you write a Silverlight application, you do not have to worry about writing specific code for Firefox, Safari, Chrome or Internet Explorer. Silverlight takes this further by supporting different desktop environments such as Mac OS and Windows.

■ **Caution** While Silverlight does handle a lot of the plumbing code for you, as a developer, you still have the responsibility of researching what the technology supports or doesn't support. For example, if you are looking to support the Linux OS while using the Lynx browser, you will find yourself out of luck. However, while Silverlight doesn't handle every possible combination, the mix of platforms and browsers that it supports covers the vast majority of platforms.

Leveraging the Power of .NET

Starting from Silverlight version 2.0, Microsoft has leveraged a subset of the powerful .NET Framework as the underlying programming environment for developers and architects. This allows .NET developers to harness their existing skills and tools in creating new Silverlight applications. Microsoft has done an excellent job in making a majority of the framework work in Silverlight. This is a major step forward, as you do not need to learn a new language syntax or change your software development processes in order to start designing on the Silverlight framework. Figure 2-2 shows a subset of the popular languages you can use in Silverlight.

Using .NET as the groundwork for Silverlight, developers gain access to a powerful development framework. The framework includes such things as the ability to use advanced data structures, multiple threads, and abstracted query languages such as LINQ all on the client. Furthermore, since Silverlight and other .NET technologies share the same framework, integration between technologies like WCF, SharePoint, and WPF is made much easier. Enterprise-level development and integration features such as dependency injection, unit testing, and functional development are also available to the developer. The fact that Silverlight runs on .NET is probably the biggest advantage this technology has.

If you work for an organization that has invested in .NET, the transition to Silverlight will be much smoother than to another RIA development platform. Many organizations have taken advantage of this already, and this is why Silverlight is sometimes called "RIA for business."

Figure 2-2. Silverlight's use of .NET allows you to code in several languages.

It's All on the Client (Well, Mostly)

The Silverlight runtime executes locally on whatever client platform it is being used with. Silverlight is a true RIA because it can provide rich media experiences with highly interactive visuals.

Silverlight has to explicitly cross the client boundary in order to get data or request processing from servers. Creating service calls, even on fast networks, can lead to delays in client responsiveness.

This client-side architecture guides developers to favor on client-side processing rather than requesting everything from the server. This makes it easier for developers to create richer experiences, as they actually have to add explicit code to cross the client boundary. Conversely, technologies like ASP.NET web forms favor execution on the server. For example, in ASP.NET, if you add a combo box, the interactions are by default posted to the web server. You have to explicitly write code to handle the interactions on the client (unless you are using an Ajax-based framework from the start). Silverlight by default is the exact opposite of that. For example, if you add a combo box in Silverlight, the interactions are done on the client, and you have to add explicit code to communicate with an outside server. This guides developers less familiar with RIA technology to work on the client rather than the server. As discussed previously, the Silverlight client closely resembles the performance of desktop applications.

Client processing is not just limited to the rendering engine. Internal memory and local persistence are managed by Silverlight as well. This allows Silverlight to access application memory and storage quickly without having to make server requests for it. Concepts like large local caching persistence layers are made possible with local execution (You will see this applied to BI data in the next chapter).

Next-Generation Interaction with Multitouch

If you have ever watched any of the forensic crime dramas on television these days, you're probably blown away by scenes where detectives analyze crime data completely using hand gestures. They zoom in, pan, pause, and select data assets by simply using a multitouch interface. Producers of these shows specifically add these visuals to make average viewers understand the insight provided by crime data. Doesn't that sound like one of the tenets of BI 2.0? While this may seem like a technology difficult to master, we are actually very close to being able to develop these types of interfaces quite easily with technology like Silverlight. The iPhone OS has a multitouch screen, and even with its small form factor, it has been very useful in a wide range of applications. Imagine what software you could design if you had access to this functionality. Start thinking, because this technology is already here!

Silverlight 4 supports multitouch hand gestures. The support for this type of interactivity is much needed for next-generation applications. Most new mobile phone manufacturers are following the iPhone's trend and adding multitouch support. Furthermore, desktop OSs like Windows 7 also supports multitouch gestures. This may seem like overkill now; however, in the next couple of years, users are going to expect applications to offer these types of interactive experiences. You will need to invest in a technology that will support responsive next-generation gestures in order to compete with upcoming solutions.

Multiple Platforms and the Cloud

I mentioned earlier that Silverlight has been designed to deliver content across multiple platforms using a proprietary model or the cloud foundation. Figure 2-3 shows Silverlight embracing five different platforms under a common technology. The following subsections describe how Silverlight is able to solve these challenges specifically.

Figure 2-3. Silverlight technology embraces a variety delivery platforms.

The Desktop

Silverlight 3 introduced a new feature called *out-of-browser mode*. This mode allows Silverlight to be run on the local desktop of the user. If a user has Silverlight 3 or Silverlight 4 installed, they do not need to install anything else to run their Silverlight applications locally. The application can also utilize local storage and function without the need of an Internet connection (if coded properly). Once a Silverlight application is installed, it can automatically check and update itself from the location it was installed originally. The best part is that out-of-browser mode is not limited to Windows workstations—it works on the Mac as well.

A developer who wishes for their application to work in local mode does not have to do much extra work. Simply editing a simple configuration file can enable this feature. The ability to target the desktop using Silverlight without having to make coding changes reinforces Silverlight's focus on design as opposed to plumbing code.

■ **Note** If you are familiar with Adobe's RIA products, you probably know about Adobe AIR, another product that allows you to run RIAs on the desktop. Adobe AIR and Silverlight's out-of-browser technologies are similar, but there are a couple of key differences. With Adobe AIR, even if you have Adobe Flash installed, you will still need to install the Adobe AIR framework in order to run an Adobe RIA locally on the desktop. By default Silverlight runs in a lower security context and makes the framework a little more secure than Adobe AIR. Silverlight 4 introduced a capability to access more of the local resources through elevated trust and additionally integrate with local COM components on Windows-based operating systems.

Linux support is unofficially provided by the open-source Moonlight project. It contains a large majority of Silverlight features contained in runtime provided by Microsoft. However, Moonlight does lack some key Silverlight 3 and 4 features.

The Web

Silverlight is a lightweight browser plug-in that can be embedded in a web page using basic HTML syntax. Silverlight is a cross-browser platform that runs on all the major browsers: Internet Explorer, Firefox, Safari, and Chrome. As mentioned earlier with Silverlight, you let Microsoft worry about the implementation and integration with the different browsers and you concern yourself about the design of your application.

Mobile

Microsoft has demonstrated Silverlight running on mobile devices in several conferences prior to 2010. During the MIX 2010 conference Microsoft finally announced the developer story for its upcoming Windows Phone 7 platform (set to be released later in 2010). The development platform is the Silverlight SDK.

Even though Windows Phone 7 devices are not available, based on the public information Microsoft has released, we can safely assume a few key features. The Silverlight runtime on mobile devices will be almost exactly the same as the runtime for the Web and desktop. A Silverlight application written for the desktop or Web will work on a mobile device using a large part of the same source code. More importantly the same design tools and programming languages can be used to develop Windows Phone 7 solutions.

Microsoft, like Apple, has its own mobile OS (Windows Phone 7) and mobile multimedia device (Zune). This allows Microsoft to design a device that will have Silverlight fully integrated into the entire user experience. The distribution of these applications will follow the Apple App Store model. Microsoft is planning on competing in the mobile app store arena with the Microsoft Marketplace for Mobile. This will make the delivery of content and applications to the mobile audience easier than prior Windows Mobile applications.

In addition, Microsoft has signed deals with several mobile device manufactures that will include the Silverlight runtime. In Figure 2-3 you may have questioned why Nokia is listed in the mobile section for Silverlight. In March 2010, Microsoft released a beta for Silverlight running on the Nokia N00 platform. Unfortunately to date this has been the only other mobile platform supported other than the Windows Phone 7. Many users and developers are requesting support for the Apple iPhone and Android.

■ **Note** Silverlight support for the Nokia S60 5th generation mobile platform currently targets the Silverlight 2 runtime. Interestingly, the Silverlight 2 runtime is available through the browser only. Conversely, for the Windows Phone 7 the Silverlight runtime is out of the browser only.

■ **Note** Silverlight support is not limited to decisions or limitations by phone carriers and operating systems. Skyfire is a third party browser that is available on the Windows Phone, Android and Symbian devices that brings Silverlight capability to the mobile device. The browser was recently submitted (April 2010) to the Apple App Store and it will be interesting if Apple allows it. For more information on the Skyfire browser, go to www.skyfire.com.

Silverlight's support for the mobile platform in the near future is very important. I hope Microsoft champions the reach of Silverlight further on more mobile devices. The platform will only be successful if more and more devices are supported. It shows that investing in Silverlight technology can net you not only the traditional desktop and web users, but also the mobile audience.

The Tablet

Microsoft has had a formal presence with tablet devices since Windows XP Tablet Edition in 2002. There are many older tablet devices that can run Silverlight 4 with the help of a stylus. Newer devices running Windows 7 can provide a richer experience using multi-touch gestures. Furthermore, there are also hybrid laptop devices on the market that act as both a tablet and a full-feature notebook.

The story for Silverlight on tablet devices is still evolving. There are several tablet devices releasing this year that will run on Windows 7. In order for Silverlight to be a viable tablet platform, more manufactures need to support Windows 7 or Silverlight needs to be ported over to different operating systems.

■ **Note** In April 2010, Microsoft-based tablets hit a roadblock. HP bought Palm and inherited the WebOS. In conjunction, HP announced it was cancelling their upcoming Windows 7 tablet called HP Slate. During that timeframe, Microsoft announced it was cancelling their stealth project called Courier which looked very promising. The perception is that Windows 7 is not a good OS for tablet devices, because it doesn't support basic features such as fast boot times and is considered "too bulky" for a tablet OS. Maybe we will see a tablet device based on a scaled-up version of the Windows 7 Phone operating system?

The Cloud

In October of 2008, Microsoft publicly announced a new OS called Windows Azure. Windows Azure is unique because it is a cloud computing platform. The entire back end is comprised of services that are hosted on virtualized servers at Microsoft data centers. The virtual servers are completely responsible for managing and scaling the resources that are running the applications.

Where does Silverlight fit into this? Services are a large part of cloud computing; however, to complete the development platform, Microsoft has integrated UI technologies in order to expose these cloud services. One of these technologies is Silverlight. Silverlight can use the Azure APIs and consume services from the cloud. This allows companies to create an application without having physical hardware for scaling. For example, if you are a small company and write an application that you think will be successful, traditionally you have to plan your hardware infrastructure accordingly. Hosting your idea on the Azure platform allows you to focus on the software. Let Microsoft worry about managing the web servers, allocating computing resources, and scaling. If your application only gets 100 users per day and it grows rapidly to over a million per day, you do not have to do anything, and the virtual servers will simply scale up automatically!

Just to reinforce what I have been repeating in previous sections, both of these technologies allow businesses to utilize their existing .NET skills and resources. Having a technology like Silverlight that is integrated with cloud computing is another advantage in delivering your content across multiple platforms.

■ **Note** Business Intelligence professionals looking for BI functionality may be interested in Azure in the near future. Microsoft is planning on including some business intelligence features from SQL Server including Reporting Services in Azure. Furthermore, Microsoft is planning on adding robust map reduce services for computing large amounts of data based on Hadoop. Consuming data via these services will be possible in Silverlight in the near future.

■ **Note** For more information on the Microsoft Azure platform and to get all the tools/SDKs that you need to start developing on the platform, go to www.microsoft.com/azure.

Silverlight vs. Other RIA Technologies

Many critics of Microsoft argue that the company is usually late to catch on to rapidly evolving technology trends. They also point out that Microsoft doesn't contribute much to the innovation of new technologies and that they would rather use their enormous cash war chest to compete via brute force. This argument has been used in the past to label the initial release of the .NET Framework as a copy of Java, and it is being argued now that Silverlight is a copy of Adobe's Flash/Flex products.

While it is true that Microsoft comes late to the game sometimes, Silverlight provides many empirical and business advantages that go well beyond what other current RIA technologies have to offer. In this section, I will cover what Silverlight technology currently brings to the next-generation applications and try to show its advantages over other RIAs.

Current State of RIA Technology

RIAs have been around for a while and are nothing new. The term *RIA* was coined by Macromedia (now owned by Adobe) who pioneered the Flash technology in the late '90s. For the purposes of this discussion, RIAs can be broken into two different groups: *true RIA technology*, which applies most or all of the RIA features, and *RIA-like technology*, which provides some of the RIA concepts but has some noticeable features missing. Figure 2-4 breaks down the different technologies that make up the different factions.

Figure 2-4. Different RIA technologies split into two groups

RIA software has the following key attributes:

- Desktop-like performance and visuals

- The ability to embed rich multimedia

- The ability to run offline or provide a relatively large local persistence layer

- The ability to support web, desktop, and mobile platforms

- The ability to use a single code base to target different platforms

There are three key true RIA products: Adobe's Flash, Flex, and Air platforms; Microsoft's Silverlight; and Sun's JavaFX. All three technologies implement all of the attributes just mentioned.

Google and Mozilla have also seen value in RIA technology, but they have taken a different approach by using the existing framework that powers the Internet—HTML and JavaScript. Google has launched an open source project called Gears that allows the creation of web applications that can run offline on the browser. Gears supports semi responsive UIs, background processing, and large local storage with SQLite. However, most RIA experts don't consider this a true RIA. Because of the similarities to HTML 5, Google decided to scrap the Gears project on February 2010 and focus on delivering RIA-like experiences via HTML 5. Likewise, the Mozilla Foundation has a technology called Prism that lets you create web applications easily. It has similar functionality to Google Gears in that it lets you quickly create web applications that can run offline using existing web technology. However, it falls short of a true RIA technology in the respect that the visuals and performance simply do not match RIAs like Flash or Silverlight.

In these ways, they are better described as frameworks that allow for Web 2.0–enhanced applications.

■ **Note** For more information on the Mozilla Prism platform, go to https://mozillalabs.com/prism.

Figure 2-4 includes other technologies based on the Web, such as Ajax, which allows developers to create applications that have some RIA features. The benefit of using these frameworks is that you can create mashable content that contains several frameworks and services working together. The upcoming

HTML 5 standard will bring enhanced support for multimedia applications and offline storage. The problem with the HTML 5 standard, however, is that it just a standard. Different browsers can decide to implement this in a variety of different ways, and the companies that own browsers have varying interests in implementing it. If HTML 5 is implemented by most browsers, it will deprecate some of the usefulness provided by frameworks like Gears and Prism. However, just like the Gears and Prism frameworks, HTML 5 alone will not provide users with a complete RIA-like experience.

Figure 2-5 illustrates this distinction between RIA and RIA-like technologies. When you chart the technologies out on an arbitrary performance vs. visual experience graph, you can see that JavaFx, Silverlight, and Flash are in a group of their own. HTML 5 is not lagging far behind. Even though most benchmarks show that HTML 5 is slower compared to Silverlight and Flash, this might change once HTML 5 hits the mainstream.

Figure 2-5. *Graph showing RIA vs. RIA-like technologies*

■ **Note** Figure 2-5 is based on several benchmarks available on the Web comparing these technologies. Some RIA experts might argue about the Silverlight vs. Flash positioning. My argument is that Silverlight is the fastest RIA in computational algorithms. Multithreading support gives Silverlight a big edge (I will discuss the topic in later chapters). Conversely, Flash has a slight upper hand in visualization rendering and overall UI performance. However, both technologies are relatively close in performance in most application scenarios.

Silverlight's Position Among RIAs

While Silverlight technology has a very strong position among the various true RIA technologies, each technology offers unique benefits, and the preference really comes down to the eye of the beholder. A Java guru is going to feel at home with JavaFX, a designer is going to love Adobe's graphical tools and wide adoption, and a .NET developer is going to prefer Silverlight. However, businesses that want to deliver content with an RIA have to be able to compare these technologies at some level in order to make a wise decision.

The Adobe Flash, Flex and AIR platforms are more mature platforms than the other two RIAs. Overall, they boast the most features. Most importantly, Flash has a huge market penetration and has versions installed on over 90 percent of desktops. Conversely, Silverlight has about a 60 percent adoption rate.

Silverlight and Adobe Flash have comparable feature sets. Silverlight 4 has caught up to almost all of the features Flash provides. However, Silverlight includes some features that Flash doesn't have, such as multithreading, sharing .NET and supporting adaptive streaming out of the box. Silverlight by no means is playing catch-up and has plans to innovate in its own path.

Sun JavaFX is late to the RIA game with version 1.0 having been released in December 2008. The JavaFX framework boasts the least amount of features among the top three RIAs. However, it does have the benefit of one of the most popular developer communities in Java. One big negative for JavaFX is that Sun was taken over by Oracle in early 2009, and questions have been raised as to whether Oracle will continue to improve the technology. After a long hiatus, JavaFX had a release in April 2010. However, it is lacking many features compared to current releases of Silverlight and Flash.

When looking at Silverlight from a high level, there aren't really any groundbreaking features that scream for a business to automatically jump to this technology. However, once you start looking at the integration opportunities with Microsoft's technology stack, it becomes clear that Silverlight has a very unique advantage over other RIA technologies.

Silverlight vs. HTML 5

HTML 5 has been receiving a lot of buzz recently, as version that "will kill RIAs". The goal of the HTML 5 specification is to reduce the need for proprietary plug-ins like Silverlight or Flash. While HTML 5 does include many new compelling features that will compete with true RIAs, HTML 5 is by no means can replace Silverlight outright.

As of this book's publication the HTML 5 spec is not complete. The specification is expected to evolve for some time. However, this has not stopped major browsers from starting to support new HTML 5 content. Current or beta versions of Firefox, Chrome and Safari support some of the HTML 5 specification. While current versions of Internet Explorer do not support HTML 5, Internet Explorer 9 is supposed to support a majority of HTML 5 features.

■ **Note** In the section below, I am just including the key features comparing Silverlight and HTML 5. I wrote a comprehensive article on the subject a couple months ago located on my main Silverlight blog. If you are interested, please visit `http://silverlighthack.com/post/2010/02/08/Top-Reasons-why-HTML-5-is-not-ready-to-replace-Silverlight.aspx`.

Key New Features of HTML 5

Some of the key new features supported in most HTML 5 compatible browsers include:

- *Audio and Video tags*: Multimedia content in the form of video and audio can be easily embedded into the HTML markup for a web page

- *Canvas and SVG support*: The new Canvas tag will allow HTML 5 to render rich user interfances comparable to Silverlight and Flash in 2D

- *Offline Storage Database*: This will allow larger data sets to be persisted locally on an end-user's workstation. This is similar to Isolated Storage in Silverlight

- *CSS 3*: Cascading style sheets is updated for the HTML 5 spec and receives many updates that makes creating RIA-like experiences easier.

Some of the key new features not yet supported in most HTML 5 compatible browsers include (spec is not defined for some of these features):

- *Web Workers*: Allows JavaScript to be executed asynchronously

- *Device tag*: The new Device tag plans to support integrating with devices like web cams natively in HTML 5

- *Web Sockets*: This is convention would bring the publish-subscribe model

- *GPU Accelerated Graphics*: Many of the RIA applications put a large tax on the CPU to render the complex layouts. This applies to complex layouts in HTML 5 as well. There is a plan to improve the rendering performance by offloading some of the tasks to the GPU, rather than always relying on the CPU.

▪ **Caution** The list above by no means Is complete. The HTML 5 specification is much larger than what is listed. I wanted to list the most compelling new features of HTML 5 to compare them to Silverlight. For a summary of all the features of HTML 5 please visit http://en.wikipedia.org/wiki/HTML_5.

HTML 5 Limitations

As you can see from the previous section HTML 5 has a lot of new features that will directly compete with Silverlight and Flash. If HTML 5 has all these features why would you still use a proprietary plug-in? This is especially true if some people's predictions come true that HTML 5 will be ready to hit the mainstream in 2 years tops.

In my opinion, HTML 5 has some key obstacles it needs to overcome before proprietary RIA plug-ins are deemed legacy.

HTML 5 is "born old": This was a comment on my Silverlight blog and I think it summarizes HTML 5 perfectly. Every new feature that HTML 5 has (even the ones not mentioned in this section) are all included in Silverlight and Flash. HTML 5 is just catching up to Silverlight. When HTML 5 is hitting the masses in 2-3 years, Silverlight will have evolved at least a couple more versions with many new features. In my opinion, the WSC will simply not move fast enough to keep up.

Internet Explorer problem: Internet Explorer is still the dominant browser on the web today with well over 66% of the market share, which is not HTML 5 compatible. 2-3% yearly drops are huge in market share and even at this pace it would take 7+ years before current versions of Internet Explorer are replaced. One question you have to ask yourself: *Is a user more likely to try a new browser or try a simple plug-in like Silverlight?*

Limitations of HTML 5 tags: Some of the new HTML 5 tags have pretty crippling limitations for some scenarios. For example, the video tag works great for simple progressive download scenarios for sites like YouTube. However, sites like Hulu and Netflix require DRM protection so the content does not get pirated easily. Furthermore, advanced streaming scenarios like adaptive streaming in full HD are not possible natively in HTML 5. Lastly, the agreed upon codec that the video tag will support is up to the browsers! Apple and Microsoft plan on supporting H.264, while Mozilla wants to support an open-source alternative. The video tag is just one example of some the features that Silverlight natively provides that will not be possible to do in HTML 5.

HTML's 5 dynamic language is still JavaScript: As you saw in the previous section, Silverlight allows you to code in any .NET compatible language. However, for HTML 5 we are still programming in JavaScript. It is not that JavaScript is a bad language, but most software design patterns have evolved well beyond the langauge's original inception. This is why you see frameworks like jQuery so popular or additional libraries that bring LINQ functionality to JavaScript. The problem with this is that when you start a complex HTML 5 project, you are going to go hunting for JavaScript frameworks first.

Productivity: HTML 5 uses a combination of technologies like: CSS 3, HTML 5, JavaScript, SVG etc., It is not hard to see that writing design tools that a non-programmer can easily use is not going to be easy. This is a great example of how Expression Blend for Silverlight provides a very rich design experience. This allows designers to not only code rich design, but add sample data and provide interactivity. Conversely, there are no good HTML 5 design tools out there. Furthermore, it is going to be difficult to provide a tool that seamlessly integrates custom JavaScript frameworks natively into the tool and provides similar behavior found in Silverlight XAML. If you think this is a simple issue, just look at today's HTML 4 editors that use HTL and CSS. Many of them have trouble generating basic clean markup to position a div tag with some CSS selectors set.

HTML 5 is going to "democratize parts of RIA functionality" and provide a way for web sites to deliver rich interactive content without relying on plug-ins. However, it is important to note that HTML 5 is not ready and does not have full support in all the browsers. In 3-4 years from now, if I am creating a simple site or blog HTML 5 will probably be the technology I will use. However, if my requirements include rich 3D with deep integration with business intelligence modules; HTML 5 might not be the right platform to deliver the solution on.

Silverlight: The Business RIA

Microsoft is one of the biggest software companies in the world. Its market includes both home users and enterprise businesses. Microsoft is positioning Silverlight as an end user technology, but more importantly as technology for business. The first two versions of Silverlight targeted the end-users with simple visuals, multimedia, and design controls. Since Silverlight version 3, Microsoft has added many compelling features for business applications. The set of features Silverlight currently possesses and the future integration plans clearly point to the fact that Microsoft wants Silverlight to become the delivery mechanism for enterprise business services. This section will cover some key areas that show why Silverlight has a distinct advantage over other RIAs in the business space.

Silverlight is a cross-browser and cross-platform UI technology. This puts Silverlight in a unique position that Microsoft can use it to deliver its own enterprise services to a much wider audience than before. If Microsoft is successful, then Silverlight can be the one-stop business UI platform.

Microsoft platform technologies like ASP.NET, WINforms, and WPF all require the full .NET Framework to display or host content from. This makes Microsoft enterprise offerings less attractive to consumers who do not want to install the large .NET Framework or want it to work on a Mac OS, for example.

The following subsections will take a look at Silverlight's specific integration opportunities with Microsoft products.

Lessons from the Past

Silverlight will likely follow an integration pattern with the Microsoft technology stack similar to the .NET Framework. The .NET Framework was released in 2002, and it didn't have strong legs in the early stages. However, when Microsoft started porting its APIs from COM and C++ into .NET, the .NET Framework gained tremendous popularity. Nowadays, every single application Microsoft releases has a .NET API or SDK. The .NET Framework has become the de facto standard for extending Microsoft-based applications. In the future, I see Silverlight as the multiplatform technology that will expose the huge amount of services that Microsoft can offer.

Leveraging Existing Development Investments

Businesses that are currently developing enterprise applications using Microsoft solutions are heavily invested in the .NET Framework. If you have a development organization with developers who are familiar with .NET, why would you want to shift their skills to another technology? Silverlight allows development organizations to learn the new technology and tools associated with it but doesn't require them to change their development processes or skill sets. This is a very important distinction Silverlight has from Adobe Flash, which uses ActionScript as its primary development language, and has its own set of development tools. The Microsoft .NET community is enormous, being several factors greater than that of ActionScript. Therefore, using .NET allows you to simply copy most existing algorithms directly into Silverlight, and they will work. Furthermore, you can share source code between Silverlight applications and other .NET assemblies. A good example of this is sharing source code between Silverlight and WPF because these two technologies share the same core architectural foundation. This allows developers to write code once and have the application build for both Silverlight and WPF.

The Silverlight development tools run on top of Visual Studio and do not require an additional license investment. This is very important as existing project layouts, source control, and code tests do not have to change to another platform to accommodate Silverlight integration. Silverlight's primary visual design tool is Expression Blend. This tool also integrates with Visual Studio and makes the integration between designers and developers easier to manage. Microsoft has realized that is not the leader in the design space (Adobe is still king); therefore, it should be comforting to know that certain Adobe graphical assets can be imported into Expression Blend. This allows imported assets to be used in Microsoft Silverlight applications.

Moving to the Cloud More Easily

As already mentioned, with Windows Azure, an organization can move its services from physical hardware to Microsoft's data centers and pay for only the resources it uses. Designing cloud services, creating a client for the cloud, and debugging and deploying the system can be done all under a single project! This is a very profound integration advantage for Silverlight. Flash can consume cloud services; however, Adobe does not have its own cloud computing initiative. This forces Flash developers to look for third-party cloud computing providers. Azure and Silverlight allow developers to do this in a single integrated solution.

Silverlight RIA applications can take advantage of the enormous amount of services that Azure provides: .NET services, SQL Server storage services, Live services, SharePoint services, and Dynamics CRM services. This list will no doubt grow. This allows businesses to be up and running much more quickly by automatically leveraging these preexisting services. Creating new applications by leveraging Azure services accentuates my earlier point about not writing plumbing code and focusing on adding value to the system for your clients.

Integrating with Microsoft Products

Microsoft offers a robust stack of applications that businesses can take advantage of. Even though Silverlight has only been around for a couple of years, we are already seeing Silverlight integrated into various applications. This will only continue to grow as the technology matures and Microsoft has time to catch up and offer products that integrate with Silverlight. Following are some examples of how you can take advantage of Microsoft integration by using Silverlight technology.

On the development side, Silverlight seamlessly leverages Microsoft's enterprise service-oriented development platform, Windows Communication Foundation (WCF). WCF allows organizations to architect robust and scalable service-oriented architectures. Silverlight's runtime and deployment configurations seamlessly integrate with WCF. Similar to the Azure integration, WCF and Silverlight integration allows developers to consolidate the back-end services and presentation layer into a single deployable solution.

One of the biggest business products for Microsoft is SharePoint Server. Many organizations use SharePoint's modular and customizable architecture to host all of their systems from a single user access portal. Silverlight is completely compatible with SharePoint 2007. You can embed Silverlight directly into your SharePoint site. In addition, you can create web parts that surface Silverlight packages. These web parts can be dynamically added by users to create custom portals with interactive Silverlight content.

■ **Note** Chapter 13 discusses Silverlight web parts (with a focus on SharePoint 2010) in more detail.

Microsoft provides value-added services with which Silverlight can integrate. One example of this is a global mapping service called Virtual Earth. Microsoft released a Silverlight control that can be used with the Virtual Earth SDK. Developers can use this control to not only display map navigation using Silverlight, but also add Silverlight content into maps. For example, you could integrate sales data for each region and show that visually using Virtual Earth inside the Silverlight control. We will look at an example of using the Virtual Earth Silverlight control in a later chapter.

Microsoft is positioning Silverlight technology as the primary platform for delivering high-definition (HD) content. Microsoft's IIS Web Server 7.0 has a free extension you can add to expose adaptive streaming content in your site. This technology can deliver HD streams in 720p and 1080p formats. The best part of this technology is that it can automatically downscale the bit rate if your Internet connection becomes slower without pausing the content. Figure 2-6 displays a video being played that is automatically adjusting based on the bit rate. This technology can also be used to provide a DVR-like experience with live content. You can also record certain parts of the stream while navigating back and forth between live sections.

■ **Note** To experience the HD smooth streaming, go to www.iis.net/media/experiencesmoothstreaming or www.smoothhd.com.

This experience is really impressive and removes the annoying buffering pauses that currently plague streaming solutions. How successful is this technology? Netflix is using Silverlight to deliver streaming rentals to its clients on the Web and on the Xbox. Furthermore, Silverlight is used to handle the hundreds of millions of media requests for the NBC Olympics.

The most intriguing feature of IIS Media Services integration with Silverlight is that there are no extra add-ons required! This is in contrast to other RIAs that need special add-ons to be able to play HD media content. An end user that has Silverlight installed on their workstation or mobile device is ready to consume HD smooth streaming. To me, that is simply a killer feature of Silverlight technology.

Note To find more information on IIS Media Services and download the extensions to IIS 7.0, go to www.iis.net/media.

Figure 2-6. HD video displayed using IIS 7.0 Media Services adaptive streaming technology

Overcoming Silverlight's Weaknesses

Silverlight is not the perfect business technology for all scenarios. The technology has some weaknesses that business applications have to account for. Some of these weaknesses are design-based and others concern missing features. One big limitation of adoption is that the Silverlight plug-in requires administrative rights on the workstation in order to be installed. For workstations in sensitive industries like finance, banking or law where users do not have administrative rights, this could be a problem. As you saw from the previous sections, not all platforms and devices support Silverlight. Therefore, there are plausible scenarios where Silverlight simply many not be a good choice to surface a business intelligence solution.

The Microsoft Business Intelligence Platform and Silverlight

Microsoft BI is built on the foundation of two core products: SQL Server and Microsoft Office. SQL Server is primarily responsible for the back-end services and providing the horsepower that runs the BI tools. Microsoft Office is responsible for exposing the services to the users. Together, these two products offer a wide range of powerful BI tools upon which organizations can build.

SQL Server BI

SQL Server is an enterprise platform that can deliver BI data to the entire organization. The SQL Server product allows companies to aggregate their data, build data warehouses, design a rich reporting infrastructure, and create multidimensional databases using a single product. This is achieved from the multiple services that make up SQL Server:

- *Integration Services*: An enterprise ETL platform that is used to integrate and aggregate data from various sources

- *Database Engine*: A database storage engine that allows the creation of data warehouses and data marts to persist and query information

- *Analysis Services*: A platform for creating OLAP databases that can be used for multidimensional analysis, querying, and forward-looking data models

- *Reporting Services*: A reporting platform for creating data, and delivering it to and sharing it with all the users in an organization

- *Master Data Services (new in SQL Server 2008 R2)*: This is a service oriented platform for creating a single version of truth for your mission critical data across the enterprise

- *PowerPivot (new in SQL Server 2008 R2 and Office 2010)*: PowerPivot is a self-service data analysis tool that allows users to derive insight from very large data sets. There is also an add-in for Excel 2010 runs locally and can scale up to millions of rows on 64-bit architectures utilizing in-memory storage.

- *StreamInsight (new in SQL Server 2008 R2)*: This engine allows SQL Server to process millions of rows of data in real-time using event data streaming. Financial services and real-time business intelligence implementations will benefit greatly from this technology

BI is a value-added proposition to the SQL Server product. When a user buys a business license for SQL Server, they will generally be able to use most of these services with no additional costs. This is different from other database vendors that have additional costs associated with different BI modules. This makes the SQL Server product very attractive to many organizations, as the licensing is relatively simple compared to the competition.

The primary users of SQL Server BI are on the back-end side: BI architects, DBAs, report authors, data warehouse developers, and so on. While SQL Server, cannot deliver a full-blown BI 2.0 solution alone; its robust amount of BI services can be consumed in Silverlight.

Microsoft Office BI

The Microsoft Office products include a variety of BI modules that surface a lot of the information stored in the SQL Server product. The Office BI modules include Excel, SharePoint Server, and SharePoint Services.

Microsoft Office BI is responsible for providing the user interface for consuming the back-end service data that comes from SQL Server BI. For example, a user could use Excel to analyze data from an Analysis Services Cube. Furthermore, a SharePoint portal could be created to include Reporting Services reports or get KPIs (key performance indicators) from a data warehouse. Microsoft Office BI includes a variety of end user tools and configuration options to make delivering BI insight easier.

The primary users of the Microsoft Office BI products are the data analysts and consumers of insight.

What Does Silverlight Have to Offer BI?

I consider most Microsoft BI products largely BI 1.0. For example, you can create excellent BI tools and present terabytes of data using them; however, they are relatively complex to set up and use. Furthermore, certain Microsoft languages, like MDX, are proprietary.

■ **Note** Not all Microsoft BI features fall into the BI 1.0 category. For example, Microsoft provides a rich set of APIs that make extending the BI modules easy. Furthermore, insight can be easily shared through built-in features like alerting, e-mail, and report distribution. Microsoft's BI offering is so robust that it can't easily be described as either BI 1.0 or 2.0. It largely depends on the implementation and the type of tools used.

Silverlight has the ability to surface data in a rich presentation format. As mentioned, Silverlight can bring applications to life using rich media content, interactivity, and multitouch capabilities. This is exactly the wow factor that Microsoft BI is missing.

Microsoft realizes that BI data using Microsoft products needs to be more easily attainable. Microsoft is applying BI 2.0 concepts into their next-generation BI products. For example, Figure 2-7 shows a concept dashboard called Microsoft Enterprise Cube (MEC), which is the epitome of BI 2.0. It provides interactive panels, geographic visualizations, sliders for manipulating timelines, and so on. All the data is located in a single place, making strategic decisions easy. This dashboard is designed such that it can easily incorporate next-generation interactivity, such as hand gestures.

Starting with Office 2010, Microsoft has started to jump on the BI 2.0 bandwagon. Both Excel 2010 and SharePoint 2010 include a new self-service tool called PowerPivot, which will be discussed in later chapters. Furthermore, SharePoint 2010 includes a lot of Silverlight tools as well.

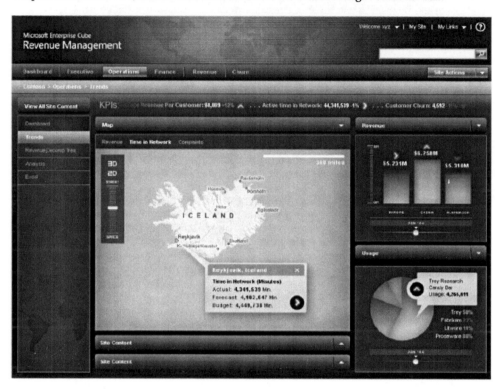

Figure 2-7. *MEC is an example of what you can do with a Silverlight RIA dashboard.*

Summary

This chapter introduced Silverlight as a potential solution to the challenges facing businesses that want to keep up with current industry trends. Businesses want to maximize the audience for their content across different platforms while keeping costs down. Silverlight answers these challenges with its portability across different platforms and integration with the Microsoft business intelligence product platform. This chapter also showed how Silverlight technology is on the forefront of leading industry trends with its integration with Microsoft's cloud computing initiative and its offering of multitouch support. The chapter concluded with a look at the Microsoft BI product technology stack and how potential Silverlight integration could enhance the delivery of BI 2.0 solutions.

Your major takeaway from this chapter should be that Silverlight is positioned very well to be the business intelligence RIA for Microsoft products and services. Because Microsoft provides a rich variety of value-added BI services, development and integration with Silverlight makes sense on multiple strategic levels.

In the next several chapters, we are going to take a look at how we can improve static and uninteresting data visualizations and make them more appealing by adding interactivity. You will see how you can integrate the Silverlight presentation layer to visualize data in interesting ways and also perform analytics on it. This is essentially what this book is about; being able to create interactive data visualizations using Silverlight technology.

CHAPTER 3

■ ■ ■

Silverlight as a Business Intelligence Client

This chapter introduces Silverlight as a potential world-class BI client. In the first two chapters, you learned about BI 2.0 concepts and Silverlight RIA technology. It is time to see how the combination of BI 2.0 and Silverlight can form very powerful applications.

In this chapter, we will start by looking at the role Silverlight plays in the overall architecture of a BI implementation. Next, we will look at how you can take advantage of distributing computation processing logic onto the Silverlight client. We will work with local data sets and manipulate them on the client.

This chapter is the first one to include programming exercises (coding scenarios). The following coding scenarios are included in this chapter:

- Working with business data using LINQ

- Decoupling business algorithms using Silverlight's data binding converters

- Caching in memory and persisting in local storage

The following table outlines the specific goals that different types of readers will achieve by reading this chapter.

Audience	Goals
Silverlight developers	Apply known concepts like LINQ querying, data caching, and business logic to BI data insight.
Business intelligence professionals	Understand the advantages of distributed architecture for BI.
	See how Silverlight can be used to offload processing from a traditional "process-on-the-server" design. This will mimic conventions used in PowerPivot.

Audience	Goals
Strategic decision makers	Discover whether Silverlight as a BI client makes sense for your products.
	Find out whether adoption of Silverlight allows you to free up server resources to add more product value.
	Understand Silverlight's client advantages in BI product delivery.

Client Distributed Architecture

Architecture of complex systems has evolved in the last decade. In Chapter 1, I touched on the monolithic size of complete BI system architectures. These architectures rely on multiple services to communicate with each other and provide data to client workstations that users can consume.

■ **Caution** Before we proceed, I want to make sure there isn't confusion between the terms *client* and *customer*. Obviously, these two terms can mean the same thing. In this book, the term *client* refers to the presentation layer application/site that is responsible for rendering content on the user's desktop workstation or mobile device, and the term *customer* refers to a business or organization purchasing a system or services from a vendor.

Distributed Architectures Defined

In the early days of BI systems, it was obvious that client workstations simply did not have the computing power to do anything other than display the relevant data to the user. The quantity of BI data required server hardware in order to be processed efficiently. The first solution was to offload the processing onto a server and allow a client to communicate with the server. The server housed the data and the client made the appropriate requests via the network. This was usually a tightly coupled two-layer model known as the client-server model (Figure 3-1). The client-server architecture worked well until it was necessary to have the system be more scalable and dependable. For example, if the server is running slowly, then the client will not receive requests in a timely fashion.

Figure 3-1. Client-server architecture

Distributed n-tier architecture was an evolution of the client-server model that aimed to solve the limitations of the original architecture. The model favored injecting tiers in between the servers that could be responsible for different functional parts of the system. This allowed for a more robust system that could easily be scaled by adding more horizontal tiers or caching layers (Figure 3-2).

Figure 3-2. Distributed n-tier architecutre

Problems with N-Tier Architecture

Distributed n-tier architecture is very successful at distributing the computational processing of business logic across different physical or virtual servers. This works well in most cases. In fact, most original web sites on the Internet were architected this way.

This is how most applications are currently designed and scaled. An application could have a database layer, a business logic layer, and a service layer. Each of these layers is responsible for doing its own individual processing and represents an application boundary. Therefore, it is easy to scale any layer onto its own server (physical tier). Figure 3-3 shows an example of scaling a system vertically and horizontally. In the example, if the database is running slowly, we can move database processing onto its own server so it can use the full resources. The server layers are scaled vertically by moving their processing onto stand-alone servers. Layers can also be scaled horizontally by load balancing and splitting out the processing for that tier into multiple servers.

All tier processing is done on a single server

Different tiers are broken into separate physical layers on different servers

Figure 3-3. Scaling an n-tier architecture

■ **Caution** I normally do not like getting into semantics; however, I'd like to briefly discuss the difference between the definitions of *n-tier* and *n-layer* architectures. N-layer architectures deal with splitting up processing into functional logical units (database processing assembly, web services assembly, etc.), while n-tier architectures deal with splitting up processing into physical functional units (e.g., database processing on its own server). If someone tells you a product is a three-tier system, this automatically lets you know that this system implementation requires three physical/virtual servers. A three-layer system, on the other hand, can be all on one server or multiple servers.

The problem with n-tier architectures is that they scale very well on the server side but not on the client. The theory with applications designed on traditional n-tier architectures is that they only need to scale on the server-processing side. This theory held up well until the client tier required the surfacing of more and more data.

Web 2.0 web sites started a trend of providing users with lots of social networking tools as well as collective intelligence data. No matter how well the back-end services scaled, it was not feasible to rebuild each page each time the page was refreshed for millions of users. The client tier became overloaded with data, and something needed to be done. As a result, Ajax techniques for background processing and rendering parts of the page that change became popular. This was a perceived improvement for the users as well because it put less stress on the main rendering thread of the web browser.

In the last several years, users started expecting more interactive applications with rich experiences. A user may want to analyze data, interact with it, and visually see it on a geographic map. In order to provide fast response times, application clients need to share some of the processing and caching responsibility locally.

CASE STUDY OF IMPROVING MYSPACE MESSAGING

MySpace is one of the biggest social networking web sites on the Internet. It allows users to submit information about themselves and share it with their friends or the entire world. The web site is highly interactive and provides large amounts of data you can share, such as photos, messages, music, and lists.

When a site on the Internet is massively successful, it needs to be able to continue to scale for growth. MySpace embraced Ajax techniques relatively quickly and started bringing enhanced user experiences to the client. However, this still meant that if a user wanted to see a new piece of data, a new request had to be submitted over the Web, processed on the server, and returned to the client. The fact that it was happening on a background process didn't really help.

MySpace decided to test its local processing components to help alleviate bandwidth and server processing problems. One of the components that MySpace decided to try moving over in 2008 was messaging. They used an open source project called SQLite (www.sqlite.org), which is a client assembly that provides SQL database functionality. Using this client database, MySpace was able to cache messages on the client locally. This reduced server requests dramatically and sped up client response times. MySpace did not stop there. Having the data locally, they were also able to provide basic data manipulation algorithms directly on the cached information. Basic operations like sorting, filtering, and searching of the messages could all be done on the client and did not require expensive calls to the MySpace server tier. On such a massive social networking site like MySpace, there are tens of millions of avid users with thousands of messages. The impact on performance when a feature like this is implemented can be dramatic.

Scaling BI with the Client Tier

BI systems rely heavily on server horsepower and storage capacity to surface data on multiple levels. In the older days of DSS and BI 1.0, it was commonly accepted that if you had more users or larger data sets, you simply had to invest in a greater amount of servers. BI software vendors have traditionally used a similar message; with more users, there will be more server requests, and the customer will have to provide a corresponding number of virtual or physical servers.

In the past, BI software vendors required their customers to have stand-alone servers. With the advent of BI 2.0, customers expect BI software to be more performant, simple to install, and in some cases, share resources with other applications.

Software vendors who implement their solutions on stand-alone servers are faced with challenges of fixed hardware resources. Figure 3-4 shows the resources being used on a fictitious BI server. In this example, the total amount of resources used at peak times is 75 percent. A BI software vendor should be very wary of adding additional features to that server, as it may start running dangerously close to the maximum amount of computing resources provided. This poses secondary problems like not being able to fulfill maintenance agreements, provide software upgrades with additional features, or fulfill custom enhancements for clients.

- Remaining Resources for Scalability — 25%

- Database Storage
- Database Processing
- Business Logic
- Handling Client Requests
- Memory Resources
- Caching, Logging — 75%

Figure 3-4. *Resources used on a sample BI server*

One way to free up additional resources on the server tier is to move some of the processing to the client tier. Moving some system processing to the client workstation is not a new idea. However, this concept has not been popular with BI for two main reasons: horsepower of client workstations and the thin client.

In the early days of BI systems, desktop applications were the presentation layer of choice. It would seem natural that these applications would have had some client processing. This was true in limited scope because computers in the late '90s were simply not what they are now. The workstations over a decade ago had a small fraction of the speed they do now in terms of raw computing resources (e.g., CPU, graphics, and RAM).

Another reason we haven't seen BI systems move some of the processing to the presentation layer is the recent popularity of thin clients. As software vendors wanted to deliver their content to more users, they started leveraging the Internet platform. The web browsers simply could not provide the same access to computing resources as a desktop could. As mentioned, Web 2.0 started to change that with frameworks speeding up JavaScript execution and local SQL databases used for caching.

The governing practice of architecture is to avoid unnecessary "preoptimization." Many systems, including the biggest systems/sites on the Web (e.g., MySpace and Facebook), follow this principle. However, as systems scale to more users, architects may need to revisit certain parts of the system. If we need to optimize our system, which types of processes can be moved to the local tier on the client?

Crossing tier boundaries is expensive no matter what messaging architecture you are employing. Messages between client and service tiers need to have a valid structure, their data needs to be deserialized/serialized for transport, they need security or a signature applied, and they need to be transformed into packets across the network. Each message starts to chip away at the available system resources, even if it is simple. Table 3-1 breaks down the different types of processing that can be placed on the client into two main areas: light business logic and cacheable items.

Table 3-1. Attributes of Client Processing

Client Processing Type	Candidates
Light business logic	Simple sorting, filtering, grouping, and searching of local data structures
	Simple statistical algorithms
	Graphic visualizations and interactions (e.g., moving a slider)
	Algorithms on higher-level data aggregates (e.g., trend analysis, predictive analytics)
	Algorithms on data that has a known maximum (e.g., analytical calculations on all of the games in the 2009 baseball season)
	Simulations that combine rich animations and interactivity with calculations (e.g., physics simulation)
Cacheable items	Data fetched on landing pages
	Data that does not change frequently
	Pre-fetching data in a paging solution (e.g., read-ahead caching)
	Data that is used in memento recovery patterns (e.g., undo)

The first step to distributing logic to the client tier is to isolate messages that are good candidates for processing on the presentation layer. This can be done by profiling your BI systems to find out what service calls can be eliminated or mitigated through client improvements. For example, if you find that users are interacting with a data grid heavily on your system, it might be a good idea to see if sorting/filtering grid operations can be moved to local processing. Another example of distributing logic to the client tier might be to cache data on a landing page for the user for minutes or even days (depending how often your BI data warehouse refreshes). Figure 3-5 shows how moving basic processing to the client can reduce the strain on a BI system. This allows for more features to be added to existing systems while giving the users increased interactivity.

Figure 3-5. Scaling processing to the client

Is Business Intelligence on the client viable?

If you are an experienced business intelligence professional, you might question the validity of implementing client distributed architecture on a workstation. Even most business intelligence professionals assume that you need very powerful servers to process large amounts of data and do all of the calculations on the server. This is a valid architecture for BI 1.0 scenarios. However, having all of the calculations reside server-side the user interface of the business intelligence modules will suffer from some latency when transferring the data locally to the user. Therefore, usually you will be unable to provide real-time visual intelligence only relying on the server. Business Intelligence data service endpoints would have to be configured in several different conventions in order to take advantage of these scenarios. For example, data services can be configured for: streaming a lot of data, transactional, bulk processing, calculating KPIs on the fly. However, rarely do you see service orientation done on the server level that allows all the different business intelligence scenarios. This is where distributed client side architecture comes in.

Microsoft and other business intelligence vendors have leveraged the evolution in hardware and software architectures and are able to provide business intelligence locally on the workstation. Improvements like being able to take advantage of: 64-bit architectures, increased access to more RAM, columnar data structures, rapid in-memory access, GPU acceleration, local storage and multi-core processors on workstations now makes it easier to surface business intelligence data.

In the next sub sections, I list several examples of business intelligence tools that take advantage of new architectural conventions to deliver business intelligence on the client.

Microsoft Excel

The first obvious comparison of a client-side business intelligence tool is Microsoft Excel. Excel is essentially spreadsheet software that can be extended to surface business intelligence data in the form of grids, charting visualizations, predictive models, Excel dashboards. Since the 2003 version, Microsoft Excel has been adding more and more tools that can be used for business intelligence.

Some of the business intelligence features found in Microsoft Excel are:

- *Pivot Tables*: Pivot tables allow analysts to create spreadsheets that include powerful multi-dimensional analysis capabilities

- *Charting Visualizations*: Microsoft Excel provides a large number or charting options to visualize the data and deliver the exact insight. Excel 2007 improved on the data visualizations and included word-sized progress bars.

- *What-If Analysis*: In Excel basic predictive analytics are possible using several different add-ins

- *Slicers (new in Excel 2010)*: Slicers are a new control that allows you to filter your data in easy and interactive manners. Slicers are an improvement over other filtering mechanisms, because they allow you to see quickly where you are in your analysis and provide multi-selection

- *Sparklines (new in Excel 2010)*: Sparklines allow business intelligence analysts to increase the amount of the data they are surfacing to the end user without sacrificing complexity. Figure 3-6 below shows the new addition of sparklines to the Excel 2010 ribbon

Figure 3-6. Excel 2010 includes two new visualization features: sparklines and slicers

As you can see Excel 2010 has evolved over the years a quite capable tool to surface business intelligence data. One of the questions that you may be asking yourself, why not just deliver business intelligence via Excel? This is actually a very common scenario to create very powerful spread sheets that include aggregate data in Excel. However, Excel has the limitation of being quite a complex tool to use. It is simply not a self-service business intelligence 2.0 tool. It can be simply summarized by asking a single question: Would you trust that your "single version of truth" has been delivered 100% correctly when an analyst created a complex spread sheet from scratch? (Figure 3-7) As you can probably guess with an "open" tool like Excel the data can lose its meaning, or worse provide completely incorrect insight.

Figure 3-7. *Excel can create powerful business intelligence dashboards. However, there is a risk that the data could contain errors.*

PowerPivot for Microsoft Excel 2010

PowerPivot (codename Gemini) is an add-in for Microsoft Excel 2010 that has been released in the SQL Server 2008 R2 timeframe. The tool's main goal is to overcome three main challenges of delivering business intelligence with traditional Excel: scaling to millions of records, ensuring the "single version of truth" is delivered and making the consumption of data analysis simpler. Many business intelligence professionals are really excited about PowerPivot and what it can provide for client-side business intelligence.

One of the key features is that PowerPivot scales to an enormous amount of data on the client. There are many demos online showing PowerPivot easily surfacing 3-15 million records in a worksheet. More importantly, the data is able to be filtered, sliced, pivoted, calculated-on very rapidly in real-time.

In the previous section (Figure 3-7) I highlighted how an analyst using Excel could potentially surface incorrect data from the "single version of truth" data stores. PowerPivot provides a data synchronization tool that brings down the data in read-only mode into the Excel spread sheet. It is not failsafe, however when a user is using PowerPivot as a data source they cannot manipulate the data.

PowerPivot uses the following client-side architecture features:

- *In-memory storage*: Loading the data into memory for aggregations and analysis is much faster than reading off of a disk drive. Even the fastest disk drives are up to 50x slower than accessing RAM directly.

- *64-bit architecture*: PowerPivot can load millions of rows into memory, because it can access more than 4 GIG of RAM. A 64-bit operating system and 64-bit version of Windows are required.

- *Optimized data structures*: Frequently data warehouses are converted from transactional data bases. While they may deformalize or flatten the data for optimal retrieval, frequently they are not converted to optimal data structures for analysis. When data comes into PowerPivot it converted into columnar data structures which optimize it for business intelligence analysis.

- *Local Storage:* How can you store so much data efficiently in a spread sheet? After the spread sheet is saved, the data is compressed using zip into the Excel file. This reduces the size of the file up to 8x.

PowerPivot allows users to access the data "offline" for analysis. If you have used Analysis Services cubes or Reporting Services, you need to be connected to the respective server. However, with PowerPivot you can analyze the data with just Excel from an airport or a remote location without the Internet.

PowerPivot is not a UI tool. It is essentially an optimized OLAP client-side data store. Therefore, you are still using native Excel features to surface the data in a visual manner as shown in Figure 3-8.

Figure 3-8. An Excel grid, slicers, charts and sparklines surfacing data from PowerPivot.

■ **Note** For more information on PowerPivot and to download the add-in for Microsoft Excel 2010 go to
`www.powerpivot.com`.

Pivot for Silverlight

In the summer of 2010, Microsoft released a visual intelligence tool called Pivot. Pivot is a control for Silverlight 4 that allows self-service analysis using visual gestures on data collections. Pivot for Silverlight is the quintessential self-service tool. The tool has limited analytical capabilities: simple search, sorting, dimensional filtering, timeframe filtering using sliders, two simple views etc. What makes this perfect is that the tool is simple to learn very quickly and does not overburden the end-user with many complex business intelligence features.

The most attractive feature is that Pivot uses visual dialogs to convey additional information about the data. In Figure 3-9, we can see the Silverlight Pivot control analyzing a data collection of Sports Illustrated covers.

Pivot for Silverlight uses the following client-side architecture features:

- *In-memory storage:* Loading the data into memory for aggregations and analysis is much faster than reading off of a disk drive. Even the fastest disk drives are up to 50x slower than accessing RAM directly.

- *GPU acceleration:* The visual animations, transitions and rendering is offloaded to the GPU in order to free up processing time on the CPU for increased analytical power.

- *Multi-touch gestures:* The ability to use fluent gestures to filter data, pan the visual dialogs and zoom in and out using hand gestures is all possible because of Silverlight client features

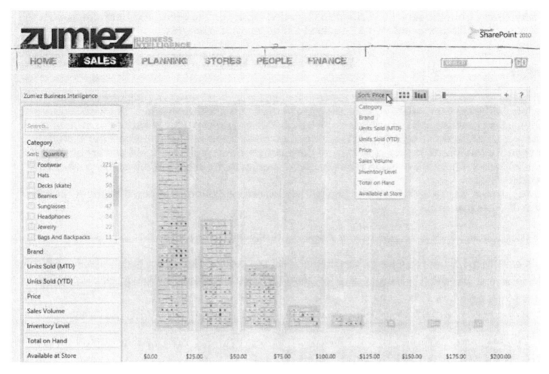

Figure 3-9. Pivot for Silverlight can provide self-service visual analysis features normally found in complex business intelligence tools.

■ **Note** Pivot for Silverlight will be discussed further in Chapter 14. For more information go to www.getpivot.com/silverlight.

Disconnected MOLAP

MOLAP is an acronym for Multidimensional Online Analytical Processing. It is a storage and processing architecture that is alternative to ROLAP (Relational Online Analytical Processing) or HOLAP (Hybrid Online Analytical Processing). In MOLAP all the leaf level data and aggregations are located in a data store and this allows for very fast data retrieval for analysis.

Disconnected MOLAP is an architecture that does not rely on a server to be present in order for the MOLAP data to be consumed by client software. If you are familiar with Analysis Services 2005 or 2008 this is analogous to local cubes. This architecture is also used by IBM Cognos PowerPlay Series 7 and 8. This allows client software to perform all of the calculations locally on the user's workstation without overburdening the server.

If you go back to Figure 3-4 and 3-5, you can see why this type of architecture is very advantageous if you have powerful local clients that can handle analysis locally. Therefore RAM, CPU, disk I/O resources are not taken away from the server and can be all handled locally on the client. Furthermore, similar to PowerPivot or Excel disconnected MOLAP enabled offline analysis scenarios.

Summary

I hope you can see via the examples listed above that client-side distributed architecture is not only possible, but being implemented by large enterprise business intelligence vendors. The same concepts, conventions, best practices can be utilized by Silverlight! Silverlight can take advantage of in-memory data structures, multi-core processing, GPU acceleration and advanced data structures in F# or C#. In the Pivot control for Silverlight, you saw some of these conventions applied in a self-service business intelligence 2.0 tool. There is no reason why Silverlight should not be able to mimic a very performant client resident BI tool.

As you proceed further into this book, you will see numerous examples of how Silverlight can take advantage of these features.

■ **Note** As of version 4, Silverlight does not support the 64-bit architecture. The hope is that this feature will come in a future version of Silverlight. This would allow Silverlight to access a very large amount of data in-memory limited only by the RAM.

Business Logic on the Silverlight Client

You already know by now that Silverlight favors local execution on the client workstation or device. Many web developers since the advent of Web 2.0 have seen the power of executing code locally. JavaScript and other frameworks based on it (e.g., jQuery) allowed for web applications to become more responsive by moving some of the user interactions locally.

Silverlight can improve on this concept dramatically. Silverlight is built on a subset of the .NET Framework which runs compiled code very efficiently. This makes executing code much faster than JavaScript. If JavaScript could power basic Ajax interactions, imagine what Silverlight can do.

BI is about manipulating, analyzing, and visualizing data sets. Silverlight provides a variety of features that specialize in this area. Following are some features of Silverlight that allow for local processing of data into meaningful insight for users.

First-Class Data Structures and Querying

The Silverlight .NET runtime exposes many first-class data structures that can aid you in designing your BI solution. Developers have the ability to use a multitude of different data structures and tailor them to specific operations like searching or aggregation. This enhances the performance of local operations. Furthermore, the use of generics allows custom data structures to be reused with different types while remaining performant.

These data structures can then be filtered, searched, grouped, and aggregated in many complex different ways using a SQL-like language called LINQ (Language-Integrated Query). Data manipulation of objects in memory is surprisingly fast using LINQ. No other RIA client comes close to providing similar features.

Local Access to the DOM

When Silverlight is hosted on a web page, it can manipulate the DOM (document object model). This allows a developer to interact with the local JavaScript implementation or manipulate the HTML layout directly. This can be done locally without any postbacks or roundtrips to the server.

Local APIs to the DOM allow for interesting integration scenarios, as you will see Chapter 11. For example, communication between two interactive Silverlight web parts can be implemented via the Silverlight HTML bridge.

Isolated Storage

Silverlight includes a local storage mechanism called *isolated storage*. This mechanism can persist any kind of serializable data locally. The amount of space available for localized storage is theoretically unlimited (maximum value of the long data type). The developer can store very large amounts of data to the user's workstation. There is no theoretical limit to the amount of data that can be persisted locally.

■ **Note** Additional third party frameworks exist that provide an abstracted data base layer on top of Isolated Storage to create "local databases". This allows for more advanced caching and offline scenarios. Furthermore, these databases provide additional features such as encrypting data and syncing with data services. An example of a Silverlight embedded database is Perst offered by McObject. More information can be found at www.mcobject.com.

Multithreading

Computational processing or business algorithms can be scaled across local workstation processor cores using Silverlight's multithreading features. Silverlight's multithreading capabilities are not as robust as the full .NET Framework; however, some operations can be scaled well over a factor of 100 percent if done correctly.

■ **Note** Chapter 10 is dedicated to concurrent programming and it covers the topic in great detail.

Open and Save Dialogs

Silverlight runs in a partial trust sandbox. Therefore, it cannot directly access local computer resources and do anything malicious without the user agreeing first. Silverlight does include Open and Save dialogs to either load content from local storage or save content to local storage. This allows for scenarios like rendering a report locally and saving it to the user's hard drive. Another popular BI scenario is to save an Excel spreadsheet export of the data being presented in the UI.

Visual Intelligence

Silverlight allows for data to presented in a variety of ways. However, for BI applications, you may want to supplement grids and lists with a more eye-friendly presentation. This allows average users (BI 2.0 consumers) to leverage data visualizations to derive analytical insight. Silverlight can be extended with the Silverlight Control Toolkit which contains many types of data visualizations (charts, tree maps, etc.).

The most important aspect of this is that the transitions between the visualizations are all done on the client. Conversely, if you drag and drop an ASP.NET chart, by default its behavior is going to require a render request on the server. This allows Silverlight visualizations to seamlessly interact with an RIA environment and quickly respond to user interactions. The ASP.NET chart can be extended with JavaScript or Ajax techniques to respond to end user interactions in real time. However, with Silverlight, this is native to the technology, and no Ajax-like extensions or wrappers are necessary.

OData Support

OData is an acronym for the Open Data Protocol used for exposing data over the web. Microsoft has started to implement these conventions in the OData protocol across a wide variety of their enterprise applications. The services and lists in SharePoint 2010 all utilize the OData protocol. The new PowerPivot add-in for Excel 2010 can consume OData as well. In fact, even the data sources in Reporting Services 2008 R2 can be consumed as OData.

OData support in WCF RIA Services is fantastic for exposing your business intelligence data over an open protocol that can be consumed by a variety of clients. Utilizing WCF RIA Services, you can easily create OData endpoints with a simple checkbox. As mentioned above, this is not just for Silverlight! OData endpoints allow you to consume your business intelligence data in SharePoint 2010, PowerPivot, ASP.NET, SQL Server 2008 R2. You can also use the OData protocol to consume data from non-Microsoft platforms and data providers such as IBM WebSphere, Palm Web OS, PHP etc.,

The OData conventions allow Silverlight to further manipulate the data using LINQ. In my book, I talk about how this pattern allows you to distribute some of the processing onto the Silverlight client rather than always having to rely on the services having the data exactly how the client expects it. This pattern works exceptionally well when creating rich business intelligence visualizations that require data to be pivoted, aggregated, and/or filtered in a variety of ways.

COM Automation Support

Silverlight 4 has evolved out of the browser support introduced in Silverlight 3. In an elevated trust scenario, you can take full advantage of the COM providers installed on the client workstation.

COM automation has excellent potential for integration with business intelligence enterprise applications. For example, you could take Excel dashboard spreadsheets or Excel PowerPivot files and provide a simpler/richer experience in Silverlight. Silverlight COM automation can also be used to extend existing business intelligence applications. For example, IBM Cognos Transformer & PowerPlay can be dramatically enhanced in Silverlight with COM automation. Why would you want to do this? If you have worked with large-scale business intelligence vendors, you will note how they are slow to evolve some of their tools. This is where Silverlight can inject business intelligence 2.0 concepts such as self-service analytics or data visualizations to the existing tools.

Printing Support

Prior to version 4, Silverlight did not support unformatted printing. Unformatted printing is essentially rendering the screen directly to the printer without having to do any special translation. Prior to Silverlight 4, if you wanted to print a chart or data from a grid, you had to translate it to an HTML control/grid. Silverlight 4 now supports unformatted printing.

This is big for business intelligence because of the rich dashboards, grids and data visualizations for obvious reasons. For example, a rich dashboard using sparklines, bullet graphs and KPIs that is ready to be printed in Silverlight 4 without having to sacrifice any of the UI or provide a formatted printing option.

F# Language Support

Silverlight 4 now runs under the Visual Studio 2010 development environment. This move has brought formal F# support to Silverlight 4. Do we need another language? Isn't F# just another choice between VB.NET or C#? The short answer is absolutely not. F# is a new functional programming language that runs on the .NET 4.0 CLR. C# is an object-oriented language and it can be used to build first-class applications. However, the recent trend in programming languages has been to use a more declarative style that is much easier to understand. This declarative style is best seen in language features such as LINQ.

Functional languages have some advantages over traditional scripting or object-oriented languages. For example, immutable data structures are great for read-only business intelligence data. Furthermore, this allows you to parallelize your data manipulation tasks. Utilizing F# assemblies for your data manipulation or business rules engine allows you to push more data on the Silverlight client. Therefore, you can take advantage of the client-side data manipulation and not always have to rely on every calculation or KPI to be in your business intelligence data stores.

Improvements to Expression Blend 4

Expression Blend 4 includes a new feature called the PathListBox. This allows you to create lists with items that follow along a path. Not only does this allow you to create static lists in creative patterns, but it also allows you to extend this functionality with Silverlight's rich animation framework. This seemingly small enhancement allows you to create immersive data visualizations that bring out the data's environment.

Expression Blend 4 includes a new Shapes section that provides the ability to create basic shapes like circles, arcs, triangles etc. that can be animated and styled. Why is this important for business intelligence? As you will see in further chapters these new shapes reduce the work that needs to be done in creating word-sized KPIs or creating push-pins for Bing Maps. Figure 3-10 shows off the available Shapes in the Expression Blend 4 asset manager.

■ **Note** The data visualization chapters will include a couple examples on how to leverage the new shapes controls for business intelligence scenarios.

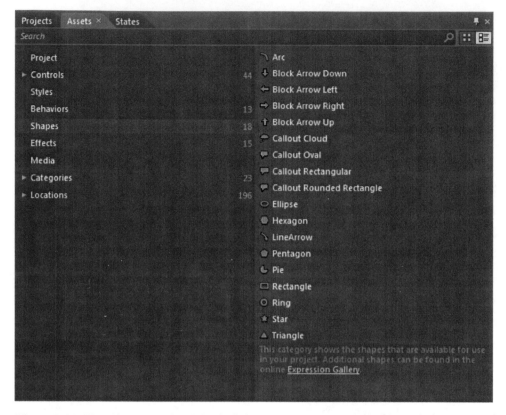

Figure 3-10. New Shapes section is included in the Expression Blend 4 asset manager.

■ **Warning** Starting from this point, the book will start to include coding scenarios. Please refer to the Introduction to ensure you have the proper tools installed if you want to follow along with the coding scenarios. The live demos of these exercises are provided on the accompanying web site at www.silverlightbusinessintelligence.com. While the coding scenarios are designed to be step by step, prior knowledge of Silverlight, C#, and .NET coding fundamentals is assumed. If you are not comfortable working with Silverlight or .NET, please use the accompanying web site to aid you in your understanding of the topics.

Common Scenarios Handled with Silverlight

By now, you have read through more than two chapters of information and theory. It is time to start applying BI 2.0 concepts to Silverlight code.

In order to be a worthy client for BI, the technology must be able to work with data effectively. To prove that it can, in this section we will challenge Silverlight with some common business data scenarios.

The scenarios are broken up into three parts: working with business data, local storage of data, and transferring data with the user. The focus on these exercises is the back-end computational processes rather than the front-end UI. Even though we are going to be building a basic UI, it will just be a vehicle to show off the computational processing.

Coding Scenario: Working with Business Data

In this scenario, we will show how Silverlight can interact with business data calculations. We will challenge Silverlight to work with a large amount of data and see how the technology holds up under pressure.

Following are the goals of this scenario:

- Understanding that Silverlight can work with very large data sets locally

- Gaining insight on how data can be manipulated quickly using LINQ locally

- Seeing how we can decouple business logic and reuse it in other locations

---

■ **Note** A live demo of this coding scenario can be found on the companion site at www. silverlightbusinessintelligence.com/Demos/SilvelightBIClient/WorkingWithBusinessData/ WorkingWithBusinessData.html.

Querying Large Data Sets with LINQ

In this step-by-step exercise, we are going to aggregate some data to perform analysis on a large data set of people. We are going to create a large data set of 1 million Person objects as our sample data. They will be our data sample for analysis. The analysis we are going to perform is going to center around the body mass index (BMI) scale.

■ **Note** The BMI scale is a measure and classification of a person's body type. The calculation uses the person's height and weight as the main input attributes for calculating this information. For more information on the BMI measurements, see http://en.wikipedia.org/wiki/Body_mass_index.

Using local processing only, we are going to show how LINQ can be used to query data very quickly. In a complete BI application, you will have data coming from a data service. However, the same concepts apply directly to those scenarios. Therefore, instead of generating the data locally, you would call a service instead.

■ **Note** LINQ is a feature that was added in .NET 3.5 and is supported by Silverlight. See
`http://msdn.microsoft.com/en-us/netframework/aa904594.aspx` for more information on this technology.

Let's begin the coding scenario:

1. Open Visual Studio 2010 and create a new Silverlight Application project called Chapter3_WorkingWithBusinessData. Click OK to allow the project to be hosted on an ASP.NET site. Ensure that Silverlight 4 is selected as the Silverlight version.

2. Once the project is created, you should see an empty canvas. We are going to add some UI content to build out our test harness for this scenario. The UI content will consist of the following content:

   • We are going to add a Generate Data button that will generate 1 million `Person` records for us.

   • We will also have a Perform Analysis button that will analyze this data. This button will kick off a calculation to find the minimum, maximum, and average BMI among the sample data. It will also calculate a count of people who are considered obese by the BMI measurement.

   • Below the Perform Analysis button, we will have a set of labels to display the findings.

   • Lastly, we will have a label with a timer to show how long it took to execute this code (in milliseconds).

3. Let's start building the UI. In your Silverlight project, add a reference to the `System.Windows.Controls.Data.Input.dll` assembly.

4. Add the code shown in bold in Listing 3-1 to your `MainPage.xaml` (or whatever your default XAML page is). Note the two sections in bold (the `Controls` namespace and the StackPanel content). The StackPanel element replaces the Grid element. Make sure you place your code as shown in Listing 3-1.

Listing 3-1. XAML for the BMI control layout (new code is highlighted in bold)

```
<UserControl
  xmlns="http://schemas.microsoft.com/winfx/2006/xaml/presentation"
  xmlns:x="http://schemas.microsoft.com/winfx/2006/xaml"
  xmlns:d="http://schemas.microsoft.com/expression/blend/2008"
  xmlns:mc="http://schemas.openxmlformats.org/markup-compatibility/2006"
  xmlns:dataInput="clr-namespace:System.Windows.Controls;assembly↵
=System.Windows.Controls.Data.Input"
  x:Class="Chapter3_WorkingWithBusinessData.MainPage"
  Width="400" Height="300">
    <StackPanel x:Name="LayoutRoot" Background="White">
      <Button x:Name="btnGenerateData" Margin="0,0,0,10" Content="Generate Data"/>
      <Button x:Name="btnPerformAnalysis" Content="Perform Analysis" Margin="0,0,0,10"/>
```

```xml
      <StackPanel Height="200">
        <StackPanel Height="25" Orientation="Horizontal">
          <dataInput:Label Content="BMI Minimum:" Width="150" HorizontalAlignment="Right"/>
          <dataInput:Label x:Name="bmiMinimum" HorizontalAlignment="Right"
      Width="50" Content="0" Margin="5,0,0,0"/>
        </StackPanel>
        <StackPanel Height="25" Orientation="Horizontal">
          <dataInput:Label HorizontalAlignment="Right" Width="150" Content="BMI Maximum:"/>
          <dataInput:Label x:Name="bmiMaximum" HorizontalAlignment="Right"
      Width="50" Content="0" Margin="5,0,0,0"/>
        </StackPanel>
        <StackPanel Height="25" Orientation="Horizontal">
          <dataInput:Label HorizontalAlignment="Right" Width="150" Content="BMI Average:"/>
          <dataInput:Label x:Name="bmiAverage" HorizontalAlignment="Right"
      Width="50" Content="0" Margin="5,0,0,0"/>
        </StackPanel>
        <StackPanel Height="25" Orientation="Horizontal">
          <dataInput:Label HorizontalAlignment="Right" Width="150" Content⤶
="Count with obese BMI:"/>
          <dataInput:Label x:Name="bmiObeseCount" HorizontalAlignment="Right"
      Width="50" Content="0" Margin="5,0,0,0"/>
        </StackPanel>
        <StackPanel Height="25" Orientation="Horizontal">
          <dataInput:Label HorizontalAlignment="Right" Width="150" Content⤶
="Peformed Analysis In:" FontWeight="Bold"/>
          <dataInput:Label x:Name="performedAnalysisIn" HorizontalAlignment="Right"
      Width="50" Content="0" Margin="5,0,0,0"/>
        </StackPanel>
      </StackPanel>
    </StackPanel>
</UserControl>
```

5. After adding the code, your project should look like Figure 3-11. The figure shows the XAML and the UI in Visual Studio 2010. At this point, perform a "sanity check" and make sure your project builds. You can try running it (If you get a warning about debugging, just click OK), and you should see something similar to the screen we were designing.

■ **Note** If you receive an error at this point stating that there is already a LayoutRoot present, you probably copied the StackPanel element into the Grid. This can cause the code-behind and the XAML UI to be out of sync. If this happens, just restart the exercise.

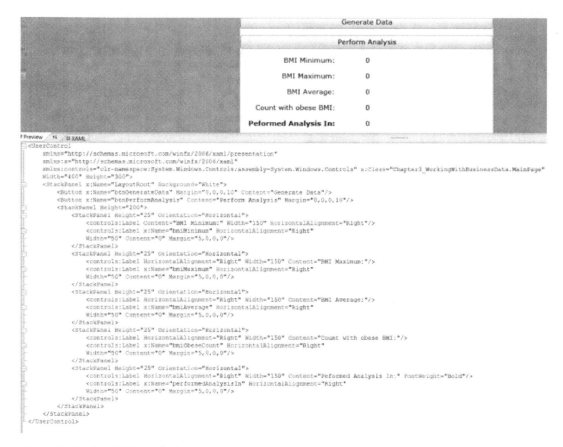

Figure 3-11. Our BMI analysis canvas

6. Now it is time to generate a class that is going to hold the actual data we are going to be working with. In Visual Studio 2010, right-click the Silverlight project, select Add, and then select New Item. Select Class from the Visual Studio templates. Name the class file `Person.cs`. Next, click the Add button to add it to the project.

■ **Note** Ensure that you did not add the class to the Web project by accident.

---

7. Add three integer properties to the class called ID, Weight, and Height. Your `Person.cs` file should look as shown in Listing 3-2.

Listing 3-2. Person C# class

```
public class Person
  {
    public int ID { get; set; }
    public int Weight { get; set; }
    public int Height { get; set; }
  }
```

8. In the next step, let's add our event handlers to the buttons so that when they are clicked, an action can be performed. This can be done several ways. I am just going to show you the easiest way. In Visual Studio 2010, navigate your cursor to the first Button element, type in **Click**, press Enter, and then select <new event handler> from the list. Figure 3-12 illustrates how to perform this. Repeat this step for the second button. Your XAML for the buttons should look like Listing 3-3.

Listing 3-3. XAML for the buttons (new code is highlighted in bold)

```
        <Button x:Name="btnGenerateData" Margin="0,0,0,10" Content="Generate Data" ↵
Click="btnGenerateData_Click"/>
        <Button x:Name="btnPerformAnalysis" Content="Perform Analysis" Margin="0,0,0,10" ↵
Click="btnPerformAnalysis_Click"/>
```

```
<StackPanel x:Name="LayoutRoot" Background="White">
    <Button x:Name="btnGenerateData" Margin="0,0,0,10" Content="Generate Data" Click=""/>
    <Button x:Name="btnPerformAnalysis" Content="Perform Analysis" Margin="0,0,0,10
    <StackPanel Height="200">
```

Figure 3-12. Adding a click event handler to the button

9. At this point, ensure that your project builds. Now we will add the logic that will generate the million-row sample data for us.

    *   In the MainPage.xaml.cs file, add a new collection field called people and initialize it like so: List<Person> people = new List<Person>();.

    *   We are going to generate 1 million records. We also want to randomize the data. To keep things simple (and somewhat accurate), I kept the height of the people between 5 and 7 feet and their weight between 85 and 320 pounds. Change the btnGenerateData_Click event handler to generate our data algorithm, as shown in Listing 3-4.

Listing 3-4. C# code to generate fake data (new changes in this step are highlighted in bold)

```
 public partial class MainPage : UserControl
 {
    // create a list that will hold the person items
    List<Person> people = new List<Person>();

    public MainPage()
    {
```

```
    InitializeComponent();
}

private void btnGenerateData_Click(object sender, RoutedEventArgs e)
{
  // clear the list
  this.people.Clear();

  // iterate through list and add Person objects
  for (int i = 0; i != 1000000; i++)
  {
    Random randWeight = new Random(DateTime.Now.Millisecond);
    int weight = randWeight.Next(85, 320);

    Random randHeight = new Random(DateTime.Now.Second * 100 + DateTime.Now.Millisecond);
    int height = randHeight.Next(5, 8);

    Person person = new Person
    {
      ID = i + 1,
      Weight = weight,
      Height = height
    };

    people.Add(person);
  }

  // show message when processing is complete
  this.btnGenerateData.Content = "Data Generated. Click again to regenerate.";
}
```

...

- After adding the algorithm, run the application and click the Generate Data button. It could take several seconds depending on the speed of your machine. Your button's text will change to "Data Generated…" once it is complete, and you will then have an in-memory data set you can use for analysis.

10. Now it's time to add some LINQ logic to perform some analysis calculations on our data. Add the bold code from Listing 3-5 inside your btnPerformAnalysis_Click event handler. The following bullet points describe what this code accomplishes:

    - We add a timer that will start recording when we click the Perform Analysis button.

    - Next, we create an iterator that holds a query with the BMI calculation for every person in our list. The BMI calculation is = weight*4.88/height^2 (This calculation provides us with a number that we can use to classify the different body types).

- Next, we calculate the minimum, maximum, and average BMI.

- Then we calculate the count of people defined with an obese BMI (> 30).

- Then we set the labels and calculate how long it took us to do this.

Listing 3-5. C# code that will perform the computational analysis

```
private void btnPerformAnalysis_Click(object sender, RoutedEventArgs e)
{
  // start the timer
  DateTime dateStart = DateTime.Now;

  // generate people iterator with BMI calculation
  var peoplewithBMI = (
  from p in people
  select new { ID = p.ID, BMI = p.Weight * 4.88 / (p.Height * p.Height) }
  );

  // calculate the min, max, and average BMIs
  var minBMI = peoplewithBMI.Min(a => a.BMI);
  var maxBMI = peoplewithBMI.Max(a => a.BMI);
  var averageBMI = peoplewithBMI.Average(a => a.BMI);

  // calculate the count of people who are considered obese (BMI > 30)
  var countOfPeopleWithObeseBMI = peoplewithBMI.Count(a => a.BMI > 30);

  // round and set the appropriate labels on the controls
  this.bmiMinimum.Content = Math.Round(minBMI, 2).ToString();
  this.bmiMaximum.Content = Math.Round(maxBMI, 2).ToString();
  this.bmiAverage.Content = Math.Round(averageBMI, 2).ToString();
  this.bmiObeseCount.Content = countOfPeopleWithObeseBMI.ToString();

  // calculate the length of analysis time and set it
  this. performedAnalysisIn.Content = DateTime.Now.Subtract(dateStart)↵
.Milliseconds.ToString() + " ms";
}
```

11. Let's run our application and see what is happening. Figure 3-13 shows the application in a state after it has generated the data and after we have clicked the Perform Analysis button and it has populated the labels for us.

Data Generated. Click again to regenerate.
Perform Analysis

BMI Minimum:	8.47
BMI Maximum:	62.27
BMI Average:	28.98
Count with obese BMI:	399975
Analysis Peformed In:	668

Figure 3-13. Our BMI analysis application at work

Lessons Learned

We just completed the first coding scenario in this book. This should give you a small taste of how you can apply a BI concept using Silverlight features and stay 100 percent in the Silverlight client. This coding scenario amplified that Silverlight can be used as a client in client distributed architecture.

This scenario proves that Silverlight is quite capable of running large data sets on the client device and doing heavy data calculations as well. We showed how a list consisting of 1 million people can have multiple calculations and aggregates performed on it in sub second time. More importantly, we were able to do this with not much code at all using LINQ. On my workstation (a dual 2.67GHz machine), I was able to perform those five separate calculations on 1 million records in about 680 milliseconds. This is very impressive performance when you realize what is going on in the system. More importantly, this proves that data processing doesn't have to be done on the server now and can be distributed to the client workstations.

■ **Note** We could have implemented this code more quickly by using simple loops. This would have bypassed an insignificant amount of overhead when using LINQ. However, there is a balance between performance and code brevity. The algorithms we were able to perform were all one line of code! Imagine if the code gets more complex. We could have also done the aggregates all in one pass of the data and perhaps used additional threads to help. There is some further optimization that can be done with this logic. However, that is for a more advanced discussion that dives into more advanced and behind-the-scenes features of LINQ.

How useful is this kind of client processing? This type of optimization depends largely on your ability to deliver the raw data to the client and how the client interacts with it. This type of client-side processing works well if you have scenarios where BI users are getting large amounts of raw data and they perform heavy data manipulations or interact with it a great deal. In this chapter, we discussed the power of distributed architecture, and there are many scenarios like this that BI applications can take advantage of.

Realistically, anything you can do in a Excel spreadsheet, you should be able to mimic with a Silverlight RIA. As mentioned in this chapter, spreadsheets are great; however, they allow users to make mistakes easily by being completely open. Applying this to BI 2.0, you can see how you can provide local client algorithms and a specific UI that users can use to perform rapid analysis on the data.

■ **Note** In Chapter 10, you will see how you can speed this processing up dramatically further using concurrent programming techniques.

Coding Scenario: Decoupling Business Algorithms

This coding scenario aims to add more information to the information you got from the previous one. In this scenario, we will take the same large data set and see how we can inject the business calculations into the UI.

Following are the goals of this scenario:

- Understanding how to decouple business algorithms that need to be displayed in a UI

- Learning how to leverage Silverlight's data binding converters to apply business algorithms

- Seeing how decoupling the business algorithms can lead to testable code

Applying Business Logic with Data Binding and Value Converters

Let us take a look at what we accomplished in the previous coding scenario. Figure 3-14 shows our business logic directly living inside our code-behind file. Furthermore, we have explicitly set the values of the labels. So inside our business algorithm, we are also setting UI code. The code right now is coupled to the procedural UI logic, and we can improve upon this.

Figure 3-14. Our business logic living inside the code-behind file and setting UI object values

Silverlight has a powerful feature called *data binding* in which the data objects are exposed along with the presentation. This can be declaratively set in the XAML (UI markup code) or in the C# code. Furthermore, Silverlight extends data binding with a feature called *value converters*. These value converters can be used to convert the data into another form before it is bound and set into a UI object. For example, you can have a data set with a male gender attribute marked with a 1 or a 0. However, it wouldn't make sense to a user to see a 1 or a 0. The user would probably rather see the words *Yes* or *No*. Conversely, you wouldn't want to change your service or database model just to accommodate a single view in your application. This is exactly what value converters do.

In our coding scenario, we are going to take the data we created and bind the resultant aggregates to the UI controls. Figure 3-15 shows how the data is manipulated by the value converter and setting the UI controls. This is the pattern we will be implementing with the value converter.

Figure 3-15. Data binding our BMI data with a value converter

Let's begin this coding scenario:

1. This project will use the previous coding scenario. Create a copy of the previous Visual Studio project and place it in a folder called DecouplingBusinessAlgorithms. Once the project is copied, open up the solution file (Chapter3_WorkingWithBusinessData.sln) in Visual Studio.

2. At this point, you should have a working solution that has the same UI, Person class, and button that generates our Person data that we built in the previous coding scenario. Now let's add the value converter. This is the object in Figure 3-15 that is going to intercept the data and aggregate it into the format we need. Add a new class and call it BMIConverter.cs.

3. This class is going to handle the conversion and querying of our data. We need to add the following using statements at the top of our code, as shown in Listing 3-6.

Listing 3-6. using statements that need to be added at the top of the BMIConverter code file

```
using System.Windows.Data;
using System.Collections.Generic;
using System.Linq;
```

4. The value converter needs to be of type IValueConverter in order to be used during the data binding process. In order to do this, simply implement the IValueConverter interface. This is done by typing **: IValueConverter** after the class name, which is BMIConverter. Next, right-click the word IValueConverter and select Implement Interface. If you implement the interface properly, you should see the code with two empty methods, as shown in Listing 3-7.

Listing 3-7. Code you should see after implementing the IValueConverter interface

```
public class BMIConverter : IValueConverter
{

  #region IValueConverter Members

  public object Convert(object value, Type targetType, object parameter,↵
System.Globalization.CultureInfo culture)
  {
    throw new NotImplementedException();
  }

  public object ConvertBack(object value, Type targetType, object parameter,↵
System.Globalization.CultureInfo culture)
  {
    throw new NotImplementedException();
  }

  #endregion
}
```

5. The implementation of the interface provides us with two methods: Convert and ConvertBack. The Convert method is called when binding data to the UI object. Conversely, the ConvertBack method is called when the UI changes the information and the data needs to be updated. In our scenario, we have a one-way binding from the data to the UI object. Therefore, we are only going to be interested in working with the Convert method. The following bullet points describe what this method will do.

    •   The method will need to analyze the value parameter and ensure it is of type IEnumerable<Person> iterator. Essentially, the value parameter is going to have the data that we are going to aggregate.

    •   The parameter parameter can be optionally passed into the converter. This can tell the value converter how to process the data specifically. We are going to use this parameter to let the converter know whether it should aggregate the data using Min, Max, Average, or a count.

- We are not going to use the targetType or culture parameters in this method.

Update your Convert method with the bold code shown in Listing 3-8.

Listing 3-8. Logic that will perform the BMI calculations

```
public object Convert(object value, Type targetType, object parameter,↵
 System.Globalization.CultureInfo culture)
{
  // Stop processing if the value is not of type IEnumerable<Person>
  if ((value is IEnumerable<Person>) == false)
    return -1;

  // Calculate the BMI
  double aggregate = 0.0;
  IEnumerable<Person> people = value as IEnumerable<Person>;

  switch (parameter.ToString())
  {
    case "AVG":
      // aggregate the data finding the average BMI calculation
      aggregate = people.Average(p => p.Weight * 4.88 / (p.Height * p.Height));
      break;
    case "MIN":
      // aggregate the data finding the minimum BMI calculation
      aggregate = people.Min(p => p.Weight * 4.88 / (p.Height * p.Height));
      break;
    case "MAX":
      // aggregate the data finding the maximum BMI calculation
      aggregate = people.Max(p => p.Weight * 4.88 / (p.Height * p.Height));
      break;
    default:
      if (parameter.ToString().StartsWith("COUNT"))
      {
        // split the optional paramter and take the second item
        // this item will let us know what body type we are looking for
        string countType = parameter.ToString().Split(';')[1];

        switch (countType)
        {
          case "OBESE":
            // obese body type is BMI over 30
            aggregate = people.Count(p => p.Weight * 4.88 / (p.Height * p.Height) > 30);
            break;
          case "NORMAL":
            // normal body type is BMI between 18.5 and 25
            aggregate = people.Count(p => p.Weight * 4.88 / (p.Height * p.Height)
              >= 18.5 && p.Weight * 4.88 / (p.Height * p.Height) < 25);
            break;
          case "UNDERWEIGHT":
```

```
            // underweight body type is BMI is under 18.5
            aggregate = people.Count(p => p.Weight * 4.88 / (p.Height * p.Height) < 18.5);
            break;
        }
    }
    break;
}

// return rounded string value
return Math.Round(aggregate, 2).ToString();
}
```

That may seem like a lot of code, but it is actually pretty simple. In summary, we are going to receive the data in the parameter named value. In the parameter named parameter, we will receive an object telling us how to aggregate the data. The logic simply aggregates the data using average, maximum, or minimum aggregates. If we pass in a count parameter, we have to pass in an additional parameter to tell us what body type we are counting. Ensure your project builds at this point.

6. The logic in this class is finished. We now need to implement the Converter in our UI. Adding binding to UI data is done in XAML. First, we need to add the namespace in XAML where our converter is (In this example, I am simply calling it local). The other piece of code is to add this converter as a resource so we can use it with our XAML markup. Navigate to MainPage.xaml and in your user control element, add the code highlighted in bold in Listing 3-9.

Listing 3-9. Adding the BMIConverter in the XAML page (new code is highlighted in bold)

```
<UserControl
  x:Class="Chapter3_WorkingWithBusinessData.MainPage"
  xmlns="http://schemas.microsoft.com/winfx/2006/xaml/presentation"
  xmlns:x="http://schemas.microsoft.com/winfx/2006/xaml"
  xmlns:d="http://schemas.microsoft.com/expression/blend/2008"
  xmlns:mc="http://schemas.openxmlformats.org/markup-compatibility/2006"
  xmlns:dataInput="clr-namespace:System.Windows.Controls;assembly⏎
=System.Windows.Controls.Data.Input"
  xmlns:local="clr-namespace:Chapter3_WorkingWithBusinessData"
  Width="400" Height="300">
  <!-- User Control Resources -->
  <UserControl.Resources>
    <!-- BMIConverter resource -->
    <local:BMIConverter x:Key="BMIConverter" />
  </UserControl.Resources>
...
```

The namespace is aliased local because it aliases the local namespace of the project. (Chapter3_WorkingWithBusinessData is the name of our project and the namespace in the project). The user control resources element includes the custom resources we want to use in this project. Inside this code, we reference the BMIConverter type (the value converter class we defined in step 6) and we give it a key name of BMIConverter. For simplicity, I kept both of these names the same. Ensure your project builds at this point.

7. We are ready to use the converter in our binding. Remember that in the first coding scenario, we explicitly set the values of the UI controls after the BMI calculations were done. Using data binding converters, we are going to be able to abstract this in the Convert method. If you are not familiar with binding converters, Figure 3-16 breaks down the different attributes we are going to set in the binding. Arrow 1 shows that the local BMIConverter resource references the local namespace we added to the user control. Arrow 2 shows the BMIConverter being used in a binding context and referencing the converter defined in the user control references.

```
xmlns:local="clr-namespace:Chapter3_WorkingWithBusinessData"
  xmlns:x="ht    schemas.microsoft.com/winfx/2006/xaml"
  xmlns:          clr-
namesp        em.Windows.Controls;assembly=System.Windows.Controls"
Width="        eight="300">
  <Us  ontrol.Resources>
    <local: BMIConverter x:Key="BMIConverter" />
  </UserControl.Resources>
...
<StackPanel Height="25" Orientation="Horizon
    <controls:Label Content="BMI Minimum:"      "150"
HorizontalAlignment="Right"/>
    <controls:Label x:Name="bmiMinimum" Horizon   ignment="Right"
    Content="{Binding Converter={StaticResource BMIConverter},
ConverterParameter=MIN, Mode= OneWay}"
    Width="50" Margin="5,0,0,0"/>
  </StackPanel>
...
```

Figure 3-16. Binding converter working together with XAML

We are going to add this converter into our respective UI elements that require the aggregate calculation to be performed on the data set. In our main StackPanel (contains the labels for the BMI results), we are going to change the Content property of the labels to be bound to data and aggregated via our converter. After this, perform a build and ensure your code compiles and runs. The new Content property is highlighted in bold in Listing 3-10.

Listing 3-10. Adding the BMI converters to each label

```
<StackPanel Height="200">
  <StackPanel Height="25" Orientation="Horizontal">
    <dataInput:Label Content="BMI Minimum:" Width="150" HorizontalAlignment="Right"/>
    <dataInput:Label x:Name="bmiMinimum" HorizontalAlignment="Right"
```

```
Content="{Binding Converter={StaticResource BMIConverter }, ConverterParameter↵
=MIN, Mode=OneWay}"
Width="50" Margin="5,0,0,0"/>
  </StackPanel>
  <StackPanel Height="25" Orientation="Horizontal">
    <dataInput:Label HorizontalAlignment="Right" Width="150" Content="BMI Maximum:"/>
    <dataInput:Label x:Name="bmiMaximum" HorizontalAlignment="Right"
Content="{Binding Converter={StaticResource BMIConverter }, ConverterParameter↵
=MAX, Mode=OneWay}"
Width="50" Margin="5,0,0,0"/>
  </StackPanel>
  <StackPanel Height="25" Orientation="Horizontal">
    <dataInput:Label HorizontalAlignment="Right" Width="150" Content="BMI Average:"/>
    <dataInput:Label x:Name="bmiAverage" HorizontalAlignment="Right"
Content="{Binding Converter={StaticResource BMIConverter }, ConverterParameter↵
=AVG, Mode=OneWay}"
Width="50" Margin="5,0,0,0"/>
  </StackPanel>
  <StackPanel Height="25" Orientation="Horizontal">
    <dataInput:Label HorizontalAlignment="Right" Width="150" Content="Count with↵
 obese BMI:"/>
    <dataInput:Label x:Name="bmiObeseCount" HorizontalAlignment="Right"
Content="{Binding Converter={StaticResource BMIConverter }, ConverterParameter↵
=COUNT;OBESE, Mode=OneWay}"
Width="50" Margin-"5,0,0,0"/>
  </StackPanel>
  <StackPanel Height="25" Orientation="Horizontal">
    <dataInput:Label HorizontalAlignment="Right" Width="150" Content↵
="Peformed Analysis In:" FontWeight="Bold"/>
    <dataInput:Label x:Name="performedAnalysisIn" HorizontalAlignment="Right"
Width="50" Content="0" Margin="5,0,0,0"/>
  </StackPanel>
</StackPanel>
```

■ **Note** For additional information on the ValueConverter syntax and examples, please look at the MSDN library. For a basic example of IValueConverter use, see http://msdn.microsoft.com/en-us/library/system.windows.data.ivalueconverter(VS.95).aspx.

---

8. At this point, we have our UI completely formed the way we need it to display our BMI analysis. In step 10 of the previous exercise, we explicitly set the data properties in our UI. The point of this exercise is to let the XAML UI handle all of this. However, we still need to notify the UI where the initial data is coming from. This can be achieved by setting the DataContext property in our UI XAML tree to our list. This will, in effect, pass our list of people to the UI and allow the converter with the XAML parameters to set all of these aggregates automatically. In our btnPerformAnalysis_Click handler, replace the code with what is shown in bold in Listing 3-11. Notice there is no procedural code anymore, other than the code that sets the timer.

Listing 3-11. Adding the BMI converters to each label

```
private void btnPerformAnalysis_Click(object sender, RoutedEventArgs e)
{
  // start the timer
  DateTime dateStart = DateTime.Now;

  // reset the data context, if it has been set
  this.DataContext = null;
  // set the data context to our list of People
  this.DataContext = this.people;

  // calculate the length of analysis time and set it
  this.performedAnalysisIn.Content = DateTime.Now.Subtract(dateStart)↩
.Milliseconds.ToString() + " ms";
}
```

We are done adding code in this coding scenario. You should be able to compile the application and run it and attain the same results as in Figure 3-8. The only difference between this method and the one from the previous coding scenario is that in this one we did not set a timer to calculate the time it takes to perform the analysis. Therefore, the Analysis Performed In number will remain at 0.

■ **Note** If you are interested in the difference in speed, note that this implementation is 30 percent faster than the previous one. The combination of using Silverlight binding and removing the sequential nature of the procedural code allowed Silverlight to slightly optimize the code. Although 200 milliseconds may not seem like a lot, keep in mind, we are processing 1 million records. If we were processing 5 million records, then a 30 percent increase in performance would be huge.

Lessons Learned

In this coding scenario, we extended the previous scenario and showed how you can use the powerful binding features of Silverlight to decouple your business logic from procedural code. Utilizing this method allows you to create business algorithms that can be reused in other pages, unit tested, and set in XAML while remaining very performant.

BI developers need to understand this concept well. Each time you mix business logic with procedural code, you are stepping closer to unmaintainable code. BI applications evolve and will add additional configurations, calculations, aggregates, and algorithms as you work with the data. Decoupling these algorithms from the main application functionality allows developers to simply plug these new algorithms into their applications without interfering with existing code that has been already verified by the users or your development quality assurance team.

■ **Note** If you are interested in implementing MVVM (Model-View-ViewModel) patterns on the client, performing basic abstractions like this will allow you to remove code from the code-behind and place it in separate business objects that can be added 100 percent in XAML UI code.

Coding Scenario: Persisting Local Data

This coding scenario aims to show how we can store the data locally in a Silverlight application using one single mechanism.

In the previous two coding scenarios, we worked with in-memory data structures. However, we accessed the data in a very procedural way. In a complex business application, you are going to want to have a single location for all of your local data access.

Following are the goals of this scenario:

- Introducing working with in-memory and isolated storage in Silverlight. This mimics techniques used in disconnected MOLAP and Pivot scenarios.

- Using the caching state bag access pattern to add, locate, and retrieve cached objects

- Understanding the benefits of working with data locally from a single cache repository

In-Memory and Isolated Storage Caching

In a typical Silverlight application, you will have the application start up and retrieve data using some kind of web service. When all of the data in a request is in our Silverlight client, it is ready to have additional manipulations done on it or be displayed in a UI. We do not want to perform these expensive web service requests each time we need data. It would be much better to cache some of this information on the local client.

Silverlight provides two different forms of caching we can utilize: in-memory and isolated storage. In-memory storage is true volatile storage that only exists for the duration of the session of the application. Silverlight isolated storage is a virtual file system that allows data to be persisted using local storage (i.e., on the hard drive). Users can have megabytes and even gigabytes of data in their isolated storage folders. This makes it a perfect feature for persisting large amounts of data and not having to request the data from the server each time. The Silverlight .NET APIs provide methods to put data into and retrieve it from this storage mechanism. However, a simple library currently does not exist that allows you to work with both forms of caching in a single location.

Figure 3-17 provides a high-level overview of what we are going to be covering in this coding scenario. We will first create a small caching library that can be used to access data in-memory or from isolated storage. Next, we will show how this library can be used to access the data from a single location. We will simulate an expensive web service call and retrieve some data. Finally, we will implement the interactions with the local data using our caching class using a common design pattern called the *caching state bag pattern*. This will show how we can access the data in-memory or in our virtual file system and how we can improve load performance by not having to rely on web services only.

Figure 3-17. *Graphical overview of our data caching scenario*

■ **Caution** This coding scenario assumes some knowledge of isolated storage and caching mechanisms. If you have worked with ASP.NET caching, Enterprise Library–based caching, or other caching forms, this will be very familiar to you. If you need additional information on isolated storage, see `http://silverlight.net/quickstarts/isolatedstorage.aspx`.

In this scenario, we are going to build a small application that will use a custom class for in-memory and local storage caching that will be manipulated with the UI. We will simulate a service call that will pause the main thread for 700 milliseconds. The UI will also have responses that will show advantages of caching using both in-memory and local storage over making direct service calls each time.

Let's begin this coding scenario:

1. Open Visual Studio 2010 and create a new Silverlight Application project called Chapter3_PersistingLocalData. Ensure Silverlight 4 is the selected version of Silverlight.

2. First, we are going to create our local cache library. Right-click the Silverlight project and select Add New Item. Select the Class template from the dialog window and name it LocalCacheManager.

3. Add a reference to the System.Runtime.Serialization assembly.

4. Add the using statements shown in Listing 3-12 at the top of the LocalCacheManager.cs file.

Listing 3-12. using statements for the LocalCacheManager.cs class

```
using System.Collections.Generic;
using System.IO;
using System.IO.IsolatedStorage;
using System.Runtime.Serialization;
```

5. Enter the code shown in Listing 3-13 to build the LocalCacheManger class.

Listing 3-13. Code for the LocalCacheManager class

```csharp
public class LocalCacheManager
{
  // local cache
  public static LocalCacheManager localCache = new LocalCacheManager();
  // dictionary of cache
  private readonly IDictionary<string, object> cacheDictionary = new Dictionary<string,
object>();
  // local cache manager folder
  private const string localCacheMangerFolder = "LocalCacheManager";

  // private constructor
  private LocalCacheManager()
  {
    using (IsolatedStorageFile isf = IsolatedStorageFile.GetUserStoreForApplication())
    {
      // create the local cache manager folder
      if (!isf.DirectoryExists(localCacheMangerFolder))
      {
        isf.CreateDirectory(localCacheMangerFolder);
      }

      // load the files from the Isolated Storage Cache
      string[] fileNames = isf.GetFileNames(localCacheMangerFolder + @"\*");

      for (int i = 0; i != fileNames.Length; i++)
      {
        this.cacheDictionary.Add(fileNames[i], null);
      }
    }
}
```

```csharp
  }

  public void AddCacheItem(string key, object value)
  {
    if (this.cacheDictionary.ContainsKey(key))
    {
      this.cacheDictionary.Remove(key);
    }

    this.cacheDictionary.Add(key, value);
  }

  public T GetCacheItem<T>(string key) where T : class
  {
    if (this.cacheDictionary.ContainsKey(key))
    {
      return (T)this.cacheDictionary[key];
    }
    else
    {
      return null;
    }
  }

  public T GetCacheItem<T>(string key, bool checkIsolatedStorage) where T : class
  {
    if (this.cacheDictionary.ContainsKey(key))
    {
      return (T)this.cacheDictionary[key];
    }
    else
    {
      return (T)this.GetFromIsolatedStorage<T>(key);
    }
  }

  public static LocalCacheManager CurrentLocalCacheManager()
  {
    return localCache;
  }

  public void Clear(bool includeIsolatedStorage)
  {
    this.cacheDictionary.Clear();

    // remove the local cache manager
    using (IsolatedStorageFile isf = IsolatedStorageFile.GetUserStoreForApplication())
    {
      if (isf.DirectoryExists(localCacheMangerFolder))
      {
        string[] fileNames = isf.GetFileNames(localCacheMangerFolder + @"\*");
```

```csharp
        for (int i = 0; i != fileNames.Length; i++)
        {
          isf.DeleteFile(localCacheMangerFolder + @"\" + fileNames[i]);
        }
      }
    }
  }
}

public bool Clear(string key)
{
  bool remove = this.cacheDictionary.Remove(key);

  return remove;
}

public bool Clear(string key, bool includeIsolatedStorage)
{
  bool remove = this.cacheDictionary.Remove(key);

  // remove the local cache manager
  using (IsolatedStorageFile isf = IsolatedStorageFile.GetUserStoreForApplication())
  {
    isf.DeleteFile(localCacheMangerFolder + @"\" + key);
  }

  return remove;
}
public bool Exists(string key)
{
  return this.cacheDictionary.ContainsKey(key);
}

public void SaveToIsolatedStorage<T>(string fileName, T objectToSave)
{
  using (IsolatedStorageFile isf = IsolatedStorageFile.GetUserStoreForApplication())
  {
    using (IsolatedStorageFileStream isfs = isf.OpenFile(localCacheMangerFolder
+ @"\" + fileName, FileMode.Create))
    {
      DataContractSerializer serializer = new DataContractSerializer(typeof(T));
      serializer.WriteObject(isfs, objectToSave);
    }
  }
}

public T GetFromIsolatedStorage<T>(string fileName)
{
  T obj = default(T);

  string localStorageFullName = localCacheMangerFolder + @"\" + fileName;
```

```
using (IsolatedStorageFile appStore = IsolatedStorageFile.GetUserStoreForApplication())
{
  if (appStore.FileExists(localStorageFullName))
  {
    using (IsolatedStorageFileStream isfs = appStore.OpenFile(localStorageFullName, ↵
FileMode.Open))
    {
      DataContractSerializer serializer = new DataContractSerializer(typeof(T));
      obj = (T)serializer.ReadObject(isfs);
    }
  }
}

return obj;
}

public IDictionary<string, object> CacheDictionary
{
  get { return this.cacheDictionary; }
}
}
```

6. At this point, your application just includes the local cache manager. Now we are going to add some XAML UI code to interface with our local cache manager. We are going to add four buttons that will manipulate caching logic. Please note that we are adding the event handlers all in one step, so the project will not build until you complete steps 6 and 7 together. Inside MainPage.xaml, add the bold code from Listing 3-14.

Listing 3-14. Bold code adds UI logic to test the LocalCacheManager functionality

```
<UserControl x:Class="Chapter3_PersistingLocalData.MainPage"
  xmlns="http://schemas.microsoft.com/winfx/2006/xaml/presentation"
  xmlns:x="http://schemas.microsoft.com/winfx/2006/xaml"
  xmlns:d="http://schemas.microsoft.com/expression/blend/2008"
  xmlns:mc="http://schemas.openxmlformats.org/markup-compatibility/2006"
  Width="400" Height="300">
  <Grid x:Name="LayoutRoot" Background="White">
    <StackPanel Orientation="Vertical">
      <Button x:Name="btnLoadFromService" Width="375" Height="25"
        Content="Load Data from Service Only" Click="btnLoadFromService_Click"/>
      <Button x:Name="btnLoadDataFromCacheThenService" Width="375" Height="25"
        Content="Try to Load Data from Cache First, then Service; insert into Cache"↵
 Click="btnLoadDataFromCacheThenService_Click"/>
      <Button x:Name="btnSaveDataToIsolatedStorage" Width="375" Height="25"
        Content="Save Data to Isolated Storage" Click↵
="btnSaveDataToIsolatedStorage_Click" />
      <Button x:Name="btnLoadDataFromIsolatedStorageCache" Width="375" Height="25"
        Content="Load Data from Isolated Storage Cache" Click↵
="btnLoadDataFromIsolatedStorageCache_Click"/>
    </StackPanel>
```

```
    </Grid>
</UserControl>
```

7. Your canvas in Visual Studio 2010 or Expression Blend 4 should look like Figure 3-18 after you have completed the previous step. In this step, we are going to add the procedural logic that will drive the tests we are going to perform. Add the code shown in bold in Listing 3-15 into your MainPage.xaml.cs code-behind file.

Figure 3-18. Our Silverlight UI to test out different caching scenarios

Listing 3-15. Bold code implements the code to test the LocalCacheManager

```
public partial class MainPage : UserControl
{
  List<string> names = new List<string>();

  public MainPage()
  {
    InitializeComponent();
  }

  private void btnLoadFromService_Click(object sender, RoutedEventArgs e)
  {
    this.names = this.loadNamesDataFromService();

    MessageBox.Show("Number of names loaded from service: "
+ this.names.Count.ToString());
  }

  private void btnLoadDataFromCacheThenService_Click(object sender, RoutedEventArgs e)
  {
    this.names = loadNamesDataFromCacheThanService();

    MessageBox.Show("Number of names loaded from cache: " + this.names.Count.ToString());
  }

  private void btnSaveDataToIsolatedStorage_Click(object sender, RoutedEventArgs e)
  {
    LocalCacheManager.CurrentLocalCacheManager()
```

```
      .SaveToIsolatedStorage<List<string>>("names", this.names);
        }

        private void btnLoadDataFromIsolatedStorageCache_Click(object sender, RoutedEventArgs e)
        {
          // reset the names collection
          this.names = null;
          this.names = LocalCacheManager.CurrentLocalCacheManager()↵
      .GetFromIsolatedStorage<List<string>>("names");

          MessageBox.Show("Number of names loaded from Isolated Storage: "↵
       + this.names.Count.ToString());
        }
        private List<string> loadNamesDataFromService()
        {
          // simulate an expensive service call
          System.Threading.Thread.Sleep(700);

          return new List<string> { "Joe", "Bob", "Ron", "Andrew", "Shane" };
        }

        private List<string> loadNamesDataFromCacheThanService()
        {
          this.names = LocalCacheManager.CurrentLocalCacheManager()↵
      .GetCacheItem<List<string>>("names");

          if (this.names == null)
          {
            this.names = this.loadNamesDataFromService();
            LocalCacheManager.CurrentLocalCacheManager().AddCacheItem("names", this.names);
          }

          return this.names;
        }
      }
```

8. You should be able to build the application now. Let's perform some tests and see what we have built:

    • Click the first button (labeled "Load Data from Service Only"). This button simulates a service call that takes 700 milliseconds to bring data back from a server. Notice that even though the request is made in subsecond time, it is still noticeable to the user. Try clicking the button several times and note that the request to get our list of names takes the same amount of time. You would see this scenario in production-level code if there were no caching present.

    • The second button (labeled "Try to Load Data from Cache First, then Service; insert into Cache") uses the cache access pattern to access the data. Look at the preceding code in the loadNamesDataFromCacheThanService method to see how this pattern is applied. First, we try to see if the data is cached in memory using our local cache manager. If it is not, then we load the data from the expensive service call and add it to the cache for future requests. Therefore, the first time you click the button, it will be slow (the same simulated 700-millisecond delay in the previous case). The subsequent requests for the data will not have to make an expensive service call, as they data can be accessed directly from memory.

- The third button (labeled "Save Data to Isolated Storage") persists our collection of names to the local storage on your workstation (i.e., hard drive). Click this button to add the names collection to isolated storage.

- The fourth button (labeled "Load Data from Isolated Storage Cache") loads the names collection directly from isolated storage. Click this button to see this in action. Note how quick it is, and that it is comparable to the performance of in-memory caching.

■ **Caution** The custom `LocalCacheManager` class we just coded is a very trivial implementation. While the class will work in basic scenarios, I recommend extending it with additional functionality to make it production ready. For example, integration among local and in-memory caching, time-based expiration, thread safety, and local storage quota handling would be some of the features you could potentially want.

Lessons Learned

In this coding scenario, we saw the benefit that using a Silverlight caching layer has when requesting data from remote data repositories. This coding scenario was trivial and used to mock a service. However, it does hone in on some very important points to take away when working with data on a Silverlight client. First, you can see that even subsecond requests can cause noticeable delays for the user. Imagine more expensive or multiple requests being made. This could make the system unusable. Second, by doing the preceding exercise, you saw firsthand how caching improves performance tremendously. In a real BI application, having larger data sets cached locally can tremendously improve the overall performance of the BI system.

If you are a web developer, you are probably familiar with back-end caching on the Web or using cache headers to minimize requests. This type of caching was probably not available to you if you did not use other plug-in technology or a client database (e.g., SQLite). Silverlight provides this front-side caching, and it is very powerful.

In the beginning of this chapter, I talked about how using distributed architecture techniques can free up resources on the BI servers. This exercise reinforced that concept. Imagine the amount of CPU, RAM, and network resources that are not used on the server as a result of the local Silverlight caching layer we have added. A well-designed local caching layer is one of the most important things you can add to improve the performance of a BI system that works with multiple or large data repositories. A next-generation BI user experience needs to have fast and responsive data sets that can be quickly used for analysis. Therefore, implementing this technique is a must for successful BI 2.0 projects.

Summary

In this chapter, you learned a vital role that Silverlight can play in a distributed BI architecture. The chapter covered several challenges that BI software vendors face when relying on servers to process all of their business intelligence data needs. Client distributed architecture is not just a theory and it is being implemented in PowerPivot, Pivot for Silverlight and disconnected MOLAP architectures.

This chapter was your first introduction to some of the conventions that enable Silverlight to deliver business intelligence 100 percent on the client workstation. In addition, this chapter showed how utilizing Silverlight technology to manipulate BI data locally can alleviate some of the resource burdens you face when trying to process a majority of the business logic on the server. The three coding scenarios included in this chapter should reinforce that Silverlight is a first-class BI client. Your main takeaway from this chapter should be that implementing a Silverlight presentation layer in a BI system can provide fast data manipulation, improve server performance, and store large amounts of data locally. This is the main reason why I believe Silverlight is a first-class RIA client for BI.

At this point, you should have a good idea of what path this book is following in terms of integrating BI concepts with Microsoft Silverlight technology.

CHAPTER 4

■ ■ ■

Adding Interactivity to Business Intelligence Data

This chapter goes over various design techniques that can make interacting with vast amounts of data simpler, more intuitive, and more performant.

In the previous chapter, you saw that the .NET runtime provides Silverlight with a powerful client environment to work with large data sets locally. In this chapter, we will look at how we can use Silverlight to create rich designs that give end users easy ways to interact with data. This chapter will cover current UI design practices of data presentation. Then we will proceed to show the features of Silverlight that simplify data interactivity. Furthermore, we will introduce various UI controls that can be used not only with the classic mouse and keyboard, but also with next-generation gestures such as touch screen monitors/tablets.

The following coding scenarios are included in this chapter:

- Lazy Loading List Box Data

- Adding dynamic and interactive data paging with the slider control

- Fluent querying and filtering with the slider

- Quick searching with the AutoComplete Box control and LINQ queries

The following table outlines the specific goals that different types of readers will achieve by reading this chapter.

Audience	Goals
Silverlight developers	Understand how Silverlight controls can be enhanced to provide fluent data manipulation.
	See how to take advantage of controls that add fluent user interactions.
Business intelligence professionals	Learn the advantages Silverlight brings to manipulating BI data easily.
	Contrast fluent interactions that Silverlight UIs provide over traditional interactivity found in current BI offerings.

Audience	Goals
Strategic decision makers	Understand if next-generation, fluent Silverlight designs can add a wow factor to your BI product demos and add additional intangible value to the product(s).
	Deduce if simpler data interactivity in your products can allow you to expand the product target audience (including less-technical users).

User Interactivity

Interactivity in a user interface is simply defined as taking a human input via a device (e.g., mouse, keyboard, or touch screen) and translating it to processing operations in software applications.

Over the years, interactions have become simpler and easier for the users. Before the mouse input became a standard, users had to input all commands via a keyboard. In the last couple of decades, most workstation users have become familiar with the mouse and keyboard. In order to make it even easier for users, software has evolved standard practices that users can expect any modern application to include. Over time, some tweaks have been made to the standard mouse input, such as the mouse wheel. However, the mouse and keyboard input tandem hasn't changed much over the last several years.

Importance of Good User Interactivity

Successful software applications need to expose elegant and simple interactions that work extremely well in surfacing business logic. Applications need to expose business logic with clear interactions. If applications require complex keyboard commands and/or mouse gestures, users are not going to bother with learning the application.

User interactions need to be planned for when designing rich interfaces. This is especially true for RIA applications where features like transitions, animations, and videos can pepper the application canvas. Many UI design patterns and standards exist to help alleviate some of these design challenges. For example, a user will expect that clicking the Tab key will place the focus on the next control in the screen. A well-designed business application will adhere to as many of these standard design practices as possible.

One of the most important design facets to consider is how to expose your business logic to the user. Static presentations such as reports or simple data forms do not have to deal with too much beyond implementing proper UI patterns. However, RIA applications (e.g., Silverlight) are dynamic and try to engage the user with enhanced interactions. This is where translating business logic into a well-designed application canvas becomes very important. It is paramount that users can quickly relate the UI interactions and how this affects business logic. This helps the users learn the application rapidly if they can relate their input and gestures to business algorithms.

Touch Interactivity

As mentioned previously, human interactions with software have not changed much beyond the mouse and keyboard. Over the last few years, developers have mainly focused on the mouse and keyboard as the primary human input and gesture devices. This is quickly changing with the advent of single-touch and multitouch interfaces. Products such as the Apple iPhone, Microsoft Surface, and Windows Tablet

PCs allow users to control software applications using their fingers or a stylus. This allows more natural and quicker gestures that users are more familiar with. Furthermore, touch interactions lend themselves to smaller form factors such as mobile devices where a keyboard or mouse doesn't need to be attached. These touch interfaces have just become popular and have not penetrated the business realm. However, touch technology is quickly maturing and proving itself as a great way to provide intuitive interactions for otherwise complex operations. Many large companies such as Apple, Microsoft, and Palm are investing serious R&D capital into this technology.

Software user interfaces have to adapt in order to accommodate the emerging touch interactions. Touch gestures usually deal with swiping, pinching, and expanding of fingers. If the interface does not support touch gestures properly, it will ruin the application experience. For example, a user interface that expects a mouse as a main source of input for a button control works well. However, on a touch screen, a classic design would be translated to a lot of poking the interface with a finger or a stylus to click a button. Obviously, this is not the desired experience we would want users to have with our application.

■ **Note** Both the new Microsoft Windows 7 OS and Mac OS X support multitouch interfaces. The Windows 7 OS (if the hardware supports it) includes several multitouch applications and supports multitouch input from Internet Explorer 8. This allows developers to write both desktop and web applications that enhance user experiences with multitouch input. Many computer stores now sell laptops that include multitouch interfaces. With Windows 7 supporting multitouch, this is set out to be a standard feature in the very near future. A large majority of businesses have opted to skip Microsoft Vista and wait for Windows 7. Therefore, the adoption rate on this OS should be fairly quick in the business space, and you will probably see Windows 7 and multitouch business applications going mainstream in 2010.

As of this book's publication, we are just starting to see both touch hardware and touch operating system combinations being prevalent on enough user desktops to explicitly code for touch environments. This does not mean that you should not factor touch gestures into your GUI design decisions. However, the story is different for Windows Phone 7. The operating system and the device will both be ready for multitouch input. Therefore, if you are planning on running your Silverlight application on a Windows Phone 7 mobile device (when Windows Phone 7 is released in the second half of 2010) or a Windows 7 tablet, you need to implement good multitouch design principles from the beginning of the software project.

THE NEAR FUTURE OF NEXT-GENERATION INTERACTIVITY

Microsoft unveiled a very exciting project during the E3 Expo 2009 conference called Kinect (formally known as Project Natal). Project Natal is a controller-free system that allows you to interact with the Xbox console completely with human gestures.

The Natal system is able to take input from three key sensors: full-body motion gestures, facial recognition, and voice recognition. The introduction of this technology dramatically changes the landscape of not just gaming but entertainment as a whole. This was amplified as Steven Spielberg was selected to introduce Project Natal to the public at the conference. He stated that this completely adds a new step to interactive entertainment.

Microsoft showed how this new interactivity will be implemented with a variety of demonstrations. First, navigating the Xbox menus is as simple as swiping your hand vertically or horizontally. Selecting a menu item is done by simply pointing at it or using a voice command. If anyone has used the Xbox, this is a huge improvement. However, the Natal interactivity system is much more than that. The full-body motion sensor is able to recognize who you are and select your Xbox avatar based on your body type. Furthermore, the system is able to tell what your mood is or even tailor the game experience to you by your facial expressions, body posture, and so on. For example, eight-year-olds who use the system could have the experience tailored to their age group by blocking certain content or making the game levels easier. Games will now include an immersive experience completely controlled by human gestures. This can include shooting, kicking, fighting, and so on. The items I described are just scratching the surface of possibilities of the technology.

Adding three simultaneous human gesture inputs for entertainment is going to revolutionize how Xbox entertainment is designed and presented to the user. Xbox developers will not be able to rely on traditional controller input and will have to plan for enhanced human gesture compatibility. For more information on Project Natal and demonstrations of the technology, see www.xbox.com/en-US/live/projectnatal.

Silverlight and Interactivity Support

Silverlight has great support for designing fluent user interfaces. As mentioned in the previous chapters, Silverlight runs on the local workstation or device. Therefore, applications can take advantage of this and provide quick and snappy responses to user input without needing server processing. Furthermore, Silverlight includes a rich set of controls that lends itself to fluid interactivity and displaying responsive content. These interactions can be enhanced by a powerful animation framework to either soften or accent user gestures even further.

■ **Note** If you are familiar with iPhone data lists, you will note how the scrolling gesture has been enhanced with inertia to soften scroll animation. An inertia physics behavior could be added to a Silverlight list control to provide more natural scrolling.

Silverlight (just like any modern, well-designed GUI) can support basic single-touch gestures. In addition, Silverlight (as of version 3) can take advantage of new hardware that supports multitouch gestures. Do keep in mind that Silverlight is just a presentation technology. Even though Silverlight supports multitouch, it still needs to be hosted on an OS and hardware that supports multitouch input. For example, a Silverlight 4 application exposed inside Windows 7 (running on multitouch-enabled hardware) or Windows 7 Mobile can take full advantage of multitouch gestures. This is a very important combination that allows for creating a new class of engaging business applications. Investing in Silverlight technology now could translate into your application being ready for touch gesture input in the near future.

The following sections and coding scenarios will cover the Silverlight features for implementing BI data interactivity in detail.

Interactivity with Business Intelligence Data

Implementing rich interactions plays a very important role when presenting data to users. This is further amplified when we present BI data that usually involves very large data sets. To refresh your memory, the main BI 2.0 paradigms were that analytical tools should be simple to use, easy to learn, available to a wider audience, and very responsive. If you want your BI application to be useful for people other than technical analysts, your application needs to implement data manipulation techniques that any user can grasp quickly. The interactions need to be clear so that a user can quickly translate them into the information the data is holding.

The goal of BI 2.0 applications is to deliver insight quickly from large amounts of data. Many BI 2.0 systems have evolved algorithms that are highly automated and can deliver the insight without much input from the human user. However, there are still many cases where users need to be able to interact with the data to swiftly attain the insight manually.

Computer systems are good at processing algorithms for which they have been explicitly designed. They can do this millions of times faster than humans. For example, a BI system hooked into a network of home improvement stores could analyze that sales of wood are above normal levels and automatically place an order for more wood. However, computer systems currently can't understand the environment they are in and make the best decisions for themselves. Therefore, there is still a great need for computer systems that present information to users so that decisions can be derived manually. For example, you would not want to have a system that automatically gave employees raises every year just based on some analytical metrics. These metrics could be used as guides for managers but would not be used exclusively. This is the main reason why you need to provide easy-to-use interactions that can translate to fast analysis.

Types of Data Interactivity

If you have worked with or developed BI software, you are very familiar with presenting information with standard data controls. Figure 4-1 shows common controls (in Silverlight) used to present data: a data grid, a list, and a tree view. Showing even large amounts of data in UI controls is straightforward. However, it could be challenging to enhance data controls with good interactivity (e.g., paging, sorting, and filtering). When the data sets are small, this is a moot point. However, when dealing with thousands of items or more, it can be nearly impossible for users to interact with the data.

Figure 4-1. Common Silverlight data controls include data grids, lists, and tree views.

In a BI 2.0 system, one of the questions a UI expert needs to answer is how users are going to find the data they want from a large data set. There are several types of data manipulation or techniques users can apply to find the data in the format they expect to make easier decisions. I will go over the main types in the following subsections.

Sorting

Sorting is one of the most basic data interaction techniques used to create custom data views. When presenting data sets that have many attributes, users will want to order the data and create views that are of analytical significance. Obviously, these attributes can order the data in either an ascending or descending manner. Furthermore, sorting multiple attributes at once is possible as well.

Sorting is a data manipulation function that is typically used as a first step in searching data. However, sorting by itself rarely isolates the exact data a user wants. But when used in conjunction with other interactions, it is usually a technique that any UI should include.

■ **Note** The Silverlight PivotViewer control does an excellent job of interactively showing a sort interaction. It amplifies that sorting is not just about the act of sorting the data behind the scenes programmatically. However, adding the extra animation and transition really help the user understand what is happening to their data.

Data Paging

Data paging is another very common data interaction technique. It is not practical to try to display thousands of items of data on a single screen. This is especially true for BI systems. Even if you could surface a great deal of information, you are limited to the finite size of monitor and screen resolutions.

Over the years, paging techniques have been developed to display smaller subsets of data from a larger source. This allows users to isolate smaller sets of data on which they want to focus. Adding paging to data on a screen seems like a trivial feature; however, this is one of the most poorly implemented features in BI applications. Developers usually apply the functionality of paging properly. However, many times developers forget that paging is a navigation technique to quickly create a view of data that users want to see.

Filtering

Filtering data is another popular data interaction that can be implemented to find matching records. Sorting and paging interactions do not limit the amount of items that are available to the end user. However, filtering operations do exactly that, by horizontally partitioning the data by removing items that do not match the filter criteria. The filters could be either numeric data (e.g., items with a purchase amount greater than $5.00) or string information (e.g., items made in Chicago).

■ **Note** Excel 2010 slicers (mentioned in the previous chapter) are a good example how to implement filtering in an interactive manner.

Searching

Sometimes users don't know what they are looking for and need a technique that will help them narrow the items further. A user might know an attribute of an item but not enough to give them the item itself. For example, a user might have an idea of a date or a phrase that an item starts with and need a control that will help them find the information.

Grouping and Pivoting Data

Even when we are presenting denormalized or aggregated data warehouse information, this data could be in data structures that are related to each other. This is why it is very important to provide a way to present data that shows the relationship between data properties. This allows users to navigate natural hierarchies derived from the relationships between the objects.

Pivoting data can be defined as providing summarized data and a condensed view with additional metrics of the data. When a user looks at a data set that is not aggregated, they may have difficulty ascertaining the key pieces of information. For example, Figure 4-2 shows a flat file inside Microsoft Excel that is displaying sales information. If you were tasked with finding the summary of sales for Boston for all the years, you couldn't easily do that without doing math in your head or using the spreadsheet calculator. However, if the data were presented in a way such as Figure 4-3, then you could easily tell what the sales numbers were.

Year	City	Sales	Cost	Profit
2002	Philadelphia	$54,000	$11,000	$43,000
2002	New York	$65,000	$33,333	$31,667
2002	Boston	$34,999	$15,000	$19,999
2002	Los Angeles	$44,444	$15,000	$29,444
2002	Chicago	$34,999	$25,000	$9,999
2002	Orlando	$65,555	$3,333	$62,222
2002	Houston	$34,999	$15,000	$19,999
2003	Philadelphia	$65,000	$3,434	$61,566
2003	New York	$34,999	$15,000	$19,999
2003	Boston	$34,000	$35,000	-$1,000
2003	Los Angeles	$34,999	$15,000	$19,999
2003	Chicago	$43,000	$15,000	$28,000
2003	Orlando	$34,999	$15,000	$19,999
2003	Houston	$41,000	$15,000	$26,000
2004	Philadelphia	$34,999	$25,000	$9,999
2004	New York	$42,000	$15,000	$27,000
2004	Boston	$34,999	$15,000	$19,999
2004	Los Angeles	$34,999	$65,000	-$30,001
2004	Chicago	$25,000	$15,000	$10,000
2004	Orlando	$34,999	$25,000	$9,999
2004	Houston	$34,999	$43,433	-$8,434
2005	Philadelphia	$34,999	$15,000	$19,999
2005	New York	$34,999	$23,232	$11,767

Figure 4-2. Snippet of fictitious sales data in a flat format in Microsoft Excel

Row Labels	Values		
	Sum of Sales	Sum of Cost	Sum of Profit
⊟ Boston	$378,229	$197,778	$180,451
2002	$34,999	$15,000	$19,999
2003	$34,000	$35,000	-$1,000
2004	$34,999	$15,000	$19,999
2005	$75,000	$15,000	$60,000
2006	$66,000	$23,233	$42,767
2007	$45,454	$54,545	-$9,091
2008	$87,777	$40,000	$47,777
⊞ Chicago	$205,219	$142,455	$62,764
⊞ Houston	$250,995	$128,888	$122,107
⊞ Los Angeles	$251,002	$265,555	-$14,553
⊞ New York	$333,107	$183,198	$149,909
⊞ Orlando	$341,451	$159,343	$182,108
⊞ Philadelphia	$315,561	$187,401	$128,160
Grand Total	$2,075,564	$1,264,618	$810,946

Figure 4-3. Sales data in an Excel pivot table showing summary totals

Pivot tables and tools have been a standard feature of software that deals with data. For example, Microsoft Excel and Access software have supported pivot tools as a standard feature for several years. Even open-source spreadsheet packages like OpenOffice Calc include rich pivot support. Pivot tables have become a standard in BI software packages.

Applying Interactivity in Business Intelligence with Silverlight

It is time to go over some explicit concepts concerning how you can present data and interact with it using Silverlight controls and features. In Chapter 3, I introduced how the client processing tier can be used to do very powerful data manipulations and apply business logic in Silverlight. However, in that chapter I purposely left out the complexities of dealing with data controls that expose larger data sets. In the following sections, I am going to cover how you can surface larger data sets and how you can add interactivity to them.

Common Silverlight Controls for Data Lists

Before covering interaction scenarios, I need to introduce some of the more common data controls that the Silverlight framework includes. If you are familiar with web or desktop UI programming, these controls will be very similar to what you have used before.

Several Silverlight data controls use a concept called *UI virtualization*. The Silverlight rendering engine will only render what is currently being viewed. For example, if you bind 1 million rows to a data grid and you are showing 20 items on the screen, Silverlight will not render 1 million rows on a screen. This keeps the performance of the UI very responsive even though there could be a large data set stored behind the scenes. This applied concept is a significant performance enhancement for BI data that could have data sets that have tens of thousands or more items.

Data Grid

The Silverlight data grid is a data control that is used to show data in a tabular format. Figure 4-4 shows the Silverlight data grid bound to a set of sales data. Following are the key BI features of the Silverlight data grid:

- It can sort interactions automatically (this is the default behavior).

- It can resize columns.

- It allows you to change the order of columns by dragging and dropping them.

- It allows for freezing columns when scrolling.

City ▲	Date Of Sale	Sales Person	Customer	Sale Amount
Chicago	June 16, 2003	Ramos, Luciana	Coho Vineyard	$10,999
Chicago	July 7, 2006	Sarin, Raman	Litware, Inc.	$10,999
Detroit	September 10, 2006	Clark, Molly	Tailspin Toys	$25.34
Detroit	May 27, 2007	Bowen, Eli	Humongous Insurance	$29.99
Los Angeles	November 5, 2003	Makovac, Zrinka	Northwind Traders	$249.99
New York	April 9, 2008	Gladkikh, Andrey	Graphic Design Institute	$10,999
New York	June 4, 2007	Hicks, Cassie	Woodgrove Bank	$100
Philadelphia	January 16, 2008	Li, Yuhong	Wide World Importers	$25.34
Philadelphia	August 9, 2006	Sato, Naoki	Adventure Works	$49.99

Figure 4-4. Sales data in a Silverlight data grid sorted by city

Following are some of the scenarios in which you should display data using a data grid:

- When you need to display a data set that has several attributes/properties (e.g., in Figure 4-4, City, Date of Sale, Sales Person, Customer, and Sales Amount).

- When you have a large data set that is bound to a data grid (e.g., over several thousand records).

- When you need to provide default features like sorting, in-place editing, column reordering, column freezing, or grouping without having too much additional code.

List Box

The Silverlight list box is a data control that is used to show data usually in a vertical format. A list box is very similar to a drop-down or a combo box, except a list of items is constantly shown and doesn't collapse. Users are shown a list of items from which they can make a selection. Figure 4-5 shows the Silverlight list box bound to the same sales data that the data grid was bound to.

Following are the key BI features of the Silverlight list box:

- It has single or multiple selection mode.

- The list box and its items can be easily styled to incorporate additional features and behaviors.

Figure 4-5. *Sales data in a Silverlight list box*

Following are some of the scenarios in which you should display data using a list box:

- When you need to display a large data set that does not need to show many properties at once

- When you want to display read-only data for which the selection of items is important

Tree View

The Silverlight tree view is a data control that is used to show hierarchical data. Figure 4-6 shows the Silverlight tree view displaying sales data with the city at the top level and the customers for each city at the second level.

Following are the key BI features of the Silverlight tree view:

- It allows you to easily to create complex dynamic hierarchy bindings. This is good for visualizing attribute or semantic hierarchy dimensional information.

- Tree view items can be easily styled to incorporate additional features and behaviors. For example, a Silverlight tree view node can host a data grid control.

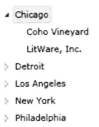

Figure 4-6. *Sales data in a Silverlight tree view showing cities and their customers*

Following are some of the scenarios in which you should display data using a tree view:

- When you need to present a data set that has a hierarchical relationship (parent/child).

- When you want to represent the hierarchy and signal presence of child items without loading the child items on initial load (lazy loading).

- When you need to group the data semantically. For example, if we grouped a series of reports by year, the first levels of the tree view would be the years, and they would contain the actual reports as children.

- When you need similar functionality to a list box.

■ **Note** Silverlight data controls provide a great baseline to present data. In most scenarios, these controls completely suffice for most data presentation needs. However, in some cases you may want to extend the out-of-the box functionality for some controls (e.g., to allow drag-and-drop functionality). In those cases, it is best to invest in a control package from a third-party vendor that provides additional functionality.

The three controls just covered are the most common controls you will need for displaying various types of lists in Silverlight. The Silverlight Control Toolkit includes additional controls that allow you to present data using charts. Those will be covered in Chapters 5 through 7. Furthermore, please note that there are several less-used Silverlight Control Toolkit controls that can be used to present lists of data, such as the accordion and wrap panel controls.

Silverlight controls are highly customizable. I have seen very interesting mashup user controls created with multiple controls with ease. Furthermore, advanced Silverlight features like attached properties, state model, animations, behaviors, and styling allow you to create very powerful and unique controls that can have customized functionality. This gives developers and designers a rich framework to create custom UIs. If that is not enough, writing custom controls is easier than doing it on the Web or Windows desktops. All of the control's visual aspects are created in XAML and abstracted from the developer. For example, there is no need to learn low-level device context like GDI+ to draw custom shapes.

The ability to create custom controls and enhance the behavior of existing ones in Silverlight lends itself very well to designing BI 2.0 applications. BI 2.0 applications that need to have simple, easy-to-learn, responsive UIs can take advantage of Silverlight's customizability by presenting data to users in better ways.

Coding Scenario: Lazy Loading List Box Data

In this coding scenario, we will show how the Silverlight list box control can be modified to load additional items once the user has scrolled to the end of the items list.

Following are the goals of this scenario:

- Understanding how data list controls can be modified to efficiently surface large amounts of BI data on demand

- Gaining insight on how controls are modified through the different style hierarchies

- Seeing how these concepts can be applied to other data controls

---

■ **Note** A live demo of this coding scenario is available on the companion site: http://silverlightbusinessintelligence.com/Demos/AddingInteractivity/LazyLoadingListBoxData/ LazyLoadingListBoxData.html.

Importance of Lazy Loading

In BI 2.0 implementations, we want to provide as much insight from data to users as possible. However, in terms of system scalability, it is simply impractical to load tens of thousands of records at once. On one hand, BI software should deliver as much data for analysis to the user as possible. On the other hand, BI software can't compromise system scalability in favor of providing everything the user wants. A balance between the two needs to be struck.

In this coding scenario, we are going to implement a list box that will load additional data as the user scrolls to the bottom of the list. This will implement the concept of lazy loading which can be defined as loading an item when it is needed.

■ **Note** As of Silverlight version 3, the list box control supports UI virtualization. This allows the list box control to bind massive amounts of items effectively. However, UI virtualization is a UI performance enhancement, and we shouldn't retrieve thousands of records if we don't have to.

Let's begin this coding scenario:

1. Open Expression Blend 4 and create a new Silverlight Application project called Chapter4_LazyLoadingListBoxData.

2. Open the project in Expression Blend 4and create a new dynamic data source called SampleDataSource. (sample data sources are covered in detail in Appendix A)

3. Perform the following steps to add items to the SampleDataSource (if you need help with Blend's data tool, see Appendix A of this book):

   - Add a collection by choosing Add Collection Property from the SampleDataSource drop-down called Companies.

   - Add a string property called AccountAcquired to the Companies collection, and use the Date format.

- Add a string property called CompanyName to the Companies collection, and use the Company Name format.

- Click the Companies collection and increase the number of items to 100.

After you complete the preceding steps, the data set should look like Figure 4-7.

Figure 4-7. *Sample data with a date and company name properties*

4. Add a list box to the main layout of the project and name it lstCompanies. Your XAML should look like Listing 4-1 in the main project (new code is highlighted in bold).

Listing 4-1. *List box added to the LayoutRoot*

```
<Grid x:Name="LayoutRoot" Background="White">
    <ListBox x:Name="lstCompanies" Height="200" HorizontalAlignment="Left"
    VerticalAlignment="Top" Width="200" Margin="10,36,0,0"></ListBox>
</Grid>
```

5. We are going to bind our list box to the sample data we created in step 2. We are going to do this step manually in code so we can easily extend it in our coding exercise. First, add the using statement shown in Listing 4-2 to the MainPage.xaml.cs file (or the code-behind file you added to the list box) in order to enable access to the sample date source you created in step 3.

Listing 4-2. using statement in the MainPage.xaml.cs file to utilize the sample data

```
using Expression.Blend.SampleData.SampleDataSource;
```

6. In the grid control (LayoutRoot), add an event handler for the Loaded event. This will create a corresponding method in the code-behind file. The change is shown in bold in Listing 4-3.

Listing 4-3. Add the Loaded event to the LayoutRoot.

```
<Grid x:Name="LayoutRoot" Background="White" Loaded="LayoutRoot_Loaded">
    <ListBox x:Name="lstCompanies" Height="200" HorizontalAlignment="Left"
    VerticalAlignment="Top" Width="200" Margin="10,36,0,0"></ListBox>
</Grid>
```

7. In the MainPage.xaml.cs file, add the following items:

- A variable called data that will access our sample data source

- A variable called page that will hold the current page of the data

- A method called bindData that will bind the Companies collection to the list box

Add code to the Loaded event handler that will call the bindData method each time the page loads. The MainPage.xaml.cs file changes are highlighted in bold in Listing 4-4.

Listing 4-4. Bind the data to the list box.

```
public partial class MainPage : UserControl
{
    // create the sample data source variable
    SampleDataSource data = new SampleDataSource();
    // create a variable that will hold the current page
    int page = 1;

    public MainPage()
    {
        InitializeComponent();
    }

    private void LayoutRoot_Loaded(object sender, RoutedEventArgs e)
    {
        this.bindData();
    }

    private void bindData()
    {
        this.lstCompanies.ItemsSource = data.Companies.Take(10 * page);
    }
}
```

8. At this point, your project should build and work. However, we need to add a data template to expose the two properties in our list box and set them as a static resource in our list box. The changes to the XAML are highlighted in bold in Listing 4-5.

Listing 4-5. Change the data template for the list box.

```
...
<UserControl.Resources>
    <DataTemplate x:Key="ItemTemplate">
        <StackPanel>
            <TextBlock Text="{Binding Path=AccountAcquired}" Margin="1"
HorizontalAlignment="Left" VerticalAlignment="Top"/>
            <TextBlock Text="{Binding Path=CompanyName}" Margin="1"
HorizontalAlignment="Left" VerticalAlignment="Top"/>
        </StackPanel>
    </DataTemplate>
</UserControl.Resources>
<Grid x:Name="LayoutRoot" Background="White" Loaded="LayoutRoot_Loaded">
        <ListBox x:Name="lstCompanies" Height="200" HorizontalAlignment="Left"
    VerticalAlignment="Top" Width="200" Margin="10,36,0,0"
    ItemTemplate="{StaticResource ItemTemplate}" ></ListBox>
</Grid>
...
```

9. We will want to test the enhancements we are going to be making to the list box with both the vertical (default) and horizontal lists. In Silverlight, there is no simple property to change the orientation. We have to add the bold code from Listing 4-6 to our list box in order to change the orientation. Note that this code will not change anything since the default layout is vertical. However, the code is needed in order to change the orientation in the following step.

Listing 4-6. Add the ItemsPanel to customize the control orientation.

```
...
<ListBox x:Name="lstCompanies" Height="200" HorizontalAlignment="Left"
VerticalAlignment="Top" Width="200" Margin="10,36,0,0"
ItemTemplate="{StaticResource ItemTemplate}">
    <ListBox.ItemsPanel>
        <ItemsPanelTemplate>
            <StackPanel Orientation="Vertical" />
        </ItemsPanelTemplate>
    </ListBox.ItemsPanel>
</ListBox>
...
```

10. Build your project and run it. You should have a list box that shows ten records with the company name and date properties showing vertically. If you want to show the list box in a horizontal manner, simply change the StackPanel orientation to horizontal, as shown in Listing 4-7.

Listing 4-7. Changing the orientation to horizontal will display the list horizontally.

```
<StackPanel Orientation="Horizontal" />
```

Note that when setting the orientation to horizontal, you should set the height of the list box to something more reasonable (e.g., 75). Figure 4-8 shows the two lists working in vertical and horizontal orientations:

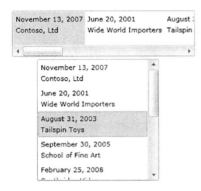

Figure 4-8. Our list boxes bound to the same data set using a horizontal and vertical orientation

11. At this point, we have our list box fully working and showing 10 records. Now it is time to add our enhanced code to our list box that will load additional pages of data as the thumb of the scroll bar is moved to the end of the list. We will want to hook into the scroll bar of the list box, and when the thumb moves to the max position, we will want to trigger an event. Take a look at Figure 4-9 for further information on how the list box scroll bar is constructed.

Figure 4-9. Our list boxes bound to the same data set using a horizontal and vertical orientation

12. The formula we are going to use to determine if the thumb has made it to the end is position of the thumb + height of the thumb + height of the decrease scroll position button + top and bottom margins of the scroll position button (thumbPositon + thumbHeight + increaseButtonHeight + increaseButtonMarginTop + increaseButtonMarginBottom). If we add all those items together and they match the rendered height of the scroll bar, then the thumb has reached the end of the scroll bar.

13. The list box control (like most Silverlight controls) is actually composed of simple layout controls (e.g., grid, StackPanel) and other simple controls like the button, rectangle, and so on. We are going to define these default styles that we need for this control. The primary reason for this is to be able to hook into the drag event for the thumb control. Go into Expression Blend 3 to edit your project and perform the following tasks:

- In Expression Blend, navigate to the Objects and Timeline section of the tool. In there, you will find our list box, lstCompanies. Right-click the list box and highlight the Edit Template menu item. Then select Edit a Copy. Figure 4-10 shows the menu that needs to be selected.

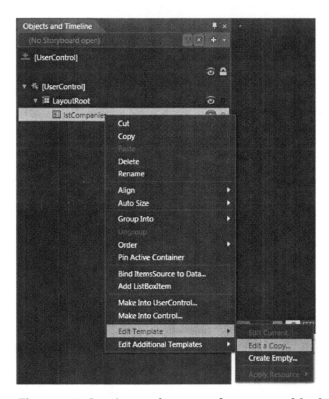

Figure 4-10. Creating a style resource from a copy of the default

- After the option is selected, a dialog box will be presented to create a style resource. Click OK on that screen. This will create a style called ListBoxStyle1, and Blend will automatically bind this resource for us. Blend will automatically show ListBoxStyle1 in the Objects and Timeline section.

- Expand the border control, and notice the ScrollViewer control. Right-click ScrollViewer and highlight the Edit Template menu item. Then select Edit a Copy. Once again, click OK on the dialog to accept the defaults. This will create a style called ScrollViewerStyle1.

- In ScrollViewerStyle1, expand the grid control, and you will find two controls, called VerticalScrollBar and HorizontalScrollBar. Right-click VerticalScrollBar and highlight the Edit Template menu item. Then select Edit a Copy. Once again, click OK on the dialog to accept the defaults. This will create a style called ScrollBarStyle1.

- We are finally in the control part we need to access. In this template, there is a thumb control called VerticalThumb. Highlight the VerticalThumb control and select the Events button from the Properties toolbox. Create an event handler for the DragCompleted event called Thumb_DragCompleted, as shown in Figure 4-11. This will create the event handler for the DragCompleted event. Note that the same event will be used for the HorizontalThumb control (described next).

Figure 4-11. *Creating an event handler for the HorizontalThumb control*

- We need to do the same for the horizontal thumb. In Expression Blend, go back up the template hierarchy by clicking the Return to Scope button (shown in Figure 4-12).

Figure 4-12. *Returning to a higher-level scope in the template hierarchy*

- Highlight the HorizontalScrollBar control. Right-click the HorizontalScrollBar and highlight the Edit Template menu item. Then select Edit a Copy. Once again, click OK on the dialog to accept the defaults. This will creates a style called ScrollBarStyle2.

- Expand the HorizontalRoot control. In this template, there is a thumb control called HorizontalThumb. Highlight the HorizontalThumb control and select the Events button from the Properties toolbox. Create an event handler for the DragCompleted event called Thumb_DragCompleted (as shown previously in Figure 4-11). This will create the event handler for the DragCompleted event.

We made a lot of style/template changes. Ensure the project still builds and runs. We have now wired up the DragCompleted events for both the horizontal and vertical list boxes.

14. This allows us to process some additional logic when the drag event has been completed. We will now add our calculation to the Thumb_DragCompleted event handler. Add the code that is in bold in Listing 4-8 to the DragCompleted method.

Listing 4-8. DragCompleted code to calculate the position of the scroll thumb to bind additional data

```
private void Thumb_DragCompleted(object sender,
System.Windows.Controls.Primitives.DragCompletedEventArgs e)
{
    // cast the sender as the thumb
    FrameworkElement thumb = sender as FrameworkElement;
    // retrieve the actual height & width of the thumb (rounded)
    double thumbHeight = thumb.ActualHeight;
    double thumbWidth = thumb.ActualWidth;

    // retrieve the thumb parent
    UIElement thumbParent = thumb.Parent as UIElement;

    // define the increase button height and default value
    double increaseButtonHeight = 16.0;
    // define the increase button width and default value
    double increaseButtonWidth = 16.0;
    // define the increase button top margin and default value
    double increaseButtonMarginTop = 1.0;
    // define the increase button bottom margin and default value
    double increaseButtonMarginBottom = 1.0;

    // retrieve parent control of the thumb control (grid)
    FrameworkElement thumbParentFrameworkElement = thumb.Parent as FrameworkElement;

    // retrieve the root control
    FrameworkElement root = thumbParentFrameworkElement.Parent as FrameworkElement;

    // retrieve the scroll bar control
    FrameworkElement scrollBar = root.Parent as FrameworkElement;
```

```
    // Find the relative postion of the thumb to the scroll grid (parent)
    GeneralTransform gt = thumb.TransformToVisual(thumb.Parent as UIElement);
    Point p = gt.Transform(new Point(0, 0));

    // Check if ListBox is vertical
    if (thumbParentFrameworkElement.Name == "VerticalRoot")
    {
        FrameworkElement verticalSmallIncrease =
            thumbParentFrameworkElement.FindName("VerticalSmallIncrease")↩
as FrameworkElement;
        increaseButtonHeight = verticalSmallIncrease.Height;
        increaseButtonMarginTop = verticalSmallIncrease.Margin.Top;
        increaseButtonMarginBottom = verticalSmallIncrease.Margin.Bottom;

        // if the thumb has reached the bottom of the list
        // increase the page number shown
        // rebind the data
        if (p.Y + thumbHeight + increaseButtonHeight + increaseButtonMarginTop↩
+ increaseButtonMarginBottom == thumbParentFrameworkElement.RenderSize.Height)
        {
            this.page++;
            this.bindData();
        }
    }
    else // if listBox is horizontal
    {
        FrameworkElement horizontalSmallIncrease =
            thumbParentFrameworkElement.FindName("HorizontalSmallIncrease")↩
as FrameworkElement;
        increaseButtonHeight = horizontalSmallIncrease.Height;
        increaseButtonMarginTop = horizontalSmallIncrease.Margin.Top;
        increaseButtonMarginBottom = horizontalSmallIncrease.Margin.Bottom;

        // if the thumb has reached the max width of the list
        // increase the page number shown
        // rebind the data
        if (p.X + thumbWidth + increaseButtonWidth + increaseButtonMarginTop↩
+ increaseButtonMarginBottom == thumbParentFrameworkElement.RenderSize.Width)
        {
            this.page++;
            this.bindData();
        }
    }
}
```

15. The preceding code is straightforward. After the drag event completes, it grabs the necessary objects from the scroll bar, retrieves the necessary height or width properties, and compares that to the rendered scroll bar. If the end has been reached, it calls the bindData method, which will rebind the data.

117

16. Build the solution and run the application. Figure 4-13 shows the list box running with additional data.

- Scroll to the bottom of the list and notice how additional items are added.

- Change the list box to horizontal orientation and notice as you scroll to the right that more items are added.

- Change the height and width of the list box to Auto and note that the behavior works by adding additional data.

Figure 4-13. *List box data with additional items dynamically added (note the smaller thumb size)*

■ **Note** In the preceding coding scenario, we dug into the internals of the control through its internal styles. This is the proper way to enhance a control. However, in a production scenario, we would want to add this interaction through a custom list box control or through an attached behavior (add behavior through composition).

Lessons Learned

In this coding exercise, we showed how we can extend a basic list box control and get it ready to handle the large data sets we are sure to encounter in BI systems. This technique is called data virtualization. Hopefully, you learned how to utilize the open templates to customize and hook into the underlying Silverlight objects easily.

Not every Silverlight control is designed with easy-to-set properties or methods. However, Silverlight XAML exposes a rich style and template model that can be used to understand the design of the control and even extend the behavior of the control itself. This allows developers to solve business problems easily through composition and extending control behaviors. This approach is favored by most developers over reverse-engineering or creating custom controls by applying OOP concepts.

In the beginning of this chapter, I talked about fluid and interactive interfaces. We could have easily solved this problem by providing a Next button that would have showed the next page or something equivalent. However, this would have compromised the fluid behavior and interactions of the list box. With this solution, the list box remains easy to scroll. Furthermore, touch interfaces can easily use hand gestures to scroll through the list items fluently.

This coding scenario used fictitious data that was loaded locally. In a real-world scenario, you would consume the data from a BI data service. The way we extended the control, we could potentially load several pages in advance as the user interacts with the current data. Furthermore, we could provide an interesting animation as the data is being requested. The best part is that we are not overwhelming the user with thousands of records, yet we are providing them with more data as they want to see it. This is a great implementation of several BI 2.0 concepts mentioned in this chapter.

Coding Scenario: Interactive Data Paging with the Slider Control

In this coding scenario, we will show how paging can be added to the Silverlight data grid control. Furthermore, we will enhance the standard paging with fluent gestures using the Silverlight slider control.

Following are the goals of this scenario:

- Understanding how simple paging can be added to the data grid

- Understanding the benefit of extending paging in a fluent and interactive way

- Seeing how fluent paging can improve a UI experience in a touch scenario

In the previous coding scenario, we looked at how a form of scrolling would allow a user to access a dynamically growing list of items. However, in that scenario, we were not able to page a full set of data all at once. As mentioned before, the Silverlight data grid includes a feature called UI virtualization which allows the user to bind large amounts of data to the grid without degrading performance. Therefore, it is completely feasible for developers to want to surface a large data set and provide a comprehensive paging solution that includes all of the items bound to the data grid.

■ **Note** A live demo of this coding scenario is available on the companion site:
http://silverlightbusinessintelligence.com/Demos/AddingInteractivity/
InteractiveDataPagingAndFiltering/InteractiveDataPaging.html.

Most people have worked with some form of paging mechanism that provides the ability to jump to another section or view of the data. Figure 4-14 shows some of the different data paging mechanisms found on the Web. For example, a user can simply click the Next or Previous link to jump to different parts of the data set.

Figure 4-14. Different paging styles with common functionality

Following are some of the problems with traditional and simple paging:

- Jumping to different pages gives you a poor context of where you are in the data. For example, where does jumping from page 1 to page 8 take you?

- Large data sets (in BI data scenarios) are hard to navigate using simple paging design patterns. Clicking links to narrow down a data set is not very responsive and could be frustrating to users.

- Fluent interactivity is broken in :touch screen scenarios. Users are left to tap on buttons/links to access different views of data.

Silverlight supports the traditional paging methods shown in Figure 4-14. This is a good UI design pattern for most data technologies. However, Silverlight is an RIA technology. This allows developers to think outside of the box and incorporate some of the key features surrounding responsiveness and local execution. By incorporating complete fluent motions, we can combine interactivity and context to improve paging for larger data sets.

This coding scenario has two parts. The first part will show how we can attach a data pager to the data grid. The second part will improve on the traditional data pager with a more fluent control (the slider). It will also cover some of the out-of-the-box features the Silverlight data grid provides, like sorting and column reordering.

Let's begin this coding scenario:

1. Open Visual Studio 2010 and create a new Silverlight Application project called Chapter4_InteractiveDataPaging.

2. Open the project in Expression Blend 3 and create a new dynamic data source called SampleDataSource.

3. Perform the following steps to create dynamic data (if you need help with Blend's data tool, see this book's Appendix):

   - Add a collection called Sales by choosing Add Collection Property from the SampleDataSource drop-down.

   - Add a string property called CompanyName to the Sales collection, and use the Company Name format.

   - Add a string property called SalesPerson to the Sales collection and use the Name format.

   - Add a number property called SalesAmount to the Sales collection, and use the Number format. Set the length to 5.

   - Add a number property called SalesForecast to the Sales collection and use the Number format and set the length to 5.

   - Click the Sales collection and increase the number of items to 100.

After you complete the preceding steps, the data set should look like Figure 4-15.

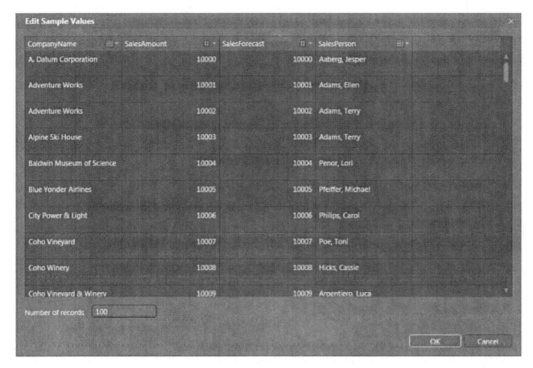

Figure 4-15. Data set for this exercise

4. Now that we have our sample :data defined, we are going to set the UI up so that it will accommodate the data controls required for this demo.

- Change the width of the user control to 600. This will show the data grid columns for our demo more cleanly.

- Change the grid LayoutRoot to a StackPanel.

Your MainPage.xaml file should look like Listing 4-9 now (the changes are highlighted in bold).

Listing 4-9. Change the height and the LayoutRoot of the control.

```
<UserControl x:Class="Chapter4_InteractiveDataPaging.MainPage"
    xmlns="http://schemas.microsoft.com/winfx/2006/xaml/presentation"
    xmlns:x="http://schemas.microsoft.com/winfx/2006/xaml"
    xmlns:d="http://schemas.microsoft.com/expression/blend/2008"↵
 xmlns:mc="http://schemas.openxmlformats.org/markup-compatibility/2006"
    mc:Ignorable="d" Width="600" Height="300">
    <StackPanel x:Name="LayoutRoot" Background="White" >
    </StackPanel>
</UserControl>
```

5. Add the Loaded event to the LayoutRoot StackPanel control (as shown in Listing 4-10).

Listing 4-10. Implement the Loaded event.

```
<StackPanel x:Name="LayoutRoot" Background="White" Loaded="LayoutRoot_Loaded">
 </StackPanel>
```

6. 'We need a control to surface the data to the UI. We are going to use a data grid control.

- In Expression Blend, drag and drop a data grid control.

- Name the data grid dgSales.

- Set the AutoGenerateColumns property to False, as we are going to manually set the columns.

- Change the column definitions: to include the four columns in our data.

- Your MainPage.xaml file should look like Listing 4-11 now (the changes are highlighted in bold).

Listing 4-11. Add the data grid to the main layout.

```
<UserControl
    xmlns="http://schemas.microsoft.com/winfx/2006/xaml/presentation"
    xmlns:x="http://schemas.microsoft.com/winfx/2006/xaml"
    xmlns:d="http://schemas.microsoft.com/expression/blend/2008"
 xmlns:mc="http://schemas.openxmlformats.org/markup-compatibility/2006"
    mc:Ignorable="d"
    xmlns:data="clr-namespace:System.Windows.Controls;assembly=System.Windows.Controls.Data"
x:Class="Chapter4_InteractiveDataPaging.MainPage"
    Width="600" Height="300">
    <StackPanel x:Name="LayoutRoot" Background="White" Loaded="LayoutRoot_Loaded">
        <data:DataGrid x:Name="dgSales" AutoGenerateColumns="False" Height="200"
Margin="0,0,0,0">
            <data:DataGrid.Columns>
                <data:DataGridTextColumn Header="Sales Person" Binding="{Binding
Path=SalesPerson}"/>
                <data:DataGridTextColumn Header="Company Name" Binding="{Binding
Path=CompanyName}"/>
                <data:DataGridTextColumn Header="Sales Amount" Binding="{Binding
Path=SalesAmount}"/>
                <data:DataGridTextColumn Header="SalesForecast" Binding="{Binding
Path=SalesForecast}"/>
            </data:DataGrid.Columns>
        </data:DataGrid>
    </StackPanel>
</UserControl>
```

▪ **Note** If you manually copied the preceding code, ensure that you have added a reference to the
System.Windows.Controls.Data assembly to the project. The data grid control is located in this assembly.

---

7.   Now that we have a data grid defined, perform the following steps:

   • Add the using statement for the SampleDataSource.

   • Define a new SampleDataSource object called data.

   • Set the data grid ItemsSource property to data.Sales.

   • After making :these changes, your code-behind file should resemble Listing
     4-12.

Listing 4-12. Bind the grid data to the data source.

```
...
using Expression.Blend.SampleData.SampleDataSource;

namespace Chapter4_InteractiveDataPaging
{
    public partial class MainPage : UserControl
    {
        SampleDataSource data = new SampleDataSource();
        ....
        private void LayoutRoot_Loaded(object sender, RoutedEventArgs e)
        {
            this.dgSales.ItemsSource = data.Sales;
        }
    }
}
...
```

8.   The application should build and look like Figure 4-16. When I introduced the
     Silverlight data grid, I mentioned that this control provides some standard
     interactions that can be valuable for BI applications. Before going further, try
     some of the standard interactions that come with the Silverlight data grid:

   • Click a column header to sort the data.

   • Drag and drop a column header on top of another one. This will switch the
     column order in the data grid and override the initial default order.

   • Drag the border of the column and change its width.

   • Click the cells and edit the items in place.

Sales Person	Company Name	Sales Amount	SalesForecast	
Aaberg, Jesper	A. Datum Corporation	10000	10000	
Adams, Ellen	Adventure Works	10001	10001	
Adams, Terry	Adventure Works	10002	10002	
Adams, Terry	Alpine Ski House	10003	10003	
Penor, Lori	Baldwin Museum of Science	10004	10004	
Pfeiffer, Michael	Blue Yonder Airlines	10005	10005	
Philips, Carol	City Power & Light	10006	10006	

Figure 4-16. Data grid with sales information sorted by Sales Person

9. At this point, we have 100 records bound to a data grid—not enough records that we would have to entertain the idea of adding paging. However, let's assume that we have many more records. In :this scenario, we are going to apply a data paging solution that adds paging interactions to our data grid.

10. Open up Expression Blend 3 and add the data pager control below the data grid. Note that the data pager control is part of the Silverlight Control Toolkit. If you do not have the toolkit installed, it may not show up in your control assets.

   - Name the data page control dgSalesPager.

   - Set the source of the data pager to {Binding}. This will allow us to dynamically set the context of the data pager.

   - Set the data pager DisplayMode to FirstLastNumeric.

The added data pager line should look like Listing 4-13.

Listing 4-13. Data pager for the data grid control

```
<data:DataPager x:Name="dgSalesPager" Source="{Binding}" DisplayMode="FirstLastNumeric"/>
```

11. We need to set the data context of both the grid and data pager to the same source. In step 8, we set the data grid source explicitly. Let's add dynamic binding to the data grid in MainPage.xaml. The code change is highlighted in bold in Listing 4-14.

Listing 4-14. Set the source for the data grid.

```
<data:DataGrid x:Name="dgSales" Height="200" Margin="0,0,0,0"
               AutoGenerateColumns="False" ItemsSource="{Binding}">
```

12. Our UI and XAML are ready to consume data. In the MainPage.xaml.cs file, let's change the Loaded event of the layout control to activate our data pager.

   - Add a using reference to System.Windows.Data.

- We need to create a special type called PagedCollectionView, which the data pager needs to consume.

- Set the collection page size to 10.

- Set the data context of our UI to the collectionView.

- The added using statement and the LayoutRoot_Loaded event should look the code in Listing 4-15 (the changed code is highlighted in bold).

Listing 4-15. Add binding for the data pager and data grid.

```
using System.Windows.Shapes;
using Expression.Blend.SampleData.SampleDataSource;
using System.Windows.Data;

namespace Chapter4_InteractiveDataPaging
{
    public partial class MainPage : UserControl
    {
        SampleDataSource data = new SampleDataSource();

        public MainPage()
        {
            InitializeComponent();
        }

        private void LayoutRoot_Loaded(object sender, RoutedEventArgs e)
        {
            // create a PageCollection view from our sales data
            PagedCollectionView collectionView = new PagedCollectionView(data.Sales);
            // set the page size
            collectionView.PageSize = 10;
            // set the data context to the page collection views
            this.DataContext = collectionView;
        }
    }
}
```

13. Our project will build now :and fully function. Build the project and try using the data pager. Once executed, the project should look like Figure 4-17.

- We can do the same interactions we have done before on the data grid.

- With the data pager, we can navigate to any page by clicking any of the page items. We can also jump to the beginning and end of the data set.

- Note that when you sort the data grid, the data pager maintains the sorted state of the data.

Sales Person	Company Name	Sales Amount	SalesForecast	
Argentiero, Luca	Coho Vineyard & Winery	10050	10081	
Perry, Brian	Contoso, Ltd	10051	10083	
Ramos, Luciana	Contoso Pharmaceuticals	10052	10085	
Barber, David	Consolidated Messenger	10053	10087	
Jamison, Jay	Fabrikam, Inc.	10054	10089	
Reid, Miles	Fourth Coffee	10055	10091	
Bowen, Eli	Graphic Design Institute	10056	10093	

|◀ 4 5 **6** 7 8 ▶|

Figure 4-17. Data grid with the data pager

14. We have achieved a pretty good paging solution thus far. The data pager grants us access to different views of the entire data set quickly. Furthermore, there was very little code we had to add in order to accommodate the data pager. It is time to extend our scenario with a more fluent data pager using a slider control:

- Add a slider control to the bottom of the data grid pager.

- Name the control `sliderPager`.

We are going to take advantage of Silverlight element binding. We will both retrieve and set the values of the data pager from the slider control.

The XAML code of the `MainPage.xaml` file is shown in Listing 4-16 (the changes are highlighted in bold).

Listing 4-16. Add binding for the data pager and data grid.

```
...
<dataControls:DataPager x:Name="dgSalesPager" Source="{Binding}"
DisplayMode="FirstLastNumeric"/>
    <Slider x:Name="sliderPager" Cursor="Hand" Minimum="0"
        Value="{Binding PageIndex, ElementName=dgSalesPager, Mode=TwoWay}"
        Maximum="{Binding PageCount, ElementName=dgSalesPager, Mode=TwoWay}" />
</StackPanel>
```

15. It was pretty simple to extend the paging with the slider using element binding, and it required no additional C# code. The slider uses two-way binding and relies on the data pager as a bridge between the slider and the data grid. The project will look like Figure 4-18.

- Note how easy it is to: page the data with the slider. It is responsive and fluid. The user quickly gains insight and a sense of context of where they are in the data.

- Notice not only that the slider can be used as input, but also that as we use the data pager, it changes the slider automatically. Both can be used in conjunction together.

Sales Person	Company Name	Sales Amount	SalesForecast	
Cook, Kevin	Margie's Travel	10030	10041	
Li, Yuhong	Northwind Traders	10031	10043	
Strande, Amy	Proseware, Inc.	10032	10045	
Makovac, Zrinka	School of Fine Art	10033	10047	
Miller, Ben	Southridge Video	10034	10049	
Orton, Jon	Tailspin Toys	10035	10051	
Zhang, Larry	Trey Research	10036	10053	

Figure 4-18. Data grid with slider that can be used as a fluent pager

Lessons Learned

This coding scenario introduced how easily we can extend the data grid and provide different paging solutions with it. Paging is a very important paradigm for creating easy-to-use data-centric applications.

In this scenario, our first implementation was using the data pager control. Even though this approach works well for most scenarios, it has some limitations when applied to BI 2.0 concepts. Furthermore, imagine using a Windows 7 Mobile device and having to tap the screen continuously to try to find the desired page of data.

The slider paging solution improved paging dramatically. A user can instantaneously gain context of where they are in the data and fluently move the slider to access the exact piece of data they want. Not only does this solution apply BI 2.0 concepts, but it also works well: with next-generation interactivity input like touch screens. On a mobile device or a touch-enabled screen, wouldn't you rather use the slider interactivity to page data? Applying this technique in a production environment, you would see a great benefit when this is used in conjunction with web services.

Possible Enhancements

The slider implementation can be enhanced in several different ways. First, we could add another display mode to the data pager (called SliderMode) which would replace the numeric list of pages with a slider control. Furthermore, we could improve the user's context of the data by adding labels for the minimum and: maximum records while the slider is being used.

Coding Scenario: Fluent Data Filtering with the Slider Control

In this coding scenario, we will extend the concepts of the preceding data paging coding scenario. This will cover how to provide easy and fluent filtering of data using the slider control.

127

Following are the goals of this scenario:

- Comprehending the value of fluent filtering in BI 2.0 scenarios

- Understanding how responsive interactions with data can give instant BI insight

- Envisioning using this technique to enhance what-if and statistical scenarios in BI applications

---

▨ **Note** A live demo of this coding scenario is available on the companion site:
http://silverlightbusinessintelligence.com/Demos/AddingInteractivity/InteractiveDataPagingAndFiltering/
InteractiveDataPaging.html.

Let's begin this coding scenario:

1. Copy the previous coding scenario to a folder, and name it Chapter4_FluentDataFiltering. Open the project in Visual Studio.

2. We are going to add two sliders to the UI (below the slider control) that will enable data filtering of the sample data source that will be surfaced on the data grid.

    - The slider minimum and maximum values are defined between 10,000 and 10,100. This is because in our sample data, we defined the numeric length of our SalesAmount and SalesForecast properties as 5. Note that Expression Blend 3 increments the number data type by 1 (This is a change from Blend 3 beta which randomly assigned numerical values).

    - The UI will consume the slider ValueChanged event with the slider_ValueChanged event handler.

    - The UI will display the value of the slider in a text block by using element binding.

3. Add the XAML highlighted in bold in Listing 4-17 to the MainPage.xaml file.

Listing 4-17. Two slider controls to interactively filter the data

```
...
<StackPanel Orientation="Horizontal" HorizontalAlignment="Stretch">
    <StackPanel Orientation="Vertical" Width="300">
        <TextBlock Text="Sales Amount"/>
        <Slider x:Name="sliderSalesAmount" Cursor="Hand" Minimum="10000"↵
Maximum="10100"
            ValueChanged="slider_ValueChanged"/>
        <TextBlock Text="{Binding Value, ElementName=sliderSalesAmount,↵
Mode=OneWay}"/>
    </StackPanel>
    <StackPanel Orientation="Vertical" Width="300">
```

```
                <TextBlock Text="Sales Forecast"/>
                <Slider x:Name="sliderSalesForecast" Cursor="Hand" Minimum="10000" ↵
 Maximum="10100"
                   ValueChanged="slider_ValueChanged"/>
                <TextBlock Text="{Binding Value, ElementName=sliderSalesForecast, ↵
 Mode=OneWay}"/>
            </StackPanel>
        </StackPanel>
     </StackPanel>
</UserControl>
```

4. We need to create a corresponding event handler that will be called when the value of either slider changes. This piece of code will execute each time a slider value has changed. We will use a simple LINQ query to filter the records that have a value greater than or equal to the value of the slider. Add the code in bold in Listing 4-18 to the MainPage.xaml.cs file.

Listing 4-18. Code-behind for the slider control to use LINQ to filter the data

```
...
private void slider_ValueChanged(object sender, RoutedPropertyChangedEventArgs<double> e)
{
    // make sure not to call the code before the data grid is rendered
    if (this.dgSales != null)
    {
        // filter the data using LINQ based on the two slider values
        // SalesAmount and SalesForecast properties are used for filtering
        this.dgSales.ItemsSource = from s in data.Sales
                          where s.SalesAmount >= this.sliderSalesAmount.Value &&
                          s.SalesForecast >= this.sliderSalesForecast.Value
                          select s;
    }
}
...
```

5. The project is ready to build and test. Once you run the program, it should look like Figure 4-19.

   - The Sales Amount and Sales Forecast sliders can be used to filter the sales data.

   - Move either of the sliders to the right and notice records being removed. This motion increases the sales amount that the records have to be greater than.

   - Move either of the sliders to the left and notice records being added. This motion decreases the sales amount that the records have to be greater than.

Sales Person	Company Name	Sales Amount	SalesForecast	
Silva, Alexandre	Lucerne Publishing	10029	10039	
Cook, Kevin	Margie's Travel	10030	10041	
Li, Yuhong	Northwind Traders	10031	10043	
Strande, Amy	Proseware, Inc.	10032	10045	
Makovac, Zrinka	School of Fine Art	10033	10047	
Miller, Ben	Southridge Video	10034	10049	
Orton, Jon	Tailspin Toys	10035	10051	

|◀ 1 2 3 4 5 ▶|

Sales Amount

10028.3737024221

Sales Forecast

10000

Figure 4-19. Sales data grid with two sliders that can fluently filter sales data

Lessons Learned

In this coding scenario, we extended the fluent interaction scenario introduced earlier in this chapter. This project showed how you could translate query operations into simple to user interactions. In BI 2.0 software, we have to translate data querying and filtering into interactions. It is difficult to translate user gestures and interactions into software processing that manipulates data. However, new technologies like Silverlight provide local processing that enables designers to be more creative. This example amplified this. We not only have a simple UI that applies BI 2.0 concepts, but we also have a design that can be presented in next-generation devices (touch screens, gesture-enabled devices, etc.).

Possible Enhancements

The project we just created skipped several key points you would want to consider in a production scenario. First, the slider labels did not round the numbers or use currency format. This could be solved by implementing converters.

In a production implementation, you are likely to link the slider interactions to data requests from web services. You would not want to call a service for every small value change. A good design would be to leverage Silverlight's local caching in combination with data services. Therefore, you could load the data from the local cache rather than making expensive web service requests.

Coding Scenario: Searching Data with the AutoCompleteBox Control

In this coding scenario, we will introduce the Silverlight AutoCompleteBox control from the Silverlight Control Toolkit. With this control, we will cover how you can easily add searching and filtering of data.

Following are the goals of this scenario:

- Understanding the functionality of the AutoCompleteBox control
- Seeing how to use the control effectively to provide basic data search scenarios

---

▨ **Note** A live demo of this coding scenario is available on the companion site:
http://silverlightbusinessintelligence.com/Demos/AddingInteractivity/SearchingDataWithAutoComplete/
SearchingDataWithAutoComplete.html.

Let's begin this coding scenario:

1. Make a copy of the previous coding scenario to a folder, and name it
   Chapter4_SearchingDataWithAutoComplete. Open the project in Visual
   Studio.

2. We are going to add an AutoCompleteBox control which is available in the
   Silverlight Control Toolkit. This control will be responsible for searching our
   Sales Persons data items. Ensure that MainPage.xaml contains the changes
   highlighted in bold in Listing 4-19. Also ensure that a reference to
   System.Windows.Controls.Input is present.

Listing 4-19. Code to add the AutoCompleteBox control to the project

```
...
xmlns:input="clr-namespace:System.Windows.Controls;assembly=System.Windows.Controls.Input"
x:Class="Chapter4_InteractiveDataPaging.MainPage"
Width="600" Height="300">
<StackPanel x:Name="LayoutRoot" Background="White" Loaded="LayoutRoot_Loaded">
    <StackPanel Orientation="Horizontal" HorizontalAlignment="Stretch">
        <TextBlock Text="Search Sales Person:    " />
        <input:AutoCompleteBox x:Name="searchSalesData" Margin="0,0,0,10"
FilterMode="Contains"
            MinimumPrefixLength="1" IsTextCompletionEnabled="False" Width="250"
        />
    </StackPanel>
...
```

3. Add the event handler for the SelectionChanged event for the
   AutoCompleteBox, as shown in Listing 4-20.

Listing 4-20. SelectionChanged event for the AutoCompleteBox control

```
<input:AutoCompleteBox x:Name="searchSalesData" Margin="0,0,0,10" FilterMode="Contains"
MinimumPrefixLength="1" IsTextCompletionEnabled="False" Width="250"
SelectionChanged="searchSalesData_SelectionChanged"/>
```

   4. The AutoCompleteBox will provide a search mechanism for our sales data.
       Therefore, we need to provide it with a data source. In addition, we need to
       create the event handler to process the SelectionChanged event of the
       AutoCompleteBox. This will allow us to rebind the data grid once we select a
       particular salesperson. Make the changes that are highlighted in bold in Listing
       4-21 to the MainPage.xaml.cs file.

Listing 4-21. Implementation of search in the AutoCompleteBox

```
...
private void LayoutRoot_Loaded(object sender, RoutedEventArgs e)
{
    // create a PageCollection view from our sales data
    PagedCollectionView collectionView = new PagedCollectionView(data.Sales);
    // set the page size
    collectionView.PageSize = 10;

    // set the data context to the page collection views
    this.DataContext = collectionView;

    // set the autocomplete box filter to the salesperson records
    this.searchSalesData.ItemsSource = data.Sales.Select(a => a.SalesPerson);
}

private void searchSalesData_SelectionChanged(object sender, SelectionChangedEventArgs e)
{
    // retrieve the selected salesperson
    string salesPerson = (sender as AutoCompleteBox).SelectedItem as string;

    if (salesPerson != null)
    {
        // if the selected sales person is not null,
        // select the person from the data
        this.dgSales.ItemsSource = from s in data.Sales
                                   where s.SalesPerson == salesPerson
                                   select s;
    }
    else
    {
        // reset the grid
        this.dgSales.ItemsSource = data.Sales;
    }
}
...
```

5. Build the project and run it. The UI will resemble Figure 4-20.

    • Start typing any letters and you will notice that a list box with names appears. You can traverse the list with arrow keys or select a salesperson manually.

    • Note that when you select a salesperson, the data grid automatically updates with the selection. Conversely, if you clear the items out of the AutoCompleteBox, it will return the data grid to its original state.

Figure 4-20. Sales data grid filtered with the AutoCompleteBox

Lessons Learned

In this coding scenario, we implemented a simple but powerful search solution in our data. Implementing this simple search technique can make other query or filter interactions secondary. Why would a user want to page or scroll through lots of data when they could just simply type a few letters and narrow the search immediately? Furthermore, a quick search option allows users to narrow the data greatly if they do not know the full information. For example, if I knew the salesperson for a particular company started with the letter *P*, I could enter this into the AutoCompleteBox and immediately be presented with possible record matches. This enhancement limits the amount of time a users spends trying to isolate particular data records.

This control can be extended to consume data from data services and lends itself beautifully to searching large BI data repositories. Optimized services indexed for search can provide rapid responses for query requests. It can do this while remaining snappy and responsive, fulfilling key tenets of BI 2.0 software.

Summary

This chapter clarified why it is important to create simple designs that allow users to manipulate data interactively. It discussed the different types of interactions a user might perform on a data set. This chapter concluded by showing four different examples of how Silverlight can enhance data-centric applications by quickly paging, querying, and filtering data sets. This chapter reinforces some of the techniques added in current Microsoft Pivot controls.

Your main takeaways from this chapter should be that Silverlight controls can be extended to provide interactive UIs for current BI solutions. You do not have to rely on the default behavior of Silverlight controls in order to provide interactivity to you data. Applying these concepts correctly allows the delivery of BI applications to many users by leveraging next-generation platforms like mobile or multitouch-enabled devices.

CHAPTER 5

■ ■ ■

Introduction to Data Visualizations

This chapter is the first chapter in a three-part series about data visualizations.

In the previous chapter, you saw how Silverlight can be used to present data using list-based controls like the data grid. This chapter builds on that foundation, introducing the concept of data visualizations. You will learn the importance of data visualizations and how they can be used to create engaging graphical representations of data. Furthermore, you will see several scenarios that show how Silverlight's rich rendering engine can be leveraged to present data graphically.

This chapter provides the fundamental knowledge you need about data visualizations in order to understand the next two chapters. This chapter covers data visualizations at a high level; the next two chapters will be a deeper dive into analysis and advanced data visualization concepts.

The following coding scenarios are included in this chapter:

- Creating charts using the Silverlight Control Toolkit chart controls

- Surfacing data with a tag cloud

- Using the Microsoft Bing Enterprise map control to expose BI information

The following table outlines the specific goals that different types of readers will achieve by reading this chapter.

Audience	Goals
Silverlight developers	Learn techniques on how to use Silverlight to create basic data visualizations.
	Understand how data visualizations deliver insight in using BI 2.0 conventions.
Business intelligence professionals	Understand that Silverlight contains a powerful rendering engine that can compete with other BI data visualization software.
	Perceive the additional value Silverlight can bring to BI software.
Strategic decision makers	Understand how data visualizations can enhance the perceived value of applications beyond simple controls.
	See how Silverlight's integration with Microsoft Enterprise Services (e.g., the Bing Map SDK) can add a big advantage to your application.

■ **Note** Additional external resources for this data visualization chapter can be found on the companion web site: `http://silverlightbusinessintelligence.com/BookResources/ExternalResources/DataVisualizations.aspx`.

What Are Data Visualizations?

In the previous chapter, you displayed data via controls that presented information using numbers formatted in a list or hierarchy. The goal of those controls was to effectively deliver insight from large amounts of data. You learned some techniques that you could implement in helping list-based controls deliver information quickly. However, in some cases, lists of data (no matter how simple the interactivity) are just not good enough to deliver key information effectively. This is where data visualization techniques come in.

Data visualizations surface information from data using graphical means. Data visualizations have the same goals as their list-based counterparts. With data visualizations, insight and key information still needs to be delivered effectively. However, data visualizations use the power of graphics rather than numbers to do this. For example, Figure 5-1 shows Microsoft's Bing visual search engine (`www.bing.com/visualsearch`) powered by Silverlight. In this image, Silverlight is used to show dog breed images in a 3D list layout to aid the user in searching for information visually. This is a great improvement over basic text keyword searches.

Figure 5-1. A list of dog breeds in a 3D Silverlight list implemented in Bing Visual Search

Data visualizations are used across different technologies and various software applications. Over the years, data visualizations have been called a number of different names in different circles. Two of the more popular names are *information visualizations* and *infographics*. In addition, some software professionals use the term *visualizations*. If you are interested in researching this topic further, you can find additional information by searching for those alternative names.

■ **Note** Data visualizations are not a new paradigm. However, as software UIs have become graphically rich, visualizations have become very popular. Many software and service vendors like throw around the latest buzzwords. Sadly, this blurs the definition of true data visualizations. You may have come across a control or a piece of software that claims to be a data visualization because it uses a data grid to "visually present data." In my opinion, this is a stretch, and loose use of this terminology can lead to confusion. This book takes a more purist approach by defining data visualizations as a means of surfacing data using graphical techniques. There are professionals on the other side of the spectrum that don't consider charts or mapping tools as true data visualizations. However, those opinions are in a very small minority. I consider charts and graphs valid data visualizations; however, they tend to be simple and don't include as much of the animations and effects that more complex visualizations do.

Data visualizations are everywhere. You see many examples of them every day. You are a consumer of data visualizations if you read magazines or newspapers or even if you watch the news. For example, when the weatherperson is presenting the five-day forecast, she shows you a list of days with the temperature shown in big bold letters. There's also a graphic that summarizes the weather: rainy days have gray clouds and droplets of rain, sunny days show the sun, and cloudy days include clouds. All news organizations present the weather in some kind of visualization format. The important properties (temperature, rain, cloudiness) are clearly presented using graphic hints. This allows the person watching the forecast to quickly narrow down the important days and discern if the weather is going to be pleasant or not.

Characteristics of a Data Visualization

In the previous section, you learned what data visualizations are. But what constitutes good data visualization? What are the key characteristics of data visualizations? The following subsections cover some basic concepts.

Respect the Data

Data visualizations are graphical techniques to present data. I cannot stress enough how important the underlying data is for data visualizations. You cannot simply create an engaging animated 3D graphic and say it is a representation of the data. The graphic has to be bound to the data and it has to be a valid representation of the information. Just because it's a graphic does not mean it can stray from presenting the data in proper way.

One of the main reasons why data visualizations are so popular is that humans are better at understanding information visually. A user can instantly process multiple colors, perspectives, sizes, animations, and so on, to be used as hints to focus on key pieces of information.

Figure 5-2 shows fictitious sales information. The visualization presents three years of data with a progress bar for each year and the amount of sales made. The width of the progress bars represent the amount of sales in a given year. Note how the progress bars and the numbers don't match. According to the graphic, the 2008 sales numbers appear to have dropped minimally compared to 2007, when in actuality they are down by almost 50 percent. This is an example of a poor visualization because it doesn't represent the underlying data accurately.

Figure 5-2. Visualizations have to represent the underlying data accurately, not just look elegant. Note that the progress bars are not scaling the underlying data properly.

One of the key aspects of a data visualization is that the context of the data it represents must be maintained and displayed accurately. Well, you say, sometimes it's hard to translate that context. In some scenarios, that's true. For example, in a visualization showing the solar system, it is hard to translate the size of the sun in proportion to the Earth accurately. However, in those cases, that should be noted on the graphic. There are solutions for presenting data that has dramatic changes. For example, if you have ever looked at stock charts with steep gains or losses, you have probably noticed that the y-axis is scaled appropriately. Glancing at it might not give the proper context; however, upon studying the chart further, you will see that the axis of the chart will effectively translate the data visually.

Data visualizations are traditionally read-only representations of the data. A user should not be provided a technique to alter the data in any way. This is different than a list-based presentation of data which sometimes offers the ability to edit data in place.

Properly designed visualizations need to represent data accurately, and under no circumstances should they present the data in such a way that would give the data an alternate meaning.

Simple and to the Point

Data visualizations are designed as an alternative way to view data and should offer insight at a high level more quickly than a data grid can. If designed properly, visualizations can complement lists and grids elegantly. This is the main reason why visualizations are so popular in dashboard scenarios.

To gauge the difference between a data grid and a data visualization, look at Figure 5-3. This figure displays some fictitious data about company expenses. The top image is a pie chart visualization of the data. The bottom image is a data grid representation of the same data. Imagine that you are an executive tasked with cutting costs. If the chart was displayed, you would immediately be drawn to the red area of the pie chart. Clearly, it is the biggest expense relative to the others. The visualization immediately draws your eyes to the largest slice of the pie. Conversely, the data grid requires you to scan all of the items. Furthermore, you don't understand the scale of each item until you take a second to think about it. You could sort the data grid and get an ordered list of expenses. However, this is an additional interaction with the data that is unnecessary with the pie chart.

Good data visualization provides quicker insight into data without having to perform additional analysis or data interactions.

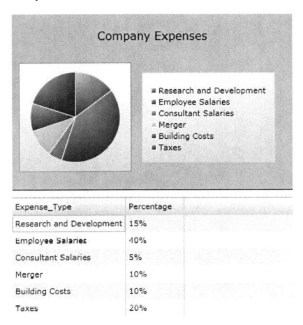

Expense_Type	Percentage
Research and Development	15%
Employee Salaries	40%
Consultant Salaries	5%
Merger	10%
Building Costs	10%
Taxes	20%

Figure 5-3. Which one allows you to more quickly gauge the biggest expense: the chart or the data grid?

Animations and Transitions

Data visualizations displayed using advanced rendering engines (e.g., Silverlight, WPF) can use animations to provide additional clues about the data to the user.

Figure 5-4 shows an example of an elegant interface used in a data visualization. This example is a screenshot from Roambi's (www.roambi.com) dynamic visualization application for the iPhone. The Roambi for iPhone application presents your custom data using its dynamic rendering engine. When you click a slice of the pie, the pie chart animates and the slice circles around to the details pointer displaying the numerically formatted data. The animation transition is very well implemented in the pie chart as an extension of the data visualization. First, the transition animation signifies that something is happening with the state of the display. This prompts the eyes of the user to focus on the detailed information.

■ **Note** The Roambi application provides additional services to business clients by presenting salesforce.com, Crystal Reports, and Excel data. Obviously, a screenshot of an animation does not do the application justice. Go to www.roambi.com to try some of the application's features. The iPhone application is available as a free download from the Apple App Store.

Figure 5-4. Roambi's dynamic data visualization iPhone application

Animations are a great way to enhance the behavior of a UI and add extra elegance to interactions. However, animations need to be used properly in data visualizations. They need to add value to the visualization and should be considered an extension of the data presentation. For example, an animation could be added when a bar chart is rendered. Initially, all of the items appear at the bottom and then they slowly grow to their proper positions. The highest bars (representing the largest pieces of data) will take the longest time to attain their resting positions, giving the user's eye an additional area to focus on. In this example, the animation is an effective extension of both the data and the graphical visualization.

Adding animations aimlessly to data visualizations for the sake of elegance could be perceived negatively by the target audience. Many times an animation is added because the designer thinks it's cool. However, designers should be respectful of the user's time. Even if you add the most beautiful transitional animation ever created, if it takes 2 or 3 seconds to complete, users are going to get annoyed by it rather quickly and want to turn it off. Furthermore, by using ineffective animations, you could block the user's ability to perform analysis or gain insight from the data visualization. This could lead to a data visualization having the opposite effect: not providing quick and simple insight by seeming cumbersome and overladen with animations.

Use of animations and transitions is optional when designing data visualizations. Animations should only be added to provide an extension of the data or the graphical visualization. Furthermore, when planning animations, you need to consider the target framework of the software. For example, Silverlight and WPF frameworks offer very powerful rendering engines while JavaScript and HTML do not offer a rich rendering framework. Concepts like 3D take a lot of additional code.

■ **Note** The next couple of data visualization chapters will cover some effective transition techniques that leverage Silverlight's animation engine.

Interactivity

Data visualizations that are displayed using advanced rendering engines and that have rich animations lend themselves well to interactivity. In the previous chapter, I discussed how to add interactions through various inputs to list-based data. This concept applies well to graphical visualizations where animations can show transitions, expansion, trends, timelines, and so on, while providing a valid context to the underlying data.

Even in simple scenarios, users expect to be able to interact with a well-presented data visualization. For example, in Figure 5-3 or 5-4, a user would probably expect to click or touch the respective pie slices and thus be taken to either a details screen or some form of drill-down.

Figure 5-5 shows a simple bar chart bound to historic data of widget sales for four regions. A slider control located on the bottom allows the user to quickly change the years and visually see the trend of the sales by noting the size of the representative bar. If you try the control online at www.silverlightbusinessintelligence.com/Demos/IntroToDataVisualizations/InteractiveDataVisualization/InteractiveBarChart.html, you can see that the control is very responsive; it adds interactivity that enhances the analytical experience.

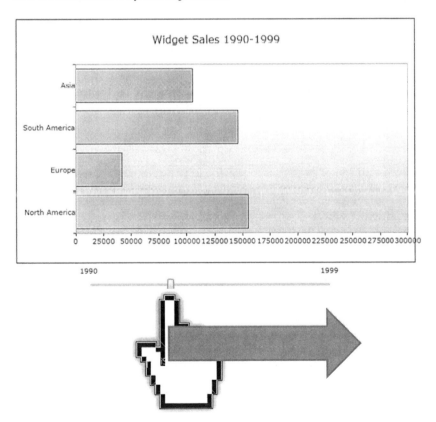

Figure 5-5. *Interactivity complements data visualizations*

Designers of data visualizations have to be cognizant of the many standard design patterns that exist when creating data-centric applications. Omitting simple interactivity such as the drill-down design pattern could leave a negative perception with the user.

In the next chapter, I will cover detailed examples of different types of interactivity that can be added to data visualizations.

Widgets and Dashboards

Data visualizations are an individual unit of functionality. Their main goal is to provide small pieces of key insight from the underlying data. This makes data visualizations good candidates to be deployed in widget form and displayed from smaller areas in a larger application. Data visualizations can also be used to enhance existing software applications without having to rearchitect the entire system. For example, if you want to enhance the user experience in a BI system, you could add some data visualization widgets or web parts in key areas of the application. Dashboard deployments are very popular; designers can create interactive controls that can be hooked into the business data and instantly provide value.

Data Visualizations and Business Intelligence 2.0

Now that you have some fundamental information about data visualizations, you can start to see how data visualizations can play an important role in BI 2.0 concepts. In these subsections, I will cover some of the BI 2.0 concepts introduced in Chapter 2 and discuss how they relate to data visualizations.

BI for the Masses

BI 2.0 targets an increased audience, and one of its goals is to provide BI to non-analytical users. The average user is not going to want to use an application that presents data via a scrolling list of data. Data visualizations can provide a much more engaging experience if graphics and symbols are used instead of rows of data. This is a much more intuitive approach to surface data for a casual user.

Controlled Analysis

One of the early problems of BI was that it wanted to be so powerful that it allowed users to do a lot. A great example of this is the spreadsheet; it's useful for creating great insight but it's too open for average users. An average user needs to be steered in the right direction so that they do not create analysis that is incorrect. Data visualizations are an excellent way to control analysis. Querying, searching, and complex business algorithms can be completely abstracted from the user with interactions that are controlled. For example, if you provide a slider that has a minimum and a maximum range, a user cannot input a string or a bad date. This limits the user from performing an action that would cause an incorrect analysis.

Ease of Use

One of the characteristics of a good data visualization is that it is simple to use and communicates only the key messages from the data. This fits right into the BI 2.0 paradigm of keeping analysis simple. By allowing the user to focus on one item and extrapolate one key piece of information from it, you keep things simple for the average user.

Rich Interfaces

BI 2.0 design techniques advocate using robust interfaces backed by technology that is fast and responsive. If you have created an interactive data visualization, you have probably already met that requirement. Good infographics require a robust rendering engine that needs to be responsive. Therefore, by investing in technology that supports data visualizations, you are on the way to selecting a platform that will probably be good for surfacing BI 2.0 software.

Challenges of Implementing Data Visualizations

Data visualizations sound great. You might be inclined to implement them all over your BI applications. However, you do have to be aware of the challenges of investing in data visualizations.

Custom Controls

When you start crafting your first data visualization, you will soon realize that you are essentially developing your own custom data control. As mentioned in the previous section, the data visualization needs to respect the underlying data. Therefore, the data visualization control should be unit tested and verified many times to ensure that it can handle all forms of changes in the data.

Many development organizations simply do not have the resources or the time to get involved in creating in-house custom controls; this is the main reason why there are so many third-party control vendors out there. Furthermore, developing custom controls requires a unique skill set from a developer that might not exist in the organization. A development organization that has not done custom control development in the past could struggle in creating data visualizations.

Frameworks that use a declarative language for their UIs (e.g., Silverlight and WPF) can reduce the pain of custom development dramatically. For example, Silverlight controls can be extended through composition, and creating mashup controls can speed up the creation of custom controls. Even though challenges with custom control development remain, adding custom in-house visualizations is more plausible than several years ago.

Need for Designers

Data visualizations are based on surfacing information and rely heavily on graphics. Any time you are dealing with graphical components, designers should be involved. Developers can usually handle creating effective and clean data UIs that are based on standard controls. However, the same cannot be said with custom visualizations since a data visualization is usually a custom design. Do you really want to leave the color palette, the animations, and the transitions in the hands of a developer?

Even simple visualizations such as charts and graphs sometimes need a designer to polish the UI. For example, the standard look and feel of a Silverlight Control Toolkit bar chart is not very appealing. It's passable, but it probably needs to be customized to fit into your overall design. More complex data visualizations that have rich animations, transitions, and 3D effects should always involve a designer's input.

This presents a challenge to development organizations, as they may have to invest in hiring a designer or use the productivity of an existing one for data visualizations.

Reinventing the Insight Wheel

A data visualization is supposed to highlight additional insight that a list or a grid cannot offer. If the visualization does not provide significant and immediate analytical comprehension, then it is probably overkill to present the data using this technique. Presenting data visually should lead to better analysis and good decisions.

One of the pitfalls of using data visualizations is that you have to be sure that a graphical representation adds significant value over traditional means. As mentioned previously, using proven means like a data grid or simple chart visualizations is usually less resource consuming than creating rich visualizations. Therefore, investing in an infographic should guarantee that it will communicate additional insight that cannot be ascertained by traditional means.

Presenting Proper Insight

One of the dangers of creating graphical representations of data is that you might create an object that is not representative of the underlying data. Going back to Figure 5-1, you can see that the progress bars do not reflect the trending information in the data. Botching the opportunity to deliver secondary insight like trending is reflective of poor design, but it could be worse. For example, you could introduce a bug in the algorithm that provides the exact opposite of what you are trying to communicate. As the business algorithms become more complex, the probability of communicating poor insight becomes greater. The problem is significant for data visualizations because users presented with bad data in list form might not be able to spot data anomalies or bad calculations. This presents a challenge to developers to maintain not only data integrity but also the insight that can be derived from a data visualization.

Not Knowing the Target Audience

The demands of users are what drive the new designs to be simpler and more engaging. However, not knowing the characteristics of your general audience could hinder how the data visualization is perceived. This is especially true in BI 2.0 scenarios where the goal is to provide BI to a large target audience. For example, not knowing that your audience prefers to surface data from a mobile device could lead to critical errors in the way the data visualization is designed. In addition, not following proper design patterns for UIs could alienate users. For example, if you don't stick with neutral color palettes, you could alienate users that are color-blind.

Data Visualizations Might Not Be Enough

As you can see from the challenges just listed, there are many things to consider before investing in data visualization technology. In some cases, even if all of the guidelines are followed, you may still need to provide a traditional mechanism for surfacing data. Providing an option to view the data in both a traditional way and in a new data visualization is a good way to transition users into next-generation user interfaces. In later versions of the software, the traditional data views could be deprecated.

Data Visualizations and Silverlight

In my opinion, Silverlight offers many features that make it an ideal platform for creating data visualizations. This section will expand on some of the Silverlight features introduced in Chapter 2 and relate them to implementing data visualizations.

Out-of-the-Box Data Visualizations

If you have been a .NET developer from the beginning, you probably know that Microsoft has been criticized for not providing a charting solution in its development tools. Microsoft has started listening to the developer community and has formally begun providing charting packages for different frameworks, including ASP.NET and Silverlight.

Silverlight's controls are extended from the Silverlight Control Toolkit project (http://silverlight.codeplex.com). In the toolkit, you will find many controls that provide enhanced functionality not found in the standard Silverlight framework. Pictured in Figure 5-6 is the data visualization section of the Silverlight Control Toolkit. The toolkit has an entire section dedicated to charting visualizations, including area, bar, bubble, column, line, pie, and scatter series chart controls.

■ **Note** If you would like to browse the Silverlight Control Toolkit visualizations online, go to

www.silverlight.net/content/samples/sl4/toolkitcontrolsamples/run/default.html.

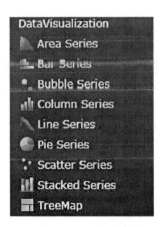

Figure 5-6. The Silverlight Control Toolkit includes several simple data visualizations.

The data visualization controls contained in the Silverlight Control Toolkit are pretty simple when compared to manually created complex infographics. However, the open nature of the Silverlight framework allows these controls to be extended rather easily with enhanced styles, animations, and behaviors. This allows you improve on the standard functionality you get from these controls. Figure 5-7 shows a screenshot of two chart visualization controls. The one on the left has the default look and feel;

the one on the right has a style theme applied to it. This shows you how the Silverlight Control Toolkit controls can be enhanced quickly to fit naturally with your particular UI.

Figure 5-7. *Chart visualizations can be quickly styled using themes. The chart on the right has a toolkit theme applied.*

One of the great benefits of using the Silverlight Control Toolkit is that it is open source, and developers do not have to pay to integrate it into their applications. This also allows you to use the code of these controls as guides for more complex custom infographics. If the toolkit controls are only missing a couple of pieces of functionality, you can use the Silverlight framework to extend them.

Rich Rendering Engine and Design Tools

Rich data visualizations require a rich rendering engine to surface all of the controls. More complex visualizations benefit from a robust rendering engine and advanced transformations such as 3D. The Silverlight rendering engine is based on the WPF version. The engine itself is very performant and can be hardware accelerated. This allows Silverlight to create immersive and media-rich experiences.

If you are familiar with advanced graphics programming, you are probably saying that this is nothing new. Well, this is true; if you wanted to, you could extend ASP.NET or the desktop .NET Framework with rich animations and pretty graphics. However, if you did that, you would have to learn GDI+ or DirectX extensions. Furthermore, tooling for these frameworks is not particularly great and doesn't integrate well at all into business applications. This is why GDI+ and DirectX are largely left to game, media, device, and control developers.

Silverlight abstracts the complexity of learning additional graphic-oriented frameworks by using XAML to declaratively control the user interface. Silverlight improves this further because you don't have to be a XAML expert to create Silverlight user interfaces. Expression Blend provides rich designer tools for creating these experiences, making editing XAML by hand rare. Figure 5-8 shows some of the tools available in Expression Blend 4 to create animation timelines, transformations, and 3D projections.

Figure 5-8. *Expression Blend 4 tools like the Objects and Timeline panel, render transforms, and 3D projections allow designers to create rich data visualizations.*

■ **Note** Silverlight 3 introduced support for pixel shader effects that provide a much more realistic rendering over traditional means. Silverlight integrates with a compiled script from the HLSL (High Level Shader Language). In order to create this, you have to be well versed in graphic rendering. Furthermore, special add-ons like the DirectX SDK are required to create shader effects. This is the only example where a designer might have to go outside the realm of XAML and Expression Blend/design tool support to create additional UI functionality.

Looking back at all the characteristics and challenges of creating good data visualizations, developers are already challenged with implementing a great deal of design patterns. Therefore, if Silverlight can make the UI much easier to work with, it could make sense to invest in data visualizations. In my opinion, Silverlight's rendering engine is going to be one of the leading factors in why data visualizations will make the leap from requiring specialized software to concepts used in mainstream development.

Data-Centric Processing

Data is extremely important to data visualizations. Without it, you just have a picture. The framework that surfaces and renders data visualizations needs to be able to work with data as well.

In the previous chapters, you have seen how powerful the local data processing functionality is in Silverlight. Silverlight is based on a subset of the .NET Framework which makes the technology really performant. Some of the data features include querying or filtering data with LINQ, using multiple threads for increased performance, and applying statistical analysis with F#. In addition, all of this data can be cached using Silverlight's large isolated storage mechanism.

There are a lot of frameworks out there that can do specialized rendering and generate elegant business graphs. However, very few of these frameworks include the robust local data processing features found in Silverlight. This is one of the reasons why Silverlight can be used to create interactive infographics with dynamic business logic powering it.

Silverlight also has the processing power to work with data that scales to BI levels. In fact, the BMI exercise in Chapter 3 was done with a record set of 1 million items. As you saw, Silverlight can process large amounts of data and surface it in data visualizations for BI scenarios.

Integration with Microsoft Enterprise Services

One of the advantages Silverlight has over other RIA frameworks is that it can integrate with a robust Microsoft enterprise services stack. Microsoft has been busy creating and reorganizing several services under their cloud computing initiative. Some of these services can be used directly to aid in the creation or surfacing of data visualizations.

The Bing Maps (previously known as Microsoft Virtual Earth) provides an enterprise service for displaying geographic information. There are other software vendors that provide a similar service. What makes Microsoft's map service unique? Microsoft provides a Silverlight assembly that allows users to navigate a world map and integrate their location data with it. The Silverlight control is optimized with additional features over the Ajax counterpart. For example, zooming in and out is much smoother and quicker. Furthermore, the Silverlight map control can zoom in several layers further than the Ajax control. Figure 5-8 shows the Bing Map Silverlight control in action. For more information, go to the Microsoft Maps web site, located at `www.microsoft.com/maps`.

This control opens up many mashup possibilities for visualizing a combination of geographic and business data. For example, if you had a list of stores in different states, you could quickly create a visualization using this control to highlight the strength of sales by using color highlighting for each state. The last coding scenario in this chapter covers how to use this control in a data visualization scenario.

Figure 5-9. The Bing Maps for Enterprise Silverlight control can be used to navigate geographic and business data together.

Descry Framework

Once you are familiar with data visualizations, Silverlight, and BI, it becomes fairly obvious that Silverlight is an ideal platform to create engaging infographic experiences. The people at Microsoft saw this and created a project that outlines how to create effective infographics with Silverlight technology. This project is called Descry.

The Descry project consists of four visualization samples that have been implemented in Silverlight. These samples can be tried out on the Descry web site (www.visitmix.com/lab/descry). All of the source code is available on the CodePlex web site (www.codeplex.com/descry). On the Descry project web site, you will also find additional data visualization resources and links to articles.

The Descry visualizations are examples of advanced infographics that include interactivity, animations, and custom assets. These are not simple controls, and a lot of thought has gone into creating them. Note that these visualizations apply best practices and visualization guidelines; thus, they are a good starting point for understanding what can be achieved with Silverlight.

Let's analyze one of these visualizations. Figure 5-10 is a screenshot of the "Obesity Epidemic" Descry visualization. This visualization aims to show how more and more people across the United States have become obese in the last two decades.

Interactive slider that allows data querying with adjusting the timeline

Short description of the data visualization

Simple sorting

Graphical indicator of obesity using colors, shape, and numbers

Alternate data visualization using progress bars

Figure 5-10. The Descry project "Obesity Epidemic" infographic implements many data visualization best practices.

Some of the key features of the visualization include:

- It includes a description and short instructions on how to use the data visualization.

- When the visualization first loads, it plays an animation that moves the slider control and presents the user additional clues on how to interact with the infographic.

- The main interactivity is performed using a slider control. This allows for fluent motion of adjusting the timeline. As the slider moves, the graphics change, providing instant insight from the data.

- Simple sorting is provided using radio buttons. The sorting control is clearly presented to the user.

- The main part of the visualization is fifty "human shirt" indicators that represent each state. Each of these graphical indicators has visual properties that change as the data changes. Color, size, and numerical labels are the properties displayed on each indicator.

- There is another chart consisting of progress bars that provides an alternate view for the data visualization. The second view is geared for users that favor a cleaner and simpler look.

Try the visualization out yourself and note how simple it is to interact with the control. The visualization communicates the information about obesity effectively and quickly. After interacting with it after a few seconds, you can see that the main message is that over the last two decades, the percentage of people that are obese has skyrocketed.

Several key BI 2.0 concepts were applied in this visualization as well. First, there was no need to provide a special guide or minitutorial to use the application. This takes care of the simple-to-use and self-service tenets of the implementation. Furthermore, the user can only control the information through either sorting or querying, and neither option lets the user to provide bad input. So there is simply no way the user could perceive an incorrect message from the infographic.

While you're there, try the other visualizations in the Descry project. If you are interested in the implementation techniques, download the source code. It provides a great starting point if you are planning a complex data visualization in Silverlight.

Coding Scenarios

This section covers three coding scenarios that will show you how to create simple data visualizations.

Chart Data Visualizations

This coding scenario will cover creating simple charting scenarios you can implement to quickly use data visualizations provided in the Silverlight Control Toolkit. In order to complete this coding scenario, you will need the Silverlight Control Toolkit installed on your development workstation.

There is a lot to cover even for simple data visualizations found in the Silverlight Control Toolkit. However, I want to provide a basic introduction to these visualization controls because you will be using them in the upcoming chapters.

■ **Note** A live demo of this coding scenario is available on the companion web site at: http://silverlightbusinessintelligence.com/Demos/IntroToDataVisualizations/ChartDataVisualizations/ChartingVisualizations.html.

The goals of this scenario are:

- Understanding the basics of how to use Silverlight data visualizations

- Seeing how the chart visualizations can be extended with simple behaviors

To begin this coding scenario:

1. Open Visual Studio 2010 and create a new Silverlight Application project called Chapter5_ChartingVisualizations. Ensure that Silverlight 4 is the selected Silverlight version.

2. Prepare your screen:

   - Set the width and height of the user control to 600 by 900.

   - Change the layout type from a grid to a StackPanel.

Your XAML should look like the code in Listing 5-1 (changes are highlighted in bold).

Listing 5-1. Initial Changes for the Layout

```
...
    Width="600" Height="900">
        <StackPanel x:Name="LayoutRoot" Background="White" >
        </StackPanel>
</UserControl>
```

3. Add the Loaded event to the StackPanel (shown in Listing 5-2).

Listing 5-2. StackPanel After the Loaded Event Has Been Added

```
        <StackPanel x:Name="LayoutRoot" Background="White" Loaded="LayoutRoot_Loaded">
        </StackPanel>
```

4. Open Expression Blend 4 and drag and drop the chart control. The chart control can be found in the Custom Controls asset library in Blend 4. Figure 5-11 shows the Chart control in the asset library. If you do not have the Chart control showing, ensure you have installed the Silverlight Control Toolkit properly and have the proper references for the toolkit in your project. After the chart is added to the MainPage.xaml, it will look like Listing 5-3.

Listing 5-3. StackPanel After Adding a Chart

```
<StackPanel x:Name="LayoutRoot" Background="White" Loaded="LayoutRoot_Loaded">
        <toolkit:Chart Title="Chart Title">
                < toolkit:Chart.DataContext>
                        <PointCollection>
                                <Point>1,10</Point>
                                <Point>2,20</Point>
                                <Point>3,30</Point>
                                <Point>4,40</Point>
                        </PointCollection>
                </ toolkit:Chart.DataContext>
                < toolkit:ColumnSeries DependentValuePath="X" IndependentValuePath="Y" ↵
```

```
ItemsSource="{Binding}"/>
        </ toolkit:Chart>
</StackPanel>
```

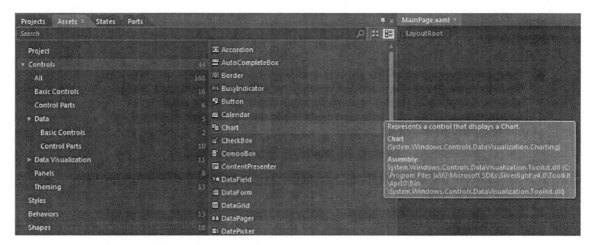

Figure 5-11. The Silverlight Control Toolkit chart control in the Expression Blend 4 asset library

5.   The chart control is just a container for the type of series that you will render.
     For example, in order to render a bar chart, you would add a bar series to the
     control. In Expression Blend, open up the XAML view or split view to access
     the XAML code. In the XAML, remove the word ColumnSeries after the cursor
     and then begin to type. Note the different series available to render. In this
     example, you are going to render a column chart, so select ColumnSeries
     (shown in Figure 5-12).

Figure 5-12. The chart control can be rendered in different ways by applying different series.

6.   Set the chart title to be Actual Sales, and the height of the chart control to 250.

7.   When you drag a new chart control, it provides you with some simple fake
     data. Remove that data by deleting the Chart.DataContext element tag. You are
     going to bind your chart to an in-memory data collection. The XAML for the
     chart control should look like Listing 5-4.

Listing 5-4. Chart After the Title and Height Have Been Changed

```
<toolkit:Chart Title="Actual Sales" Height="250">
        <toolkit:ColumnSeries DependentValuePath="X" IndependentValuePath="Y"↩
ItemsSource="{Binding}"/>
</toolkit:Chart>
```

8. You are going to create a list collection of Sale objects. The Sale object is going to have three properties: a string CompanyName, a double SalesActual, and a double SalesForecast. This sample data is going to contain a small list of companies and the sales that have been made during the period, as well the forecasted sales numbers.

- Create a Sale class with the previously listed properties.

- In the Loaded event, create a list of five Sale objects with all three properties populated.

- Set the DataContext property of the user control to the collection of Sale objects.

Your codebehind file should look like Listing 5-5 (the changes are highlighted in bold).

Listing 5-5. Codebehind to Create and Bind the Sales Data

```
...
    private void LayoutRoot_Loaded(object sender, RoutedEventArgs e)
    {
        this.DataContext = new List<Sale>
        {
            new Sale { CompanyName = "Contoso", SalesActual= 15000.0,↩
SalesForecast = 25000.0},
            new Sale { CompanyName = "Magie's Travels", SalesActual= 30000.0,↩
SalesForecast = 50000.0},
            new Sale { CompanyName = "Joe's Tires", SalesActual= 50000.0,↩
SalesForecast = 70000.0},
            new Sale { CompanyName = "World Wide Traders", SalesActual= 75000.0,↩
SalesForecast = 55000.0},
            new Sale { CompanyName = "Iono", SalesActual= 10000.0, SalesForecast = 5000.0}
        };
    }
}

public class Sale
{
    public string CompanyName { get; set; }
    public double SalesActual { get; set; }
    public double SalesForecast { get; set; }
}
```

9. At this point, you need to provide binding for the column series. In a column series, there are two main parts: the dependent and independent properties that you need to set. The *independent property* is the value that stands by itself and doesn't change. In your example, that is the `CompanyName` property. The *dependent property* is a value that depends on another value. The `SalesActual` and `SalesForecast` properties depend on the `CompanyName` property to give it proper context. For example, if you show data that says $15,000, what does that mean? If it is stated that $15,000 depends on the Contoso company, that means something.

   - Set the `DependentValuePath` to `SalesActual`.

   - Set the `IndependentValuePath` to `CompanyName`.

   - Set the title of the series to Sales Actual. This will set the title in the legend.

   Your chart XAML should look like the XAML in Listing 5-6. The changes are highlighted in bold.

Listing 5-6. Changes to the Column Series

```
...
<toolkit:Chart Title="Actual Sales" Height="250">
        <toolkit:ColumnSeries Title="Sales Actual" DependentValuePath="SalesActual" ↩
  IndependentValuePath="CompanyName" ItemsSource="{Binding}"/>
</toolkit:Chart>
...
```

The project is ready to build. After running the project, it should look like Figure 5-13. Note that the x-axis is showing the company names and the y-axis is showing the information from the `SalesActual` property.

Figure 5-13. A chart rendered using column series showing sales information

10. Now that you have built a simple chart, add a second chart below that will compare your sales information and the sales that you forecast. This visualization will try to communicate how well you did with forecasting your sales vs. actual sales.

   - Copy the chart XAML from earlier and add it below the first chart (do not remove the first chart; you will use it in a comparison exercise later).

- Change the title of the chart to Sales Actual vs. Forecast.

- Add a line series below the column series.

- Set the `DependentValuePath` to `SalesForecast`.

- Set the `IndependentValuePath` to `CompanyName`.

- Set the title of the series to be Sales Forecast.

Your chart XAML should look like the XAML in Listing 5-7. The changes are highlighted in bold.

Listing 5-7. Changes to the Column Series

```
...
<toolkit:Chart Title="Sales Actual vs. Forecast" Height="250">
    <toolkit:ColumnSeries Title="Sales Actual" DependentValuePath=↵
"SalesActual" IndependentValuePath="CompanyName" ItemsSource="{Binding}" />
    <toolkit:LineSeries Title="Sales Forecast"  DependentValuePath=↵
"SalesForecast" IndependentValuePath="CompanyName" ItemsSource="{Binding}"/>
</toolkit:Chart>
...
```

11. The project should build now and your second chart should look like Figure 5-14. You changed a few properties and added a second series that you can use to compare the information.

Figure 5-14. A chart rendering two different series that you can use to compare information

12. The developers of the Silverlight Control Toolkit have left the majority of the styling to you. However, there are some nice simple properties that allow you to extend some of the rendering of the chart. Let's change the way each item in the series is rendered by walking through each item from beginning to end. In both series, set the `AnimationSequence` property to `FirstToLast`.

Your Chart XAML should look like the Listing 5-8. The changes are highlighted in bold.

Listing 5-8. Changes to the animation sequence

```
...
<toolkit:ColumnSeries Title="Sales Actual" DependentValuePath="SalesActual"
    IndependentValuePath="CompanyName" ItemsSource="{Binding}"
    AnimationSequence="FirstToLast"/>
<toolkit:LineSeries Title="Sales Forecast"  DependentValuePath="SalesForecast"
    IndependentValuePath="CompanyName" ItemsSource="{Binding}"
    AnimationSequence="FirstToLast"/>
...
```

13. Build and run the project and compare the rendering of the two charts. The first chart loads the column bars in one swoop. However, the second chart loads each item individually in sequence from first to last (like the setting name implies).

Lessons Learned

In this very light introduction into simple data visualizations, you saw how you can use the out-of-the-box data visualizations from the Silverlight Control Toolkit. Hopefully, you saw that the charting visualizations are pretty simple to use and offer some simple properties for extending the look and feel of the controls.

These simple visualizations do not provide the immersive and engaging experiences that custom infographics can. However, these controls can be used to help you in communicating effective insight from your data.

Building a Tag Cloud

This coding scenario will show you how to build one of the most popular data visualizations on the Web: the tag cloud. In Chapter 1, you saw a great implementation of a tag cloud in Figure 1-8. You are not going to implement anything that exciting in this control; however, you will stay true to the features of the tag cloud.

A tag cloud presents a list of objects, usually text that is classified in levels of importance. Objects with greater levels of importance are displayed prominently in the tag cloud via a larger size. Less important objects are shown less prominently. The level of importance can be a property (e.g., sales amount or body weight) or the frequency of times a particular object appears in a list of items. There is not much more you need to know to implement a basic tag cloud.

The goals of this scenario are:

- Understanding how to turn existing controls into new controls that provide additional functionality

- Understanding how a basic tag cloud works

■ **Note** A live demo of this coding scenario is available on the companion web site at:
www.silverlightbusinessintelligence.com/Demos/IntroToDataVisualizations/BuildingATagCloud/
TagCloud.html.

Let's begin this coding scenario.

1. Open Visual Studio 2010 and create a new Silverlight Application project called Chapter5_TagCloud. Ensure that Silverlight 4 is the selected version of Silverlight.

2. You are going to use a wrap panel control as the baseline for your tag cloud. The wrap panel positions objects from left to right and automatically wraps into new lines as necessary.

   - Drag a wrap panel control from the asset library (this will add the necessary namespace).

   - Name the wrap panel control wrapPanelSales.

   - Change the height to 200 and the width to 400.

   Your XAML should look like that in Listing 5-9 (the changes are highlighted in bold).

Listing 5-9. User Control After Adding the Wrap Panel

```
<UserControl
    xmlns="http://schemas.microsoft.com/winfx/2006/xaml/presentation"
    xmlns:x="http://schemas.microsoft.com/winfx/2006/xaml"
    xmlns:d="http://schemas.microsoft.com/expression/blend/2008"
    xmlns:mc="http://schemas.openxmlformats.org/markup-compatibility/2006"
    mc:Ignorable="d"
    xmlns:toolkit="http://schemas.microsoft.com/winfx/2006/xaml/presentation/toolkit"
    x:Class="Chapter5_TagCloud.MainPage"
    d:DesignWidth="400" d:DesignHeight="300">
  <Grid x:Name="LayoutRoot">
        <toolkit:WrapPanel x:Name="wrapPanelSales" Height="200" HorizontalAlignment="Left"↵
 VerticalAlignment="Top" Width="400"/>
  </Grid>
</UserControl>
```

3. Add the Loaded event to the LayoutRoot. Ensure the codebehind event handler is created. The new XAML is shown in Listing 5-10.

Listing 5-10. Grid After Implementing the Loaded Event

```
<Grid x:Name="LayoutRoot" Loaded="LayoutRoot_Loaded">
```

4. It is time to define your data collection and consume it in the data. In Listing 5-11, you will perform the following tasks:

- Add a Sale class that will hold a property for SalesAmount and CompanyName.

- Create a collection of Sale data to be consumed by the wrap panel.

- Add a list of text block controls that alternate colors and represent each company name.

The changed area of the codebehind file should look like Listing 5-11 (the changes are highlighted in bold).

Listing 5-11. Implementing the Data Binding

```
...
private void LayoutRoot_Loaded(object sender, RoutedEventArgs e)
    {
        // define a list of sales
        List<Sale> sales = new List<Sale>
        {
            new Sale { CompanyName = "Contoso", SalesAmount= 15000.0},
            new Sale { CompanyName = "Magie's Travels", SalesAmount= 15000.0},
            new Sale { CompanyName = "Joe's Tires", SalesAmount= 16000.0},
            new Sale { CompanyName = "World Wide Traders", SalesAmount= 15000.0},
            new Sale { CompanyName = "Iono", SalesAmount= 15000.0},
            new Sale { CompanyName = "Nokes", SalesAmount= 25000.0},
            new Sale { CompanyName = "Bob's Repair", SalesAmount= 15000.0},
            new Sale { CompanyName = "Tara's Plumbing", SalesAmount= 15000.0},
            new Sale { CompanyName = "Smitty Funs", SalesAmount= 16000.0},
            new Sale { CompanyName = "Granpeeda", SalesAmount= 45000.0},
            new Sale { CompanyName = "Tyo", SalesAmount= 115000.0},
            new Sale { CompanyName = "Weeebo", SalesAmount= 155000.0},
            new Sale { CompanyName = "Vic's Bagels", SalesAmount= 15000.0},
            new Sale { CompanyName = "Wrenchmaniacs", SalesAmount= 15000.0},
            new Sale { CompanyName = "Fan Fixers", SalesAmount= 85000.0},
            new Sale { CompanyName = "Jemo Holdings", SalesAmount= 15000.0},
            new Sale { CompanyName = "TAC Bank", SalesAmount= 70000.0},
            new Sale { CompanyName = "Finite Metals", SalesAmount= 5000.0},
            new Sale { CompanyName = "Smitty Coins", SalesAmount= 15000.0},
            new Sale { CompanyName = "Target Tootsies", SalesAmount= 7000.0}
        };

        // add items to the wrap panel
        for (int i = 0; i != sales.Count; i++)
        {
            // define a new text block control
            TextBlock textBlock = new TextBlock
            {
                // set the text to the company name
                Text = sales[i].CompanyName,
                // alternate the colors
```

```
                    Foreground = i % 2 == 0 ? new SolidColorBrush(Colors.Red) ⏎
    : new SolidColorBrush(Colors.Blue),
                    // apply a uniform margin
                    Margin = new Thickness(2)
                };

                this.wrapPanelSales.Children.Add(textBlock);
            }
        }
    }

    public class Sale
    {
        public string CompanyName { get; set; }
        public double SalesAmount { get; set; }
    }
    …
```

5. You have enough information to build your application, having added 20 text block controls to your wrap panel. Each one is set to the name of the company in your data list. Furthermore, you have broken the items up nicely using alternating colors. When you run the application, it should look like Figure 5-15.

Contoso Magie's Travels Joe's Tires World Wide Traders Iono Nokes
Bob's Repair Tara's Plumbing Smitty Funs Granpeeda Tyo Weeebo
Vic's Bagels Wrenchmaniacs Fan Fixers Jemo Holdings TAC Bank
Finite Metals Smitty Coins Target Tootsies

Figure 5-15. The wrap panel shows the company names on your sales list.

6. This is a good start, but now you need to implement the prominence of the companies that have had strong sales using the SalesAmount property. This will implement the tag cloud functionality. In Listing 5-12, you are performing the following steps:

   - You get the minimum and maximum values for the SalesAmount. This will serve as the range for your data.

   - You define a minimum and maximum font size for your text block.

   - You will scale the text blocks proportionally to the SalesAmount properly.

   The changed part of the codebehind file should look like Listing 5-12 (the changes are highlighted in bold).

Listing 5-12. *Adding Data Processing to Change the Font Size Based on the Data*

```
...
// define min and max sales amounts
double minSalesAmount = sales.Min(a => a.SalesAmount);
double maxSalesAmount = sales.Max(a => a.SalesAmount);
// calculate the sales delta
double salesAmountDelta = maxSalesAmount - minSalesAmount;

// define the min and max font sizes
double minFontSize = 10.0;
double maxFontSize = 30.0;
// calculate the font size delta
double fontSizeDelta = maxFontSize-minFontSize;

// add items to the wrap panel
for (int i = 0; i != sales.Count; i++)
{
    // define a new text block control
    TextBlock textBlock = new TextBlock
    {
        // set the text to the company name
        Text = sales[i].CompanyName,
        // alternate the colors
        Foreground = i % 2 == 0 ? new SolidColorBrush(Colors.Red) : new↲
SolidColorBrush(Colors.Blue),
        // apply a uniform margin
        Margin = new Thickness(2),
        // set the font size
        FontSize = minFontSize + sales[i].SalesAmount * fontSizeDelta / salesAmountDelta
    };

    this.wrapPanelSales.Children.Add(textBlock);
}
...
```

7. Your tag cloud is complete. Build the project; it should look like Figure 5-16. Note how the company names with the highest sales amounts are displayed prominently in the control. Building on top of this functionality, like providing a sorting mechanism, would be straightforward.

Contoso Magie's Travels Joe's Tires World Wide Traders Iono

Nokes Bob's Repair Tara's Plumbing Smitty Funs Granpeeda

Tyo Weeebo Vic's Bagels Wrenchmaniacs

Fan Fixers Jemo Holdings TAC Bank Finite Metals

Smitty Coins Target Tootsies

Figure 5-16. Your tag cloud communicates effectively the companies with the biggest sales amounts.

Lessons Learned

A tag cloud is a great visualization because it quickly communicates the most important items a user should focus on via the size of the text objects. You saw how easy it was to leverage existing Silverlight layout controls and applying BI functionality to create the tag cloud control.

This small demonstration could easily be enhanced with animations, drill-downs, dynamic filtering, and other behaviors.

Possible Improvements

The tag cloud control you just built is trivial and static in nature. Tag clouds can be dramatically enhanced by using the full Silverlight framework. A great example of fully interactive tag clouds that can be rendered in numerous styles is Tagxedo created by Hardy Leung. Tagxedo is based on the Silverlight runtime. This word cloud tool allows you to create word clouds using your own custom text and organize them using custom artwork.

Figure 5-17 below shows the Tagxedo – Creator tool editing a word cloud in the shape of Abraham Lincoln. The word cloud can be fully customized with different themes, fonts, rendering options, etc.

Figure 5-17. Tagxedo can create Silverlight word clouds using custom shapes.

■ **Note** If you are interested in trying Tagxedo go to http://www.tagxedo.com.

Using Geographic Visualizations

Microsoft provides a control for Silverlight that presents Microsoft map data. This control is great way to provide geographic visualization mashups in your BI applications. In this coding scenario, you will learn how to get started with the Bing Maps Silverlight map control.

The goals of this scenario are:

- Understanding the basics of geographic data visualizations

- Seeing how the Bing Silverlight map control can be used to enhance applications by integrating geographic data into your applications

■ **Note** A live demo of this coding scenario is available on the companion web site at:
www.silverlightbusinessintelligence.com/Demos/IntroToDataVisualizations/
UsingGeographicVisualizations/SilverlightBingMaps.html.

Before you get started with this coding scenario, you need to acquire the Bing Maps Silverlight control. As of this book's writing, version 1.0 of the control is available on the Bing Maps portal site (www.bingmapsportal.com). The control is offered as a free download; you just need a Windows Live account. On the web site you will find information on how to use the control, an interactive SDK for the control, and a place to monitor your map credentials. Figure 5-18 illustrates Bing Map key management on the portal. You will need a key in order to use the control without any annoying pop-up messages.

Figure 5-18. Map keys for the Bing Maps Silverlight control can be managed on the portal site.

This control hooks into Microsoft geographic data services for the images that are rendered on the screen, so you will need an active Internet connection when performing this exercise. Microsoft provides an interactive SDK that lets you to try the control and see some code samples without having to install the control. I highly encourage you to check it out.

As mentioned, this control is provided free of charge for non-commercial use. Microsoft encourages developers to get familiar with the control before determining if it is good for them to use in an application. If you do decide to use the control, check the license agreement before using it in commercial applications. Most likely, there is a fee for such use.

In this coding scenario, you are creating a geographic data visualization. This infographic will assist a fictitious taxi cab driver who is trying to determine which areas of Manhattan provide the highest taxi fares. Assume that his taxi is equipped with a GPS, and each time he starts a fare, it records the latitude and longitude positions. Now that his shift is over and the data has been recorded, it is time for you to create a data visualization to spot a potential pattern of high or low fares.

Before starting, you need to understand how the architecture of the Silverlight map control. By default, the map control includes a single read-only layer that shows geographical assets. You cannot edit this layer but you can add multiple transparent editable map layers on top of the default layer. These editable layers are where you add custom content. Figure 5-19 illustrates the architecture of the map control. All these layers work together in sync when the map control is zoomed or panned. This gives the illusion that the controls you add are part of the map.

Map layer
that allows
controls to
be added

Read-only
geographic
assets

Figure 5-19. *The Silverlight map control uses multiple layers to integrate custom controls.*

Once you have the control downloaded, you can begin the coding scenario.

1. Open Visual Studio 2010 and create a new Silverlight Application project called Chapter5_SilverlightBingMaps.

2. The first step is to add a reference to the control to your application. Navigate to the location of the Silverlight control assembly. The default location of the Bing Maps Silverlight control assemblies is C:\Program Files (x86)\Bing Maps Silverlight Control\V1\Libraries\; however, if you have chosen to install the control in another location, check there. Add a reference to both the Microsoft.Maps.MapControl.dll assembly and the Microsoft.Maps.MapControl.Common.dll assembly.

3. Increase the user control canvas to a width of 900 and height of 600. This will give you a nice-sized canvas to interact with. Add a Loaded event to the LayoutRoot grid.

4. Now that you have added references to the Bing Maps control assemblies in your project, you should see the Map control in the asset manager. If you cannot find it, try searching for it in the Expression Blend 4 asset manager (shown in Figure 5-20 below). Once you find it, drag over the map control onto the design canvas.

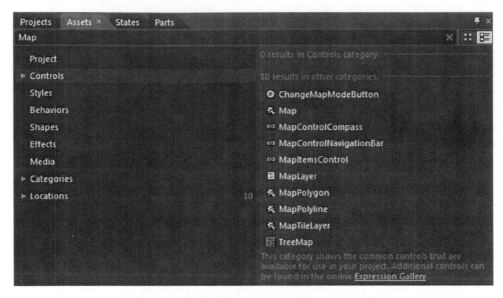

Figure 5-20. Expression Blend 4 Assets manager filtered on the Map controls.

5. The XAML file should resemble Listing 5-13

Listing 5-13. Initial Layout of the XAML File

```
<UserControl x:Class="Chapter5_SilverlightBingMaps.MainPage"
    xmlns="http://schemas.microsoft.com/winfx/2006/xaml/presentation"
    xmlns:x="http://schemas.microsoft.com/winfx/2006/xaml"
    xmlns:x="http://schemas.microsoft.com/expression/blend/2008"
    xmlns:x="http://schemas.openxmlformats.org/markup-compatibility/2006"
    xmlns:Microsoft_Maps_MapControl="clr-namespace:Microsoft.Maps.MapControl;assembly⤸
=Microsoft.Maps.MapControl"
    Width="900" Height="600">
    <Grid x:Name="LayoutRoot" Background="White" >
        <Microsoft_Maps_MapControl:Map d:LayoutOverrides="Width, Height"/>
    </Grid>
</UserControl>
```

6. Add a Loaded event to the LayoutRoot (shown in bold in Listing 5-14).

Listing 5-14. Adding Data Processing to Change the Font Size Based on the Data

```
<Grid x:Name="LayoutRoot" Background="White" Loaded="LayoutRoot_Loaded">
```

7. That is all you need to present a fully functional and interactive geographical map. Build the project and try interacting with the map. Note how responsive and smooth the transitions are. However, without any additional data, this control holds no true business value. Let's build out this example.

8. Change the name of the map control to silverlightMapControl.

9. In your coding scenario, you need two things:

   • A map that is focused on Manhattan, NY.

   • To be able to add symbols where your taxi pickups happen. In the Bing Maps Silverlight control, this is done through adding a map layer.

   Make the changes highlighted in bold in Listing 5-15.

Listing 5-15. Adding Coordinates to Center the Map on Manhattan, New York

```
<UserControl x:Class="Chapter5_SilverlightBingMaps.MainPage"
    xmlns="http://schemas.microsoft.com/winfx/2006/xaml/presentation"
    xmlns:x="http://schemas.microsoft.com/winfx/2006/xaml"
    xmlns:x="http://schemas.microsoft.com/expression/blend/2008"
    xmlns:x="http://schemas.openxmlformats.org/markup-compatibility/2006"
    xmlns:map="clr-namespace:Microsoft.VirtualEarth.MapControl;assembly↵
=Microsoft.VirtualEarth.MapControl"
    Width="900" Height="600">
    <Grid x:Name="LayoutRoot" Background="White" Loaded="LayoutRoot_Loaded">
        <!--Center the map on Manhattan, New York -->
        <Microsoft_Maps_MapControl:Map x:Name="silverlightMapControl"
        Center="40.71,-74.013" ZoomLevel="15" Mode="AerialWithLabels">
            <Microsoft_Maps_MapControl:Map.Children>
                <!--Add a map layer for adding our visualizations -->
                <Microsoft_Maps_MapControl:MapLayer x:Name="TaxiPickUpLayer">
                </Microsoft_Maps_MapControl:MapLayer>
            </Microsoft_Maps_MapControl:Map.Children>
        </Microsoft_Maps_MapControl:Map>
    </Grid>
</UserControl>
```

10. Build and run the project. You will see that the map control is zoomed in and focused on Manhattan, as shown in Figure 5-21.

Figure 5-21. The Bing Silverlight map control centered on Manhattan, New York

11. Now add data that includes the location of the pickups that the taxi made as
     well as the fares it has received. In the code in Listing 5-16, you do the
     following things:

     • Add the following using statements:

        using Microsoft.Maps;

        using Microsoft.Maps.MapControl;

        using Microsoft.Maps.MapControl.Common;

        using Microsoft.Maps.MapControl.Core;

        using Microsoft.Expression.Shapes;

     • Create a class called TaxiPickup that holds the latitude and longitude
        positions of the pickup as well as the taxi fare that was received.

     • Create a collection of TaxiPickup items that will be displayed in the map
        control.

     • Iterate over the collection of TaxiPickup items and add them to the
        TaxiPickupLayer layer of the map control.

     • Add a tool tip of the fare amount to the pickup indicator.

- If the fare is over \$35, create a green KPI. If the fare is below \$35, create a red KPI.

The codebehind file is shown in Listing 5-16 with the changes highlighted in bold.

Listing 5-16. Adding Data Points to the Map with the Logic to Add the Appropriate KPIs

```
...
using Microsoft.Expression.Shapes;

namespace Chapter5_SilverlightBingMaps
{
    public partial class MainPage : UserControl
    {
        public MainPage()
        {
            InitializeComponent();
        }

        private void LayoutRoot_Loaded(object sender, RoutedEventArgs e)
        {
            // create the fictitious data
            List<TaxiPickup> taxiPickups = new List<TaxiPickup>
            {
                new TaxiPickup{ FareAmount = 25.0,
                    PickupLocationLatitude = 40.7091, PickupLocationLongitude = -74.012},
                new TaxiPickup{ FareAmount = 45.0,
                    PickupLocationLatitude = 40.712, PickupLocationLongitude = -74.01},
                new TaxiPickup{ FareAmount = 25.0,
                    PickupLocationLatitude = 40.710, PickupLocationLongitude = -74.012},
                new TaxiPickup{ FareAmount = 75.0,
                    PickupLocationLatitude = 40.7123, PickupLocationLongitude = -74.013111},
                new TaxiPickup{ FareAmount = 20.0,
                    PickupLocationLatitude = 40.7111, PickupLocationLongitude = -74.01222},
                new TaxiPickup{ FareAmount = 105.0,
                    PickupLocationLatitude = 40.71255, PickupLocationLongitude = -74.01},
                new TaxiPickup{ FareAmount = 125.0,
                    PickupLocationLatitude = 40.713, PickupLocationLongitude = -74.012},
                new TaxiPickup{ FareAmount = 15.0,
                    PickupLocationLatitude = 40.71111, PickupLocationLongitude = -74.0122},
                new TaxiPickup{ FareAmount = 20.0,
                    PickupLocationLatitude = 40.7111, PickupLocationLongitude = -74.01222},
                new TaxiPickup{ FareAmount = 150.0,
                    PickupLocationLatitude = 40.7134, PickupLocationLongitude = -74.0155},
                new TaxiPickup{ FareAmount = 175.0,
                    PickupLocationLatitude = 40.7133, PickupLocationLongitude = -74.00},
                new TaxiPickup{ FareAmount = 100.0,
                    PickupLocationLatitude = 40.7137, PickupLocationLongitude = -73.999},
                new TaxiPickup{ FareAmount = 95.0,
                    PickupLocationLatitude = 40.7136, PickupLocationLongitude = -73.998},
```

```
        new TaxiPickup{ FareAmount = 15.0,
            PickupLocationLatitude = 40.7141, PickupLocationLongitude = -74.00},
        new TaxiPickup{ FareAmount = 42.0,
            PickupLocationLatitude = 40.7139, PickupLocationLongitude = -73.995},
        new TaxiPickup{ FareAmount = 55.0,
            PickupLocationLatitude = 40.714, PickupLocationLongitude = -73.997},
        new TaxiPickup{ FareAmount = 25.0,
            PickupLocationLatitude = 40.7065, PickupLocationLongitude = -74.0155},
        new TaxiPickup{ FareAmount = 5.0,
            PickupLocationLatitude = 40.7062, PickupLocationLongitude = -74.0152},
        new TaxiPickup{ FareAmount = 15.0,
            PickupLocationLatitude = 40.7063, PickupLocationLongitude = -74.0148},
        new TaxiPickup{ FareAmount = 25.0,
            PickupLocationLatitude = 40.7083, PickupLocationLongitude = -74.013},
        new TaxiPickup{ FareAmount = 25.0,
            PickupLocationLatitude = 40.7071, PickupLocationLongitude = -74.011},
        new TaxiPickup{ FareAmount = 66.0,
            PickupLocationLatitude = 40.7066, PickupLocationLongitude = -74.010},
        new TaxiPickup{ FareAmount = 59.0,
            PickupLocationLatitude = 40.7062, PickupLocationLongitude = -74.011}
};

// iterate through the taxi pickup data
// add a green circle for a taxi pickup that netted over 35 dollars
// add a red circle for a taxi pickup that netted less than 35 dollars
foreach (var taxiPickup in taxiPickups)
{
    Shape kpiShape = null;

    if (taxiPickup.FareAmount > 35.0)
    {
        // create a (green KPI) circle indicator
        Ellipse ellipse = new Ellipse
        {
            Height = 25,
            Width = 25,
            Fill = new SolidColorBrush(Colors.Green),
            Cursor = Cursors.Hand,
            Stroke = new SolidColorBrush(Colors.Black)
        };

        kpiShape = ellipse;
    }
    else
    {
        // create a (red KPI) circle indicator
        RegularPolygon polygon = new RegularPolygon
        {
            Height = 25,
            Width = 25,
            Fill = new SolidColorBrush(Colors.Red),
```

```
                    Cursor = Cursors.Hand,
                    PointCount = 4,
                    Stroke = new SolidColorBrush(Colors.Black)
                };

                kpiShape = polygon;
            }

            // add a tooltip for the circle indicator
            ToolTipService.SetToolTip(kpiShape, String.Format("{0:c}", ↵
taxiPickup.FareAmount));
            // set the location for the KPI
            Location location = new Location();
            location.Latitude = taxiPickup.PickupLocationLatitude;
            location.Longitude = taxiPickup.PickupLocationLongitude;

            // add the circle indicator control to the map layer
            (this.silverlightMapControl.FindName("TaxiPickUpLayer") ↵
as MapLayer).AddChild(kpiShape, location);
        }
    } // end of LayoutRoot_Loaded

    public class TaxiPickup
    {
        public double FareAmount { get; set; }
        public double PickupLocationLatitude { get; set; }
        public double PickupLocationLongitude { get; set; }
    }
}
```

12. This project is now complete. Execute it and interact with the results. When
    the application is running, you should see a visualization similar to Figure 5-
    22. Note the green and red circles that pepper the Manhattan map. You can
    zoom in and out to see the exact location of the pickup points. Furthermore,
    you can hover over each circle indicator and quickly see the exact taxi fare.

Figure 5-22. Your geographic visualization indicating which areas net the best fares (color shown in e-book version only). However, since you also used different shapes for the KPIs, it is easy to distinguish between the two.

From the preceding data visualization, your taxi operator can quickly deduce that there is a pattern in the northern areas; they seem to have the highest fares. (High fares are defined as anything over $35.). This is another example of how Silverlight can enhance the delivery of insight by leveraging integration with enterprise tools (Bing Maps).

■ **Note** If you receive an error message stating "Invalid Credentials...", enter your Bing Maps key in the CredentialsProvider property for the map control.

Lessons Learned

As you can see, the powerful Bing Maps Silverlight map control allows you to extend your BI application with geographic visualizations. Not only can you visualize geographic data, but you can implement all of the features that you have learned about in Silverlight. Furthermore, this amplifies my statement that Silverlight poses a key advantage in integrating with Microsoft's enterprise services.

Realistically, this control is only going to be used for larger-scale data sets. Smaller BI implementations might not have geographic data. Therefore, in order to use geographic data visualizations, you need to have a valid context and proper data.

Summary

This chapter introduced the fundamentals of data visualizations. You saw how Silverlight and BI 2.0 concepts can be implemented together to form data visualizations. In the next two chapters, I will build on the information introduced here and cover more advanced topics of data visualizations that focus on interactivity and engaging visualizations. The web site accompanying this book (www.silverlightbusinessintelligence.com) also includes resources and Internet links for creating data visualizations.

The main takeaway from this chapter should be understanding the value of data visualizations in BI software. Data visualizations can truly change the usability and feature set of BI software. They can be added into software for a wow factor or to gain a strategic advantage over the competition. Another main takeaway should be the unique advantages Silverlight technology brings in designing and implementing data visualization concepts successfully.

CHAPTER 6

■ ■ ■

Creating Data Visualizations for Analysis

In this chapter, we continue our conversation about data visualizations. The previous chapter introduced you to the fundamentals of using infographics to present data visually. However, we did not cover the required steps and best practices to design visualizations as good analytical tools for business intelligence.

The focus on this chapter is creating simple and effective data visualizations that are best suited for visual analysis. While reading this chapter, you will understand that not all visualizations deliver insight in the same manner. Furthermore, sticking to simple visualization guidelines will allow your BI offering to deliver insight more effectively.

The visualizations that we will compare in this chapter have been created in Silverlight (unless otherwise noted). While reading this chapter, you will see that the Silverlight framework is capable of creating visual analytical tools that compare with enterprise-level business graphics software.

This chapter covers data visualization concepts like key performance indicators (KPIs), sparklines, column-charts, reference lines, and data standardization using Silverlight technology. This should amplify the incentive to use Silverlight as a potential environment for BI visual analytics to deliver a wide array of visual analytical tools.

This chapter includes a variety of Silverlight code samples embedded within the chapter. Therefore, a separate coding scenario was not included in this chapter.

The following table outlines the specific goals that different types of readers will achieve by reading this chapter.

Audience	Goals
Silverlight developers	Discover the basics of the science behind designing proper visualizations for data analysis.
	Understand the available Silverlight visualizations and how they can apply BI 2.0 analysis best practices.
Business intelligence professionals	Understand why Silverlight is a good choice to design data visualizations and how it can easily apply BI 2.0 conventions.
	See how current data visualization tools can be built in Silverlight using KPIs, sparklines, column charts etc.

Audience	Goals
Strategic decision makers	Work out if your visualizations are delivering the proper insight. Does your visualization package need an upgrade?
	See if Silverlight can provide a more flexible framework for delivering analytical insight.

Choosing a Visualization for Analysis

As you saw in the previous chapter, visual graphics can be used as tools to deliver the insight more quickly than looking at lists of numbers. However, the previous chapter did not focus on creating data visualizations whose purpose was to provide specific analytical value. This chapter aims to cover the conventions of creating data visualizations for the purpose of delivering quick data analysis insight.

You have probably heard the saying "A picture is worth a thousand words." The reason this cliché makes sense is because the brain has an ability to understand visuals more quickly than lists of text. Therefore, using visualizations for analysis leverages the brain's ability to process visual symbols quickly.

When designing tools for analysis, choosing the appropriate visualization depends on what type of knowledge we want to be able to deliver. Therefore, over the years many graphical representations have been accepted as a standard mechanism for representing data relationships and comparisons. For example, a pie chart has been generally accepted as a great way to show data that is part of a whole. Everyone with basic business acumen can read, understand, and analyze a pie chart. However, you will see later on in this chapter that choosing the appropriate visualization for data analysis is not always as simple as picking one that looks professional.

Figure 6-1 shows the available charting (visualization options) available to an Microsoft Office Excel user. Note that there are over 70 different chart visualizations available.

Figure 6-1. *Various charting visualizatons available in Microsoft Excel 2007& 2010.*

In Report Builder 3.0 (a report authoring tool for SQL Server 2008 R2), there is a similar amount of charting options. In addition to providing charting visualizations, Report Builder 3.0 includes a number of gauges that can be used for data analysis as well. This is shown in Figure 6-2.

Figure 6-2. *Gauge visualizations available in SQL Server Reporting Services Report Builder 2.0*

You might be asking yourself why you should care about data visualizations in these products. Both Excel and Report Builder are popular BI tools that provide rich visualizations. As you can see, there are a lot of visualization options to choose from in these products. Which visualizations you pick would probably depend on the data or type of analysis you were trying to do. Even then, trying to narrow down the ideal visualization from over 90 default choices can be difficult. BI professionals have gone through this process numerous times and eventually this becomes second nature. The same science that is behind choosing the suitable data visualization in a report, dashboard, or spreadsheet applies to Silverlight BI 2.0 applications.

Designing a BI 2.0 data visualization that delivers insight effectively, simply, and quickly requires much more than binding a data set to any visualization that looks appealing or cool. Over the years, best practices have been defined on which visualizations make the most sense for the delivery of different types of data analysis.

Choosing an incorrect visualization can cause a number of issues for a BI application. I covered a lot of these challenges in Chapter 1. However, it does not take a seasoned BI professional to understand that if you took the same data set and applied to a variety of visualization options, this data would tell an entirely different story. For example, take a look at Figure 6-3. In this figure, you can see four different charting visualizations bound to the same data set showing four quarters of sales information. Each visualization illustrates a picture of the sales information differently. A user looking at these visualizations could interpret the data differently and walk away with a different perception of the information. The example illustrated in Figure 6-3 is pretty simple. However, more complex visualizations try to answer more than one question, include interactivity, or include custom graphics. In those cases, choosing the proper baseline data visualization becomes even more important when you want to apply BI 2.0 governance (simple to use, easy to understand, requires little or no training, easy enough for an average user, etc.)

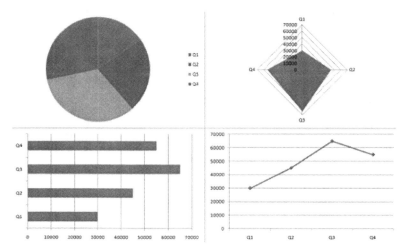

Figure 6-3. Four simple charting visualizations can tell a different story even if they are bound to the same data set.

Microsoft has acknowledged that sometimes choosing the correct visualization is not always easy. This is especially true for developers or analysts just starting out with business intelligence. For example, (shown in Figure 6-4) in Report Builder 3.0 Microsoft added a new feature that explains the different charting visualizations in the charting wizard. This aids the users in choosing the correct visualization from the ones provided.

Figure 6-4. *Descriptions help report authors select the appropriate charting visualization for their data.*

Determining Types of Analysis for Silverlight Visualizations

This section will discuss choosing appropriate data visualizations for common data analysis scenarios. This section will focus on the data visualization options available in the Silverlight SDK, Silverlight Control Toolkit, and third-party add-ons. In the previous chapter, I touched on the basics of what Silverlight technology can offer for data visualizations. However, I did not go into the details of applying different visualizations to data analysis.

Covering ambiguous design, programming, or architecture topics is always difficult in absolute terms because the typical answer is "it depends" with lots of caveats. I personally do not like "it depends" answers without a full description or guide. Therefore, the goal of this section is to provide you with a guide for when to choose common data visualizations for a Silverlight BI application.

■ **Note** This section covers this topic from the standpoint of best practices and keeping it simple for BI 2.0 software. However, there is a science behind a lot of these best practices, dealing with how the brain perceives the colors, visual objects, layout, size, and so on, and translates them into trends, comparisons, and scale. There are entire books dedicated to explaining visual analysis with scientific methodology. If you are interested in this, please visit the companion web site (www.silverlightbusinessintelligence.com) for these detailed resources.

Comparing Parts of a Whole

Parts of-a-whole analysis is done when you have multiple data objects that make up an entirety together. For example, if I have a company that sells five products, the sales summed up for each individual product make up a whole. I could illustrate the products in a data visualization that would allow a user to compare the individual products to each other using a simple pie chart visualization.

A pie chart is one of the most popular parts-of-a-whole visualization techniques. The structure of the visualization lends itself to displaying and comparing parts effectively. Figures 6-3 and 6-5 include examples of pie charts.

A typical pie chart that is used in parts-of-a-whole comparison includes the following.

- Slices of the pie represent individual parts.

- The area of each slice is representative of the part of the whole in the data set.

- Each slice can be identified quickly using a color legend.

- Hovering over a slice provides a tool tip that usually includes a value and/or label.

Optional features of pie charts include the following:

- Annotations for the data to be displayed with each slice

- Drill-through capability (clicking on a slice displays details data)

- A grid with the source data set (in addition to or in lieu of a legend)

Pie charts are usually the starting point for a visual designer or a BI professional. It is usually a great starting point because, as mentioned before, pie charts are readily understood by almost all users. Furthermore, a pie chart delivers insight on part-to-whole analysis very effectively.

Pie charts are effective visualizations when these conditions are met:

- There are no more than six to ten parts to visualize (depends on the size of the pie slices).

- Pie slices are large enough to be noticeable when rendered in a pie chart.

- Colors can be used effectively to distinguish slices.

Pie chart visualizations are an excellent choice when the data fits the mold of visualization. However, in data-driven applications, this is not always the case. Figure 6-5 illustrates two scenarios where pie chart visualizations make very poor implementation choices of part-to-whole analysis. On the left-hand side, we see a pie chart that includes pie slices that are barely legible. On the right-hand side, we see a pie chart that includes so many slices that it makes finding the appropriate slice within the legend very difficult.

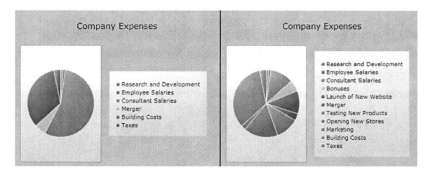

Figure 6-5. *Pie chart visualizations with small pie slices or a large number of slices can hamper visual analysis.*

Following are some of the challenges of using pie chart visualizations:

- The slices of a pie chart must add up to 100 percent. By definition, a pie (circle) cannot represent more than 100 percent correctly. However, software charting solutions are often forgiving, and this causes designers to improperly expose the dynamic data in a pie chart. For example, a 50 percent pie slice that represents a 120 percent total is going to take less than half of the area (which is clearly incorrect visually).

- Very small slices can be hard to see in a pie chart.

- Small slices can make it frustrating for the user to get additional information or perform an action (e.g., hovering to see a tool tip or clicking for drill-down).

- Large number of slices can degrade analysis and cause annotations (labels) to overlap.

- Pie charts rely on colors to clearly identify slices. If there are a large number of slices or a color cannot be used (e.g., when printing to paper), this will negate using a color-based legend. Furthermore, the color requirement could cause problems for users that are color-blind.

The challenges with pie charts are further complicated with dynamic data. During prototype, development, and testing phases, pie chart visualizations may look great and professionally describe the data. However, when it comes time to bind the chart to production data, you may encounter issues such as those shown in Figure 6-5.

One way to mitigate the uncertainty of how data may look inside a pie chart is to provide a secondary view of the data. This could be visual or in a list format. Figure 6-6 shows the same data as the Company Expenses pie chart (Figure 6-5) accompanied by a data grid for additional information. Another technique is to provide annotations (labels) on the pie chart itself. This technique works great for simple pie charts. However, annotations tend to overlap and become hard to read when there are a lot of smaller pie slices shown in the pie chart.

■ **Note** The Silverlight Control Toolkit does not provide annotations (labels) for charts out of the box. The chart control can be extended with annotations; however, it is not very straightforward. For examples on how this can be done, please visit the companion web site.

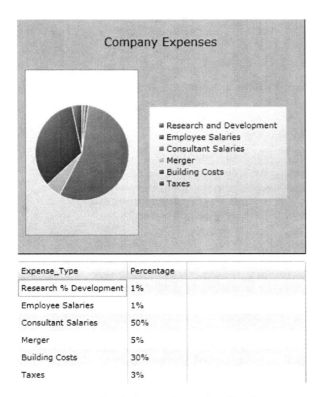

Expense_Type	Percentage	
Research % Development	1%	
Employee Salaries	1%	
Consultant Salaries	50%	
Merger	5%	
Building Costs	30%	
Taxes	3%	

Figure 6-6. *A Silverlight pie chart visualization accompanied by a data grid can provide a secondary view into the data being presented.*

Providing a secondary view of data does not solve the problem of the pie chart visualization. Secondary views are a good approach when a pie chart will suffice and the view is only needed as a backup. However, the nature of dynamic data can cause the pie chart to be useless for analysis some of the time. In those cases, we need to investigate alternatives that can provide better visual results.

When comparing parts of a whole, the individual items are discrete pieces that are mutually exclusive. From looking at our example data (Figure 6-6), building costs are independent of employee salaries. Since we can treat individual items independently, we can look at visualizations that facilitate the same meaning in the data. Another type of visualization that can be used for part-to-whole analysis is a bar or column chart. Each bar or column represents an individual item. The size (length) of the column illustrates the value of the item that is being compared. Therefore, as the items are rendered on the screen, their individual sizes can be compared to each other. Bar or column charts are usually used to compare the items to each other. However, with small tweaks to the axis, we can use the bar or column visualizations to compare the parts of a whole.

The Silverlight Control Toolkit supports both bar and column series visualizations for the chart. Furthermore, custom styles and properties can be set to override the default behavior of the charts to enhance it for analysis. Figure 6-7 displays the data for the Company Expenses visualization in a bar chart.

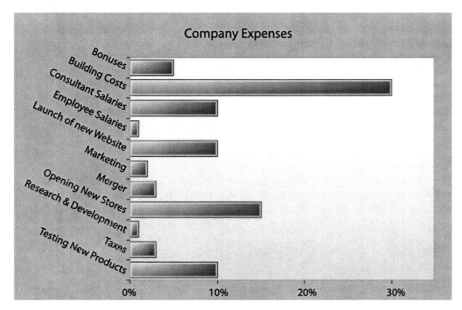

Figure 6-7. *A Silverlight bar chart visualization can be used to effectively compare parts that constitute a whole.*

Take a minute and compare Figure 6-6 and Figure 6-7. Which one do you think your users would prefer to use for visual analysis? In my opinion, the bar chart visualization provides a cleaner and simpler view into the data. Furthermore, I believe that analytical insight can be reached faster from the bar chart visualization. Following is a list of advantages that you may have picked up on that distinguish the analytical value of the two visualizations.

- Labels are easily attached to the bar chart. This requires no additional visual cues. A user does not have to look to a legend, read the color, and then locate the color on the pie chart.

- Colors in bar visualizations are optional. There is no need to provide additional colors for the bar chart in Figure 6-7 (unless additional series are presented). In the pie chart visualization, an entire color palette is required.

- Very small bars are more visible and legible than very small pie slices.

- Scale can be dynamically set. This can make very small values appear more prominently in visualization. Note that in Figure 6-7, the scale ends at 35 percent. However, in a pie chart visualization, 100 percent of the pie needs to be displayed.

- In rare situations where the part of the whole is over 100 percent, bar visualizations excel over pie chart visualizations. For example, visualizing a budget that is 20 percent over previous estimates (120 percent) can easily be done in bar chart visualizations.

- Ordering the items in ascending or descending order can make analysis even easier.

The key point to remember in part-to-whole analysis is to provide an easy way for the user to visually compare items and deliver insight on the comparison.

Pie charts are a good tool to use when you know the individual slices number less than about nine, there are no very small values, colors can be used, and the whole adds up to 100 percent exactly. Providing a list view of the data can mitigate some of the problems with pie chart visualizations. However, if the dynamic data does not meet the criteria for a pie chart, bar visualizations are a great alternative for part-to-whole analysis. Obviously, there are other visualizations that are good for comparing items as well. For example, scatter plots can be used effectively to compare parts of a whole.

Applying Chart Styles in Silverlight

If you are not familiar with extending the Silverlight Control Toolkit, you may be wondering how the styled bar chart in Figure 6-7 was achieved. In order to analyze what was changed, take a look at what the chart visualization would have looked like by default. This is shown in Figure 6-8 (note that the title was added).

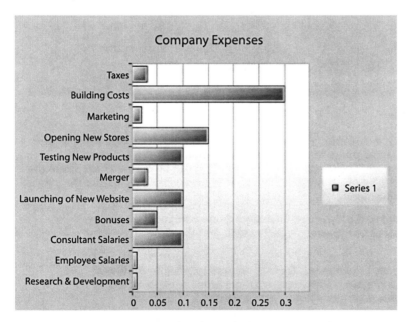

Figure 6-8. The default look of a Silverlight bar chart visualization

There are several key changes that can be seen, when comparing Figure 6-6 and Figure 6-7:

- The series legend has been removed. It is unnecessary for this type of visualization.

- The x-axis (dependent axis) has been formatted to include percentages.

- Grid lines were removed. This is an optional step; however, I feel the chart renders cleaner without grid lines. Grid lines do provide the context of the value for the user. However, in interactive tools such as Silverlight, simply hovering over the bar can provide the exact value being represented.

- The labels were transformed to rotate them 30 degrees. This is completely optional; however, if your data contains long names, this can save a bit of real estate for the labels. If this were a column chart (labels on the bottom), you would have to perform this step, as the labels would overlap horizontally.

Listing 6-1 shows the changes made (shown in bold) to the default bar chart (Figure 6-8) to achieve the cleaner presentation shown Figure 6-7.

Listing 6-1. Styling a bar chart visualization to add a formatted axis and orienting the labels

```
<toolkit:Chart x:Name-"mcChart3"
        Width="600"
        Background="LightSteelBlue" Title="Company Expenses" Height="400"⏎
Margin="0,0,0,100">
    <toolkit:BarSeries Title="" IndependentValueBinding="{Binding Key}"⏎
DependentValueBinding="{Binding Value}" Margin="0">
        <toolkit:BarSeries.DependentRangeAxis>
            <toolkit:LinearAxis Minimum="0" Maximum=".35" Interval="0.1" Orientation="X">
                <toolkit:LinearAxis.AxisLabelStyle>
                    <Style TargetType="toolkit:AxisLabel">
                        <Setter Property="StringFormat" Value="{}{0:p0}"/>
                    </Style>
                </toolkit:LinearAxis.AxisLabelStyle>
            </toolkit:LinearAxis>
        </toolkit:BarSeries.DependentRangeAxis>
        <toolkit:BarSeries.IndependentAxis>
                <toolkit:CategoryAxis Orientation="Y" RenderTransformOrigin="0.5,0.5"⏎
SortOrder="Descending" AxisLabelStyle="{StaticResource SlantedLabelStyle}"⏎
HorizontalAlignment="Right" />
        </toolkit:BarSeries.IndependentAxis>
    </toolkit:BarSeries>
</toolkit:Chart>
```

The SlantedLabelStyle in the code determines the look of the labels on the y-axis. The code in Listing 6-2 shows the render transform performed in order to achieve the slanted label look.

Listing 6-2. Applying a rotation on the labels to give it a slanted look

```
<UserControl.Resources>
        ...
        <Style x:Key="SlantedLabelStyle" TargetType="toolkit:AxisLabel">
                <Setter Property="IsTabStop" Value="False"/>
```

```xml
                        <Setter Property="StringFormat" Value="{}{0}"/>
                        <Setter Property="Template">
                                <Setter.Value>
                                        <ControlTemplate TargetType="toolkit:AxisLabel">
                                                <TextBlock TextAlignment="Right"↵
Text="{TemplateBinding FormattedContent}" Width="150" VerticalAlignment="Center"↵
HorizontalAlignment="Right" Margin="0,5,5,0" RenderTransformOrigin="1,0.5">
                                                        <TextBlock.RenderTransform>
                                                                <TransformGroup>
                                                                        <ScaleTransform/>
                                                                        <SkewTransform/>
                                                                        <RotateTransform↵
Angle="30"/>
                                                                        <TranslateTransform X="1"↵
Y="1"/>
                                                                </TransformGroup>
                                                        </TextBlock.RenderTransform>
                                                </TextBlock>
                                        </ControlTemplate>
                                </Setter.Value>
                        </Setter>
                </Style>
                ...
</UserControl.Resources>
```

This style might seem complex. However, you will be happy to note that it does not have to be coded by hand. In Expression Blend 4, you can edit the template directly by simply selecting it and creating a blank copy to edit. Therefore, in a chart where you have created a specific chart series, you can edit the label style and apply many different types of formatting to the labels. Figure 6-9 illustrates how to create an editable axis label style for customization inside Expression Blend 4.

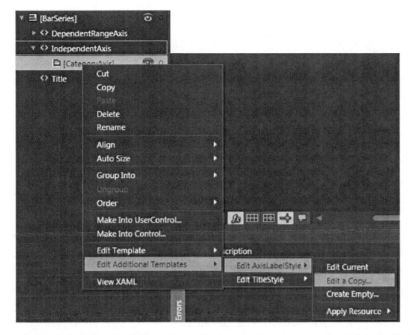

Figure 6-9. Selecting Edit a Copy allows you to customize the AxisLabelStyle of a series for a Silverlight chart.

Once the template is selected, the designer can change the color, layout, or animation, or transform the labels. Figure 6-10 shows the slanted label style selected with the applied transformation. Using the tools in Expression Blend 4 will yield the XAML shown in Listing 6-2. You cannot see the text in the TextBlock control; however the text would be following the path on the line shown below.

Figure 6-10. Editing the AxisLabelStyle by applying a 30 degree angle RenderTransform

---

■ **Note** The complete source code and project to achieve Figure 6-7 is available on the companion web site.

Visualizing Trend Analysis

Trend analysis is spotting visual patterns in continuous data sets that signify growth, decline, or stagnation. The visual patterns derived from the analysis are the insight that is delivered from the visualization. Depending on the data, more than one trend could be derived from the data set.

As mentioned, trend analysis depends on continuous data. The makeup of continuous data relies on the data entities being related. For example, "sales of bikes in 2003" can be related and compared to "sales of bikes in 2004." However, comparing "sales of bikes in 2003" to "salary costs in 2004" makes no sense when trying to derive a trend or analytical pattern. Therefore, continuous data that can be related makes a good candidate to perform trend analysis.

Trend analysis is usually performed over some historical period of time. This can be days, months, years, business quarters, and so on. In a trend visualization, the timeframe usually makes up the x-axis on the chart and is displayed chronologically. If the data is discrete, nonchronological, and cannot be related, other visualizations like a pie chart or bar chart are better options for analysis.

Trends can be visualized a number of ways. Usually, the best candidates for visual trend analysis are line, area, or stack graphs. Silverlight supports visualizing these trend scenarios in the Silverlight Control Toolkit. Silverlight includes both line series and area series charts that can display trend information. In the previous chapter, we covered a coding scenario that showed a line series.

Visualizing trends is one of the simplest forms of analysis that can be done that provides powerful insight to users. If the chart visualization is clear, almost everyone can interpret the information and determine if the trend is growing, declining, or stagnant. Trend analysis becomes more interesting when you are comparing multiple data sets and comparing the trends themselves. Figure 6-11 displays a line chart of three fictional mutual funds and their index prices over the last six months.

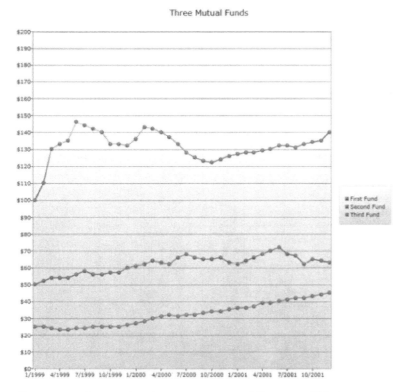

Figure 6-11. Comparing three separate trend lines even if their ranges are close can be difficult.

▦ **Note** Bar (column) visualizations can also be used to show trend information. An individual can interpret the difference in bar sizes and derive trending insight. For example, many statistical programs use bar chart visualizations to show distribution trends in data. However, bar chart visualizations are used as secondary options to analyze trends because they do have some drawbacks. The spaces between the bars and bars with similar values can sometimes make trend analysis a little more difficult than lines. In the Chapter 9 coding scenario, you can find an example of a bar chart used to visualize a statistical distribution that provides secondary trending intelligence.

In Figure 6-11, an individual can probably compare each series and tell you the trend at a given point in time. However, it is difficult to compare the trends to each other. For example, based on Figure 6-11, it isn't clear which mutual fund performed the best or worst in a given timeframe. In order to give a better comparison, the data needs to be normalized so it can be analyzed easier. Figure 6-12 shows an example of standardizing the same data into percentages. Now we can clearly analyze individual trends of each mutual fund and compare the trends to each other because the data has been standardized to a relatable format.

■ **Note** A live demo of improving trend analysis using Silverlight data visualizations can be found on the companion web site. (`http://silverlightbusinessintelligence.com/Demos/ CreatingDataVisualizationsForAnalysis/ImprovingTrendAnalysis/ImprovingTrendAnalysis.html`).

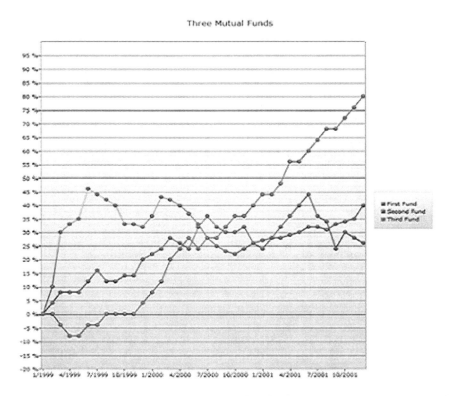

Figure 6-12. *Comparing the three mutual funds after the values have been standardized to a relatable axis is much easier.*

In the preceding example, using the same data set as before, we standardized the chart for percentages. However, the chart can be standardized to an index with a common starting point. For example, all the mutual fund prices could have started at an index value of 100. This would have given the same net effect as standardizing to preceding percentages.

In this section, we looked at one example of improving a data visualization for analysis. However, advanced BI visualizations usually provide additional tools for trending analysis. Some of the key trending features included are:

- The ability to add annotations (labels) to key pieces of information to the chart. As the data is updated with newer information, the annotations keep their "marked" location when the chart is rendered.

- The ability to zoom in on key trends and isolate specific time spans (x-axis)

- The facility to drill down and isolate key trends

- The potential to analyze data points and autosummarize key changes with the rendered data. Combined with annotations, this can display trend findings on a chart visualization.

- The ability to analyze historical data to predict future trends in predictive analytics modules

The Silverlight framework and the Silverlight Control Toolkit obviously do not come prepackaged with these trending tools. However, as you have seen in many examples, Silverlight can be extended with these analytical features. There are many samples online and in the Silverlight Control Toolkit that demonstrate the power of extending charting visualizations with interactive analytical features.

Extending the Silverlight framework with analytical features for data visualizations can be challenging. Luckily there are high-quality third-party vendors that provide a tested foundation with some analytical functionality built in. Figure 6-13 shows a trend analysis chart provided by ComponentOne that allows zooming and isolating key trends interactively using a dual slider technique.

Choosing a visualization package is usually a really good choice when the desired functionality is complex. This is especially true for business intelligence scenarios. What seems like simple functionality like annotations, zooming in, drilling in can take several weeks for a developer to add and for the features to go through the complete software development lifecycle. While you will see more powerful examples of Silverlight controls being extended to create complex visualizations, do not fall into the trap that everything "should be" done this way. You can easily create months of expensive development and testing work on "plumbing code", when a more cost efficient solution was available via a third-party vendor.

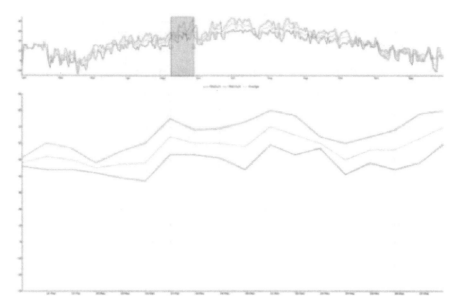

Figure 6-13. The ComponentOne chart data visualization provides rich interactivity including zooming in on key trends that is not available out of the box in the Silverlight Control Toolkit.

■ **Note** ComponentOne provides a wide array of visual components for .NET including Silverlight. Their Silverlight offering includes a healthy number of controls. Furthermore, they include controls that are important for visual analysis such as gauge controls, hierarchy controls, charting visualizations, and so on. For more information, see www.componentone.com.

Comparing Ratios (Before and After)

In some cases, you have a small amount of data points that you want to illustrate in a visualization. This is common when surfacing information that is aggregated at a high level. Comparing ratios is one type of analysis that is performed on highly summarized information. In this type of analysis, the goal is to compare the state of the summarized values.

Comparing ratios can be done using several techniques. One obvious choice would be to use a charting visualization. If the values add up to 100 percent, a pie chart could be a good potential choice. A bar chart visualization is also an option to compare two to four values in different states. The lengths of the bars would be used to perceive different ratios.

Creating custom controls to present data in Silverlight is another option for comparing ratios. Figure 6-14 shows a custom data visualization that I created in Silverlight. The data visualization displays the total home values in a fictitious city in the United States over three years. The area of each circle indicates the home values in a given year. Using the area formula for a circle (πr^2), we can calculate the required radius of a circle we should render. This is important as we want the area of the circle to properly represent the value of a given year.

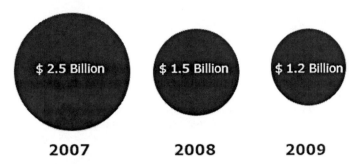

Total Value of Homes in Somewhere, USA

$ 2.5 Billion

$ 1.5 Billion

$ 1.2 Billion

2007   2008   2009

Figure 6-14. A custom data visualization created in Silverlight that can be used for ratio analysis of a small set of values

The custom infographic provides an effective way to compare ratios over three years. You can clearly see that the sizes of the circles bring an appropriate perspective to the labels of the data.

■ **Note** A live demo of improving trend analysis using Silverlight data visualizations can be found on the companion web site. (`http://silverlightbusinessintelligence.com/Demos/CreatingDataVisualizationsForAnalysis/ComparingRatios/ComparingRatios.html`).

Text Data

Text visualizations play an important role in visual analysis. The combination of being able to position a set of text labels and style the labels can be used as an effective form of visual analysis. It is a misconception that visualizations require glyphs, geometry, charts, or other visual cues in order to be useful. In the previous chapter's coding scenario, we designed a tag cloud that used color, size, and font weight to highlight the frequency of a metric. A tag cloud can deliver insight very effectively with simply styled text. Improvements to tag clouds include animations and 3D layouts to improve the analysis experience. Another example of visual analysis with text data was shown in Chapter 1 in the form of the Wordle chart.

Geographical Data

If your data sets include geographic or spatial data, visualizing them on a geographical map is ideal. As you saw in Chapter 5's coding scenario, Silverlight can be extended with the Silverlight Bing Map control to overlay geographical data on top of various map locations.

The key feature of integrating the map control with Silverlight is the dramatic performance over other Ajax map solutions. The control is much more interactive and performs much better. Furthermore, Silverlight's powerful multimedia and animation frameworks can easily overlay on top of the maps and provide rich experiences with spatial data sets. For example, charting visualizations can be added on top of the map control.

Hierarchical Data

If you have a background in BI, you have probably come across multidimensional or hierarchical data relationships. Hierarchical data sets contain several levels of parent-child relationships that can prove to be difficult to visualize if there is a lot of data or the levels are deep.

Hierarchies with their levels can be visualized a number of common ways. A common way is to visualize a hierarchy using a tree view control. Figure 6-15 shows a Silverlight tree view control that displays three levels of a hierarchy.

◢   Frank Sinatra

     ◢   In The Wee Small Hours

         ♪   *In The Wee Small Hours Of The Morning*

         ♪   *Mood Indigo*

         ♪   *Glad To Be Unhappy*

         ♪   *I Get Along Without You Very Well*

         ♪   *Deep In A Dream*

     ▷   You Do Something To Me

▷   African Wind

▷   Johnny Cash

Figure 6-15. *A Silverlight tree view that displays a three-level hierarchy (sample from the Silverlight Control Toolkit)*

A tree view is an effective way to display labels in a hierarchical fashion. This is similar to how dimension hierarchies would be presented in SQL Server Analysis Services. However, where is the data? In order to display the data, we need to attach additional visualizations (tables, infographics) to display the corresponding selection. Furthermore, displaying hierarchical data that includes many levels is ineffective, as all the nodes have to be expanded. This can take up a lot of real estate.

■ **Warning** The Silverlight tree view implements hierarchies using the HierarchicalDataTemplate. This template suffers from major performance problems when rendering the control with more than two levels expanded even for a nominal amount of records. Applying concepts like "data virtualization" can mitigate the performance impact on larger lists. For a tree view surfacing hierarchical data this would be done via delay loading the leaf level information.

A *tree map* control is a type of data visualization optimized for showing hierarchical data. The control works by drawing a series of rectangles while nesting them recursively to display parent-child relationships. This technique allows the tree map to present a large number of hierarchy levels and large data sets while not requiring a huge amount of real estate.

A basic tree map uses the size of the rectangles to display a value of a metric. A larger value would be visualized with a larger rectangle. Conversely, smaller values would be shown with smaller rectangles. A tree map control does not stop there. It can also use color to display a secondary metric value. Therefore, a single-tree map control can display a nested hierarchy while displaying two metrics using size and color. Figure 6-16 illustrates a tree map control that uses rectangle size to compare the points attained by NHL teams. Furthermore, it uses color to distinguish the rank of the teams.

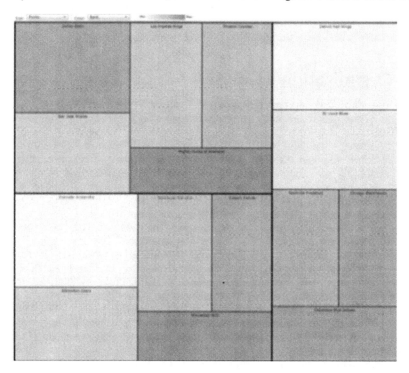

Figure 6-16. A Silverlight tree map control can present hierarchical data while displaying two metric values.

As you can see from this visualization, it is pretty easy to isolate outlier data on a tree map. Additional annotations can be provided in the form of labels inside rectangles or as tool tips when the user hovers over a rectangle. This is similar to hovering over a pie slice or a bar in a bar chart.

Even though tree maps are effective, they can be hard to understand initially by a user. This does not make them great BI 2.0 self-service implementations. Tree maps should be the implementation choice for displaying large amounts of hierarchical data with metrics in a visual form.

Other Visualization Types

I did not cover every type of data set relationship format in this section. If you are familiar with business visualization or statistical software, there are some visualization types that you might wonder if Silverlight supports.

Silverlight has a rich and growing community that provides a lot of additional visualizations that I did not cover. Furthermore, I cannot stress enough the power of the Silverlight framework. A lot of developers incorrectly treat the framework as an API and figure that they can only call the provided public functionality. Silverlight is built on the .NET framework, which has been designed for extensibility. As you saw in the examples in this section, by simply tweaking styles or leveraging the graphical rendering, we were able to extend basic charts into BI 2.0 data visualizations that were optimized for delivering wisdom. In summary, if Silverlight does not support the exact visualization, do not despair. You can probably replicate it with ease using the Silverlight framework.

Comparing Metrics to Organizational Goals

Measuring metrics against goals is one of the keys of providing analytical value to a data set in an organization. This type of analysis allows an organization to track the success of various metrics that are important to the health of the business.

Key performance indicators (KPIs) have been used in BI software to measure the progress of various metrics against business goals. As the name suggests, KPIs are a set of important metrics that summarize the overall success of an organization's goals. KPIs have become very popular for BI analysis because they provide quick and visual insight into measurable objectives. KPIs are usually found as features in performance management software, executive dashboards, and scorecard modules.

The key aspect of KPIs is that they are quantifiable and measurable against another value. For example, a KPI described as "Increase customer retention by 10 percent over the next year" can be easily quantified with underlying data. A data visualization can be created to illustrate if the organization is tracking to meet the goals of the customer retention. KPI. The KPI describes what is being measured, the target of success, and the timeframe to achieve success. Furthermore, we can use the timeframe to track if we are progressing positively toward the goal. However, ambiguous and unquantifiable metrics do not make good KPI candidates and often cause confusion. In the previous example, if the KPI had been defined as "Increase customer retention," it would be an incomplete KPI. We know the metric but we do not know the target (goal) or the timeframe that would indicate a success or failure of the goal. The target and the timeframe of the KPI are left to the interpretation of the user. Having unclear goals and timeframes impairs the ability to do proper analysis.

Comparing metrics to goals (KPIs) can be visualized a number of ways. Classic KPI visualizations include gauges, reference lines, progress indicators and KPI lists. KPIs are not new to BI 2.0, and they have been around for several years now. In fact, most BI software has standardized the way KPIs are surfaced. KPI visualizations have matured to the point that alternatives are presented to compare metrics to goals. For example, bullet graphs are becoming much more popular in BI 2.0 applications as they do not require complex and colorful visuals. Therefore, they look great when you print them. Furthermore, they take up much less real estate than traditional KPI gauges and can be used as word-sized visualizations.

■ **Note** KPI examples visualized with bullet graphs, gauges, and KPI lists can be found on the accompanying web site (www.silverlightbusinessintelligence.com).

Reference Lines

Measuring goals can be added to charting visualizations as well. A common technique to add KPI functionality to a chart is to provide a reference line that symbolizes the goal. Figure 6-17 shows an aggregate trend line chart of a player's HRs (home runs) during the baseball season. Notice that a reference line indicates the season HR goal of the baseball player. A secondary reference line is added that signifies the average for the top ten HR leaders. Using this information, you can see how the baseball player is tracking toward the goal to hit 50 HRs in the season and how he compares to the top ten HR leaders average.

The visualization in Figure 6-17 can be improved by including other visual cues for analysis. For example, a range could be added to show the minimum/maximum number of HRs the player has hit in his career. Making this visualization dynamic with a number of KPIs (reference lines) would be easy. For example, a list box could be added with selections to determine which reference lines to display on the chart. This way, the user could determine how to analyze the data.

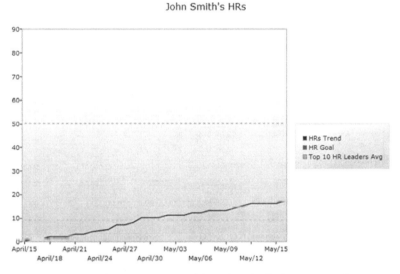

Figure 6-17. *Tracking an HR trend for a baseball player toward a 50-HR goal. A secondary reference line compares the player's trend to the top ten HR leaders average.*

The reference lines are simply added as a line series with start point and endpoint that are constant. The data points were removed from the reference lines as they do not denote actual data points on the graph. The chart's grid lines were also removed so as not to interfere with the horizontal reference lines. The XAML that was used to create this visualization is shown in Listing 6-3.

Listing 6-3. *Silverlight XAML used to create the chart in Figure 6-17*

```
<toolkit:Chart Margin="0" Title="John Smith's HRs" x:Name="HRs" Height="500" Width="700">
    <toolkit:Chart.Axes>
        <!-- Y Axis (number of HRs) -->
        <toolkit:LinearAxis Orientation="Y" Minimum="0" Maximum="90" ShowGridLines="False">
        </toolkit:LinearAxis>
```

```xml
        <!-- X Axis (date axis) -->
        <toolkit:DateTimeAxis Orientation="X">
            <toolkit:DateTimeAxis.AxisLabelStyle>
                <Style TargetType="toolkit:DateTimeAxisLabel">
                    <Setter Property="StringFormat" Value="{}{0:MMMM/dd}"/>
                </Style>
            </toolkit:DateTimeAxis.AxisLabelStyle>
        </toolkit:DateTimeAxis>
</toolkit:Chart.Axes>
<!-- HR Trend Line -->
<toolkit:LineSeries Title="HRs Trend"  DependentValuePath="Value"
            IndependentValuePath="Key" ItemsSource="{Binding}">

    <toolkit:LineSeries.DataPointStyle>
        <Style TargetType="Control">
            <Setter Property="Visibility" Value="Collapsed" />
            <Setter Property="Opacity" Value="0" />
            <Setter Property="Background" Value="Blue" />
        </Style>
    </toolkit:LineSeries.DataPointStyle>

</toolkit:LineSeries>

<!-- HR Goal Reference Line -->
<toolkit:LineSeries Title="HR Goal"  DependentValuePath="Value"
            IndependentValuePath="Key" ItemsSource="{Binding}">

    <toolkit:LineSeries.DataPointStyle>
        <Style TargetType="Control">
            <Setter Property="Visibility" Value="Collapsed" />
            <Setter Property="Opacity" Value="0" />
            <Setter Property="Background" Value="Green" />
        </Style>
    </toolkit:LineSeries.DataPointStyle>

    <toolkit:LineSeries.PolylineStyle>
        <Style TargetType="Polyline">
            <Setter Property="Opacity" Value="0.85" />
            <Setter Property="StrokeDashArray" Value="4" />
            </Style>
    </toolkit:LineSeries.PolylineStyle>
</toolkit:LineSeries>

<!-- Top Ten HR Leaders Reference Line -->
<toolkit:LineSeries Title="Top 10 HR Leaders Avg"  DependentValuePath="Value"
            IndependentValuePath="Key" ItemsSource="{Binding}">

    <toolkit:LineSeries.DataPointStyle>
        <Style TargetType="Control">
            <Setter Property="Visibility" Value="Collapsed" />
            <Setter Property="Opacity" Value="0" />
        </Style>
```

```
        </toolkit:LineSeries.DataPointStyle>

        <toolkit:LineSeries.PolylineStyle>
            <Style TargetType="Polyline">
                <Setter Property="Opacity" Value="0.85" />
                <Setter Property="StrokeDashArray" Value="4" />
            </Style>
        </toolkit:LineSeries.PolylineStyle>
    </toolkit:LineSeries>
</toolkit:Chart>
```

In this example, you can see how adding a simple reference line can provide additional insight to a charting visualization. This charting visualization doesn't just a show trends anymore; it can now answer comparison questions. Furthermore, in the spirit of BI 2.0 governance, the solution is simple and easy for the average user to interpret.

Creating Visual KPIs for Scorecard Dashboards

KPIs in for scorecard scenarios more traditional types of KPIs found in many dashboards. Dashboards attempt to provide a quick summary view of the performance of the organization. The role of a visual KPI is to provide a visual object that can symbolize the state of a given metric with a quick glance. Rendering the KPI using different colors, shapes, and orientation allows the user to translate that into insight very quickly.

Visual KPIs come in several different forms. Figure 6-18 illustrates several different types of KPIs available in SQL Server 2008 R2. As you can see, just like charting visualizations there are many different types of indicators available to surface different type of information.

In this section we are going to look at how to create some of these indicators in Silverlight. Specifically we are going to create stoplight indicators (Shapes in Figure 6-18), trend KPIs (Directional in Figure 6-18) and progress indicators (Ratings in Figure 6-18) in Expression Blend 4.

■ **Note** If you are not familiar with KPI fundamentals, please visit the Wikipedia site for an additional summary to key performance indicators (http://en.wikipedia.org/wiki/Key_performance_indicator).

Figure 6-18. Different types of indicators (KPI visuals) provided in SQL Server 2008 R2 Report Builder 3.0

Shape KPI Visuals (Stoplight indicators)

The most common type of KPI is a shape indicator or stoplight KPI. It commonly surfaces three different types of values: has met or is exceeding desired goal, is partially meeting goal or is below desired goal. The green color is used to signify a KPI in the desired range. The yellow color is used to signify a KPI in the warning/partially meeting goal range. Lastly, the red color is used to render a KPI that is not meeting the desired goal (or is at high risk).

These types of KPIs used to be known as stoplight KPIs. The term came from a traffic light and its use of three colors (green, yellow and red). In some business intelligence applications you will still see that term used. However, that term is largely deprecated for current and BI 2.0 applications. Stoplight KPIs essentially tried to mimic the traffic light look. These indicators looked great in on a color monitor, however users had a problem distinguishing the difference between the different colors when the stoplight KPIs were printed on a non-color laser printer. Figure 6-19 compares a stoplight KPI to explicit shape-based indicator. If you are reading this book in paperback, it is probably hard to distinguish which KPI is which color. Furthermore, you can imagine this problem being amplified for those that are colorblind.

Figure 6-19. Stoplight KPI visuals (shown on left) are hard to distinguish when printed on a non-color printer

The best practice is to utilize the explicit shape indicators are your primary KPIs when comparing a value to a desired goal. The explicit shapes plus colors provide two mechanisms to indicate to the user the current value of a KPI. A red diamond is used to highlight "bad metrics" that are not meeting the desired goals. A yellow triangle is used to highlight a "metric in warning" that is at risk of not meeting the goal. A green circle is used to highlight a "metric meeting or exceeding" the desired goal. When you print the explicit shape KPIs on a non-color printer, the shape itself remains the mechanism of identifying the status of the KPI metric.

Neither Silverlight 4 nor Expression Blend 4 provides KPI visualizations natively. However, just as you have seen in the earlier chapters the basic tools exist in Silverlight 4 and Expression Blend 4 to style and manipulate base controls to look render like the shape indicators shown in Figure 6-18.

As mentioned in Chapter 3, Expression Blend 4 includes a new Shapes section in the asset panel (shown in Figure 6-20). In the shapes asset panel, you can see there are various base shapes that can be used to create our shape indicators (diamond, triangle and ellipse). Studying Figure 6-20, we can see that there are several good candidates that can server as a base for our shape KPIs. We are going to create the shape indicators (KPI visuals) using this simple process:

- Start with a base Shape.

- Set "dark base color" for the stroke brush (outline of the shape)

- Set a "light base color" for the starting point of the gradient

- Set a gradient offset starting from the "light base color" ending with the "dark base color" (optional)

- Added a shadow effect with the color stroke of the "dark base color"

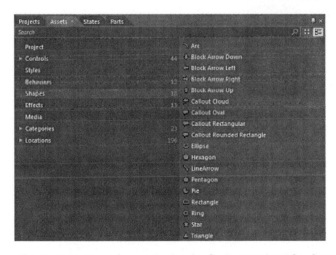

Figure 6-20. *New Shapes section in the Expression Blend 4 asset panel*

Using this technique, I was able to replicate all three shape KPIs and surface them on a list (shown in Figure 6-21). As you can see, the Silverlight KPIs are accented with an optional gradient and shadow effect to give the indicator an additional look of depth. The KPI visuals in SharePoint Server or Report Builder 3.0 are raster-based images. Conversely, these are vector-based user controls in Silverlight, which can scale to very small or very large sizes without losing visual fidelity.

Figure 6-21. Professional-looking KPIs can quickly be created using the base shapes in Expression Blend 4.

The "good KPI visual" (green circle) and "warning KPI visual" (yellow triangle) are self-explanatory in the way they were created. However, the "goal not met/high risk KPI" has an additional step. In Expression Blend 3 or earlier, you could have used a rectangle and performed a rotate transform on the control. This is still a viable approach in Expression Blend 4; however, there is a more performant approach by simply using the new Hexagon shape from the asset panel. Figure 6-22 below shows how the shapes have additional properties that can be set to tweak the appearance of these controls. The hexagon has a PointCount property that controls how many "corners" the shape has. Simply setting this to a value of 4 renders the "diamond KPI" shape for us without having to perform a rotate transform. I recommend using the hexagon approach because for large KPI lists, this will render much faster. Furthermore, this allows you to add animations and complex transitions easier without having to worry about the rotate transform "interfering" with the rendering tree.

Figure 6-22. Setting the PointCount property value to 4 will render a diamond-like shape, which can be used as a shape indicator (KPI visual).

The XAML to create this KPI is pretty straightforward. It is only between 10-15 lines of XAML (depending on how you lay out your code). The XAML is a lot simpler than going off and creating your own KPI controls that have complex paths. This sample is obviously not productized and you would want to create a single KPI control that utilizes the VisualStateManager to move between states. For example, you would have a "Goal met" state that would surface the green circle UI element. Furthermore, you would want to abstract the style setters in a separate resource. The XAML for the "bad KPI" can be seen in Listing 6-4 below.

Listing 6-4. Silverlight XAML used to create the red diamond shape indicator.

```
<ed:RegularPolygon Height="60" InnerRadius="1" Margin="241,198,339,0"
        PointCount="4" Stroke="#FFBA1313"
        UseLayoutRounding="False" VerticalAlignment="Top" Width="60">
        <ed:RegularPolygon.Effect>
                <DropShadowEffect Color="#FFBA1313"/>
```

```
                </ed:RegularPolygon.Effect>
                <ed:RegularPolygon.Fill>
                        <LinearGradientBrush EndPoint="0.658,0.974"
                                MappingMode="RelativeToBoundingBox" StartPoint="0.342,0.026">
                                <GradientStop Color="#FFE5AD93" Offset="0.194"/>
                                <GradientStop Color="#FFE51616" Offset="1"/>
                        </LinearGradientBrush>
                </ed:RegularPolygon.Fill>
        </ed:RegularPolygon>
</ed:RegularPolygon>
```

▪ **Note** In the previous chapter's coding scenario, you saw how shape KPIs can be used in geographic visualizations (Figure 5-22).

Trend KPI Visuals (Directional indicators)

In addition to basic state KPIs, you can use the shape assets to create KPIs that visualize trending information. These types of KPIs are valuable when you want to provide additional trending insight to static aggregate numbers. For example, a report may say "Q1 numbers for North American sales are 43 million". Is that better, worse or about the same from last year? An executive may want to have that information so they don't have to reference an another report from last year to compare progress. Trend KPIs can be easily created the new block arrows in the shapes asset panel shown in Figure 6-23.

Figure 6-23. Block arrow shapes in shapes asset panel in Expression Blend 4

Using the same process we did in the previous section, I created a sample list that uses the block arrows as directional indicators. I added additional styling properties like drop shadow, gradient colors and stroke to allow the KPIs to provide additional visual insight with color. This is reflected in the figure below.

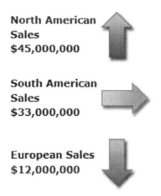

North American
Sales
$45,000,000

South American
Sales
$33,000,000

European Sales
$12,000,000

Figure 6-24. Directional indicators (trend KPI visuals) created using block arrows.

Progress KPI Visuals (Rating indicators)

Progress KPI visualizations surface a visual symbol that clearly identifies many possible states. If you go back to Figure 6-18, you can see many different rating indicators that include various graphical symbols for multiple states. What makes these indicators different from the previous shape indicators or directional indicators is that multiple states can be visualized. For example, in Figure 6-18 you can see a visual rating control with states ranging from 0 to 5. However, the visual control can also represent a state value of 3.5 or a value of 4.75 (with the stars partially colored in).

A terrific example of a progress KPI is the single pie slice visualization. This KPI is usually represented by a pie chart with a single slice that represents the state of progress from 0% to 100%. The color of the pie is usually a solid black color. For example, a progress KPI that would indicate 25% could be implemented using a single pie slice that is one-quarter of the way full using a single black color.

The Expression Blend 4 asset panel includes a Pie shape control that can draw a pie chart that surfaces a single pie slice. This is exactly what we need to implement a progress indicator. Just like the previous Shape examples, the pie shape has several interesting properties that can be set that can aid in easily surfacing a KPI indicator (shown in Figure 6-25). Properties like start angle, end angle, arc thickness unit and arc thickness can be bound to data to surface the pie shape in several different ways.

Figure 6-25. Adjusting the StartAngle or EndAngle properties allows Pie control to render pie slices differently.

How would you use the pie shape in a business intelligence scenario? As mentioned above, the pie shape is great for showing progress on an individual metric (since the pie shape only surfaces a single pie slice). This could be used to further amplify progress being made, most current data point or final result of a series of events. In Figure 6-26 you can clearly understand a business intelligence user could easily guide their eyes down the list and pick out the projects that are far from completion by just focusing on the pie slices. Additional KPI-like insight could be added by using color. For the sake of clarity, you will want to use a common start angle for your pie shape. This will allow the user a single point of reference when comparing the pie slices. I chose 360 as the end angle and this makes calculating the pie EndAngle property easy. For example, 75% completion would be .75*360 = 270. This also makes binding calculations easier. In Chapter 3, we implemented a simple ValueConverter in one of the coding scenarios. The same concept could be applied to find the EndAngle property to allow the Pie shape to be data bound.

Progress of Development Projects

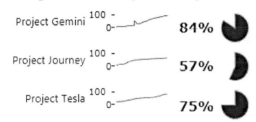

Figure 6-26. An example of a data visualization surfacing the state of several development projects. Sparklines provide trending information, while the KPI progress indicator easily surfaces the current state of the project.

■ **Note** The source code for this example is included in the zip file found on the companion web site.

Advantages of Silverlight KPIs

After reading this section, you might be wondering "Why use Silverlight, when other business intelligence tools provide much of these indicators as self-service tools?" Silverlight (in its current version) cannot compete with easily creating KPIs in a self-service manner like in Report Builder 3.0. However, Silverlight KPIs have several advantages that I did not cover:

- High degree of customization using various directional, shape or rating indicators (anything is possible)

- Easily style the KPI visualizations to match a corporate or professional dashboard theme

- KPI visualizations are vector based and scale without losing graphical fidelity when zooming in or zooming out

- Silverlight KPIs can be animated with transitions or loading animations

- Interactive scenarios (covered in Chapter 4 or Predictive Analytics) can utilize Silverlight KPIs to provide real-time insight to the data sets or calculations.

Word-Sized Chart Visualizations

So far in the two data visualization chapters, we have looked at the benefits that data visualizations bring to visual BI 2.0 analytics. Therefore, it is understandable to want to start incorporating data visualizations in many areas to aid in the delivery of knowledge. However, as you have noticed, many of these visualizations can take up a great deal of real estate on a screen in order to be effective. A BI professional often has to make tough decisions on which visualizations make the most sense. This usually results into the logical splitting of the layout into multiple screens. This can cause the data visualizations to lose some of their effectiveness as the entire analytical picture is delivered in pieces (multiple screen layouts) as the user jumps between layout windows.

Word-sized visualizations are created in order to provide the visual analysis benefits of data visualizations while not having to sacrifice a great deal of real estate. As the name implies, word-sized visualizations are much smaller in size. Their dimensions don't take up more space than the average sentence fragments. This makes word-sized visualizations very unique as they can be embedded into lists, tables, or spreadsheets with ease. Combining number lists (tables) with a visual context increases the potential insight that can be derived in a smaller footprint.

■ **Note** Word-sized charts are very popular in BI applications. They are a feature that many people have constantly asked Microsoft to include. Excel 2010 supports word-sized charts natively in the product. Previously, a user had to go through the trouble of manually designing them into spreadsheets or use third-party products. Excel 2007 partially supported word-sized visualizations using data bars.

Types of Word-Sized Chart Visualizations

In this section, we will cover common examples of word-sized chart visualizations. Furthermore, we will continue to elaborate on how Silverlight charting controls can be extended to create word-sized visualizations with ease.

Sparklines

Sparklines are small, simple word-sized line charts that provide visual context to labels or numerical information. A sparkline's primary focus is to effectively show a historical trend visually. Therefore, the line itself is the only object required to convey the information. Additional items such as data points, x-axis, and y-axis are omitted on purpose to enhance the focus on the trend patterns in the line graph.

Before discussing sparklines in further detail, let's take a look at an example of a simple list. Figure 6-27 shows a simple list of web domains with the current number of page views displayed.

domain1.com: 45k visitors

domain2.com: 33k visitors

domain3.com: 60k visitors

Figure 6-27. List of domains and their current number of page views

Note that this list only provides the user the current value. With this list, the user is not aware of past performance, trends, or any other historical information. Contrast this with Figure 6-28, which shows an example of a sparkline graph embedded in the previous list.

domain1.com: 45k visitors

domain2.com: 33k visitors

domain3.com: 60k visitors

Figure 6-28. Sparklines can provide valuable visual context to data labels.

In addition to providing the current value of page views, there is insight gained from embedding a sparkline graph. Not only do you have the current value of the page views for each domain, but you can also see past trends. For example, you can note that domain1.com has been trending downward. In addition, you can see that domain2.com has a repeating pattern of peaks and valleys.

The most important part is that we were able to perform this extra analysis even though both axes have been removed. For this type of analysis, the exact values in the past are not really important to evaluate trending context.

When using sparkline visualizations, it is important to take note of the following guidelines:

- Ensure both the x- and y-axes' labels are removed to focus the attention on the trend of the line chart rather than the values.

- Do not include the data points.

- Do not include a title or legend.

- Only a single series should be shown at a time.

- Use a label to display the current value (end value) of the sparkline chart. The label can optionally symbolize trend information (e.g., use red to show a downward trend, use an up arrow glyph to show an upward trend, etc.). It is very important to provide context (labels) to sparklines because they usually don't contain all of the members of a fully rendered chart.

- Do not clutter the sparkline visualization. The most important part of the sparkline is that it gives you the ability to interpret trending information. Do not use background colors, borders, or nonprimary colors for the line chart. Essentially, anything that takes away focus from the main trend line can take away from the value of a sparkline.

There are exceptions to the sparkline rules just listed. Figure 6-29 shows an example of effectively combining a reference line with a sparkline to highlight a starting location or a KPI. Notice the reference line was styled using a light dotted line that does not take away from the primary trend in a sparkline.

domain1.com: 60k visitors

domain2.com: 45k visitors

domain3.com: 33k visitors

Figure 6-29. Sparklines can be extended with reference lines to provide additional value.

■ **Note** A live demo of the different sparkline layouts presented in this section can be found on the Demos section of the companion web site (www.silverlightbusinessintelligence.com/Demos/ CreatingDataVisualizationsForAnalysis/WordSizedChartsSparklines/ WordSizedChartsSparklines.html).

Another exception is that sometimes the axis, if formatted properly, can provide additional context to the range of data. Figure 6-30 shows an example of enabling the y-axis for the domain1.com list item.

100k-

           domain1.com: 60k visitors

0k-

Figure 6-30. Sparkline with reference line and y-axis formatted

In the figure, note that the axis is formatting the thousand values with a *k* symbol. This makes the axis labels unobtrusive with the trend line. However, as you can clearly see, the sparkline is starting to get a little busy. If you start making exceptions to the sparkline guidelines, ensure that what you add is of analytical value. It would make no sense to enable the y-axis labels if the range is not going to provide additional insight. Furthermore, the sparkline sizes may differ for your visualization requirements. Larger sparklines may have the real estate for you to add additional items such as axis labels, reference lines, and annotations.

■ **Note** The term *sparkline* is often used as an umbrella term for all word-sized graphics. If you search the term *sparkline* on the Internet, you will often see word-sized bar charts, pie charts, bullet graphs, whisker charts, and so on included in this term. Sparklines were the original micro-sized visualizations, and others have followed. This is why you see the term *sparkline* to describe all types of word-sized graphics. In my opinion, the term *sparkline* specifically describes word-sized line charts. In my opinion, other word-sized visualizations have individual names, and it's incorrect to use the term *sparkline* to describe them all. Please note both Excel 2010 and Report Builder 3.0 (SQL Server 2008 R2) both use the term *sparkline* as an umbrella term for all word-sized graphics.

Sparkline visualizations are not limited to a line series chart. You can also create an area series sparkline using the same concepts. Figure 6-31 illustrates a Silverlight area series sparkline that is used to surface a stock's trendline. Notice in the figure below the area series amplifies the main trend line to enhance the peaks and troughs for analysis.

Financial area series sparklines can be made to look fantastic in Silverlight, because of the ability to enhance the visualization with transitions. For example, a popular enhancement to these types of charts is to display a cross-hair as the day progresses to indicate the current value of the stock.

Figure 6-31. *Area series sparklines can be used in Silverlight to create dynamic financial widgets.*

Applying Sparklines in Silverlight

All the sparklines the previous figures were rendered in Silverlight. As you can see, Silverlight charts can be extended with styles in order to render sparkline visualizations. It is important to note the Silverlight Control Toolkit framework did not require special add-ons to be able to render these charts.

Looking back at the previous figures, note that the following items were changed in order to render the chart as a word-sized visualization in Silverlight:

- Chart dimensions were made small (word-sized).

- The x- and y-axes do not display values.

- The line series thickness was made thinner.

- The line series does not display data points.

- The line series is a primary black color.

- Items like the border, title, and background are not displayed.

- A reference line was added by a secondary line series. The secondary line series has a reduced opacity level so it does not conflict with the primary line series. Furthermore, the line series is rendered using a dashed (dotted) brush.

Listing 6-5 shows the code changes in bold in order to render a sparkline chart.

Listing 6-5. Silverlight XAML code that renders a sparkline graph

```
<toolkit:Chart Width="100" Height="25" Margin="0">

        <!-- Hide the border edges -->
        <toolkit:Chart.Template>
            <ControlTemplate TargetType="toolkit:Chart">
                    <chartingPrimitivesToolkit:EdgePanel x:Name="ChartArea">
                        <Grid Canvas.ZIndex="-1" />
                    </chartingPrimitivesToolkit:EdgePanel>
```

```
            </ControlTemplate>
        </toolkit:Chart.Template>

    <!-- Format the axes for a sparkline -->
        <toolkit:Chart.Axes>
                <toolkit:DateTimeAxis Orientation="X" MaxHeight="1" Opacity="0"↵
Minimum="2008/07/07" Maximum="2008/09/08"/>
                <toolkit:LinearAxis Orientation="Y" Opacity="1" Minimum="20" Maximum="85"/>
        </toolkit:Chart.Axes>

    <!-- Reference Line Series -->
    <toolkit:LineSeries
                ItemsSource="{Binding Domain3ReferenceLine}"
                IndependentValueBinding="{Binding Date}"
                DependentValueBinding="{Binding NumberOfHits}">

        <!-- DataPointStyle -->
        <toolkit:LineSeries.DataPointStyle>
            <Style TargetType="Control">
                <!-- Collapase the data points -->
                <Setter Property="Visibility" Value="Collapsed"/>
        <!-- Collapase the data points -->
                <Setter Property="Opacity" Value="0"/>
                <!-- Set color to black -->
                <Setter Property="Background" Value="Black"/>
            </Style>
        </toolkit:LineSeries.DataPointStyle>

        <!-- Use dashes for reference line -->
        <toolkit:LineSeries.PolylineStyle>
            <Style TargetType="Polyline">
                <Setter Property="Opacity" Value="0.75"/>
                <Setter Property="StrokeDashArray" Value="2" />
                <Setter Property="StrokeThickness" Value="0.75" />
            </Style>
        </toolkit:LineSeries.PolylineStyle>
    </toolkit:LineSeries>

    <!-- Data Line Series -->
    <toolkit:LineSeries
                ItemsSource="{Binding Domain3}"
                IndependentValueBinding="{Binding Date}"
                DependentValueBinding="{Binding NumberOfHits}" >

                <!-- DataPointStyle -->
                <toolkit:LineSeries.DataPointStyle>
                        <Style TargetType="Control">
                                <!-- Collapase the data points -->
                                <Setter Property="Visibility" Value="Collapsed"/>
                                <!-- Set color to black -->
                                <Setter Property="Background" Value="Black"/>
```

```
            </Style>
        </toolkit:LineSeries.DataPointStyle>

    <!-- Use thin primary line -->
    <toolkit:LineSeries.PolylineStyle>
        <Style TargetType="Polyline">
            <Setter Property="StrokeThickness" Value="0.75" />
        </Style>
    </toolkit:LineSeries.PolylineStyle>
    </toolkit:LineSeries>
</toolkit:Chart>
```

This code may seem complex; however, it is essentially just tweaking the Silverlight styles and applying the sparkline concepts defined. The important point is that there are no third-party objects, custom objects, or additional C#/Visual Basic programming that had to be done in order to achieve this. Part of styling the Silverlight Control Toolkit charts is understanding the styling framework and knowing where things are located. For example, knowing that the edge panel (border) is rendered above the chart is important if you need to hide it. Furthermore, knowing that the line series has a PolylineStyle object that can be overridden with custom properties is valuable to be able to style the reference line (opacity, thickness, and dashed lines).

Column Charts

Word-sized column charts share many similarities with sparklines. Essentially, they are miniature versions of simple column charts without the x- and y-axes defined. However, column charts rendered in a word-sized format cannot display labels (annotations) effectively. Therefore, word-sized column charts essentially need to graph continuous data sets (similar to sparklines). For example, the chart in Figure 6-7 would not be good as a word-sized column chart since the discrete columns need to have individual labels. This is not an option in a micro-format.

Word-sized column charts can effectively display continuous data, distribution analysis, and true or false trends, or act as alternatives to sparkline visualizations. Figure 6-32 shows an example of a word-sized column chart that is used to provide visual context to a typical standings table for four soccer teams.

Team Name	W-L-T	Goal Diff	Goal Diff (Last 10)
Team 1	12-8-3	+14	
Team 2	10-10-3	+4	
Team 3	7-11-5	-4	
Team 4	5-15-2	-15	

Figure 6-32. Example soccer standings with a word-sized column visualization

In this figure, I embedded a bar chart visualization in the Goal Differential column for the last ten matches for the four teams. What extra knowledge can be derived from this visual context? Following is a short list of items that you can immediately gauge from the Goal Diff visualization column:

- Trend of goal differentials for the last ten games
- Trend of wins and losses for the last ten games

- Margin of victory or losses for the last ten games

- Visual comparison to other team wins, losses, and margin of victory/loss trends

---

■ **Note** Word-sized column visualizations that show only true/false/null values are referred to as "win/loss charts." For a sample implementation, please take a look at Excel 2010.

This example should strengthen your perception of word-sized chart visualizations. You can clearly see that a fair amount of extra insight was provided from simply adding this visualization to the standings table. This example also highlights the concept of maximizing analytical value. I could have easily added a column that was "Last Ten Wins/Losses." This would have provided us wins/losses trending and comparison. However, from the goal differential margin, we can derive both victory/loss margins as well as win/loss trending.

Best practices for word-sized column charts are as follows:

- Ensure both x- and y-axes are removed to focus the attention on the individual columns.

- Only a single column series should be shown at a time.

- Try to use a primary color for the word-sized column charts to make the individual columns stand out.

- Labels can be used to summarize the column chart. For example, if the column chart is a list of values, the label could be an addition of all the values. In the chart shown in Figure 6-22, we could have added a column called "Goal Diff (Last 10)" that was simply the +/– goal differential summary of the last ten games.

- Do not clutter the column chart visualization.

■ **Note** I mentioned earlier in this chapter that both the line and bar series can be used for trend analysis. One distinct advantage that word-sized column charts have over sparklines is interactivity. Even though the surface area of a word-sized column is smaller, a user can still hover over each column for tool tips or actionable drill-downs. Sparklines lose that ability once the data points are removed. Even though we could manually extend the sparkline with line selection, it would not be recommended because the points are so close together. The gaps in the columns provide the distinction between individual items. In addition, when a user hovers over a column, the particular column is highlighted with a different color.

Similar enhancements can be made to the word-sized column chart as we made to the sparkline visualizations. A popular enhancement to word-sized bar charts is to highlight positive and negative values clearly. Positive values are usually highlighted in green. Conversely, negative values are highlighted in red. This paints a clearer picture to the user and associates the green and red colors properly with success or failure. This is yet another example where the flexibility of the charting framework shines. Figure 6-33 illustrates our word-sized column chart enhanced with positive and negative coloring (this can only be see in the e-book version).

Team Name	W-L-T Goal Diff	Goal Diff (Last 10)
Team 1	12-8-3 +14	
Team 2	10-10-3+4	
Team 3	7-11-5 -4	
Team 4	5-15-2 -15	

Figure 6-33. Column chart visualizations enhanced with positive and negative colors (color shown in e-book version only)

This is a great enhancement as it improves the analysis capabilities dramatically. The positive and negative column positions on the axis combined with colors associating success or negative outcome truly simplify deriving intelligence.

In the preceding examples, you saw some of the ways that word-sized column charts can be used. What is really powerful about even small column charts is that they don't lose much of their analysis ability. Distribution analysis like finding gaps, skews, trends, and outliers still can be done effectively using word-sized column visualizations.

Applying Word-Sized Column Visualizations in Silverlight

In order to create word-sized column visualizations, similar changes have to be made to the style that we created when we made the sparkline visualizations. For the preceding examples, here is a list of best practices that were applied in order to render word-sized column visualizations in Silverlight:

- Chart dimensions are small (word-sized).

- X-axis and y-axis do not display values.

- Column series use a basic color (black).

- Items like the border, title, and background are not displayed.

- Positive and negative colors were added by setting the binding from the data. If the goal differential were positive, the color on the rectangle fill would be set to green brush. Conversely, if the goal differential were negative, the color on the rectangle fill would be set to red brush.

The styling of the visualization is done in two steps. First, we need a baseline that creates a chart with a column series that has small dimensions, as shown in Listing 6-6.

Listing 6-6. Silverlight XAML code highlighted in bold shows what is needed to create a baseline for a word-sized column visualization.

```
<toolkit:Chart Width="100" Height="25">
        <toolkit:Chart.Template>
                <!-- Hide the border -->
```

```
<ControlTemplate TargetType="toolkit:Chart">
        <chartingPrimitivesToolkit:EdgePanel x:Name="ChartArea">
                <Grid Canvas.ZIndex="-1" />
        </chartingPrimitivesToolkit:EdgePanel>
</ControlTemplate>
</toolkit:Chart.Template>
<!-- Format the axes -->
<toolkit:Chart.Axes>
        <toolkit:DateTimeAxis Orientation="X" MaxHeight="1" Opacity="0"↵
Minimum="2008/08/27" Maximum="2008/09/08"/>
        <toolkit:LinearAxis Orientation="Y" Height="25" MaxWidth="2" Opacity="0"↵
Minimum="-5" Maximum="5"/>
</toolkit:Chart.Axes>
<toolkit:ColumnSeries
        ItemsSource="{Binding GoalDiffTeam4}"
        IndependentValueBinding="{Binding Date}"
        DependentValueBinding="{Binding Diff}"
        />
</toolkit:Chart>
```

If you want a basic word-sized column visualization, you are done. However, the default styling of the columns includes gradients that do not look great when they are shrunk to smaller sizes. In order to be able to create a solid primary color, we need to edit the DataPointStyle of the ColumnSeries. Right-clicking the column series associated with the chart will bring out the menu structure in Expression Blend shown in Figure 6-34.

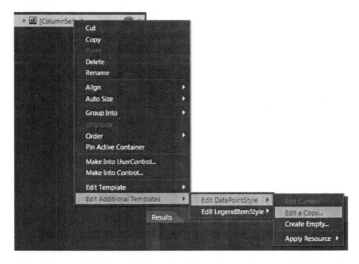

Figure 6-34. Editing the DataPointStyle template will allow the columns to be styled.

After creating the new style, the following changes need to be made (as shown in Listing 6-7):

- The border of the column control template needs to be removed.

- The rectangle that represents the column itself needs to have a primary color set (removing the gradient).

- The border of the rectangle can optionally be removed to give the columns a solid single-color look.

Listing 6-7. The Silverlight XAML code in bold shows what is needed to create a column DataPointStyle that will create a word-sized bar chart with solid black colors.

```
<Style x:Key="ColumnDataPointStyle1" TargetType="chartingToolkit:ColumnDataPoint">
        ...
        <Setter Property="Template">
                <Setter.Value>
                        <ControlTemplate TargetType="chartingToolkit:ColumnDataPoint">
                                <!-- Set BorderThickness to 0 -->
                                <Border x:Name="Root" Opacity="0"
BorderBrush="{TemplateBinding BorderBrush}" BorderThickness="0">
...
<ToolTipService.ToolTip>
        <ContentControl Content="{TemplateBinding FormattedDependentValue}"/>
</ToolTipService.ToolTip>
<Grid Background="{TemplateBinding Background}">
        <!-- Remove the Gradient Fill
        <Rectangle>
                <Rectangle.Fill>
                        <LinearGradientBrush>
                                <GradientStop Color="#77ffffff" Offset="0"/>
                                <GradientStop Color="#00ffffff" Offset="1"/>
                        </LinearGradientBrush>
                </Rectangle.Fill>
        </Rectangle>
        -->
        <!-- Add Black Fill -->
        <Rectangle Fill="Black" />
        <!-- Remove the Border Brush
        <Border BorderBrush="#ccffffff" BorderThickness="1">
                <Border BorderBrush="#77ffffff" BorderThickness="1"/>
        </Border>
        -->
```

The style in Listing 6-6 will create a word-sized column visualization that renders similarly to Figure 6-22 when bound to a data set. Extending this example further in order to dynamically pick the appropriate color based on business logic is actually pretty simple. All you need to do is to remove the hard-coded black color fill and set it to the binding of the property that contains the desired color to fill the brush. Listing 6-8 shows how this can be accomplished in the DataPointStyle template.

Listing 6-8. Setting the Fill property to a binding brush can dynamically set the color of the column.

```
<!-- Add Black Fill -->
<Rectangle Fill="{Binding Brush}" />
<!-- Remove the Border Brush
```

```
<Border BorderBrush="#ccffffff" BorderThickness="1">
    <Border BorderBrush="#77ffffff" BorderThickness="1"/>
</Border>
-->
```

The fill is bound to a property in our data that determines the brush to use. This is shown in Listing 6-9.

Listing 6-9. Calculate the brush color of the column in a property that will be data bound.

```
public SolidColorBrush Brush
{
    get
    {
        // if goal differential is less than zero
        if (this.Diff < 0)
        {
            return new SolidColorBrush { Color = Colors.Red };
        }
        else
        {
            return new SolidColorBrush { Color = Colors.Green };
        }
    }
}
```

Embedding business logic for the UI (brush color) in your data objects is not a good idea if you are writing production code. Alternatively, a value converter could be created that contains the business logic and can derive the appropriate color from the data passed into it. If you remember, this is the same approach we took in Chapter 3 when I covered the benefits of abstracting business logic into converters that can be shared among different objects.

Data Bars

Data bars are simple rectangular visualizations that can be used effectively in word-sized form. Data bars resemble the progress bar control. Furthermore, both data bars and progress bars are used in the same manner for analytics; by comparing the qualitative length to suggest a progress metric. A data bar's goal is to simply convey the progress of the measured value. This makes progress bars a great fit to embed as word-sized visualizations because they convey the message simply. Data bar visualizations can also be extended with KPI-like functionality (measuring against a goal) using color hues. This way, progress bars can effectively deliver insight on the progress of a given measure and track against predefined goal.

■ **Note** I did not include a code sample for data bar visualizations because creating word-sized progress bars is easy compared to other word-sized visualizations. The progress bar is a separate control in the Silverlight SDK that can simply have the length and color hue bound to the value to determine its look. For examples of progress bars used in lists, please visit the companion web site.

Other Candidates for Word-Sized Charts

Not all visualizations make good candidates as word-sized visualizations. Visuals that require rich detail, have lots of colors, are interactive, or are complex would not be good choices for word-sized visualization. Even simple chart visualizations like pie charts could make terrible word-sized visualizations. Remember the challenges of pie charts as described in this chapter. Could you imagine trying to decipher small slices on a word-sized pie chart? Discretion should be used when attempting to shrink a chart visualization to the size of a sentence fragment.

Summary

This chapter built on Chapter 5, the introductory data visualization chapter. The key information to understand is that creating data visualizations for analysis requires a basic understanding of what we are trying to analyze and show. Different types of visual analyses can have certain requirements that demand visualizations to be structured in a particular way. Understanding visual analysis best practices and knowing your data is vital to creating simple data visualizations for BI 2.0 software.

Silverlight is a powerful framework that is very flexible. Throughout this chapter, you saw several ways that we were able to extend the visualizations to enhance the delivery of BI insight to the user. This gives the Silverlight developer the ability to extend, create, and apply best practice analysis concepts without having to reach out to other technologies. You have seen throughout this chapter how we can utilize the Silverlight framework to create powerful business intelligence visualizations such as KPIs, sparkline charts, complex charting visualizations etc.

This chapter should amplify my assertion in the introductory chapter that Silverlight technology is a first-class environment for delivering rich data visualizations that can rival professional visualization software.

CHAPTER 7

■ ■ ■

Enhancing Visual Intelligence in Silverlight

The previous data visualization chapters showed some of the fundamental data visualization features and highlighted the rich customizability of the presentation from a charting perspective. In this chapter, you will learn how visual intelligence can be enhanced using unique characteristics of Silverlight technology to visualize almost any type of analytical data assets for different environments.

Silverlight provides a rich graphics framework that facilitates creating complex, custom, interactive data visualizations. Leveraging the power of vector rendering lends itself to creating a rich analytical environment using various graphical assets. As you will see in this chapter, complex analytical visualizations can be created by combining various techniques with ease. Furthermore, you will appreciate how the power of executing code locally enhances the real-time insight feedback, truly creating next-generation BI experiences.

The following coding scenario is included in this chapter:

- Using storyboard animations as transitions for configuration or providing visualization choices

The following table outlines the specific goals that different types of readers will achieve by reading this chapter.

Audience	Goals
Silverlight developers	Understand how the Silverlight animation framework can be incorporated into data visualization analysis.
	Have the ability to create composite data visualizations that come to life using interactivity and environmental techniques.
Business intelligence professionals	Extend your knowledge of interactive data visualizations and how they are applied in Silverlight.
	Gain a better understanding of Silverlight as a BI environment by contrasting the interactive capabilities of the technology.

Audience	Goals
Strategic decision makers	Answer the question "Will Silverlight technology improve the look and feel of our BI visualizations?"
	See how Silverlight's client execution provides a true BI 2.0 experience over other web alternatives.

Workflow Visualizations

A series of activities that describe business or organizational processes is hard to understand without good visualizations. These processes lend themselves to be visualized using workflow (flowchart) tools that connect and show relationships between different activities. Programs such as Microsoft Visio are a great example of flowchart software.

If you have used Microsoft Expression Blend 4, you don't have to look much further beyond SketchFlow to notice a workflow implemented using XAML. Figure 7-1 shows an example of an Expression Blend SketchFlow workflow. SketchFlow is a tool included with Expression Blend 4 that is used to help with creating prototype applications. The collaboration of the assets is displayed in SketchFlow using a workflow implementation.

Figure 7-1. SketchFlow workflows can visualize the flow of the application and how the page assets are related to each other.

■ **Note** Expression Blend 4 SketchFlow has been designed in XAML in WPF (Windows Presentation Foundation). However, the same principles apply to Silverlight since it too uses XAML vector-based rendering.

Workflow visualization tools have two primary goals: create and visualize. The first is the ability to create a workflow on a blank canvas. This is usually done by dragging predefined visual glyphs that symbolize input, output, types of process, connectors, and so on onto a workflow canvas. As the assets are arranged, organized, and connected, they represent a set of activities or processes. The goal is to create workflows so they can be analyzed at a later time.

In Figure 7-1, you can see rectangles with different colors and labels representing different types of windows. Furthermore, the connectors represent the association between each individual window. You can clearly see the sequence of events in the preceding diagram map. A nontechnical person could probably describe the sequence of events that will transpire from beginning to end without having any knowledge of the code or looking at the screens.

A workflow is a great example of a BI 2.0 implementation. Workflows allow users to organize and describe complex activities visually. Modern workflow software uses simple graphical assets, so the user does not need to be familiar with programming or analytical symbols to understand what is being visualized.

There are many examples of workflows used in BI software. However, they have just started being embraced in BI 2.0 principles. Once software vendors figured out how to visualize collaboration processes in a simple manner, this allowed for packaging of electronic, machine, or human processes into workflow visualizations. For example, machine operators that work with heavy lathes started benefiting from increased productivity by using workflows. Modern lathes now include screens that show a small workflow of the progress and state of the lathe job being processed. This allows front-line machine operators to understand quickly the progress of a job scheduled on a lathe. Several years ago, you would not imagine manual labor workers using business visualizations to help them in their jobs.

Workflows in Silverlight

A workflow canvas can effectively be displayed using Silverlight technology. Silverlight's rendering engine is based on vectors which are essentially math equations that are used to display graphics. This allows a Silverlight developer to create various workflow assets by applying math formulas to calculate the layout of the workflow assets on the canvas. For example, calculating the midpoint of the top rectangle in order to figure out the x and y coordinates for the connector is much easier to do in a vector-based world than having to do this with raster-based graphics (e.g., PNG). This allows Silverlight to digest data files using business rules and turn them into workflow visualizations.

A great example of a Silverlight workflow is SnapFlow. SnapFlow is a company that aims to simplify workflow creation by bringing workflow to the masses. As described in the Introduction, this is one of the cornerstones of BI 2.0: making analytical processes simple enough for average users. This is exactly what SnapFlow has done with the product it has implemented with Silverlight technology. Figure 7-2 shows an example of a SnapFlow project that illustrates a typical hiring process workflow. You can clearly see action items with connectors describing the activity sequence.

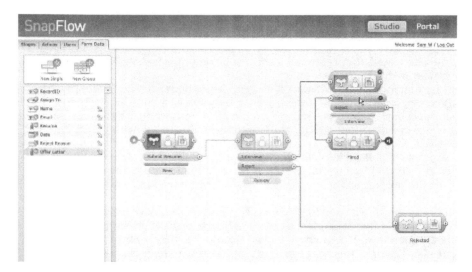

Figure 7-2. SnapFlow workflows are an example of a Silverlight and BI 2.0 software implementation.

The SnapFlow product allows the user to create powerful and complex workflows and then autogenerate forms of data from the workflow using data entity attributes. These workflows are created in Silverlight; therefore, they are easily embedded into web sites or collaboration portals like SharePoint using the plug-in object tags.

■ **Note** For more information and demos of SnapFlow's workflow product, go to `www.snapflow.com`.

Using Graphical Symbols

In the previous chapter and the preceding section, you saw several examples of how simple primitive symbols can be used to form complex visualizations. For example, in Silverlight there are no "workflow asset" controls. In cases where the Silverlight SDK does not contain the exact visual control, they can be created from much simpler objects. Furthermore, in some cases you may want to integrate a data visualization into the overall style or theme of a web site. This section will look at how simple symbols can improve the overall context of the infographic.

Assume that you are tasked with creating a data visualization that compares the weapon caches of two fictitious armies from 2010 (e.g., Army North vs. Army South). For simplicity, the weapon inventories consist of artillery, tank, missile, and plane assets.

You could create a simple list or use a charting visualization to display the comparison of the armies, but a list would not properly deliver the scope of the differences to the user. Comparison insight can be delivered much more effectively using visual symbols. However, a charting visualization could be effective but deliver a businesslike, structured look.

Creating Graphical Assets

In a rich environment such as Silverlight, you should embrace the graphical rendering flexibility it provides. In this example, you can easily create graphical symbols that represent the various army components as simple user controls. Then you can use these simple graphical objects in layout containers to render a much more meaningful and clear analytical visual tool.

The first step is to create the graphical symbols that are going to be used as visual assets in the data visualization. Figure 7-3 shows the four different symbols that will represent military equipment.

Figure 7-3. *Simple graphical symbols (user controls) created from rectangles and ellipses*

Each of these assets was created from primitive shapes available in the Silverlight SDK. For example, the missile user control is simply a rectangle topped with an ellipse. Listing 7-1 shows the XAML code used to create the plane glyph.

Listing 7-1. *The plane glyph was created using primitive controls like the rectangle and ellipse.*

```
<UserControl
    xmlns="http://schemas.microsoft.com/winfx/2006/xaml/presentation"
    xmlns:x="http://schemas.microsoft.com/winfx/2006/xaml"
    xmlns:d="http://schemas.microsoft.com/expression/blend/2008"
 xmlns:mc="http://schemas.openxmlformats.org/markup-compatibility/2006"
 x:Class="ArmyDataVisualization.ArmyAssets.Plane"
    Width="200" Height="300" mc:Ignorable="d">
    <Grid x:Name="LayoutRoot" Background="White">
        <Grid.RowDefinitions>
            <RowDefinition Height="0.3*"/>
            <RowDefinition Height="0.7*"/>
        </Grid.RowDefinitions>
        <Rectangle Fill="Black" Stroke="Black" HorizontalAlignment="Center"
Margin="0,0,0,-10" Width="50" Grid.Row="1"/>
        <Ellipse Fill="Black" Stroke="Black" Margin="75,18,75,-56"/>
        <Rectangle Fill="Black" Stroke="Black" HorizontalAlignment="Left"
Margin="38.099,13.808,0,54.156" Width="38.576" RenderTransformOrigin="0.5,0.5"
UseLayoutRounding="False" Grid.Row="1" d:LayoutRounding="Auto">
            <Rectangle.RenderTransform>
                <TransformGroup>
                    <ScaleTransform/>
                    <SkewTransform/>
                    <RotateTransform Angle="32.527"/>
                    <TranslateTransform/>
                </TransformGroup>
            </Rectangle.RenderTransform>
        </Rectangle>
```

```
                            <Rectangle Fill="Black" Stroke="Black"↵
HorizontalAlignment="Right" Margin="0,13.808,36.424,54.156" Width="38.576"↵
RenderTransformOrigin="0.5,0.5" UseLayoutRounding="False" Grid.Row="1"↵
d:LayoutRounding="Auto">
                <Rectangle.RenderTransform>
                    <TransformGroup>
                        <ScaleTransform/>
                        <SkewTransform/>
                        <RotateTransform Angle="-32.527"/>
                        <TranslateTransform/>
                    </TransformGroup>
                </Rectangle.RenderTransform>
            </Rectangle>
        </Grid>
</UserControl>
```

■ **Note** Using a polyline is another way to implement simple glyphs. Polylines are a series of connected lines. These can be organized to form shapes. One of the benefits of polylines is that they dramatically reduce the XAML code. The code in Listing 7-1 could be reduced to three or four lines of XAML. However, one drawback of using polylines as glyphs is that it is hard to manipulate them without a visual tool like Expression Blend.

Each of these graphical assets is an individual user control that is in the project. Figure 7-4 shows each control in the ArmyAssets folder. Since you created these as individual Silverlight user controls, you can simply add them to the canvas manually. Conversely, you can add the assets to a layout container that will properly reflect each army's respective data set. For example, if Army A has 2,000 tanks, you don't need to show 2,000 tanks. Instead you can use a key, such as one tank symbol equals 100 tanks.

Figure 7-4. Each graphical symbol is a separate Silverlight user control.

Visualization Layout

Now that you have your graphical components designed, it's time to think about how you are going to lay this data visualization out on the screen. This data visualization is simple; however, it still should consist of the following pieces:

- A meaningful and clear title

- A short description of the story behind the visualization

- Labels for each army

- Labels for each army asset type

- A legend

- Container controls that can lay out the army asset symbols appropriately

This visualization could be laid out several different ways. However, to keep things simple, you could lay out the graphical symbols in tabular format. One potential look of this is shown in Figure 7-5. The visualization contains the items listed previously to aid the user in understanding the story being told and how it can be used to derive knowledge from the visuals.

■ **Note** In Figure 7-5, the Silverlight ViewBox control is used to lay out the symbols in a manner that keeps their perspective while changing the scale. The controls were designed in 300 by 300 resolution, and the ViewBox container autoscales them to the desired size. This is a simple trick to use when you need to quickly scale visual layouts to a preferred size. This can also be used in fluid layouts where resolution changes between widescreen and standard monitors. Using the ViewBox is not a substitute for properly designing visualizations, but it does the job well when you need to make your layout scale fluidly quickly.

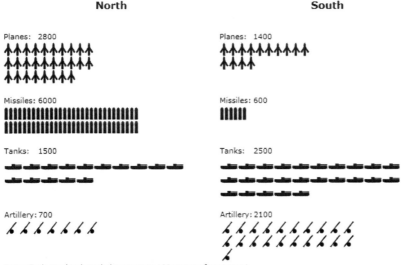

Figure 7-5. *Graphical symbols immediately provide context to the data visualization and deliver insight more quickly.*

■ **Note** A live demo of this coding scenario is available on the companion web site at `http://silverlightbusinessintelligence.com/Demos/EnhancingVisualIntelligence/DataVisUsingGraphicalSymbols/DataVisUsingSymbols.html`. The full source code for this example is located in the bonus section of the source code zip file.

The data visualization in Figure 7-5 tells a story while delivering insight. This is the power of creating custom infographics with graphical symbols. It's also an example of organized and simple use of symbols in a data visualization. By glancing at this visualization, the user is instantly drawn to the variances in the data set. Furthermore, by using the military symbols, you don't even need to explain to the user what the data is trying to express. If necessary, labels are present as a secondary apparatus to provide exact data values. Imagine what this implementation would look like in a bar chart. It wouldn't be very exciting, and it would start to get messy with four separate column series showing a different military equipment type. In cases like this, Silverlight really stands out by being able to highly customize the context of the environment.

More complex types of visualizations require more creativity from the developer or designer. Because you quickly start moving to the art aspect of the infographic design, there are no true guidelines when you step out of the norm and start creating composite glyphs or custom layouts for analysis. In BI projects that reach out to a large number of users, it is usually a good idea to pass the visualization ideas by a user experience expert and focus groups to ensure that the intended analysis and insight are delivered properly.

Silverlight can be used to create custom visualizations for analysis. However, this does not mean you should use that path as an option every time. As you saw in the previous chapter, even simple visualizations like pie charts have their faults. Therefore, even if you come up with a fantastically engaging visualization, it doesn't mean your users will understand it or use it properly for analysis.

In this section, you saw how easy it is to create graphical Silverlight user controls and use them to represent data items for delivering contextual visual analysis. The simple baseline of each control could be enhanced by adding states, interactivity, fade-in animation, tool tips, and so on to provide a more immersive visualization. Since each user control is separate, this provides a simple abstraction from the main layout control used to display the data visualization. For example, this could be used to show military losses in the future by fading the symbol slightly.

Creating Composite Visuals for Analysis

So far you have seen a good variety of Silverlight's data visualization capabilities. Out of the box, the Silverlight SDK and the Silverlight Control Toolkit provide many analytical visualizations that can be customized by styling. Combining these steps with layouts, custom symbols, 3D perspectives, animations, and interactivity allows for creating new composite controls for BI software.

Creating a Cross-Tab Data Visualization

If you are a BI professional, you have probably created cross-tab or matrix reports in the past. These types of reports allow for visualizing multidimensional data using dimensions and metrics. Metric values intersecting the rows and columns are summarized. For example, software in the Microsoft BI stack (including Access, Excel, Reporting Services, Integration Services, and Analysis Services) provides the ability to create cross-tab visualizations.

Silverlight can be used to surface simple cross-tab reports easily. It could be as simple as consuming a data service from a data warehouse or Analysis Services with the data delivered in cross-tab form. Furthermore, as you have learned in previous chapters, LINQ is available to you as a powerful tool to structure data sets in cross-tab form on the local client. Figure 7-6 shows page view information for four domains across three different regions. This report could provide some analytical value, but it is considered a very trivial BI visualization. Any developer worth their weight could develop a similar visualization in their favorite development environment.

Domain Name	USA Region	Europe Region	Other Region
Domain1.com	75000	55000	55000
Domain2.com	34000	66000	22000
Domain3.com	45000	34000	34000
Domain4.com	65000	32222	23000

Figure 7-6. A simple Silverlight cross-tab visualization displaying regions as columns and products as rows.

The metric that is being analyzed is a summary of page views for a domain. This metric is summarized at every intersection (column/row) and displayed in a grid cell. For example, the page views (hits) for Domain1.com in the USA region were 75,000 in a given region. The preceding visualization is quite simple and it can be used for basic analysis. Comparing a couple of domain values across regions or products would be the typical use of this visualization.

There are obvious drawbacks to using tabular visualizations. It is very hard to compare multiple items concurrently, and because the information is nonvisual, it takes longer for the brain to process the information displayed. This would be especially true if there were many regions and domains to compare. What if we wanted to display trending information? For example, let's say that instead of showing a single value for the whole year for the Domain1.com/USA region intersection, you wanted to see the 12 months of sales that constitute that number. One potential solution would be to nest smaller grids into the grid cells. Another solution would be to provide drill-down functionality; a click in a cell would bring up a details view of the page views for that intersection. Nesting grids into cells can get very chaotic, especially if the dimensions (e.g., number or regions or products) increase; real estate can become a problem. In the end, this will leave you with a bloated spreadsheet interface. Drill-down functionality is a good option when the user is going to be shown a great amount of additional detail. However, it is not a best practice to split analysis into separate dialogs or different pages, as this breaks the smooth path to delivering insight. In order to provide additional insight in a single analysis tool, you need to add visual items.

Silverlight Cross-Tab Implementation

Silverlight does not include a visual implantation of a cross-tab control. To solve this challenge, you can apply some of the concepts you learned in the previous data visualization chapters. One solution would be to create a composite cross-tab control that consists of small charts embedded in the data grid cells. The charts could be used to surface trending information and for parallel comparison analytics. In the previous chapter, you learned how you can skin Silverlight charts into word-sized graphics. This approach would be ideal to provide visual analysis and fit in a data grid. Figure 7-7 shows how the simple tabular cross tab was enhanced with word-sized visualizations to provide additional analytical wisdom in the control.

The visualization in Figure 7-7 is a Silverlight data grid with cell visualizations styled as word-sized charts in cross-tab format. I will refer to this implementation as a *cross-tab visualization*. These types of visualizations have been around for quite some time and have other names as well. In 1983, Edward Tufte coined the term *small multiples* for this type of visual implementation. In addition, these visualizations are very popular among visual intelligence software vendors and are known as *trellises*.

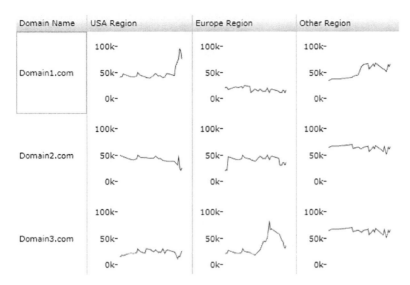

Figure 7-7. A cross-tab data visualization can provide an abundance of anaytical insight.

Look at Figure 7-7 and note how much more effective this visualization is at delivering insight than the alternative tabular data format shown in Figure 7-6:

- A user can compare multiple dimensions in parallel.

- Trending wisdom is easily discerned and can be compared between regions and/or domains.

- The vertical and horizontal layouts allow for scale comparisons.

- Small labels on axis provide scale of data.

This visualization can answer many more analytical questions more quickly than a traditional grid because it incorporates a simple, clean layout with visual graphics. In the cross-tab data visualization, note that the following best practice implementation concepts were followed:

- A clean layout without much use of colors is used (similar to the word-sized graphics approach).

- Scale is provided and is unobtrusive to the visualization.

- Scale for all of the charts is identical. This is very important, as it allows users to move their eyes up and down and quickly derive comparison knowledge. If the scales were different, this visualization would not deliver insight effectively.

- The end result implements BI 2.0 concepts of self-service and simplicity of use, as the visualization does not require too much explanation or training on how to understand it.

The cross-tab visualization was implemented using three main features of Silverlight:

- The high flexibility and customizability of the Silverlight data visualizations to create word-sized implementations (for details, see Chapter 6).

- LINQ on the local client to query the data repository to put the data in a cross-tab format.

- The ability of the Silverlight data grid cells to host complex template content such as charting visualizations.

Using the data grid as a baseline for this visualization is a good option to organize the charts in a tabular format to conform to a cross-tab layout. You will utilize the ability for the Silverlight data grid to include custom columns for the layout. The first column will be a simple text column. The latter three columns will use the cell template functionality to host a charting visualization. In addition, note that the row colors have been removed and the autogeneration of the columns has been set to False to accommodate a custom layout.

Figure 7-8 illustrates the high-level layout of the XAML that makes up the cross-tab grid showing the custom columns and the charts hosted within the cell templates. This shows a somewhat cleaner layout than the fully written-out XAML.

```
<data:DataGrid x:Name="CrossTabReport" Margin="0,0,0,0" AlternatingRowBackground="White"
    RowBackground="White" AutoGenerateColumns="False" Height="400">
    <data:DataGrid.Columns>
        <data:DataGridTextColumn Header="Domain Name" Binding="{Binding DomainName}"/>
        <!-- USA Region -->
        <data:DataGridTemplateColumn Header="USA Region">
            <data:DataGridTemplateColumn.CellTemplate>
                <DataTemplate>
                    <chartingToolkit:Chart...>
                </DataTemplate>
            </data:DataGridTemplateColumn.CellTemplate>
        </data:DataGridTemplateColumn>
        <!-- Europe Region -->
        <data:DataGridTemplateColumn Header="Europe Region">
            <data:DataGridTemplateColumn.CellTemplate>
                <DataTemplate>
                    <chartingToolkit:Chart...>
                </DataTemplate>
            </data:DataGridTemplateColumn.CellTemplate>
        </data:DataGridTemplateColumn>
        <!-- Other Region -->
        <data:DataGridTemplateColumn Header="Other Region">
            <data:DataGridTemplateColumn.CellTemplate...>
        </data:DataGridTemplateColumn>
    </data:DataGrid.Columns>
</data:DataGrid>
```

Figure 7-8. The cross-tab data visualization uses the data grid as a baseline for the composite control.

Listing 7-2 displays the XAML of the Silverlight cross-tab implementation. If you are a Silverlight developer, you have probably done this before. Note, however, that here you style the chart in sparkline format, which you learned in the previous chapter.

■ **Note** I omitted the last two chart column implementations to conserve space. The full source code for the cross-tab sample is available on the accompanying web site for this book. A live demo of the Cross-Tab implementation can be found at http://silverlightbusinessintelligence.com/Demos/ EnhancingVisualIntelligence/CrossTabDataVisualization/CrossTab.html.

Listing 7-2. XAML to create a cross-tab control using the Silverlight data grid as a baseline

```
<data:DataGrid x:Name="CrossTabReport" Margin="0,0,0,0" AlternatingRowBackground="White"
    RowBackground="White" AutoGenerateColumns="False" Height="400">
        <data:DataGrid.Columns>
        <!-- Domain Name column -->
            <data:DataGridTextColumn Header="Domain Name" Binding="{Binding⏎
DomainName}"/>

        <!-- USA Region -->
        <data:DataGridTemplateColumn Header="USA Region">
            <!-- Cell that will host the chart -->
            <data:DataGridTemplateColumn.CellTemplate>
                <DataTemplate>
                    <!-- Word-Sized Chart -->
                    <chartingToolkit:Chart x:Name="Domain1Chart" Width="125"⏎
Height="75" Margin="10,20,10,20"
                        d:LayoutOverrides="Width, Height" VerticalAlignment="Top">
                        <chartingToolkit:Chart.Template>
                            <ControlTemplate TargetType="chartingToolkit:Chart">
                                <chartingPrimitivesToolkit:EdgePanel x:Name="ChartArea">
                                    <Grid Canvas.ZIndex="-1" />
                                </chartingPrimitivesToolkit:EdgePanel>
                            </ControlTemplate>
                        </chartingToolkit:Chart.Template>
                        <chartingToolkit:Chart.Axes>
                            <chartingToolkit:DateTimeAxis Orientation="X"⏎
MaxHeight="1" Opacity="0"
                                Minimum="2008/07/07" Maximum="2008/09/08"/>
                            <chartingToolkit:LinearAxis Orientation="Y"⏎
Opacity="1" Minimum="0" Maximum="100">
                                <chartingToolkit:LinearAxis.AxisLabelStyle>
                                    <Style TargetType="chartingToolkit:AxisLabel">
                                        <Setter Property="StringFormat" Value="{}{0:0k}"/>
                                    </Style>
                                </chartingToolkit:LinearAxis.AxisLabelStyle>
                            </chartingToolkit:LinearAxis>
                        </chartingToolkit:Chart.Axes>

                        <!-- Data Line -->
                        <chartingToolkit:LineSeries
                        ItemsSource="{Binding USAHits}"
```

```
                              IndependentValueBinding="{Binding Date}"
                              DependentValueBinding="{Binding NumberOfHits}"
                              PolylineStyle="{StaticResource SparklinePolyStyle}">

                            <!-- DataPointStyle -->
                            <chartingToolkit:LineSeries.DataPointStyle>
                                <Style TargetType="Control">
                                    <!-- Collapase the data points -->
                                    <Setter Property="Visibility" Value="Collapsed"/>
                        <!-Set the Opacity of the data points -->
                                    <Setter Property="Opacity" Value="0"/>

                                    <!-- Set color to black -->
                                    <Setter Property="Background" Value="Black"/>
                                </Style>
                            </chartingToolkit:LineSeries.DataPointStyle>
                        </chartingToolkit:LineSeries>
                    </chartingToolkit:Chart>
                </DataTemplate>
            </data:DataGridTemplateColumn.CellTemplate>
        </data:DataGridTemplateColumn>
        <!-- Europe Region -->
        <data:DataGridTemplateColumn Header="Europe Region">
            <data:DataGridTemplateColumn.CellTemplate>
                <DataTemplate>
                    <!-Chart goes here -->
                </DataTemplate>
            </data:DataGridTemplateColumn.CellTemplate>
        </data:DataGridTemplateColumn>
        <!-- Other Region -->
        <data:DataGridTemplateColumn Header="Other Region">
            <data:DataGridTemplateColumn.CellTemplate>
                <DataTemplate>
                    <!-Chart goes here -->
                </DataTemplate>
            </data:DataGridTemplateColumn.CellTemplate>
        </data:DataGridTemplateColumn>
    </data:DataGrid.Columns>
</data:DataGrid>
```

Note that you are using nested binding to data bind the collection of page views for each intersecting region. For example, the object property USAHits is a collection of page view data and the dates the page view occurred. This information is used to render the independent and dependent axes on the charts.

As discussed earlier, LINQ was used on the Silverlight client to create the cross-tab format of the data. Essentially, each intersection needs to be summarized and the values extracted to display the appropriate values in the chart. This can be done a variety of ways, but for simplicity, each intersection is aggregated into a list object. Listing 7-3 shows the object that holds the collections for each region and the LINQ query used to create a cross-tab representation.

Listing 7-3. LINQ can be used in Silverlight to transform relational data into multidimenstional form (e.g., cross tab, matrix).

```
public class CrossTabReport
{
    public string DomainName { get; set; }
    public IEnumerable<Hits> USAHits { get; set; }
    public IEnumerable<Hits> EuropeHits { get; set; }
    public IEnumerable<Hits> OtherHits { get; set; }
}

....
public IList<CrossTabReport> CrossTabData
{
    get
    {
        List<CrossTabReport> reportData = new List<CrossTabReport>();
        reportData.Add(
            // Domain1.com data
            new CrossTabReport
                {
                    DomainName = "Domain1.com",
                    USAHits = Domain1.Where(a => a.HitRegion == Region.USA),
                    EuropeHits = Domain1.Where(a => a.HitRegion == Region.Europe),
                    OtherHits = Domain1.Where(a => a.HitRegion == Region.Other)
                });

        reportData.Add(
            // Domain2.com data
            new CrossTabReport
            {
                DomainName = "Domain2.com",
                USAHits = Domain2.Where(a => a.HitRegion == Region.USA),
                EuropeHits = Domain2.Where(a => a.HitRegion == Region.Europe),
                OtherHits = Domain2.Where(a => a.HitRegion == Region.Other)
            });

        reportData.Add(
            // Domain3.com data
            new CrossTabReport
            {
                DomainName = "Domain3.com",
                USAHits = Domain3.Where(a => a.HitRegion == Region.USA),
                EuropeHits = Domain3.Where(a => a.HitRegion == Region.Europe),
                OtherHits = Domain3.Where(a => a.HitRegion == Region.Other)
            });

        return reportData;
    }
}
```

The preceding example is fairly simple; however, imagine if you had complex business rules or aggregations that needed to be visualized. The ability to use LINQ to query data structures efficiently is a really powerful tool when implementing client-side Silverlight BI functionality. You will see in Chapter 10 that this can be extended to work with very large data sets by applying multithreading functionality. This should amplify the advantage a Silverlight implementation has over other development alternatives.

Why a Cross-Tab Implementation?

In this example, you may be wondering why I chose a cross tab as the solution. If you think about it, this visualization is the most scalable solution in a dynamic data scenario. Imagine if you had five regions or many more domains to analyze. With this implementation, the data grid can scroll both vertically and/or horizontally. If you implemented this by using multiple line series on a single graph, the analytical value could be deprecated very quickly. Looking at five or more line series on a chart with overlapping values could confuse the user.

In this example, I used a data grid to aid with laying out the charts. By using a data grid as a container for the cross tab, I gain several key features:

- Data can scroll vertically and horizontally if the data set grows.

- The Silverlight data grid utilizes the concept of UI virtualization. This renders only the content that is visible on the screen. Therefore, if the data is bound to ten domains and the screen only shows three rows, the data grid will not waste processing cycles on data that is not being shown.

- The Silverlight data grid provides additional analytical functionality for a cross-tab implementation. For example, in Silverlight you can freeze columns to aid in analysis. This allows a user to effectively compare data in a side-by-side fashion.

- By leveraging the data grid, you don't have to invest time in writing a custom layout container for the cross tab.

Improving the Implementation

The Silverlight cross tab in Figure 7-7 is a good implementation and may suffice for your needs. The data visualization provides a lot of analytical value; however, it is not complete. The visualization does not provide proper context of the data ranges. This could be solved with a simple title and description. Furthermore, this visualization could be enhanced with KPIs (organizational goals) to deliver extra insight. Adding reference lines to each sparkline could answer questions like "Is Domain1 meeting its traffic goals in the Europe region?" Lastly, when you updated the cross-tab visualization to use charts, you lost the ability to see the sum of the page views for the given time frame. Figure 7-9 shows the cross-tab visualization enhanced with the items mentioned previously.

Domain Performance Report

This report illllustrates the performane of our domains summarized across our main distribution regions from 7/8/2008 to 9/8/2008

Figure 7-9. An example of a more complete cross-tab data visualization that provides additional analytical context and detailed information including trending, KPIs, scales, and multiple dimensions.

Using this visualization, you can now analyze the trending information, retrieve the exact number of page views, and understand if your daily page view goals are being achieved. Equally important is the visualization context which describes to the user what you are looking at and the associated time frames. This single cross-tab data visualization packs an enormous analytical punch.

I want to emphasize how LINQ makes aggregating data structures easier. Listing 7-4 shows the LINQ query that was used to summarize the page views for each intersection and filter the appropriate goal for each domain. Note that you are also formatting the sum of the page views directly in the query. Without LINQ, traversing data structures with multiple loops or functions would turn the aggregation code into an unreadable spaghetti code. Even without being a pro at LINQ, you can quickly understand what is going on with the aggregation code because of LINQ's declarative and functional nature.

Listing 7-4. Using LINQ in Silverlight makes even complex data summary operations manageable.

```
...
// Domain1.com data
new CrossTabReport
    {
        DomainName = "Domain1.com",
        USAHits = Domain1.Where(a => a.HitRegion == Region.USA),
        USAHitsSum = string.Format("{0:0,0k}",
                    ((from domain in Domain1
                    where domain.HitRegion == Region.USA
                    select domain.NumberOfHits).Sum())),
        USAHitsGoal = Domain1Goal.Where(a => a.HitRegion == Region.USA),
```

```
            EuropeHits = Domain1.Where(a => a.HitRegion == Region.Europe),
            EuropeHitsSum = string.Format("{0:0,0k}",
                        ((from domain in Domain1
                          where domain.HitRegion == Region.Europe
                          select domain.NumberOfHits).Sum())),
            EuropeHitsGoal = Domain1Goal.Where(a => a.HitRegion == Region.Europe),
            OtherHits = Domain1.Where(a => a.HitRegion == Region.Other),
            OtherHitsSum = string.Format("{0:0,0k}",
                        ((from domain in Domain1
                          where domain.HitRegion == Region.Other
                          select domain.NumberOfHits).Sum())),
            OtherHitsGoal = Domain1Goal.Where(a => a.HitRegion == Region.Other)
        });
    ….
```

Visualizations for the Environment

Data visualizations can be displayed in different environments, not just business applications. BI 2.0's main tenet is to design simple and effective tools for the masses. We are seeing more and more of these small statistical visual tools in newspapers, magazines, and news broadcasts. In order for these visualizations to be accommodating and pleasing to the user, they cannot look like boring business charts.

Imagine you are a BI consultant working for an extreme sports site. The owner wants to highlight some information about the durability of their equipment using data from lab tests in the form of visualizations. The target audience of this statistical information is probably a younger audience. Therefore, delivering knowledge in visualizations that look clinical is probably going to turn off a large majority of them. As a BI consultant, you want to create a visualization that stands out and is immersive to the extreme sports audience. Firing up Excel and binding the lab data is not going to be enough in this situation. This is where good design and development tools that allow you to replicate the analytical functionality of a data visualization while integrating it into the appropriate environment are essential.

The data visualization mentioned in the previous example amplifies the fact that visual tools play a small piece in delivering analytics. They can be embedded in web sites, newspaper articles, and news broadcasts to break up large sets of text and draw the attention of the consumer. In these cases (as mentioned previously), it is important to have a visualization that can deliver insight and blend seamlessly with the integrated environment.

Figure 7-10 shows an example of a data visualization created in Silverlight that is enhanced with environmental variables that provide an immersive experience.

Figure 7-10. An example of a data visualization that integrates the chart seamlessly into the environment, providing additional context.

The preceding data visualization displays information about items that were purchased in anticipation for the current school year. The data itself is not important; however, the structure of the data visualization is what I wanted to highlight. In order to provide a more integrated feel of the visualization, the following design functions were performed:

- A background image of a notebook was used to provide the school location environment.

- The font for the title and the axis labels was changed to use a more cursive style that reminds the user of the style taught in grammar school.

- The bar series chart was styled to remove all the unnecessary items and blend with the surrounding elements.

- A pencil glyph was added. This further enhances the school location feel and provides a behavior as if the pencil is interacting and drawing the visualization.

- The visualization has an applied rotation transformation to give it a look as if is lying on a slanted school desk.

■ **Note** I have covered most of the techniques to create this visualization in the past chapters; therefore, I am not going to cover the implementation in detail. If you are interested in how this was done, please download the source code from the accompanying web site with this book.

Another example of immersing a data visualization in an environment is leveraging 3D transformations in order to give depth to visualizations. For example, Figure 7-11 shows the Silverlight coverflow from my companion web site. The data visualization provides a nice 3D transition effect while browsing through the different objects. In the figure you will also notice soft touches like gradients and shadows that blend the visual with the background environment. This could have been easily replaced with a background that softly highlighted the environment of the data visualization. For example, you have probably seen stock chart visualizations presented on financial programs. Next time you see one, notice that they "immerse" the stock chart into a financial environment by providing business or financial backgrounds and symbols.

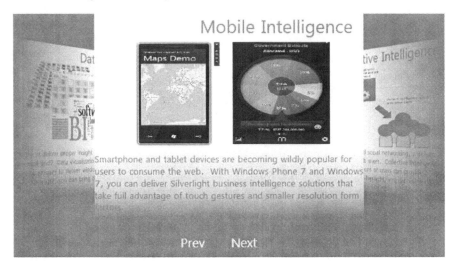

Figure 7-11. *An example of a data visualization that uses 3D transformations to place artifacts that are not in focus in the background of the visual.*

The preceding example shows you how environmental elements that surround the data assets can engage an average user. When delivering BI 2.0 for the masses, you have to realize that not everyone comes from a business environment. Business-looking presentations can frustrate users that are not familiar with them. In addition, users who have failed when using business tools may stay away from the data visualization entirely. Making data visualizations inviting and interesting increases the probability that average users will engage in the analytical conversation with the infographic.

Comparing Non-Silverlight Solutions

You might be asking yourself how Silverlight compares to other development environments or professional visual intelligence vendors. In this subsection, I'll do a brief comparison of Silverlight's key attributes in delivering BI 2.0 visually.

Other Development Environments

In the last three chapters, you have seen some of the advanced capabilities of Silverlight for visualizing intelligence. Before moving on to other BI topics, let's do a small recap and compare this in more detail to non-Silverlight solutions.

You might be asking yourself, "Couldn't I do this all using ASP.NET or other web development tools?" The answer is "Absolutely." However, it could take longer and include additional components that are not integrated to the primary development environment. The examples in the data visualization chapters extended the Silverlight charting controls, developed custom controls quickly, used LINQ to aggregate data, enhanced visualizations with animations, wrote client-side logic to control client behavior, and so on. All of this functionality is hard to mimic completely on other development platforms.

The visual and client components are not easy to come by in other solutions. For example, if I want the ability to easily query data structures on a web client, I would have to download third-party (or open source) query implementation for JavaScript. Does your web platform support a rich and extensible charting solution? Even ASP.NET (which has been around since 2002) did not include a free and integrated charting solution until recently. You can obviously diminish the gap in visualization functionality by purchasing third-party components or using open source software. But then your implementation relies on other developers to deliver the required functionality exactly as you need it. In complex BI projects, the desired functionality will be hard to achieve from a single visualization vendor.

Visual Intelligence Vendors

There are several vendors of visual intelligence software that provide a rich environment for creating data visualizations for BI deployments. If you are a BI professional, you may have worked with some of these tools in the past. These vendors are an excellent choice for a BI organization that does not have the development resources to create a custom solution. However, you still need a BI consultant or technical analyst to learn the software and be able to query the data repositories to create the appropriate visualizations for the consuming user. Therefore, even though development resources are not needed to create a rich UI, you still need BI experts to deploy this software effectively.

Another issue with implementing a custom visualization package is that many visual intelligence vendors provide various integration points. Some examples of provided integration points include a custom dashboard, a web service that exposes a picture of the data visualization, widgets/web parts, custom portal tools, and APIs. These vendors usually provide several integration points, and you will be limited as to how you can expose the visualization depending on which ones are included in the software package.

Professional visualization software can be very expensive. You can download a product that creates the appropriate data visualization with ease; however, if you need to publish it or scale to millions of records, this may include expensive server components. As reinforced through this book, Silverlight executing on the client allows you to distribute your architecture business rules to the client, thereby reducing the server footprint.

■ **Note** For a list of visual intelligence vendors, please go to www.silverlightbusinessintelligence.com. There are multiple vendors that offer solutions in this field with varying functionality, and it would not be appropriate to list them all here.

Silverlight as a Visual Intelligence Engine

Through the last three chapters, you have seen how you can create simple, custom, effective, and rich visualization solutions using Silverlight technology. Comparing Silverlight to other BI vendors or other development environments can be challenging because each choice is different. For this reason, here's a list of bullet points detailing when Silverlight makes a good choice as a visual intelligence environment:

- *When developer resources are available:* Developers have an understanding of how to create custom controls and are likely to be familiar with .NET development. If developers are not familiar with .NET, time needs to be allotted for training or learning the new technology.

- *When data repositories are factored to data services:* Silverlight requires data services as a primary way to retrieve data and cannot connect to data warehouses or Analysis Services cubes natively. Therefore, if you have a large data warehouse in a silo environment, Silverlight will not be a good choice to visualize your information. Most large organizations that have implemented MDM (master data management) or SOA (service-oriented architecture) initiatives should be OK to use Silverlight as a UI.

- *When creating embedded business intelligence is important:* Silverlight is exposed via a plug-in model and it can be used in web parts, dashboards or portals, or embedded into web sites directly. Silverlight applications can also be hosted in other domains, making Silverlight a great option in SaaS solutions. Silverlight data visualizations can be embedded more easily than other web architectures without having to change the methodology to code the Silverlight application.

- *When the BI infrastructure is based on Microsoft products:* While Silverlight can communicate with all sorts of data types, Microsoft is going to start releasing interfaces in the near future that are consumed by Silverlight. For example, SharePoint 2010 enhances the capabilities to host Silverlight content by including a Silverlight host web part and being able to consume SharePoint data via OData endpoints.

- *When rich custom visualizations are required:* Silverlight can be used to create rich custom visualizations with animations and interactions. Silverlight runs on the client computer; this makes interactivity snappy and feel like a Windows desktop or WPF application. Even commercial visual intelligence vendors cannot compete with full customizability of the Silverlight framework effectively.

Coding Scenario: Providing the User Visualization Options

This coding scenario will cover how to create an interactive visualization that provides the user a choice of which visualization they prefer to use for analysis.

The goals of this scenario are to:

- Learn how to integrate the animation framework into data visualization displays.

- Understand why providing an option to users is important for analysis.

• Leverage this technique in situations where configuration options or information is needed.

In this coding scenario, you will create a simple interface (resembling a mobile intelligence application) that will display a chart and a grid. A button will trigger an animation that will alter the displays between the chart and the grid. There will be two animations. The first animation will rotate the control 90 degrees and the second will rotate it back. You can implement this using a single animation; however, you are going to use the completed event of the first animation to switch the display of the visualization. This will provide a fluid feel to the control.

■ **Note** A live demo of this coding scenario is available on the companion web site at `http://` `silverlightbusinessintelligence.com/Demos/EnhancingVisualIntelligence/ProvidingDataVisOptions/` `SilverlightRotateTransition.html`.

The data and the actual presentation of the visualizations is not important. The focus of this coding scenario is on learning a simple technique that can be used to improve the analysis for users.

1. Create a new project in Visual Studio 2010 and name it Chapter7_DataVisualizationOptions.

2. Add the XAML in the MainPage.xaml file show in Listing 7-5. This will create a static data visualization container that will host your two data visualizations.

Listing 7-5. XAML code that defines a small static data visualization container

```
<UserControl x:Class="Chapter7_DataVisualizationOptions.MainPage"
    xmlns="http://schemas.microsoft.com/winfx/2006/xaml/presentation"
    xmlns:x="http://schemas.microsoft.com/winfx/2006/xaml"
    xmlns:d="http://schemas.microsoft.com/expression/blend/2008"
  xmlns:mc="http://schemas.openxmlformats.org/markup-compatibility/2006"
    mc:Ignorable="d" d:DesignWidth="300" d:DesignHeight="400">
    <StackPanel x:Name="LayoutRoot" Height="400" Width="300" Background="#FF848181">
        <Canvas x:Name="Header" Height="50" Background="#FF000000">
            <Rectangle Fill="#FF4B3E3E" Stroke="#FF000000" Height="25" Width="300"
HorizontalAlignment="Stretch"/>
            <TextBlock x:Name="Title" HorizontalAlignment="Stretch" Canvas.Left="65"
Canvas.Top="10" FontSize="18"
                        Foreground="#FFFFFFFF" Text="Data Visualization"
TextWrapping="Wrap">
            </TextBlock>
                    <Button x:Name="ButtonFlip" Content="Flip" Canvas.Top="12"
Canvas.Left="250" Padding="10,5,10,5" Cursor="Hand"/>
        </Canvas>
        <StackPanel x:Name="RotatePanel" Height="350" HorizontalAlignment="Stretch"
Width="Auto" Background="#FFD9D7D7" RenderTransformOrigin="0.5,0.5">
        </StackPanel>
    </StackPanel>
</UserControl>
```

3. Create an event handler for the LayoutRoot Loaded event and a click handler for the ButtonFlip button. The changes are shown in bold in Listing 7-6.

Listing 7-6. XAML code with event handlers defined

```
...
<StackPanel x:Name="LayoutRoot" Loaded="LayoutRoot_Loaded" Height="400" Width="300"↩
Background="#FF848181">
        <Canvas Height="50" Background="#FF000000">
                <Rectangle Fill="#FF4B3E3E" Stroke="#FF000000" Height="25" Width="300"↩
HorizontalAlignment="Stretch"/>
                <TextBlock HorizontalAlignment="Stretch" Canvas.Left="65" Canvas.Top="10"↩
FontSize="18"
                        Foreground="#FFFFFFFF" Text="Data Visualization" TextWrapping="Wrap">
                </TextBlock>
                <Button Content="Flip" Click="Button_Click" Canvas.Top="12"
                        Canvas.Left="250" Padding="10,5,10,5" Cursor="Hand"/>
...
```

4. Add a reference to the System.Windows.Controls.DataVisualization.Toolkit assembly.

5. This coding scenario is about providing visualization transitions, so I won't focus on the data visualizations. You want to mimic the transition between two visualizations. Add two charts to the StackPanel called RotatePanel. One will be a regular bar chart and the other will be a pie chart to differentiate the visualizations. In Blend, simply drag over two charts and place them in the RotatePanel StackPanel. Change the series of the second to a pie series. If you did this via copy and paste, ensure you add the proper namespaces on the top as well. Listing 7-7 shows the relevant code.

Listing 7-7. Adding two data visualizations to your rotating StackPanel

```
xmlns:mc="http://schemas.openxmlformats.org/markup-compatibility/2006"
mc:Ignorable="d"
xmlns:chartingToolkit="clr-namespace:System.Windows.Controls.DataVisualization.↩
Charting;assembly=System.Windows.Controls.DataVisualization.Toolkit"
x:Class="Chapter7_DataVisualizationTransitions.MainPage"
d:DesignWidth="300" d:DesignHeight="400">
...
    <StackPanel x:Name="RotatePanel" Height="350" HorizontalAlignment="Stretch"
        Width="Auto" Background="#FFD9D7D7" RenderTransformOrigin="0.5,0.5">
        <chartingToolkit:Chart x:Name="BarChart" Title="Bar Chart">
            <chartingToolkit:Chart.DataContext>
                <PointCollection>
                    <Point>1,10</Point>
                    <Point>2,20</Point>
                    <Point>3,30</Point>
                    <Point>4,40</Point>
                </PointCollection>
            </chartingToolkit:Chart.DataContext>
```

```
                <chartingToolkit:ColumnSeries DependentValuePath="X" ↵
IndependentValuePath="Y"
                ItemsSource="{Binding}"/>
        </chartingToolkit:Chart>
        <chartingToolkit:Chart x:Name="PieChart" Title="Pie Chart">
                <chartingToolkit:Chart.DataContext>
                        <PointCollection>
                                <Point>1,10</Point>
                                <Point>2,20</Point>
                                <Point>3,30</Point>
                                <Point>4,40</Point>
                        </PointCollection>
                </chartingToolkit:Chart.DataContext>
                <chartingToolkit:PieSeries DependentValuePath="X" IndependentValuePath="Y"
                ItemsSource="{Binding}"/>
        </chartingToolkit:Chart>
</StackPanel>
...
```

6. It's time to ensure the solution builds. Compile and run the solution, and you should see a graphic similar to Figure 7-12.

Figure 7-12. Your simple data visualization container with two charting visualizations

7. You're now going to initially set the pie chart visualization visibility to Collapsed. When the animation executes, it will enable the hidden visualization when the panel is 90 degrees (sideways), and this will appear to be a smooth transition. Listing 7-8 shows the relevant code to hide the second visualization. You will accomplish this in two animations.

- The first animation (SbFlip) will rotate the panel 90 degrees.

- When this SbFlip animation completes, you will switch the visibility of the charts.

- After the visibility of the charts is switched, you will then rotate the panel back to the original position using the SbFlipBack animation.

Listing 7-8. Hiding the second data visualization (changes are shown in bold)

```
<chartingToolkit:Chart x:Name="PieChart" Title="Pie Chart" Visibility="Collapsed">
    <chartingToolkit:Chart.DataContext>
….
```

8. Now it is time to add a storyboard that will flip the RotatePanel containing the visualization on its side. In Expression Blend, create a new storyboard and call it SbFlip (Figure 7-13).

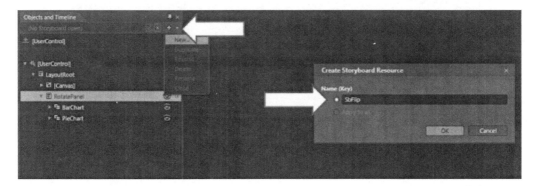

Figure 7-13. Creating a new storyboard animation

9. After the storyboard is created, highlight the RotatePanel in the Objects and Timeline window and click the Add Keyframe button. Drag the yellow timeline indicator and create a second keyframe at the 0.3 second mark (Figure 7-14).

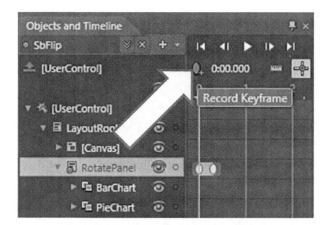

Figure 7-14. New storyboard with keyframes

10. In the Objects and Timeline window, move the time frame indicator to the 0.3 second marker. With the RotatePanel selected, change the scale of the X and Y properties of the control to 0.85. Then change the ending angle to –90 degrees. When this animation is run, it will shrink the panel and rotate it. This shrinking makes it so the corners won't be cut off by the main container (Figure 7-15).

Figure 7-15. The SbFlip animation will change the scale and roation of the panel.

11. Now that the animation is defined, you need to trigger it. In the Button_Click event handler, start the storyboard animation by adding the code shown in Listing 7-9.

Listing 7-9. Code that will trigger the SbFlip storyboard

```
private void Button_Click(object sender, System.Windows.RoutedEventArgs e)
{
    this.SbFlip.Begin();
}
```

12. Build the solution so far and run the code. Clicking the Flip button should trigger the animation and rotate the panel.

13. Now you need to define the storyboard that will flip the panel back. Similar to step 7 earlier, create a storyboard called SbFlipBack.

14. After the storyboard is created, highlight the RotatePanel in the Objects and Timeline window and click the Add Keyframe button. Drag the yellow timeline indicator and create a second keyframe at the 0.3 second mark (similar to step 9 earlier).

15. In this step, you are going to do the opposite of step 10 earlier. You want the animation to appear natural so you are going to cheat and flip the angle; otherwise, the panel would come back on the incorrect side. Ensure the time frame marker is on the 0.0 second mark now to set the initial state. Select the RotatePanel, and set the initial angle to 90 degrees (not –90) and the initial scale to 0.85 for the X and Y values (as shown in Figure 7-16).

Figure 7-16. The SbFlipBack animation initial state needs to have the Y angle set to Y and the scale to where the SbFlip animation left it. This will give a natural animation.

16. In the Objects and Timeline window, move the time frame indicator to the 0.3 second marker. With the RotatePanel selected, change the scale of the X and Y properties of the control to 1.0. Then change the ending angle to 0 degrees. This will place the panel back to the original state (similar to step 9).

17. Now you'll add the code that will flip the animation back when the original completes. When the first flip action completes, you will hide the current visualization and show the other one. Listing 7-10 shows the relevant code that needs to be added.

Listing 7-10. Code that will trigger the SbFlip storyboard

```
private void LayoutRoot_Loaded(object sender, RoutedEventArgs e)
{
    // add event handler to trigger method when initial animation is completed
    this.SbFlip.Completed += new EventHandler(SbFlip_Completed);
}

void SbFlip_Completed(object sender, EventArgs e)
{
    // change the visibility of the chart
    if (this.BarChart.Visibility == Visibility.Collapsed)
    {
        this.PieChart.Visibility = Visibility.Collapsed;
        this.BarChart.Visibility = Visibility.Visible;
    }
    else
    {
        this.PieChart.Visibility = Visibility.Visible;
        this.BarChart.Visibility = Visibility.Collapsed;
    }

    // flip the panel back
    this.SbFlipBack.Begin();
}
```

18. Now run the application. If you did everything correctly, you should see the panel animate, then change the chart visibility, and then rotate back. This is illustrated in Figure 7-17

Figure 7-17. Animation transiton that shows the rotation of the panel and switching the visibility of the charting visualization

If your animations are not working quite right, ensure that your XAML for the two storyboards looks similar to Listing 7-11. You can replace your XAML located in UserControl.Resources with that shown.

247

Listing 7-11. Storyboard code for the two animations

```
<UserControl.Resources>
        <Storyboard x:Name="SbFlip">
                <DoubleAnimationUsingKeyFrames BeginTime="00:00:00"↵
 Storyboard.TargetName="RotatePanel" Storyboard.TargetProperty=↵
"(UIElement.RenderTransform).(TransformGroup.Children)[3].(TranslateTransform.X)">
                        <EasingDoubleKeyFrame KeyTime="00:00:00" Value="0"/>
                        <EasingDoubleKeyFrame KeyTime="00:00:00.3000000" Value="0"/>
                </DoubleAnimationUsingKeyFrames>
                <DoubleAnimationUsingKeyFrames BeginTime="00:00:00"↵
 Storyboard.TargetName="RotatePanel" Storyboard.TargetProperty=↵
"(UIElement.RenderTransform).(TransformGroup.Children)[3].(TranslateTransform.Y)">
                        <EasingDoubleKeyFrame KeyTime="00:00:00" Value="0"/>
                        <EasingDoubleKeyFrame KeyTime="00:00:00.3000000" Value="0"/>
                </DoubleAnimationUsingKeyFrames>
                <DoubleAnimationUsingKeyFrames BeginTime="00:00:00"↵
 Storyboard.TargetName="RotatePanel" Storyboard.TargetProperty=↵
"(UIElement.RenderTransform).(TransformGroup.Children)[0].(ScaleTransform.ScaleX)">
                        <EasingDoubleKeyFrame KeyTime="00:00:00" Value="1"/>
                        <EasingDoubleKeyFrame KeyTime="00:00:00.3000000" Value="0.85"/>
                </DoubleAnimationUsingKeyFrames>
                <DoubleAnimationUsingKeyFrames BeginTime="00:00:00"↵
 Storyboard.TargetName="RotatePanel" Storyboard.TargetProperty=↵
"(UIElement.RenderTransform).(TransformGroup.Children)[0].(ScaleTransform.ScaleY)">
                        <EasingDoubleKeyFrame KeyTime="00:00:00" Value="1"/>
                        <EasingDoubleKeyFrame KeyTime="00:00:00.3000000" Value="0.85"/>
                </DoubleAnimationUsingKeyFrames>
                <DoubleAnimationUsingKeyFrames BeginTime="00:00:00"↵
 Storyboard.TargetName="RotatePanel" Storyboard.TargetProperty=↵
"(UIElement.Projection).(PlaneProjection.RotationY)">
                        <EasingDoubleKeyFrame KeyTime="00:00:00" Value="0"/>
                        <EasingDoubleKeyFrame KeyTime="00:00:00.3000000" Value="-90"/>
                </DoubleAnimationUsingKeyFrames>
        </Storyboard>
        <Storyboard x:Name="SbFlipBack">
                <DoubleAnimationUsingKeyFrames BeginTime="00:00:00"↵
 Storyboard.TargetName="RotatePanel" Storyboard.TargetProperty=↵
"(UIElement.Projection).(PlaneProjection.RotationY)">
                        <EasingDoubleKeyFrame KeyTime="00:00:00" Value="90"/>
                        <EasingDoubleKeyFrame KeyTime="00:00:00.3000000" Value="0"/>
                </DoubleAnimationUsingKeyFrames>
                <DoubleAnimationUsingKeyFrames BeginTime="00:00:00"↵
 Storyboard.TargetName="RotatePanel" Storyboard.TargetProperty=↵
"(UIElement.RenderTransform).(TransformGroup.Children)[0].(ScaleTransform.ScaleX)">
                        <EasingDoubleKeyFrame KeyTime="00:00:00" Value="0.85"/>
                        <EasingDoubleKeyFrame KeyTime="00:00:00.3000000" Value="1"/>
                </DoubleAnimationUsingKeyFrames>
                <DoubleAnimationUsingKeyFrames BeginTime="00:00:00"↵
 Storyboard.TargetName="RotatePanel" Storyboard.TargetProperty=↵
```

```
"(UIElement.RenderTransform).(TransformGroup.Children)[0].(ScaleTransform.ScaleY)">
                    <EasingDoubleKeyFrame KeyTime="00:00:00" Value="0.85"/>
                    <EasingDoubleKeyFrame KeyTime="00:00:00.3000000" Value="1"/>
                </DoubleAnimationUsingKeyFrames>
        </Storyboard>
</UserControl.Resources>
```

Lessons Learned

By now, you may be thinking that this was just an animation tutorial. This coding scenario can seem that way. However, proper management of real estate is very important when dealing with multiple data visualizations. Many dashboards suffer from the problem of showing visualizations that display the same analytical content—for example, if you decided to show the same data in two visualizations. This coding scenario attempted to show you how to leverage the animation framework in Silverlight to transition smoothly between different visualizations.

You might have noticed the container of this coding scenario is very similar to a mobile interface. I did this on purpose to highlight an issue that you will face when writing Silverlight mobile applications. The real estate on handheld devices is minimal, and techniques like the one shown here will help you transition between different views of the data effectively.

This technique can be applied to more than just transitioning between different visualizations. Setting up a help button that transitions to a description of the data visualization would be a great option. Another possible use of this technique would be to provide preference options or configuration options for the data visualization (e.g., setting the time frame or the default chart to show when the page loads).

In some instances, BI consultants often try to appease their clients' requests, which leads to poor design decisions. For example, I have seen instances where multiple views of the same data are presented multiple times on the same screen. If those situations arise, either the visualization isn't properly conveying all the insight or real estate is not being utilized properly. Furthermore, great designs over time become bloated with features and cause an analytical mess as features are blindly added. Leveraging Silverlight's animation framework to hide unwanted visuals and keeping things simple are ways to maintain a BI 2.0 solution that delivers great insight.

Possible Improvements

In this coding scenario, you hardwired the implementation to the control. For a custom control or a one-off implementation, this is OK. However, to provide consistent behavior across all developed controls, this animation should be abstracted to a higher functionality.

Silverlight 4 includes a feature called *behaviors* which allow pieces of functionality to be attached to UI elements. The flip animation would make a fantastic candidate as a behavior that could be attached to all controls that require a transition. This would allow the designer to provide a consistent look across all controls. Furthermore, a behavior implementation would work great in MVVM scenarios because it would eliminate codebehind logic.

Summary

This chapter advanced your knowledge of the previous data visualization concepts. It covered various advanced visualization scenarios that showed off Silverlight's capability to present composite visual intelligence scenarios to increase the amount of insight delivered for the visualizations.

In this chapter, you saw not only that Silverlight is good for presenting styled data visualizations, but that the Silverlight environment can present visual intelligence controls that are on par with enterprise commercial BI software. Examples of advanced Silverlight visualizations such as workflows, environmental visualizations, and cross-tab data visualizations amplified that the Silverlight is a very capable framework to surface complex business intelligence data in user-friendly infographics.

In the following chapters, you will see how these interactive visual controls aid in applying predictive analytics and collective intelligence scenarios.

CHAPTER 8

■ ■ ■

Applying Collective Intelligence

In this chapter, we will introduce collective intelligence as a form of BI 2.0. Collective intelligence is a form of knowledge that allows applications to be dynamically shaped by the respective users. It is a paramount feature for BI 2.0 applications that you want to tailor to a larger audience (beyond business analysts).

This chapter will introduce the features of collective intelligence and why it is important in today's applications that deal with large amounts of user data. Furthermore, I will guide you through various examples and implementations of collective intelligence you have used hundreds of times on numerous current-generation web sites.

The following coding scenarios are included in this chapter:

- Working with the Silverlight rating control to gather and surface user data

The following table outlines the specific goals that different types of readers will achieve by reading this chapter.

Audience	Goals
Silverlight developers	Grasp the fundamentals of collective intelligence.
	Apply collective intelligence in Silverlight by creating simple input and output controls.
Business intelligence professionals	Understand how collective intelligence extends BI 2.0 in today's web environments.
	Recognize the features of collective intelligence that apply to bringing BI to a larger audience (BI 2.0 for the masses).
Strategic decision makers	Understand how implementing collective intelligence can make your applications become more dynamic and deliver additional insight from content generated by the users.
	See if your applications need to apply collective intelligence in order to compete with current and upcoming semantic web trends.
	Implement advantages of collective intelligence to minimize the cost of creating new content and keep your applications more up to date.

What Is Collective Intelligence?

Collective intelligence has its roots in various sociology studies of human collaboration extending into other live organisms like animals and plants. Scientists over the years have proven over and over that large arrays of organisms exhibit mass intellect and enterprise communication patterns that can only be attributed to their ability to collaborate together to not only survive but also create healthy living environments.

An excellent example of mass collaboration is how large colonies of bees or ants create an elaborate collaboration system that sustains millions of individual members. Each bee or ant has sensors that gather information and pass that information to others. This information is then gathered and analyzed (which is still largely a mystery) to determine how the entire colony behaves. From all of these millions and millions of gathered inputs, a form of actionable knowledge emerges. For example, if a bee finds a large deposit of nectar, it returns to the colony and performs a bee dance, giving other bees in the colony the important location. With this knowledge provided by a single bee, other bees can seek out and provide food for the colony. Note that while the single bee is out gathering food, others are collecting other information, which is vital for the survival of the colony. This is the main reason why a single bee or ant can't survive alone in nature. Even a small cluster will not survive, as it depends on large amounts of data to be gathered by many individual members.

From the example that occurs in nature, we can start to form a basic definition of collective intelligence. Collective intelligence can be defined as the knowledge that is derived from the participation or teamwork of many individuals working together.

In the next few sections, we will see how collective intelligence concepts can provide enormous benefits to business applications that depend on users to generate content.

Collective Intelligence and Web 2.0

The current generation of web sites on the Internet today depends largely on collective intelligence. Without collective intelligence, we would not have an Internet that could dynamically adapt fast enough to the user's needs. Allowing users to participate in shaping the content that is presentenced to them is a fundamental feature of current web applications.

The User Is Always Right

In the early days of the Web, we were presented with largely static content that was determined by the sites' designers. Improvements were made as the content became more dynamic and updates to the web sites could be made more frequently. However, the content was still determined by the administrators and designers of the respective web sites. The users had very little input as to how they wanted their information displayed. It was thought that the site administrators knew what was best for the users. Controlling content was thought of as the best way to provide the most professional experience.

Users demanded more power and wanted to create their own content. Furthermore, they didn't just want to create the content for themselves; they also wanted to share this content with the world or individuals they trusted. However, these users needed the tools to be able to create and share this content easily. Not everyone can create professional web pages using HTML and/or JavaScript with data stores.

The Web 2.0 paradigm facilitated an explosion of user-generated content and knowledge. Many Web 2.0 sites started with the single purpose of facilitating the creation and sharing of content by individual users. This was a fundamental shift from before, as web sites began to value the contributions of their users. The tools on these web sites allowed users to find answers to questions provided by their peers, not individual experts or sample studies.

In Web 2.0, the individual user became a highly valued member of the community. Not only did web sites want users to input their content, they trusted users to determine the personality and knowledge environment of their sites.

Web site designers and owners finally understood that if a hundred or several thousand users were interested in a particular topic, maybe a million users would be interested in it as well. Site administrators, experts, and designers played less of a role in generating the content. However, the roles changed into how to facilitate the creation of content by the users.

THE DIFFERENT PERSONALITIES OF MYSPACE AND FACEBOOK

MySpace and Facebook are two social networking sites with millions of users. These sites are in a pitched battle for adding new users every month. As these sites have added more and more users, an interesting phenomenon has taken place. These sites themselves have created a collection of people that have discernable attributes.

MySpace started in 2003 by several young founders. It quickly became a hit and one of the leading Web 2.0 sites. Soon to follow was Facebook, started by Mark Zuckerberg in 2004 on Harvard's campus. It was also an instant hit, and after its initial launch, almost the entire campus was hooked on the new platform. Initially, both sites provided a similar service: a set of open tools and services for users to create their own content free of charge. There were some smaller features that were different, and the UIs looked and behaved differently. However, at a higher level, both sites provided a similar social networking experience.

Fast-forward about five years and you can start to see how these two web sites have been shaped by their users' content. The communities have started to take separate paths and have taken their respective users with them. The millions of individual users have created a subculture that exists on these sites that is different enough to be measurable. MySpace users tend to be younger. Conversely, Facebook—in part because it started out on a college campus—tends to have a more educated and an older audience. Many different people have done analyses comparing these two sites, focusing on how different they have become. Many analysts point to the topics of discussion, submitted images, and language as some of the key differences between the two sites.

The differences between the MySpace and Facebook communities show how collaboration and user-generated knowledge can shape entire communities of millions of users. This essentially gives a personality to each respective social networking platform.

Content *Is* the User

Take a second before proceeding to the next sentence and name some large Web 2.0 sites that may come to your head. If you thought of a web site like LinkedIn, Flickr, or Twitter, note what they all share in common. Almost all of the inherent value of these sites is generated from millions and millions of individual users. For example, what would Twitter be without user-generated content? Not only do all of these sites depend on the users, they would simply not exist without user-generated content. There would simply be no point in visiting these sites if there weren't many active users generating fresh content on a daily basis.

The primary goal of these sites is to allow the users to express themselves in as many ways as possible. This could be by simply typing a small message and interacting with peers. However, most of the time this includes rich interactions like uploading images, personal videos, and blog posts; interacting with other data; and tagging content of interest. The user content is persisted in a data store (usually a database) that can be retrieved later.

The following two figures show the path that administrator/expert-generated content takes vs. user-generated content. Figure 8-1 describes a typical path content takes when it is generated by the application owners. Note that users are simply consumers of content, and the flow of information is in a single direction.

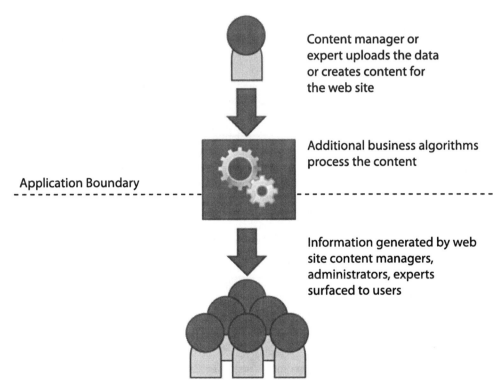

Figure 8-1. Content generated by application owners is delivered to users in a linear path.

Figure 8-2 shows how content that is generated by the user is returned in the form of derived intelligence back to the users. The flow of the information is bidirectional and individual users are both content creators and consumers of content knowledge. Obviously, some systems can be a hybrid of both, where some content is provided from internal sources and user-generated content is mixed in. An example of this is the recent trend of online news sites which will provide news stories from internal sources and mix content from user blogs, user polls, uploaded videos, and so on.

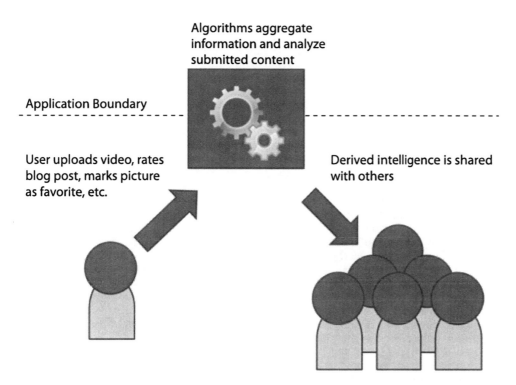

Figure 8-2. *Content generated by indivdual users is stored, aggregated, and sometimes processed, and then displayed to other users in the form of intelligence.*

The principal concept of collective intelligence to facilitate creating, processing, and presenting user-generated content can be seen in the implementation of social networking sites. These sites encourage the building of large user communities that author large amounts of content that can then be derived to provide value to a large number of other users. One of the intents of Web 2.0 social networking sites is to be as open as possible. A lot of the web sites present their content via free APIs that allow applications to be formed as extensions of the site content itself. Many applications use the open Twitter APIs to run their own custom algorithms that provide additional insight into the Twitter community. For example, there are several applications that can tell you what the current popularity of an item is based on, what Twitter mentions or what the next emerging hot topic is.

Collective intelligence concepts have been applied with great success in Web 2.0 social networking sites. For many people, these sites exposed users to their first taste of how collective intelligence can add value. However, these concepts can be applied to any application that can trust its user base to generate content that is valuable to other users.

Classifying Collective Intelligence Data

At this point, you still might be confused as to what this user-generated content that makes up collective intelligence actually is. Isn't everything technically collective intelligence data since some human users must input this into the system? In collective intelligence, user-generated data strictly refers to the content created by the application's audience. In Figures 8-1 and 8-2, I drew an application boundary line that general users cannot cross. For example, if a social networking site only allows you to upload pictures and share them, then the collective intelligence of that application is made up of the attributes of the uploaded pictures and the insight that can be derived from them. If the site contains proprietary videos that are provided by the web site, this would not be considered user-generated data.

In order to make this a little clearer, let's imagine a simple fantasy baseball application. In this application, users can compete in leagues of drafted players based on the players' historical statistics. How did the statistical data get there? This data had to be input by humans that were watching each particular game. This data eventually made it into some scoring system, and business algorithms eventually aggregated the data to present year-end averages and summaries. This is not collective intelligence because the people inputting the data are not acting as members of the audience of the fantasy application. They are simply recording the events into a scoring system. When it comes time to draft players for the fantasy league, users can use this historical data in order to help them derive insight on a player's future performance during the year. This can aid them in the decision whether to select or skip a particular player. What I have mentioned so far is not collective intelligence, as the fantasy application audience has not generated any of the data.

Collective intelligence in this particular example would be tracking the actionable decisions users make from the historical data. For example, the fantasy application can record the amount of times a player is selected on draft day by all the users. Furthermore, it can also provide a rating system that users can use to see if they think that a particular player will have a better season than last year. This content can be displayed in a grid format and provide additional insight to other users that have not held a fantasy baseball draft. Figure 8-3 shows a mix of internally generated statistics with user-generated insight. Other audience members can use both pieces of information to attain additional insight and determine the overall value of a player for their fantasy leagues.

Data columns such as batting average, hits, home runs, and RBIs all come from the statistical system. However, columns such as Percent Own and Will Improve From Last Year? are aggregated from user input or behavior of the user. As each user selects a player, this event is recorded and we can aggregate this information to determine the percentage of times a player appears in all the different user leagues in a system. In our application, we could provide a small widget next to each player's name and allow users to vote whether each player will improve. This could be presented as an aggregate per player in the Will Improve From Last Year? column.

Collective intelligence user-generated data is classified as information that is determined based on the input or behavior of the collaboration of many individuals in a particular environment (e.g., social networking web site).

Player Name	BattingAverage	Hits	HR	RBI	Percent Own ▾	Will Improve From Last Year?
Reid, Miles	231	130	45	134	99	12
Sarin, Raman	245	115	23	78	98	65
Cook, Kevin	376	200	24	128	96	34
Cook, Kevin	245	165	22	100	95	65
Poe, Toni	312	199	32	95	93	23
Gladkikh, Andrey	365	215	11	95	87	45
Perry, Brian	255	145	35	90	77	23
Reid, Miles	222	97	9	60	67	55
Kane, John	276	75	5	49	60	92
Gladkikh, Andrey	300	10	38	87	44	23

Figure 8-3. *The grid shows fictitious data from a fantasy baseball application. Note that the data is a mix of content from an internal system and user-generated data (highlighted with a rectangle).*

Collective Intelligence as BI 2.0 Applied

How does collective intelligence fit in with BI? In the earlier chapters when I introduced BI 2.0 features, I mentioned one of the goals of next-generation BI applications is to make these tools available to larger audiences, thus providing BI for the masses. Collective intelligence can be thought of as an extension of this BI 2.0 concept.

BI 2.0 simply defines that applications should empower the average user. How exactly does one empower the individual user in a BI application beyond making applications simple to learn and use? This is where collective intelligence features fill in the ambiguous gap that BI 2.0 defines. As you can see from what we have covered, it is much more than simply providing a simple interface or an analysis tool that is quick to learn. Applying collective intelligence concepts truly empowers the average user by allowing them to shape the insight that is delivered in a BI system.

Advantages of Applying Collective Intelligence

By now, you should have a high-level view of what collective intelligence is. However, you should be asking what collective intelligence is used to achieve in software applications. How will your applications benefit from implementing collective intelligence concepts?

Following is a list of advantages of applying collective intelligence in your software:

- *Empowering the user*: Not every user can participate in the software design process. Persons coming into the application after it has been designed sometimes can feel powerless and trapped by the closed set of features. Collective intelligence principles open up the application to user content. This means that users are going to be more receptive to trying to learn the new application.

- *Keeping users coming back*: With collective intelligence, users feel that their actions are directly contributing to the overall health of the system. Therefore, users often get a sense of ownership of the data and feel more responsible, as their direct input and actions often depend on the success of the application. For example, take a look at how active users manage their Twitter accounts. Users keep coming back to post information about their lives to maintain the interest of the people following them. If they post low-value content or post infrequently, others may not pay attention to the information they are trying to disseminate.

- *Generating better data*: A main principle of collective intelligence is that system designers or experts don't always know their users as much as they think they do. Allowing individual users to create, vote on, tag, and present their own data usually improves the overall data in the system. For example, take a look at Figure 8-3 again which shows two user-generated columns that additional insight in the displayed grid. How could you create those two columns without user input? You could have an expert or a computer algorithm predict what the users would do; however, that data is prone to statistical error. Gathering and presenting collective intelligence data can give your system a competitive edge, as it can generate data that is difficult to create without users.

- *Keeping the system current*: Once applications are released to the public, new features and/or content are needed to keep the overall feel of the system current. Adding new content to the application can be expensive. However, by applying collective intelligence principles properly, new content can be added at any time by the users themselves. Facilitating the creation of new content by users in masses is always going to be several factors cheaper than maintaining experts. This keeps the system current, and if there are many active users, the content will rarely get stale.

- *Achieving a better understanding of the system*: Users are usually not technical. Therefore, they sometimes have trouble grasping concepts like where the data comes from, and this can scare a user. As shown previously in Figure 8-2, with collective intelligence, the data comes back full-circle to the user. This allows users to get a little more understanding of the underlying system and how their interactions affect what is being displayed. Users can quickly learn and adapt to how the overall system reacts to their actions because the input of the data is a little more open.

- *Collaborating with humans*: Using a predefined set of tools that a developer created can be great in some cases. However, tools may have bugs or may be unclear. By opening the avenue of human users interacting and collaborating, they can help one another to use the application more effectively. Imagine yourself as a user and being told to follow a specific workflow in order for some application process to succeed. For example, collective intelligence principles can be injected into these types of applications which allow users to agree and collaborate on user-generated workflows that are more efficient.

- *Personalizing the user experience*: If the system knows some of a user's past interactions, the experience can be personalized for the user. For example, if a user has marked as favorites several videos they have seen in the past, the next time they visit the site, a list of similar videos that share similar tags can be displayed to the user. With the implementation of favorite links, these links are not just random or new links but are tailored to the user's past preferences.

I listed the more important benefits of implementing collective intelligence prospects in a system. As you can see, a lot of these benefits are largely intangible and can be hard to justify implementing.

Adding a full social networking or user collaboration architecture is not trivial. Even for existing systems, this could be a very large task.

Understanding the advantages of collective intelligence is one of the biggest obstacles many business software architects need to overcome. Web 2.0 and social networking sites have pioneered and have been thriving off of user-generated content for several years now. The benefits of collective intelligence have not been properly translated to many business offerings or have been slow to materialize as value-added features. I think this presents itself as an opportunity not fully applied in current business software. This is especially true for BI applications that are just starting to embrace BI 2.0 principles.

Measuring Collective Intelligence

Inferring the best strategy to utilize collective intelligence can be challenging. You can think of collective intelligence as a set of governing principles that need to materialize into features in your software system. These features (just like any asset in an application) need to be well planned for before the system is designed. Furthermore, after the application is designed, instrumentation (e.g., logging) needs to be in place in order to track the success of the collective intelligence features.

Not adding proper instrumentation features for collective intelligence is one the biggest design flaws in failed social networking projects. How will you know if your users are creating bad data? How will you know if your UI input tools and processes confuse users to create improper user data?

Luckily, a lot of the advantages of collective intelligence concepts can be easily quantified. With simple methods like logging and user reviews, you can quickly determine if your collective intelligence strategy is working. This allows you to directly evaluate how successful your collective intelligence strategy is and how receptive your user community is to the new collective intelligence features.

■ **Warning** If you are an expert in collective intelligence, you are probably noting how I left some important topics out of the discussion on collective intelligence instrumentation. I considered adding more information to this topic; however, it would have taken us on a path of back-end system architecture. If you are interested in more information on collective intelligence instrumentation and measuring techniques, please seek out those resources on the web site accompanying this book (www.silverlightbusinessintelligence.com) or elsewhere online.

Collecting and Displaying User Content

This section is going to cover the details of collecting and presenting collective intelligence content. The material covered here will go into more specific examples of how collective intelligence is implemented on the client.

In the previous sections, we talked about how collective intelligence can be broken down into two main parts: consuming data generated by users and presenting data generated by users. Figure 8-2 amplifies the high-level flow of the information from the user and then back to the user(s). In this section, we will look at the various techniques and examples that can be used to work with collective intelligence data.

Collecting User-Generated Data

The main goal of implementing collective intelligence in an application is to facilitate the ability for users to express themselves, materialize the expressions into data, and store this data into some kind of data store.

A collective intelligence system can collect user-generated data into two main ways: explicitly and implicitly. Figure 8-4 shows a graphical breakdown of the differences between the two styles. When the collective intelligence system collects data explicitly from a user, the user knows they are directly inputting information and acknowledges that this information will be used by the system. Conversely, implicit collection of data does not always make it clear that the user input is being monitored or collected.

Figure 8-4. *Differences between explicit and implicit user-generated content with collective intelligence*

Keeping It Simple

It sounds simple to start creating UI controls and processes to start collecting and presenting your information. If you are responsible for software design, you probably can think of numerous ways you would want users to input information. With collective intelligence, you have to adhere to some of the BI 2.0 principles outlined in Chapter 1. Remember that in BI 2.0 applications, you are probably targeting casual users and want them to be engaged as much as possible with the overall system. Therefore, collecting data needs to be clear and intuitive and provide as few obstacles to the user as possible.

Take a look at Figure 8-5, which shows a simple UI data form where the user is asked a series of questions about a movie they have just seen. The data form might be clear to most users, but the input is not standardized. What would your answer be for the second question? It could be five out of five stars or it could be ten out of ten. This nonstandard contains the same drawbacks a paper form contains. Some person will need to be involved and take the input and translate into a standard form. This is an example of a poor way to gather information from users.

Did you like the movie?:

What would you rate the movie?:

How much would you pay to see the movie?:

Figure 8-5. Free-form input data forms can lead to nonstandard input from casual users.

Investing in creating additional UI controls for data input has some associated cost. A design team needs to develop these controls and run them through the entire SDLC (Software Development Life Cycle) process. Furthermore, you have to facilitate both the collecting and presenting of the user-generated data. In order to mitigate development cost, a popular tactic has been to create controls that can act as both input and output controls.

The following two sections will cover techniques that adhere to these rules. The focus is on maintaining an enjoyable experience for the casual user while promoting a UI that encourages user interaction.

▓ **Note** The focus of this book is business software, which is an electronic format. However, collecting data for a collective intelligence system does not have to be electronic. You can collect data verbally, on pieces of paper, and using other types of human-to-human interactions. In fact, many of the "paper" forms follow the same principles that electronic forms do. These user inputs can then be entered into a system that presents this data back to the users.

Explicit Data Collection

If you have been on any social networking site in the last several years, you have probably used a rating control. The goal of a rating control is to allow users to rate the content they are being shown or described. Furthermore, a rating control allows users to input information and also serve as an output of derived collective intelligence. Figure 8-6 shows a rating control that is part of the Silverlight 4 Control Toolkit. The control contains five star shapes that the user can automatically associate with a rating. Furthermore, the user can probably discern that lower ratings are poor and the higher ratings are better. The control can be used in two modes (collect and surface mode) at the same time. In *collect mode*, the UI control accepts input from the user. This is activated when the mouse hovers over the rating control, allowing the user to choose the appropriate rating. In *surface mode*, the control simply displays the output of the derived intelligence from the collective intelligence system.

Figure 8-6. A rating control is a control used in collective intelligence UIs that allows for both gathering and surfacing of user-generated content.

A rating control is a great example of explicit data collection, as the user has to create the gestures and confirm their input in order to express their action. The control can be used in numerous areas where the system wants to engage the user and ask for their opinion (rating) on a particular topic. Figure 8-7 shows a page with a video element that displays collective intelligence information using a rating control. Notice that this particular video has a rating of three out of five stars and the user intuitively can use the control with simple input gestures in order to submit his opinion on that particular video.

Figure 8-7. A simple Silverlight page that shows a video. Both implicit and explit forms of collective intelligence gathering and surfacing are shown.

■ **Note** We are going to create a simple rating control in a coding scenario at the end of this chapter using Silverlight 4.

Input controls should also be designed to guide the user's input to minimize the creation of bad data. Previously you saw how a rating control limited the ability for the user to only be able to "input" a rating from one to five stars. The user couldn't type in 5 or put in a value like 100 that didn't make sense. However, in some instances, you will want to provide users with the freedom to enter free-form text. In most situations, it is recommended to provide some form of guidance to the user so they do not input bad data.

Tagging is a common example of attaching metadata attributes to the generated content. For example, if a user creates a blog post and wants to share this information, we would want the user to provide some additional high-level attributes about what they created. This could include basic concepts covered in the blog post. This would allow the blog to automatically be related with similar posts that share the same content. Figure 8-8 shows a simple category creation system that is included on my blog that is used when a new post is created. Note that the user can input the category manually; however, the tag control allows them to simply use a check box control instead of typing a tag that already exists. This is a perfect example of reducing bad data by complementing free-form input with previously created categories.

Categories [_____] [Add]
☐ .net ☐ Blend ☐ Book ☐ Enterprise ☐ entrepreneurial ☐ F# ☐ General ☐ iPhone ☐ Mobile ☐ MultiThreading ☐ Security ☐ Silverlight ☐ Silverlight 3 ☐ SQL Server 2008 ☐ Video Games ☐ Visual Studio ☐ Visual Studio 2010 ☐ WCF

Figure 8-8. Minimizing bad user input is important when providing flexible ways of collecting user-generated content.

Silverlight includes several controls that can be used to reduce bad data collection. One example is the AutoCompleteBox control. This control can be used as a search box, filter, or combo box. The primary function of this control is to provide a list of suggestions based on the input. The behavior of this control increases the chance that the user will select one of the predefined list items and select a valid choice. This is usually the preferred result, rather than having the end user enter free-form text.

■ **Note** Examples of the AutoCompleteBox control can be found on the Silverlight Control Toolkit samples page (www.codeplex.com/silverlight). This control has been covered in very fine detail by the Silverlight developers.

Implicit Data Collection

Implicit data collection from users is transparent instrumentation of collective intelligence that monitors and tracks how a user interacts with the system. The key part of implicit data collection is that users are not aware that their actions are being tracked. Therefore, facilitating implicit data collection focuses more on creating proper UI instrumentation rather than additional UI controls. For example, go back to Figure 8-7, which is a Silverlight page that shows a video control. Each time this page is shown to the user, logging code could run in a background that increments the amount of viewers this particular video has had. Other examples of implicitly collecting data include tracking clicks on links, monitoring the frequent zones in an application, timing completion of workflow scenarios, and so on.

Obviously, monitoring user behavior has been around for several years now. Even many first-generation web sites contained some forms of logging to track user interactions. Furthermore, many pieces of software for web analytics have existed to facilitate this. How is this different for collective intelligence? For the most part, the same best practices for transparent user monitoring apply to collective intelligence. However, collective intelligence principles do tweak the instrumentation as they encourage tracking user input that can be displayed back to the users. This is a key difference from applying simple logging techniques. Previously, instrumentation data on users was kept internally and analyzed by application administrators. Applications designers several years ago never thought of sharing this data with their users and closely guarded this data. Therefore, instrumentation architecture never planned for easily querying aggregated data that was implicitly collected and surfacing it on the application. Collective intelligence systems require instrumentation implementations that not only collect data but also integrate into a queryable system that can present the data back in the application. Furthermore, implicit data collection should remain as unobtrusive as possible with the overall performance of the system. The users should not even be able to perceive that data is being collected on their actions.

How much data should be gathered depends on the requirements of the system. If the data is collected properly, then it can be useful in the future. You can never have enough information. Data attributes that are not useful in current collective intelligence implementations might be important in the future for additional metrics. When applying implicit gathering strategies, it is important to not overburden the system.

■ **Warning** When designing a collective intelligence system that collects user behavior and shares it with other users, you have to be careful of privacy laws. You cannot simply start tracking every single user behavior and use that data in any way. Many companies go to great lengths in creating end user license agreements (EULAs) that clearly state that the application is tracking user actions and that they own the data. Therefore, even though the user may not know what exactly is being monitored, the user knows that their actions are subject to being recorded and persisted. Some collective intelligence platforms gather user-generated input; however, they protect the user by not tying the actions to a specific identity. The gathered data essentially goes into an aggregate pool.

Data Collection in Silverlight

For the longest time collecting data based on user interactions whether explicit or implicit had to be manually implemented in Silverlight. No framework existed that easily plugged into Silverlight that could facilitate collective intelligence needs. Architects and developers had to rely on existing frameworks like Google Analytics and leverage the HTML JavaScript bridge in order to communicate event streams for data collection.

Data collection based off of user events, has become much easier with the release of the Microsoft Silverlight Analytics Framework. The Microsoft Silverlight Analytics Framework (MSAF) was announced during the MIX 2010 conference in March 2010. The MSAF framework plugs in directly to Silverlight and it allows you to translate user events into data structures that can be collected and logged using analytics services. The best part is you don't have to write your own analytics service. The MSAF works with several analytics services such as: Google Analytics, Quantcast, Comscore, and so on. Therefore, if you have an existing site that uses Google Analytics to track user "movement" on your site you can leverage your existing web analytics infrastructure.

The framework has been released as an open source project, which is available at http://msaf.codeplex.com. The MSAF includes many great features. The analytics services provide a design time library for Expression Blend. This allows designers to easily create tracking items for events they want tracked without writing any kind of code. This is achieved through behaviors. MSAF also includes support for Silverlight 4 features such as off-line scenarios (where the application is disconnected from the Internet or server) and out of the browser scenarios.

If you are designed a business intelligence application and you want to derive collective intelligence on how users interact with your analytical tools, which ones are less effective or if users are taking too many steps in processes the Microsoft Silverlight Analytics Framework is a must include feature.

Displaying User-Generated Data

Once the data is collected from the users, it is persisted in data stores. BI processes then aggregate, filter, and scrub the user-generated data and present the collective intelligence data in the form of insight. A list of users that clicked a particular video provides little insight into the behavior of the system. However, presenting aggregated information like "this video was viewed 100,000 times in the past day" provides some insight that users of a system have provided you implicitly. Taking the video example further, you can then run more complex algorithms to find behavior correlations like "users who viewed this video also viewed this one."

■ **Note** The architecture of deriving collective intelligence from user-generated data is a complex topic that is not covered in this book. This book focuses on the BI of the client. If you are interested in additional information on this topic, please visit the accompanying web site of this book (www.silverlighbusinessintelligence.com).

Surfacing collective intelligence data should follow the same principles mentioned in the previous topic of collecting user information. The visuals that are used to surface collective intelligence data should adhere to BI 2.0 best practices and be easy to understand to the casual user. You do not want to overload the user with too much information, and you usually want to convey a few key pieces of insight from the collaboration of all the users.

There are many examples of ways to present derived knowledge to casual users. The controls can be visual or text based. Some examples include:

- *Tag clouds*: Tag clouds are a great way to provide a list of items that amplify particular attributes. For more information on tag clouds, refer back to Chapter 5.

- *Rating controls*: These controls provide simple visual cues that users can quickly analyze to relate the information in their heads.

- *KPI visuals*: Traffic light visuals have their roots in street traffic lights. Everyone knows what the red, yellow, and green symbols in a street traffic light represent.

Examples of these controls include KPIs which can present collective intelligence data using graphical symbols. These visualizations are popular in BI scorecard scenarios (covered in detail in Chapter 6).

- *Aggregate lists and text:* Simple lists or text boxes that display aggregates and summarize the collective intelligence content as a whole can be very effective. For example, text such as "65 percent of people recommend this book" displayed next to a book conveys collective intelligence insight very effectively and to the point.

Collective intelligence controls can also benefit from unique visualization overlays. For example, take a look at Figure 8-9, which shows a percentage of clicks that the main menu receives on my blog. The labels display the aggregate percentage of clicks. However, what is interesting is that the labels are positioned on top of the location of the clicked links. This provides additional location insight into the user-generated data automatically.

Figure 8-9. *Overlaying the percentage of clicks generated from my web site header on top of my actual blog site provides valuable insight into where users are clicking.*

One key aspect to note is that collective intelligence information doesn't have to remain in the domain of the application. Today's collective intelligence applications not only want to share the data with their users, they also want to share their data with other user-generated content. Users also demand the ability to share data outside the application domain and surface that content in their own ways.

A great example of sharing collective intelligence data across domains is the Microsoft Xbox Gamertag system. In Figure 8-10, I am showing my friend's Xbox Gamertag, which provides many points of insight into his gaming history.

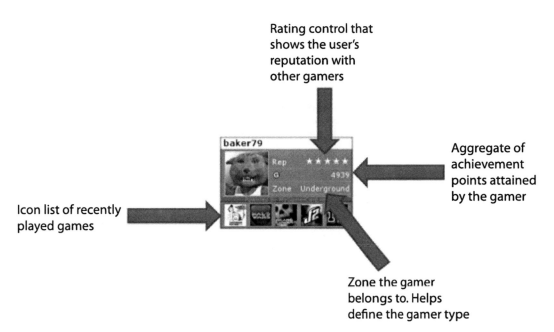

Rating control that
shows the user's
reputation with
other gamers

Aggregate of
achievement
points attained
by the gamer

Icon list of recently
played games

Zone the gamer
belongs to. Helps
define the gamer type

Figure 8-10. Xbox 360 Gamertags present a variety of information collected from a gamer, both explicitly and implicitly.

■ **Note** If you are an Xbox gamer or know a friend's Gamertag and want to look it up, go to
`http://gamercard.xbox.com`. You can append the Gamercard name with the `.card` suffix to generate the
Gamercard image shown in Figure 8-10. For example, the URL `http://gamercard.xbox.com/BartC78.card` will
generate a visual Gamercard for my Xbox account.

It is interesting to note how much information is being displayed in a single Xbox Gamertag control.
This Gamertag control is an example of a composite collective intelligence control that contains several
key pieces of collective intelligence insight and displays it in a single visualization. Let's analyze some of
the collective intelligence pieces:

- *Reputation*: The reputation is displayed in the Gamertag control using a rating
  control. This information is collected about the gamer from other users that have
  played with this person online. Users that have good experiences playing online
  with this user will rate the person higher. Reputation is collected explicitly via a
  rating control using the Xbox.

- *Achievement score*: This value is an aggregate sum of all the individual scores
  achieved on each Xbox game this person has played. This information is collected
  implicitly from the user as they gather more achievements as they play more Xbox
  games.

- *Zone*: The zone label is metadata a gamer provides about themselves. This information is provided by the gamer when the Gamertag is initially created. Gamers can use this to determine what type of an Xbox player the person is. Is he a hardcore player or just a casual gamer? This information is gathered explicitly from the user.

- *Game icons*: The five icons at the bottom represent the last five games the gamer has played. This provides additional information about the kinds of games the person is playing. This information is gathered implicitly as the gamer plays more games.

This Gamertag consolidates all of the critical information about a gamer into a small composite visualization that can be added on a social networking site like Facebook or inserted into a blog. This makes all of the Xbox user collaboration and individual user information defined in the Xbox domain able to be displayed in other application domains. This is why I think it is one of the best implementations of collective intelligence today.

■ **Note** One of the exercises I planned for this chapter was to show how to create a Gamertag using live Xbox services. Unfortunately, these APIs are not freely available, and you need to purchase access from resellers. I have created sample code on the web site accompanying this book (`www.silverlighbusinessintelligence.com`) that shows how you can create a simple Gamertag using live services and querying the data with LINQ.

Example of Collective Intelligence in Blogs

The popularity of blogs has exploded in recent years. Blogging software exists to allow users to express themselves and share the content with others very easily. Blogs are also a great way to see many collective intelligence UI features implemented. I don't want to specifically talk about what blogging is and how blogging software is architected. However, I do want to highlight how multiple collective intelligence features can work together to improve the user experience inside blogs.

Figure 8-11 shows a large screenshot of my blog (`www.silverlighthack.com`). The arrows highlight some of the many collective intelligence areas.

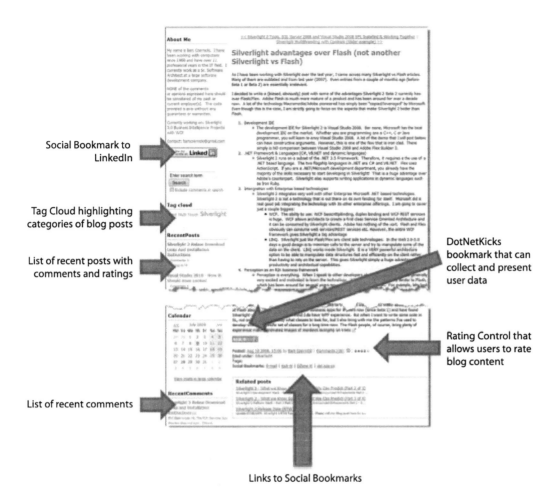

Social Bookmark to LinkedIn

Tag Cloud highlighting categories of blog posts

List of recent posts with comments and ratings

List of recent comments

DotNetKicks bookmark that can collect and present user data

Rating Control that allows users to rate blog content

Links to Social Bookmarks

Figure 8-11. *Blogs are great examples of collective intelligence UI implementations.*

Imagine the blog without all of the collective intelligence controls and user-generated data. The blog would be a pretty boring site and not very engaging. Collective intelligence features allow both the authors and readers to engage one another in collaborating on posted topics.

Collective Intelligence UIs with Silverlight

Where does Silverlight technology fit into designing a collective intelligence UI experience? Silverlight needs to be able to implement collective intelligence principles easily in order to be considered a potential technology for user collaboration. The combination of controls, integration with the Web, and being a visually appealing technology makes Silverlight a great fit for collective intelligence projects. Many of the same features I introduced in Chapter 1 that make Silverlight a great BI tool apply to collective intelligence. However, I wanted to note a few key items that make Silverlight an especially good choice for collective intelligence integration.

- *Control development*: Silverlight 4 includes several controls that make collecting data easy. For example, the Silverlight Control Toolkit includes a rating control that can be styled in several different ways and used for gathering and presenting user-generated content. In Chapters 5 through 7 on data visualization, you saw how easy it is to make a control like the tag could. Silverlight's rich interactivity and animation framework can make the collective intelligence processes easier. This makes Silverlight a great candidate because custom controls that are simple for the casual user can be created fairly quickly. These controls can be easily ported as web parts into collaboration portals such as SharePoint server.

- *Integration with the Web*: Silverlight is not the technology that powers the Web today. Today's web applications are predominantly HTML/JavaScript/CSS. Many JavaScript extensions and links already exist that facilitate user collaboration. Silverlight includes a powerful HTML/JavaScript bridge that can integrate with preexisting web tools. This minimizes the cost of implementing a collective intelligence–based solution in Silverlight, as many of the preexisting foundations can simply be leveraged.

- *Widgets that are portable*: In the Xbox Gamertag example (Figure 8-10), you saw a small widget that was created with the goal of porting user-generated content across application domains on the Web. Silverlight modules can be made very portable. This makes Silverlight an ideal technology for embedding small widgets into preexisting applications. In professional user collaboration environments (e.g., Microsoft SharePoint Server), Silverlight can implement portable collective intelligence in the form of web parts.

There are other reasons why you would want to use Silverlight to implement collective intelligence features; however, many of them are just normal functions of RIA technology. I am not advocating that Silverlight was designed for collective intelligence; however, it can be used for this purpose.

Your main takeaway should be that Silverlight will not limit your collective intelligence integration projects. If you are planning a new Silverlight application and want to facilitate collective intelligence features, you should feel comfortable that the technology can facilitate your needs.

Collective Intelligence in the Enterprise

Collective intelligence isn't just for social networking, blogs, and Web 2.0 sites. I hope you can see the many benefits of user collaboration in professional environments as well. These collective intelligence features can be applied directly to other concepts (e.g., BI) to expand their reach and effectiveness.

In BI 2.0 implementations, users want to be able to not only create reports but also share them with their peers easily. Users will want to use analytical tools, and once they find some interesting derived intelligence or insight, they will want to share that information. Currently, many organizations do not facilitate this easily, and users try to collaborate using network shares or e-mail. Finding intelligence usually means searching through e-mail, opening attachments, or searching network drives. This is why collaboration software has made major strides in enterprise-level implementations. This can put information and intelligence right in front of the users without them having to resort to manual searches or individual maintenance of documents.

One of the more popular enterprise collaboration servers is Microsoft SharePoint. This server software has been the fastest Microsoft product to reach over $1 billion in revenue, and its popularity is increasing dramatically. In fact, many consulting and software companies sprung up recently just focusing on SharePoint implementations and development. The Microsoft SharePoint product allows organizations to implement many collective intelligence features such as wikis, intelligence web parts, collaboration workflows, favorites lists, and so on. Furthermore, creating an expansive collective intelligence infrastructure is largely not needed, and the product can handle a large majority of the collective intelligence features out of the box. This enables users to share their ideas and make their document management easier. Users empowered with other user content can make better decisions from an increased number of intelligence sources. This leads to better ROI from BI implementations as users make wiser decisions from BI software that helps run the organization.

Collaboration software and server packages are becoming increasingly popular in the enterprise. Large organizations are beginning to see value in user-generated content that was popularized by Web 2.0. It is very important to understand that collective intelligence is not just for a blog or a social networking site.

Coding Scenarios

One could write an entire book on collective intelligence integration with Silverlight. There are numerous examples to fully show how collective intelligence principles could be implemented in Silverlight. I chose one topic that highlights Silverlight's features when working with user-generated data.

Coding Scenario: Working with the Rating Control

This coding scenario will cover the rating control that I mentioned multiple times in this chapter. The Silverlight Control Toolkit contains a rating control that is highly customizable and flexible to work in a variety of different scenarios. You will see why the rating control is a first-class tool in Silverlight for applying collective intelligence scenarios.

Following are the goals of this scenario:

- Understanding how to gather information using the rating control

- Understanding how to present information using the rating control

In this coding scenario, we are going to create a user control that rates movies. The user will be presented with a list of movies and see the rating associated with each movie that has been collected from the user community. We will use the Silverlight rating control to surface the ratings. Furthermore, a user will be allowed to rate each individual movie.

■ **Warning** This coding exercise requires the Silverlight 4 Control Toolkit assemblies. Please install the proper assemblies before proceeding with this coding scenario. A full working demo of this coding scenario is available on the companion web site: `http://silverlightbusinessintelligence.com/Demos/` `ApplyingCollectiveIntelligence/WorkingWithRatingControl/WorkingWithRatingControl.html`

---

1. Open Visual Studio 2010 and create a new Silverlight Application project called Chapter8_WorkingWithTheRatingControl.

2. Open the project in Expression Blend 4 and perform the following steps to set up the UI features:

   - Change the width of the user control to 640 and the height to 700.

   - Add a Loaded event to the LayoutRoot (which will add a corresponding event handler method in the code-behind file).

   - Add a list box named lstMovies that has a width of 250 and height of 500.

   - Add an open binding to the list box (ItemsSource={Binding}).

   - Your MainPage.xaml file should look like Listing 8-1 (the changes are highlighted in bold).

Listing 8-1. Initial look of our XAML (changes are shown in bold)

```
<UserControl x:Class="Chapter8_WorkingWithTheRatingControl.MainPage"
    xmlns="http://schemas.microsoft.com/winfx/2006/xaml/presentation"
    xmlns:x="http://schemas.microsoft.com/winfx/2006/xaml"
    xmlns:d="http://schemas.microsoft.com/expression/blend/2008"
    xmlns:mc="http://schemas.openxmlformats.org/markup-compatibility/2006"
  mc:Ignorable="d" Width="640" Height="700">
 <Grid x:Name="LayoutRoot" Loaded="LayoutRoot_Loaded">
  <ListBox x:Name="listMovies" Margin="0" ItemsSource="{Binding}"
  Width="250" HorizontalAlignment="Left" VerticalAlignment="Top" Height="500"/>
 </Grid>
</UserControl>
```

3. Before proceeding, ensure that the Loaded event handler was added in the code-behind.

4. In Visual Studio 2010 create a new Movie class in the Silverlight project with the following properties:

   - Name the class Movie.

   - Add a string property called MovieName.

   - Add a double property called AverageRating.

   - Add an integer property called RatingsCount.

5. The class should look like the one shown in Listing 8-2.

Listing 8-2. A Movie class that will hold three properties: MovieName, AverageRating (average rating from all users), and RatingsCount (which counts how many ratings have been made). The relevant code is highlighted in bold.

```
namespace Chapter8_WorkingWithTheRatingControl
{
```

```
public class Movie
{
  public string MovieName { get; set; }
  public double AverageRating { get; set; }
  public int RatingsCount { get; set; }
}
}
```

6. In Visual Studio, open the code-behind file (`MainPage.xaml.cs`) and make the following changes in Listing 8-3 (the changes are highlighted in bold):

    • Add a method called `GetListOfMovies()` that returns a mock list of movies.

    • In the LayoutRoot, set the `ItemsSource` property of `lstMovies` to the `GetListOfMovies()` method.

Listing 8-3. Add a method that creates a mock list of movies and set the lstMovies list box.

```
...
public IList<Movie> GetListOfMovies()
{
  // returns a list of fictitious Movies
  return new List<Movie> {
    new Movie { MovieName = "Viva Silverlight", AverageRating = 0.5, RatingsCount = 1332 },
    new Movie { MovieName = "Collective Intelligence Returns", AverageRating = 0.25,↵
RatingsCount = 3 },
    new Movie { MovieName = "RIA Raiders", AverageRating = 0.75, RatingsCount = 3500 },
    new Movie { MovieName = "Flash of RIA", AverageRating = 0.6, RatingsCount = 343343 },
    new Movie { MovieName = "Weekend at Silverlight 4", AverageRating = 0.4, RatingsCount↵
= 4 }
  };
}

private void LayoutRoot_Loaded(object sender, RoutedEventArgs e)
{
  // bind the list to the set of movies
  this.listMovies.ItemsSource = this.GetListOfMovies();
}
...
```

7. Build the project and run it. Since we did not add a proper list box template, the project will look like Figure 8-12.

```
Chapter7_WorkingWithTheRatingControl.Mo
Chapter7_WorkingWithTheRatingControl.Mo
Chapter7_WorkingWithTheRatingControl.Mo
Chapter7_WorkingWithTheRatingControl.Mo
Chapter7_WorkingWithTheRatingControl.Mo
```

Figure 8-12. The list box after completing step 5 (the list box still isn't not styled)

8. Now it is time to add an ItemTemplate to our list box to make it look presentable. With the project open, navigate to Expression Blend 4 (you can launch Expression Blend 4 from Visual Studio 2010 by right-clicking on the MainPage.xaml and selecting the Open Expression Blend option) and make the following changes:

- In the Objects and Timeline section, right click the lstMovies list box. Next, select Edit Additional Templates, and then select Edit Generated Items (ItemTemplate). Finally, select Create Empty. A dialog box will appear; click OK to confirm the creation of the new style. The selection is shown in Figure 8-13.

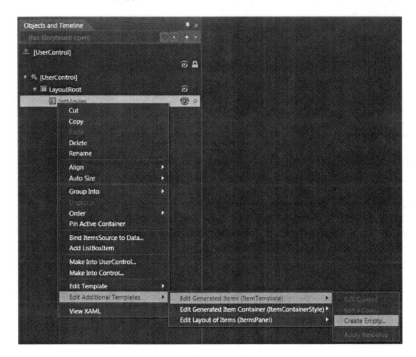

Figure 8-13. Creating an empty data template

- This will create an empty data template that we can use to design how the individual items are rendered in the list box. The changes in the MainPage.xaml.cs file are highlighted in bold in Listing 8-4.

Listing 8-4. XAML code that shows the data template added to the list box (added through the action in Step 7)

```
...
  mc:Ignorable="d" Width="640" Height="700">
      <UserControl.Resources>
              <DataTemplate x:Key="DataTemplate1">
```

```
            <Grid/>
          </DataTemplate>
      </UserControl.Resources>
  <Grid x:Name="LayoutRoot" Loaded="LayoutRoot_Loaded">
   <ListBox x:Name="listMovies" Margin="0" ItemsSource="{Binding}"
   Width="250" HorizontalAlignment="Left" VerticalAlignment="Top" Height="500"
ItemTemplate="{StaticResource DataTemplate1}"/>
   </Grid>
</UserControl>
```

9. Now we can edit the data template and add our changes. After you completed step 6, Blend should have taken you into a mode to edit DataTemplate1. Your Objects and Timeline window should look like Figure 8-14.

Figure 8-14. Editing the list box data template

- If you are not in this mode, in the Objects and Timeline section, right-click the lstMovies list box. Next, select Edit Additional Templates and then select Edit Generated Items (ItemTemplate). Finally, select Edit Current. This should make your Objects and Timeline section appear properly.

10. Make the following changes to the data template:

- Right-click on the Grid item (under DataTemplate), select Change Layout Type, and select StackPanel.

- Drag over a text block and name it MovieName. Set the FontSize property to 13 and the FontWeight property to Bold. The text block should be nested inside the StackPanel.

- Select the StackPanel again, add another StackPanel inside it, and name the new StackPanel RatingPanel. Change the Orientation property to Horizontal and both the width and height to Auto.

- Select the layout StackPanel again, add another StackPanel inside it, and name the new StackPanel RatingCountPanel. Change the Orientation property to Horizontal and both the width and height to Auto.

- Select the StackPanel named RatingPanel and add a text block. Set the Text property of the text block to Average Rating. Name the control labelAverageRating. Set the right margin to 5.

- Select the StackPanel named RatingPanel (same control as before) and add a rating control. Set the Name property of the rating control to AverageRating. If you cannot find the rating control, Figure 8-15 displays the location of the control in the Blend 4 asset library.

- Set the cursor of the AverageRating control to Hand. This will let the user know that they can input information.

Figure 8-15. The rating control can be found in the asset library if the Silverlight Control Toolkit is installed in the devloper environment.

- Select the StackPanel named RatingCountPanel and add a text block. Set the Text property of the text block to "Amount of users voted." Name the control labelRatingsCount.

- Select the StackPanel named RatingCountPanel, add a text block control, and name it RatingsCount.

11. After performing the preceding steps, the Objects and Timeline section should look like Figure 8-16.

Figure 8-16. The updated Objects and Timeline object tree for the data template

12. We will now want to make the following changes to the data template to facilitate binding the UI controls to the respective properties of the Movie class:

   • Bind the MovieName text block Text property to the MovieName property of the Movie class.

   • Bind the AverageRating rating control Value property to the AverageRating property of the Movie class.

   • Bind the RatingsCount text block Text property to the RatingsCount property of the Movie class.

   • The MainPage.xaml changes in steps 9 and 10 are highlighted in bold in Listing 8-5.

Listing 8-5. The necessary changes to the data template to present our list of movies

```
...
xmlns:toolkit="clr-
namespace:System.Windows.Controls;assembly=System.Windows.Controls.Input.Toolkit"
x:Class="Chapter8_WorkingWithTheRatingControl.MainPage"
  Width="640" Height="700">
<UserControl.Resources>
        <DataTemplate x:Key="DataTemplate1">
                <StackPanel>
                        <TextBlock x:Name="MovieName"
                                Text="{Binding MovieName}"
                                TextWrapping="Wrap" FontWeight="Bold" FontSize="13"/>
                        <StackPanel x:Name="RatingPanel" Orientation="Horizontal">
                                <TextBlock x:Name="labelAverageRating" Text="Average↵
Rating:" TextWrapping="Wrap"/>
                                <toolkit:Rating x:Name="AverageRating" ItemCount="5"↵
Cursor="Hand"
                                        Value="{Binding AverageRating, Mode=TwoWay}"/>
```

```
                                </StackPanel>
                                <StackPanel x:Name="RatingCountPanel" Orientation="Horizontal">
                                        <TextBlock x:Name="labelRatingsCount" Text="Amount of↵
    users voted:" TextWrapping="Wrap" Margin="0,0,5,0"/>
                                        <TextBlock x:Name="RatingsCount"
                                                Text="{Binding RatingsCount, Mode=TwoWay}"↵
    TextWrapping="Wrap"/>
                                </StackPanel>
                        </StackPanel>
            </DataTemplate>
</UserControl.Resources>
...
```

13. Build the project, and the screen should look similar to Figure 8-17. Take a note of several key items:

   • The rating control visually displays the average rating from the Movie class.

   • You can mouse over the ratings and change the rating of any movie seamlessly (you do not have to add additional code to do that).

Viva Silverlight
Average Rating: ★★✦☆☆
Amount of users voted: 1332

Collective Intelligence Returns
Average Rating: ★☆☆☆☆
Amount of users voted: 3

RIA Raiders
Average Rating: ★★★★☆
Amount of users voted: 3500

Flash of RIA
Average Rating: ★★★☆☆
Amount of users voted: 343343

Weekend at Silverlight 3
Average Rating: ★★☆☆☆
Amount of users voted: 4

Figure 8-17. *The rating control project at step 10 is functional but misssing some key points.*

At this point, the project can add features in several ways. In a production-quality application, you would have a service that submits the user ratings. Once the transaction was deemed successful, then the service would return and update the average rating and increment the amount of users voted. Furthermore, proper security would be needed for tracking IP addresses and user credentials of the users voting on each movie. Obviously, adding the entire infrastructure for this exercise would be overkill. However, in the next steps, we are going to add the following features to mimic some of the concepts you would design in a collective intelligence system:

   • A user will only be allowed to vote on a movie once.

   • When the user casts a vote, the rating control will become read-only.

   • A message will appear signifying a successful rating submission.

- A calculation will calculate the new average rating (including the user's submission) and increment the total vote count.

14. Go to `MainPage.xaml` in Expression Blend 4 and add a handler to the ValueChanged event for the AverageRating control inside the list box data template. The XAML should look like Listing 8-6 (the changes are highlighted in bold). This should add a corresponding event in the code-behind file.

Listing 8-6. The AverageRating control project XAML with the ValueChanged event added

```
<toolkit:Rating x:Name="AverageRating" ItemCount="5" Cursor="Hand"
        Value="{Binding AverageRating, Mode=TwoWay}"
        ValueChanged="AverageRating_ValueChanged"/>
```

15. In this step, we are going to implement all of the changes we planned in step 11. For the sake of simplicity, I added all of the code into the event handler. This is by no means production-quality code. The AverageRating_ValueChanged event handler should include the code shown in Listing 8-7 (it is not highlighted in bold, as it is all new).

Listing 8-7. Additional processing and calculations that occur when a user votes on a movie

```
private void AverageRating_ValueChanged(object sender,
  System.Windows.RoutedPropertyChangedEventArgs<System.Nullable<double>> e)
{
  // check to make sure this is not the initial binding
  if (e.OldValue != null)
  {
    // retrieve the rating control
    Rating ratingControl = sender as Rating;
    // define the amount of ratings
    int rateCount = 0;

    StackPanel panel = ratingControl.Parent as StackPanel;
    StackPanel panelParent = panel.Parent as StackPanel;

    // iterate over the parent to
    // access the second RatingCount StackPanel
    for (int i = 0; i != panelParent.Children.Count; i++)
    {
      // cast the panel to a FrameworkElement to access name property
      FrameworkElement element = (FrameworkElement)panelParent.Children[i];

      if (element.Name == "RatingCountPanel")
      {
        StackPanel ratingCountPanel = (StackPanel)element;

        // retrieve the value from the RateCount text box
        for (int j = 0; j != ratingCountPanel.Children.Count; j++)
        {
          // cast the panel to a FrameworkElement
```

```
            TextBlock textBlock = (TextBlock)ratingCountPanel.Children[j];

            if (textBlock.Name == "RatingsCount")
            {
              // retrieve count
              rateCount = Convert.ToInt32(textBlock.Text);

              // remove the ValueChanged event handler
              ratingControl.ValueChanged -= this.AverageRating_ValueChanged;

              // calculate the rating
              ratingControl.Value = ((rateCount * e.OldValue) + e.NewValue) / (rateCount + 1);

              // update the count and increment it by one (user's vote)
              textBlock.Text = (rateCount + 1).ToString();

              // thank the user for the vote
              MessageBox.Show("Thank you for your vote", "Vote Confirmation",↵
    MessageBoxButton.OK);
            }
          }
        }
      }

    // mark the control as read-only
    ratingControl.IsReadOnly = true;
    // set the curor to arrow (let's user know that action is not possible)
    ratingControl.Cursor = Cursors.Arrow;
    // set the transperancy to 0.6
    ratingControl.Opacity = 0.6;
  } // end of if statement
}
```

16. Build and run the project. Note that you can vote on the different movies and you get a message box that lets you know you have submitted a vote. This clearly confirms to the user that they are submitting content. Another way to handle this would have been with an animation that transitioned the control to another color. Furthermore, note that when a user votes, the control becomes read-only and more transparent, and the cursor ceases to be a hand.

Lessons Learned

This coding scenario covered an intermediate task of allowing a user to vote on a list of movies. The coding scenario introduced you to the Silverlight Control Toolkit rating control. The rating control was used to apply the collective intelligence UI concept of explicitly gathering and presenting user-generated data. I hope you have learned that Silverlight can facilitate creating rich collective intelligence scenarios easily. You should compare the simplicity of the rating control with the error-prone data form inputs shown in Figure 8-5. Understanding implementations like the one covered in this project ensure that you will design BI 2.0 applications that encourage your users to participate in the software applications.

Possible Improvements

As mentioned in the beginning of this coding scenario, the entire service portion of the collective intelligence back end was left out for simplicity. However, this scenario showed you how you could code a majority of the collective intelligence UI.

The rating control is very flexible and allows you to do more than just an implementation using five-star objects (which is the default). The rating control can be skinned to include different colors and items. Furthermore, the selection of objects can be made mutually exclusive or can include the selection of partial objects (e.g., selecting half a star and voting for 3.5 out of 5 stars). This coding scenario was just a simple introduction, and I encourage you to check out the many examples of what is possible in the Silverlight Control Toolkit.

Summary

This chapter introduced collective intelligence concepts as an extension of BI 2.0. You have probably been using implementations of collective intelligence on numerous social networking web sites for some time now without even knowing it. Collective intelligence principles facilitate the creation of engaging applications that users want to use. Applied properly, collective intelligence can make your applications stand out and grow vibrant communities of users that constantly provide valuable content to the overall application.

The goal of this chapter was to also show you how to consume and present user-generated data using Silverlight technology. You should have grasped that Silverlight includes many controls that can be used to surface and collect collective intelligence data. Furthermore, the Microsoft Silverlight Analytics Framework allows you to specify which events should be passed on to enterprise scale analytics services.

Implementing Collective Intelligence scenarios for your business intelligence applications is crucial to understand how your users are interacting with the rich Silverlight BI 2.0 tools you have created. Furthermore, these collective intelligence conventions applied for business intelligence allow you to quickly enhance your data sets with the wisdom of your user community.

I hope you can see how you can harness the power of collective intelligence in your BI applications to make your users feel like they are empowered, entrusted, active contributors.

CHAPTER 9

■ ■ ■

Predictive Analytics (What-If Modeling)

This chapter covers creating and applying BI models that are forward looking. In the past chapters, we focused on business intelligence concepts that applied to past or current data. However, BI 2.0 applications can extend the functionality of that data by injecting analytical models that can leverage historical data in order to predict future outcomes. Because of the incredible value that predictive analytics brings to business intelligence software, it is one of the hottest implemented convention in BI 2.0.

This chapter will cover predictive analytics and how it applies to BI 2.0 by making analysis simpler and deliver forward-looking insight more quickly to the masses. Furthermore, we will learn how Silverlight technology possesses the power to make predictive analytics applicable to BI software utilizing fluent and real-time interfaces.

This chapter includes one coding scenario:

- Applying the statistics Poisson distribution to baseball data to predict a player's performance for a given day or season

The following table outlines the specific goals that different types of readers will achieve by reading this chapter.

Audience	Goals
Silverlight developers	Understand the BI 2.0 concept of predictive analytics and creating predictive models.
	Know how to create simple what-if models using statistics, interactivity, and the full power of the Silverlight client.
Business intelligence professionals	Extend previous information in chapters on how Silverlight can apply BI 2.0 concepts.
	Recognize that Silverlight can be used to create complex statistical models with easy-to-understand UIs.
Strategic decision makers	Gain insight into how predictive analytics can extend the value of your existing BI data.

Audience	Goals
	See if Silverlight is the right technology to implement predictive analytics in your software.
	Understand that leveraging forward-looking models can be cost-effective ways to add features to your software by leveraging existing data.

What Is Predictive Analytics?

This section will cover the fundamentals of an emerging subset of BI 2.0 called predictive analytics.

Predictive Analytics Overview

In a nutshell, predictive analytics is about creating analytical models that leverage existing historical data sets in order to make predictions on future behavior.

Predictive analytics is known by many other names, including data mining, what-if analysis, predictive modeling, forecasting, decision mining, and sensitivity analysis. If you are familiar with this concept, note that these names are interchanged frequently. BI purists will argue that there are some semantic differences between the implementations and nature of what these terms truly mean. However, in my opinion (even though there are slight differences), many of these terms can be brought under a single umbrella since their goal is to predict future outcomes using analytical tools.

Predictive analytics, like the term BI, is an abstract concept and theory. Applications and implementations of forward-looking analytics are called models or scenarios. Therefore, you may have a predictive analytics model to predict future sales or gauge how many cars a dealer might sell at some point in the future. How are these models created? Predictive analytics leverage past and current data repositories. However, one important difference between predictive analytics and classic BI is that predictive analytical models include an additional step. They inject algorithms in the analytical process to predict future events. Figure 9-1 illustrates how predictive analytics data processes differ over classic BI algorithms. In these processes, the same data repositories and data transformation algorithms still exist. However, note that in a predictive model the data passes through an additional algorithm to provide future scenarios. In BI applications, a request is made from data repositories, and then additional BI processes aggregate that information. In a predictive analytics model, that data is then run through an additional algorithm on the back end or on the client, which represents some kind of future scenario. For example, let's assume that we created a simple report that shows sales information from the last quarter. The report simply queries the data repository (e.g., data warehouse) and renders the data after filtering and aggregating the information. What if we wanted to show what the sales would be in the next quarter based on the current sales trends? An additional step would need to be applied after the data has been aggregated in order to calculate future quarter sales based on some algorithm that can gauge probability of sales.

Predictive models have been used by a number of industries for quite some time in order to help organizations and their employees make better business decisions. Government, financial, insurance, and health care are just some of the areas that use predictive models to improve the way they make decisions. Forecasting for future events and trying to make better decisions are not alien to large industries. In Chapter 1, I talked about how the power of BI was being displayed to average users through simpler interfaces (BI 2.0). The same is happening with predictive models. You do not have to look far on the Web to find widgets that expose simple predictive analytical models. For example, if you navigate to most car dealer or mortgage web sites, they probably have some kind of payment calculator tool. This simple predictive model can take the loan amount and interest and calculate the payments in a snap. Even more complex predictive models for users can be found in the investment industry. Average users want to have simple tools to allocate their investments accordingly (e.g., 401K) to achieve their retirement goals. Without creating simple tools around predictive models, this would not be achieved easily.

Figure 9-1. Data in predictive analytics passes through additional statistical algorithms that allow the creation of scenarios that try to predict future events.

BI applications that implement the full scope of BI 2.0 concepts will include predictive analytical models as features. BI 2.0 governance defines that analysis should look into the future, not just focus on historical data. Therefore, predictive analytical models have become popular recently as a way to implement forward-looking analytical tools.

■ **Note** Predictive analytics (just like most topics in this book) deserves its own dedicated resources in order for you to fully appreciate its application. Please navigate to the companion web site (www.silverlightbusinessintelligence.com) for further general resources on the topic.

Classic Predictive Analytics with What-If Analysis

Instead of writing a lot of theory behind predictive analytical models, I thought it would be a good idea to cover a simple example in one of the most popular spreadsheet tools. Microsoft Excel 2007 includes a What-If Analysis section that allows users to apply future-looking models in their Excel spreadsheets.

The What-If Analysis section is located on the Data tab in the Excel 2007 (same in Excel 2010) ribbon (shown in Figure 9-2). The tool includes three main tools: Scenario Manager, Goal Seek, and Data Tables. In this section, we will focus on the Goal Seek tool.

Figure 9-2. The What-If Analysis section in Excel 2007& Excel 2010 includes three tools that can be used to create predictive models in Excel spreadsheets.

In this example, we will create a simple spreadsheet that includes a predictive model using the Goal Seek tool. In this scenario, let's say we are in the market for a car. Based on a fictitious budget, let's assume the following conditions are true:

- You can afford to spend about $400 per month on car payments.

- The trade-in value of your current car is $5,000.

- The dealer is running a special for 2.9 percent financing for a 60-month deal.

Before you go to the dealer, you want to find out what kind of money you can spend on a car. After entering the preceding information and applying the payment calculation, you are ready to use the Goal Seek What-If Analysis tool. The Goal Seek tool allows you to set a certain goal in a cell by changing another cell's value. In this example, your goal is to pay a maximum of $400 per month on a new car, and you want the Excel Goal Seek to find the maximum. Therefore, the Goal Seek tool will change the car value cell until it finds a number that matches your $400 payment. The result is shown in Figure 9-3. Based on the created scenario, you can afford a car no more than about $27,300 if you want to keep payments under $400 per month.

■ **Note** The Goal Seek model illustrated in the figure is available on the companion web site (www.silverlightbusinessintelligence.com) for this book.

Figure 9-3. Using the Goal Seek tool, we can create simple predictive models such as a payment calculator for a loan.

How easy would it be for you to replicate this model? Could you alter this model to find out what the payments would be on a higher interest rate? The answers might depend on your background. If you are familiar with Excel and/or financial calculations or are somewhat technical, creating a payment calculator should be effortless for you. However, there is a reason why mortgage web sites do not include an empty mini-spreadsheet for the user. An average user might make more mistakes in creating this model and attain a misleading result. That is one of the worst things that could happen.

Figure 9-4 shows a diagram of some of the paths that can be taken from creating such a model. Even for such a simple model, the user can take many incorrect steps that can lead to delivering incorrect insight. There are many more paths of failure than there are paths to successful insight where the correct goal is achieved.

Some of the reasons why a user could take a misleading path not leading to successful insight are as follows:

- Poor familiarity with Excel

- Entering incorrect information or using the wrong formula

- Not having Excel available

- Using incorrect decimal places

- Not being able to translate the model into using different variables

Figure 9-4. *A user that uses a free-form spreadsheet can create models that provide incorrect insight.*

Another problem with creating this model is the time it can take. For an average user, this can take additional research and can take several minutes (if not more) to create. If I had asked you to create this model, would you be able to without spending a few minutes researching this on the Internet?

Even though we created a simple predictive analytics model using What-If Analysis in Excel rather easily, you can see that this might be too complex for average users. Microsoft Excel can be a great BI tool that allows users the freedom to create any model. However, with that freedom to create anything, you create the requirement of knowing how to use the tool. If your company's business depended on accurate forecast models, would you feel comfortable on relying on the user to create the model correctly?

Delivering Predictive Analytics Faster with BI 2.0

As mentioned earlier in this chapter, predictive analytics is a subset of BI 2.0 governance. In the previous What-If Analysis example, I illustrated a valid example of a payment calculator model that could be used to forecast future payments. The problem with this model was that average users would experience a high failure rate in re-creating this model. Furthermore, users don't want to spend their time creating the model.

This is exactly where BI 2.0 governance comes in. Chapter 1 covered the topic of making simple-to-use BI analytical tools that empower the user to get insight faster. By applying BI 2.0 concepts, how could the process diagram in Figure 9-4 be improved?

- You could create a tool that took user input and validated it (e.g., no negative numbers).

- You could remove the need for Excel.

- You could remove the need to create a model, and embed the calculation algorithm in the tool.

- You could extend the model to allow for a range of information. The model could provide additional insight beyond what the user was looking for.

Figure 9-5 shows the process interaction with the predictive model. Note that the time to insight is much faster because the user does not have to create the model. Furthermore, the incorrect paths are mitigated since the model explicitly delivers the desired insight. Obviously, some users might not understand the tool or even input the data correctly. However, these straying paths can be removed through proper encapsulation of the design of the tool. Most importantly, the tool can deliver additional insight beyond what is desired. In the What-If Analysis tool, only a single goal is being sought. Exposing multiple knowledge points in a model allows the tool to provide additional wisdom beyond the original goal.

Successful Insights

Figure 9-5. *A predictive model applying proper BI 2.0 concepts can reduce incorrect paths and deliver insight more quickly to the user.*

Figure 9-6 displays an example of a simple Silverlight UI that implements some of the BI 2.0 concepts. It allows the user to input the various amounts and calculate them. However, the sliders allow the user to dynamically adjust any variable piece of information in the model. This allows not only the user to get the answer they are looking for, but potentially get answers to insight such as, What if my dream car is $28,000? How bad will the payments be? What if I get less than I anticipate for my trade-in? This is a perfect example of a predictive analytical tool that can provide multiple points of wisdom. Furthermore, using data validation for input and sliders, this completely mitigates the user from inputting bad information. For example, the user can't slide the dealer financing percentage to a ridiculous amount (e.g., 100 percent). Even though these enhancements seem simplistic, they contribute to delivering the BI goal(s) more quickly.

Car Value:	27000.00
Current car trade-in value:	5000.00
Payments Per Month:	394.33
Dealer Financing	0.029
Number of Payments:	60

Figure 9-6. *Improving the payment calulator with a UI that allows the user to quickly adjust all of the metrics with ease.*

Choosing Correct Data Sets for Predictive Models

As you saw in Figure 9-1, predictive analytics combines historical data sets and statistical algorithms to create predictive models. This is the most popular form of forecasting performed on medium- and smaller-sized data. Furthermore, this is the only type of model that can be created by user workstations (since they won't scale to billions of records). Many experts in the field would argue that I am only describing part of the story here. That is absolutely true.

There is a large science in predictive analytics that deals with larger data warehouses, neural networks, and more granular data. For example, in Chapter 8, we looked at how individual user information can be used as a whole for analysis. Individual pieces of information usually make poor choices for predictive models. You are never going to see a forecast analysis done on a single entity. For example, creating an analytical model on a single invoice or single salesperson's data provides little analytical value. However, taking these individual pieces and building relationships around them and creating sophisticated behavioral models can be valuable. For example, a web algorithm determining whether a video that has been rated 3 out of 5 stars by 10 million people is worth showing on the main page is a type of predictive analysis. However, at what point is it more collective intelligence or predictive analysis—or both? This resource simply cannot cover these types of deep analytical combinations and focuses on the simple predictive models that are defined from statistical models applied to data.

Ensuring that you have the correct data sets is the first step in creating predictive models that deliver the most potential insight. I listed a few fundamental points that have to be understood about the data first before predictive models are created:

- Does this data exist, and where does it come from?

- Does this data exist in the correct granular format? For example, if we are doing a forecast on average global temperatures and we have data for every individual city in the world, scanning millions of records as opposed to, say, several hundred could cause a performance problem.

- Can the data be exposed to the model via an interface (e.g., service, data feed, Analysis Services cube)? This is actually a huge problem for BI implementations that are silos and haven't implemented true MDM (master data management) and SOA (service-oriented architecture) concepts. For example, if two data silos can't communicate with each other, it might not be very easy to surface the data.

- Is the data current? What is an acceptable time frame in the data? If you are doing analysis on a future event, you can't use data from 1980. That is an obvious example that makes no sense to do. However, look at a more ambiguous example with sporting statistics. If you are halfway into the sports season and are trying to predict future behavior, can you afford to just look at last season's data? Wouldn't the model be more accurate if it incorporated both the past and current seasons? Using stale data or incorrect time frames is one of the easiest ways to create predictive models that deliver incorrect insight.

Implementing the Proper Tier for Predictive Analysis

After the proper data is chosen for a predictive model, the BI architect needs to determine the proper tier where the model resides. This model performs some kind of forward-looking algorithm on the data. Is it appropriate to put this algorithm on the server or client tier? Following I listed some criteria to determine the tier for the predictive model.

- Do the predictive analysis algorithms require large amounts of data? Would the cost of transferring the data locally be too expensive? Does the workstation have enough horsepower to process the algorithm? If any of these cases are true, there might be no choice but to create predictive analysis models on the server tier.

- Do the predictive analysis algorithms have dependencies on other components on different tiers? It makes sense to extend existing algorithms or models rather than move all of them to different tiers.

■ **Note** Silverlight is based on the .NET Framework. If you have designed business algorithms that are on either tier, the code should be designed to be sharable among both the full framework and the Silverlight subset. This powerful concept is largely overlooked in improving the maintenance of business applications. This allows the code to be written, tested and maintained in a single place.

- Does the predictive model need to be highly interactive? Does the user expect immediate results? In highly interactive models, it makes sense to keep the data local. The cost of continuously bringing down results from the server to the client can be much more expensive than distributing this down to the client. Furthermore, surfacing the model from the server tier might simply be to slow. In an interactive visualization, it would be very frustrating to the user for a "Loading" message to appear every time analysis parameters are changed.

- Are the predictive models cornerstones of intellectual property? If you have complex algorithms that you do not want reverse-engineered, they should remain on the server tier. Placing algorithms on the client tier can increase your "hack footprint."

Benefits of Applying Predictive Analytics

In this section, we will list the benefits of implementing predictive analytics modules in your software applications. Applying forward-looking analytical models can add cost-effective enhancements to decision-making processes by simply leveraging existing data stores.

Bringing Out Additional Value to Existing Data

Assume you have a large repository of data that is being used for a variety of BI offerings. You have used these data repositories to create a robust BI solution that includes visualizations, enterprise reports, cubes, and so on. Many of these solutions only use historical or current (real-time) data in order to deliver insight. If this is the case, then you are only exposing half of the value of data to your users. Even if your users have interactive and dynamic views into the data, they still will not have insight into predicting future events without proper predictive models.

Predictive analytical tools usually do not need new data repositories and can use the existing historical data. Adding predictive analytical models (e.g., statistical models, data mining algorithms, etc.) on top of existing historical data injects new value into the data. Data is not simply visualized in different ways. It is used to build entire new forward-looking scenarios that make the data more valuable. The original investment in creating these repositories gains importance and raises its ROI (return on investment) dramatically. For example, if you create a system that exposes historical analytics and you can use the same data to create additional forward-looking models, in effect, you increase the value of the original investment in the data repositories.

Users of predictive models use tools that inherently tie the past information to future events. This allows the end user to understand the data better and how individual pieces of information interact together. For example, let's imagine a user is working with a model that can predict sales in the next quarter. In the model, the application allows the user to adjust the Research and Development (R&D) and salary costs. As the user adjusts R&D and salary information, they can understand the impact of this for profits. R&D costs might be a fraction of salary costs, and lowering them might not impact profits the same way that lowering sales costs would. In this example, a user can quickly build a relationship of ratios and impact between the data into future scenarios. This adds additional value to the data, as it can be used as a tool for understanding the data better that can lead to better decision making. In classic BI, the complex algorithms on the back end (e.g., for data warehouses and services) are usually a "black box" to the user. However, interactive predictive analytical models can shed insight on the data relationships by providing a complete view of the data interaction in all aspects of the time frame (past, present, and future).

Translating Assumptions into Decisions

Many executives and analysts always try to stay ahead of their competitors. In order to do this, they usually theorize possible strategies that could help their particular organization. Assumptions without being able to visualize their impact clearly are just speculation and theory. However, if you can translate an assumption into a realistic future scenario, then this can materialize into a strategy or a probability. This is exactly the role that predictive models play in BI software. Therefore, one of the main goals of predictive analytical software is to be able to translate theory into probability. Tools such as these can reduce decision-making risk and provide a solid foundation for strategies. This can be applied to a large-scale scenario like a decision to acquire a company. Conversely, it can be applied to an individual problem like purchasing a car.

Being Proactive Instead of Reactive

Utilizing predictive analytics inside your decision-making processes allows your choices to be more proactive than reactive. If analysts are just looking at the past historical or current data, then they are making decisions based on the past. Since the event has already happened, they are making a reactive decision. Because they are reacting to what has happened in the past, sometimes it is too late to change the outcome for the better.

Assume a large bank receives a report with a list of persons who will be foreclosing on their homes. The decision is then made based on that list to begin the foreclosure process. Therefore, a reactive decision is made by the bank based on the fact that a foreclosure event has occurred. Going through a foreclosure is a costly process to the bank and one they would like to avoid if possible. What if a bank had a predictive model that analyzed its portfolio of mortgages and predicted (based on a variety of metrics) which ones are in danger of going into foreclosure? The bank then could take proactive steps to work with the people in danger of foreclosing on their homes. For example, the loan could be restructured to prevent a costly foreclosure. This is an example of how using tools that aid in making proactive decisions can mitigate costs and help the business dramatically.

■ **Note** A good example of predictive analytics using BI 2.0 techniques is stock buying software for day traders. You have probably seen commercials for this type of software on many financial sites or on TV. Essentially, this type of software analyzes stock patterns and trends and makes predictions on how the stock will fare in the future. The implementation of BI 2.0 techniques translates the complex algorithms into a simple visualization for the user in a manner of green (buy), yellow (hold), and red (sell). Applying BI 2.0 concepts, historical data, and predictive analytics together allows nontechnical users to make predictions on the stock market with ease.

Gaining Competitive Advantage

As you have read some of the benefits of predictive analytics, you have probably guessed that applying these models can net a competitive advantage in either your software offering or your business decision-making processes.

If you are a software organization, adding predictive analytical tools into your applications is a great way to leverage the existing data investment and provide additional value to your customers. This can net a competitive advantage over other organizations that are only using the data for past or current analysis. Implementing predictive models inside your software can dramatically add to the value to the current offering.

In the preceding bank mortgage example, you saw how a predictive model can be used to lessen costs and prepare for future scenarios. If your organization has robust analytical tools that can create scenarios into the future, this allows the executives to make well-researched decisions that examine a range of different probabilities. Many organizations have had these types of tools at executive levels; however, predictive analytics is just starting to make inroads at lower-level jobs that can benefit from this. Typical executives have had the luxury of having teams that could research this information and explain the different scenarios. However, this is not true for everyone in the organization. Providing predictive models implemented in simple tools empowers average users to use this information in their day-to-day decisions. Having a large part of the organization (not just the executive levels) empowered with the right tools nets an overall competitive advantage over those who do not implement predictive analytical tools.

Predictive analytics tries to ensure that the decisions that the organization makes will prepare it to overcome any obstacles to achieve its future objectives. If you are a software vendor, your customers would probably love this functionality. If you have an internal BI system, this can help with your organization's strategies.

Applying Forward-Looking Models in Silverlight

In Chapters 1 and 2, we discussed some of the great features of Silverlight that make it a good fit as a BI client. In this section, I wanted to highlight some of the key areas that make Silverlight a great technology for not only creating predictive models, but also exposing them to the users. The previous topics that we covered for general Silverlight BI 2.0 implementations apply to predictive analytics as well.

Using a Functional Language (F#)

If you are a seasoned BI developer, you have probably come across functional or statistical languages to create forecasting models. Functional languages are closely related to mathematics. This makes these types of languages ideal for statistics, recursive computations, data transformation, and functional calculations. Therefore, being able to use BI packages that allow for the injection of statistical functions is paramount for creating complex predictive analytical tools.

Silverlight (based on .NET) can use other languages in addition to C# or VB.NET. One of them is F# which is a new functional language introduced with .NET 4.0 and Visual Studio 2010. Since F# is a first-class language that gets all the love from the .NET CLR (Common Language Runtime), you can use it inside Silverlight to build complex statistical models on the client. Some experienced developers would argue that the functionality of F# overlaps with the new features of C# and LINQ. However, F# has some very interesting features that make it ideal for BI applications for Silverlight:

- It has a noticeable performance boost in mathematical operations compared to C#/VB.NET. The F# syntax compiles more quickly to IL (intermediate language) and executes calculations up to 20 to 30 percent faster in some cases.

- The syntax is terser for calculations. For example, passing functions into functions just works in F# without having to deal with the delegate memory leak headaches of C# or VB.NET. In F#, functions are first-class citizens (contrast this with C#/VB.NET in which objects are first-class citizens).

- F# is based on immutable structures (meaning they cannot change value) by default. This is great for read-only data operations which are included in large majority of BI applications. This makes multithreading synchronization easier since the values cannot change.

- Mapping multidimensional data is easier with F# than C# 3.0 (however, this isn't the case for C# 4.0). For example, if you have a multidimensional data set that comes from Analysis Services, you can utilize F# tuples to quickly group pieces of data together. Therefore, piecing together dimensions and measures is easier than in another language.

There is a very good reason why Microsoft is including F# as a first-class language in .NET 4.0. It provides a great functional alternative to object-oriented languages such as C#. F# has great applications in finance, mathematics, and statistics. Being able to leverage the power of this language in the Silverlight client is a great asset.

■ **Note** Please visit the companion web site of this book to download an example of a probability function created in F# in a Silverlight application. For more information on the F# language, see `http://research.microsoft.com/en-us/um/cambridge/projects/fsharp`.

Designing Predictive Models Using Silverlight

After getting this far in this book, you should be fully aware that Silverlight is a highly capable framework for creating rich client applications. Throughout this book, you have seen many examples of large data sets presented with interactive visuals that simplify BI analysis for the average user. I won't repeat all of these topics in this section; however, I want go over an example of how one could architect a more complex predictive model in the Silverlight framework.

Figure 9-7 illustrates a sample Silverlight predictive model that powers a simple profit forecasting tool. This tool allows an executive to take previous year sales and costs and adjust them to estimate the potential profits for this year. Sliders are available at the leaf level of the application to adjust the percentage change from last year's numbers. As the sliding gesture is performed in either direction, profitability calculations are quickly performed and rendered in the progress bars to show the future expectations of the profit based on this model. Imagine you are a user of this predictive model. Wouldn't this be a great way to try to forecast next year's numbers instead of crunching through a series of spreadsheets? Inside a spreadsheet, a user could make a model just as powerful and add visual graphs as well. However, the visual interactivity in this application allows you to learn about the profit data, build impact relationships between the sales information, and deliver multiple key points of insight all from a single tool. Furthermore, the simple interactions can create multiple insight paths quickly.

The following subsections will cover the key aspects of how this model was designed. This is not a coding scenario.

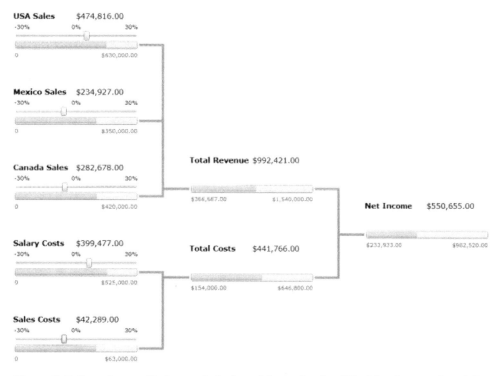

Figure 9-7. Complex predictive analytical models can be simplified for the users by adding visual and interactive elements.

■ **Note** A live demo of the Silverlight profit forecasting model is available on the companion web site (http://silverlightbusinessintelligence.com/Demos/PredictiveAnalytics/ProfitSalesForecast/ ProfitSalesForecast.html). The source code for the project is available in the bonus section of the source code zip file.

Predictive Models with Aggregated Data Sets

What data feeds do we need to implement this predictive model? In one of the first sections in this chapter, I stated that this is one of the first steps you need to look at before jumping into creating a predictive analysis model.

As you can see from Figure 9-7, we are retrieving five key pieces of information broken down into two main sections: Sales and Costs. The Sales section includes the USA, Mexico, and Canada sales information. The Costs section includes salary and sales costs. We are going to be adjusting the percentage amounts on these five pieces of information. If we need to increase USA sales by 5 percent, do we need to get every single row that made up the USA sales, or is the aggregate of the information enough? It makes no sense to bring down every single sales invoice or salary in order to adjust it. In this case, all we need to request is five objects with the key information points. This data could have come from a cube, service request, or data warehouse, for example. However, it should be summarized at the appropriate aggregate levels.

This is one of the main reasons why creating predictive models is a great fit on Silverlight. Even if you want your models to drill down into deeper levels, the data sets should remain small and perform great in Silverlight. Obviously, Silverlight can't scale to do millions of calculations per second; however, with predictive models based on summarized data, this is not necessary.

When this model loads, we simply bind the preceding data to the five leaf-level forecast controls. This will initially set the values using a historical data repository.

Building the Profit Forecast Control

As you can see from Figure 9-7, we are reusing a lot of the same UI. It would make no sense to have to create a copy of the same UI in multiple places. Therefore, this repetition is a good candidate to be abstracted into a control that can be reused.

In Silverlight, one of the quickest ways to create custom controls is through mashup user controls. Essentially, you can use other controls as building blocks for more complex controls. This concept can be applied here. Figure 9-8 illustrates some of the simple components that were used to build this forecasting control.

The control is pretty simple to create visually. After that, the interactions are hooked in together. For example, if the slider value changes, a business algorithm needs to process the percentage difference on the original value. This can be done inline or you can use value converters that were shown in Chapter 2.

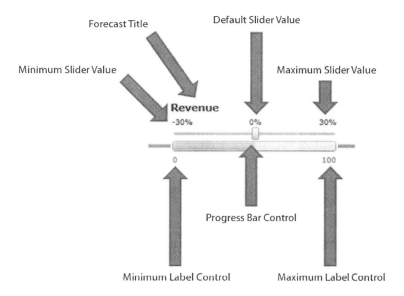

Figure 9-8. Complex controls such as the forecasting control can be easily created using existing standard Silverlight controls.

The forecast control includes multiple states to denote the connection mechanism. If the control is read-only, then only the leaf-level controls have sliders available. As you can see from Figure 9-7, only the leaf-level controls have sliders available. The other controls are read-only since their numbers strictly depend on the previous calculations. I did not want to create two separate controls, but I did want them to look and function differently when they were in these two different modes. In order to achieve this, I created multiple states (in Expression Blend 4) for the control shown in Figure 9-9. This allows for the separation of the functionality and design of the control. This becomes very useful when you have a complex control that a graphics designer should edit while allowing the developer to code the control behavior.

Figure 9-9. *Multiple states for the forecasting control translate to different renderings of the forecast control. Note that the ReadOnly state hides the slider and slider annotations.*

■ **Note** If you are a third-party control vendor or want to take advantage of advanced control designs, custom controls might be a better option. Custom controls allow the developer and designer to have explicit command overall design, behavior, and rendering. However, I find that creating custom controls is much more tedious and should only be left to more advanced developers and designers.

Communicating Between Local Controls

Control communication in Silverlight is accomplished using very similar techniques to Windows Forms programming. A Silverlight developer usually doesn't have to worry about posting back to the Web and having to maintain the session on both the server and client. For this model, I simply exposed an event for each control that is triggered when the value changes. For example, when a user uses the slider and moves it to another position, an event is fired by the control. Other user controls can subscribe to this event. Listing 9-1 shows the event definition used to communicate between controls. This event is defined in the forecast control.

Listing 9-1. *When this event is triggered, it will pass the ForecastEventArgs arguments to the other controls.*

```
public event EventHandler<ForecastEventArgs> ForecastChanged = delegate { };
```

■ **Note** If you have declared events before, you might be asking yourself what the `delegate {}` line is doing there. This is a great trick using a feature in both Silverlight and .NET 2.0 to create an empty delegate call. Essentially, an empty delegate is always assigned to this event. This prevents null exceptions from being thrown when there are no subscribers to a particular event. Without this declaration, you have to wrap the events with proper thread-safe null-checking logic. The performance hit of adding this code is negligible (i.e., it's only noticeable when you fire an event thousands of times per second).

Now that we have defined the event, we need to trigger it when the value of the control changes. This is shown in Listing 9-2.

Listing 9-2. *When the value of the control changes, trigger the event so that other subscribers are notified. This code is encapsulated in the CurrentValue property.*

```
public double CurrentValue
{
  get
  {
    return this.currentValue;

  }
  set
  {
    this.currentValue = value;
    // set the value of the progress bar
    this.Progress.Value = this.currentValue;
    // set the label display of the control
    this.Value.Text = String.Format("{0:C}", Math.Round(this.currentValue), 0);
    // trigger the ForecastChanged event
    this.ForecastChanged(this, new ForecastEventArgs { ForecastModelValue↩
 = this.currentValue });
  }
}
```

How do we set up the publisher and subscriber model? A best practice implementation would create an abstraction of the publisher-subscriber (pub-sub) model using weak references to ensure no memory leaks. For simplicity, I simply pass in the references of the dependent controls to the resultant controls. Then I wire up the ForecastChanged events. This is shown in Listing 9-3. In our forecasting example (Figure 9-7), the Revenue control is dependent on three controls: USA Sales, Mexico Sales, and Canada Sales. We can simply pass these references to the Revenue control and have the events wire up.

Listing 9-3. *The DependentForecastModels receives a list of dependent controls on application load. It wires up the ForecastChanged events with an event handlder so it can be notified of any changes.*

```
public List<ForecastModel> DependentForecastModels
{
```

```
get
{
  return this.forecastModels;
}
set
{
  this.forecastModels = value;
  double currentValues = 0;

  foreach (ForecastModel model in this.forecastModels)
  {
    model.ForecastChanged += new EventHandler<ForecastEventArgs>↵
(DependentForecastChanged);
  }
}
}
}
```

We are almost there. Now we have our controls communicating and notifying each other when one changes. This is where we inject our predictive model algorithm to determine what happens when a change is received. For the Revenue control, we simply need to add up the current values for the USA, Mexico, Canada controls. That is the algorithm for that first step.

This step can be done a plethora of ways. The proper way would be to leverage the powerful LINQ expressions to dynamically build calculations. This method allows predictive models to be dynamically injected to any control via a value converter. To keep this simple, I took a shortcut and simply used an explicit LINQ query to summarize the values from the dependent controls (Listing 9-4). I used a parameter to tell the control what type of operation is expected. The operation that is expected is sum.

Listing 9-4. Aggregate the forecast model values each time one of them changes.

```
void DependentForecastChanged(object sender, ForecastEventArgs e)
{
  if (this.DependentOperation == "sum")
  {
    // sum up the current values for the dependent forecasts
    this.CurrentValue = this.forecastModels.Sum(a => a.CurrentValue);
  }
  ...
```

▓ **Note** In Chapter 11, you will learn how to communicate between controls that are located in different Silverlight applications. This will also be further extended in the SharePoint web part section of the book.

Key Highlights

In this overview, I wanted to highlight the key components of creating a predictive model in Silverlight. I did not cover placement of the controls, slider ranges, loading data from a service, and so on. However, these items have less to do with predictive analytics and more to do with Silverlight development. Please download the code from the companion web site if you are interested in the implementation of this scenario.

I wanted to mention that this model can be improved dramatically. The end result should be a Silverlight forecasting control that can take any data set and allow the user to create a dynamic UI. This would make the tool a self-service BI application that would allow end users to create powerful models themselves. I have plans in the future to create a series of tutorials on how to create this type of tool for a production-ready BI environment.

Deployment Using the Plug-In Model

Being able to present small predictive analytical models using the Silverlight plug-in model is a great way to enhance services. In the What-If Analysis example, we discussed how a mortgage web site could display a small payment calculator to help its customers. Silverlight shines by allowing the developer to design the predictive model without knowing where it might be deployed. This allows modular, user-friendly, predictive models to leverage the Silverlight plug-in to enhance functionality on web sites, mobile devices, and the cloud. This is obviously not limited to the masses of average users. In Chapter 2, I also talked about how Silverlight can utilize the web part framework as a wrapper to expose content in portals such as Microsoft SharePoint. Leveraging this type of deployment allows predictive analytical models to target the corporate audience as well.

■ **Note** One of the reasons that I highlighted the Silverlight plug-in model again in this chapter is that I have found that forward-looking models are usually created as secondary or value-added modules in BI offerings. Even in BI 2.0, having a solid foundation of past data is usually the cornerstone of a BI solution. However, designing an application modularly that can be enhanced with these predictive analytics is also important. This is where the Silverlight plug-in model can be taken advantage of architecturally to add predictive analytical models as widgets or web parts to existing BI offerings.

Coding Scenario: Applying a Statistical Model to Predict Future Behavior

In this coding scenario, we will create a simple predictive analytics model to determine the probability of a baseball player having multiple hits in a game. Furthermore, we will then extend the model by adding interactivity to increase the probability of delivering multiple points of insight.

Following are the goals of this scenario:

- Understanding how to apply statistical algorithms in Silverlight and C#

- Gaining knowledge on how to combine interactions, visuals, data, and algorithms to create a complete predictive analytics experience

In this task, we will attempt to predict the probability of a batter in a baseball league to attain a certain number of hits in a given day. We will predict this information only knowing how many hits he had in the past season. Therefore, our predictive analytics model will use a single variable. This will make the model very simple to comprehend. This is a classical example of using recent historic data to predict the outcome of a future event.

There are many statistical algorithms that we can use in order to predict this event. Some are simple and some are more complex and provide varying degrees of good insight. In order to forecast the future, this coding scenario will use the Poisson probability distribution in order to provide a good "researched guess" of a certain event happening. This statistical distribution is a great way to predict simple future events having known the average number of times these events happened in a past time frame. In our scenario, we will know how many hits the batter has had in the past season.

The Poisson distribution function is defined in Figure 9-10. If you are not familiar with the formula, it might look scary, but it is actually pretty simple.

■ **Note** A live demo of this coding scenario is available on the companion site for this book located at: `http://silverlightbusinessintelligence.com/Demos/PredictiveAnalytics/` `ApplyingStatisticalModelForPredictiveAnalytics/ImplementingPoissonDistribution.html`.

$$P(x) = \frac{\lambda^{\kappa} e^{-\lambda}}{\kappa!}$$

Figure 9-10. The Poisson distribution function allows us to predict how many times a certain event will occur knowing its occurrence in a given time frame in the past.

For those who are not familiar with the Poisson distribution, this is a breakdown of the formula:

- The λ (lambda) variable is a number that signifies the mean (average) of the particular event.

- K signifies the number of successful events.

- e is a constant base of a natural logarithm (2.718).

- $K!$ is the factorial of K. For example, a factorial of 5! is equal to 1 * 2 * 3 * 4 * 5, or 120.

Essentially, we just need to plug in the single variable we have in our data (hits in a season) and the amount of expected successes into the model. Let's assume our fictitious baseball player has 200 hits during the season. Our goal is to estimate the likelihood the batter will attain a certain amount of hits. Defining the variables in the model nets us the following:

- The λ (average mean) is 200 hits/162 games in a season. The batter on average has 1.2345 hits per game.

- K is the amount of successful hits we expect the hitter to have. Let's use the number 1 to calculate the probability of the hitter having a single hit in the game.

- $K!$ becomes 1!, which translates to 1.

The formula is illustrated in Figure 9-11 after the numbers are entered into the Poisson calculation. The answer to our problem is 35.9 percent. The full answer is that the probability of a batter with 200 hits in a season to have a 1 hit in a game is 35.9 percent.

$$P(x) = \frac{1.2345^1 2.718^{-1.2345}}{1}$$

Figure 9-11. The Poisson calculation with the numbers entered into the formula

---

▓ **Note** You can use Microsoft Excel's statistical Poisson calculation to double-check your results.

The Poisson distribution formula is cornerstone of the coding scenario. Once you understand this part, you are ready to proceed to implement this model in a Silverlight application.

▓ **Note** The latter part of the coding scenario includes a chart data visualization. This requires the Silverlight Control Toolkit to be installed.

Part 1: Creating the UI and Applying a Static Predictive Model

1. Create a new Silverlight 4 application in Visual Studio 2010 and call it Chapter9_ImplementingPredictiveAnalytics.

2. Add references to the `System.Windows.Controls.Data` and the `System.Windows.Controls.Data.Input` assemblies to the main Silverlight project.

3. We are going to build a simple UI that includes the following items:

    • A StackPanel (which the LayoutRoot will be changed into)

    • A title for the predictive model

    • A label and input text box for the number of hits in a season

    • A button to trigger the calculation

    • A data grid to display the probability results

4. Add a reference to the `System.Windows.Controls`, `System.Windows.Controls.Data`, and `System.Windows.Controls.Data.Input` assemblies to the Silverlight project.

5. The XAML for the application should look like Listing 9-5.

Listing 9-5. The basic UI that will display the Poisson calculation results (code changes are highlighted in bold)

```
<UserControl x:Class="Chapter9_ImplementingPredictiveAnalytics.MainPage"
  xmlns="http://schemas.microsoft.com/winfx/2006/xaml/presentation"
  xmlns:x="http://schemas.microsoft.com/winfx/2006/xaml"
  xmlns:d="http://schemas.microsoft.com/expression/blend/2008"
  xmlns:local="clr-namespace:Chapter9_ImplementingPredictiveAnalytics"
  xmlns:data="clr-namespace:System.Windows.Controls;assembly=System.Windows.Controls.Data"
  xmlns:dataInput="clr-namespace:System.Windows.Controls;assembly=↵
System.Windows.Controls.Data.Input"
  Width="640" Height="480">
  <StackPanel x:Name="LayoutRoot">
    <dataInput:Label x:Name="Title" HorizontalAlignment="Center" FontSize="18.667"↵
Content="What is the probability of a batter having a hit in the next game?"/>
      <StackPanel Orientation="Horizontal" HorizontalAlignment="Center">
        <dataInput:Label Content="Hits during a 162-game season:"/>
        <TextBox Text="200" TextWrapping="Wrap" Width="50" Margin="10,0,0,0"↵
x:Name="NumberOfHits"/>
        <Button x:Name="Calculate" Width="75" Content="Calculate" Margin="5,0,0,0"↵
Cursor="Hand"/>
      </StackPanel>
    <data:DataGrid x:Name="GridResults" HorizontalAlignment="Center"↵
VerticalAlignment="Center" Width="400" AutoGenerateColumns="False" ItemsSource="{Binding}">
      <data:DataGrid.Columns>
        <data:DataGridTextColumn Header="Number of Hits" IsReadOnly="True"↵
Binding="{Binding NumberOfEvents, Mode=OneWay}"/>
        <data:DataGridTextColumn Header="Probability of Success" IsReadOnly="True"↵
Binding="{Binding ProbabilityOfSuccess, Mode=OneWay}"/>
      </data:DataGrid.Columns>
    </data:DataGrid>
  </StackPanel>
</UserControl>
```

6. Add two event handlers to the UI: a Loaded event for the LayoutRoot StackPanel and a Click event for the Calculate button. The changes to the XAML are highlighted in bold in Listing 9-6.

Listing 9-6. Add event handlers to the LayoutRoot and Calculate buttons.

```
…
<StackPanel x:Name="LayoutRoot" Loaded="LayoutRoot_Loaded">
  <dataInput:Label x:Name="Title" HorizontalAlignment="Center" FontSize="18.667"↵
  Content="What is the probability of a batter having hit the next game?"/>
  <StackPanel Orientation="Horizontal" HorizontalAlignment="Center">
    <dataInput:Label Content="Hits during a 162 game season:"/>
    <TextBox Text="200" TextWrapping="Wrap" Width="50" Margin="10,0,0,0"↵
x:Name="NumberOfHits"/>
    <Button x:Name="Calculate" Width="75" Content="Calculate" Margin="5,0,0,0"↵
Cursor="Hand" Click="Calculate_Click"/>
…
```

7. Ensure the project builds. After running the scenario, the UI should look like Figure 9-12.

What is the probability of a batter having hit the next game?

| Hits during a 162 game season: | 200 | Calculate |

Number Of Hits	Probability of Success	

Figure 9-12. The UI so far for displaying our predictive analytics model

8. Now it is time to implement the Poisson calculation defined in Figure 9-11. Plus we will also implement a helper method to calculate the factorial of a number (the numerator part of the Poisson calculation in Figure 9-11). In your MainPage.Xaml.cs file, add the methods highlighted in bold in Listing 9-7. The code is a simple direct translation of the code in C#.

Listing 9-7. Two methods that are used to implement the Poisson distribution in C#

```
public static double CalculatePoissonProbability(double mean, int numberOfSuccesses)
{
  // calculates an indiviudual Poisson Distribution
  double result = (Math.Pow(mean, numberOfSuccesses)) * (Math.Pow(Math.E, -mean))↩
 / Factorial(numberOfSuccesses);

  return result;
}

public static int Factorial(int x)
{
  int factorial = 1;
  int i = 1;

  // multiply results returning a factorial
  while (i <= x)
  {
    factorial *= i;
    i++;
  }

  return factorial;
}
```

9. Now that we have the calculation implemented, we need to create an object that will hold our results. As you can see in Figure 9-12, we have two columns. One column is the number of hits we want to determine the probability the batter will attain. The second column is the probability of success of the result.

- Add a new class to the Silverlight project and name it ProbabilityResults.

- Add an integer property and call it NumberOfEvents.

- Add a double property and name it ProbabilityOfSuccess.

10. The ProbabilityResults code file should look like Listing 9-8.

Listing 9-8. The ProbabilityResults class holds information on two properties.

```
public class ProbabilityResults
{
  public int NumberOfEvents
  {
    get; set;
  }

  public double ProbabilityOfSuccess
  {
    get; set;
  }
}
```

11. It is time to hook in the calculation code with our UI.

- Our UI will calculate the list when the page loads (Loaded event).
- The Calculate click button should also calculate the set of probabilities when clicked (Click event).

12. Add the code shown in Listing 9-9. The new code is highlighted in bold.

Listing 9-9. The code calculates the probability of a hitter getting zero to six hits on a given day knowing how many hits he is averaging during a season or has hit last season.

```
...
// field to hold the results
List<ProbabilityResults> results;

public MainPage()
{
  InitializeComponent();
}

private void LayoutRoot_Loaded(object sender, RoutedEventArgs e)
{
  // calculate the probability on load
  calculateProbability();
}

private void Calculate_Click(object sender, RoutedEventArgs e)
{
  // calculate the probability on button click
  calculateProbability();
}
```

```
private void calculateProbability()
{
  // retrieve the number of hits from the text box
  int numberOfHits =
    Convert.ToInt32(this.NumberOfHits == null ? "200" : this.NumberOfHits.Text);
  // calculate the mean for the Poisson distribution
  // season hits / season games
  double mean = Convert.ToDouble(numberOfHits) / Convert.ToDouble(162);

  // build a list of probability event out comes
  // note the Poisson calculation used
  this.results =
      new List<ProbabilityResults>{
      new ProbabilityResults{ NumberOfEvents = 0,
        ProbabilityOfSuccess = CalculatePoissonProbability(mean, 0)},
      new ProbabilityResults{ NumberOfEvents = 1,
        ProbabilityOfSuccess = CalculatePoissonProbability(mean, 1)},
      new ProbabilityResults{ NumberOfEvents = 2,
        ProbabilityOfSuccess = CalculatePoissonProbability(mean, 2)},
      new ProbabilityResults{ NumberOfEvents = 3,
        ProbabilityOfSuccess = CalculatePoissonProbability(mean, 3)},
      new ProbabilityResults{ NumberOfEvents = 4,
        ProbabilityOfSuccess = CalculatePoissonProbability(mean, 4)},
      new ProbabilityResults{ NumberOfEvents = 5,
        ProbabilityOfSuccess = CalculatePoissonProbability(mean, 5)},
      new ProbabilityResults{ NumberOfEvents = 6,
        ProbabilityOfSuccess = CalculatePoissonProbability(mean, 6)}
    };

  // set the list as a data context
  this.DataContext = this.results;
}
```

13. It's time to build our application and see if it works. If you added everything successfully, you should see a Silverlight page that looks similar to Figure 9-13.

   - Try putting in a new value for the amount of hits and click the Calculate button.

   - Note that as you put in larger amounts, the probability of the batter getting a hit or multiple hits goes up.

   - Using our model, if a batter is averaging 200 hits per season, the mean is 200 / 162 = 1.2345. Using the Poisson distribution, the batter has a probability of 29 percent of having no hits in a game, 35.9 percent of having a single hit, and so on.

Figure 9-13. *The functional predictive analytics model UI so far*

We have completed a basic predictive analytics model that can predict a future event (having a certain amount of hits in a game). However, note that the Probability of Success column is not formatted correctly. In order to do this, we need to add a value converter. If you want to skip the next steps until Part 2 of this coding scenario, please do so.

14. Add a new class called `PercentageValueConverter`.

15. In this class, we will implement a simple conversion from a double to a string formatted as a percentage. The value converter should include the code shown in Listing 9-10.

■ **Note** Don't forget the `using` statement for the value converter.

Listing 9-10. *PercentageValueConverter class that converts the input value into a percentage*

```
...
using System.Windows.Shapes;
using System.Windows.Data;

namespace Chapter9_ImplementingPredictiveAnalytics
{
  public class PercentageValueConverter : IValueConverter
  {
    public object Convert(object value, Type targetType, object parameter,↵
System.Globalization.CultureInfo culture)
    {
      // format the double as a percentage with two decimal points
      return String.Format("{0:P2}", value);
    }
```

```
    public object ConvertBack(object value, Type targetType, object parameter,↵
System.Globalization.CultureInfo culture)
    {
        throw new NotImplementedException();
    }
  } // end of PercentageValueConverter class
} // end of namespace
```

16. It is time to implement the value converter as a resource in our user control. This is shown in Listing 9-11.

Listing 9-11. Implementing the value converter in the MainPage.xaml file (adding the resource is shown in bold). Remember that you will need to add the Chapter9_ImplmentingPredictiveAnalytics namespace as well.

```
x:Class="Chapter9_ImplementingPredictiveAnalytics.MainPage"
xmlns="http://schemas.microsoft.com/winfx/2006/xaml/presentation"
….
mc:Ignorable="d" Width="640" Height="480">
<UserControl.Resources>
  <local:PercentageValueConverter x:Key="PercentageValueConverter" />
</UserControl.Resources>
…
```

17. After the resource has been added, we can use the value converter in the binding definition for the Probability of Success column, as highlighted in bold in Listing 9-12.

Listing 9-12. Implementing the value converter in the DataGrid

```
<data:DataGrid.Columns>
  <data:DataGridTextColumn Header="Number Of Hits" IsReadOnly="True" Binding=↵
"{Binding NumberOfEvents, Mode=OneWay}"/>
  <data:DataGridTextColumn Header="Probability of Success" IsReadOnly="True"
  Binding="{Binding ProbabilityOfSuccess, Converter={StaticResource↵
PercentageValueConverter}, Mode=OneWay}"/>
</data:DataGrid.Columns>
```

18. After adding the code successfully, the Probability of Success column should be formatted as a percentage properly. This is shown in Figure 9-14.

What is the probability of a batter having hit the next game?

Hits during a 162 game season: 200   [Calculate]

Number Of Hits	Probability of Success
0	29.10 %
1	35.92 %
2	22.17 %
3	9.12 %
4	2.82 %
5	0.70 %
6	0.14 %

Figure 9-14. The data grid displaying the predictive model results with properly formatted columns

Part 2: Creating an Interactive and Visual Predictive Model

Up until this point, we have succeeded in creating a good implementation of a simple predictive model. This works pretty well. The user can input a value and click the Calculate button, and the UI will update. However, if you have been alert in paying close attention to BI 2.0 principles, you will note that this model is lacking a couple of best practice implementation guidelines:

- Input of the data is tedious and requires multiple steps: text input and clicking a button. Testing multiple values would require too many keyboard and mouse interactions.

- The noninteractive nature of the UI does not lend itself to highlighting changes and differences in results easily. Insight is not delivered as quickly as it could be.

- The nonvisual nature of the UI makes it hard to gauge the distribution and trending of the data.

- The UI would not be a great choice for a next-generation touch application (e.g., Windows Mobile 7, a multitouch tablet, etc.). Users of this type of application would be frustrated with our implementation.

- There is no validation check on the data input. For example, a user could input negative values. Furthermore, non-realistic values are also allowed. For example, no player is going to have 500 hits in a 162-game season.

In this section, we are going to make a couple of slight improvements to the UI to make the experience better. After all, this is a book about next-generation BI software, so we should deliver our analytical tools in the same manner.

1. Our first improvement is going to be replacing the Calculate button trigger with a slider that will interact with the calculations. As the slider changes, it will automatically change the number of hits per season (changing the mean and recalculating the Poisson results). The code changes are highlighted in bold in Listing 9-13.

- Add a slider into your StackPanel. Bind the value of the slider using element binding to the text box. As the slider changes values, it will update the text box.

- Set the visibility of the button to Collapsed, as we are not going to be using it anymore.

Listing 9-13. Add a slider to drive the calculations of our model.

```
...
<dataInput:Label x:Name="Title" HorizontalAlignment="Center" FontSize="18.667" Content=
"What is the probability of a batter having hit the next game?"/>
<StackPanel Orientation="Horizontal" HorizontalAlignment="Center">
  <dataInput:Label Content="Hits during a 162 game season:"/>
  <Slider x:Name="SliderNumberOfHits" Cursor="Hand" Width="150" Maximum="350"
SmallChange="1" Value="200" />
  <TextBox Text="{Binding Value, ElementName=SliderNumberOfHits}"
      TextWrapping="Wrap" Width="50" Margin="10,0,0,0" x:Name="NumberOfHits"/>
  <Button x:Name="Calculate" Width="75" Content="Calculate" Margin="5,0,0,0" Cursor=
"Hand" Click="Calculate_Click" Visibility="Collapsed"/>
</StackPanel>
...
```

2. Add an event handler for the ValueChanged event for the slider shown in Listing 9-14.

Listing 9-14. Add the ValueChanged event handler.

```
...
  <Slider x:Name="SliderNumberOfHits" ValueChanged="SliderNumberOfHits_ValueChanged"
    Cursor="Hand" Width="150" Maximum="350" SmallChange="1" Value="200" />
...
```

3. In the added event handler (in the MainPage code file), add a process that will calculate the Poisson distribution each time the value is changed. This is shown in Listing 9-15.

Listing 9-15. Handling the ValueChanged slider event. This will update the calculations each time the slider value changes.

```
...
private void SliderNumberOfHits_ValueChanged(object sender,
 RoutedPropertyChangedEventArgs<double> e)
{
  this.calculateProbability();
}
...
```

4. Before we run the application, we will need to add a converter that will round the value of the slider to the bound text box. If we don't do this, the values from the slider will be decimal numbers. Create a new class called IntegerValueConverter, as shown in Listing 9-16.

Listing 9-16. Value converter that will convert the slider position to an integer value

```
...
using System.Windows.Shapes;
using System.Windows.Data;

namespace Chapter9_ImplementingPredictiveAnalytics
{
  public class IntegerValueConverter : IValueConverter
  {
    public object Convert(object value, Type targetType, object parameter, ↵
  System.Globalization.CultureInfo culture)
    {
      return System.Convert.ToInt32(value);
    }

    public object ConvertBack(object value, Type targetType, object parameter, ↵
  System.Globalization.CultureInfo culture)
    {
      throw new NotImplementedException();
    }
  } // end of class
} // end of namespace
```

5. In the MainPage XAML file, add the value converter to UserControl.Resources (shown in Listing 9-17).

Listing 9-17. Add the value converter to the XAML page. We do not have to add the local namespace, since that was added in prior to the MainPage.xaml (Listing 9-11).

```
...
<UserControl.Resources>
  <local:PercentageValueConverter x:Key="PercentageValueConverter" />
  <local:IntegerValueConverter x:Key="IntegerValueConverter" />
</UserControl.Resources>
...
```

6. Change the element binding of the slider and text box controls to include the value converter. This is illustrated in Listing 9-18.

Listing 9-18. Implementing the value converter in the text box

```
...
<TextBox Text="{Binding Value, Converter={StaticResource IntegerValueConverter}, ↵
 ElementName=SliderNumberOfHits}"
     TextWrapping="Wrap" Width="50" Margin="10,0,0,0" x:Name="NumberOfHits"/>
...
```

7. Now it is time to run the application and try our new interactive predictive model. It should look like Figure 9-15. Note how easy it is to get real-time insight from the model and quickly determine the probability values. The user can set the NumberOfHits variable with a fluid interaction and quickly match it up to the desired value.

What is the probability of a batter having hit the next game?

Number Of Hits	Probability of Success
0	20.72 %
1	32.61 %
2	25.67 %
3	13.47 %
4	5.30 %
5	1.67 %
6	0.44 %

Hits during a 162 game season: 258

Figure 9-15. Interactive predictive model delivers real-time insight

8. Hopefully you have learned by now that data visualizations provide additional wisdom that cannot be gathered from grids and lists. As you have learned in the data visualization chapter, trending and distribution of the data is hard to see using a grid. This is especially true when we have a rapidly changing set of data.

9. In order to achieve a graphic, we are going to use a column series chart from the Silverlight Control Toolkit. In order to start the process, add a reference to the System.Windows.Controls.DataVisualization.Toolkit assembly. Next, in the MainPage.xaml file, add the code shown in Listing 9-19.

Listing 9-19. Import the Control Toolkit into the XAML file.

```
...
xmlns:dataInput="clr-namespace:System.Windows.Controls;assembly=
System.Windows.Controls.Data.Input"
xmlns:toolkit="http://schemas.microsoft.com/winfx/2006/xaml/presentation/toolkit"
Width="640" Height="480">...
```

10. It is time to add the column chart to the project. Simply enter the code below the grid in the XAML file shown in Listing 9-20. The code includes additional formatting to show the y-axis as a percentage.

Listing 9-20. Add a charting visualization to our predictive model (code changes are highlighted in bold).

```
...
    </data:DataGrid.Columns>
  </data:DataGrid>
```

```
    <toolkit:Chart x:Name="ChartResults" Title="" Width="425" Height="175">
      <toolkit:ColumnSeries DependentValuePath="ProbabilityOfSuccess"↵
IndependentValuePath="NumberOfEvents"
        ItemsSource="{Binding}" TransitionDuration="00:00:00">
        <toolkit:ColumnSeries.DependentRangeAxis >
          <toolkit:LinearAxis Minimum="0" Maximum="1" Interval="0.3" Orientation="Y">
            <toolkit:LinearAxis.AxisLabelStyle>
              <Style TargetType="toolkit:AxisLabel">
                <Setter Property="StringFormat" Value="{}{0:p0}"/>
              </Style>
            </toolkit:LinearAxis.AxisLabelStyle>
          </toolkit:LinearAxis>
        </toolkit:ColumnSeries.DependentRangeAxis>
      </toolkit:ColumnSeries>
    </toolkit:Chart>
  </StackPanel>
</UserControl>
...
```

11. That is all we need to get the chart fully functioning with our model because we set the DataContext earlier in the code-behind. Build the application, and it will look like Figure 9-16.

Figure 9-16. The model now includes both a grid and visual representation of the calculation results.

12. Use the slider and move it around. Look how quickly you can get the answer you are looking for. Furthermore, the bar chart data visualization provides additional insight into trends and distribution, as the calculations are being processed in real time.

One thing you will probably note is that the column chart can be given a cleaner look. Furthermore, by default Silverlight charts have an animation that delays the rendering slightly. While animations look nice, such features should be removed in this example to deliver insight without any unnecessary delays. You should never sacrifice analytical value for a fancy presentation.

If you download the source code on the accompanying web site (www.silverlightbusinessintelligence.com), you will see the much cleaner-looking visualization shown in Figure 9-17. The style for the chart is simply too big to copy and paste and would actually take up over three pages. The rendering animations were removed as well.

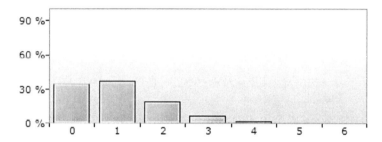

Figure 9-17. Column chart styled more professionally for the predictive model

Lessons Learned

In this coding scenario, you learned how to create a simple predictive analytical model in Silverlight. This model took a single variable, and we were able to run that variable through a statistical algorithm to predict potential future events. Next, we applied BI 2.0 concepts that improved the model by adding interactivity and visualization to provide a secondary insight stream in the model.

I hope you can see why Silverlight is a great environment to implement predictive models. The combination of interactivity, visualizations, and processing power can create pretty interesting forward-looking models that can compete with the best statistical environments on the market.

Possible Improvements

This model is a great baseline for enhancements and is surprisingly accurate. Try taking the model and comparing it to real-world statistics. Pick a player and look at their game log data. You will notice that the percentage predicted off of the mean is pretty close to what our model results predict. This model is not just attributed to hits. It could be used for home runs, at bats, strikeouts, and so on.

One of the misconceptions about predictive modeling is that it needs to include multiple variables to be accurate. That is not true. Using a funneling technique, we can improve our model to include "weighted portions" of other variables. For example, a batter's mean is 1.2345 hits per game. However, let's assume that the batter performs 10 percent less on hot days and he playing in a ballpark where his numbers are down significantly. Do we create additional models and combine them somehow in a more complex model? That is one approach. However, we could take the baseline mean (1.2345 hits/game) and adjust this 15 percent down to come up with a new mean of about 1.05 and use that as the mean that will drive the probability of the model. Remember, predictive analytics has some educated guessing and art to it. It is not all science, and you simply cannot take into account every single possible variable. The technique of funneling into single variables is popular for slightly improving the accuracy of the forecasting models by estimating the impact other variables have in terms of a net percentage on the main model (see Figure 9-18).

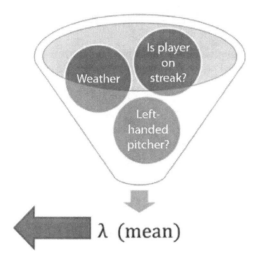

Figure 9-18. *Using the funnel approach in our predictive model, we adjust the percentage of the core variable accordingly.*

Summary

In this chapter, you learned about looking forward with data using predictive analytics. Creating applications that just look at the past show only part of the story in BI 2.0 modules. Therefore, the predictive analytics concepts covered in this chapter are important to understand in creating complete BI 2.0 solutions.

Silverlight is a great technology for creating rich predictive analytical models. These models can combine visual elements and interactive components to create tools that deliver insight more quickly to the user. Crafting forecasting tools in modular analytical tools is a great way to enhance existing BI applications. It adds another dimension and value to your existing data. Since most forward-looking models use aggregated data, this makes Silverlight a great technology to implement predictive models all locally on the client workstation.

In summary, predictive analytical models allow information to be understood in different dimensions that historical data sets simply don't provide. This can empower users to understand the data and predict future events with clarity. Therefore, having an organization or software offering that simplifies forward-looking decisions with predictive analytics is a very valuable asset.

CHAPTER 10

∎ ∎ ∎

Improving Performance with Concurrent Programming

In this chapter, you will learn how to get the most performance from Silverlight BI deployments by using concurrent programming techniques. This will allow you to deliver visual intelligence, predictive analytics, and other BI 2.0 topics with real-time performance on the end user's workstation.

This chapter will introduce the importance of using multiple threads on current processor architectures. After an overview of basic concurrency and multithreading concepts, I will cover what type of threading support is included in the Silverlight framework. Using secondary threads can help your applications remain responsive while they retrieve data, render complex graphics, and execute computational algorithms. I will cover several common asynchronous coding patterns that can be applied to business algorithms.

BI applications with complex algorithms and large data sets can be demanding of local client resources. The two coding scenarios in this chapter will help you understand the value that multithreading implementation can bring to composite BI applications.

The following coding scenarios are included in this chapter:

- Improving UI responsiveness with multiple threads

- Improving business algorithms with multithreading concepts

The following table outlines the specific goals that different types of readers will achieve by reading this chapter.

Audience	Goals
Silverlight developers	Grasp the fundamentals of multithreading benefits for RIA technology.
	Recognize the parallel programming features and limitations in Silverlight 4.
Business intelligence professionals	Understand the importance of multithreading for current-generation processors.
	Recognize how BI algorithms and data sets can benefit from concurrent programming.

Audience	Goals
Strategic decision makers	Understand how adding multithreading applications can make your product offerings function better than the competition.
	See if your applications can add more features or scale to bigger clients with the additional performance benefits of concurrent programming.

Concurrent Programming Defined

Concurrent programming is a paradigm for designing applications with the goal of achieving simultaneous execution across several processors. Breaking up algorithms and scheduling them across multiple processors can lead to improved performance and dramatically increased application scalability.

Several years ago, writing code that could execute operations in parallel was considered a black art. Writing applications that could execute algorithms concurrently was considered difficult and was truly mastered by only a limited amount of developers properly. Back then, local client workstations consisted of single-core CPU architectures. Additional threads would be executed sequentially on the same CPU; client workstations did not have the proper hardware to benefit from parallel coding techniques. As a result, concurrent programming techniques were limited to servers that ran large back-end processes and services. The challenges and serviceability of designing applications that could execute code in parallel limited this design's effectiveness. Many developers who were unfamiliar with concurrent programming techniques simply did not want to venture down that path.

The evolution of higher-level languages and the trend of modern day workstations to include multiple cores have changed the demand for concurrent programming. Newer languages that are based on declarative and functional styles lend themselves to concurrent programming much more easily than before. Mistakes that were hard to debug and avoid are now less of a problem. Furthermore, as modern user devices (e.g., laptops, workstations, and mobile phones) evolve to include multiple cores in their processor architectures, applications need to include parallel instructions in order to maximize application efficiency. These two trends have aided in the popularity of applying concurrent algorithms from the start.

Processor Architecture Shift to Multiple Cores

Decades ago, computer systems were designed to perform explicit tasks following a sequential path. Programmers would write applications in the form of a series of instructions and then the computer would process them in order. This model existed for a long time. However, as operating systems introduced improved graphics and multitasking, the hardware was expected to keep pace. Computers were challenged with performing more and more tasks on single processing units. This meant that multiple tasks had to be sequenced and scheduled to give the illusion that the CPU was handling multiple things at once. Figure 10-1 shows a graphic of multiple tasks being sequenced into a series of processing instructions on a single-core processor.

Figure 10-1. *A high-level overview showing multiple processing tasks being queued for sequential processing on a processing unit with a single CPU*

Computer processors had to allocate resources to constantly manage the selection of tasks that needed processing. Up until several years ago, it was thought that making the processing units faster would solve these problems. That worked fairly well for a long time. As the CPUs got faster, they could queue and execute algorithms more quickly. However, the core problem remained: CPUs were spending time managing resources. Furthermore, single-core CPUs suffer from other bottlenecks like limited access to primary cache and I/O bus speeds. It was becoming apparent that simply making the CPUs faster to process everything synchronously was not going to be enough. In addition, it was becoming harder for microprocessor manufacturers to continue raising processor frequencies while trying to limit the generated heat.

Processor manufacturers came up with the strategy of offering multiple CPU or multicore CPU architectures that allowed for the parallel execution of tasks. Now, multiple tasks could be queued up among multiple CPUs, as shown in Figure 10-2.

■ **Note** An individual CPU consists of at least one processing unit called a *logical core*. A multicore computer can either have multiple CPUs—each with one core—or a single CPU that consists of multiple cores. You have probably heard the terminology *dual-core* or *quad-core processor*. Different multiprocessor architectures implement this in different ways. For example, you can have a quad-core workstation that has two physical CPU sockets with two cores each, or you can have a single physical CPU socket with four cores. A multicore workstation can have any of these implementations, and the specifics are immaterial for this chapter.

Figure 10-2. A high-level overview showing multiple processing tasks being queued for sequential processing on a processing unit with multiple CPUs

Note that each CPU still needs to process the tasks individually and sequentially. The difference with multicore or multi-CPU architectures is that there are multiple CPUs instead of one. Just as there is overhead for a single-core CPU to queue up tasks, there is additional overhead for multiple CPUs when negotiating how to break up the algorithms among themselves. Furthermore, multicore architectures are still limited by some bottlenecks and, in some cases, have to share primary memory. This is the main reason why the benefit of adding CPUs does not net linear increases in performance. For example, adding a second CPU might net close to double in performance improvement. However, adding a seventh or eighth CPU will not result in performance that is equivalent to a factor of eight over a single-core CPU. It is also important to understand that multithreading is not just about hardware solutions. The OS and the software that is executing the tasks both have to be designed to support multiple threads effectively. For example, the expensive processes you wrote in Chapter 3 can't magically scale themselves to different CPUs. How does the software know how to split up the process across several CPUs and bring it back together to derive the correct solution? The answer is that software needs to be architected properly in order to take advantage of multiple cores.

If you have bought a desktop or laptop in the last couple of years, chances are that you have a computer that includes two or more cores. Even current-generation mobile devices are starting to include multiple-core architectures. The shift to adding more and more cores is only going to pick up steam. The plan by processor manufacturers is to add more and more processing cores to improve performance and meet the challenges of software and OSs that have to handle an increasing amount of tasks.

■ **Note** I wanted to include a basic introductory brief on hardware multiprocessing for those of you who may not be familiar with the current multiprocessing trends. A vast amount of detail was left out, so the preceding section should not be thought of as a definitive guide to multiprocessing architecture.

Developers of GPUs have followed the shift to parallel processing architectures as well. For example, NVIDIA has released the CUDA (Compute Unified Device Architecture) that allows parallel processing on GPUs. This allows software applications to be crafted by offloading common tasks to the GPU. GPUs are not just for gaming or creating visual effects. Very complex and memory intensive mathematical computations can be performed by a GPU very effectively. This is especially true for mid- to high-end graphics cards that have fast (DDR3 or better) and large amounts of memory (1 GB).

■ **Note** The NVIDIA CUDA SDK is a C++ API. However, on Windows machines it does expose COM interfaces. This allows Silverlight 4 to interact with the CUDA SDK to parallelize tasks to the GPU.

Taking Advantage of Multicore Architectures

Computing hardware that includes multicore architecture is only part of what you need in order to engineer software that can scale across all execution cores. Operating systems running on multiple cores can do a good job of scaling out multiple tasks across the available hardware. For example, if there are two critical applications running simultaneously, they can target separate CPU cores individually. However, good multicore scalability is not automatically achieved for individual applications.

An application is a set of instructions that runs in a process in an OS. If you use Microsoft Windows, you can see a complete list of processes in Windows Task Manager. Individual processes consist of at least one main execution thread and possibly more. The individual threads on each process are the units of work that can be scheduled on a processor core. These threads are responsible for executing the assigned pieces of code.

Figure 10-3 highlights two processes that have a different thread makeup. Process One was started with a single thread, and the OS can schedule that single thread on any individual CPU core. Conversely, Process One is made up of two threads (one main and one secondary). Since Process Two consists of two threads, there are two pieces of individual work that can be scheduled by the OS.

Process one in Figure 10-3 cannot scale beyond a single processor core because the OS can only allocate processor time based on individual threads. Therefore, if a process consists of a single thread, it will execute its algorithms on a single core. However, if a process consists of multiple threads, a possibility exists that the OS can schedule the threads on different processor cores, potentially improving performance.

■ **Note** It is very important to understand that creating programs (processes) that include multiple threads does not automatically guarantee that these threads will scale across multiple cores. A particular piece of client hardware may not include multiple cores. The OS scheduler may decide not to use multiple cores or the processor affinity of a particular process may be limited to a single core. Therefore, do not assume creating multiple threads in an application translates into multicore scalability.

Figure 10-3. Processes (computer programs) that consist of multiple threads (Process Two) allow the OS to potentially schedule these individual units of work across processor cores.

Developers can take advantage of multicore architectures by creating processes that consist of multiple threads. Almost all current programming languages and developer frameworks allow for the creation and management of processes that consist of more than a single thread. The patterns used by developers to create applications that consist of multiple threads and concurrency techniques are called *multithreading*. Developer frameworks usually include APIs that allows developers to manage threads explicitly. However, each development framework can include different implementations of how threading is handled and the options that are available to a developer.

Multithreading vs. Parallelism

The previous section covered some essential information about multithreading and concurrency programming basics. Another term that is used in concurrent programming is *parallelism*. You might equate this term with multithreading. In my opinion, it is wrong to exchange "parallelism" with "multithreading" and vice versa. These concurrent programming concepts are different in the way the code is designed and executed on computing hardware.

Multithreading

When we speak about multithreading, developers usually understand concurrency concepts like using the ThreadPool, calling a service asynchronously, and keeping the UI responsive while some background work is being done. However, what happens to that secondary thread and where does it get executed? Does that secondary thread execute on another processor core? If the server has eight cores, how many are used to execute the process? These are the questions that parallelism provides interfaces for and gives the developer explicit control over.

Take a look at Listing 10-1. In this small piece of C# code, a secondary thread is created and executes a method concurrently. In the multithreading paradigm, a developer only has control over the imperative threading logic. In the code in Listing 10-1, the developer only knows that they created a secondary thread in the application process. The developer cannot be sure how that piece of code is executed or scheduled by the OS. Furthermore, differences in hardware where the program executes could lead to completely different behaviors in how the threads are managed by the OS. In fact, multithreaded code executed two different times on the same exact machine could produce different execution schedules on processing cores. Therefore, multithreaded code execution is largely left to the programming framework, OS, and hardware on which it is executing.

Listing 10-1. A second thread is started in a program that does not have explicit control over how the thread is managed. (Note that this code will work in Silverlight.)

```
private void LayoutRoot_Loaded(object sender, RoutedEventArgs e)
{
  // create a second thread
  Thread secondThread = new Thread(this.DoWorkOnSecondThread);
  // start the thread
  secondThread.Start();
}

public void DoWorkOnSecondThread()
{
  // Mimic doing real expensive work
  Thread.Sleep(200);
}
```

Parallelism

Parallelism extends the programming concurrency model beyond thread management. True parallelism is a fine-grained control over how multiple threads interact in solving algorithms concurrently on hardware that supports simultaneous processing. The first key difference in parallelism compared to multithreading is that parallelism techniques are used in environments that support true simultaneous execution. As stated before, the developer cannot be sure the secondary thread will be scheduled on another processor core using multithreading techniques. If the hardware environment does not include multiple cores, the code can still use multiple threads; however, the performance gain will be negligible, if not adverse. Parallelism techniques can analyze the environment and will not create additional concurrency execution if they will not help the execution of the algorithms. For example, there are Windows APIs that allow developers to explicitly set processor affinity masks on both physical and logical processors. This is analogous to setting the affinity mask manually on a process in Windows Task Manager, as shown in Figure 10-4.

■ **Note** If you are interested in how to set the processor affinity mask using Microsoft Windows APIs, go to http://msdn.microsoft.com/en-us/library/ms686223%28VS.85%29.aspx.

Figure 10-4. The Processor Affinity mask in Windows Task Manager showing a process that will use all four logical CPUs if necessary.

Having explicit control over how threads are managed in a hardware environment is a very important tuning option for enterprise-level applications. A software deployment is not a one-size-fits-all solution in today's age of multicore and virtualized servers. Microsoft SQL Server is an enterprise-level database server that is a great example of a business server product that allows a variety of options to tune execution on the different processors. Figure 10-5 displays a screenshot of the processor settings available in SQL Server. An administrator can set options for processor affinity, I/O affinity, maximum worker threads, thread priority boosting, and so on.

Figure 10-5. Various processor threading options available in SQL Server 2005

Parallelism techniques are usually declarative in nature. This allows the developers to "design" concurrency techniques in their system and provides them with explicit control over a variety of threading attributes. For example, a developer can ask a parallel framework to execute an algorithm on four cores, explicitly set processor affinity, or set a higher priority on the threads. Listing 10-2 shows how a simple LINQ query can be executed in a concurrent way by simply appending the AsParallel() extension method at the end of a LINQ query in .NET 4.0. Furthermore, using WithDegreeOfParallelism, a developer can declare how many concurrent tasks to use in order to execute the query.

■ **Note** *PLINQ* is an acronym for *Parallel Language Integrated Query*. It is essentially the LINQ language introduced in .NET 3.5 plus additional extension methods that allow for parallel execution of queries. PLINQ is officially supported in .NET 4.0 with the Visual Studio 2010 release.

Listing 10-2. PLINQ in .NET 4.0 allows for declarative control over threads (new parallelism options of PLINQ are highlighted in bold)

```
var parallelQuery = from u in data.Users.AsParallel().WithDegreeOfParallelism(4)
        where u.IsActive == true
        orderby u.LastName
        select u;
```

Listing 10-2 displays a form of fine-grained control that parallelism frameworks can provide. In the code listing, the program will attempt to scale the algorithms across four thread tasks (which could translate to four threads scheduled onto four logical or physical processor cores). Note that the code doesn't have to start three additional threads or manage the thread synchronization. The code simply declaratively asks to be executed using four separate tasks and leaves the complex threading management to the library. This is the key difference between imperative and declarative thread management. Back in Listing 10-1, the code creates a secondary thread and has to manage it from beginning to end. The code in Listing 10-1 was simple. However, if there were a requirement to show a message box on the UI thread after the thread completed, the code would get more complex. Dispatching is needed to guarantee that the thread would not step on objects that were previously rendered with the UI thread (shown in Listing 10-3).

Why go through the hassle of managing all of the aspects of threading yourself? As you can see, certain parallelism extensions like PLINQ in .NET 4.0 abstract the "concurrency plumbing" code away from the developer, allowing the developer to focus on the business logic. Listing 10-2, shown previously, is a perfect example of simply telling the framework what type of parallelism the task requires and nothing more.

Listing 10-3. The highlighted code shows how imperative multithreading code can get complex very quickly.

```
private void LayoutRoot_Loaded(object sender, RoutedEventArgs e)
{
  // create a second thread
  Thread secondThread = new Thread(this.DoWorkOnSecondThread);
  // start the thread
```

```
  secondThread.Start();
}

public void DoWorkOnSecondThread()
{
  // Mimic doing real expensive work
  Thread.Sleep(200);

  // Dispatch the message box to the thread to the UI
  Dispatcher.BeginInvoke(() =>
    MessageBox.Show("I am back on the main UI thread.")
);

}
```

Parallelism-based programming techniques are extremely beneficial when the hardware environment is static. This may not hold true for many PC workstations because they can include various hardware components. However, on hardware such as game consoles or mobile devices, the hardware is largely not upgradable and thus remains static. For example, a developer can optimize and tailor algorithms manually for an application knowing that they will have four processing cores available. If a software engineer knows exactly how the code will perform on every single device (because the hardware environment is identical), he can provide dramatic increases in performance using explicit parallelism techniques.

In summary, the main differences between multithreading and parallelism programming paradigms are:

- In multithreading scenarios, the developer is doing exactly what the name implies: managing multiple threads with the hope that it will improve algorithm performance or the user experience.

- In the multithreading paradigm, the developer has only explicit control over managing threads. The environment is tasked with scheduling the threads across the available processor cores.

- In the parallelism paradigm, the developer can have explicit control over both thread tasks and how these threads are managed on the available processor cores.

- Parallelism programming is usually performed declaratively, not imperatively. This abstracts the creation of complex locking, synchronization, and management of threads.

- Parallelism framework APIs allow the developer to control threading concepts such as thread management, setting processor affinity (which cores are used in the available environment), setting the thread priority, enforcing concurrency, and so on.

- Parallelism frameworks can dynamically create concurrent code based on the environment. Therefore, code should only be optimized for concurrency if the hardware supports it.

.NET 4.0 PARALLEL LIBRARIES

.NET 4.0 and Visual Studio 2010 include several new features that simplify the designing of software that takes advantage of multiple cores. These APIs and tools give software engineers fine-grained control over advanced concurrency concepts.

The .NET 4.0 Framework includes new parallelism libraries. The main managed libraries for parallelism are called *parallel extensions for .NET*. These extensions include parallel LINQ (PLINQ), Task Parallel Library (TPL), and Coordination Data Structures (CDS). The addition of these managed extensions allows for the parallelizing of data queries and invoking methods using concurrency concepts. The most exciting addition is probably PLINQ, which offers a declarative way of creating parallel data queries. Making existing LINQ queries into parallel LINQ queries can be as simply appending an extension method.

Visual Studio 2010 includes tooling improvements in order to facilitate the new parallelism additions to the .NET 4.0 Framework. Visual Studio 2010 also allows developers to debug parallel tasks and parallel stacks. Furthermore, Visual Studio 2010 provides the necessary tools to profile how the parallelized algorithms are executing in the environment.

Microsoft is taking the hardware shift to multicore processors very seriously. It is providing developers additional libraries and tools that make creating advanced parallelism scenarios easier. For more information on the .NET 4.0 parallel libraries, go to `http://msdn.microsoft.com/en-us/concurrency/default.aspx`.

Silverlight Concurrent Programming Features

The previous sections covered concurrent programming on a very high level—the topic is much too broad and complex to cover in a single chapter. Since this book's main technology is Silverlight, this section will cover the concurrency programming options available in this technology.

Multithreading Support

Silverlight applications run under the STA (single-threaded apartment) application model. This means that one single thread is responsible for creating and running the entire application. This is the default behavior in Silverlight. If an application adds business logic to Silverlight, a single thread will be responsible for managing the entire application. In order to take advantage of multiple cores and concurrent execution, a developer needs to use the Silverlight multithreading objects.

■ **Note** The opposite of the STA model is the MTA (multithreaded apartment) model. It is sometimes referred to as the loose threading of free-threaded models. If you have coded Windows Forms applications, you may have noticed the STAThread attribute located above the main entry point of a Windows application. This initializes the application with a single thread, and external communication is done on this main thread. This is very similar to the default application behavior in Silverlight.

As mentioned, Silverlight is based on a subset of the .NET framework. Therefore, it includes some of the APIs and objects that can facilitate concurrent programming that are available in the full .NET Framework. Silverlight is cross-browser and cross-OS plug-in. Therefore, some of the concurrency programming options have been streamlined in order to work smoothly across these environments.

Silverlight has solid support for multithreading techniques. However, as of Silverlight version 4, it does not include a rich parallelism framework. Therefore, the multicore programming (concurrent programming) support that Silverlight includes can be best described as multithreading rather than parallelism. My hope in the near future is for Microsoft to include some of the parallel extensions in Silverlight so that we as developers can design multicore applications rather than just write expensive plumbing code. The following subsections cover the main multithreading features of Silverlight 4.

■ **Note** The following sections assume some previous knowledge of .NET multithreading features. You should only use these multithreading objects if you understand the full implications of concurrent programming. If you aren't familiar with some of the topics, please consider consulting other resources outside of this book. Multithreading is a programming concept that should not be approached without a deep understanding of the developer environment, programming framework, and implications of intermittent issues.

Silverlight Multithreading Essentials

Silverlight's main multithreading support is located in the System.Threading namespace. This namespace includes basic thread management, timers, wait handles, callback pattern classes, the ThreadPool, and synchronization management. Figure 10-6 shows a comparison between the System.Threading namespace in Silverlight and the one available in a Windows Forms application. While Silverlight includes a nice multithreading API, it is not as robust as the full .NET Framework. Using the various constructs in this namespace, a Silverlight developer has the essential tools for creating multithreaded algorithms.

Silverlight

Windows Forms

Figure 10-6. Silverlight 4 includes good support for multithreading; however, not all of the advanced multithreading features are available.

A Silverlight application launching with the STA model has certain implications in how the secondary threads interact with the main application thread. The STA model is also the default in Windows Forms applications. If you have created a Windows Forms application, you are probably aware of the golden rule of not allowing your secondary threads to manipulate UI objects (since they were created with the main application thread). This synchronization rule also applies to Silverlight development.

Listing 10-4 shows a simple example of a cross-thread exception. In the LayoutRoot_Loaded event, a secondary thread is started. The second thread calls the DoWorkOnSecondThread method. The problem with this code is that the program is still on the second thread and it tries to display a message box. This is an example of a secondary thread accessing an asset created with the main thread.

Listing 10-4. The code in bold will cause a cross-thread exception.

```
private void LayoutRoot_Loaded(object sender, RoutedEventArgs e)
{
  // create a second thread
  Thread secondThread = new Thread(this.DoWorkOnSecondThread);
  // start the thread
  secondThread.Start();
}
```

```
public void DoWorkOnSecondThread()
{
    // Mimic doing real expensive work
    Thread.Sleep(200);

    // this will cause a cross-thread exception
    // still on the secondary thread
    MessageBox.Show("This will cause a cross-thread exception!");
}
```

If you try to run the code in Listing 10-4, it will error out with a UnauthorizedAccess exception, as shown in Figure 10-7. The secondary thread that you started to run your DoWorkOnSecondThread method cannot manipulate the UI objects that belong to the UI thread.

Figure 10-7. Invalid cross-thread access will occur when a secondary thread tries to manipulate UI objects created with the main application thread.

Silverlight has a class called Dispatcher that includes methods to guarantee that the code executed within it will be run on the main application thread (you can remember this by thinking of dispatching the secondary thread to the main app thread). This allows developers to create asynchronous code that can report status to the UI or notify other objects on the main thread. For example, you need to show a message box on the main application thread, so you can "wrap" the message box code with the Dispatcher class in order to execute it on the application thread. Listing 10-5 highlights the necessary code to do this.

Listing 10-5. Wrapping code with the Dispatcher guarantees it will execute on the main application thread.

```
public void DoWorkOnSecondThread()
{
    // Mimic doing real expensive work
    Thread.Sleep(200);

    // Dispatch the message box to the thread to the UI
    Dispatcher.BeginInvoke(() =>
    MessageBox.Show("I am back on the main UI thread."));
}
```

The Dispatcher class is not the only way to marshal a secondary thread back to the main application thread. Silverlight offers the SynchronizationContext class which is also found in the System.Threading namespace. Those who are familiar with WPF multithreaded programming and have made the transition to Silverlight will be familiar with this class. Listing 10-6 shows how you can force the execution of a task on the main application thread.

Listing 10-6. Executing a piece of code on the main thread using the SynchronizationContext in Silverlight

```
...
SynchronizationContext syncContext = SynchronizationContext.Current;

private void LayoutRoot_Loaded(object sender, RoutedEventArgs e)
{
  // create a second thread
  Thread secondThread = new Thread(this.DoWorkOnSecondThread);
  // start the thread
  secondThread.Start();
}


public void DoWorkOnSecondThread()
{
  // Mimic doing real expensive work
  Thread.Sleep(200);

  this.syncContext.Post(param => MessageBox.Show("I am back on the main UI thread."), null);
}
```

Many professional developers feel that using the SynchronizationContext class is a best practice in marshaling threads, as it provides more options when dealing with advanced scenarios. Furthermore, note that the Dispatcher class is a UI object located in the System.Windows.Threading namespace in both Silverlight and WPF. Therefore, a developer creating libraries of objects that need synchronization will need to reference a heavy UI assembly (System.Windows) in order to provide thread marshaling. However, when comparing the Dispatcher and the SynchronizationContext for brevity, the Dispatcher object does its job in a single line of code. This is because the SynchronizationContext object needs to have its state cached from the main application thread in order to be used properly while inside the secondary thread. You should always try to use the SynchronizationContext class over the Dispatcher class whenever possible.

Using the BackgroundWorker Class

The BackgroundWorker class has been around in the full .NET Framework since version 2.0. This class abstracts some of the tedious behavior of managing threads and having to worry about thread synchronization to the main application thread. This class uses a simple event model in order to execute and report status to the application. Listing 10-7 illustrates how you can use the BackgroundWorker class to execute a process on a second thread and then display a message box. Note that this method is much more verbose than the previous multithreaded methods shown. You created the object scoped at the class level so the events could be created. Furthermore, two methods were created in order to facilitate the fired events. Although it is a few extra lines of code, this type of event programming model is familiar to most developers who have created event-driven UIs (e.g., wired up a click event on a button). Furthermore, you didn't have to worry about marshaling threads. The code is simply placed in the correct event handler, and the BackgroundWorker object does the rest for you.

Listing 10-7. The BackgroundWorker uses an event-based design to abstract certain complexities of multithreading from the developer.

```
// instantiate a background worker object
BackgroundWorker backgroundWorker = new BackgroundWorker();

private void LayoutRoot_Loaded(object sender, RoutedEventArgs e)
{
  // wire up the event that will be called on the secondary thread
  this.backgroundWorker.DoWork += new DoWorkEventHandler(backgroundWorker_DoWork);
  // wire up the event that will be called when the process is finished
  this.backgroundWorker.RunWorkerCompleted += new↵
RunWorkerCompletedEventHandler(backgroundWorker_RunWorkerCompleted);

  // execute the background worker
  this.backgroundWorker.RunWorkerAsync();
}

void backgroundWorker_RunWorkerCompleted(object sender, RunWorkerCompletedEventArgs e)
{
  // code here runs on the UI
  MessageBox.Show("I am back on the main UI thread.");
}

void backgroundWorker_DoWork(object sender, DoWorkEventArgs e)
{
  // code here runs on the secondary thread
  Thread.Sleep(200);
}
```

The BackgroundWorker is a very basic abstraction of multithreaded programming. Developers who are not familiar with multithreaded concepts should start with the BackgroundWorker first. While this object makes working with asynchronous processes easier, it is not recommended for heavy-duty use in production code because you are essentially limited to longer-running processes on one secondary thread. If you want to scale the code to additional threads, this requires creating additional BackgroundWorker objects which tends to be very verbose. Furthermore, poor use of event-driven objects is one of the biggest causes of memory leaks in Silverlight applications.

Asynchronous Workflows in F#

As mentioned in the earlier chapters, Silverlight 4 includes first class support for the F# programming language. F# is a functional programming language that includes some very interesting features that are exposed via the functional language paradigm. A functional language tries to guide the developer to write code using immutable conventions, which can lead to code that does not respond to side effects from secondary threads.

Asynchronous workflows allow you split up a series of tasks on secondary threads in a nice declarative way. For example, in a business intelligence scenario you may have a dashboard that requires the data to be aggregated four different ways. As a result, you have a workflow of four tasks that need to be processed. Using the asynchronous workflows feature, you can allocate these four tasks to be allocated on four separate cores. That is the essence of asynchronous workflows in F#. You could replicate this functionality in C# or VB.NET, but it would require writing plumbing code. F# compiles into the same IL as C# and VB.NET, so you can call assemblies written in F# via C#.

■ **Note** Asynchronous workflows in F# are an advanced feature that requires understanding of parallel programming and the F# functional language. These topics are well beyond the scope of this book. An example of F# asynchronous workflows in Silverlight can be found on my Silverlight blog: `http://silverlighthack.com/post/2009/11/04/Silverlight-3-and-FSharp-Support-in-Visual-Studio-2010.aspx`.

Using the Network Stack Asynchronously

All network communication in Silverlight is done asynchronously. Microsoft does not simply just recommend this pattern—a Silverlight developer must do this in order to retrieve data across the network. Whether you are calling a WCF REST service, downloading a file, or calling an RSS feed, all types of network communication has to be done asynchronously. All of the Silverlight networking APIs use the asynchronous callback pattern. A network request is made, and a second thread waits until a response is retrieved. When the response is retrieved, the callback method is called (see Listing 10-8).

■ **Warning** If you are an experienced web developer, you have probably created numerous Ajax data requests. These requests are done via JavaScript which Silverlight has access to via the HTML bridge. Therefore, you can probably deduce that you could create an instance of the `XmlHttpRequest` object and call it via the HTML bridge and attain synchronous requests. This pattern does work; however, it is emphatically not recommended. Essentially, it's a hack. First, you are breaking the asynchronous services rules that Microsoft has set. Making a network request this way will lock up the Silverlight UI. Furthermore, any cross-domain issues are now your problem since the networking policy files do not apply to this workaround. Lastly, using this can also break the cross-browser compatibility in your application. Ajax requests are done differently in Chrome, Safari, Firefox, and Internet Explorer. Using the non-Silverlight methods that Microsoft has verified is another reason why it is not a good idea to try to force synchronous services.

Listing 10-8. All networking communication in Silverlight is done asynchronously (try this code yourself in a Silverlight application).

```
private void LayoutRoot_Loaded(object sender, RoutedEventArgs e)
{
  // create a URI with the message resource
  Uri uri = new Uri("http://www.silverlighthack.com/message.txt");
  // Instantiate a web client object
```

```
  WebClient webClient = new WebClient();
  // Wire up the download string completed event
  webClient.DownloadStringCompleted += new⏎
 DownloadStringCompletedEventHandler(webClient_DownloadStringCompleted);
  webClient.DownloadStringAsync(uri);
}

void webClient_DownloadStringCompleted(object sender, DownloadStringCompletedEventArgs e)
{
  // retrieve the message results
  string message = e.Result;
}
```

This asynchronous network pattern is not limited to just the developer. Internally the Silverlight framework respects this pattern. All application assets and assemblies are brought down to the client using asynchronous patterns. Furthermore, when Silverlight is used to stream media elements, those bits are brought down on secondary threads as well. This improves the performance of launching and the overall experience of a Silverlight application.

Initially, many developers thought it was overkill that Microsoft forced developers to use asynchronous network patterns everywhere. Many developers prefer to have the choice how to implement network requests. While I agree having more choice is always good, in this case, Silverlight applications simply will always have to follow best practices. This prevents developers from releasing an application that is rushed or coded lazily. Consider the numerous applications for the iPhone. The iPhone SDK gives developers a choice to create synchronous or asynchronous network requests. I have an iPhone 3G and I get annoyed when my entire phone locks up because a developer is making an expensive network request in their loading screen. Even though Apple strongly recommends creating network requests asynchronously, some developers simply do not follow that pattern. No doubt if Microsoft gave developers a choice, the same would happen on the Silverlight platform. Some developers would release applications that locked the entire browser and this could give Silverlight a bad name in the RIA space.

Retrieving data asynchronously over the network is technically not really true multithreading. However, it is important to note that the multithreading concepts apply even when using the networking communication stack. The asynchronous callback pattern is similar to other multithreaded techniques. Furthermore, in order to guarantee that network callbacks are resolved on the main application, thread marshaling is required.

Concurrency and Rendering

The previous section covered some Silverlight multithreading examples that can be used for business algorithms and to improve the user experience. However, Silverlight 4 includes some additional concurrency improvements that involve other processing types.

Silverlight's rendering engine is fully optimized for multicore workstations. Silverlight 4 can utilize up to eight processor cores (physical or logical) at once to improve the rendering of the application. As a developer, you do not have access to manipulate these settings explicitly in Silverlight. However, when comparing Silverlight application deployments, note that you may see additional improvements on workstations that have multiple cores.

Silverlight 3 introduced a new feature called GPU (graphics processor unit) acceleration. This allows Silverlight to offload some of the rendering processing from the CPU to the GPU using DirectX (Windows) or OpenGL (Mac). The GPU acceleration is a declarative opt-in model that can be turned on in the Silverlight application. Once turned on, a developer can declaratively select portions of the UI that she wishes to be cached using the video card's resources. Technically, this is not multithreading or concurrent programming. However, it does facilitate moving resources from the CPU to another processing unit core. It can improve performance tremendously on complex UIs, free up CPU resources, and improve the user experience—advantages similar to those of multithreading.

■ **Note** Adobe Flash 10 includes a feature called Pixel Bender that allows Flash developers to offload graphical computations to the GPU. This is very similar to Silverlight GPU acceleration. A GPU can be used more than for just graphical effects; it's actually pretty good at performing very complex math operations. Clever Flash developers have used the Pixel Bender feature to mimic multithreading. Using this workaround does not overcome the limitations of not having true multithreading in Flash, but it does amplify how important GPU acceleration is for RIA technologies.

Enabling GPU acceleration for Silverlight content is very easy and can be done in two steps. First, the Silverlight application needs to have the enableGPUAcceleration parameter set to true. This is shown in Listing 10-9. This does not automatically turn GPU acceleration on; it simply enables acceleration to be potentially used in the Silverlight application.

Listing 10-9. Enabling GPU acceleration in a Silverlight application via object parameters (the relevant code is highlighted in bold).

```
<object data="data:application/x silverlight 2," type="application/x silverlight 2"
width="100%" height="100%">
  <param name="enableGPUAcceleration" value="true" />
  <param name="source" value="ClientBin/GPUAcceleration.xap"/>
  <param name="onError" value="onSilverlightError" />
  ...
```

The next step is to select a UIElement that you want to cache. Good candidates for GPU acceleration are UI objects that do not change dramatically with transforms. For example, you can set the CacheMode property of a media element (that plays a movie) to BitmapCache, as shown in Listing 10-10. This will utilize the GPU in order to offload some of the rendering calculations from the CPU. That is all that's needed in order to use the GPU! It's a very simple declarative opt-in model that allows you to fine-tune the performance of a Silverlight application. In addition, the GPU caching provides a "visual" debugger of sorts to let the developer know what components of the user interface are being cached. This can be enabled by setting EnableCacheVisualization parameter to true. When this parameter is turned on, it will render the Silverlight application normally; however any user interface not benefitting from the GPU caching will be rendered with a red background. This tells the developer exactly which components are either not configured correctly or can't benefit from a GPU.

Listing 10-10. Setting the CacheMode property on a media element to BitmapCache can minimize the required resources on the CPU.

```
<Grid x:Name="LayoutRoot">
      <MediaElement x:Name="MyVacationTrip" Margin="68,44,195,153"
      Source="/Vacation.wmv" Stretch="Fill" CacheMode="BitmapCache" />
</Grid>
```

Improving Business Application Performance

It is imperative to note that GPU acceleration is not just for Silverlight games and media-rich applications. Many developers overlook GPU acceleration as a concurrency optimization feature. Business applications can dramatically improve their performance using GPU acceleration as well. As you have seen throughout this book, BI 2.0 applications are very visual. Therefore, application modules that use charts, gauges, data grids, or complex data visualizations can use GPU acceleration effectively. When architecting several Silverlight line-of-business (LOB) applications, I have used this technique to free up as much as 40 percent of CPU resources on BI applications.

In Chapter 5, you programmed a coding scenario that showed how to use charting visualizations. That scenario simply showed two charts in a Silverlight application. The way the scenario was coded, all of the rendering was performed on the CPU. Let's use Silverlight's GPU acceleration to allow both the CPU and GPU to concurrently render the UI. As mentioned in the preceding section, enabling GPU acceleration is done in two steps: enabling it in the Silverlight application and then declaratively opting in on GPU rendering on selected UI objects. The enableGPUAcceleration property can be set as a parameter on the Silverlight object in the HTML or ASPX page. After that, all that needs to be done is to set the CacheMode properties on each chart (shown in Listing 10-11).

Listing 10-11. Setting the CacheMode property on the two charts in Silverlight can improve rendering performance.

```
...
<chartingToolkit:Chart Title="Actual Sales" Height="250" CacheMode="BitmapCache">
  <chartingToolkit:ColumnSeries Title="Sales Actual" DependentValuePath="SalesActual"
  IndependentValuePath="CompanyName" ItemsSource="{Binding}"/>
</chartingToolkit:Chart>
<chartingToolkit:Chart Title="Sales Actual vs. Forecast" Height="250"↵
  CacheMode="BitmapCache">
  <chartingToolkit:ColumnSeries Title="Sales Actual" DependentValuePath="SalesActual"
...
```

■ **Note** The enableGPUAcceleration property is an example of a high-level property that exists in Silverlight 3 and 4 only. Some Silverlight developers prefer to use the Silverlight 2 SDK and the ASP.NET control in C# to control higher-level Silverlight application properties. This property was not available in Silverlight 2; therefore, you need to use the object parameter instantiation in order to take advantage of GPU acceleration in Silverlight 4 applications.

I decided to benchmark CPU utilization of the application by reloading it 15 times and then removing the GPU acceleration. Figure 10-8 illustrates a noticeable drop in CPU utilization when GPU acceleration is turned on. The figure shows two processor cores in Windows Task Manager. The application was run 15 times with GPU acceleration and then 15 times without GPU acceleration. The application still performs the same, except now Silverlight rendering processes receive help from the GPU. This test was not very scientific, but you can see that even two simple chart objects benefit from GPU acceleration. If this were a more complex data visualization, the benefit would be very noticeable on the end user's workstation.

Figure 10-8. *GPU acceleration can be used to improve chart control rendering and animations. A GPU accelerated XAML design takes a noticably less amount of CPU processing resources.*

Silverlight Concurrent Programming Limitations

Silverlight supports a robust multithreading framework; however, it does have some limitations that software engineers need to be aware of. These limitations must be considered when designing the overall application and individual modules.

No Parallel Extension Support

Even though Visual Studio 2010 includes rich support for parallel programming, Silverlight 4 does not support the Parallel Extension library found in the full .NET 4.0 Framework. Therefore, many of the advanced parallelism patterns cannot be taken advantage of in Silverlight without writing custom code. Furthermore, writing PLINQ queries on the Silverlight client is not possible out of the box. As a result, if you have projects that share code between full .NET and Silverlight assemblies, you will have to account for this in your application design. Using the multithreading support as a common denominator is a best practice if you need to share concurrency programming techniques across projects.

■ **Note** Asynchronous workflows support in Silverlight does provide some declarative programming support similar to parallel extensions. However, it is not as complete.

Missing Concurrency Programming Essentials

Earlier in this chapter, Figure 10-6 illustrated the differences between the objects available in the System.Threading namespace of the Silverlight runtime and the full .NET Framework. A closer investigation will note that Silverlight is missing some objects that are deemed best practices in creating locking mechanisms. For example, the System.Threading.ReaderWriterLockSlim is missing. This class is an extension of the locking pattern that creates thread-safe objects that do not hold exclusive locks on read operations. This can prevent larger solutions from sharing source code files.

Do Not Block the UI Thread

In Silverlight, the main UI thread is not just tied to the Silverlight plug-in. The UI thread is also the thread that runs the web browser process. Therefore, you can completely ruin the user experience if you use concurrency patterns incorrectly.

For example, Listing 10-12 shows a UI that is creating a secondary thread from the ThreadPool and blocking the UI until the method completes.

Listing 10-12. Blocking the main application thread (UI thread) is a very bad practice in Silverlight applications.

```
...
ManualResetEvent mReset;

...

private void LayoutRoot_Loaded(object sender, RoutedEventArgs e)
{
  // Initialize the manual reset event
  this.mReset = new ManualResetEvent(false);
  // Queue up another thead to process work
  ThreadPool.QueueUserWorkItem(this.DoWork);
  // Block the UI thread until the the DoWork method completes
  this.mReset.WaitOne();
  // tell the user processing is finished
  MessageBox.Show("Finished");
}

private void DoWork(object state)
{
  // Mimic doing expensive work
  Thread.Sleep(5000);
  // Set the Manual ResetEvent
  this.mReset.Set();
}
```

▨ **Note** If you create a blank Silverlight application and add the Loaded event to the LayoutRoot control, you can run this test yourself by adding the code from Listing 10-12.

When the code in Listing 10-12 executes, it blocks the main Silverlight thread for 5 seconds. During that time, the browser becomes unresponsive. You have probably seen this same pattern used in Windows Forms applications where the screen goes gray while the UI thread is blocked. It is true that many classic Windows applications suffered from long processes blocking the main thread. Even though this could be frustrating, the user could simply wait out the process. In Silverlight applications hosted on the Web, this problem is amplified because blocking the UI thread will block both the Silverlight application and the browser hosting it! Imagine if you are a user with several tabs open for browsing and your Silverlight web site locks up the entire browser. You will not have a good user experience on that site. If a developer is lazy, they might get away with it in a local Windows application; however, bringing down the entire browser is many times worse.

The code in Listing 10-12 can be improved by blocking the secondary thread instead of the main thread. Therefore, if you require a pattern that needs to wait for background threads to complete, place the blocking content on a secondary thread. The first coding scenario in this chapter shows this technique which can be used with filtering large data sets.

Missing Implementations in the Framework

Because Silverlight runs on a subset of the .NET Framework, Microsoft seems to have left some holes in the APIs in order to maintain Silverlight's compatibility with the full .NET Framework. These omissions appear in more obscure and advanced scenarios. For example, the code in Listing 10-13 uses a Func delegate to calculate a sum of numbers. This is done synchronously (using Invoke) and asynchronously (using BeginInvoke). This exact code will work in an ASP.NET, WPF, or Windows Forms application. However, the asynchronous execution (BeginInvoke) will not work in Silverlight.

Listing 10-13. IntelliSense and the API both have the BeginInvoke method available in the Silverlight SDK. Even though the code will compile, it will throw an exception at the location highlighted in bold.

```
Func<int, int, int> addNumbers = null;

private void LayoutRoot_Loaded(object sender, RoutedEventArgs e)
{
  this.addNumbers = (int one, int two) => one + two;
  // this works fine because it was executed synchronously
  int result2 = addNumbers.Invoke(5, 10);
  // this doesn't work in Silverlight
  addNumbers.BeginInvoke(5, 10, this.asyncResult, null);
}

private void asyncResult(IAsyncResult ar)
{
  int result;

  if (ar.IsCompleted)
```

```
  {
    // retrieve the result
    result = this.addNumbers.EndInvoke(ar);
  }
}
```

The interesting part is that the preceding code works in Visual Studio and compiles. The problem is that the BeginInvoke method requires the System.Runtime.Remoting namespace which is not fully implemented in the Silverlight .NET version of the framework. It would have been nice if the BeginInvoke method at least gave compile warnings instead of waiting until the program executed. When designing advanced concurrency scenarios, ensure that your strategy uses the lowest common denominator that will work in Silverlight.

Coding Scenarios

Before you begin the coding scenarios, I'd like to offer a word of caution: in order to get a full understanding of the coding scenarios in this chapter, I highly recommend performing them on a workstation that has multiple cores. Any laptop, desktop, or sever with at least two cores will amplify the improvements to using concurrency techniques. If you do not have a multicore workstation, I still recommend that you follow the coding scenarios. However, you might only see a negligible performance increase (or, in some old processors, a decrease) in performance.

Coding Scenario: Improving the Performance of the UI

This coding scenario will show how concurrent programming techniques can be used to improve the performance of the UI, giving the user a good user experience with BI tools.

The following are the goals of this scenario:

- Understanding how business algorithms can slow down fluent interactions

- Seeing how to improve user interactions coupled with complex business algorithms by minimizing the number of executions

---

■ **Note** A fully working demo of this scenario is available online on the companion web site: http://silverlightbusinessintelligence.com/Demos/ImprovingPerfWithConcurrentProgramming/ImprovingUIPerf/UIPerf.html

---

In this coding scenario, you will create a series of slider controls. The first slider will not be bound to any algorithm. The second slider will be bound to a mock algorithm that takes 150 milliseconds to complete. The default behavior of Silverlight is to run everything on a single thread; note how painful this experience can be for the user. The last slider in the series will be bound to the same business algorithm except it will be executed on a secondary thread. The user experience using the last slider should be improved dramatically.

1. Open Visual Studio 2010 and create a new Silverlight Application project called Chapter10_ImprovingUIPerformance.

2. Open the project in Expression Blend 4 and set the UI as follows:

   • Change the LayoutRoot to a StackPanel.

   • Add a Loaded event to the LayoutRoot (which will add a corresponding event handler method in the codebehind file).

3. You are going to build a control that looks like Figure 10-9. The control's important pieces include a slider, a label for the value of the slider, and the number of times the event was executed.

Slider with little work

Slider Value: 0

Number of times event fired:

0

Figure 10-9. *Simple slider control that lets you know the current value and the number of times it was executed*

4. The XAML in your main page should have code similar to that shown in Listing 10-14. The changes from Step 2 are highlighted in bold.

Listing 10-14. *XAML code to render a simple slider control*

```
  mc:Ignorable="d" d:DesignWidth="640" d:DesignHeight="480">
  <StackPanel x:Name="LayoutRoot" >
    <StackPanel Height="Auto" Margin="10,0,0,0" Width="Auto" Orientation="Vertical">
      <TextBlock Height="Auto" HorizontalAlignment="Left" Margin="0,0,5,5" Width="Auto"⤶
Text="Slider with little work" TextWrapping="Wrap"/>
      <StackPanel Height="Auto" Width="Auto" HorizontalAlignment="Left"⤶
VerticalAlignment="Stretch" Orientation="Horizontal">
        <Slider Cursor="Hand" Height="18" x:Name="SliderSimple" Width="175"⤶
Margin="0,0,10,0"/>
        <TextBlock Height="Auto" Width="Auto" Text="Slider Value:" TextWrapping="Wrap"⤶
Margin="0,0,10,0"/>
        <TextBlock Height="Auto" Width="Auto" Text="0" TextWrapping="Wrap"⤶
x:Name="txtSliderSimpleValue"/>
      </StackPanel>
      <TextBlock Height="Auto" HorizontalAlignment="Left" Margin="0,0,0,5" Width="Auto"⤶
Text="Number of times event fired:" TextWrapping="Wrap"/>
      <TextBlock Height="Auto" Width="Auto" Text="0" TextWrapping="Wrap"⤶
HorizontalAlignment="Left" x:Name="txtSliderSimpleNumberEventFires"/>
    </StackPanel>
  </StackPanel>
</UserControl>
```

5. Implement the Loaded event for the LayoutRoot and the ValueChanged event for the slider, as shown in Listing 10-15. The corresponding method will be created in the codebehind. Handling this event will allow you to track when this event has been fired and set the value of the slider.

Listing 10-15. Adding Loaded and ValueChanged events to the XAML code

```
<StackPanel x:Name="LayoutRoot" Loaded="LayoutRoot_Loaded">
  <StackPanel Height="Auto" Margin="10,0,0,0" Width="Auto" Orientation="Vertical">
    <TextBlock Height="Auto" HorizontalAlignment="Left" Margin="0,0,5,5"
        Width="Auto" Text="Slider with little work" TextWrapping="Wrap"/>
    <StackPanel Height="Auto" Width="Auto" HorizontalAlignment="Left"
        VerticalAlignment="Stretch" Orientation="Horizontal">
    <Slider Cursor="Hand" Height="18" x:Name="SliderSimple"
        Width="175" Margin="0,0,10,0" ValueChanged="SliderSimple_ValueChanged"/>
```

6. In the codebehind, you are going to write a simple instrumentation harness in order to track when the slider moves and its current value.

- Declare an integer field to hold the count of how many times the event was fired.

- In the ValueChanged event handler, set the value of the slider to the text box.

- In the ValueChanged event handler, increment the count of the simple slider event and set it to the text box.

7. The codebehind file should look like that shown in Listing 10-16.

Listing 10-16. Simple slider code to set its value and how many times the event was triggered (highlighted in bold)

```
// declare count variables
int countSliderSimple = 0;

...

private void SliderSimple_ValueChanged(object sender, ↵
 RoutedPropertyChangedEventArgs<double> e)
{
  // increment simple slider event count
  this.countSliderSimple++;
  // set the slider value to its text box
  this.txtSliderSimpleValue.Text = this.SliderSimple.Value.ToString();
  // set the count on the text box
  this.txtSliderSimpleNumberEventFires.Text = this.countSliderSimple.ToString();
}
```

8. Let's do a sanity check to ensure your application builds properly and performs as expected. Build the application and try moving the slider around. The slider should move with ease. As you move the slider, the value changes, and you can see the number of times the ValueChanged event is triggered. Figure 10-10 shows the control in action.

■ **Note** If your control isn't displaying the slider value properly or isn't incrementing the event count, please go back to the previous steps and ensure the event handler has been created and the code was properly added before proceeding.

Slider with little work

Slider Value: 3.10975609756098

Number of times event fired:

12

Figure 10-10. The simple slider control displaying the slider value and the number of times the event triggered

From the preceding steps, you created a simple slider control. You can see how fluidly it operates. As you move the slider from end to end, the number of events fired adds up quickly. What would happen if you had a business algorithm that needed to be calculated each time the slider thumb's position changed? This would obviously impact the slider since everything is executed on a single thread.

In the following steps, you are going to create the same control layout as before. However, this time you will mock the execution of a business algorithm.

9. Add the XAML highlighted in bold in Listing 10-17 under the previous StackPanel we created before.

Listing 10-17. Adding the UI for the slider that will mimic the execution of a complex business algorithm

```
...
</StackPanel>

<!-- Single Threaded Section -->
<StackPanel Height="Auto" Width="Auto" Orientation="Vertical" Margin="10,10,0,5">
        <TextBlock Height="Auto" HorizontalAlignment="Left" Margin="0,0,5,5" Width="Auto"↵
Text="Slider with 150ms delay (single threaded)" TextWrapping="Wrap"/>
        <StackPanel Height="Auto" Width="Auto" Orientation="Horizontal">
                <Slider Cursor="Hand" Height="18" x:Name="SliderSingleThreaded"↵
Width="175" Margin="0,0,10,0"/>
                <TextBlock Height="Auto" Width="Auto" Text="Slider Value:"↵
TextWrapping="Wrap" Margin="0,0,10,0"/>
                <TextBlock Height="Auto" Width="Auto" Text="0" TextWrapping="Wrap"↵
x:Name="txtSliderSingleThreadedValue"/>
```

```
    </StackPanel>
        <TextBlock Height="Auto" HorizontalAlignment="Left" Margin="0,0,0,5" Width="Auto"↵
Text="Number of times event fired:" TextWrapping="Wrap"/>
        <TextBlock Height="Auto" Width="Auto" Text="0" TextWrapping="Wrap"↵
HorizontalAlignment="Left" x:Name="txtSliderSingleThreadNumberEventFires"/>
</StackPanel>
```

10. Add a ValueChanged event to the new slider. The change is highlighted in bold in Listing 10-18. This will create the corresponding event handler in the codebehind file.

Listing 10-18. Adding the ValueChanged event to the single-threaded slider

```
<Slider Cursor="Hand" Height="18" x:Name="SliderSingleThreaded"
    ValueChanged="SliderSingleThreaded_ValueChanged" Width="175" Margin="0,0,10,0"/>
```

11. Now it is time to add an instrumentation harness similar to the one added in the simple slider, except now you will put the main thread to sleep for 150 milliseconds to mimic a business algorithm. The code changes are highlighted in Listing 10-19.

Listing 10-19. Adding an instrumentation harness and mocking a business algorithm with slow behavior highlighted in bold)

```
// declare count variables
int countSliderSimple = 0;
int countSliderSingleThreaded = 0;

….
private void SliderSimple_ValueChanged(object sender,↵
 RoutedPropertyChangedEventArgs<double> e)
{
  // increment simple slider event count
  this.countSliderSimple++;
  // set the slider value to its text box
  this.txtSliderSimpleValue.Text = this.SliderSimple.Value.ToString();
  // set the count on the text box
  this.txtSliderSimpleNumberEventFires.Text = this.countSliderSimple.ToString();
}

private void SliderSingleThreaded_ValueChanged(object sender,↵
 RoutedPropertyChangedEventArgs<double> e)
{
  // increment single threaded slider event count
  this.countSliderSingleThreaded++;
  // set the slider value to its text box
  this.txtSliderSingleThreadedValue.Text = this.SliderSingleThreaded.Value.ToString();

  // add a fake delay of 150 milliseconds (3/20 of a second)
  System.Threading.Thread.Sleep(150);
```

```
    // set the count on the text box
    this.txtSliderSingleThreadNumberEventFires.Text↵
 = this.countSliderSingleThreaded.ToString();
}
```

12. If everything was added properly, the project should build, and you will see the two sliders with a layout similar to Figure 10-11.

   • Try moving the second slider around. Note how the slider jumps positions and "locks up" easily. The interaction has been severely degraded with the addition of business logic. Furthermore, note that the number of times the event is processed is much fewer. The processing of the business algorithm takes time away from the UI to efficiently handle user interaction. This would be considered highly unusable by most users.

Slider with little work

Slider Value: 3.71951219512195

Number of times event fired:

20

Slider with 150ms delay (single threaded)

Slider Value: 4.75609756097561

Number of times event fired:

5

Figure 10-11. The slider coupled to a complex business algorithm is a lot less responsive.

In the next steps, you will take a look at how you can improve the responsiveness of the UI by using a simple concurrency programming technique. Figure 10-12 shows a visual diagram of what is occurring in the two sliders when you move the thumb and cause the triggering of three ValueChanged events. Essentially, both sliders follow the same execution pattern on a single thread. However, the second slider has to spend 150 milliseconds each time the event fires in order to process the mock business algorithm you injected. Therefore, the main UI thread has less time to allocate for a response to UI gestures. Note that Figure 10-12 does not represent the exact ratio of the time elapsed to scale.

Slider 1: Main Thread

Slider 2: Main Thread

> Time elapsed for processing UI

> Time elapsed for processing event handler

Figure 10-12. *Slider 1's thread has much more time to spend to allocate for the UI, making it much more responsive. Slider 2's thread time is allocated to processing the business logic in the event handler.*

How can you improve the user experience using a secondary thread? The goal is to process the business logic on a secondary thread and leave the main thread free to handle other work associated with the program. This allows the UI to remain responsive, thus the user thinks the UI is working more quickly. Figure 10-13 shows the main thread splitting the work with the secondary thread. The secondary thread processes the business algorithm while the main thread remains responsive.

Slider 2: Main Thread

Slider 2: Secondary Threads

> Time elapsed for processing UI

> Time elapsed for processing the event handler and threading

Figure 10-13. *Slider 2 optimized can utilize secondary threads for the business logic. The main thread has more time to process UI gestures, animations, and other logic.*

▨ **Caution** It is wrong to assume that no work should be done on the main thread. The event is still handled on the main thread. Threading has to be scheduled, and after the business logic is done, the result processing is dispatched to the main UI thread. However, this work is negligible and only slightly more resource intensive than the first slider.

---

13. Going back to your project in Visual Studio 2010, add the XAML in Listing 10-20 below the second slider. This XAML code, shown in Listing 10-20, will add the UI for the third slider.

Listing 10-20. Adding the UI for the third multithreaded slider

```
...
</StackPanel>

<!-- Multi Threaded Section -->
<StackPanel Height="Auto" Width="Auto" Orientation="Vertical" Margin="10,10,0,5">
        <TextBlock Height="Auto" HorizontalAlignment="Left" Margin="0,0,5,5" Width="Auto"↵
Text="Slider with 150ms delay (multi threaded)" TextWrapping="Wrap"/>
        <StackPanel Height="Auto" Width="Auto" HorizontalAlignment="Stretch"↵
Orientation="Horizontal">
<Slider Cursor="Hand" Height="18" x:Name="SliderMultiThreaded" Width="175"↵
HorizontalAlignment="Left" Margin="0,0,10,0"/>
                <TextBlock Height="Auto" Width="Auto" Text="Slider Value:"↵
TextWrapping="Wrap" Margin="0,0,10,0"/>
                <TextBlock Height="Auto" Width="Auto" Text="0" TextWrapping="Wrap"↵
x:Name="txtSliderMultiThreadedValue"/>
        </StackPanel>
        <TextBlock Height="Auto" HorizontalAlignment="Left" Margin="0,0,0,5" Width="Auto"↵
Text="Number of times event fired:" TextWrapping="Wrap"/>
        <TextBlock Height="Auto" Width="Auto" Text="0" TextWrapping="Wrap"↵
HorizontalAlignment="Left" x:Name="txtSliderMultiThreadNumberEventFires"/>
</StackPanel>
```

14. Add the event handler for the third slider, as shown in Listing 10-21. This will create the corresponding codebehind method.

Listing 10-21. Adding the event handler for the third slider (highlighted in bold)

```
<Slider Cursor="Hand" Height="18" x:Name="SliderMultiThreaded"↵
ValueChanged="SliderMultiThreaded_ValueChanged"
    Width="175" HorizontalAlignment="Left" Margin="0,0,10,0"/>
```

15. Now it is time to add the multithreaded business logic and the instrumentation harness to the third slider. This will implement the pattern outlined in Figure 10-13. You will use the BackgroundWorker object in order to create the second thread for processing your expensive business algorithm. The tasks are as follows:

- A BackgroundWorker are added to the project. Then the DoWork and RunWorkerCompleted events are added.

- The DoWork event processes the business logic on the second thread.

- The RunWorkerCompleted event ensures the instrumentation harness items are processed. Furthermore, it ensures that the business logic has processed the correct position when the slider has stopped.

- In the SliderMultiThreaded_ValueChanged event handler, add instrumentation code and logic that will fire off the DoWork method on the secondary thread (if the background worker isn't busy).

- Use a property to hold the last value processed to see if you need to reprocess to catch up.

Listing 10-22. Code that will enable the third slider to execute code on the secondary thread while the UI remains responsive (highlighted in bold)

```
...
using System.ComponentModel;

namespace Chapter10_ImprovingUIPerformance
{
  public partial class MainPage : UserControl
  {
    // declare count variables
    int countSliderSimple = 0;
    int countSliderSingleThreaded = 0;
    int countSliderMultiThreaded = 0;
    // last value
    double lastMultiThreadedSliderValue = 0.0;
    // declare background worker
    BackgroundWorker bw = new BackgroundWorker();

    public MainPage()
    {
      InitializeComponent();
    }

    private void LayoutRoot_Loaded(object sender, RoutedEventArgs e)
    {
      // wire up RunWorkerCompleted event
      // This will fire when the business logic has completed
      this.bw.RunWorkerCompleted +=
        new RunWorkerCompletedEventHandler(bw_RunWorkerCompleted);
      // Wire up the DoWork event
      // This will fire each time we need to process the "business logic"
      this.bw.DoWork += new DoWorkEventHandler(bw_DoWork);
    }

    void bw_DoWork(object sender, DoWorkEventArgs e)
```

```csharp
  {
    //NOTE: The logic here is processed on the secondary thread

    // add a fake delay of 150 milliseconds (about 1/7 of a second)
    // this mocks an expensive business algorithm
    System.Threading.Thread.Sleep(150);
  }

  void bw_RunWorkerCompleted(object sender, RunWorkerCompletedEventArgs e)
  {
    //NOTE: The logic here is processed on the main thread

    // set the slider value to its text box
    // notice this is set here, as it guarantees that the value is now officially set
    // setting it in the SliderMultiThreaded_ValueChanged event, the 2nd thread would↵
have to catch up to the UI
    this.txtSliderMultiThreadedValue.Text = this.SliderMultiThreaded.Value.ToString();

    // Run the background worker again in case the slider value needs to catch up
    // If you stop the slider at the end for example, it might be still processing the↵
previous event
    // you want to make sure that where the slider is stopped (last event fired) matches↵
what was processed by the 2nd thread
    if (!this.bw.IsBusy)
    {
      // if the values are not in sync, then the 2nd thread needs to catch up to the UI
      if ((this.SliderMultiThreaded.Value != this.LastMultiThreadedSliderValue) &&↵
(this.LastMultiThreadedSliderValue != 0.0))
      {
        // run the process again if the last value set has not been run by the second↵
thread
        this.bw.RunWorkerAsync();
        // set the value to 0.0
        this.LastMultiThreadedSliderValue = 0.0;
      }
    }
  }

  public double LastMultiThreadedSliderValue
  {
    get
    {
      object objLock = new object();
      lock (objLock)
      {
        return this.lastMultiThreadedSliderValue;
      }
    }
    set
    {
```

```
    // lock the setter so multiple threads do not leave the value inconsistant
    object objLock = new object();
    lock (objLock)
    {
      this.lastMultiThreadedSliderValue = value;
    }
  }
}

private void SliderMultiThreaded_ValueChanged(object sender, ↵
RoutedPropertyChangedEventArgs<double> e)
  {
    // increment multi threaded slider event count
    this.countSliderMultiThreaded++;
    // set the last value set compared to the current value
    this.LastMultiThreadedSliderValue = this.SliderMultiThreaded.Value;

    // If the BackgroundWorker is free,
    // execute the business logic on the second thread
    if (!bw.IsBusy)
    {
      bw.RunWorkerAsync();
    }

    // set the count on the text box
    this.txtSliderMultiThreadNumberEventFires.Text↵
= this.countSliderMultiThreaded.ToString();
  }
```

16. Now build the project. You'll see three sliders, as illustrated in Figure 10-14. Move the third slider around. Note that even though you still have the 150 millisecond business algorithm processing, the UI code and the sliding motion remains very responsive. Isn't this user experience much better than the single-threaded experience in slider 2?

Slider with little work

———————————⬚——————— Slider Value: 5.12195121951219

Number of times event fired:

13

Slider with 150ms delay (single threaded)

—————————⬚————————— Slider Value: 4.8780487804878

Number of times event fired:

4

Slider with 150ms delay (multi threaded)

—————————⬚————————— Slider Value: 5.18292682926829

Number of times event fired:

22

Figure 10-14. Three sliders in the final build of the coding scenario emphasize the need to use concurrent programming techniques for expensive business logic.

Lessons Learned

This coding scenario created a simple program optimizing the UI by moving expensive processing to the secondary thread. This type of pattern is a something that any serious Silverlight developer creating BI 2.0 solutions needs to be aware of. In your scenario, Sliders 2 and 3 essentially do the same thing; however, the user experience is completely different.

This type of pattern can be applied to any UI events that require expensive processing on the client. This is a concurrency technique that allows Silverlight to process large-scale computations on the client without needing a large BI server implementation. After completing this scenario, hopefully you have a better appreciation for the power of multithreading in Silverlight.

Possible Improvements

In this scenario, you used a lot of logic to handle the synchronization between the UI and the threads in order to ensure that the processing represented the last stop of the slider. Using a number of different techniques, this should be abstracted into binding, value converters, or behaviors. Secondly, you also used the BackgroundWorker object to simplify the multithreading aspects of processing. The BackgroundWorker is a powerful tool but doesn't scale well, and you will rarely find it used in Silverlight production environments.

■ **Caution** Many Silverlight and WPF architects are quick to jump to "best practice" patterns such as MVVM and the Prism framework without taking into consideration optimizations such as the one covered in this scenario. Implementing the MVVM pattern is not straightforward. Not only do you have to architect the solution properly, but your developers have to adhere to the MMVM patterns. For example, take a look at the commanding mechanisms employed in MVVM to facilitate the communication of the View (the *V* in *MVVM*) with the ViewModel (the *VM* in *MVVM*). This works well for synchronous patterns; however, asynchronous patterns are much more complex. You would have to create an asynchronous commanding pattern. This is where I find myself at a fork in the road when architecting Silverlight applications. Ask yourself how much plumbing code you'll have to write in order to fit into the best-practice mold and whether this will prohibit you from adding concurrency optimizations. Remember that with almost all design patterns, you will write more code. The ROI on the investment of MVVM has to outweigh the time it takes to write the increased amount of code plus the time it takes to test it.

Coding Scenario: Improving Computational Processing Performance

This scenario will cover how you can use several threads in order to improve the performance of a computational business algorithm. This example will revisit the coding scenario from Chapter 3 and improve it via additional threading techniques.

The following are the goals of this scenario:

- Understanding the technique of using multiple threads to solve a large data problem

- Seeing how a Silverlight multithreaded algorithm can scale well beyond just one or two threads

- Learning that applying concurrent techniques relies on testing your scenarios

- Gauging the benefit of providing configuration parameters for concurrency algorithms

■ **Note** A fully working demo of this scenario is available online on the companion web site: http://silverlightbusinessintelligence.com/Demos/ImprovingPerfWithConcurrentProgramming/ImprovingComputationalPerf/ComputationalPerf.html.

This coding scenario is a little different from the others. I don't want to start from scratch, so let's reuse the previous coding scenario from Chapter 3 for calculating the BMI for a million records on the Silverlight client. If you didn't complete the scenario or don't have it handy, just download it from the companion web site for this book (www.silverlightbusinessintelligence.com).

Because this scenario is long, it's broken up into three parts:

- *Getting the Project Ready for Concurrency*: This will start with the basic UI for the project and add some additional configuration and instrumentation.

- *Designing a Two-Thread Solution to Improve Performance*: This part will cover creating a two-threaded design for improving performance.

- *Dynamic Concurrency and Performance Analysis*: This part will cover making the threads dynamic and analyze what you did in this coding scenario.

Part 1: Getting the Project Ready for Concurrency

1. After downloading the Chapter3_WorkingWithBusinessData project, open the solution with Visual Studio 2010. Ensure the project builds by compiling and running it. You are going to make two improvements to this project. First, you're going to improve the performance of the data generation algorithm using concurrent threads.

2. Let's add some basic instrumentation and parameters to the tool:

    - Ensure the height of the canvas is 400.

    - Add a text box that will be used to input how much data is generated.

    - Add a second button to generate the data using a concurrent technique.

    - Add a label that will display how long it took to generate the data using multithreaded and non-multithreaded techniques.

3. The XAML in the project should look like that shown in Listing 10-23.

Listing 10-23. Code for a UI for testing your project with single-threaded and mulithreaded techniques

```
...
Width="500" Height="400">
  <StackPanel x:Name="LayoutRoot" Background="White">
  <StackPanel Height="25" Orientation="Horizontal">
    <dataInput:Label HorizontalAlignment="Right" Width="200" Content="Amount of Records↵
  to Generate:" FontWeight="Bold"/>
    <TextBox x:Name="numberOfRecordsToGenerate" HorizontalAlignment="Right" Text="1000000"
    Width="75" Margin="5,0,0,0"/>
  </StackPanel>
    <Button x:Name="btnGenerateData" Margin="0,0,0,10" Content="Generate Data"↵
Click="btnGenerateData_Click"/>
    <Button x:Name="btnConcurrentGenerateData" Margin="0,0,0,10" Content="Generate Data↵
Concurrently" />
    <Button x:Name="btnPerformAnalysis" Content="Perform Analysis" Margin="0,0,0,10"↵
Click="btnPerformAnalysis_Click"/>
    <StackPanel Height="200">
      <StackPanel Height="25" Orientation="Horizontal">
        <dataInput:Label Content="BMI Minimum:" Width="150" HorizontalAlignment="Right"/>
        <dataInput:Label x:Name="bmiMinimum" HorizontalAlignment="Right"
```

```
      Width="50" Content="0" Margin="5,0,0,0"/>
    </StackPanel>
    <StackPanel Height="25" Orientation="Horizontal">
      <dataInput:Label HorizontalAlignment="Right" Width="150" Content="BMI Maximum:"/>
      <dataInput:Label x:Name="bmiMaximum" HorizontalAlignment="Right"
    Width="50" Content="0" Margin="5,0,0,0"/>
    </StackPanel>
    <StackPanel Height="25" Orientation="Horizontal">
      <dataInput:Label HorizontalAlignment="Right" Width="150" Content="BMI Average:"/>
      <dataInput:Label x:Name="bmiAverage" HorizontalAlignment="Right"
    Width="50" Content="0" Margin="5,0,0,0"/>
    </StackPanel>
    <StackPanel Height="25" Orientation="Horizontal">
      <dataInput:Label HorizontalAlignment="Right" Width="150" Content="Count with obese↵
BMI:"/>
      <dataInput:Label x:Name="bmiObeseCount" HorizontalAlignment="Right"
    Width="50" Content="0" Margin="5,0,0,0"/>
    </StackPanel>
    <StackPanel Height="25" Orientation="Horizontal">
      <dataInput:Label HorizontalAlignment="Right" Width="150" Content="Data Generated↵
In:" FontWeight="Bold"/>
      <dataInput:Label x:Name="dataGeneratedInPerformedIn" HorizontalAlignment="Right"
    Width="50" Content="0" Margin="5,0,0,0"/>
    </StackPanel>
    <StackPanel Height="25" Orientation="Horizontal">
      <dataInput:Label HorizontalAlignment="Right" Width="150" Content="Peformed↵
Analysis In:" FontWeight="Bold"/>
      <dataInput:Label x:Name="performedAnalysisIn" HorizontalAlignment="Right"
    Width="50" Content="0" Margin="5,0,0,0"/>
    </StackPanel>
    <StackPanel Height="25" Orientation="Horizontal">
      <dataInput:Label HorizontalAlignment="Right" Width="250" Content="Concurrent Data↵
Generated In:" FontWeight="Bold"/>
      <dataInput:Label x:Name="concurrentDataGeneratedInPerformedIn"↵
HorizontalAlignment="Right"
    Width="50" Content="0" Margin="5,0,0,0"/>
    </StackPanel>
  </StackPanel>
</StackPanel>
```

4. Add the click event handler for btnConcurrentGenerateData (shown in Listing 10-24). The corresponding event handlers should be created for you in the codebehind file.

Listing 10-24. The highlighted code shows the click event handlers for two concurrency buttons.

```
...
<Button x:Name="btnConcurrentGenerateData" Margin="0,0,0,10"
    Content="Generate Data Concurrently" Click="btnConcurrentGenerateData_Click"/>
<Button x:Name="btnPerformAnalysis" Content="Perform Analysis" Margin="0,0,0,10"
 Click="btnPerformAnalysis_Click"/>
...
```

5. Build the project and ensure that the UI looks like Figure 10-15 after adding the code for Steps 2 and 3.

Amount of Records to Generate:	1000000

Generate Data

Generate Data Concurrently

Perform Analysis

BMI Minimum: 0

BMI Maximum: 0

BMI Average: 0

Count with obese BMI: 0

Data Generated In: 0

Analysis Peformed In: 0

Concurrent Data Generated In: 0

Figure 10-15. The UI for tesing the concurrency improvements

6. Take a look at the current event handler for the btnGenerateData_Click event. It's currently reporting the time, generating data, and reporting completion all in one event handler. You need to move that code out into a separate method so it can be called by multiple threads.

   - Create a new method called CreatePersons that will return a List<Person> collection in the MainPage code-behind file.

   - The method will take two parameters. The first parameter will be called Start and will determine at which point to seed the random value. The second parameter will be called numberOfPersons and will determine the amount of members to create in this collection.

   - The method should look like the code shown in Listing 10-25.

Listing 10-25. The new CreatePersons method can now be called by multiple threads and create individually scoped collections.

```
private List<Person> CreatePersons(int start, int numberOfPersons)
{
    // number of person to genereate = seed point + number to generate
    numberOfPersons += start;
    // create a locally scoped collection
    List<Person> personList = new List<Person>(numberOfPersons);

    // add the people to the list
    for (int i = start; i != numberOfPersons; i++)
    {
        Random rand = new Random(i);

        int weight = rand.Next(85, 320);
        int height = rand.Next(5, 8);

        Person person = new Person
        {
            ID = i + 1,
            Weight = weight,
            Height = height
        };
        personList.Add(person);
    }

    // return the list of Person objects
    return personList;
}
```

7. You are going to use the original data generation procedure as a comparison. Change the procedure to use the number of records to generate from the text box shown in Listing 10-26. Then add instrumentation so that you can tell how long it will take to generate the data.

Listing 10-26. The code changes highlighted in bold make the code generation dynamic and report the time to complete.

```
private void btnGenerateData_Click(object sender, RoutedEventArgs e)
{
    // start the timer
    DateTime dateStart = DateTime.Now;

    int numberOfRecordsToGenerate = Convert.ToInt32(this.numberOfRecordsToGenerate.Text);

    // clear the list
    this.people.Clear();

    for (int i = 0; i != 1000000; i++)
```

```
{
  Random rand = new Random(i);

  int weight = rand.Next(85, 320);
  int height = rand.Next(5, 8);

  Person person = new Person
  {
    ID = i + 1,
    Weight = weight,
    Height = height
  };
  people.Add(person);
}

this.btnGenerateData.Content = "Data Generated. Click again to regenerate.";

// calculate the length of analysis time and set it
this.dataGeneratedInPerformedIn.Content↩
= DateTime.Now.Subtract(dateStart).TotalMilliseconds.ToString();
}
```

8. Run the project and click Generate Data. This should build a list of data and report how long it took to the UI.

Part 2: Designing a Two-Thread Solution to Improve Performance

1. This is the hardest part of this scenario. It's time to design how you want to add concurrency to this process. In this step, you are going to use two secondary worker threads to split up the data generation and then synchronize it into one master list. This should speed up the improvement dramatically, as one thread will not be responsible for creating all of the data. This should, in theory, cut the time almost in half. Obviously, there is overhead in creating worker threads, combining the data from the list, and dispatching the results to the main UI thread. However, the performance increase should be about double. Figure 10-16 shows the process visually.

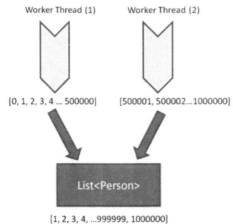

Figure 10-16. Two worker threads will generate the data independently. After the data sets are generated, they will be placed into a master Person collection. This collection can then be used by the Perform Analysis process.

At this point, you should be clear on what you're trying to achieve. However, it is not clear how to make this process come together. Figure 10-17 illustrates one possible solution to this problem. Each step is annotated with a number and description.

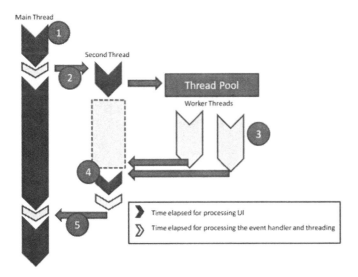

Figure 10-17. A simple workflow of the mulithreaded data generation process. It may look complex at first, but it isn't too hard to comprehend.

- In Step 1, you create instrumentation that handles when the worker threads are complete using reset events. This is done on the main UI thread.

- In Step 2, you create a second thread that manages the data creation process.

- In Step 3, you create two worker threads that process a subset of the total data. It is important to note that the threads are created from the ThreadPool. For now, you split the process evenly between threads.

- Step 4 blocks the thread and wait for the processes to complete. You put instrumentation in that waits for a signal for the worker threads to notify the second thread when they are done. It waits to proceeding until both threads are complete.

- Step 5 executes after both threads have finished. This then dispatches code to the main UI thread and lets the user know that you're done.

2. Add a using System.Threading namespace to the MainPage.xaml file, as shown in Listing 10-27.

Listing 10-27. Adding the System.Threading namespace to the project page

```
...
using System.Windows.Media.Animation;
using System.Windows.Shapes;
using System.Threading;
```

3. Add the code shown in Listing 10-28 to the event handler for the concurrent data generation. The code steps are labeled to match the steps in Figure 10-17.

Listing 10-28. Concurrent code generation process added to the event button event handler

```
private void btnConcurrentGenerateData_Click(object sender, RoutedEventArgs e)
{
  // start the timer
  DateTime dateStart = DateTime.Now;

  // retrieve number of records to generate from the text box
  int numberOfRecordsToGenerate =
    Convert.ToInt32(this.numberOfRecordsToGenerate.Text);

  this.people = new List<Person>(numberOfRecordsToGenerate);

  // STEP ONE
  // create a list of AutoResetEvents
  // We are going to queue two worker threads, therefore
  AutoResetEvent[] autoEvents = new AutoResetEvent[]
  {
    new AutoResetEvent(false),
    new AutoResetEvent(false)
  };
```

```csharp
// STEP TWO
// create a second thread to manage the data generation process
new Thread(new ThreadStart(delegate
{
  // STEP THREE

  // Queue worker thread from ThreadPool.
  // using the ThreadPool is a good practice, not to overwhelm
  // the environment with too many threads
  ThreadPool.QueueUserWorkItem(
    delegate(object o)
    {
      // process the first half of the List
      people.AddRange(CreatePersons(0, numberOfRecordsToGenerate/2));
      // set the AutoResetEvent to signal process is complete
      autoEvents[0].Set();
    }
  );

  // Queue worker thread from ThreadPool.
  // using the ThreadPool is a good practice, not to overwhelm
  // the environment with too many threads
  ThreadPool.QueueUserWorkItem(
    delegate(object o)
    {
      // process the second half of the List
      people.AddRange(CreatePersons(numberOfRecordsToGenerate / 2,↵
numberOfRecordsToGenerate/2));
      // set the AutoResetEvent to signal process is complete
      autoEvents[1].Set();
    }
  );

  // STEP FOUR
  // This blocks the current thread (the second one)
  // Thread is blocked until all the queued worker items complete
  WaitHandle.WaitAll(autoEvents);

  // STEP FIVE
  // Dispatch that the processing has finished
  // This has to be done on the UI thread
  this.Dispatcher.BeginInvoke(delegate
  {
    this.btnConcurrentGenerateData.Content = "Data Generated concurrently.↵
Click again to regenerate.";
    // calculate the length of analysis time and set it
    this.concurrentDataGeneratedInPerformedIn.Content↵
= DateTime.Now.Subtract(dateStart).TotalMilliseconds.ToString();
  });
```

```
        })).Start();
}
```

4. Build the project and execute the scenario. If it builds, you have just improved the computational process using Silverlight multithreading! Now you can try out some different scenarios to see if you truly improved the processing time.

5. With the project running, click the Generate Data button. After it completes, click the Generate Data Concurrently button (it's important not to click them together, as it will skew the results). Note the difference in times. On my workstation, the single-threaded option took about 5200 milliseconds, while the concurrent option took about 3000 milliseconds. As you can see, this cut the processing almost in half. Note that your results will vary depending on your hardware.

   - Rerun the project to get a good baseline.

   - Iincrease the number to 2 or 3 million. The time gap between the two processes becomes greater and greater, but the percentage improvement should remain rather constant.

6. With the project running, change the number of items to generate between 100 and 1,000 items. Note that when dealing with this few items, the difference in time is actually inverted. Remember that there is a slight overhead in creating this multithreaded process. Therefore, small data sets are not going to benefit as much from multithreaded optimizations. Adding all this pre-optimization code would actually be a hindrance and could introduce unnecessary defects into your code.

Part 3: Dynamic Concurrency and Performance Analysis

1. You improved the performance of the data generation using two hard-coded threads. Can you do better? What if the user has a four- or eight-core workstation? More threads could improve the process further. Let's add code for making this process more configurable. In the code in Listing 10-29, you add a text box that you can use to determine how many threads will be used to perform the data generation process.

Listing 10-29. Adding a text box to control the number of threads that will be executed (highlighted in bold).

```
<StackPanel x:Name="LayoutRoot" Background="White">
  <StackPanel Height="25" Orientation="Horizontal">
    <controls:Label HorizontalAlignment="Right" Width="200" Content="Amount of Records↩
 to Generate:" FontWeight="Bold"/>
    <TextBox x:Name="numberOfRecordsToGenerate" HorizontalAlignment="Right" Text="1000000"↩
Width="75" Margin="5,0,0,0"/>
  </StackPanel>
<StackPanel Height="25" Orientation="Horizontal">
  <dataInput:Label HorizontalAlignment="Right" Width="175" Content="Number of Threads↩
 to Use:" FontWeight="Bold"/>
```

```
<TextBox x:Name="numberOfThreadsToUse" HorizontalAlignment="Left" Text="2" Width="30"↵
Margin="5,0,0,0"/>
</StackPanel>
...
```

2. Now it is time to make the data process dynamic by utilizing the input text box to control the number of threads that will be used. Note that the process outlined in the main workflow (Figure 10-17) will not change except that instead of always having two threads in Step 3, you could have more, depending on the input.

3. Make the changes shown in bold in Listing 10-30.

Listing 10-30. Making the mulithreaded code dynamic by removing the hard-coded values and replacing them with multithreaded alternatives.

```
private void btnConcurrentGenerateData_Click(object sender, RoutedEventArgs e)
{
  // start the timer
  DateTime dateStart = DateTime.Now;

  // retrieve number of records to generate from the text box
  int numberOfRecordsToGenerate =
    Convert.ToInt32(this.numberOfRecordsToGenerate.Text);
  // retrieve number of threads to generate
  int numberOfThreadsToGenerate =
    Convert.ToInt32(this.numberOfThreadsToUse.Text);

  this.people = new List<Person>(numberOfRecordsToGenerate);

  // STEP ONE
  // create a list of AutoResetEvents
  // We are going to queue two worker threads, therefore
  AutoResetEvent[] autoEvents = new AutoResetEvent[numberOfThreadsToGenerate];

  // add a list of auto reset events
  for (int i = 0; i != autoEvents.Length; i++)
  {
    autoEvents[i] = new AutoResetEvent(false);
  }

  // STEP TWO
  // create a second thread to manage the data generation process
  new Thread(new ThreadStart(delegate
  {
    // STEP THREE

    // determine how many records to place on each thread
    int numberOfRecordsToGenerateForEachThread =
      numberOfRecordsToGenerate / numberOfThreadsToGenerate;
```

```csharp
    // Queue worker thread from ThreadPool.
    // using the ThreadPool is a good practice, not to overwhelm
    // the environment with too many threads
    for (int j = 0; j != numberOfThreadsToGenerate; j++)
    {
      // add this to the delegate closure
      int currentThreadNumber = j;

      ThreadPool.QueueUserWorkItem(
        delegate(object o)
        {
          // process the appropriate subset
          this.people.AddRange(CreatePersons(
            // calculate the starting point
            (numberOfRecordsToGenerate / (currentThreadNumber + 1)) * currentThreadNumber,
            // pass in the number of records to generate for each thread
            numberOfRecordsToGenerateForEachThread)
            );
          // set the AutoResetEvent to signal process is complete
          autoEvents[currentThreadNumber].Set();
        }
      );
    }

    // STEP FOUR
    // This blocks the current thread (the second one)
    // Thread is blocked until all the queued worker items complete
    WaitHandle.WaitAll(autoEvents);

    // STEP FIVE
    // Dispatch that the processing has finished
    // This has to be done on the UI thread
    this.Dispatcher.BeginInvoke(delegate
    {
      this.btnConcurrentGenerateData.Content = "Data Generated concurrently.↵
Click again to regenerate.";
      // calculate the length of analysis time and set it
      this.concurrentDataGeneratedInPerformedIn.Content =↵
DateTime.Now.Subtract(dateStart).TotalMilliseconds.ToString();
    });

  })).Start();
}
```

4. Test this solution passing in a number of different threads and note the performance gains. If you have a multicore processor, you should see a performance gain directly proportional to the amount of logical processors on the computer. Figure 10-18 displays two charts.

   • The two graphs show three series, each representing how many millions of records were generated (1, 3, or 5 million). The number of threads used is on the x-axis and the time (in milliseconds) is on the y-axis.

- The chart on the left displays the program running on a single physical CPU with four logical cores.

- The chart on the right displays the program running on a dual physical CPU (with four cores for each CPU), giving it a total of eight logical cores.

Figure 10-18. The mulithreaded code is dynamic after you remove the hard-coded values.

5. After analyzing the chart, you should note the following:

- The maximum point of concurrency optimization is directly proportional to the number of logical cores on a workstation or server. The current multicore architectures from the major multiprocessor vendors behave the same. In the future, multiprocessor vendors are planning to improve the performance ratio of threads to logical core.

- As you approach the point of maximum optimization by adding more threads, the net performance gain becomes smaller. For example, note that the percentage in improvement for adding a second thread is much greater than adding a third, and so on.

- Every laptop, workstation, and server is different. Making concurrency optimization configurable is paramount in making sure you get the best performance. You are probably thinking that it would be crazy for an average user to know the exact number of physical cores they have available. This is true especially in Silverlight which doesn't have access to local environment APIs, so this information can't just be pulled from the OS. However, one possible solution would be to provide a process that can self-optimize and pick the right configuration by running the algorithms.

Lessons Learned

This coding scenario was one of the most complex and longest in this book. You saw that adding concurrency can greatly improve the performance of data algorithms. However, it is not easy, and you have to know your way around threading techniques in order to write the code properly.

The latter part of the scenario showed the importance of adding concurrency code that is dynamic. In the analysis of the program, you saw a direct relationship between threads and logical processor cores. This means that not all workstations will behave the same way. Your applications should provide configuration or processes that auto-tune for best performance gains.

The most important takeaway from this example is to understand the importance of concurrent programming benefits for data-driven scenarios like client-side BI. Every single scenario considered up until this point can be enhanced using these techniques. Utilizing multiple cores allows an application to process more data, render more graphics, and design the most complex analytical tools using Silverlight.

Possible Improvements

This scenario left out a lot of the complexities of Silverlight multithreading (this might be hard to believe because the code is pretty advanced). However, note that you are still writing code in the UI, and it would be much better to have this code abstracted to business objects. Furthermore, proper locking and thread-safety techniques were not implemented for simplicity. This code should not be thought of as production ready. It was meant as a lesson on how to implement advanced concurrency techniques in Silverlight.

Additional Coding Scenarios on the Companion Web Site

I could not add every business scenario as an exercise in this book. Arguably, one could write an entire book on Silverlight multithreading techniques alone as this topic is quite advanced and very immersive. Therefore, on the companion web site (www.silverlightbusinessintelligence.com), I have added additional projects for download that consist of some of the code shown in the listings in this chapter. This way, you can see some of the improvements that additional coding scenarios provide. Furthermore, I have updated some of the earlier chapter scenarios and created more complex representations with concurrency techniques built in. In addition, I plan on adding some small projects that show a developer how to abstract concurrency algorithms in business objects (e.g., thread-safe collections and multithreaded extension methods). Please visit the companion web site for additional information.

Summary

This chapter covered the important topic of utilizing concurrent programming patterns in Silverlight technology. The chapter began with an overview of basics of multicore architecture and processes. Then it covered multithreading concepts that any professional software engineer developing on current hardware should understand.

There are several vital takeaways from this topic. You should understand the unique advantages that Silverlight and .NET multithreading technology bring to RIA software. Furthermore, after reading the chapter, you should note how multithreading optimization can be a very powerful tool in your arsenal to give your software a competitive edge. The two coding scenarios, covering UI and computational concurrency processing, applied the power of Silverlight's multithreading features in simple business scenarios.

In summary, BI software clients can be very resource demanding. Implementing multithreading concepts on Silverlight can help optimize performance and dramatically improve the user experience. Applying concurrent programming techniques in Silverlight allows you to create highly visual analytical BI modules that remain responsive and process algorithms quickly.

■ ■ ■

CHAPTER 11

Integrating with Business Intelligence Systems

Over the past ten chapters, you have learned that Silverlight is a powerful technology that can deliver BI 2.0 concepts. Hopefully, the past content has made a compelling argument that Silverlight can successfully surface BI 2.0 modules. It is time to cover how to design Silverlight applications so they can be successfully integrated and deployed across BI systems. In this chapter, you will learn what enterprise components are required to be able to deploy Silverlight effectively. Furthermore, you will learn the various architecture options associated with Silverlight.

Silverlight being a plug-in technology opens up a variety of architecture strategies that can be used to deploy Silverlight almost anywhere (e.g., the Web, an Azure instance, the desktop, a mobile app, etc.). This unique feature allows Silverlight modules to be used as full applications or individual components that integrate with existing BI systems. Do you want to deploy a full Silverlight BI application? Do you want to integrate Silverlight in your existing system? Do you want to deploy Silverlight modules without losing the interactivity? Do you want your Silverlight applications to communicate with each other? These are the questions this chapter aims to answer.

There are no coding scenarios included in this chapter. However, there are several code samples that highlight Silverlight business intelligence architecture integration strategies. These samples will highlight integration into existing or brand new business intelligence systems.

This chapter will be a high level introduction to integration techniques that I will look at more in detail in the upcoming chapters. You will see how concepts in this chapter apply to SharePoint 2010, mobile devices, and the Silverlight Pivot control in the upcoming chapters.

The following table outlines the specific goals that different types of readers will achieve by reading this chapter.

Audience	Goals
Silverlight developers	Learn how to architect Silverlight applications for integration strategies.
	Understand the pros and cons of different integration options.
	See how separate Silverlight applications communicate and interact with each other.
Business intelligence professionals	Learn how Silverlight can potentially integrate with existing BI deployments.

Audience	Goals
	Understand the role Silverlight BI modules can play in BI systems.
Strategic decision makers	See if investing in Silverlight will allow you to integrate with existing BI investments.
	Understand if Silverlight is a good fit for business strategies, including using portals, web parts, and SaaS (Software as a Service).

Architecting for Business Intelligence Systems

Investing in Silverlight to deliver BI content is much more than just learning the technology and implementing it. As discussed in previous chapters, the Silverlight plug-in model and the technology itself present a series of opportunities and challenges that need to be understood in the planning phase of the development life cycle.

Infrastructure and Software Requirements

In BI systems, data artifacts are the most important parts of the system. The data is collected, cleansed, and aggregated from a variety of sources and usually placed in a central repository that is the "single version of truth" for the BI system. This repository guarantees that the data contained is accurate, complete, precise, and fully representative of the purpose of the system. In BI, these repositories are usually implemented using data warehousing, master data management (MDM), customer data integration (CDI), and other enterprise data architecture techniques. In these systems, data governance policies provide the structure for data access.

In classic BI (BI 1.0) systems, the importance of data architecture was not well understood. Some of the original implementations were treated as disparate systems, and the data quality, integration, accuracy, and data lineage were different across the data repositories. As BI implementations matured, enterprise architecture practices evolved to improve the data synchronization across the different repositories. Figure 11-1 illustrates a hub-and-spoke (data hub) model that uses the aforementioned central repository that is the "single version of truth" as the hub. The spokes of the hub are interfaces that expose specific data views of the main repository.

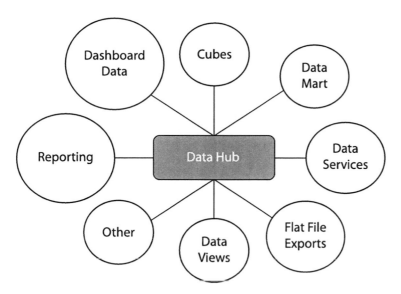

Figure 11-1. *A BI hub-and-spoke architecture for exposing data assets as interfaces*

This is a popular architecture of exposing customized data endpoints to specific applications. For example, if you have a data warehouse (hub) that includes 30 years of data, there's no point in exposing all of this data if your reporting data needs span only the last couple of years. The data hub model allows the data architect to have a single reliable source (single version of truth) of data and provide different data views as data interfaces. This keeps the interfaces lightweight and able to scale while having them build off of a data repository that has been certified as the single version of truth for the organization. This architectural style promotes reuse of the main data repository and of the individual interface spokes across different applications.

Figure 11-2 illustrates an example of a spoke using the data provided in multiple applications. In this figure, you can see that the data for the year 2009 is exposed as a spoke that is a source for web parts, executive dashboard, reports etc. Partitioning the data by a timeframe (in this example, a year) is just one strategy. The spokes could be partitioned by regions (i.e., North America, South America) or different summary levels of aggregation (i.e., invoice level, customer level). This dramatically mitigates the amount of data that needs to be scanned and sent to a Silverlight application.

Figure 11-2. An interface spoke can provide data to several applications in larger BI environments.

The integration and interface architecture is very important when deciding to use technologies such as Silverlight. Silverlight can only consume data from data service interfaces. In Figure 11-1, Silverlight would only be able to be used to surface content from the data services interface spoke and the flat file exports interface (if upload functionality were written in a Silverlight application). Silverlight cannot talk to proprietary protocols easily and consume data from a database or a multidimensional cube directly. Even current Microsoft BI offerings (e.g., Analysis Services, Reporting Services, etc.) do not provide the appropriate service interfaces to consume their data in Silverlight. An organization that has not invested in exposing a large amount of content via data services will simply not be able to use Silverlight effectively to present BI content.

Organizations using internal and external BI systems came to realize that having different technology implementations as their spokes was a problem. This caused more issues when new technologies were introduced as integration points. How do you deal with these differing interfaces using different technologies? For example, if a BI software vendor builds a series of Analysis Services cubes, they can be consumed by users using software that knows how to communicate with the ADOMD.NET protocol or the Microsoft proprietary MDX query language (multidimensional expressions). These interfaces could include business processes that provide value to the data. In the preceding example, if the client wanted to understand the underlying data or business processes better, they would have to understand proprietary protocols or query languages in order to achieve this. Each spoke (interface) faces the same problem. This problem becomes amplified when data security, availability control, and data quality issues arise. How can you control data quality when a customer is writing custom SQL code against your data repository to access the information?

▪ **Note** As mentioned in the previous chapters, Microsoft is opening up access to all of their systems (SQL Server Reporting Services, SharePoint 2010, and others) using the OData protocol, which can be consumed by Silverlight 4. In the near future, I fully expect that the entire SQL Server business intelligence platform to surface data and content using these open conventions that make data consumption easier.

In current BI architectures, service-oriented architecture (SOA) complements the data integration strategies in order to provide common interfaces. This allows the master data assets to be made available through consistent and singly defined service endpoints. Common interfaces (e.g., service APIs) allow the consumers to access the data, workflows, and business processes that are central to the data hub and its interfaces. Furthermore, this architecture can be extended in complex data integration scenarios to replace ETL (extract-transform-load) and other load processes that make up the data integration hubs themselves. The next generation of enterprise data integration architecture has evolved into MDM, which is a set of architecture and framework principles that provide data artifacts in a common methodology to the enterprise (internal and external) across different applications and business processes.

MDM architectures, along with SOA, allow the creation of master data repositories that expose interfaces with commonly defined services. This allows data interfaces to be consumed in a single manner using an implementation that is technology neutral for the consuming client. Furthermore, MDM and SOA centralize the interfaces, which allows data governance principles to be applied to the interfaces easily. Data governance such as security, data availability, instrumentation, data entity management, and so on can be applied across the entire system in a shared service bus, giving the system complete control over how the data is used.

MDM implementations use the data integration hub models. There are various architectural hub implementations that determine how the data is stored and synchronized with secondary repositories. Figure 11-3 shows a donut of data services that expose all the information for all the interface spokes. Data services are not a substitute for implementing specific interface spokes (e.g., cubes). However, they are used in conjunction with the data hub spokes to provide endpoints for consuming the underlying information and business logic in a common standard mechanism.

■ **Note** MDM, SOA, and data governance are the current evolving frontiers in BI 2.0 systems. Applying these principles in enterprise data integration systems is an evolution over previous data warehousing techniques. If you are a stakeholder in BI software development, I highly encourage you to become familiar with these concepts. Please visit the accompanying web site for more resources on these topics.

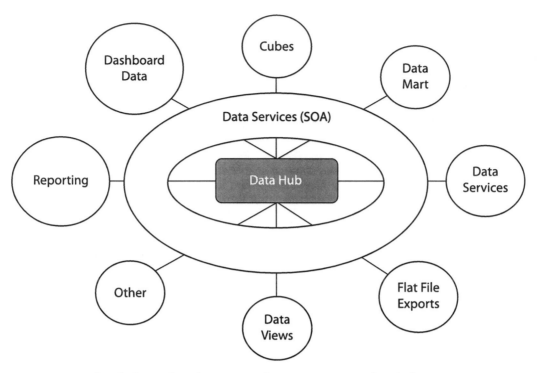

Figure 11-3. A data hub interface that exposes data services as interface endpoints

The maturity of the data integration architecture in the underlying BI system is important in order to deploy technologies like Silverlight to present information. You need data services that expose a single version of truth of your data and business processes in order to effectively use Silverlight in BI analytical tools. Having a complete SOA will allow a BI architect to expose any content across your master data hub. Without the investment in proper data integration management, Silverlight can only be used sparingly to implement specific or one-off pieces of functionality which would raise many red flags for an enterprise data architect.

Non-Microsoft Infrastructures

One of the big misconceptions about Silverlight is that it requires a robust investment in a Microsoft stack in order to be deployed effectively. Nothing could be further from the truth. While it is true that Silverlight is based on .NET and requires a .NET-based development environment, it does not require a Microsoft host server or a Microsoft BI infrastructure (e.g., SharePoint, Analysis Services, Integration Services, or SQL Server).

As discussed in the Introduction, a Silverlight application is just a compressed file (XAP package) that gets transferred to the client and executed locally in the browser or on the desktop. Nothing about Silverlight requires it to run on a Windows Server, ASP.NET, or Internet Information Services (IIS). You can host Silverlight on the Apache web server and integrate with it using PHP or other dynamic languages that can interface with the HTML on the client. Silverlight can integrate with certain Microsoft features. For example, high-definition (HD) smooth streaming works on IIS 7.0 only. However, I would guess that this is not of primary concern for BI software. Portal integration strategies like web parts (discussed later in this chapter) do require ASP.NET; however, if you are not using Microsoft SharePoint or ASP.NET web parts, you will not be clamoring for this feature.

In the preceding section, I highlighted the importance of data services for Silverlight deployments. Silverlight benefits from WCF (Windows Communication Foundation) integration. This allows Silverlight to consume advanced service-binding configurations like streaming and duplex polling. However, in BI systems, you rarely need transactional, streaming, or polling service consumers. This is the main reason why MDM service interfaces are exposed in technology-neutral endpoints. For example, exposing an RSS feed in XML or a service using RESTful principles is advocated, as it maximizes the amount of potential consumers. This is especially important in CDI (client-facing MDM architecture) scenarios where a BI system has to work and comply with technology consumers that are different from the system implementation or that might change in the future. Silverlight can be implemented successfully in BI systems that use other enterprise BI vendors such as SAP, IBM, or Oracle. The only requirement is that the data service endpoints need to be implemented in a manner that allows nonproprietary technologies to retrieve the data. Most current enterprise MDM software vendors provide mechanisms that expose data services in an open paradigm that allows different technologies to consume the information.

The BI architect needs to do the proper research when attempting to integrate Silverlight into the system. There are articles on the Web that lead developers to believe that Silverlight cannot be used with complex or non-Microsoft services. Obviously, integration with proprietary protocols and custom services (custom SOAP services) will not be possible without a lot of development effort. However, there are very few technologies out there that allow you to connect everywhere to anything with ease.

New BI 2.0 Applications

Silverlight is a great technology that can deliver complete end-to-end, next-generation BI solutions. Many existing application samples do not highlight the fact that Silverlight is much more than just a small module or media player. Full-blown BI dashboards, analytical engines, and visual intelligence tools can be created as self-reliant business applications that do not need help from other supporting technologies. The Silverlight development environment and included controls allow developers to create a wide range of business applications. In the past chapters, you have seen how flexible the Silverlight environment is when extending existing visualization controls or creating new interactive BI 2.0 analytical tools. As a BI professional or application architect, you should feel comfortable by now that a Silverlight solution can implement BI 2.0 concepts and deliver insight from data effectively.

Creating an entire BI application in Silverlight is appropriate when you do not have many existing or planned integration points. A large Silverlight screen that takes up a majority of real estate would be hard to integrate as a small web part or place in an existing portal. Items like this need to be thought out carefully before deciding to go this route.

There are several benefits to creating full Silverlight BI applications:

- Application development is faster because all of the components reside in a single application using a single code base using a common language and shared components.

- A single technology is being used to deliver the content which frees developers from worrying about integration with other technologies (i.e. mixing Java with .NET code).

- The full scope of inner control communication can be taken advantage of with Silverlight. This means that controls can communicate with each other in real time and provide immediate insight to the user in BI applications.

- The entire Silverlight application can be treated as a single deployable module. This means that integration into custom portals such as Cognos 8 or SharePoint 2010 is much easier.

Figure 11-4 illustrates a sample dashboard laid out using Silverlight Backlight controls and implemented completely in Silverlight. The individual charting and grid controls share the same data collections and can communicate with the preceding filter controls. This provides real-time feedback to the user without the page posting back to the server.

Figure 11-4. A simple dashboard implemented completely in a Silverlight application

This dashboard also illustrates how easy it is to create a rich analytical environment while maintaining a good amount of real estate. The dynamic nature of the docking controls allows the dashboard controls to be scaled appropriately without having to jump to another screen or popping out a window of details. Figure 11-5 illustrates the pie chart visualization maximized while the grid is minimized to the bottom-right corner. The dashboard remains fully functional and interactive. Therefore, all of the concepts of interactivity, real-time analytical insight, and client-distributed architecture can work together seamlessly in a dashboard that is implemented in a homogenous technology such as Silverlight.

Figures 11-4 and 11-5 do not do the dashboard justice. A demo of this simple dashboard and the corresponding source code are available on the accompanying web site (www.silverlighbusinessintelligence.com).

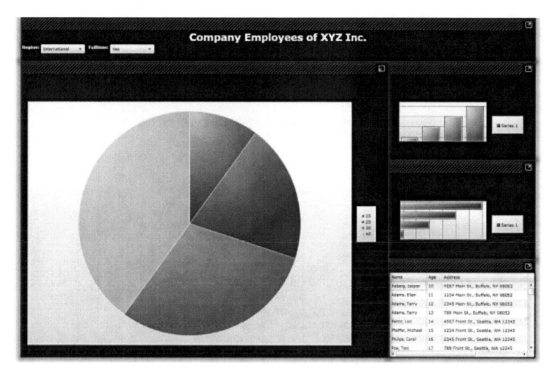

Figure 11-5. Silverlight dashboard with a charting visualization maximized

---

■ **Note** Silverlight Backlight controls are a great way to create composite dashboards for BI. If you are interested in using these controls for your project, see http://backlight.codeplex.com.

Integrating with Existing BI Investments

An investment in BI systems is expensive since these systems include many tiers and components that have to work together. As technology evolves, these systems can look dated just a few years after their initial design. It is very expensive to rewrite entire complex systems with new technologies.

Silverlight's plug-in model provides flexible options that can extend the life of the original BI system investment. As shown in previous chapters, Silverlight can be used in a BI environment to provide a distributed architecture performance, implement visual intelligence (data visualizations), provide interactive BI modules, and implement predictive analytics and collective intelligence concepts. Original BI 1.0 systems that lack these next-generation BI 2.0 features can be extended by injecting Silverlight properly. For example, an existing executive dashboard that has static charting visualizations can be extended with a Silverlight module that provides an interactive predictive sales model, like the one described in Chapter 9. This is one of the major advantages of having Silverlight technology implemented as a browser plug-in model.

Basic Integration

One of the easiest and most effective ways to integrate a Silverlight solution into an existing web site is to simply leverage the plug-in model architecture. You have probably seen web sites that provide you with HTML tags that allow you to embed the site's widgets, videos, lists, and other content in your own web site. This is essentially how Silverlight BI modules can be integrated into existing web BI investments. Figure 11-6 diagrams a simple example of how Silverlight can be embedded into an HTML page using a div that contains the Silverlight object. Using CSS and fluid design techniques, this can be customized to integrate the Silverlight module seamlessly into the web site.

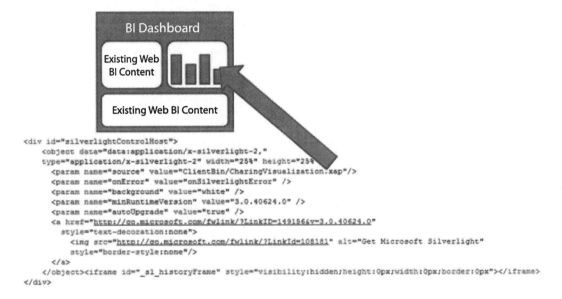

Figure 11-6. Silverlight content can be integrated at a basic level using the HTML plug-in model.

This type of integration is very basic, and I would only recommend it for one-off modules. For example, in Chapter 9, you created an interactive Silverlight module that predicted the success of a batter getting a hit. This is a great example of a simple analytical tool implemented in Silverlight that could be integrated into an existing BI solution. The Silverlight solution could be used to modernize parts of the BI solution without having to re-architect the entire web site.

Communicating Between Separate Silverlight Applications

As you add more Silverlight modules, you will probably want them to communicate with each other. You do not want to lose the interactivity between Silverlight modules. Figure 11-7 adds an additional Silverlight module to your existing BI dashboard. Now you have two Silverlight components, and one of them has a data filter. You want these two visualizations to be in sync when the filter is changed.

Figure 11-7. *Silverlight 4 includes a LocalCommunication API to facilitate inner Silverlight application communication.*

Silverlight includes a LocalCommunication API feature that allows communication between two completely separate Silverlight applications (XAP files). Up to 1MB of string data can be sent between two applications (which can be serialized or deserialized to objects). In most cases, you probably just want to send the filter parameter(s) and allow the consumer to retrieve the associated data from a data service.

Figure 11-8 illustrates an HTML page that has two separate Silverlight applications hosted together. The left Silverlight application includes a grid and a combo box that allows the user to select a region. Once the region is selected, the grid is updated accordingly. However, you want to keep the data across these two applications in sync so that when someone selects a region, the corresponding charting visualizations are bound to the proper region.

Figure 11-8. *Two separate Silverlight applications (XAP files) that need to communicate to keep the data in sync.*

Before you get into the implementation, you need to define what the actionable control is and how the communication is going to flow. The Silverlight application on the left is a publisher of data and will be sending the selected region information to the Silverlight chart visualization on the right. The charting visualization will be a simple consumer and will not be sending data back to the Silverlight application on the left. Therefore, you have a simple publisher-subscriber (pub-sub) model, and the subscriber simply needs to listen to changes that are made on the publisher Silverlight application.

Listing 11-1 shows the code necessary for the publisher application that implements the LocalCommunication API. Note that the code for the publisher is very simple and only requires two lines of code related to the Silverlight LocalCommunication API. There are essentially two parts to set up the publisher part. First, you need to instantiate a LocalMessageSender object and pass in the type of communication (in your example, it is Region). The second step involves sending the message using the SendAsync method with the message content formatted as a string. In this example, you are simply sending the selected region from the combo box (i.e., North, South, and International).

Listing 11-1. The Relevant LocalCommunication Message Provider Code is Highlighted in Bold.

```
public partial class MainPage : UserControl
{
    // collection of sales data
    List<Sale> sales = new List<Sale>();

    // set up the sender to send Region type information
    LocalMessageSender msgSender = new LocalMessageSender("Region");

    public MainPage()
    {
        InitializeComponent();
    }

    private void ComboBox_SelectionChanged(object sender, ↵
System.Windows.Controls.SelectionChangedEventArgs e)
    {
        ComboBoxItem item = e.AddedItems[0] as ComboBoxItem;

        if (this.Grid != null)
        {
            // bind the grid initially
            this.Grid.ItemsSource = this.sales.Where(a => a.Region ==↵
item.Content.ToString());

            // send selected region
            msgSender.SendAsync(item.Content.ToString());
        }
    }
...
```

Now that you have the provider set up, the consumer needs to be set up to receive messages (see Listing 11-2). On the consumer application, you need to instantiate an instance of the LocalMessageReceiver class. This object has two important tasks: listening for incoming messages and, when incoming messages are processed, doing something with them. In this example, when you receive a message that the region has changed, you will simply filter the data based on that region using a local

LINQ query. In a real production application, this would call a data service and retrieve the information from there using an asynchronous data retrieval pattern.

Listing 11-2. Relevant LocalCommunication Message Consumer Code is Highlighted in Bold.

```
public partial class MainPage : UserControl
{
    // collection of sales
    List<Sale> sales = new List<Sale>();

    public MainPage()
    {
        InitializeComponent();
    }

    private void LayoutRoot_Loaded(object sender, System.Windows.RoutedEventArgs e)
    {
        // Set up receiver to listen to messages of type Region
        LocalMessageReceiver receiver = new LocalMessageReceiver("Region");

        // Add an event handler when a message is received
        receiver.MessageReceived +=
            new EventHandler<MessageReceivedEventArgs>(receiver_MessageReceived);

        // Receiver listens to incoming messages
        receiver.Listen();

        // bind the chart initially on load to the North region
        this.DataContext = sales.Where(a => a.Region == "North");
    }

    void receiver_MessageReceived(object sender, MessageReceivedEventArgs e)
    {
        // This method is called when a message is received
        // Filter the sales data based on selected region from provider
        this.DataContext = sales.Where(a => a.Region == e.Message);
    }
...
```

■ **Note** A full demo and source code for the application is available on the companion web site for this book (www.silverlighbusinessintelligence.com).

The LocalCommunication API allows the BI developer to create individual modules that can communicate between each other. I cannot stress enough how fast this communication bridge is. Fully interactive communication is possible among multiple controls for providing real-time feedback. For example, moving a slider thumb's effects in one application can be immediately seen in the second

Silverlight application. This feature, introduced in Silverlight version 3, allows for a true implementation of BI 2.0 theory.

Silverlight in the SaaS Model

SaaS (Software as a Service) is a popular architectural model for organizations to provide their solutions as a service. This type of model has become a very popular mechanism to deliver software to customers in license form. Customers benefit because they only license the modules or services they need, paying only for what they use. As the customers need extra licenses, more users, or increased functionality, they can increase their investments and purchase higher-level solutions from the vendor. Vendors benefit from SaaS models because they can deliver their solutions from a centralized location to a wide range of customers that previously could not implement the solution.

SaaS for BI

Traditional customer BI solutions involve installing enterprise software on servers. These servers house the data repositories, ETL processes, and applications that the internal client's users would use. This required on-site presence of multiple servers obviously has an associated infrastructure cost. Not all customers can afford this type of infrastructure or have an IT staff to maintain the hardware. As a result, small businesses have been unable to take advantage of BI.

The delivery of BI is changing rapidly. As mentioned, BI 2.0 is about delivering BI to the masses and average users. This includes smaller organizations or industries that have not traditionally used BI. In addition, this includes single users. Smaller organizations or individual users simply cannot afford to host servers in-house. Therefore, delivering BI solutions as a service has become an increasingly attractive model for software vendors. BI vendors can now offer a subset of their enterprise products as services and collect revenue from "down-market" clients that they were previously ignoring.

SaaS Features Implemented in Silverlight

The SaaS model implementations vary depending on which expert you talk to. The SaaS model is rapidly evolving and thus is not fully mature yet. New cost-cutting technologies like cloud computing and virtualization are further enhancing the model and making it more attractive to businesses. In the next couple of sections, I will talk about how Silverlight can be used to implement key SaaS model features.

Centralized Management of Service Delivery

The cornerstone of the SaaS model is the ability to deliver software and services from a centralized location. This includes hosting, maintaining, and updating the service in that central location. In the Web 2.0 age, this means delivering content on the Internet from domains that do not belong to the consumer.

The Silverlight plug-in model facilitates the SaaS model natively. As mentioned, a Silverlight application can be as simple as just one XAP file. All that is needed to host this XAP file is a properly formatted HTML Silverlight object with the proper parameters. Figure 11-9 illustrates how a Silverlight XAP file is hosted on a web page and delivered to the client workstation.

SomeServiceDomain.com

HTML Page

Silverlight XAP
Package

Figure 11-9. Silverlight XAP packages are brought down to the client's workstation where the application executes locally.

SaaS models are usually implemented using web technologies hosted on the vendor's server on their domain. This allows the web site to be managed centrally and updated as needed. What Silverlight provides natively is another level of abstraction and separation of concerns in the SaaS model. Therefore, if the vendor needs to update a particular piece of functionality, it might only have to make a single change to the Silverlight XAP package which will be reflected on the client's workstation. The other key benefits of using Silverlight in a SaaS model is that you gain the performance of a desktop application without having to install complex software on the user's workstation. As discussed in previous chapters, architects can implement advanced caching and distributed architecture mechanisms that can dramatically improve the performance of the entire system. Web applications can only offload so much processing using Ajax and JavaScript techniques. Silverlight takes this to another level which makes the Silverlight SaaS models even more scalable.

Let's take a look at a more complex SaaS model example. Figure 11-10 displays an example model for a software vendor that provides interactive Silverlight BI components with data services. Instead of just providing an RSS or data feed, this vendor uses the power of Silverlight to visualize the information in various controls. These controls are then sold to various other web sites that incorporate the Silverlight BI components in their custom web sites.

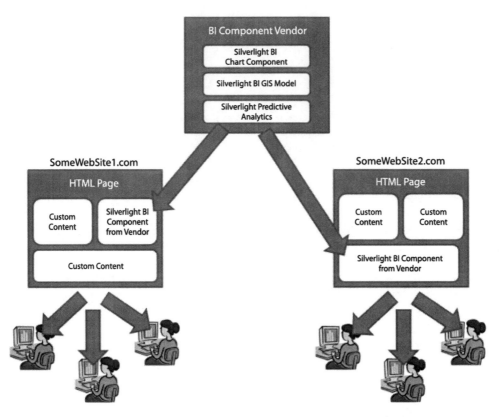

Figure 11-10. *Silverlight components can be provided by a vendor for reuse on different web sites.*

The figure illustrates a model similar to the popular widget model provided by a lot of web sites. This allows content from different network locations to be hosted on different domains. You can see from the example that two web sites (who are customers of the BI component vendor) are exposing the Silverlight components to their customers without hosting the components themselves. They simply have a pointer HTML tag to the component location on the BI component vendor's web site.

This is a fundamentally powerful concept for SaaS. If the vendor wants to update the version of the component or provide additional functionality, this can be done very easily. Nothing extra has to be done to the Silverlight application for this to work in most scenarios.

In order to reinforce this concept, I took a sample Silverlight package from a previous chapter and placed the XAP file on my domain at `www.silverlighthack.com/sample/sample.xap`. To follow along, simply open Visual Studio, create a new Silverlight project, and call it TestSaaS. In `TestSaaSTestPage.aspx`, you are going to change the reference of the Silverlight application from the project to the one located on my domain. Listing 11-3 shows the new code highlighted in bold.

Listing 11-3. *Silverlight Object Tag Receiving an Application from a Remote Domain*

```
<div id="silverlightControlHost">
    <object data="data:application/x-silverlight-2," type="application/x-silverlight-2"↵
 width="100%" height="100%">
```

```
<param name="source" value="http://www.silverlighthack.com/sample/sample.xap"/>
<param name="onError" value="onSilverlightError" />
<param name="background" value="white" />
```

When you run the application locally, the Silverlight application will be transferred from the silverlighthack.com domain. Figure 11-11 shows the Internet profile of the TestSaaS application. Notice that the HTML and JavaScript files are hosted on the local web server. However, the sample.xap file is brought down from silverlighthack.com via a reference in the local HTML file and executed on the client workstation.

URL	Status	Timestamp	Response Size	Connection Time	Response Time
http://localhost:56524/TestSaaSTestPage.aspx	200	9/13/2009 3:16:18 AM	3,079	00:00:0000	00:00:0000
http://localhost:56524/Silverlight.js	200	9/13/2009 3:16:18 AM	7,680	00:00:0000	00:00:0000
http://www.silverlighthack.com/sample/sample.xap	200	9/13/2009 3:16:18 AM	56,653	00:00:0000	00:00:0000

Figure 11-11. Sample Silverlight application brought down from a remote host

One very important note to take away is that I did not change the XAP file at all from its original creation when the exercise was coded. Again, I did not do anything special code-wise. Furthermore, I did not have to do anything different to compile or deploy it. This cross domain reference just worked. Compare this with deployment options like ClickOnce for WPF which does require additional changes to be made in order to work vs. a traditional WPF desktop application.

In a real SaaS environment, you would obviously not reference Silverlight XAP files directly. The SaaS vendor would provide their customers with an API key and service reference that would process the licensing, security, and client information before allowing the Silverlight application to be downloaded. In addition, a Silverlight BI SaaS model would probably include data service components that needed to be called. This would be another SaaS artifact that would not be referenced directly, and appropriate security and licensing mechanisms would be applied between the customer and SaaS vendor.

■ **Note** The full scope of implementing SaaS model topics is well beyond the scope of this book. However, if you are familiar with delivering software/services in the SaaS model, the same concepts that apply to web applications apply to Silverlight SaaS model deliveries. If you are new to SaaS architecture concepts, I recommend that you read current content. In my opinion, SaaS models that do not incorporate virtualization or cloud computing are legacy architecture foundations.

SaaS Maturity Model

SaaS architectures are classified into groups based on how the SaaS model is implemented and executed by the SaaS vendor. There are many variables that depend on how a SaaS vendor is classified. The key attributes are how well the SaaS model scales, whether the baseline supports all of the client needs, and whether the application is dynamically configurable. As the SaaS model supports all of these attributes in an automated fashion, it is classified in higher maturity levels.

Mature SaaS models are highly configurable models with a common baseline that can support the needs of all the clients while maintaining a high degree of scalability and the ability to grow almost indefinitely. The goal for most SaaS vendors is to be able to claim that their baseline software and their services can achieve the highest degree of maturity as a SaaS deployment.

■ **Note** For more information on SaaS maturity model levels and what they mean, see `http://blogs.msdn.com/architectsrule/archive/2008/08/18/saas-maturity-model-according-to-forrester.aspx`.

This is another area where Silverlight technology truly shines. You have seen that Silverlight allows different XAP files to be delivered to customers based on licensing (this would be the lowest SaaS maturity level). However, Silverlight's architecture allows for Silverlight applications to be created dynamically on the fly from assemblies in remote locations! This allows SaaS architects to model composite applications from multiple features for customers. The highest level of SaaS maturity dictates that a common software foundation is used to deliver scalable services that are customizable for each customer instance.

Silverlight's deployment model allows you to defer the loading of some client assemblies until they are needed. For example, in a SaaS model, Client1234 could have an application with additional menu options providing additional functionality for which the client has paid. Furthermore, dynamic composite applications allow for individual pages or components to be delivered differently among clients.

This can be implemented a number of ways. One way is to implement dynamic assembly loading in the codebehind in the Silverlight application. In a SaaS model, the Silverlight client could call a service that would determine what assemblies and which versions are loaded for a particular client. These assemblies can be loaded dynamically. Using basic OOP principles or reflection, the customized assemblies can be seamlessly integrated into the baseline code. Listing 11-4 shows some basic C# code that makes a service request in order to get a list of required assemblies and then loads these assemblies from remote locations. The code is not production ready, but it can be further enhanced to provide a good baseline for achieving dynamic module loading (this is made much easier with the MEF/Prism frameworks described later in this chapter).

Listing 11-4. Dynamically Loading Assemblies from Locations Provided by a Service

```
...
// list of assembly locations
List<string> assemblyLocations = new List<string>();

public MainPage()
{
    InitializeComponent();
}

private void LayoutRoot_Loaded(object sender, RoutedEventArgs e)
{
    // Call the service to retrieve a list of assembly locations

    // set the service URL
    string url = "http://silverlighthack.com/Assemblies/0232;343434";

    // perform the REST call async
```

```
    WebClient assemblyService = new WebClient();

    assemblyService.DownloadStringCompleted +=
        new DownloadStringCompletedEventHandler(assemblyService_DownloadStringCompleted);

    assemblyService.DownloadStringAsync(new Uri(url, UriKind.Absolute));
}

void assemblyService_DownloadStringCompleted(object sender, ↵
 DownloadStringCompletedEventArgs e)
{
    // serialize the string JSON result to a list of assemblies
    this.assemblyLocations = this.deserializeListOfAssemblies(e.Result);

    // download the list of assemblies
    this.loadAssemblies();
}

private List<string> deserializeListOfAssemblies( string jsonString )
{
    using( MemoryStream ms = new MemoryStream( Encoding.Unicode.GetBytes( jsonString ) ) )
    {
        DataContractJsonSerializer serializer -
            new DataContractJsonSerializer( typeof( List<string> ) );

        return ( List<string> )serializer.ReadObject( ms );
    }
}



private void loadAssemblies()
{
    // iterate through the assembly locations and download them from the web site
    foreach (string assemblyUrl in this.assemblyLocations)
    {
        WebClient wcAssembly = new WebClient();

        wcAssembly.OpenReadCompleted +=
            new OpenReadCompletedEventHandler(wcAssembly_OpenReadCompleted);

        wcAssembly.OpenReadAsync(
            new Uri(assemblyUrl, UriKind.Relative));
    }
}

void wcAssembly_OpenReadCompleted(object sender, OpenReadCompletedEventArgs e)
{
    if ((e.Error == null) && (e.Cancelled == false))
    {
        // load the assembly into the Silverlight project domain
        AssemblyPart assemblyPart = new AssemblyPart();
```

```
        assemblyPart.Load(e.Result);
    }
}
```

This technique works for Silverlight 2 through Silverlight 4. Silverlight 3 extends this functionality by introducing a technique called *assembly caching*. The purpose of this feature is to reduce the size of the main Silverlight application by providing the network locations where the additional components can be located. This is controlled by the application manifest file (AppManifest.xaml) that is embedded with every Silverlight XAP application. What is great about this feature is that this does not require manually writing code to figure out what assemblies to load and how.

Using this feature in a SaaS model is pretty obvious if you understand how the Silverlight XAP application is packaged. Figure 11-12 shows a Silverlight XAP package open in a compression tool which illustrates that the XAP package is simply a compressed file (using ZIP compression) of the assemblies that constitute the application. This compressed file (XAP package) is then decompressed on the client and loaded into memory.

These assemblies can take up a lot of space that needs to be downloaded initially. This is especially true for assemblies that contain font glyphs. For example, integrating a complete font assembly (alpha characters, numbers, etc.) in Silverlight can easily take up over 1 MB of space!

File	Size	Modified	Type
..	<UP--DIR>	9/13/2009 1:59:20 PM	Local Disk
AppManifest.xaml	1,335	9/13/2009 1:50:38 PM	Windows Markup File
SaaSDynamicAssemblies.dll	9,728	9/13/2009 1:59:16 PM	Application Extension
System.ComponentModel.DataAnnotations.dll	75,640	6/23/2009 10:12:2...	Application Extension
System.Data.Services.Client.dll	325,480	6/23/2009 10:12:2...	Application Extension
System.Json.dll	51,016	6/23/2009 10:12:2...	Application Extension
System.ServiceModel.PollingDuplex.dll	141,168	6/23/2009 10:12:2...	Application Extension
System.ServiceModel.Syndication.dll	116,592	6/23/2009 10:12:2...	Application Extension
System.Windows.Data.dll	71,512	6/23/2009 10:12:2...	Application Extension
System.Windows.Interactivity.dll	45,056	7/14/2009 6:56:12 PM	Application Extension
System.Xml.Linq.dll	124,752	6/23/2009 10:12:2...	Application Extension
System.Xml.Serialization.dll	321,376	6/23/2009 10:12:2...	Application Extension
System.Xml.Utils.dll	108,368	6/23/2009 10:12:2...	Application Extension

Figure 11-12. The contents of a Silverlight XAP application include assemblies and a AppManifest.xaml file.

Back-end SaaS services can be created to customize Silverlight XAP packages for clients. A combination of IIS HttpModules and services could automatically inject the proper AppManifest.xaml file for each Silverlight application for individual SaaS customers. This would allow for a high-maturity SaaS level implementation because a common baseline could be dynamically customized for each customer with ease. Listing 11-5 shows an AppManifest.xaml file with the dynamic assembly section highlighted in bold. If the objects in these assemblies are well factored and abstracted, the dependency injection pattern can be used to inject objects of varying implementations across the application in a similar fashion.

Listing 11-5. Assembly Packages Located in the ExternalParts Element will be Loaded Dynamically by a Silverlight Application.

```xml
<Deployment xmlns="http://schemas.microsoft.com/client/2007/deployment"
xmlns:x="http://schemas.microsoft.com/winfx/2006/xaml"
EntryPointAssembly="SaaSDynamicAssemblies"
EntryPointType="SaaSDynamicAssemblies.App"
RuntimeVersion="3.0.40624.0">
  <Deployment.Parts>
    <AssemblyPart x:Name="SaaSDynamicAssemblies" Source="SaaSDynamicAssemblies.dll" />
    <AssemblyPart x:Name="System.ComponentModel.DataAnnotations"
 Source="System.ComponentModel.DataAnnotations.dll" />
    <AssemblyPart x:Name="System.Data.Services.Client"
Source="System.Data.Services.Client.dll" />
    <AssemblyPart x:Name="System.Json" Source="System.Json.dll" />
    <AssemblyPart x:Name="System.ServiceModel.PollingDuplex"
 Source="System.ServiceModel.PollingDuplex.dll" />
    <AssemblyPart x:Name="System.ServiceModel.Syndication"
 Source="System.ServiceModel.Syndication.dll" />
    <AssemblyPart x:Name="System.Windows.Data" Source="System.Windows.Data.dll" />
    <AssemblyPart x:Name="System.Windows.Interactivity"
 Source="System.Windows.Interactivity.dll" />
    <AssemblyPart x:Name="System.Xml.Linq" Source="System.Xml.Linq.dll" />
    <AssemblyPart x:Name="System.Xml.Serialization" Source="System.Xml.Serialization.dll" />
    <AssemblyPart x:Name="System.Xml.Utils" Source="System.Xml.Utils.dll" />
  </Deployment.Parts>
  <Deployment.ExternalParts>
    <ExtensionPart Source="/Client234/CustomBusinessLogic.zip" />
    <ExtensionPart Source="/Client234/CustomVisualizations.zip" />
    <ExtensionPart Source="/Client234/CustomInteractions.zip" />
  </Deployment.ExternalParts>
</Deployment>
```

Enterprise Composite Applications

Large Silverlight business applications should be architected using the enterprise composite application patterns in order to be hosted in SaaS models. Designing a framework that can encompass all of the composition, scalability, communication, and abstraction processes yourself is not recommended. Luckily for Silverlight architects, there are a couple of enterprise application frameworks that allow for modular and dynamic composition of Silverlight content into large-scale applications. These frameworks are ideal for hosting Silverlight content in a SaaS model because loosely coupled components can make up client-specific deliverables in a dynamic fashion. This allows Silverlight applications to be delivered with specific client functionality depending on security, licensing, version, and so on, which is the ideal answer for SaaS implementations. Two of the most popular Silverlight composite application frameworks are the Managed Extensibility Framework (MEF) and Composite Application Guidance Libraries (Prism):

- *Managed Extensibility Framework*: This framework simplifies the creation of extensible enterprise applications. The primary function of this framework is for third parties to extend application functionality from a common baseline. Application contracts can be exported to interfaces that can later be dependency injected dynamically to create composite applications. As of Silverlight version 4, MEF is now part of the Silverlight framework. For previous versions of Silverlight (Silverlight 3) visit www.codeplex.com/MEF for the MEF assemblies. One of the benefits of this framework is that it uses aspect oriented programming patterns (AOP) that allows you to code your components as you normally would; the developer is responsible for only "decorating" the artifacts with proper attributes and attribute properties. This makes the framework very unobtrusive to your business logic.

- *Composite Application Guidance Libraries (Prism)*: Prism is a set of related libraries provided by Microsoft to aid in creating loosely coupled applications. This allows architects to design composite applications like MEF. However, Prism includes a richer set of libraries that contain important features like loosely coupled communication, which is missing in MEF. Prism also allows you to share code between WPF and Silverlight solutions. For more information, see www.codeplex.com/CompositeWPF.

The best feature about these composition frameworks is that they can be used together. In fact, individual functionality can be leveraged from each framework. This allows you to use these frameworks in a lightweight fashion (pick the features you need). For example, The Managed Extensibility Framework (MEF) contains features like application composition that makes dynamically loading assemblies trivial without writing the "plumbing code" that you did in Listing 11-4.

▪ **Note** I encourage you to research information on both of these frameworks if you intend to create Silverlight applications hosted in a SaaS model. You should spend your time designing applications rather than writing frameworks or plumbing code.

SaaS in the Virtualized Cloud

Virtualization of SaaS software and services is a very important facet of providing a model that can scale to an ever-increasing amount of clients. All current SaaS strategies and architectures account for virtualization. While the plug-in model can make deploying Silverlight applications easier, there is no specific feature of Silverlight that aids in virtualization. However, Silverlight is a first-class citizen in the Microsoft cloud OS, Windows Azure. Silverlight applications and their services can be deployed to Windows Azure and scale as needed based on client volume. So, if you signed a large customer and need four additional servers to handle the user load, this can be done almost instantly for you. In the future, Windows Azure is going to be extended with enterprise business intelligence services such as reporting and map reduce aggregations. This will allow small teams or even individual developers with good ideas to compete with large software vendors by providing custom software for these services. Furthermore, architects and developers can focus on developing software rather than plumbing architecture such as hardware infrastructure.

Summary

This chapter covered the common architecture scenarios that you may encounter when investing in Silverlight as a technology to deliver BI content. If you want to take advantage of what Silverlight has to offer, you absolutely need to understand whether the technology is a right investment for you.

Proper data service integration architecture is essential in being able to deliver Silverlight BI modules across the enterprise. Without this in place, Silverlight's effectiveness in delivering BI insight will be mitigated dramatically.

In this chapter, you also saw some key Silverlight integration strategies. Silverlight provides architects with many integration options across the enterprise. In fact, some integration points such as web parts and hosted SaaS models highlight a key integration advantage Silverlight has over other technologies.

CHAPTER 12

■ ■ ■

Mobile Intelligence

This chapter is dedicated to applying the business intelligence 2.0 concepts you learned earlier to mobile devices. The popularity of mobile devices such as smartphones and tablets has exploded. As a result, software that has been traditionally distributed via desktops or laptops now has a new audience of mobile consumers, leaving many software companies scrambling to deliver their content to mobile devices. Business Intelligence software is no different: we are starting to see many business intelligence implementations on smartphones and tablets. (Business intelligence software implemented on a mobile device is called *mobile intelligence*.)

This chapter will convey how mobile intelligence can be applied to Silverlight-enabled mobile devices. This category includes Windows tablets, Windows Phone 7, Symbian phones, and Windows Compact Embedded 7 tablets.

Throughout this chapter, topics from previous content such as word-sized visualizations, predictive analytics, data visualizations, self-service applications, and interactivity will be applied to delivering mobile intelligence on Silverlight-enabled devices. Note that the primary focus of the examples will be the Windows Phone 7 platform.

The main goal of this chapter is for the reader to understand that business intelligence 2.0 concepts applied on a mobile device will guarantee a successful mobile intelligence implementation. The following table outlines the specific goals that different types of readers will achieve by reading this chapter.

The following coding scenarios are included in this chapter:

- Using the Bing Maps Silverlight control on the Windows Phone 7 platform

- Improving interactivity performance using concurrent programming techniques on the Windows Phone 7 platform

Audience	Goals
Silverlight developers	Understand how existing Silverlight business intelligence components can be re-used on Silverlight mobile devices.
	Understand that fundamentally mobile intelligence is just BI 2.0 on mobile devices.
	Grasp the challenges and unique features of the mobile platform.
Business intelligence professionals	Find out how business intelligence concepts can be applied to Silverlight enabled devices.
	Understand the key paradigms of BI 2.0

Audience	Goals
Strategic decision makers	Discover if mobile intelligence on Silverlight is a plausible source for additional revenue or for your organization to distribute their content.
	See how your company can leverage an investment in Silverlight to deliver mobile intelligence.
	Understand Microsoft's mobile strategy and if investing in Silverlight and mobile intelligence is logical.

What is Mobile Intelligence?

Mobile intelligence (MI) is an abstract term much like business intelligence. Mobile intelligence is an encompassing term that expresses patterns that should be followed to deliver business intelligence tools on current mobile devices. With the dramatic growth of powerful smart phones and tablet devices, mobile intelligence is gaining dramatic traction in the business intelligence community. Devices released in the last couple years are capable of storing large amounts of data, providing rich interactivity, accessing networks quickly, and visualizing complex data. This allows many best practices of business intelligence to be implemented on mobile devices.

In my opinion, mobile intelligence can be simply defined as business intelligence 2.0 for mobile devices. BI 2.0 patterns call for simple, interactive, provide real-time feedback, self-service (easy to learn) modules that can be used by casual users. Mobile devices like the Windows Phone 7 or the Apple iPhone are perfect examples of this.

One of the key differences between mobile devices (tablets, smart phones) and desktops is the large difference between input and interactivity. Mobile devices, for the most part, are not designed to be alternatives to quickly typing on a keyboard or the sensitivity a mouse provides for drawing. A large majority of the interactions on a mobile device are done to retrieve information. Figure 12-1 illustrates the level of interactivity between desktops and mobile devices.

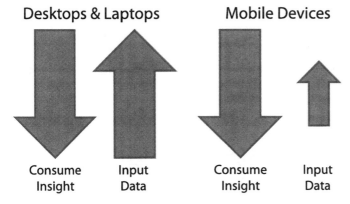

Figure 12-1. Different levels of data input and output. Mobile devices are designed as consumers of data or insight. The primary interactions and gestures on mobile devices are to retrieve data.

Mobile devices like smartphones or tablets obviously provide virtual keyboards. Some even can accept external USB input devices like keyboards and mice. However, you will find that a very large majority of these devices are not used for data input because data input is much simpler and faster to do on a desktop. This is where the principles of business intelligence 2.0 stand out in mobile intelligence implementations. You won't want to design an interface that requires frequent tapping, large text input, non-validated data, or non-real-time feedback as this will frustrate the casual user. For example, if you wrote an application that provided real-time analytics on a baseball game, you could have the user input the data play-by-play or implement a service that does this for them. This way the user focuses on only consuming business intelligence interactions.

It isn't by accident that devices like Windows Phone 7, Android Phone, or the iPad are grouped as "consumer devices" as they are essentially consumption devices.

Mobile Intelligence for the Consumer

Even though a large majority of mobile devices include enterprise services, these devices are primarily targeting the consumer market. Knowing that a large number of non-analytical users will be using this platform, you may have some concerns in creating a business intelligence solution for it.

How viable is a mobile device to surface business intelligence if it is primarily for the average consumer? Throughout this book I have mentioned that BI 2.0 is all about *business intelligence for the masses*. The concepts that were outlined earlier directly apply in creating simple to use, self-service, and easy to understand analytical tools. This is precisely why BI 2.0 paradigms are vital if you want to craft a mobile intelligence solution that effectively targets average consumers.

But just how popular is mobile intelligence for consumer phones? Looking at the Apple App Store, you can see many examples and ideas of successful business intelligence, analytical, and statistical applications that provide rich and interactive experiences to consumers. Figure 12-2 shows a screenshot of Roambi's iPhone application, which allows the user to interact with local data sets and perform analysis right on their phone utilizing hand gestures. Notice the interface is simple and non-cluttered, allowing for quick delivery of business intelligence insight. Furthermore, the menu buttons let the user to share this insight (e-mail), filter, and create different views without a relying on a large amount of input.

Mobile intelligence does not have to be delivered as a "business intelligence only" application. Mobile Intelligence can be surfaced as modules that are part of an application or enhance additional functionality. For example, a Windows Phone 7 app could be created that manages web domains for an infrastructure engineer. The main features of the application would be the domain management functionality. The core functionality could be extended with predictive analytics to determine if the hardware can handle future visitor loads and possibly recommend a hardware upgrade.

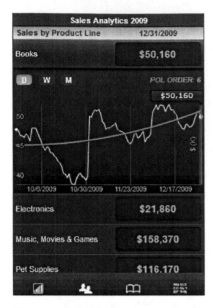

Figure 12-2. Sales Analytics visualized using Roambi's iPhone application.

In this brief introduction of mobile intelligence you should understand the following things:

- The current primary audience of mobile devices is the consumer. iPad, iPhone, Android and Windows Phone 7 devices are absolutely applicable to business; however, you should be aware that your audience will likely be a casual user.

- Applying BI 2.0 principles will allow you to deliver mobile intelligence to "the masses" of casual users. A user that downloads a simple application will not bother with a multi-page manual. Therefore, it is absolutely necessary to implement self-service and easy to use applications

- Interactions on mobile devices are different than on desktops or laptops. Mobile intelligence applications should not incorporate heavy use of data entry and should focus on read-only or interactions that consume insight. Furthermore, multitouch gestures should be heavily utilized for filtering, panning, zooming, or pivoting data grids or visualizations.

Silverlight Mobile Intelligence Platforms

If you have a product that relies on Silverlight or are planning on delivering mobile intelligence with Silverlight, you need to have a good understanding of what mobile devices currently support Silverlight.

Figure 12-3 depicts a visual matrix of the different mobile platforms that run Silverlight; these will be discussed in the next several sections.

Figure 12-3. Various mobile device platforms that can surface the Silverlight runtime

Windows Phone 7

Apple and Google have made major progress in creating powerful smartphone platforms. For the longest time Microsoft seemed to be in disarray with their mobile strategy. Finally in early 2010, Microsoft officially announced the new consumer mobile platform called Windows Phone 7.

Windows Phone 7 is a new mobile platform from Microsoft that makes a clean break from the previous architectures defined in Windows Mobile versions 4.x through 6.x. Similarly to the Apple iPhone, the Windows Phone 7 platform targets the consumer. Applications for the Windows Phone 7 will be made available via the Windows Marketplace (similar to the Apple App Store).

■ **Note** This chapter only covers some details of the platform. For more information on the Windows Phone 7 developer story, register for the Marketplace, access the forums, and download the developer tools from `http://developer.windowsphone.com`

Developing for the Windows Phone 7

In order to take a closer look at the development story for the Windows Phone 7 OS we need to look at the hardware features the development tools.

The Windows Phone 7 Operating System has the following key minimum hardware specifications:

- *Processor.* The processor minimum for the Windows Phone 7 OS is a 1 GHz processor. However, a more compelling feature is that a majority of the newer mobile CPUs actually include multiple cores that enable concurrent programming techniques.

- *Hardware acceleration*: Silverlight applications will be able to utilize GPU hardware to accelerate rendering and free the CPU. In addition, the GPU can be used to cache rendered graphics.

- *Big Touchscreen and Multitouch*: The minimum hardware specs call for a large touch screen with good resolution that will be able to handle multitouch gestures (pinch, expand).

From the previous list of requirements, you can clearly see that the Windows Phone 7 platform is a very capable modern mobile OS. For this reason, Microsoft needed to create a compelling SDK that is able to take advantage of the concurrent programming, hardware acceleration, multitouch gestures, etc. Microsoft essentially had three choices: Silverlight, WPF, or start over.

The popularity of .NET and community of millions developers essentially dictated Microsoft releases a .NET based SDK and API. Even though the Windows Phone 7 packs a powerful punch, it's still is a mobile device, so WPF and running the full .NET framework did not make sense. The Silverlight runtime is much smaller than WPF. Furthermore, as of Silverlight version 3, Silverlight can utilize up to eight processing cores (covered in Chapter 10), utilize hardware acceleration, and take advantage of multitouch gestures. The development environment for Silverlight has always been Visual Studio and a subset of the .NET framework. This made Silverlight a no-brainer as the SDK for the Windows Phone 7 platform.

One important note: Microsoft states that Silverlight on the Windows Phone 7 is equal to the full Silverlight runtime. This is mostly true. However, there are some limitations of Windows Phone 7 Silverlight implementation:

- *Out of the browser only*: Windows Phone 7 Silverlight applications only run in out of the browser mode on the phone. What does this mean? The Silverlight application must be purchased and installed via the Microsoft Marketplace. Using the Windows Phone 7 browser to launch a Silverlight web application will not work. Third-party browsers like Skyfire already allow Silverlight on the phone! Microsoft has hinted that there will be an enterprise mobile OS based on Windows Phone 7 that bypasses the Microsoft Marketplace. However, it is not coming until the second half of 2011.

- *Silverlight version 3 plus some Silverlight 4*: The feature set of the Windows Phone 7 Silverlight runtime is based on version 3. There are some Silverlight 4 features like CompositeTransform that were added for performance. Silverlight 4 assemblies cannot be referenced in Windows Phone 7 applications and must be Silverlight 3 (i.e., Bing Maps Silverlight controls is based on Silverlight 3).

- *Compact Framework base*: The Silverlight runtime on Windows Phone 7 executes on a newer (to be released with Windows Phone 7) version of the Compact Framework. The compact framework has several limitations that remove functionality from the full Silverlight runtime. A complete list of changes can be found at `http://msdn.microsoft.com/en-us/library/ff426930(VS.96).aspx`

- *Currently C# only*: The current preview of the Windows Phone 7 SDK is C# only. I think this limitation will change, eventually including VB.NET. However, because of the limitations of the Compact Framework, don't expect full F# or dynamic language support anytime soon.

Even though there are some limitations placed on the Silverlight runtime for the Windows Phone 7 platform, a large majority of your Silverlight 3 or Silverlight 4 code should be compatible. The development and design environment remains Visual Studio 2010 and Expression Blend 4. Furthermore, you will see in the examples and coding scenarios in this chapter that for the most part Silverlight assemblies will work in Windows Phone 7 projects by simply adding the proper reference.

■ **Note** Windows Phone 7 includes a rich development environment for building smartphone games that is based on the XNA framework. Because this SDK is tailored for game development, I did not cover it in this chapter. However, there are some very compelling 3D visuals that can be created to surface data visualizations for mobile intelligence. The powerful processor on the Windows Phone 7 platform is capable of utilizing ray tracing to create images simulating virtual 3D worlds. These techniques will become very popular with the addition of augmented reality.

Windows XP OS and Windows 7 OS Tablets

Even though tablets have become popular in 2010, it is not a new technology. Windows based tablets have been around since Windows XP Tablet Edition was released in 2003.

Over the last eight years, various manufactures including DELL and HP have released Windows based tablets. Older Windows XP tablets rely on a stylus for input and do not provide the new multitouch gestures. However, this does not mean these devices cannot execute Silverlight code effectively. Some of these devices are very capable of effectively surfacing Silverlight content. Figure 12-4 below shows a Windows XP tablet executing the coding scenario from the predictive analytics chapter. Notice the stylus is interacting with the slider. Because the interaction is a fluid slide gesture, the interaction of the control is quite easy to work with. This example amplifies that consuming insight in a tablet is much easier than inputting data.

Figure 12-4. The stylus is still an effective tool for interacting with Silverlight BI 2.0 modules. Fluid interactions are possible with the stylus if the data visualizations provide fluent interactions.

Several manufactures have released Windows 7 tablets; however, the OS is a heavy drain on battery life because it's a full OS with many desktop features, so it doesn't make a great tablet OS. Windows 7 based tablets are probably not going to gain much traction. However, new Windows 7 based tablets will obviously be able to surface the full Silverlight 4 runtime and take advantage of multitouch capabilities.

Windows Embedded Compact 7

Windows Embedded Compact 7 is part of the Windows Embedded line of Microsoft operating systems that targets embedded platforms such as kiosks, tablets, and point of sale devices. Windows Embedded Compact 7 operating system was announced at the Computex conference in June 2010. Microsoft is positioning it as the successor of Microsoft's Windows CE line of products.

The Windows Embedded Compact OS is quite powerful. It will run a form of Silverlight embedded, offer hardware acceleration for HD movie playback, and support next generation multitouch gestures. The operating system was created to be powerful enough to run next-generation user interfaces without requiring powerful laptop-like hardware.

The user interface of this operating system will be powered by Silverlight. OEMs can create custom user interfaces and completely tailor the experience to their product. For example, imagine going to a car dealer and being presented with a kiosk device that surfaces statistical information about a car's safety ratings. This functionality will make this OS a compelling choice to deliver mobile intelligence patterns. In fact, Microsoft is positioning many of its Silverlight components such as Bing Maps, DeepZoom, and the Silverlight Pivot Viewer control to be tablet friendly.

I think this platform is very interesting because it will allow OEMs to create custom tablet experiences. Imagine being able to create an analysis tablet for a particular genre. For example, you could create a tablet to helping a car buyer pick the best cars based on their budget or desired specifications. These types of custom tailored tablet experiences will be available on the Windows Embedded Compact 7 platform.

The first Windows Embedded Compact 7 devices are expected to ship in early 2011. A few tablet devices were demoed at the 2010 Computex conference showing off the tablet OS capabilities. This has garnered positive initial impressions; in fact, Windows Embedded Compact 7 has been compared to an Apple iPad.

■ **Note** More information on the Windows Embedded Compact 7 operating system can be found on the Windows CE site at www.microsoft.com/windowsembedded/en-us/products/windowsce/compact7.mspx

---

Other Platforms

Silverlight mobile intelligence can be implemented on various other secondary platforms. The SkyFire mobile browser enables Silverlight 2 content on it. Currently, the SkyFire browser runs on Android, Symbian Series 60, and Windows Mobile 5 and 6. The SkyFire browser has submitted an iPhone application as well. The main reason I place SkyFire in the "Other" category is because the browser is relatively unknown. Furthermore, only the Silverlight 2 runtime is supported, which is two versions behind the current Silverlight version. This makes the delivering Silverlight mobile intelligence on SkyFire very hacky.

Microsoft has made the Silverlight Symbian 1.0 runtime available for Nokia 60 series phones. This platform is also largely based on the Silverlight 2 runtime and is thus rather limited in functionality. The popularity and the restricted functionality limit this framework's effectiveness in delivering Silverlight mobile intelligence.

Implementing Silverlight Mobile Intelligence

This section will cover examples on how to implement mobile intelligence on the Windows Phone 7 platform. Many of the familiar examples that you saw in past chapters will be implemented using the Silverlight for Windows Phone 7 SDK.

■ **Warning** The business intelligence paradigms behind these scenarios were covered in previous chapters. I will not be repeating the same material; instead I will specifically focus on the mobile intelligence implementation caveats.

Adding Interactivity

Chapter 9 introduced fluid interactions as BI 2.0 mechanism to limit data input and provide real-time insight in business intelligence modules. Interactivity is very important in mobile intelligence scenarios because of the nature of consuming insight. Users will be using their fingers to manipulate data visualizations to garner wisdom from the data.

The same controls that are available to us in the full Silverlight 4 are available to us on the Windows Phone 7 platform SDK. Figure 12-5 illustrates a replicated predictive analytics coding scenario as a Windows Phone 7 application. While the form factor of the application has changed, the idea of fluid interactivity remains the same. A slider control is used to track the amount of hits a batter has over the season. This is used to determine the probability of that batter attaining a hit in a given at bat.

The functionality of the two applications is identical. However, since we are dealing with explicit resolutions I can cheat a little and layout the controls relying on a WYSIWYG design. Instead of a heavy charting control, I simply rendered five separate progress bars.

■ **Note** The source code for this example is available on version 3.0 of the source code zip file on the web site.

Figure 12-5. Chapter 9's predictive analytics coding scenario implemented on the Windows Phone 7

The key point I stressed during Chapter 9's coding scenario was the ease of use when using the slider to change the values of input and provide real-time insight. This is amplified on the Windows Phone 7 platform because the data input takes slightly longer. For example, if I tap into the text box control that hosts the value of the hits in a season, I will see a virtual keyboard (shown in Figure 12-6). I will have to delete the previous number and tap in the digits that I want the value to be. Common sense will tell you that this type of interaction is clearly faster and easier to do on a keyboard. This is a clear example of the mobile intelligence paradigm that mobile devices are best suited for fluid interactivity and consuming insight, not data entry. However, presenting different keyboard layout types depending on the expected type input is a great way to make information entry on a mobile device much simpler.

It is important to note that not every interactive gesture is a good idea in mobile intelligence. For example, if you have used the Windows Mobile 5.x or 6.x OSes you probably noticed a context menu and right-click interactivity. This type of gesture is considered obsolete and you should stay away from hidden functionality. Remember that BI 2.0 calls for simple interfaces that are easy to use without much documentation. Hidden controls and complex interactions prevent the user for learning the application quickly and effectively. Say a casual user downloaded your application from the Microsoft Marketplace. Your application has only several minutes to convince the user to purchase the full application or subscribe to a paid service. If you have a great mobile application but many of the features are hidden or are hard to surface, you have a lower probability of receiving payment for your application.

Other examples in this book show that data interactivity can be implemented in the very same manner shown here. Interactive controls that facilitate real-time insight and rapid changes of values will be a popular choice when designing mobile intelligence interfaces on the Windows Phone 7 platform.

Figure 12-6. *Setting input focus on the text block will cause a virtual keyboard to appear for user input. The control is formatted for number input, so it will default to numbers.*

Word-Sized Visualizations

In the data visualization chapters you learned about the importance of word-sized data visualizations. You saw many examples where business intelligence insight was maximized because of the small footprint of the word-sized data visualizations. Word-sized visualization implementations play an important role on smartphone devices because they maximize the amount of business intelligence wisdom that can be surfaced on the screen.

Figure 12-7 shows an example of maximizing the insight delivered using several bullet graph controls (covered in Appendix B) as KPI indicators. Notice that each bullet graph control surfaces multiple pieces of mobile intelligence insight. Achieving this level of business intelligence information would be difficult to do using traditional additional gauges or other larger data visualization controls.

Figure 12-7. A Windows Phone 7 application surfacing a list of custom bullet graph user control

Mobile Dashboards

If you have seen some of the demos of the Windows Phone 7 platform, you have seen videos or screen shots of the Pivot and Panorama controls. These controls allow you to surface a large area control surface in the small form factor of a mobile device.

Figure 12-8 illustrates a simple example of a mockup of a mobile intelligence dashboard implemented using a Pivot control. Notice there are three tabs or headers that consist of regions: Americas, Europe, and Asia. Europe is rendered in a darker color because it is the active tab. Each region page presents a list of metrics that surface trending, KPIs, and a current value for the metric. The casual user can simply scroll through the regions by flicking the finger to the left or to the right. Conversely, selecting the header will present the region's page on the mobile screen. Notice how this mobile dashboard page makes heavy use of word-sized data visualizations. Sparklines represent trending information and KPI indicators give a visual status of the current value versus the organizational goal.

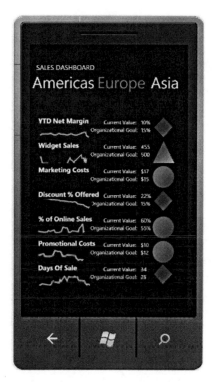

Figure 12-8. Mobile dashboards can be easily set up by combining mobile layout controls like the Pivot or Panorama control and word-sized data visualizations (sparklines, KPIs, labels).

This type of control is a fantastic way to mimic dashboard concepts for mobile intelligence. You can clearly see that surfacing business intelligence metrics for different categories (i.e., region pages in Figure 12-8) provides intuitive navigation for a mobile device user. This allows you to maximize the real-estate on a mobile device and you don't have to cram everything into a single mobile screen. Furthermore, the navigation is not elusive or hidden. Therefore, even if the user is not trained on the application, she will probably understand that clicking on a header or flicking to the left or right will take them to the next dashboard page.

■ **Note** As of the publication of this book, the Pivot and Panorama controls are not officially available from Microsoft. This should change by the time the final phone SDK is released. There are several Pivot and Panorama third party implementations available online. A control like this is not easy to design. The developer has to have good knowledge of memory management, caching, data virtualization, and other advanced concepts. Please be aware of this before attempting to create your own or leveraging a non-vetted control in your mobile applications.

Leveraging Microsoft Services and Components

In the past chapters you learned that one of the main advantages of Silverlight is the integration of Microsoft enterprise services in order to enhance business intelligence. This applies to Silverlight on the Windows Phone 7 as well. Enterprise services such as SharePoint and Windows Azure can be consumed on the Windows Phone 7. Furthermore, existing Silverlight components can be used on the Windows Phone 7 platform, such as the Silverlight Bing Maps control.

Coding Scenarios

This chapter includes two coding scenarios that focus on the Windows Phone 7 platform. Throughout this chapter you saw the numerous practices that I introduced in the previous chapters applied to delivering mobile intelligence. I picked two compelling coding scenarios that reinforce the applicability of BI 2.0 concepts and how they can apply to delivering mobile intelligence on the Windows Phone 7 platform.

These coding scenarios will require that you have downloaded the Windows Phone 7 development tools in order to follow along. The developer software necessary is located on the Windows Phone 7 developer website at http://developer.windowsphone.com. The following software is required:

- *Windows Phone 7 Developer Tools*: This package installs the Windows Phone 7 software emulator and Silverlight for Windows Phone 7. In addition, the proper project types will be registered in Visual Studio 2010.

- *Expression Blend 4 Windows Phone Add-In*: This add-in makes it possible to design, debug, and deploy Windows Phone 7 applications using Microsoft Expression Blend 4.

■ **Warning** As of the publication of this book, the final release of the Windows Phone 7 SDK is not available. There is a great likelihood that the steps outlined might be outdated. Please visit the web site for the latest source code and any updates for the following two coding scenarios. In addition, these coding scenarios have not been tested on actual Windows Phone 7 hardware, just the software emulator.

The Bing Maps Silverlight Control on Windows Phone 7

In Chapter 5, you learned how to use the Bing Maps Silverlight Control to surface geographic data. This coding scenario will show you how the same exact Bing Maps Silverlight Control assemblies can be used on the Windows Phone 7 platform using the same strategies shown in Chapter 5.

In order to proceed with this coding scenario you will need to download the Bing Maps Silverlight Control (outlined in Chapter 5) in addition to the Windows Phone 7 developer tools. Also, y must be connected to the Internet in order to debug the solution. The aerial and road geographic images are downloaded from Microsoft servers.

> ■ **Warning** If you have skipped this coding scenario in Chapter 5 or are not familiar with the Bing Maps Silverlight Control, please go back to Chapter 5 before proceeding. This coding scenario is not an introduction to the Bing Maps Silverlight Control.

Follow the steps below when you are ready to proceed with the coding scenario.

1. Open Visual Studio 2010 or Microsoft Expression Blend 4 and create a new Windows Phone Application project called Chapter12_WindowsPhoneBingMaps (see Figure 12-9).

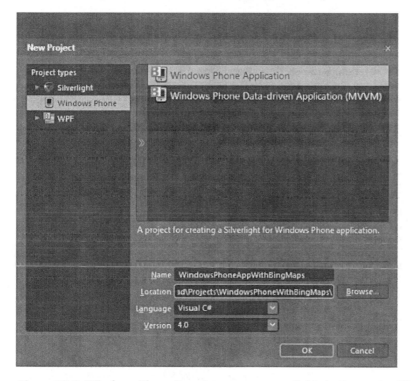

Figure 12-9. Windows Phone 7 project types are available in Expression Blend 4 when the Windows Phone 7 SDK is installed.

2. Add a reference to the control to your application. Navigate to the location of the Silverlight control assembly. The default location of the Bing Maps Silverlight control assemblies is C:\Program Files (x86)\Bing Maps Silverlight Control\V1\Libraries\; however, if you have chosen to install the control in another location, look there. Add a reference to both the Microsoft.Maps.MapControl.dll assembly and the Microsoft.Maps.MapControl.Common.dll assembly (Figure 12-10).

Figure 12-10. *Adding references to the Bing Maps Silverlight assemblies to the Windows Phone project*

3.   Now that you have added references to the Bing Maps control assemblies in your project, so you should see the Map control in the asset manager. If you cannot find it, try searching for it in the Expression Blend 4 asset manager (shown in Figure 12-11). Once you find it, drag the map control onto the design canvas. Ensure that the Map control is taking up the entire design canvas so you can easily see all of the map components.

Figure 12-11. *The Map control is available in the Expression Blend 4 assets after the proper references are added.*

4.   Now you can build the project. However, notice that there is an error shown in Figure 12-12.

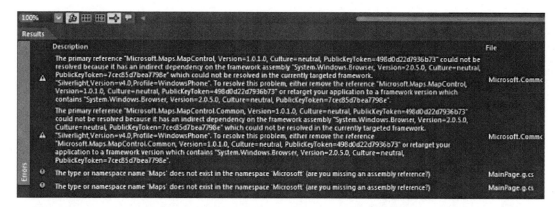

Figure 12-12. *Adding the Bing Maps Silverlight control to a Windows Phone 7 project can cause this build error to appear.*

5. In order to fix this error, follow the directions stated in the error. Add a reference to the System.Windows.Browser.dll assembly, which is located at C:\Program Files (x86)\Microsoft Silverlight\4.0.50524.0\. The project should now build and you should be able to debug your application. The emulator can take about 2-3 minutes to start for the first time. Once the Windows Phone 7 emulator has been started, it's a good idea to not close it. This will prevent the startup penalty each time you would like to debug the application.

6. Looking at the Figure 12-13 below, you will notice a lot of additional components cluttering up the Map interface, including a white bar and an out-of-place navigation control. These two components are highlighted with two arrows. Even though some components obstruct the map view, the application is completely functional. On the Windows Phone 7 platform, the navigation is performed using hand gestures, so the navigation component is not required. On the Windows Phone 7, you can pan the map using the flick finger gesture.

Navigation control seems out of place in the middle. Do we really need it since the user will want to pan with their fingers?

What is this thing?

Figure 12-13. Two components are obstructing the complete view of the Windows Phone 7 map application.

7. Remove the navigation control by setting the visibility of the control to collapsed on the loaded event. This is shown in Listing 12-1. If you build the project now, you will notice that the navigation control has been removed from the Map control.

8. In order to remove the white bar across the Map, add your credentials to the Bing Maps Silverlight controls (this is covered in the Chapter 5 coding scenario).

9. You can also remove additional components like the Microsoft Copyright information and the Bing logo. This will result in an interface that looks like Figure 12-14.

Figure 12-14. Removing the optional components and adding the security credentials cleans up the map interface.

Lessons Learned

This coding scenario was important because it showed several key facets of implementing mobile intelligence on the Windows Phone 7 platform. In this coding scenario you saw that you can leverage existing Silverlight 3 assemblies that were designed for the full version of Silverlight on the Windows Phone 7 platform. Furthermore, this coding scenario presented the use of Microsoft enterprise services in order to surface business intelligence. Finally, if you have a Windows Phone 7 device, you can test the control using multitouch gestures. Panning, zooming out, and zooming in is done using completely different gestures than on a desktop or laptop.

In Chapter 5 a Bing Maps Silverlight control was used as solution to help cab drivers find the best locations with the greatest fares. Mobile devices make this scenario more realistic. Imagine leveraging additional Windows Phone 7 services such as GPS to make the locations of cab pick-ups dynamic. This is yet another way that a mobile device can enhance traditional business intelligence modules.

Concurrent Programming on Windows Phone 7

In Chapter 10 you learned how to use several different concurrent programming techniques in order to improve the performance of interactive slider controls as well as the business logic processing in Silverlight. In this coding scenario, you will apply the same principles learned in Chapter 10 to the Windows Phone 7 platform.

■ **Warning** If you have skipped this coding scenario in Chapter 10 or are not familiar with the multithreading in Silverlight, please go back to Chapter 10 before proceeding. This coding scenario will not be an introduction to the multithreading techniques in Silverlight.

Follow the steps below when you are ready to proceed with the coding scenario.

1. Open Visual Studio 2010 or Microsoft Expression Blend 4 and create a new Windows Phone Application project called Chapter12_WindowsPhoneConcurrencyProgramming.

2. Open the project in Expression Blend 4 and set the UI as follows:

   - Change the ContentGrid to a StackPanel.

   - Add a Loaded event to the LayoutRoot (which will add a corresponding event handler method in the codebehind file).

   - Add a ValueChanged event to the Slider.

   - Optionally, you can change the name of the page and list title.

You are going to build a control that looks like Figure 12-15. The control's important pieces include a slider, a label for the value of the slider, and the number representing the number of times the event was executed.

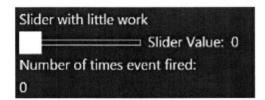

Figure 12-15. Simple slider interface to track events fired

3. The XAML in your main page should look similar to that shown in Listing 12-1. The changes from Step 2 are highlighted in bold.

Listing 12-1. XAML code to render a simple slider control

```xaml
<Grid x:Name="LayoutRoot" Background="{StaticResource PhoneBackgroundBrush}"↩
 Loaded="LayoutRoot_Loaded">

    <Grid.RowDefinitions>
        <RowDefinition Height="Auto"/>
        <RowDefinition Height="*"/>
    </Grid.RowDefinitions>

    <!--TitleGrid is the name of the application and page title-->
    <Grid x:Name="TitleGrid" Grid.Row="0">
        <TextBlock Text="Multithreading" x:Name="textBlockPageTitle" Style=↩
"{StaticResource PhoneTextPageTitle1Style}"/>
        <TextBlock Text="Sliders" x:Name="textBlockListTitle" Style=↩
"{StaticResource PhoneTextPageTitle2Style}"/>
    </Grid>

    <!--ContentGrid is empty. Place new content here-->
    <StackPanel x:Name="ContentGrid" Grid.Row="1">
                <StackPanel Height="Auto" Margin="10,0,0,0" Width="Auto"↩
Orientation="Vertical">
                    <TextBlock Height="Auto" HorizontalAlignment="Left" Margin="0,0,5,5"↩
Width="Auto" Text="Slider with little work" TextWrapping="Wrap"/>
                    <StackPanel Height="Auto" Width="Auto" HorizontalAlignment="Left"↩
VerticalAlignment="Stretch" Orientation="Horizontal">
                    <Slider Cursor="Hand" Height="18" x:Name="SliderSimple" Width="175"↩
Margin="0,0,10,0" ValueChanged="SliderSimple_ValueChanged"/>
                    <TextBlock Height="Auto" Width="Auto" Text="Slider Value:"↩
TextWrapping="Wrap" Margin="0,0,10,0"/>
                    <TextBlock Height="Auto" Width="Auto" Text="0" TextWrapping="Wrap"↩
x:Name="txtSliderSimpleValue"/>
                    </StackPanel>
                    <TextBlock Height="Auto" HorizontalAlignment="Left" Margin="0,0,0,5"↩
Width="Auto" Text="Number of times event fired:" TextWrapping="Wrap"/>
                    <TextBlock Height="Auto" Width="Auto" Text="0" TextWrapping="Wrap"↩
HorizontalAlignment="Left" x:Name="txtSliderSimpleNumberEventFires"/>
                </StackPanel>
    </StackPanel>

<!-- End of LayoutRoot -->
</Grid>
```

4. In the codebehind, you are going to write a simple instrumentation harness in order to track when the slider moves and its current value.

- Declare an integer field to hold the count of how many times the event was fired.

- In the ValueChanged event handler, set the value of the slider to the text box.

- In the ValueChanged event handler, increment the count of the simple slider event and set it to the text box.

The codebehind file should look like that shown in Listing 12-2.

Listing 12-2. Simple slider code to set its value and how many times the event was triggered (the changes are highlighted in bold)

```
// declare count variables
int countSliderSimple = 0;

...

private void SliderSimple_ValueChanged(object sender, RoutedPropertyChangedEventArgs↵
<double> e)
{
  // increment simple slider event count
  this.countSliderSimple++;
  // set the slider value to its text box
  this.txtSliderSimpleValue.Text = this.SliderSimple.Value.ToString();
  // set the count on the text box
  this.txtSliderSimpleNumberEventFires.Text = this.countSliderSimple.ToString();
}
```

5. Now it is time to do a sanity check to ensure your application builds properly and does what you want. Build the application and try moving the slider around. You should see the slider moving with ease. As you move the slider, the value changes, and you can see the number of times the ValueChanged event is triggered. Figure 12-16 shows the control in action.

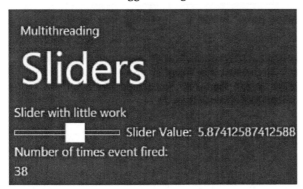

Figure 12-16. The simple slider control displaying the slider value and the number of times the event triggered

6. Similar to how you added a second slider to mimic single-threaded processing, you will add another slider below this one that will have a time delay to mimic processing. Add the XAML highlighted in bold in Listing 12-3 under the previous StackPanel.

Listing 12-3. Adding the UI for the slider that mimics the execution of a complex business algorithm

```
...
</StackPanel>

<!-- Single Threaded Section -->
<StackPanel Height="Auto" Width="Auto" Orientation="Vertical" Margin="10,10,0,5">
        <TextBlock Height="Auto" HorizontalAlignment="Left" Margin="0,0,5,5"↵
Width="Auto" Text="Slider with 150ms delay (single threaded)" TextWrapping="Wrap"/>
        <StackPanel Height="Auto" Width="Auto" Orientation="Horizontal">
                <Slider Cursor="Hand" Height="18" x:Name="SliderSingleThreaded"↵
Width="175" Margin="0,0,10,0"/>
                <TextBlock Height="Auto" Width="Auto" Text="Slider Value:"↵
TextWrapping="Wrap" Margin="0,0,10,0"/>
                <TextBlock Height="Auto" Width="Auto" Text="0" TextWrapping="Wrap"↵
x:Name="txtSliderSingleThreadedValue"/>
        </StackPanel>
        <TextBlock Height="Auto" HorizontalAlignment="Left" Margin="0,0,0,5" Width="Auto"↵
Text="Number of times event fired:" TextWrapping="Wrap"/>
        <TextBlock Height="Auto" Width="Auto" Text="0" TextWrapping="Wrap"↵
HorizontalAlignment="Left" x:Name="txtSliderSingleThreadNumberEventFires"/>
</StackPanel>
```

7. Add a ValueChanged event to the new slider. The change is highlighted in bold in Listing 12-4. This will create the corresponding event handler in the codebehind file.

Listing 12-4. Add the ValueChanged event to the single-threaded slider

```
<Slider Cursor="Hand" Height="18" x:Name="SliderSingleThreaded"
    ValueChanged="SliderSingleThreaded_ValueChanged" Width="175" Margin="0,0,10,0"/>
```

8. Now add the similar instrumentation harness you added in the simple slider, except now you will put the main thread to sleep for 150 milliseconds to mimic a business algorithm. The code changes are highlighted in Listing 12-5.

Listing 12-5. Adding an instrumentation harness and mocking a business algorithm with slow behavior

```
// declare count variables
int countSliderSimple = 0;
int countSliderSingleThreaded = 0;

....
private void SliderSimple_ValueChanged(object sender, RoutedPropertyChangedEventArgs↵
```

```
<double> e)
{
  // increment simple slider event count
  this.countSliderSimple++;
  // set the slider value to its text box
  this.txtSliderSimpleValue.Text = this.SliderSimple.Value.ToString();
  // set the count on the text box
  this.txtSliderSimpleNumberEventFires.Text = this.countSliderSimple.ToString();
}

private void SliderSingleThreaded_ValueChanged(object sender, ↵
 RoutedPropertyChangedEventArgs<double> e)
{
  // increment single threaded slider event count
  this.countSliderSingleThreaded++;
  // set the slider value to its text box
  this.txtSliderSingleThreadedValue.Text = this.SliderSingleThreaded.Value.ToString();

  // add a fake delay of 150 milliseconds (3/20 of a second)
  System.Threading.Thread.Sleep(150);

  // set the count on the text box
  this.txtSliderSingleThreadNumberEventFires.Text =↵
 this.countSliderSingleThreaded.ToString();
}
```

9. If everything was added properly, the project should build, and you will see the two sliders with a layout similar to Figure 12-17.

10. Try moving the second slider around. Note how the slider jumps positions and "locks up" easily. The interaction has been severely degraded with the addition of business logic. Furthermore, note that the number of times the event is processed is much fewer. The processing of the business algorithm takes time away from the UI to efficiently handle user interaction. This would be considered highly unusable by most users.

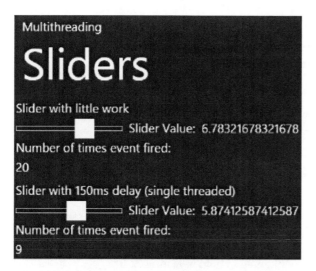

Figure 12-17. The performance of the two sliders can be compared. The second slider will be significantly slower and provide a jumpy and non-fluid motion.

■ **Warning** The multithreaded logic used in this coding scenario is explained in detail in Chapter 10.

> 11. Going back to your project in Visual Studio 2010, add the following XAML the second slider in order to add the UI for the third slider. The code is shown in Listing 12-6.

Listing 12-6. Adding the UI for the third multithreaded slider

```
...
</StackPanel>

<!-- Multi Threaded Section -->
<StackPanel Height="Auto" Width="Auto" Orientation="Vertical" Margin="10,10,0,5">
        <TextBlock Height="Auto" HorizontalAlignment="Left" Margin="0,0,5,5" Width="Auto"↵
 Text="Slider with 150ms delay (multi threaded)" TextWrapping="Wrap"/>
        <StackPanel Height="Auto" Width="Auto" HorizontalAlignment="Stretch"↵
Orientation="Horizontal">
<Slider Cursor="Hand" Height="18" x:Name="SliderMultiThreaded" Width="175"↵
HorizontalAlignment="Left" Margin="0,0,10,0"/>
                <TextBlock Height="Auto" Width="Auto" Text="Slider Value:"↵
 TextWrapping="Wrap" Margin="0,0,10,0"/>
                <TextBlock Height="Auto" Width="Auto" Text="0" TextWrapping="Wrap"↵
x:Name="txtSliderMultiThreadedValue"/>
        </StackPanel>
```

415

```
        <TextBlock Height="Auto" HorizontalAlignment="Left" Margin="0,0,0,5" Width="Auto"↵
    Text="Number of times event fired:" TextWrapping="Wrap"/>
        <TextBlock Height="Auto" Width="Auto" Text="0" TextWrapping="Wrap"↵
    HorizontalAlignment="Left" x:Name="txtSliderMultiThreadNumberEventFires"/>
    </StackPanel>
```

12. Add the event handler for the third slider, as shown in Listing 12-7. This will create the corresponding codebehind method.

Listing 12-7. Add the event handler for the third slider (highlighted in bold). This will create the corresponding event handler in the codebehind file.

```
<Slider Cursor="Hand" Height="18" x:Name="SliderMultiThreaded"↵
    ValueChanged="SliderMultiThreaded_ValueChanged"
        Width="175" HorizontalAlignment="Left" Margin="0,0,10,0"/>
```

13. Now add the multithreaded business logic and your instrumentation harness to the third slider (the code changes are highlighted in bold in Listing 12-8). You will use the BackgroundWorker object in order to create the second thread for processing your expensive business algorithm. The tasks that will be completed are as follows:

   - A BackgroundWorker will be added to the project. Then the DoWork and RunWorkerCompleted events will be added.

   - The DoWork event will process the business logic on the second thread.

   - The RunWorkerCompleted event will ensure the instrumentation harness items are processed. Furthermore, it will ensure that the business logic has processed the correct position when the slider has stopped.

   - In the SliderMultiThreaded_ValueChanged event handler, you will add instrumentation code and logic that will fire off the DoWork method on the secondary thread (if the background worker isn't busy).

   - You will use a property to hold the last value processed to see if you need to reprocess to catch up.

Listing 12-8. Code changes that enable the third slider to execute code on the secondary thread while having the UI remain responsive.

```
...
using System.ComponentModel;

namespace Chapter12_WindowsPhoneConcurrencyProgramming
{
  public partial class MainPage : UserControl
  {
    // declare count variables
    int countSliderSimple = 0;
    int countSliderSingleThreaded = 0;
```

```
    int countSliderMultiThreaded = 0;
    // last value
    double lastMultiThreadedSliderValue = 0.0;
    // declare background worker
    BackgroundWorker bw = new BackgroundWorker();

public MainPage()
{
    InitializeComponent();
}

private void LayoutRoot_Loaded(object sender, RoutedEventArgs e)
{
    // wire up RunWorkerCompleted event
    // This will fire when the business logic has completed
    this.bw.RunWorkerCompleted +=
        new RunWorkerCompletedEventHandler(bw_RunWorkerCompleted);
    // Wire up the DoWork event
    // This will fire each time we need to process the "business logic"
    this.bw.DoWork += new DoWorkEventHandler(bw_DoWork);
}

void bw_DoWork(object sender, DoWorkEventArgs e)
{
    //NOTE: The logic here is processed on the secondary thread

    // add a fake delay of 150 milliseconds (about 1/7 of a second)
    // this mocks an expensive business algorithm
    System.Threading.Thread.Sleep(150);
}

void bw_RunWorkerCompleted(object sender, RunWorkerCompletedEventArgs e)
{
    //NOTE: The logic here is processed on the main thread

    // set the slider value to its text box
    // notice this is set here, as it guarantees that the value is now officially set
    // setting it in the SliderMultiThreaded_ValueChanged event, the 2nd thread would⤶
have to catch up to the UI
    this.txtSliderMultiThreadedValue.Text = this.SliderMultiThreaded.Value.ToString();

    // Run the background worker again in case the slider value needs to catch up
    // If you stop the slider at the end for example, it might be still processing the⤶
previous event
    // you want to make sure that where the slider is stopped (last event fired) matches⤶
what was processed by the 2nd thread
    if (!this.bw.IsBusy)
    {
        // if the values are not in sync, then the 2nd thread needs to catch up to the UI
        if ((this.SliderMultiThreaded.Value != this.LastMultiThreadedSliderValue) &&⤶
(this.LastMultiThreadedSliderValue != 0.0))
```

417

```
            {
                // run the process again if the last value set has not been run by the second
    thread
                this.bw.RunWorkerAsync();
                // set the value to 0.0
                this.LastMultiThreadedSliderValue = 0.0;
            }
        }
    }

    public double LastMultiThreadedSliderValue
    {
      get
      {
        object objLock = new object();
        lock (objLock)
        {
          return this.lastMultiThreadedSliderValue;
        }
      }
      set
      {
        // lock the setter so multiple threads do not leave the value inconsistant
        object objLock = new object();
        lock (objLock)
        {
          this.lastMultiThreadedSliderValue = value;
        }
      }
    }
}

private void SliderSimple_ValueChanged(object sender, RoutedPropertyChangedEventArgs
<double> e)
{
    // increment simple slider event count
    this.countSliderSimple++;
    // set the slider value to its text box
    this.txtSliderSimpleValue.Text = this.SliderSimple.Value.ToString();
    // set the count on the text box
    this.txtSliderSimpleNumberEventFires.Text = this.countSliderSimple.ToString();
}

private void SliderSingleThreaded_ValueChanged(object sender,
 RoutedPropertyChangedEventArgs<double> e)
{
    // increment single threaded slider event count
    this.countSliderSingleThreaded++;
    // set the slider value to its text box
    this.txtSliderSingleThreadedValue.Text = this.SliderSingleThreaded.Value.ToString();

    // add a fake delay of 150 milliseconds (3/20 of a second)
```

```
        System.Threading.Thread.Sleep(150);

        // set the count on the text box
        this.txtSliderSingleThreadNumberEventFires.Text =↵
    this.countSliderSingleThreaded.ToString();
    }
        private void SliderMultiThreaded_ValueChanged(object sender,↵
    RoutedPropertyChangedEventArgs<double> e)
        {
          // increment multi threaded slider event count
          this.countSliderMultiThreaded++;
          // set the last value set compared to the current value
          this.LastMultiThreadedSliderValue = this.SliderMultiThreaded.Value;

          // If the BackgroundWorker is free,
          // execute the business logic on the second thread
          if (!bw.IsBusy)
          {
            bw.RunWorkerAsync();
          }

          // set the count on the text box
          this.txtSliderMultiThreadNumberEventFires.Text =↵
    this.countSliderMultiThreaded.ToString();
        }
```

14. Build the project and you will see three sliders (as illustrated in Figure 12-18). Move the third slider around and note that even though you still have the 150 millisecond business algorithm processing, the UI code and the sliding motion remain very responsive. Isn't this user experience much better than the single-threaded experience in Slider 2?

419

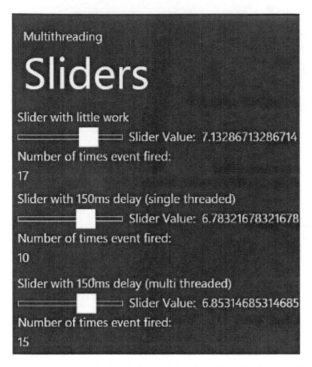

Figure 12-18. *Three sliders in the final build of the coding scenario emphasize the need to use concurrent programming techniques for expensive business logic.*

Lessons Learned

It may have surprised you that this coding scenario is applicable on a mobile intelligence device. As mentioned earlier, even mobile processors can take advantage of multiple cores in order to implement important features such as multitasking. Note that although the processor on a Windows Phone 7 device is powerful, it's still a mobile class processor. A single thread is limited on how much processing can be pushed through the CPU efficiently. Taking advantage of multiple cores is crucial in order to implement business intelligence modules that require complex processing with real-time insight. Fluid interactivity is a cornerstone when delivering successful mobile intelligence applications.

Note also that you were able to use the same exact code line for line from Chapter 10. Earlier in this chapter, I mentioned that Silverlight for Windows Phone 7 has less functionality than the full runtime. However, the Windows Phone 7 hardware platform and the Silverlight SDK both support concurrent programming techniques and you should implement them when you can.

Summary

In this chapter, you learned how business intelligence 2.0 concepts delivered on mobile devices define the emerging mobile intelligence paradigm. This chapter focused on how mobile intelligence can be delivered via the Silverlight runtime on various mobile platforms.

You saw how business intelligence 2.0 concepts from the past chapters have come together to create successful mobile intelligence modules. In this chapter's samples and coding scenarios you implemented fluid interactivity, word-sized data visualizations, geographic visualization services, concurrent programming, and custom controls in Silverlight mobile intelligence. This amplified the definition of mobile intelligence as business intelligence 2.0 on a mobile device.

The knowledge garnered in this chapter ought to clarify how to deliver mobile intelligence using Silverlight enabled mobile devices.

CHAPTER 13

■ ■ ■

Surfacing Silverlight Business Intelligence in SharePoint

This chapter covers how to surface Silverlight business intelligence modules in SharePoint 2007 and SharePoint 2010. It will not introduce new business intelligence or specific Silverlight topics. Instead, it's dedicated to showing you how to use SharePoint server to deploy your existing Silverlight business intelligence investments. This chapter is broken down into two main sections. The first section will cover how to integrate with SharePoint Server 2007 and the second section will cover SharePoint 2010.

The content covered is very important if you are leveraging SharePoint, Silverlight, or invested in Microsoft business intelligence. The following table outlines the specific goals that different types of readers will achieve by reading this chapter. Microsoft's strategy is to use SharePoint functionality in order to expose existing business intelligence services (i.e., PerformancePoint), back-end data services (i.e., Analysis Services, SQL Azure), visual business intelligence (i.e., Reporting Services), etc. The topic of integrating Silverlight business intelligence modules with other Microsoft business intelligence tools is very important. Therefore, I decided to extend the information covered in Chapter 11 and dedicate an entire chapter to this critical topic.

The following coding scenario is included in this chapter:

- Self-Service Silverlight application hosting

Audience	Goals
Silverlight developers	Grasp the process of deploying Silverlight applications to SharePoint Server 2007.
	Recognize how Silverlight is a first-class citizen in Microsoft SharePoint 2010 and the tools that make development easier.
Business intelligence professionals	Understand how you can surface Silverlight business intelligence applications inside SharePoint server.
	Recognize that Silverlight business intelligence applications can co-exist with existing Microsoft business intelligence modules or SharePoint data lists.

Audience	Goals
Strategic decision makers	Understand that Silverlight can work with SharePoint Server 2007 and SharePoint 2010 with little or no additional changes to the Silverlight applications.
	See how an investment in SharePoint server can surface Silverlight content on potential client portals or SaaS hosted solutions.

Why SharePoint for Business Intelligence?

Since Microsoft started competing in the business intelligence market, the company has done a good job providing small- and enterprise-scale back-end business intelligence solutions. Products like Analysis Services, Integration Services, Reporting Services, StreamInsight, Master Data Services, and Microsoft AppFabric are extremely popular business intelligence solutions. However, from the late 1990s and largely through the 2000s Microsoft lacked a central location where to surface the data, reports, and service endpoints these services where exposing. Some solutions like Reporting Services and PerformancePoint Server could act as a "UI hub" but were very limited in the functionality. For example, publishing data from various data providers was very intensive or impossible to do. Microsoft needed to resolve this issue in order to remain competitive with other business intelligence vendors like IBM Cognos, SAP (Business Objects), and Oracle who did offer complete business intelligence solutions that surface the BI data in a central user interface (i.e., dashboard, portal).

Microsoft listened to the feedback from business intelligence clients and started marketing a central repository that would act as the business intelligence UI hub. Since SharePoint Server 2007, Microsoft developed a very serious strategy about utilizing the SharePoint platform as a hub for surfacing the content provided by their business intelligence solutions. The SharePoint product provides numerous features like document management, search, modular portals, collaboration, enterprise search, etc. It makes sense to expose business intelligence content via a portal that business users are already familiar with and use during their daily work operations. Microsoft has since deprecated or stopped supporting products that competed with SharePoint (i.e. PerformancePoint Server 2007 is a service in SharePoint 2010).

SharePoint 2007 Business Intelligence Capabilities

Microsoft SharePoint Server 2007 is largely seen as the "1.0 version" of SharePoint that exposes business intelligence content. Previous versions of SharePoint could expose business intelligence content; however, the business intelligence story was very erratic and did not take proper form until SharePoint 2007 was released.

Microsoft SharePoint Server 2007 is highlighted with the following unique business intelligence features:

- *Report Center*: The Report Center is a central place for business intelligence where users can access reports, document lists, and data from multiple sources in a single location.

- *Excel Services*: Excel Services is a new feature that lets users to store an Excel spreadsheet and its data on the server, making the content discoverable by SharePoint search. Furthermore, owners of the spreadsheet can expose some or all of the data on a SharePoint site. Excel Services is a great place to store complex spreadsheet insight in a read-only manner to business or casual users.

- *Key Performance Indicators (KPIs)*: KPIs were surfaced in SharePoint 2007 via KPI lists. This allows business users to combine data and create visual indicators to allow them to see how the organization was tracking to organizational goals.

- *System Connections*: SharePoint administrators can create data connections to multiple data sources and expose them to business users for consumption in SharePoint services or lists.

- *Modular dashboards*: SharePoint Server 2007 exposes various business intelligence web parts that allow users to compose dashboards from these modules. Business intelligence web parts include filter web parts, KPI lists, Excel, Analysis Services, etc.

- *Easy collaboration*: Creators and owners of business intelligence can easily share the content without having to resort to e-mail attachments or letting sensitive data out beyond the SharePoint security perimeter. This allows business users a self-service manner to control business intelligence access.

- *Basic Mobile Intelligence*: Certain SharePoint lists can be viewed on mobile devices using mobile templates in SharePoint. This allows remote business intelligence users to consume the same SharePoint data on their mobile devices.

SharePoint Server 2007 provided a good foundation for exposing business intelligence content. A business user could create a dashboard, KPI lists, and upload and share Excel spreadsheets. However, the 2007 version of SharePoint lacked key self-service business intelligence, Silverlight, and other Microsoft business intelligence product integration.

■ **Note** There are many third party SharePoint extensions as well as very flexible API for SharePoint 2007 that pretty much allow an administrator or SharePoint architect to do anything. However, the "out of the box" business intelligence capabilities that are provided in SharePoint 2007 are listed above.

SharePoint 2010 Business Intelligence Capabilities

Microsoft SharePoint 2010 enhances the business intelligence user interface hub and greatly improves the amount of business intelligence sources and applications that can be easily integrated. In fact, Microsoft has rebranded the SharePoint 2010 business intelligence capabilities as Insights.

Insights for Microsoft SharePoint 2010 truly follows the business intelligence 2.0 tenets taught throughout this book. The primary goal for the SharePoint 2010 Insights platform is to separate the function of the business department and the backend IT department. If you are familiar with SharePoint 2007, it requires a lot of administrator privileges to do a lot of tasks. This can be crippling if you are a business user that wants to surface data in a simple list using a database as a data source. For example, deploying a web part in SharePoint 2007 requires all kind of access to the GAC (global assembly cache), installing features, and even editing configuration files; this prevents the business user from using the product in a self-service manner. Essentially Microsoft has created a series of services and tools that empowers business users to utilize business intelligence how they want to without involving the SharePoint administrators from the IT department. This fundamental shift is to self-service business intelligence 2.0 and empowering casual SharePoint users is labeled as Insights for SharePoint 2010.

Microsoft SharePoint 2010 offers the following unique business intelligence features:

- *Collective Intelligence*: SharePoint 2010 brings many new collective intelligence features to the SharePoint platform. Almost any piece of data can be shared, rated, and tracked using new social networking features. Furthermore, this allows for clear business intelligence data accountability and tractability.

- *Self-Service PowerPivot*: PowerPivot Excel spreadsheets can be saved in SharePoint 2010. A PowerPivot gallery can be used to surface the in-memory analytics engine. The entire process from data source selection, creation, collaboration, and maintenance of PowerPivot and SharePoint 2010 can be done without the need for IT department involvement.

- *Visio Services*: Visio Services empowers users to create and share complex data visualizations in SharePoint 2010. Complex business intelligence workflow or flowchart visualizations can be created using Visio Services.

- *PerformancePoint Services*: Many features found in PerformancePoint Server 2007 are now included in SharePoint 2010 as PerformancePoint Services. This allows casual users to create rich and interactive business intelligence solutions. PerformancePoint Services includes tools like data integration, data visualization, and dashboard creation.

- *Chart Web Parts*: The power to create simple chart data visualizations is in the hands of the casual user in SharePoint 2010. Users can use a wizard that will walk them through creating a chart web part from available shared data sources.

- *Silverlight Support*: Silverlight is a first-class citizen in SharePoint 2010 and can be found in various menu and navigation tools (i.e., Pivot Gallery). Furthermore, sharing and surfacing a Silverlight application could not be easier in SharePoint 2010.

- *Business Connectivity Services (BCS)*: BCS is a set of services that allows SharePoint to consume data from a variety of data sources. This is important for business intelligence solutions that host the "single version of truth" of data in data stores outside of SharePoint. Essentially, this allows the BI architect to "mash-up" external BI data with SharePoint lists, web parts, etc.

SharePoint 2010 has added many compelling features surrounding self-service business intelligence. Microsoft sees this as a differentiator that empowers the business user without impacting the IT department. The business intelligence story in SharePoint 2010 has become much more mature and Microsoft decided to market this as "SharePoint 2010 Insights".

■ **Note** For more information on Insights for SharePoint 2010, please visit
`http://sharepoint.microsoft.com/en-us/product/capabilities/insights/Pages/default.aspx`.

SharePoint 2007 and Silverlight Integration

SharePoint 2007 was released prior to the release of Silverlight 1.0. Therefore, SharePoint 2007 does not have native Silverlight support and out of the box tooling to help with Silverlight deployment. However, SharePoint 2007 exposes a rich development model and the nature of Silverlight makes it possible to deploy Silverlight applications to SharePoint Server 2007.

Silverlight applications can be integrated with SharePoint 2007 in the following ways:

- *Object (plug-in) HTML tag*: SharePoint 2007 is a web product that essentially renders dynamic HTML content. Simple Silverlight applications can easily be incorporated into SharePoint 2007 using this basic technique.

- *Custom Web Parts*: SharePoint Server 2007 includes a modular UI development model called the web part framework. This allows users to expose specific pieces of business content in a web part. A custom web part can include Silverlight content.

Silverlight deploys as a separate application that essentially consists of a XAP file, JavaScript helper, and other optional resources. Therefore, the Silverlight XAP file can be any Silverlight version you chose, whether it is version 1.0 or 4.0. That is an important point: the SharePoint version does not dictate with version of Silverlight you have to deploy and vice versa.

Object HTML Tag

Many Silverlight and SharePoint developers constantly miss this obvious integration point. All of the SharePoint 2007 content that you see (i.e., lists, document libraries, navigation, menus) is HTML. Since (in simple terms) SharePoint Server 2007 renders HTML, Silverlight can be embedded into the HTML using the object tag.

You can embed Silverlight content as navigation menus, master page content, edit menus, static pages in workflows, etc. This Silverlight content can call various data services and behave like a dynamic control in SharePoint 2007. Furthermore, initialization parameters can be passed into the Silverlight modules to properly initialize the application. For example, an initialization parameter could be the Windows ID of the user that is logged into the SharePoint site. This could be passed into the Silverlight application, which can in turn call a service to retrieve the relevant data for the user.

Object HTML tag integration is the simplest form of integrating Silverlight content in SharePoint Server 2007. However, it is also very limited. SharePoint 2007 does not include any special tools to help with integrating Silverlight. The biggest downside is this type of integration usually requires a developer with administrative privileges.

Custom Web Parts

Web parts are ASP.NET controls that surface visual content. Web parts are Microsoft's implementation of the "web widget;" they allow for the development of modular user interface components so that web sites can be "composed" dynamically by a developer or even a casual user.

Two Types of Web Parts

Figure 13-1 illustrates the two different kinds of web parts a developer can create. ASP.NET web parts allow you to create portal components that can be used in proprietary ASP.NET portals as well as SharePoint. Conversely, SharePoint 2007 web parts can only be deployed to SharePoint Server. There is an important functionality distinction that many resources do not make clear. Even Microsoft, as late as 2006, was describing this in simple technical talk without making a proper recommendation to developers. The problem with SharePoint web parts is that they can only be used in SharePoint deployments. This might be OK if you are developing a custom in-house solution specifically for SharePoint. However, if you are a component vendor or want to maximize the points of integration, ASP.NET web parts provide the most flexibility.

.NET Web Parts

ASP.NET	SharePoint
• Work in both .NET and Sharepoint • Supported since .NET 2.0 • Minor tooling and deployment functionality missing as compared to SharePoint web parts	• Only work in SharePoint environment • Supported since 2003 • Provide an upgrade path from previous SharePoint web parts • Extra SharePoint designer, features, and SharePoint-specific functionality

Figure 13-1. Two kinds of .NET web parts provide slightly different functionality.

It is important to understand that ASP.NET web parts are the recommended and preferred way of developing web parts. However, Silverlight can be displayed in both types of web parts effectively using the same techniques. SharePoint Server 2010 includes a specific Silverlight hosting web part that allows a designer to simply point it to a XAP file and surface it with no code (if advanced features like communication are not required).

The Relationship between Silverlight and Web Parts

Web parts can be viewed as simple widget wrapper controls that allow for modular design of composite applications. Figure 13-2 illustrates how a Silverlight application is hosted in a web part.

Figure 13-2. Silverlight XAP package referenced inside the web part container

Web parts are wrappers around Silverlight applications. As you saw in previous sections, all you need to do to expose Silverlight content in an HTML page is to properly define the object tag parameters and provide a valid location to the Silverlight XAP file. That is all that is required to host a Silverlight application within a web part.

■ **Warning** There are many advanced scenarios that require proper architecture when designing Silverlight web parts. One example is the communication mechanism. If you plan on having your Silverlight web parts communicate to both non-Silverlight and Silverlight web parts, you should consider extending the web part communication framework. This will allow you to communicate to web parts in all scenarios: Silverlight to Silverlight, Silverlight to non-Silverlight, and vice versa. I plan on posting some advanced Silverlight web part scenarios on the companion web site.

Why Silverlight Web Parts?

Silverlight web parts are some of my favorite integration points for rich client BI 2.0 solutions. Silverlight web parts actually provide several key advantages that should not be overlooked by technical architects:

- *Simplified web part life cycle.* Designing web parts properly is not simple. It gets very complicated when you have three or more levels of communication between multiple web parts where web parts act as both providers and consumers. Maintaining state on post backs and intercepting inter–web part messages is difficult to architect.

- *Local client communication*: As you saw in Chapter 11, you can use the LocalCommunication API to send and receive messages locally between multiple web parts. This allows web part communication to occur without expensive post backs. Web parts of the SharePoint type include capabilities for local client communication. With Silverlight, this is available to ASP.NET web parts as well.

- *Removing the update mess*: If you have worked with web parts in SharePoint, deployment and maintenance can be a mess. .NET web parts need to be installed locally on the client with their assemblies and code locally stored on the server. This usually works fine for the first installation; however, upgrades can cause major problems. If you release an updated version of the web part assemblies, the assemblies need to be uninstalled, referenced SharePoint web part pages need to be removed, and assemblies need to be reinstalled. Then you need to redo the web part pages. This can be automated; however, it is a major pain without third-party software. SharePoint Server was designed with hard references across the tiers, and it is not simple to maintain updates across a SharePoint farm (multiple servers). Silverlight actually solves this very nicely. If you have a Silverlight web part and the only updates are to the Silverlight application, all you need to do is exchange the XAP file! It is that easy. This feature alone makes Silverlight web parts a fantastic implementation strategy.

- *SaaS in SharePoint*: As you saw in Chapter 11, Silverlight supports the SaaS model effectively. You can install a .NET web part locally on a SharePoint server and have it reference a remote location of the Silverlight XAP file. This in effect allows that XAP application to be hosted, maintained, and upgraded over time by a completely different vendor. This very powerful SharePoint integration concept means that portions of the SharePoint 2007 services can be outsourced or maintained by a third party without them having any direct access to the SharePoint 2007 server.

- *Interactive BI*: Previous chapters demonstrated the strength of the relationship between Silverlight and BI 2.0. Having fully interactive analytical tools available across all your users in a single SharePoint environment is truly a powerful implementation. In trying to replicate rich BI functionality, many developers resort to injecting asynchronous web parts or Ajax. This complicates the web part development model because maintaining state and communication is even more complicated. Silverlight makes this much easier.

SharePoint 2010 and Silverlight Integration

Microsoft released SharePoint 2010 in May of 2010. In the meantime, Silverlight had gone through three iterations due to its fast release cadence. Microsoft had time between the SharePoint 2007 and Silverlight 1.0 release to enhance the Silverlight integration options.

Silverlight applications can be integrated with SharePoint 2010 in the following ways:

- *Object (plug-in) HTML tag*: (same as SharePoint 2007) SharePoint 2010 is a web product that essentially renders dynamic HTML content. Simple Silverlight applications can easily be incorporated into SharePoint 2007 using this basic technique.

- *Custom Web Parts:* (same as SharePoint 2007) SharePoint Server 2010 includes a modular UI development model called the web part framework. This allows users to expose specific pieces of business content in a web part. A custom web part can include Silverlight content.

- *Silverlight Web Part:* The Silverlight Web Part is a new web part that is part of SharePoint 2010. This web part allows you to host one single Silverlight application (XAP file). Its main feature is that you do not have to write a custom web part to host a Silverlight application like you did in SharePoint 2007.

- *Client Object Model:* SharePoint 2010 includes a client-side API that allows the developer to query remote SharePoint 2010 data. This is an excellent integration option if you want to consume data that is exposed in SharePoint.

- *SharePoint 2010 Development Story:* The Visual Studio 2010 tools for SharePoint 2010 are leaps and bounds better than Visual Studio 2008 and SharePoint 2007. The tools allow for easier deployment and debugging of Silverlight solutions into SharePoint 2010. Furthermore, the developer can use a non-server workstation (Windows 7 x64) to perform development tasks instead of relying on remote debugging or a server operating system.

■ **Note** The object HTML tag and custom web part integration options are, for the most part, the same between SharePoint 2007 and SharePoint 2010. The SharePoint 2010 Designer includes additional options that make surfacing Silverlight content easier, but it is the same in principle, so those two topics will not be covered again in this section.

Silverlight Web Part

The Silverlight Web Part is a new web part that comes out of the box with Microsoft SharePoint 2010. This is essentially a simple "wrapper" for a Silverlight application (XAP file). The primary function of the Silverlight web part is to provide an easy mechanism to host a Silverlight application (XAP file).

The Silverlight web part can be found in the "Media and Content" category in SharePoint 2010. Figure 13-3 depicts the location of the Silverlight web part.

Figure 13-3. The Silverlight web part can be found in the Media and Content category after clicking "Insert – Web Part" in SharePoint 2010.

There are two unique parameters of the Silverlight web part. The first is the location of the XAP file. The XAP file location is a URI where XAP file is hosted. This is usually a local resource (i.e., document library URI) or it can be a remote location. Figure 13-4 shows the simple two-step process of using the Silverlight web part to host an existing Silverlight application. In SharePoint 2010, while in edit mode, select to insert a new web part. Then click on the Silverlight Web Part and hit add. A dialog appears to select the location of the Silverlight XAP file. Select a remote location (I selected http://silverlightbusinessintelligence.com/Demos/IntroToDataVisualizations/BuildingATagCloud/ClientBin/Chapter5_TagCloud.xap, as shown in Figure 13-4). Then click OK. The Silverlight web part grabs the XAP file and is able to host the remote Silverlight application on the local SharePoint 2010 server.

Figure 13-4. A Silverlight web part can host local or remote Silverlight applications.

In addition to being able to set generic web part properties, the Silverlight web part exposes a "Custom Initialization Parameters" property (see Figure 13-5). This property passes in one more initialization parameter to the Silverlight web part. This comes in handy if you want to create a control that behaves differently in SharePoint 2010 than in a regular ASP.NET site. In that case you could create an IsInSharePoint parameter and set it to yes. This parameter is completely optional.

Figure 13-5. A Silverlight web part can be edited by changing the location of the XAP file or providing additional Custom Initializtion Parameters.

As you can see, the Silverlight web part is limited in the features it exposes; however, it is very easy to use. One the key missing features this web part an implemented provider and consumer web part communication model. Furthermore, if you want to extend the Silverlight web part with additional custom parameters, you will have to develop your own custom web part. The SharePoint 2010 Silverlight web part serves its purpose very well, but in a limited fashion.

■ **Note** The Silverlight web part functionality can be very easily mimicked for SharePoint 2007 by writing your own custom web part wrapper for Silverlight.

Client Object Model

The Silverlight Web Part is a new web part that comes out of the box with Microsoft SharePoint 2010.

The client object model allows developers to write Silverlight applications that interact with the SharePoint 2010 artifacts. This allows you to do basic things like query lists and document libraries or advanced things like manipulating and creating new SharePoint 2010 artifacts.

The client object model is packaged in two .NET client assemblies called Microsoft.SharePoint.Client.Silverlight.dll and Microsoft.SharePoint.Client.Silverlight.Runtime.dll. Instead of referencing both of these assemblies, a developer can reference the

Microsoft.SharePoint.Client.xap, which is cached on the server. This way the assemblies do not have to take up additional size in your Silverlight application and you do not pay the "download penalty" each time.

Why would a developer want to create a Silverlight application that communicates with SharePoint 2010? There are many possible answers to this. As you have seen throughout the chapters, Silverlight is a great framework that features interactivity, data visualizations, rapid UI responses, etc. Therefore, Silverlight is a great framework for automating tedious operations in SharePoint 2010. For business intelligence scenarios, the answer is much simpler. Imagine if you have created a self-service list of important data and you want to visualize that data or provide an interactive tool to the SharePoint data; Silverlight could be a great option.

SharePoint 2010 Development Story

The development story for SharePoint 2010 is much improved over SharePoint 2007. The Visual Studio 2010 IDE is the primary development environment for SharePoint 2010. The SharePoint 2010 projects now include several SharePoint project types that make development and deployment much easier. A SharePoint 2010 solution that includes a Silverlight application can now be natively debugged in Visual Studio 2010. This is a huge productivity enhancement for Silverlight developers. SharePoint includes a project type that can automatically package up a Silverlight project and automatically deploy it to a SharePoint 2010 server. This is another great feature, because in SharePoint 2007 you had to write your own or rely on a third party solution.

SharePoint 2010 is the first SharePoint version that allows an installation on a non-server operating system. This allows developers to run local instances of SharePoint 2010 if they have a Windows 7 64-bit operating system (or better). For Silverlight designers and developers who have all their tools installed on their local workstations this is a huge development productivity boost.

Implementing Silverlight Business Intelligence Scenarios in SharePoint

Up to this point you should be familiar with the business intelligence capabilities of SharePoint 2007 and 2010 and how you can surface Silverlight content in both versions. In this section, I will cover some common Silverlight business intelligence scenarios in SharePoint.

Adding Silverlight to an existing SharePoint BI SharePoint Site

A common business intelligence scenario (covered in Chapter 11) is when you have an existing investment in a dashboard or portal and want to enhance it with a "fresh" Silverlight application. In both SharePoint 2007 and SharePoint 2010, Silverlight web parts can co-exist with non-Silverlight web parts. Figure 13-6 illustrates a sample SharePoint 2010 dashboard that includes two Chart web parts and a Silverlight web part.

Figure 13-6. A Silverlight web part can co-exist and function normally even though there are non-Silverlight web parts present.

This is a very common scenario where business intelligence architects want to inject some business intelligence 2.0 tools into a fully functional SharePoint business intelligence portal. Obviously, if you invested several months or years creating a portal that everyone uses, you would not re-write the entire site to add a simple BI 2.0 component. Silverlight can be a very inexpensive way to add a couple modular BI 2.0 tools without losing the previous investment. In SharePoint 2010, this is accomplished using the Silverlight web part and hosting the Silverlight application. In SharePoint 2007, this takes a little more work; first you create a web part wrapper and then you host the Silverlight application file.

One key point to remember is that Silverlight web parts are downloaded and then executed on the user's workstation. If you have a dashboard consisting of web parts that constantly post back and require server processing, this may depreciate the value a Silverlight business intelligence tool can bring to a SharePoint dashboard.

Exposing Complete Silverlight BI tools in SharePoint

Another scenario covered in Chapter 11 is when you have a "feature complete" Silverlight business intelligence tool that a client wants or you want to expose in SharePoint. The integration options are exactly the same as the previous section; you simply host the entire Silverlight application inside SharePoint. The only difference is that the Silverlight application may take up a larger amount of real-estate or be the sole focus on the page. This leaves the responsibility of rendering all the different states of the application to Silverlight and not SharePoint. Figure 13-7 illustrates this with a mini-Silverlight dashboard exposed in SharePoint 2010. Notice that the dashboard consists of multiple panels that minimize, maximize, and change the rendering of the data visualizations. This is all handled inside the single Silverlight application.

Figure 13-7. A full Silverlight dashboard running inside SharePoint 2010. Notice the children panels inside the dashboard are fully managed inside the Silverlight application.

This integration option is a great solution if you have a complete Silverlight business intelligence solution that you want to expose "as is" inside SharePoint. Again, it would make no sense to re-write an existing dashboard to add a little Silverlight module; it would also make no sense to re-write a fully working Silverlight application in smaller pieces if it has been proven it works.

This type of integration is very interesting for SaaS models. Imagine you are a software business intelligence vendor and want to integrate your product into an existing SharePoint 2007 or 2010 portal. Silverlight is an absolutely perfect fit in this scenario. As you saw in Figure 13-4, you could host a completely remote Silverlight business intelligence module inside a local SharePoint server by simply referencing the XAP file location. This would allow you to provide four different levels of SaaS maturity to all your clients while hosting the content inside their existing SharePoint investment.

■ **Note** I dramatically simplified the steps needed to deploy a production level SaaS solution, but the concept outlined above is accurate.

In the sections that listed all of the business intelligence capabilities of SharePoint 2007 and 2010, you probably noticed a lot of features that allow you to surface data from different sources. In an earlier chapter, you created a simple PivotViewer control that surfaced content provided by Microsoft Bing. Figure 13-8 below shows an example of the PivotViewer Silverlight control running inside SharePoint 2010. This amplifies the reoccurring theme that content surfaced in SharePoint 2010 can be from various data sources. This is in line with other enterprise business intelligence solutions like SAP Business Objects, Oracle Hyperion, and IBM Cognos.

■ **Note** Microsoft offers a concept tool called PivotViewer Extensions for Reporting Services. This allows you to surface visual data from Reporting Services in an interactive PivotViewer tool powered by Silverlight. This concept tool integrates very nicely into SharePoint 2010 and there are few examples of how this works.

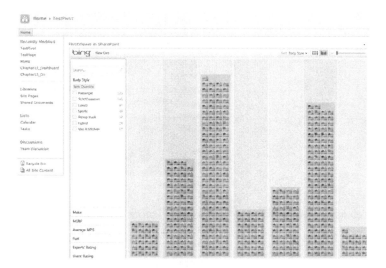

Figure 13-8. The PivotViewer Silverlight control running inside SharePoint 2010. This is an example of a control that is retrieving data from an external data source.

Communication Between Silverlight Web Parts

One of the most common implementation of regular ASP.NET web parts is to leverage the web part communication model. This allows web parts to communicate between one another. This communication is facilitated through the ASP.NET post back model that sends an agreed upon interface data between the web parts. This model will not work for Silverlight web parts for several reasons. Could you imagine an interactive web part causing a flicker and post back each time you move a slider? We need to leverage a client communication model that allows communication outside the ASP.NET post back model.

In Chapter 11, you learned that two separate Silverlight web parts can communicate between each other using the Silverlight messaging API. This messaging API is 100 percent compatible on Silverlight applications hosted on a SharePoint site. Figure 13-9 illustrates a SharePoint 2010 page that surfaces two Silverlight web parts (they were added the same manner as in the examples in this chapter). Once they are added, the messaging API takes over and allows the controls to communicate.

■ **Note** The two Silverlight XAP files used in the example below are included in the source code. If you have SharePoint 2010 installed, you can re-creating this example yourself by simply adding the two XAP files to a SharePoint 2010 page. If you change the value in the drop down, you'll notice the second Silverlight application receiving the changes and updated the chart.

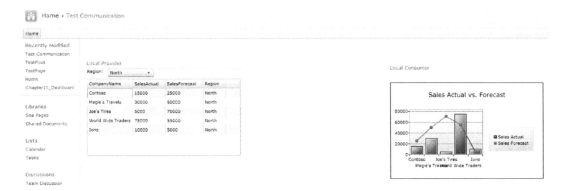

Figure 13-9. Two individual Silverlight web parts communicating between each other using the local messaging API.

The example above is the simplest way you can enable local communication between multiple Silverlight web parts. Notice that you did not have to consume interfaces, use attributes, or leverage post backs in ASP.NET. However, this code is not production ready. There are several ways to make this more dynamic.

- *Use Init Parameters*: Init parameters can be used in order to pass in the type of messaging to send and to which controls. This can be done dynamically or by setting the parameters when adding the control to a page. This is a good way to have some control over Silverlight web part communication, but it does not allow full customizability.

- *Custom Silverlight Web Part*: By creating a custom web part, you can route the communication between Silverlight web parts dynamically. This can also be extended to use the native SharePoint web part connections manager. This would allow an end-user to dynamically create connections between Silverlight web parts without having to know anything about programming. Therefore, the custom Silverlight web part would use the web part manager to connect the web parts on initial load or post back. However, once connected, the local message API would take over the communication. If you want to maximize the flexibility of Silverlight web part connections and comply with the SharePoint connections model, this is the best option in order to surface modular Silverlight web parts that can communicate with one another.

Coding Scenarios

■ **Note** These coding scenarios require access to a SharePoint 2010 installation. If you have MSDN access and a Windows 7 x64 workstation, you can install SharePoint 2010 locally to follow along with these coding scenarios.

Coding Scenario: Self-Service Silverlight Application Hosting

This coding scenario will show you how a casual user can take an existing local Silverlight application file and host it inside a new SharePoint 2010 page. Imagine you are a business user of a business intelligence SharePoint 2010 portal. A business intelligence developer created fantastic data visualization in Silverlight. You have used it in the past and you want to add to the SharePoint 2010 site to share with other colleagues. What do you do?

The goals of this scenario are to:

- Understand the steps to upload, host, and surface a local Silverlight application file in SharePoint 2010.

- Recognize how a casual user could use these steps to quickly build a business intelligence solution using existing Silverlight applications.

Follow these steps:

1. Locate a sample Silverlight application (XAP file). If you do not have a XAP file available, use any of the XAP files included with the Version 3.0 of the source code of this book. For simplicity, I will use the tag cloud XAP file located in the Chapter 5 folder in the source code zip file.

2. Open up the default SharePoint 2010 site:

   - Click on Home.

   - Select the Shared Documents document library (shown in Figure 13-10).

Figure 13-10. *The Shared Documents document library will host the Silverlight application (XAP file).*

3. Open up the default SharePoint 2010 site:

   - Click Add Document.

   - The Upload Document dialog will appear (shown in Figure 13-11). Browse for the XAP file on your local or network drive and click OK.

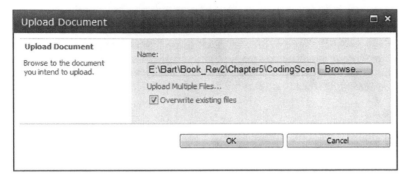

Figure 13-11. Uploading the Silverlight application (XAP file) to the SharePoint 2010 server.

4. After this is done, you should see the XAP file added to the Shared Documents library. The XAP file is now being hosted by SharePoint 2010.

5. The next step is to make this XAP file addressable with a URI. The nice thing about SharePoint is that any document, list, etc. is URI addressable. You need the URI address of the XAP file so you can pass it in as a parameter to the Silverlight web part.

    •   Hover over the XAP file and right-click and select copy shortcut (Figure 13-12).

    •   The URI shortcut of the XAP file is now in the clipboard memory.

Figure 13-12. Retrieving the URI location of the Silverlight application

6. Create a new page in SharePoint 2010 by clicking Site Actions and then selecting New Page (Figure 13-13). Enter the new page name. You should now be taken to that page.

Figure 13-13. Creating a New Page to host the Silverlight application.

7. In that new page, you will insert a Silverlight web part.

- Under the orange Editing Tools tab, click the Insert button.

- In the ribbon below, select web part.

- A list of available web part categories will appear. Select the Media and Content category and then select the Silverlight Web Part.

8. Inside the dialog, you will want to paste in the URI shortcut you copied in Step 5 (Figure 13-12). In my case, the URI was http://bartwin7desktop/Shared%20Documents/Chapter5_TagCloud.xap. In your case, the name of the server will be different. However, the URI should end with ".xap". If it doesn't, you probably copied the URI incorrectly.

9. Click OK and you should see the Silverlight application rendered inside the web part. Since you successfully deployed a Silverlight app to SharePoint 2010, you can grant access to it to your colleagues.

Lessons Learned

This coding scenario amplified the self-service business intelligence capabilities of SharePoint 2010. You clearly saw that an end-user can easily surface a Silverlight business intelligence tool for either themselves or colleagues. In SharePoint 2010, this type non-requirement of a SharePoint administrator or the IT department is commonplace. It allows the business user to focus on surfacing content rather than playing the role of facilitator or project manager liaison to the IT department.

Summary

This chapter covered the role that the SharePoint platform plays in Microsoft's business intelligence strategy, the capabilities of the last two versions or SharePoint, and possible integration strategies with Silverlight applications. While this chapter did not introduce new Silverlight business intelligence topics, this chapter is very important in understanding what options are available when surfacing Silverlight content in SharePoint server.

In summary, SharePoint is the business intelligence "user interface" hub for Microsoft products. Over the next few years you will see many organizations leveraging SharePoint's capabilities to surface business intelligence content. In this chapter, you learned how you can augment SharePoint business intelligence by deploying Silverlight business intelligence modules.

CHAPTER 14

■ ■ ■

Using the Silverlight PivotViewer

The PivotViewer is a Silverlight 4 control that allows you to interact with a great deal of data in a visual and interactive manner. This chapter is dedicated to understanding the PivotViewer control and how it can be used to implement Silverlight business intelligence 2.0 scenarios.

In the past chapters, you have learned how to implement BI 2.0 tenets by crafting self-service, simple, interactive and visual controls. This chapter will introduce you to the Silverlight PivotViewer control. You will see how Microsoft implemented some of the BI 2.0 paradigms into this control to surface and interact with large amounts of visual data.

This chapter will cover the user interface components of the PivotViewer control. You will learn how to create static collections easily using the Microsoft Excel 2010 Pivot Collection add-in. You will become familiar with the PivotViewer control by surfacing sample PivotViewer collections available on the Internet. The following table outlines the specific goals that different types of readers will achieve by reading this chapter.

This chapter includes two coding scenarios. They are not presented at the end of the chapter because they are not used to reinforce material already introduced in the chapter. Instead, I placed the coding scenarios in the middle of the chapter so you can learn about the tool as you use it. This is a much more effective way than reading a knowledge dump of all the properties of the PivotViewer control and PivotViewer collections. The two coding scenarios included in this chapter are:

- Consuming an existing PivotViewer Collection (inside the a Silverlight PivotViewer application)

- Using the Pivot Collection Tool for Microsoft Excel

Audience	Goals
Silverlight developers	Learn to use the PivotViewer control inside existing Silverlight 4 applications.
	Understand how to create custom PivotViewer collections.
	See how separate Silverlight applications communicate and interact with each other.
Business intelligence professionals	See how the PivotViewer control implements key business intelligence 2.0 tenets such as interactivity, data visualizations, real-time feedback, in-memory analysis, etc.
	Understand how the PivotViewer control can be used as an entry point or replacement for a light analysis business intelligence module.

Audience	Goals
Strategic decision makers	See how the PivotViewer control can add the "wow factor" to your product demos and spike the interest of potential customers.
	Appreciate the functionality the PivotViewer control surfaces and how it can make your static data appear dynamic.

What is the PivotViewer?

The Silverlight PivotViewer is a Silverlight web control that allows a casual user or analyst to interact with large amounts of visual data. The PivotViewer is not a traditional analysis control because it surfaces visual data that can be interacted with using next-generation interactions such as panning, zooming in and out. This control can be used to host massive amounts of data like the entire collection of Wikipedia articles or collections as small as one record.

The Silverlight PivotViewer was generated to expose visual data for various scenarios including business intelligence, retail, point of sale, academic research, web search, etc. While all of these scenarios are important, I will focus on how the PivotViewer can be used for business intelligence analytics and surfacing data visualizations.

Which Pivot Technology is this?

Before I proceed with an overview of the Silverlight PivotViewer, it is important to understand what technology I am going to cover. The term "pivot" is thrown around loosely in some business intelligence communities and I want to make sure that you understand that the Silverlight PivotViewer should not be confused with other Microsoft "pivot technologies." Furthermore, understanding the functionality of some of these tools will help you understand the underlying concepts that allowed the PivotViewer control to come to fruition.

■ **Note** I personally do not like the name "Silverlight PivotViewer." As you will see in the next several subsections, Microsoft has multiple technologies that use the "pivot" label. I would have preferred a name like Silverlight Data Collection Viewer or Silverlight Data Visualizer. Essentially, anything but the name "pivot" would have been great.

PivotTable

PivotTable is the Microsoft trademarked data tool in Microsoft Office Excel. PivotTable is Microsoft's implementation of pivot tables, which are multi-dimensional analysis tools for sets of data in spreadsheet programs.

The PivotTable in Microsoft Excel allows users to create data summarization views on flat data sets. This allows flat relational data to be analyzed as a multi-dimensional cube. In fact, Excel PivotTables can be used to surface OLAP data from SQL Server Analysis Services.

PivotTable is a free value-add tool inside Microsoft Excel. Figure 14-1 illustrates the added dimensionality, filter, and aggregation capabilities available when the tool is used on a flat data set. If you are not familiar with PivotTable, note that it makes data summarization and analysis simpler as the user does not have to sift through pages of tabular data.

Figure 14-1. *Microsoft Excel PivotTable in action, providing dynamic analysis capabilities*

Power Pivot

PowerPivot is a new Microsoft Excel 2010 add-in that allows users to surface business intelligence data in a self-service manner. The add-in was released during the SQL Server 2008 R2 release timeframe. PowerPivot is meant to be a simpler alternative to creating complex Analysis Services or data mining models in SQL Server. PowerPivot can work with multiple different data sources and does not require a server backend. Therefore, you can consume data from SQL Server databases, Analysis Services, Windows Azure, and other data sources.

The imported data is stored in a columnar database. When PowerPivot is inactive, the data is compressed into the Excel spreadsheet. However, when the data is active, it's loaded into memory. This allows PowerPivot to perform data interactivity operations very quickly. For example, sorting several million records in memory is very responsive, and that operation takes less than a second to complete. Note that Microsoft recommends a x64 operating system in order to take advantage of very large data sets.

PowerPivot should be looked at like an in-memory database for Excel. It does not provide any additional API or intrinsic analytical functionality. Additional aggregations and Excel-like operations can be created using the DAX language. However, you will primarily be using Excel 2010 charting,

PivotTable, slicers, and other functions in order to manipulate the data. I like to think of PowerPivot as a "disconnected MOLAP" solution, because it essentially can be used to replace workstation resident cube technology (i.e., Cognos 8 MOLAP cubes).

■ **Note** For more information on PowerPivot, please go the Microsoft PowerPivot website at `www.powerpivot.com`

PivotViewer Components & Architecture

A PivotViewer application consists of two primary components.

The first component is the Silverlight PivotViewer control. As the name implies, this is a Silverlight control exposed via several assemblies. This control provides the user interface, interactivity, and analytical functions in order to surface visual data. Additional Silverlight components like Deep Zoom are used to provide a rich user experience when working with high quality images.

The current 1.0 version (released June 2010) of the PivotTable control is *locked down* user experience. This means that the control surfaces multiple different interactivity functions automatically for the developer. However, it is the developer's job to provide the data in order for these interactions to function properly. This leads us to the second component of the PivotViewer, which are the PivotViewer collections. PivotViewer collections are the data that you want to expose using the PivotViewer. PivotViewer collections consist of two parts: XML files and binary image files. The XML files host the metadata and the data itself in text format. The image files are images, photographs, symbols, or data visualizations that represent the data in the XML file. You can think of the XML file as a small static database that has pointers to image files.

Figure 14-2 illustrates the different components in a PivotViewer module. One key point to remember is that the PivotViewer control is not an "open" control that can be manipulated to host any forms of data. While there is an API, the API is limited to interacting with existing PivotViewer collections. Therefore, the PivotViewer must have the data formatted exactly as the PivotViewer schema defines it.

Figure 14-2. A PivotViewer module consists of the Silverlight PivotViewer control and the PivotViewer collection files.

In order to use the PivotViewer control, you must host it inside a Silverlight 4 application. While the PivotViewer is a complex control that demands a large amount of page real estate, it is still just a control like a data grid or a text box. Therefore, creating a PivotViewer page is as simple as dragging over the control on the design canvas of the Silverlight page.

The second step is to make the control functional by referencing a PivotViewer collection. This is usually done via a static URI. Figure 14-3 shows the architecture of the PivotViewer components working together. At a high architectural level, hosting the PivotViewer control inside a Silverlight 4 application and referencing a PivotViewer collection URI location (described in the coding scenarios) is all that is required to create a working PivotViewer module. As stated before, the developer does not need to perform any additional analytical design steps; the PivotViewer control handles all that.

Figure 14-3. *Architecture of a Silverlight PivotViewer module*

Installing the PivotViewer Platform

The PivotViewer control is an interactive and very visual control. Therefore, it is easier to learn the functionality of the control by using it while learning the functionality. In order to proceed with this chapter effectively, I would highly recommend downloading the PivotViewer platform in order to follow along with the next sections.

Prerequisites

- *Visual Studio 2010 and Silverlight 4*: The Silverlight PivotViewer control is built on the Silverlight 4 runtime. Therefore, Visual Studio 2010 is required in order to create embedded PivotViewer applications and Silverlight 4 is required in order to consume the application on a workstation.

- *Silverlight Control Toolkit*: The PivotViewer control references several of the assemblies found in the control toolkit. The April 2010 release is the minimum release required in order for the PivotViewer application to work.

PivotViewer & Pivot Collection Tools

- *Silverlight PivotViewer*: The Microsoft Silverlight PivotViewer can be downloaded from the Silverlight site at www.silverlight.net/learn/pivotviewer/. The installation includes the PivotViewer assemblies and a sample application. The installation is an MSI installation file. The PivotViewer will be installed in this default location: C:\Program Files (x86)\Microsoft SDKs\Silverlight\v4.0\PivotViewer\

- *Collection Tool for Microsoft Excel*: The collection tool for Microsoft Excel will allow you to create PivotViewer collections directly inside Excel. The collection tool is ideal for creating small and static PivotViewer collections that are smaller than 3,000 items. The collection tool can be downloaded from the Pivot site at www.getpivot.com/developer-info/tools.aspx.

■ **Note** The PivotViewer files include a folder called Sample. This includes an html file and the sample Silverlight application (XAP file). However, because of the nature of the PivotViewer control this will not work off of your hard drive. If you try to run it, you will get a blank screen.

Running the Sample Silverlight PivotViewer Application

The PivotViewer MSI file includes a sample Silverlight 4 application that references a web collection of automobiles. The sample application is a Visual Studio 2010 project located at C:\Program Files (x86)\Microsoft SDKs\Silverlight\v4.0\PivotViewer\Jun10\Source\PivotViewerSampleXapCode.zip.

Unzip the compressed file. Running the existing project under the Visual Studio 2010 Cassini development web server will surface errors. Host the project in IIS in order to be able to view the project without errors.

In order to host the PivotViewerSample project under IIS, you need to add the following three MIME types (you need to add these depending if you are hosting on IIS 5.x – 7.x; if you are on IIS 7.x, you probably don't have to do this step):

- CXML – text/xml

- DZC – text/xml

- DZI – text/xml

If you copied the web compiled PivotViewer web folder and added the MIME types, you should be able to launch the sample by simply referencing the virtual directory name and PivotViewerSample.html file. In order to run the sample, you will need an internet connection because the entire PivotViewer collection XML data needs to be downloaded from the hosted site. If you have deployed the PivotViewerSample project correctly to IIS, you should see a picture similar to Figure 14-4. If you see a blank figure or have an exception, either the internet connection is down or there was a problem with the way you deployed the sample to the IIS web server.

Figure 14-4. The PivotViewerSample project includes a collection of new cars provided by Bing.

PivotViewer User Interface

This section will interactively look at the PivotViewer user interface. I will cover the included functionality that is available for analysis. Note that you'll be using the sample the PivotViewer sample with the "Bing New Car" collection to learn about the PivotViewer control.

■ **Note** If you were not able to successfully deploy the PivotViewerSample for any reason, you still can follow along the chapter's sections by using any public PivotViewer collection. The exact screen shots that will be used in this chapter will not match exactly. All you need is to have Silverlight 4 installed. Multiple samples of collections are provided on the Silverlight PivotViewer site.

PivotViewer User Interface Components

The first thing you will notice when launching the PivotViewer with data is that it requires a great deal of space on a page in order to be effective. This is primarily due to the amount allocated to rendering the images for the data.

The PivotViewer consists of four primary user interface components:

- *Top Bar*: The top bar is a small strip on top of the PivotViewer control that includes the collection name, a sort dropdown, a grid and graph toggle, and a zoom option.

- *Filter Panel*: The filter panel is located on the left-hand side of the PivotViewer. This panel includes a search text box, list of facet categories, and facets grouped together. Each facet category includes different types of filter options depending on the data type of the facet.

- *Imagery Canvas*: This is the large canvas in the middle of the PivotViewer that hosts all the imagery data.

- *Info Panel*: This is a panel that appears on the right-hand side of the PivotViewer control when one of the image items is selected from the canvas. The info panel includes the item name, description, and additional properties for the item.

Top Bar

Figure 14-5 below illustrates the top bar PivotViewer component. In that figure, notice the components of the top bar. The first item you see is the read-only label of collection name of "New Cars." Just to the left of the label is a logo (in this case, the Bing logo), which is optional. In a corporate intranet environment, this could be a company logo.

Figure 14-5. *The top bar of the PivotViewer includes the collection name, Sort Order drop down, grid/graph view toggle and the zoom slider.*

The left-hand side of the top bar includes interactive controls that manipulate the image data on the imagery canvas. Clicking on the sort order drop down will open up a list of facet categories (this will be explained later) that can be used to sort the image data. Try selecting something other than "Body Style" and you will notice the immediate visual feedback as the data images move to their proper location. The grid and graph view toggle allows you to organize the data in either a grid or graph of hierarchies. Figure 14-6 shows the difference between a grid view and a graph (hierarchical) view. Notice switching between the two views is seamless and very responsive. This view is very beneficial when trying to garner insight from a large data set. For example, notice the additional insight that the Graph view provides over the Grid view. The data images are grouped together by body style. This grouping allows for easy qualitative analysis (visual interpretation), because you can compare the sizes of the graph columns. In Figure 14-6, you can see that two columns are more pronounced than others. If you have the "Bing new cars" collection open, you can clearly tell that the Passenger and SUV/Crossover are the top two body types.

Grid View   Graph View

Figure 14-6. *The Grid and Graph views compared in the PivotViewer.*

The last option on the PivotViewer top bar is the zoom slider. Moving the slider to left and right adjusts the zoom level of the imagery canvas. Try zooming in and out and you can focus on a set of items or one particular item. This is a valuable tool when the image items have additional data that you want to see. For example, Figure 14-7 is zoomed in on a set of four luxury cars. As you zoom in, you can clearly make out several pieces of qualitative data from each image item (i.e., price, gas mileage). Furthermore, you're presented with a picture of the car and the logo of the car manufacturer.

Figure 14-7. *Using the zoom slider in the top bar allows the user to clearly make out the properties of the PivotViewer data items on the imagery canvas.*

Filter Panel

Figure 14-8 below illustrates the filter panel Pivot Viewer component. The filter panel appears on the left-hand side of the PivotViewer control. The filter panel components are automatically generated from the XML data that is located in the PivotViewer collection. The developer only has to create the collection in the appropriate manner and the PivotViewer will render the filter panel appropriately. Because the control is very "self-service," it doesn't require much programming, so it could be designed by an analyst or a designer. However, the dynamic rendering of the control limits the configuration and rendering flexibility.

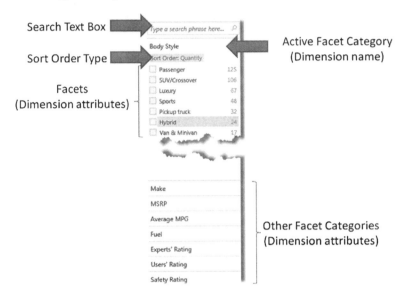

Figure 14-8. The filter panel includes several components like searching and facet filtering that allow you to locate the desired data elements on the imagery canvas faster.

Search Text Box

The topmost component of the filter panel is the search text box, which allows you filter the data by a simple text search. You can search any of the facet categories as well as the data items themselves. In addition, the text box provides auto-complete help for the user. For example, if the user starts typing BMW, she will be presented with an additional context menu of possible matches shown in Figure 14-9. The search text box is not a new implementation and you have probably used this type of control hundreds of times. One interesting difference between this control and traditional web search boxes is that this is searching a local Silverlight PivotViewer collection database and not calling a web service.

Figure 14-9. *The search box provides auto-complete to aid in searching facet categories and data items.*

Select the BMW option and this will narrow down the items shown on the imagery canvas to only the BMW make. This is an example of searching a on a particular facet ("Make" is the facet category and "BMW" is a facet that is part of the Make facet category). In addition to searching facets, you can also search on particular data items. Go back to the search box and select "BMW 5-Series" from the type-ahead drop down menu and you will notice that the imagery canvas will automatically trim the image data rendered to only show the two available BMW 5-Series models. In that example, you searched the lowest level (leaf level) of the PivotViewer data set, which are the individual items.

One interesting visual tool you may have noticed is the ability to clear applied filters on the filter panel. Figure 14-10 illustrates a search applied on BMW. Notice that the right-hand side of the facet includes a circle with a red X. This is in two locations. The first location is a Clear All button that will remove all of the filters applied from multiple facet categories. Another is an individual button that will clear either a search or an applied filter to a facet category. This is useful when you have a complex set of filters and you want to only remove a specific applied filter. The Clear All filter is automatically applied any time a single filter is created on either a search or facet category. This is a very useful way to understand if your data has any filters applied to it.

Figure 14-10. *Filters can be removed very easily using the Clear All or the red x buttons.*

By default there is always one active facet category. Usually this is the first facet category in the PivotViewer collection. The active facet category shows all of its facet categories below. If you look back at Figure 14-8, you will notice that the "Body Style" facet category is active since we can see the several facets directly below it. Other facets in Figure 14-8 are not active. Clicking on the facet category will enable the selection of facet filters. There can be only one active facet at a time in the PivotViewer. Remove any filters (click the Clear All button) and then try selecting another facet category such as MSRP or Fuel. Notice the previous filter category becomes hidden and the selected one becomes active and surfaces the facets (filters).

While selecting various facet categories you should have noticed that the filters of the facets are shown in different manner. Filter 14-11 contrasts the filters in the "Make" facet category and the "MSRP" facet category. Notice that the "Make" facet category includes simple facet filters that are essentially on/off filters. However, the MSRP facets are not individually listed. Instead a word-sized graph view data visualization is shown that includes a slider on the bottom. This slider can be move around to filter the facets.

Figure 14-11. String based facet categories enable simple on/off filtering of facets. Numerical facet categories provide an interactive slider that can be used to specify ranges.

String Facet Categories

String facet categories are based on string values. Imagine if you are looking at a database or spreadsheet column that includes states in the USA (i.e., New York, New Jersey, Pennsylvania, etc.). These states could be repeated several different times for each row. For example, New York could appear ten times. When that type of data is loaded into the PivotViewer a distinct list is built with the count. For example, in Figure 14-11 the Luxury facet in the "Body Style" facet category appeared in a list 67 times.

String facet categories include a simple UI that provides the user the ability to filter individual facets (facet items) in a mutually exclusive method. In addition to providing a checkbox next to each facet (shown in Figure 14-11) that turns off and on the filters, the counts of each facet are provided in a label on the right. Checking off the Luxury item will automatically filter the imagery canvas with just the Luxury facets.

It is important to note that the facets are individual filters. This means that you can easily apply filters from multiple facet categories and they will be filtered based on a summary of those properties; for example, if you select the "Body Style – Luxury" facet and then you additionally filter on another facet in a completely different facet. If you are a developer, you can think of this as a SQL query that applies two independent where clauses with a logical and operator (PivotViewer uses dynamic LINQ to query these data structures).

The filter panel provides some additional help when you are performing analysis in multiple categories. In Figure 14-12, the before and after is shown after a filter is applied (bottom facet category) of the facet counts. When a filter is applied, you can clearly notice that the counts of the other facets are automatically updated. Furthermore, notice that some facets are completely removed. For example, the Honda facet is removed from the "Make" facet category because they do not make a luxury automobile (according to this collection). This is an important feature to note when a user is trying to search for items in the PivotViewer control, because facets may seem to disappear from the collection when filters are applied.

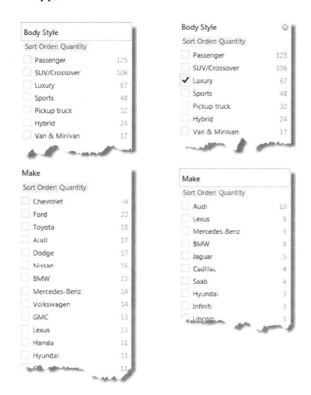

Figure 14-12. Filtering on facets can effect the counts of facet counts as well as the rendering of the facet name itself.

Numerical Facet Categories

Looking at Figure 14-11 you may be asking yourself "Why are the facet categories filtered using different mechanisms?" If you think about this from an business intelligence analysis perspective, this makes perfect sense. For example, say you are a casual user looking for a car that is under $50,000. Would it make sense to have a list of individual prices and have to check several off that are all under $50,000? This would not be a good implementation of BI 2.0 principles. Instead you have an interactive word-sized data visualization that you can interactively filter by simply using the two-thumb slider.

Figure 14-13 depicts two facet category images. In the left image, the leftmost slider thumb has been moved to the right and the rightmost thumb has been moved to the left. This allows you to narrow the start and end range for the MSRP. In addition, you can take the defined range and move the entire range left or right. You can achieve this by hovering over the slider range (not the slider thumb) and move it around the slider (shown in the right image of Figure 14-13). Interacting with the slider will automatically filter the data on the imagery canvas. Notice as you limit the range of the MSRP, an additional label is created to note the actual filtered range.

Figure 14-13. A numerical facet category can have its range adjusted a number of ways. The start and end thumbs can be used to adjust the start and end range of the numerical range. Dragging the slider bar will move the pre-defined range across the slider.

Interacting with a numerical facet category causes some interesting visual controls to appear or modify.

- *Actual filtered range*: As soon as the numbers in the range are changed, a label that notes the actual filtered range will appear directly under the Facet category name. It is interesting to note that the label logic is smart enough to understand when the begin range is not set. Figure 14-12 (right picture) shows MSRP "under $50,069" and doesn't list it as "$0 - $50,069".

- *Clear filter button*: Similarly to the Clear filter button that appears when search text is applied, when a range is applied the facet category surfaces a Clear filter button.

- *Greyed-out hierarchy bars*: Notice in Figure 14-13 that certain columns are grayed out to signify that this data does not participate in the filtered range of the slider.

■ **Warning** Numerical facet categories suffer from some analytical limitations. For example, it would be nice to hover over individual graph bars to tell what range grouping they each represent. Furthermore, the word-sized graph view does not match up directly to the main graph view on the imagery canvas. Looking at Figure 14-12, notice that the filter is MSRP "under $50,069" and not "under $50,000." There is no way to input specific numerical filters currently. This could be a problem when performing analysis on records that are very specific or if there is a very large amount of records.

Imagery Canvas

The imagery canvas is the main area in the center of the Pivot Viewer control that renders all of the image items. If you have been using the top bar and filter panel filter components, you probably are well aware of how the imagery canvas works.

The imagery canvas serves two main purposes. The first is to render the images based on the selected view using the applied filters. It is essentially a read-only data visualization of images. You can interact with the image canvas in several ways:

- *Panning*: Holding the left mouse button down, you can pan around the imagery canvas. This control leverages the Silverlight DeepZoom implementation that provides additional features like inertia so that the panning interaction feels fluid.

- *Zooming in and out*: Using the mouse wheel you can zoom in and out of the imagery canvas. This is in addition to the top bar – zoom slider control. The PivotViewer is said to have multitouch gestures exposed. I have not tested this, but on a tablet it presumably would allow you to pinch and expand with two fingers to zoom. In addition, clicking between the images will zoom the imagery canvas completely out.

- *Item selection*: Individual data items can be interacted with by either hovering over them or clicking on them. These additional interactions have to be added via the PivotViewer API. The only default action provided by the PivotViewer is the click select interaction. Clicking on an item in the imagery canvas will bring up the Info Panel.

Info Panel

The info panel is a hidden control that appears on the right side of the PivotViewer when a data item is selected. The info panel hosts additional properties that may not be surfaced on the data image. For example, Figure 14-14 shows facets like "Expert's Rating" and "Body Style" that are not rendered on the image. This paints a more complete picture of the individual item.

The info panel also includes some limited interactive functionality. You can navigate to the previous and next data item using the Previous and Next Row buttons. You can close the info panel clicking the double arrow button in the corner. Additional interactivity is optional by providing web links. For example, a user can click the name of the data item and be taken to a web page for additional information (in this case, maybe the Jaguar web site).

Figure 14-14. The info panel is actived when a data item is selected from the imagery canvas.

At this point, you should be comfortable with the PivotViewer user interface. This topic was introduced before you looked at PivotViewer collections because, as you will see in the upcoming sections, collection design is a trial-and-error and learn-by-doing process. It is difficult to get the collection designed perfectly the first time. You will most likely have to tweak the collection when you see it rendered. Therefore, understanding all the components of the PivotViewer is essential in order to create great PivotViewer collections.

PivotViewer Collections

PivotViewer collections are the second main component of a complete PivotViewer application. In the previous section, you saw all the functionality that the PivotViewer user interface exposes. Now it's time to look at the data aspect of the PivotViewer and how to create your own collections.

There are three types of PivotViewer collection architectures: simple, linked, and Just in Time collections. Figure 14-15 shows a data visualization that depicts each collection attributes. Essentially, the choice between the different collection architecture depends on the amount of data items you want to surface and expose to the PivotViewer. Collections that have less than 3,000 items can be easily created in a single static XML file that is a simple collection. If you need to surface additional items, it is recommended to use a linked collection, which is several XML files hosted on a server. A linked collection can surface up to several thousand data items. The Just in Time collection for enormous amounts of content (up to millions of records) is a just in time collection. This collection requires a server component that can dynamically build the XML responses for the PivotViewer; this is essential for collections that are the size of Wikipedia articles. Obviously these are the most complex collections to create.

Types of PivotViewer Collections

- • Easiest to create
- • Most common
- • Static XML file
- • Less than 3,000 items

- • Medium difficulty to create
- • Not very common
- • Several static XML files
- • Between 3,000-50,000 items

- • Difficult to create
- • Not very common
- • Dynamic XML files generated on the server
- • Over several hundred thousand items, millions of items

Figure 14-15. Three different types of PivotViewer collection architectures

---

■ **Warning** Linked and Just in Time collections are well beyond the scope of this book. We will focus on the simple collections, so you can become familiar with the collection architecture and how it works. Additional resources for the advanced collections can be found at

www.silverlight.net/learn/pivotviewer/collection-design/.

The PivotViewer collection is an XML document that applies the collection schema. This is why it is usually referred to as CXML (Collection XML). To create a simple CXML document, all you have to do is create a simple text document that adheres to the CXML schema. The CXML namespaces and XSD files are all publicly available on the PivotViewer web site:

- • *Overview of the CXML Schema*:
  http://www.silverlight.net/learn/pivotviewer/collection-xml-schema/

- • *PivotCollection XSD file*: http://www.getpivot.com/collection-code/pivotcollection.xsd

Instead of publishing the schema definition in this book, please refer to it online. There is a great chance that there may be enhancements, changes, or bugs in the currently published 1.0 version of the documentation.

Figure 14-16 shows the CXML hierarchy. The collection node is the root node that hosts two children FacetCategories and Items. Each of these nodes has their own children. Not shown in Figure 14-16 are the additional data types (string, date time) that determine the filter panel rendering visualizations. The figure below should give you a good understanding of the CXML data structure without covering the schema in detail. This is enough to proceed with this chapter.

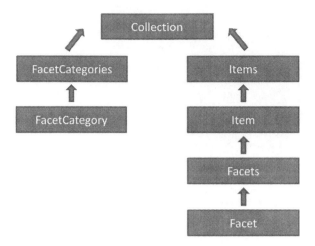

Figure 14-16. Collection XML (CXML) schema high level hierarchy. Individual nodes shown in this figure contain more children nodes.

Listing 14-1 shows a very simple CXML document that observes the schema definition. You can clearly notice that all of the CXML main hierarchy members are present. Essentially, the CXML document defines properties of the collection, a collection of FacetCategories and their properties, and a collection of items. The collection of items makes up the bulk of the CXML file size, since each facet value must be included in the CXML file. This should make clear why advanced PivotViewer collections are a single XML file, because adding millions of records to a single file would simply not work.

Listing 14-1. A simple CXML schema

```xml
<?xml version="1.0" encoding="utf-8"?>
<Collection xmlns:p="http://schemas.microsoft.com/livelabs/pivot/collection/2009"
SchemaVersion="1.0" Name="New Collection1"
xmlns="http://schemas.microsoft.com/collection/metadata/2009">
  <FacetCategories>
    <FacetCategory Name="Date Taken" Type="String" p:IsFilterVisible="true"↵
  p:IsWordWheelVisible="true" p:IsMetaDataVisible="true" />
  </FacetCategories>
  <Items ImgBase="New Collection1_files\k145q2qg.lu5.xml">
    <Item Id="0" Img="#0" Name="Hydrangeas">
      <Description>Flower</Description>
      <Facets>
        <Facet Name="Date Taken">
          <String Value="12/23/2009" />
        </Facet>
      </Facets>
    </Item>
    <Item Id="1" Img="#1" Name="Lighthouse">
      <Description>Nice pic of lighthouse</Description>
      <Facets>
        <Facet Name="Date Taken">
```

```
          <String Value="02/23/2010" />
        </Facet>
      </Facets>
    </Item>
    <Item Id="2" Img="#2" Name="Penguins">
      <Description>Penguins having fun</Description>
      <Facets>
        <Facet Name="Date Taken">
          <String Value="12/23/2001" />
        </Facet>
      </Facets>
    </Item>
...
```

Learning Coding Scenario: Consuming an existing PivotViewer Collection

So now you have a good understanding of the PivotViewer user interface as well as the basics of a PivotViewer collection. In the prior sections, you learned that the PivotViewer does a lot of hand holding for a developer and automatically generates a rich and interactive UI based on the pivot collection. Therefore, the easiest way to create a PivotViewer application is to consume a public PivotViewer Collection that is on the Internet. This section goes through the high level steps in consuming a PivotViewer collection published to the Internet:

1. Create a new Silverlight 4 solution and ensure that you create a web site to host the Silverlight project.

2. The assemblies are installed with the PivotViewer SDK and are located at: C:\Program Files (x86)\Microsoft SDKs\Silverlight\v4.0\PivotViewer\Jun10\Bin\. Ensure you add a reference to all of five assemblies.

3. As you have seen, the PivotViewer control is pretty large control. Increase the size of the layout to 1024×768 so the view is maximized. One limitation of the 1.0 PivotViewer control is that it does not support fluid layouts. Therefore, if you embed the PivotViewer control in a dynamic layout where width and height is calculated during the render process, the images on the image canvas may not render properly.

▦ **Note** Appendix B covers fluid layouts in more detail. In it, I cover creating a custom Silverlight business intelligence control.

---

4. The PivotViewer control is named PivotViewer. You should be able to filter for it in the Expression Blend 4 assets window, if you added the reference properly in Step 2 (see Figure 14-17). Drag it on to the layout root and give it a good explicit size (i.e., 1024×768). Name the PivotViewer control "PivotViewer".

Figure 14-17. The Silverlight PivotViewer control is located in the System.Windows.Pivot.dll assembly file.

5. Create a Loaded eventhandler for the loaded event for the LayoutRoot control and add the code that is shown in Listing 14-2. Inside the loaded event, you are calling the LoadCollection method on the PivotViewer object. The method takes two parameters. The first is the URI location of the hosted CXML file and the second is an optional ViewerState parameter.

Listing 14-2. All the code that is necessary to load an existing hosted PivotViewer collection

```
...
public partial class MainPage : UserControl
{
        public MainPage()
        {
                // Required to initialize variables
                InitializeComponent();
        }

        private void LayoutRoot_Loaded(object sender, System.Windows.RoutedEventArgs e)
        {
        // TODO: Add event handler implementation here.
        this.PivotViewer.LoadCollection("http://content.getpivot.com/Collections/↵
bingnewcars/bingnewcars.cxml",
            string.Empty);
        }
}
...
```

6. Run the project. You should see the PivotViewer load the "Bing new cars" collection. This project is very simple and does not include the extra buttons and Add to cart enhancements that are included in the sample project. If you don't see any data inside the PivotViewer, ensure you have a proper Internet connection and the event handler was properly created.

■ **Note** The source code for this example is available in Version 3.0 of the source code zip file on the www.silverlightbusinessintelligence.com web site.

Lessons Learned

This small exercise showed you that consuming an existing PivotViewer collection is quite trivial. More importantly, you saw that the PivotViewer control does a lot of work for the developer. All the interactivity is provided inside the PivotViewer control and derived from the CXML file and imagery files that are downloaded from a web server. You should be able to see all the images, facet categories, and facets just like you saw in the previous section's sample.

Learning Coding Scenario: Using the Pivot Collection Tool for Microsoft Excel

The CXML schema is not complex. However, you would not want to attempt to design a collection using Notepad or a XML tool. It could be done, but it would take a long time and it would be very prone to error. Microsoft realized this and has provided an add-in to Excel that makes creating static/simple collections much easier. The Pivot Collection Tool for Microsoft Excel is a free download that adds Pivot collection creation capabilities to Microsoft Excel.

■ **Note** If you have not done so already, download and install the Pivot Collection Tool for Microsoft Excel from www.getpivot.com/developer-info/tools.aspx.

If you have downloaded and installed the Pivot Collection Tool, you will have a new tab in the Microsoft Excel ribbon that will allow you to create new and manipulate existing PivotViewer collections. Figure 14-18 illustrates an active Pivot Collections tab and shows the different options available. By exposing the Pivot collection tool inside Microsoft Excel, editing a PivotViewer collection is a simple as working with an Excel spreadsheet.

Figure 14-18. The Pivot Collection Tool for Microsoft Excel allows you to easily use Excel to create simple collections. Adding images, facets, descriptions and data types is easy if you are familiar with Microsoft Excel.

The best way to learn about the tool is to use it to create a pivot collection that you can host and add to a PivotViewer project. In the same spirit of the previous section, you'll leverage some of the functionality of the Pivot Collection Tool for Microsoft Excel to create a new pivot collection and host it inside a Silverlight 4 application.

■ **Note** The source code for this example is available in Version 3.0 of the source code zip file on the www.silverlightbusinessintelligence.com web site.

Follow these steps:

1. First, create a new Silverlight solution that will host your new PivotViewer collection. Then create a web site to host the Silverlight project. Name the solution SilverlightHostingCustomPivotViewerSample.

2. The assemblies are installed with the PivotViewer SDK and are located at: C:\Program Files (x86)\Microsoft SDKs\Silverlight\v4.0\PivotViewer\Jun10\Bin\. Ensure you add a reference to all of five assemblies.

3. As you have seen, the PivotViewer control is pretty large control. Increase the size of the layout to 1024x768 so the view is maximized. One limitation of the 1.0 PivotViewer control is that it does not support fluid layouts. Therefore, if you embed the PivotViewer control in a dynamic layout where width and height is calculated during the render process, the images on the image canvas may not render properly.

4. The PivotViewer control is named PivotViewer. You should be able to filter for it in the Expression Blend 4 assets window if you added the reference properly in Step 2. This is shown in Figure 14-17 below. Drag it on to the layout root and give it a good explicit size (i.e., 1024x768). Name the PivotViewer control "PivotViewer".

5. Open Microsoft Excel 2010 and navigate to the Pivot Collections tab. If you do not have the tab, you need to install the Pivot Collections Tools for Microsoft Excel mentioned earlier in this chapter. With the tab open, click the New Collection button. You should see a new Excel Window resembling Figure 4-19 appear.

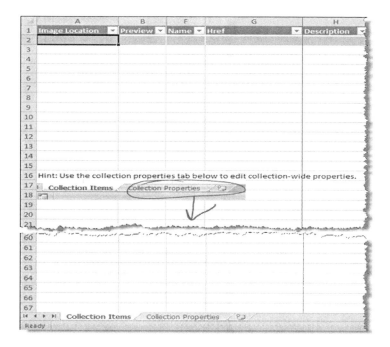

Figure 14-19. *Clicking the New Collection button will create two WorkSheets. The first one is the Collection Items where the actual items will be placed. The second is called Collection Properties where general property settings can be tweaked.*

6. As you have seen throughout the chapter, the PivotViewer is a very visual control. It is much easier to add images first than descriptions to the collection tool. Inside the Pivot Collection tool click the Import Images button. This will bring up a dialog that will ask you for the location of images. If you have some images handy, you can use those. However, I will use the images that are installed with Windows 7. They are located at C:\Users\Public\Pictures\Sample Pictures\. Add all the images in that folder. Figure 14-20 depicts the Collection Items worksheet after the images have been added.

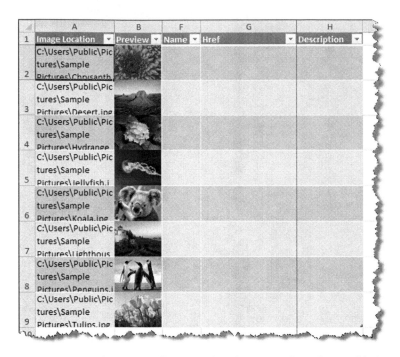

Figure 14-20. The Pivot collection after the images have been added

7. Now that the images are loaded, you can add additional properties like filling out the Name and Description cells. You can add whatever you want to those fields. I just filled out the cells with the obvious information. For example, for the Name cell, I just used the name of the file.

8. Click on the second worksheet named Collection Properties and fill out the collection name property.

9. Now that you have a very simple collection created, you can publish it. You are going to host the collection in the Silverlight application that you created in Step 1. Click the Publish Collection button and select Publish Collection To... (see Figure 14-21; if the button is grayed out, click on any of the cells in the blue section of the Collection Items worksheet—this should activate the button). This step is very important: make sure that the publish location is the SilverlightHostingCustomPivotViewerSampleSite folder because this is where your Default.html page is located. The CXML collection needs to be on the web project folder. Name the collection "SampleCollection" and click Save.

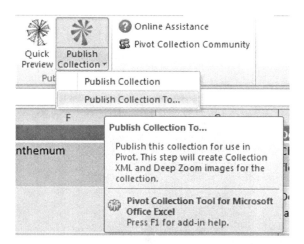

Figure 14-21. Publishing the Collection to a location on the hard drive. This will create the CXML file and the appropriate image partitions required for the imagery canvas component for the PivotViewer.

10. Navigate to the folder where you published the collection. You will notice that there are two main components created. The first is a file called SampleCollection.cxml, which hosts all of the data items and schema. The second component is created as a folder called SampleCollection_items, which holds all of the images required to surface the images for the PivotViewer.

11. Go back to the Visual Studio 2010 or Expression Blend 4 application and create a Loaded event handler for the Loaded event for the LayoutRoot control. Inside it (the same way you did in step 5 of the previous coding scenario), you will add the location of the CXML file. The CXML file is going to be hosted locally. Therefore, you will be using a localhost plus port address for the URI. You can find out the port number by either looking at the web project properties or by running the application and locating what the dynamic port number is. Listing 14-3 shows an example of my loaded event (remember your port number will be different).

Listing 14-3. Loaded event that hosts the custom Pivot Collection

```
...
public partial class MainPage : UserControl
{
    public MainPage()
    {
        // Required to initialize variables
        InitializeComponent();
    }

    private void LayoutRoot_Loaded(object sender, System.Windows.RoutedEventArgs e)
    {
        // TODO: Add event handler implementation here.
        this.PivotViewer.LoadCollection("http://localhost:1882/SilverlightHostingCus
```

```
                      tomPivotViewerSampleSite/SampleCollection.cxml", string.Empty);
        }
    }
    ...
```

12. After you have added the URI location of the SampleCollection.cxml, you can now build and run the project. If you have followed the steps correctly, you should see a PivotViewer with your loaded collection as shown in Figure 14-22 (if you used different images, yours will obviously be different).

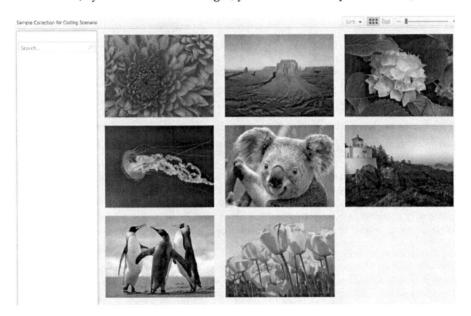

Figure 14-22. A custom Pivot Collection hosted inside a Silverlight PivotViewer control

13. Note that you can interact with the PivotViewer control normally. However, you have probably noticed that there are no Facet Categories and no facets. This is because you did not create any. The name and description are just properties of the items and not custom facets. In order to do so, you will need to add additional columns to the Collection Items worksheet.

14. Go back to the Microsoft Excel Pivot Collections tab in the worksheet. You will add two simple Pivot Collection columns that will be used to create facets. Right click on the Description column and select Insert Table column to the right. Add two columns. Name the first column "Year" and the second column "Magazine." Fill the first column with numerical dates like 1999 through 2002. In the Magazine column, add fake names of some magazines, but group them together. Figure 14-23 shows and example of the data I used for the two columns. The two names for the columns added will be the facet categories. A distinct list of the facet categories will be the facets that will be used for PivotViewer control.

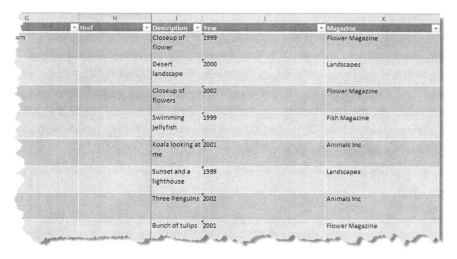

Figure 14-23. Collection Items with two new facet categories: Year and Magazine

15. Now that the collection has been updated, re-publish it to the same location by clicking the Publish Collection button and selecting the same location and file name as before (select yes to replace it). Once the collection is republished, go into Visual Studio or Expression Blend 4 and start the application. You will now notice the two additional facet categories (Year and Magazine) are added to the collection.

Year

Sort: Quantity

☐ 1999   3

☐ 2001   2

☐ 2002   2

☐ 2000   1

Figure 14-24. By default, the data types of the facets are string based.

16. It was that simple to add two new facets. However, you will notice that the Year facet category is treated like a string (shown in Figure 14-24) and you would really like it to have a numerical slider so you can select a range. As you learned in the previous sections, this requires the data type to be changed to a numerical or date data type. To accomplish this, go back to the collection Items worksheet. Select the Year column and change it to a number format with zero decimal spaces. Republish the collection and run the application. Notice that the Year facet category is surfaced with a numerical range slider (similar to Figure 14-13). The Pivot Collection tool automatically infers the data type and properly writes the proper XML. You can double check this by opening the CXML file in Notepad.

▓ **Tips** When creating larger (over 2,000 records) PivotViewer collections, start with a smaller subset (around 300). This will speed up the generation of the imagery and CXML dramatically, while you are creating the all the facet categories and formats. Another big performance boost is to remove the Preview column from the Collection Items worksheet. The preview column eats up a ton of memory in Excel. On my workstation, removing the Preview column saved me several hundred MB of RAM when working on a large PivotViewer collection. If you have a 64-bit operating system, I would also recommend installing the 64-bit version of Microsoft Office 2010. This will help you tremendously if you have to load a large collection into Microsoft Excel.

Lessons Learned

In this coding scenario, you learned how easy it is to create a custom pivot collection using the Pivot Collection Tool for Microsoft Excel. You created a very simple collection; however, you can apply these principles to create more advanced collections. I have used the Pivot Collection tool to create collections that have several thousand records. I accomplished this through automating the creation of the imagery and the facets. I let the Pivot Collection tool to handle the grunt work of creating all of the necessary CXML and proper image shapes for the PivotViewer.

This coding scenario should have also amplified the concept that the hardest part in creating a good PivotViewer module is the collections. As soon as the collection had the proper facets and format, the PivotViewer was able to render the imagery, filter, and info panels automatically.

Creating custom collections is a try-by-doing process. You are not going to get all the collection items, images, facets, or properties correct on the first try. This is why you should rely on this tool to help you get started with creating PivotViewer applications.

PivotViewer and Business Intelligence 2.0

I chose to end this book with the PivotViewer because it is a fantastic example of business intelligence 2.0 control. Over the past 13 chapters, you learned about business intelligence 2.0 tenets and you saw numerous examples of how to apply BI 2.0 in Silverlight. To reinforce these lessons, here's a list of the most important of the BI 2.0 paradigms and how the PivotViewer control applies them:

- *Simple to use & learn*: The PivotViewer is a control that a casual user should have no problem learning. All of the possible interactions are in front of the user (no hidden right-click menus) and there is no complex analysis involved.

- *Rapid Feedback*: All of the interactions and filters provide very rapid feedback to the user. There is no typical web flicker or an Ajax wait control. The PivotViewer is very responsive so the user can quickly see the impact of their interactions.

- *Data Visualizations*: The Pivot Viewer is a very visual control. Obviously the control makes heavy use of images, but this is not the only visual aspect of the tool. The graph view organizes the data in a columnar format that allows for qualitative comparison. Furthermore, the filter panel utilizes a word-sized graph view in order to help with qualitative analysis and filtering the appropriate ranges.

- *Next-Generation Interactivity*: The PivotViewer makes very good use of several interactivity controls. The search box allows the user to quickly narrow down the collection of items. Furthermore, the zoom slider and numerical facet sliders allow for fluid interactivity with the control. Lastly, the imagery canvas is fully interactive with panning and zooming gestures. On a multitouch tablet, the PivotViewer shines by allowing the user to interact with the data using primarily their fingers.

- *Beyond the CPU*: The PivotViewer control utilizes GPU acceleration for caching the images on the imagery canvas. In Chapter 10, you learned how to leverage the GPU and this control is a great example of that.

- *Not expensive to implement*: In the first chapter you learned that classic business intelligence (BI 1.0) had a major drawback because it required large systems to be in place for analytical tools to be effective. In contrast, this tool is a perfect example of a self-service tool that is easy to implement. With the ease of the Expression Blend 4 designer tools and the Pivot Collection tool for Microsoft Excel, you can have a simple but effective analytical tool up and running in no time. Notice that you did not need to invest in complex server hardware or enterprise business intelligence software (i.e., SharePoint or SQL Server 2008 R2).

- *Ease of integration & modularity*: Because the PivotViewer control is a Silverlight control, it can be easily embedded into an existing HTML page. More advanced integration options such as creating a PivotViewer web part are also possible with little or no work. As you learned in Chapter 11, business intelligence tools that can be used outside the scope of their application have a better chance of being adopted by casual users.

Summary

This chapter covered the key components, architecture and how to get started with the new Silverlight PivotViewer control. After reading this chapter, you should be familiar with the architecture of the PivotViewer control, PivotViewer collections. Furthermore, you should know how to consume an existing collection or create a new PivotViewer collection from scratch.

The PivotViewer control is a great example of how to apply business intelligence 2.0 concepts. It is a highly visual, simple to use, simple to learn (self-service), responsive, and interactive control that can provide a great deal of analytical value. While the PivotViewer will not replace traditional analytical tools, it can provide a great wow factor when demoing a business intelligence solution.

■ ■ ■

Prototyping Applications with Dynamic Data

In the Appendix, we will cover the dynamic data feature in Microsoft Expression Blend 4. Version 4 of Expression Blend includes many features for designers and developers that allow them to prototype business applications without the need to consume production data services. Throughout this book, I took advantage of this feature in the coding scenarios to simulate realistic-looking data. Instead of providing detailed instructions each time we use dynamic data in our coding scenarios, I thought it would be easier to provide an appendix that could be used as a resource.

The Appendix covers the fundamentals of using the dynamic data feature in Expression Blend. Furthermore, it provides all of the knowledge you need in order to understand how to create realistic-looking collections that are used in some of the coding scenarios.

Dynamic data is a feature that is part of the prototyping tools added into Microsoft Expression Blend 4. Both Visual Studio and Blend can be used to manipulate all the objects inside a Silverlight solution. Since version 1.0, Expression Blend has provided additional UI tools for designers that could manipulate the solution XAML and code-behind files. One of the biggest additions in version 3 was the addition of tools that could create realistic dynamic data integrated with a Silverlight or WPF project.

The dynamic data feature of Expression Blend 4 is a set of UI tools that generates the necessary classes and bindings that can be quickly generated in a development prototype environment.

■ **Note** Expression Blend versions 1 and 2 do not include the dynamic data feature. Only versions 3 and 4 of Expression Blend supports this feature.

Blend's Dynamic Data Tools

This section will cover the features of the dynamic data tools. If you create a new or open an existing new Expression Blend 4 project, next to the Properties and Resources tab you will find the Data tab. Figure A-1 shows the location of the Data tab in Expression Blend.

Figure A-1. *The Data tab in Expression Blend 4 allows you to manage and create data sources*

The Data tab provides the developer two key pieces of functionality. It allows the developer to create data sources from dynamic or live data sources. Furthermore, it allows the developer to explore and manage data sources defined in the application or in the selected document. On the right-hand side, you can see two database icons with plus signs. The one on the left is used to create a local sample data source. Figure A-2 shows the menu that appears when a user clicks the "Create sample data source" icon.

Figure A-2. *Menu options available when creating a sample data source*

In the context menu that appears, you have two options:

- *New Sample Data*: This feature allows you to define sample data manually.

- *Import Sample Data from XML*: This feature allows you to take a well-defined XML file and import the data as a local data source.

- *Create Sample Data from Class*: This feature allows you to take a sample class with defined properties and create a sample data set from it

Defining New Sample Data

To define new sample data, the designer needs to perform the following steps:

1. Navigate to the Data tab (shown in Figure A-1).

2. Click the "Create Sample Data" icon (which is a database icon shown on the left with a plus sign).

3. Click the *New Sample Data* menu item , which will bring up the New Sample Data dialog box. The dialog box is shown in Figure A-3.

Figure A-3. The New Sample Data dialog box allows the developer to set some data source properties.

The Define New Sample Data dialog box allows you to create three key properties:

- *Data source name:* This is the name of the data source.

- *Create data source in:* This property determines the scope of the sample data. The Project scope allows the data to be used in the entire application across all XAML pages. "This document" scopes the data source for the current XAML file selected.

- *Enable sample data when application is running:* This property determines if the data is instantiated automatically when the application is running. Most of the time, you want this property selected. Why is there an option to turn this off and on? This property should be turned off when an application goes into production because resources are consumed to instantiate sample data sources.

■ **Warning** Not checking "Enable sample data when application is running" is one of the biggest mistakes I have seen when trying to figure out why your application is not presenting data. When attempting any of the coding scenarios in this book, always ensure that you have this option checked.

---

4. After clicking OK, you will see that a dynamic data source has been created in the Data tab. In the Data tab in the data source management list, you will see the newly created sample data source. The sample data source includes a default collection and property, as shown in Figure A-4.

Figure A-4. A default sample data source is created with a collection with a single property.

Customizing Sample Data Sources

A sample data source can be thought of as a minidatabase in which a developer can define multiple collections, custom properties, property data types, data type lengths, and the format of the data. This section will cover the options related to modifying sample data sources.

When you have created a sample data source, several management options are available to you. By default, a Collection property is created that holds a simple string property. One of the first things you will want to do is rename or remove these objects. You can double-click any of the property names, and this will make the text of the property editable. Figure A-5 shows the Collection property in edit mode. When a property is in edit mode, the name can be changed.

Figure A-5. Collection property in edit mode

■ **Warning** When naming your properties, try to stay away from certain keywords. For example, naming a property "Name" will cause problems for you when the property is used in a binding in the application.

The sample data source provides several management options to configure a data source. These options can be displayed as drop-down menu items from the right-hand side. Figure A-6 highlights the available data source management options.

Figure A-6. Data source management options

At the highest level is the data source object. Clicking the database icon with the wrench displays the menu shown in Figure A-7. The sample data source management options available to you are as follows:

- *Reimport Sample Data from XML*: This option allows you to refresh your data from an XML file.

- *Enable When Running Application*: This option is equivalent to the "Enable sample data when application is running" option that selected when you created the data source. This option allows you to manage whether the data source is enabled when the application is running.

- *Remove "[sample data source name]"*: This option removes the sample data source from the project.

Figure A-7. Sample data source management options

The second level in the data source hierarchy is the data source class. In this section, you manage the collections and properties that belong to a data source. Clicking the plus icon (Add Simple Property) brings up the menu shown in Figure A-8.

Figure A-8. The Add Simple Property menu allows you to add data objects to the data source.

The Add Simple Property menu options are as follows:

- *Add Simple Property.* This option adds a property of a basic type (e.g., string or number). There are four simple properties available to you: String, Number, Boolean, and Image.

- *Add Complex Property.* This option adds a complex type (custom class) to the data source.

- *Add Collection Property.* This option adds a collection of items to the data source.

- *Convert to Hierarchical Collection.* This option converts a collection of collections etc. Collections of items will be nested within other collections. If you drag a hierarchical collection onto the canvas it will create a nested tree view control.

In order to remove a property from a data source or collection, simply right-click the property and select the Remove "[name of property]" ("Collection") menu item, as shown in Figure A-9.

Figure A-9. Right-clicking a property allows you to remove it from a data source.

Customizing Properties

Properties have their own individual settings that can be set by the designer to change the shape and format of the data. Clicking the "Change property type" icon (shown as an ABC graphic) allows you to customize property options in the menu window shown in Figure A-10.

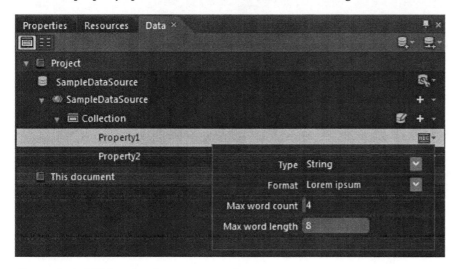

Figure A-10. *Editing simple property settings*

This window allows you to change the following common settings:

- *Type*: This option allows you to change the data type. Four default data types are provided for simple properties: String, Number, Boolean, and Image.

- *Format*: This is the format of the data. It determines what data Blend uses to provide realistic data. For example, you can format your strings to look like names of people or addresses. This gives the data a more realistic look. There are different formats provided depending on the type of the property.

Individual properties may have additional settings. For example, in Figure A-10, notice how the dynamic String format allows you set the "Max word count" and "Max word length" settings. This gives you the ability to create flexible data sets that are pretty realistic and resemble real data.

Customizing Collections

Collection properties are needed if you want to work with data sources that have more than one value. Collections consist of multiple simple or custom properties. Furthermore, collections can also include nested collections and simple data hierarchies.

After adding several simple properties to a collection, you probably want to view what you have created or even edit the individual values. The "Edit sample values" icon (database icon with a pencil), shown in Figure A-11, allows you to view and edit the collection data you have created.

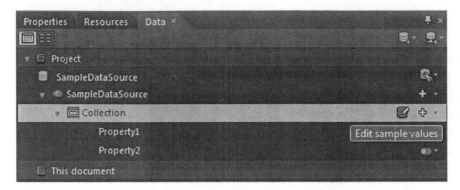

Figure A-11. Clicking the "Edit sample values" icon on a collection will bring up the Edit Sample Values dialog box.

Editing collection values is done in the Edit Sample Values dialog box, as shown in Figure A-12. The following changes can be made to a collection in this dialog box:

- Clicking the property header icons allows you to change the property type settings.

- The values can be directly edited inside the grid and you can override the default generated formatted values.

- The "Number of records" input slider allows you to change the amount of records inside the collection. The default maximum is set to 100.

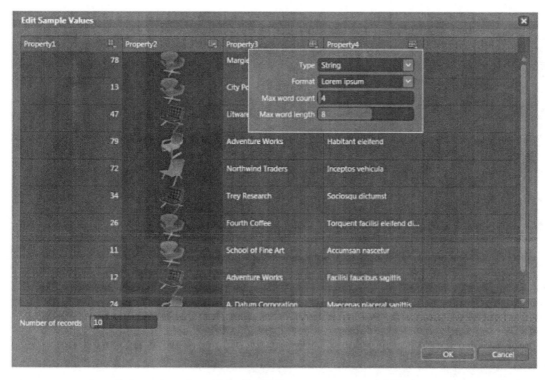

Figure A-12. *The Edit Sample Values dialog box allows you to view and customize collection properties in a data grid format.*

Generating data from image collections

As you can see from Figure A-12, sample properties can be set to generate sample data. What if you wanted to use your own images in an image column instead of using the generic chair images that you get with Expression Blend 4. Expression Blend allows you to modify the source of the collection of images used. Figure A-13 shows you that when you specify an image property you can provide a path to the location of the images.

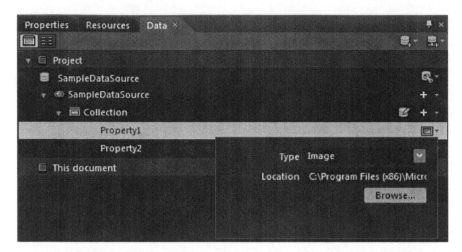

Figure A-13. The image property allows you to set your own location of images.

This is a really nice feature if you want to provide images for business intelligence scenarios like KPIs, trending indicators, sample chart images etc. I pointed my location to the Visual Studio 2010 graphics library and you can see the results below in Figure A-14. Note that Expression Blend 4 will automatically copy the images and add them to your Silverlight project.

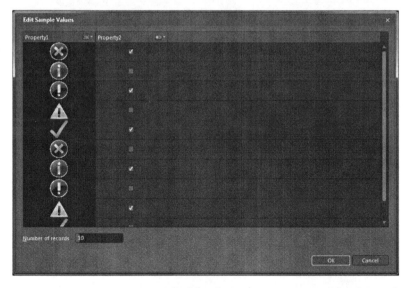

Figure A-14. Custom images used for the image property in Blend sample data

Behind the Scenes of Dynamic Data

Expression Blend provides a set of tools to create dynamic data. However, there are some important things that happen to the project that a designer needs to understand.

Autogenerated Files

Adding a sample data source modifies the Silverlight project in your solution. Figure A-13 shows you the folders added to the Silverlight project. These files are dynamically generated and maintained by Expression Blend. You can manually edit these files and provide your own enhancements. For example, by editing the files manually, you can get around the 100 record limit Expression Blend imposes. Be careful editing these files manually, as your changes will be lost if you use Blend to manipulate the sample data source.

Figure A-15. _Silverlight Application project that shows the generated resources after adding a sample data source_

The following items are added to a Silverlight project when you add a sample data resource:

- The SampleData folder is added to the root of the Silverlight project.

- A folder with the name of your data source is added in the SampleData folder. For example, if your data source is called SampleDataSource, then a folder called SampleDataSource is created in the SampleData folder.

- If resource properties are created, then an additional folder named [data source name]_Files will be added to the resource folder. For example, Figure A-13 shows a property that has an image resource as the source.

- There are three files generated with the name of the sample data source. A XAML file is created that contains the generated data. A corresponding code-behind file is generated that contains all of the types of the collections and properties. The code-behind file includes additional code for two-way binding and property notifications. Figure A-14 shows the data XAML file and the corresponding code-behind file.

■ **Note** Removing a data source in Expression Blend will delete all of the autogenerated files from the Silverlight project. You could configure a custom build that will include this data for debugging or QA testing. A production or release build would have this data removed to keep the Silverlight application (XAP file) smaller.

```
<SampleData:SampleDataSource34 xmlns:SampleData="clr-namespace:Expression.Blend.Sampl
  <SampleData:SampleDataSource34.Collection>
    <SampleData:Item Property1="Sociosqu suscipit interdum" />
    <SampleData:Item Property1="Placerat pulvinar" />
    <SampleData:Item Property1="A
    <SampleData:Item Property1="P
    <SampleData:Item Property1="S
    <SampleData:Item Property1="E
    <SampleData:Item Property1="T
    <SampleData:Item Property1="V
    <SampleData:Item Property1="S
    <SampleData:Item Property1="M
  </SampleData:SampleDataSource34
</SampleData:SampleDataSource34>
```

```
namespace Expression.Blend.SampleData.SampleDataSource34
{
    using System;

    public class SampleDataSource34 : System.ComponentModel.INotifyPropertyChanged
    {
        public event System.ComponentModel.PropertyChangedEventHandler PropertyChanged;
        protected virtual void OnPropertyChanged(string propertyName)
        {
            if (this.PropertyChanged != null)
            {
                this.PropertyChanged(this, new System.ComponentModel.PropertyChangedEventArgs(propertyName));
            }
        }

        public SampleDataSource34()
        {
            try
            {
                System.Uri resourceUri = new System.Uri("/SilverlightApplication1;component/SampleData/SampleDataSo
                if (System.Windows.Application.GetResourceStream(resourceUri) != null)
                {
                    System.Windows.Application.LoadComponent(this, resourceUri);
                }
            }
            catch (System.Exception )
            { }
        }

        private ItemCollection _Collection = new ItemCollection();
        public ItemCollection Collection
        {
            get
            {
                return this._Collection;
            }
        }
    }

    public class Item : System.ComponentModel.INotifyPropertyChanged
    {
        public event System.ComponentModel.PropertyChangedEventHandler PropertyChanged;
```

Figure A-16. Generated XAML and corresponding code-behind file

Using the Dynamic Data

Dynamic data can be used in several ways.. Expression Blend 4 allows designers to set up bindings without having to write any code or understand anything about data binding methodologies. For example, a designer can take a collection and drag and drop it onto the design canvas. Expression Blend will automatically create a list and a template binding all of the defined properties that can be styled. In another example, a designer can create a skeleton UI containing combo boxes, text boxes, lists, and so on, and then simply drag over collections or properties, and it will automatically bind the sample data to the controls. Figure A-15 shows a simple UI created by simply dragging and dropping collections onto UI controls. No programming was required. This amplifies how dynamic data empowers designers to design software with realistic data without having to know anything about data programming.

Developers can benefit from the dynamic data feature as well. A developer can programmatically present the data source collection's properties. This allows developers to alter the structure of the data using LINQ.

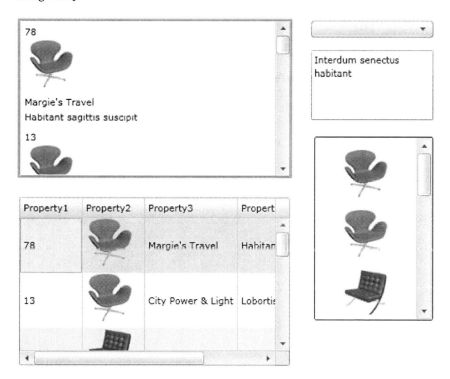

Figure A-17. *Various UI controls bound to sample source data using only drag-and-drop gestures in Expression Blend 4*

A developer can work with a sample data source by accessing any of the public objects available in the dynamic data source code-behind file. A developer can simply investigate the generated class objects to see how to interface with them. If you have a generated sample data source, you have to do two things to access the object programmatically:

- Add the appropriate using statement to the class (e.g., `Expression.Blend.SampleData.SampleDataSource`).

- Instantiate the data source. The name of the object will be the name of the data source. For example, a data source named SampleDataSource will need to be instantiated with this code: `SampleDataSource SampleData = new SampleDataSource();`.

The collections and properties will appear in IntelliSense, and the objects can be edited or manipulated just like normal objects in .NET.

Summary

This Appendix covered using the dynamic data feature of Microsoft Expression Blend 4. The dynamic data feature allows you to quickly prototype applications that interact with data. The UIs created using sample data sources generate data binding statements that are created using best practices. This allows you to create a shell of an application that can be swapped out with live data services without having to redo any of the UI.

If you have prototyped data-centric applications before, you will love this feature in Expression Blend 4. There aren't very many settings, and you can learn all of the options in less than a couple of hours. I highly encourage developers and designers to leverage this functionality in their software development life cycles.

APPENDIX B

■ ■ ■

Creating a Bullet Graph User Control

In the Appendix, you will be shown how to create a custom bullet graph user control from scratch using Expression Blend 4 and Silverlight.

First, I'll introduce the bullet graph data visualization as an alternative presentation of KPI (Key Performance Indicator) data. I will cover the bullet graph control components as well as how it compares to traditional gauge data visualizations.

The second part of this chapter is devoted to creating a specification for the bullet graph control. This specification will include what functionality, properties, and design approaches will be used. Detailed concepts like fluid layouts and dependency properties will be introduced in the implementation part of the chapter.

The remaining part of this Appendix is dedicated to showing how a custom control can be easily built by leveraging the user control mash up capabilities; you will use primitive and simple Silverlight controls as building blocks of this control. Furthermore, you will use features like scaling transformations and bindings to build a bullet graph control. Lastly, you'll see some simple uses of the bullet graph control in real-world business intelligence scenarios to prove out the bullet graph implementation.

The primary goal of this Appendix is to demonstrate to you how Silverlight 4 and Expression Blend 4 tools can come together to help build custom business intelligence controls. Table 7-1 outlines the specific goals that different types of readers will achieve by reading this chapter.

Table 7-1. Audience Types and the Different Goals of Each

Audience	Goals
Silverlight developers	Apply user control design paradigms in order to create a custom business intelligence user control utilizing a fluid layout, dependency properties, and best practice design patterns.
	Understand the fundamentals, components, and how to use a bullet graph.
Business intelligence professionals	Understand that Silverlight 4 can be used to implement custom business intelligence user controls that compliment enterprise business intelligence tools.
	See how a bullet graph compares to a traditional dashboard gauge.

Audience	Goals
Strategic decision makers	Discover how easy it is to create Silverlight user controls that can enhance your strategic business intelligence vision.
	Find out how a bullet graph can provide more insight faster than traditional indicator gauges or meters.

What is a Bullet Graph?

The bullet graph is a data visualization control that was created by Stephen Few in 2005. Stephen Few developed the control as a next-generation replacement for the gauge and meter controls commonplace in business intelligence dashboards. The primary goal of the bullet graph control is to provide a concise view in a simple visual control of the data ranges and comparison metrics without all the glitz. Figure B-1 shows a sample bullet graph implementation.

Figure B-1. *A bullet graph that surfaces profitability margin information using ranges to signify progress versus the organizational goals.*

If you are not familiar with a bullet graph, you might be wondering what the colors, ranges, shapes, and lines are trying to symbolize. Figure B-2 provides a breakdown of the main components of a bullet graph data visualization.

Figure B-2. *The bullet graph is a data visualization consisting of several simple components such as text labels, data bars, and rectangular symbols.*

■ **Note** As mentioned, the bullet graph control was developed by Stephen Few. I do want to stress that this is not my own creation. Throughout this chapter, you will be creating a custom implementation of the bullet graph control. Stephen has posted a public specification of the bullet graph control that can be used for various business intelligence implementations. The language that I will use for the components of the bullet graph control comes from this specification, located on his site at http://perceptualedge.com/articles/misc/Bullet_Graph_Design_Spec.pdf.

In Figure B-2 you can see that the bullet graph has the following components:

- *Text Label*: the label describes what KPI data (measure) is being presented in the bullet graph. Units of measure can be presented as well in the label.

- *Quantitative Scale*: This is a linear scale along an either X or Y axis that includes tick marks at equal intervals. Tick marks and their corresponding labels allow you to determine or estimate the value of the featured measure, comparative measure, and qualitative ranges.

- *Featured Measure*: This is a rectangular data bar (progress data bar) that visually depicts the value of the measure being shown. This bar usually begins at either end of the scale and extends to the position of the value it is showing.

- *Comparative Measure*: This is an optional measure visualized with a black rectangular indicator that shows the desired goal. It's optional because in some cases the background good scale range suffices.

- *Qualitative Ranges*: There are between two to five background optional ranges (scales) using different color shades. In conjunction with the quantitative scale, range colors show the start and end of a particular range. Typically there are three ranges in a bullet graph to signify a bad range, satisfactory range, and good range (as shown in top of Figure B-2 and noted by the bad, satisfactory, and good colors). However, as you will see in the section below, you can have a single range and still have an effective bullet graph control (even though the specification says that you should have at least two). Darker colors symbolize ranges that symbolize poor performance (bad range) while lighter colors symbolize more favorable ranges (good or excellent range).

■ **Note** Do not get the two concepts of "quantitative" and "qualitative" confused. When reading and trying to comprehend the information, sometimes the letters tend to blur. These terms have different meanings when talking about data. Quantitative information deals with explicitly assigned values or numbers. For example, the quantitative scale explicitly assigns the numbers to the tick marks. Conversely, qualitative information is data that is observed, such as a color or size of a range. Therefore, the scale ranges are qualitative since their attributes (color, size, contrast, position) are all observed. Qualitative and quantitative data work together to paint the full picture for analysis.

The bullet graph specification includes additional guidelines on the colors, positions, shade intensity, borders, tick marks, and measure markers that should be implemented. Please visit the design guide internet page for the detailed information. Even though the details are not listed, the general spirit of the specific guidelines is to make the bullet graph as easy and legible as possible by using basic colors and avoiding glitzy effects.

Using the Bullet Graph to Gain Business Intelligence Insight

If you have never used or implemented a bullet graph visualization, you may not be familiar with some of the ways it can be used to deliver insight. This section covers some basic ways a bullet graph can be configured and rendered. I will cover the important components of each sample, so you can feel familiar with the visualization. If you are familiar with bullet graphs, feel free to skip this section.

The first example shows realistic data surfaced via a bullet graph control.

Figure B-3. In this bullet graph, all of the components end on labled tick marks on the quantitative scale.

Figure B-3 shows a bullet graph that depicts an arbitrary net margin percentage metric. The net margin bullet graph has the following component characteristics:

- *Text Label*: The label clearly states "Net Margin" as the measure name. The units of measure percent represented by the % symbol. This label is clear and easily legible.

- *Quantitative Scale*: This is a linear scale on X axis that begins with 0% and ends with 60%. This scale could have started at a negative value such as -30%. In fact, the quantitative scale could start and end with any value but the interval tick marks need to be spaced out so that the scale values can easily be discerned.

- *Featured Measure*: You can see a black data bar that starts at 0% (beginning of the quantitative scale) and ends at 48%. The location where the featured measure ends is the value of the featured measure. Therefore, the net margin percentage value is 48%.

- *Comparative Measure*: Note the small black rectangular marker at the 36% location of the quantitative scale. This can be interpreted as the organizational goal was to have a net margin achieve or exceed 36%.

- *Qualitative Ranges*: In this bullet graph you can clearly see that there are three distinct ranges in the background. The darkest range begins at 0% and end at 12%. The medium hue range starts at 12% and ends at 24%. The lightest range begins at 24% and finishes at the end of the quantitative scale at 60%. The darkest range is the Bad performance range; the medium dark range is the Satisfactory performance range, and the lightest range is the Good performance range.

The bullet graph in Figure B-3 would be analyzed by a user visually as offering the following insight: The net margin percentage measure has a scale from 0 to 60 percent. The organization is currently tracking at a 48% net margin. Based on that value, the measure falls into the Good range (lightest color hue range). The organization is 24% over the minimum of the Good range and they have attained their goal of a 36% net margin percentage (comparative measure).

As highlighted in Stephen Few's specification, the comparative measure is optional. Therefore, you could start your Good performance range as the comparative measure location. The beginning of the Good range would indicate the organizational goal. This would eliminate the need for the comparative measure marker, because as soon as the featured measure crosses the Good performance range, the organization has attained the goal. Figure B-4 illustrates the same data as Figure B-3. However, note that the comparative measure marker is no longer visible and that the Good performance range starts at 24%. The insight delivered between Figure B-3 and Figure B-4 is identical. The user can clearly still see the value of the featured measure and that the organizational goal has been achieved.

Figure B-4. The bullet graph can be rendered without the comparative measure. When rendering a bullet graph without a comparative measure, the beginning of the qualitative Good range acts as the organizational goal. In this example, it would be a net margin value of 24%.

Bullet graphs can vary in the number of tick marks rendered. Figure B-5 illustrates the same bullet graph with additional tick marks. The greater amount of tick marks allows for a more granular analysis of the ranges and measures. The bullet graph specification does not mention the amount of tick marks that should be rendered. This depends on the range and density of the data that you are surfacing. A good implementation of a bullet graph control will allow this to be configurable.

Figure B-5. The bullet graph can be rendered with a dynamic number of tick marks in the qualitative scale. The values of the labels should be rounded and spaced evenly for legible analysis.

Figure B-6 illustrates another bullet graph with slightly different characteristics. This bullet graph aims to deliver insight to a doctor on how many patients she has each day. The "Number of Patients" bullet graph has the following component characteristics:

- *Text Label*: The label clearly states "Number of Patients" as the measure name. Below the label is the units of measure percent represented by the word count and a date of 6/20/2010. This label is clear and easily legible.

- *Quantitative Scale*: This is a linear scale on X axis that begins with 0 and ends with 200.

- *Featured Measure*: The black data bar starts at 0 (beginning of the quantitative scale) and ends at 125. The location where the featured measure ends is the value of the measure. Therefore, the number of daily patients is 125.

- *Comparative Measure*: You can see a small black rectangular marker at the 100 location of the quantitative scale. This can be read as the organizational goal is to have at least 100 patients per day.

- *Qualitative Ranges*: In Figure B-6, there are no ranges shown. Sometimes a bullet graph doesn't need ranges because they serve no analytical purpose and don't bring any additional insight. In such cases, there is no need to render any background range. The user of this bullet graph simply concerns themselves with the value of the featured measure and how it compares to the organizational goal symbolized by the black comparative measure marker.

Figure B-6. *The bullet graph can be rendered without any qualitative ranges if they do not provide analytical value. In this example,the user is explicitly looking to see if she made the organizational goal or not.*

The bullet graph in Figure B-6 would be analyzed by a user visually and she would gain the following insight: The scale shows that she typically see between 0 and 200 patients per day. On 6/20/2010 this doctor's office saw 125 patients, which is 25 more patients than her daily goal of 100.

The reasons for using this type of bullet graph may vary. Inthis case, say the doctor's office gets a flat fee from each patient's insurance company. 100 patients might be their break-even point for profitability.

Later in this chapter you will see how this type of rendering of the bullet graph can be used for word-sized data visualizations (sparklines).

Comparing the Bullet Graph to Traditional Gauges

Bullet graphs were developed to improve the analytical capabilities of gauges. Therefore, it is valid to compare bullet graphs to a typical dashboard gauge. This should help you to see how bullet graphs have some intrinsic advantages over traditional gauges.

Figure B-7 illustrates a bullet graph and traditional dashboard gauge. The gauge in Figure B-7 is from SQL Server 2008 R2 Reporting Services and it includes the identical components found in the bullet graph. The components for both visualizations have the same values, so the comparison between the two will be trivial.

Figure B-7. *A SQL Server 2008 R2 gauge compared to a bullet graph rendered with the same measure and range values.*

Looking at Figure B-7, you might be thinking to yourself that there is not much of a difference between the two visualizations. The dashboard gauge looks nicer and has a factor of glitz. Conversely, the bullet graph looks like a simpler visualization that may have come out of Microsoft Excel. You may also find the bullet graph slightly easier to read, because the axes are linear and not circular. However, the design of the bullet graph has some additional benefits over a traditional dashboard gauge:

- *Smaller form factor*: the form factor of the bullet graph is much smaller than the gauge. Surfacing one or two gauges usually is not a problem. However, when you want to visualize several metrics on a single dashboard a smaller form factor has distinct advantages.

- *Qualitative ranges do not rely on colors*: As you have learned in the previous sections about the bullet graph, you know that the bullet graph relies on different shades of a single color to define the good, satisfactory, and bad ranges. This has multiple advantages. First, color blind users are not affected by different colors. If you are a color blind, you can still make out the strength/hue of a color. This allows a color blind person to determine which range the featured or comparative measures fall in. Since bullet graphs do not rely on a rich color palette, these controls can be printed using black and white printers and still deliver analytical insight effectively.

- *Rendering Performance:* The bullet graph control is a much simpler control than a traditional dashboard gauge. There are far less components. Furthermore, rendering components such as shadows, 3D effects, and borders does not take place. The simplicity of the bullet graph control has a dramatic impact on rendering performance when compared to a traditional dashboard gauge.

- *Word-Sized Rendering:* In the data visualization chapters, you learned about the analytical significance of word-sized charts (sparklines). This type of analytical insight can be presented in a bullet graph. By turning off the scale and quantitative ranges you can shrink down the size of a bullet graph and still deliver business intelligence insight in a word-sized visualization.

- *More substance and less filler:* If you look at Figure B-7 in detail, you can appreciate how much simpler the bullet graph control is over its gauge counterpart. This makes the implementation much easier on the eyes. Furthermore, this allows the user to focus on the gaining insight since every component symbolizes an important range, measure, or value.

If you are an experienced business intelligence professional, you may challenge the assertion that gauges or meters are too rich or too noisy when compared to a bullet graph. While it is true that you can turn off a lot of the extra features and make gauges or meters render simply. they just don't look as natural as a bullet graph. Figure B-8 shows a stripped down version of a gauge and a meter without extra features. As you can see, the control looks like it's missing something. That's because it wasn't designed to look this way. If you look on any component vendor's site, they show demos of pretty and appealing data visualizations to catch the eye. This is the main reason why stripping out optional components on a gauge or meter makes the controls inelegant.

Figure B-8. Stripped down versions of the SQL Server 2008 R2 Reporting Services gauge and meter controls

SQL Server 2008 R2 Reporting Services includes an implementation of a bullet graph. However, the default style of the bullet graph includes unnecessary borders, shadows, and gradients that take away from the main point of the bullet graph, which is to deliver analytical insight in a simple control. All the extra items do look nice and demo well, but they do not improve the analytical behavior of the control. Figure B-9 below shows the default look of a SQL Server 2008 R2 Reporting Services bullet graph.

Figure B-9. *The default implementation of a SQL Server 2008 R2 bullet graph includes uncessary components that do not add analytical value. These options can be turned off.*

Specification of the Silverlight Bullet Graph

This section is dedicated to building your Silverlight implementation of Stephen Few's bullet graph design specification in Silverlight 4 using Microsoft Expression Blend 4.

The goal of the specification is to give you a clear picture of how you will be implementing the control, before you even start coding the control. I want to make sure the ideas are presented clearly beforehand and not intertwined with code. The specification in this section will outline what you will implement from the design specification, what controls will be used to create the rendering, and how the controls will be presented on the control surface. If you are a developer or an architect, this is not a formal development specification.

▨ **Warning** If you have not done so, familiarize yourself with the bullet graph specification online. The bullet graph design specification can be located on Stephen Few's site at http://perceptualedge.com/articles/misc/ Bullet_Graph_Design_Spec.pdf.

Implementation Roadmap

This chapter will not have a full production-ready implementation of the bullet graph control. Anytime you are designing a control from scratch, there will be a lot of features that need to be added in order to compete with enterprise based controls. While this control is usable, it will not serve as a full replacement without adding key features.

Looking at Figure B-10, the complexity of the property dialogs that exist for a SQL Server 2008 R2 Reporting Services gauge is depicted. The amount of configuration options is simply staggering, but necessary for an enterprise level control like this. There are well over several hundred individual properties that can be configured and bound to different data values or calculations. While it is possible to implement a full bullet graph with all the features seen in Figure B-10 (and more), that is not the purpose of this chapter. Covering all of the configuration options and replicating them all in a bullet graph would easily span over several chapters. Therefore, I selected the key features from Stephen Few's bullet graph design specification to make a working bullet graph control implementation. If you are

495

interested in building a control that includes all of these properties for a production-ready control, the implementation in this chapter will have to be extended quite heavily.

Figure B-10. SQL Server 2008 R2 Reporting Services includes a robust configuration model for controlling how a gauge is rendered. Two dialogs are shown that control the pointer and scale properties. There are over six property dialogs for an SSRS gauge that contain many individual properties.

Below is a list of features that you will implement in the bullet graph:

- *Dynamic & fluid form factor*: The form factor of the bullet graph will be able to scale to different width and height. It will be able to scale to explicit dimensions and be contained in layout controls such as a StackPanel. The fluid layout will allow the control to be stacked or used in a word-sized rendering format.

- *Text & unit labels*: The text and unit labels of the control will be set through control element binding. This will allow these properties to take full advantage of Expression Blend 4 and Silverlight 4 tooling for binding. The text and unit labels will be separate controls to allow for independent configuration.

- *Qualitative ranges*: Three qualitative scales will be implemented in this control. The bullet graph specification mentions the ability to render between two to five scales. Most business intelligence gauges or meters only render two (good and bad) or three (good, satisfactory, bad) ranges. All three ranges can be turned off and on. This will allow for various configurations, including the ability to use the bullet graph as a word-sized (sparkline) visualization. The quantitative scales will have their values exposed as dependency properties, so that Expression Blend 4 binding tooling can facilitate the configuration of the control.

- *Quantitative scale*: The bullet graph will include a linear scale on the bottom control. The scale will expose a minimum and maximum for the range. The scale will be dynamically rendered and adjust itself properly as the bullet graph control changes dimensions. There will be a default of five tick marks rendered that will provide a mechanism for the user to locate the values of the quantitative scales, featured and comparative measures. The scale will also expose a "visible" or "show" property that will hide the scale from the user.

- *Featured measure*: A black progress bar will be used to render the featured measure component of the bullet graph. The featured measure will expose a dependency property for its value to determine the rendering position on the bullet graph control.

- *Comparative measure*: A rectangular shape will be used to render the comparative measure artifact of the bullet graph control. The comparative measure component will expose a dependency property to allow a value to be bound to the component.

Below is a list of features that you will *not* be implementing:

- *Vertical rendering*: Horizontal rendering is the only one being implemented in this chapter. In the specification, you will note that the bullet graph can also be rendered vertically.

- *Right to left rendering*: The bullet graph specification specifies right to left rendering for measures that have "good ranges or good values" that are better when they are lower.

- *Formatting of tick mark labels*: The tick mark labels will not be formatted for currency or percentages. The control can be extended with this functionality if it is necessary.

Looking at the bullet graph specification, you can see that you are implementing a lot of features of the bullet graph. While the control is not being fully realized to spec, the components that you will add in the upcoming sections will allow for a practical bullet graph control. This bullet graph implementation could be used in a business intelligence scenarios to replace a gauge or meter visualization.

Mashing Up the Control with Silverlight Controls

The implementation of the bullet graph control will be a mash up control that will leverage existing primitive and complex controls to render this control exactly how you want it to look. Essentially, you create a custom user control and use existing Silverlight controls as components of the bullet graph.

You need to make a decision on how you want to mash up this bullet control from existing Silverlight components. This is where you may have ideas that are different or better than the ones outlined in this book. I am by no means advocating that these components are the best ones to use, or that this will be the fastest or least resource intensive implementation. Very similar Silverlight components have pros and cons. Lighter weight controls tend to have less functionality, but render faster and requires less resources. However, lightweight controls usually have less features. For example, compare a label versus a textblock control, both of are used to display text. Without diving into too much detail, you could argue that they could be used interchangeably. However, once you delve deeper into the control hierarchy and how the controls are created you will notice that the label control contains more features, allows more flexibility for templating, can present content rather than just strings (like a Button control), etc. Figure B-11 illustrates the template for a Silverlight Label. The same template does not exist for a TextBlock control.

Figure B-11. *The Silverlight label control has additional children controls that provide configuration and rendering options at the expense of being more complex than a TextBlock control. Pictured is a hierarchy tree of a template that includes a Grid, Border, and ContentControl.*

For simplicity, select Silverlight controls that have obvious responsibilities to act as simple components in the bullet graph control implementation. Figure B-12 pictures a bullet graph control and highlights the candidates for components. You can tell that Figure B-12 is a mash up Silverlight user control:

- *TextBlock:* This will be used to surface the labels for the bullet graph and the tick marks for the quantitative scale.

- *ProgressBar:* This will be used to render the qualitative ranges as well as the featured measure data bar.

- *Rectangle:* This will be used to render the small comparative measure symbol.

Figure B-12. *The bullet graph control will use three Silverlight controls that already exist in the framework.*

Is that really it? You are going to create a bullet graph with only three Silverlight controls? The simplicity of the bullet graph control truly streamlines the rendering process and components of the control. If you look at Figures B-7 or B-9 that show the SQL Server 2008 R2 Reporting Services gauges, you can clearly tell that implementing those controls would not be as simple. This is one of the reasons why the bullet graph control has gained so much popularity recently in business intelligence dashboards. In the upcoming sections, you will see in detail how these controls are going to be transformed, laid out, styled, and calculated to create the bullet graph control.

Creating a Fluid Layout

From the examples, the design specification, and from other dashboard implementations, you have to create a control that is very flexible and can be rendered in various ways. The control has to not only render well but also deliver proper business intelligence insight This can become challenging when you do not know how a developer will use your control. The control can have explicit widths, can be really wide or tall, it can have dynamic dimensions etc. The best approach for any custom control is to create a fluid layout that will satisfy most implementations.

The best way to explain this is through example. Focus on Figure B-13 and notice how the button control is rendered with several different dimensions but still maintains a valid consistency. The content label "Button" is always in the center of the button control. The control can be explicitly rendered with width and height dimensions. Automatic layouts are also shown that dynamically calculate the position of its children. For example, in Figure B-13, the buttons in the StackPanel are not given explicit dimensions and are calculated dynamically.

▒ **Caution** The button control trivializes some of the concepts that go into creating a fluid and dynamic control layout. However, these concepts are very similar to creating fluid layouts in HTML web programming for different screen resolutions.

Figure B-13. The Silverlight bullet graph implementation should be able to render in simple and complex layouts.

To create a fluid layout, several key features in the Silverlight framework will be used. The first key feature that will be used are Silverlight layout controls: the Canvas, StackPanel, and Grid. These layout controls will allow the control to shape the location of the bullet graph components. The second feature is Silverlight render transformations. These transformations will allow us to dynamically space out, scale, and translate the children components in complex layouts without having to rely on setting explicit dimensions.

▪ **Warning** When I mention that you will create a completely fluid control, please take that with a grain of salt. Obviously not everything can be made dynamic. In some cases, it doesn't even make sense. For example, look at Figure B-13. Notice that even though there are buttons of various sizes, the font size is exactly the same in all of them. If someone sets an explicit font size for a label, why would you dynamically scale that? Other components of the control like margins, borders, corners, or stroke thickness do not usually scale. Please keep that in mind as you do deeper into your implementation of the bullet graph.

Leveraging the Silverlight Layout Controls

The first step in implementing a fluid layout is selecting the suitable layout control design. Just like in the previous section when you picked the Silverlight controls to make up the bullet graph controls, now you have to select the appropriate layout controls.

Figure B-14 illustrates a breakdown of how you want to layout or internal components. As you can see, the bullet graph control is broken into four separate quadrants. Each quadrant will be responsible for hosting various children controls that will be the internal components of the main bullet graph control.

Figure B-14. Breaking the control into quadrants helps with the design layout and selecting the correct layout controls.

The control in Figure B-14 looks pretty good for an initial guess. However, as you can see, the tick mark labels on the bottom of the quantitative scale would be cut off if you only had four quadrants. One option would be to create a margin between the right border. Other options are to create a whitespace quadrant that will not host any controls but act as a buffer or to use right alignment for all tick marks. This will make the dynamic math calculations much easier. After adding the whitespace buffer, you will have six quadrants that look like Figure B-15.

Figure B-15. The bullet graph layout now has four quadrants that host the children components and two whitespace buffers.

Separating the bullet graph layout implementation into four quadrants, we can see which controls belong into which section:

- *Quadrant 1*: The first quadrant hosts three qualitative range progress bars, the featured measure progress bar, and the comparative measure rectangle.

- *Quadrant 2*: The second quadrant hosts the bullet graph label, which will be surfaced using a TextBlock control.

- *Quadrant 3*: The third quadrant hosts the units label, which will be surfaced using a TextBlock control

- *Quadrant 4*: The fourth quadrant hosts the quantitative scale. An important note is that both Quadrant 1 and Quadrant 4 have to be aligned so that the quantitative scale tick marks match the location of the progress bars in Quadrant 1.

■ **Note** Quadrant 3 could have been left empty—you could have put both the text and unit labels in Quadrant 2. This part of the design is less important; you can improvise in this part if you like.

How do you translate the quadrants into a fluid layout? As mentioned, in Silverlight you have three main options to host children controls: Canvas, Grid, and the StackPanel. If the task was to create a simple control that always had a width of 400 and height of 150, this selection would not matter. However, since your goal is to create a dynamic layout based on various control dimensions, you have to select the outer control that makes the most sense. In this case, the best control for the layout is a Grid layout control.

The Silverlight Grid container will create a layout that is essentially composed ratios using column and row definitions. In this implementation, the main layout of the bullet graph will be a Grid composed of three columns and two rows. This will render a quadrant. Now that there are four quadrants with controls, the next step is to select the ratios the quadrants will maintain as the control is scaled to different sizes. As you can tell from Figure B-14, the quantitative ranges and scale will be the most prominent horizontal components. The label and the quantitative ranges (top two quadrants) are the most prominent vertical components. Therefore, Quadrant 1 and Quadrant 2 will take up the most area in the bullet graph control.

Stephen Few's design specification is not explicit in the dimensions or the ratios that need to be used when laying out the internal components. If you do want to be specific, you could measure the graphics in the spec and use that in the implementation. I chose to guesstimate the layout. Figure B-16 shows a Grid layout control with six sections defined, four of which host the bullet graph components.

```
1   <UserControl
2       xmlns="http://schemas.microsoft.com/winfx/2006/xaml/presentation"
3       xmlns:x="http://schemas.microsoft.com/winfx/2006/xaml"
4       x:Class="QuadrantShow.MainPage"
5       Width="450" Height="50">
6
7       <Grid x:Name="LayoutRoot" Background="White">
8           <Grid.RowDefinitions>
9               <RowDefinition Height="3*"/>
10              <RowDefinition Height="2*"/>
11          </Grid.RowDefinitions>
12          <Grid.ColumnDefinitions>
13              <ColumnDefinition Width="4*"/>
14              <ColumnDefinition Width="15*"/>
15              <ColumnDefinition Width="1*"/>
16          </Grid.ColumnDefinitions>
17          <Rectangle Fill="#FF59595E" Margin="0" Stroke="Black"/>
18          <Rectangle Fill="#FF909099" Margin="0" Stroke="Black" Grid.Column="1"/>
19          <Rectangle Fill="#FFBBBBC2" Margin="0" Stroke="Black" Grid.Row="1"/>
20          <Rectangle Fill="#FF424250" Margin="0" Stroke="Black" Grid.Column="1" Grid.Row="1"/>
21          <Rectangle Fill="#FF1E1E25" Margin="0" Stroke="Black" Grid.Row="2" Grid.Column="2"/>
22          <Rectangle Fill="#FF5E5E6C" Margin="0" Stroke="Black" Grid.Column="2"/>
23      </Grid>
24  </UserControl>
```

Figure B-16. *The Grid container control can use a star based layout to control the ratios of the columns and rows.*

In the XAML code section of Figure B-16, you defined the Grid row and column definitions using the star layout. The star layout methodology is a complex algorithm that uses relative layouts. It can get really hard to understand if you include auto and explicit widths in addition to star-sized width or heights. However, if all of the rows and columns use star layouts, the grid container will simply render everything in relative ratios. This is exactly what you will do for the bullet graph.

The layout in Figure B-16 uses whole number ratios. The top row of the bullet graph has a 3:2 ratio advantage in size. Therefore, the top row takes up about 60 percent of the height of the bullet graph control. The columns are also whole number ratios. The first column has a 4:20 ratio, which is about 20 percent of the control. The quantitative range and scales (Quadrant 1 and 4) take up about 75 percent of the horizontal area (15:20 ratio). The remaining whitespace buffer columns takes up 5 percent of the real estate (1:20 ratio).

You start to visualize the bullet graph control components fitting into the selected ratios quite nice. What did you attain by using this type of layout? Figure B-17 shows the layout of the user control in varying dimensions. You can clearly see that the ratios are being maintained automatically for you. Therefore, this is a piece that the Silverlight framework will handle for you during the layout rendering process. You will only be responsible for laying out the controls in the individual quadrants.

Figure B-17. *The star layout in the Grid container will maintain the ratios created even if the widths and heights change dramatically.*

Inside Quadrant 1 and Quadrant 2, additional layout containers will be created to further control the positioning of the child controls. However, the decision of what type of internal layout control has much less impact then selecting the root layout container. For simplicity, you will add a Grid container to both Quadrant 1 and Quadrant 2 instead of adding the component controls directly to a single root layout Grid container. This will become clearer in the implementation sections of this chapter. At this point in the chapter, you should know the overall design and where the controls will lie in the layout.

Bullet Graph Configuration Properties

By now you have seen how the bullet graph is used, the components that make up the control, how your implementation will work, and how it will be laid out. Now it's time to determine which configuration options you will make discoverable and settable.

Earlier in this section in Figure B-10 you saw just a small sample of the hundreds of properties that SSRS 2008 R2 exposes for its gauge configuration. In the same manner, based on our implementation we want to expose a set of public properties on the main bullet graph control that will render the control appropriately. Based on the outlines spec, these are the properties you will implement:

- *FeaturedMeasure*: This property will control the value of the featured measure. This property will be responsible for rendering the end value of the progress bar to match the quantitative scale tick marks. This property will be exposed as a double data type.

- *ComparativeMeasure*: This property will control the value of the comparative measure. This property will be responsible for rendering the end value of the rectangle to match the quantitative scale tick marks. This property will be exposed as a double data type.

- *TextLabel*: This string property will control the text label of the bullet graph.

- *UnitLabel*: This string property will control the unit label of the bullet graph.

- *QualitativeRangeBad*: This property will determine the end value of the progress bar that symbolizes the bad qualitative range to match the quantitative scale tick marks. This property will be exposed as a double data type.

- *QualitativeRangeSatisfactory*: This property will determine the end value of the progress bar that symbolizes the satisfactory qualitative range to match the quantitative scale tick marks. This property will be exposed as a double data type.

- *ScaleMinimum*: This double property will control the end value of the quantitative scale.

- *ScaleMaximum*: This double property will control the start value of the quantitative scale.

- *QualitativeRangeBadColor*: This property will determine the Brush (color) used to render the bad qualitative range.

- *QualitativeRangeSatisfactoryColor*: This property will determine the Brush (color) used to render the satisfactory qualitative range.

- *QualitativeRangeGoodColor*: This property will determine the Brush (color) used to render the good qualitative range.

- *ShowComparativeMeasure*: This Boolean property will determine whether to render (show) the comparative measure.

- *ShowQuantitativeScale*: This Boolean property will determine whether to render (show) the quantitative scale.

- *ShowLabels*: This Boolean property will determine whether to render (show) the text and unit labels of the bullet graph.

- *ShowQualitativeRangeBad:* This Boolean property will determine whether to render (show) progress bar that symbolizes the bad qualitative range.

- *ShowQualitativeRangeSatisfactory:* This Boolean property will determine whether to render (show) progress bar that symbolizes the satisfactory qualitative range.

- *ShowQualitativeRangeGood:* This Boolean property will determine whether to render (show) progress bar that symbolizes the good qualitative range.

In your bullet graph implementation, you are going to implement 17 properties that will allow for the control to be configured by a developer or designer. While this is not an abnormal amount for an enterprise scale data visualization control, the amount is quite a lot for trying to teach the material in a technical book chapter. The pattern that will surface these 17 properties will be a little repetitive; therefore the implementation should not be too complicated. Therefore, I will not implement every single property and cover every single line of code in this chapter's text, as it spans over 1,000 lines of code.

Implementing Dependency Properties

If you are familiar with Silverlight or WPF custom control development, you already know that you can't simply expose a bunch of public properties and expect everything to work like other Silverlight controls. There are additional steps that need to be implemented to make this bullet graph control usable in a business intelligence scenario. A designer or developer will expect the following functionality from any public control:

- *Data Binding*: Setting the properties programmatically in code is a deprecated method of implementing dynamic configuration of controls. Silverlight exposes a full data binding framework that allows developers to data bind the controls declaratively in XAML as well as using advanced options like converters, data validation, or element binding. These 17 bullet graph properties should take full advantage of the Silverlight data binding framework.

- *Design Time Experience*: If you have set properties, styles, and templates in Expression Blend 4 or Visual Studio 2010 on a control in design time, you have noticed that these controls are immediately responsive. This is especially true in Silverlight 4. The designer expects that what they see during design time is what they will see during the control's runtime. Therefore, if a designer changes a configuration property, the control should re-render on the design surface to give the designer immediate feedback on the impact of the change.

- *Expression Blend 4 Tools & Design Best Practices*: Designers expect the configuration properties to work with the designer tools in Expression Blend 4. This lets designer avoid having to write code or complex XAML syntax. The available tools in Expression Blend 4 should allow the designer to easily manipulate the bullet graph control.

In order to take full advantage of the Silverlight framework and how it bridges the interactions of data and controls, dependency properties will be implemented for each CLR property. Dependency properties are a special type of property that is wrapped by a .NET CLR property. Dependency properties allow the Silverlight framework to use a regular CLR property and accept values based on other inputs for animation, data binding, or styling. This essentially extends the functionality or regular CLR properties beyond a get and set calculation of a value.

■ **Warning** The dependency property system in Silverlight is a complex topic that requires a good understanding of CLR property interaction, value precedence, dependency property functionality, lifecycle during property changes, data binding, etc. This is well beyond the scope of this book. I plan on introducing a basic level of dependency properties to get you by the creation of the bullet graph control. If you are not familiar with the dependency property system in either Silverlight or WPF, please start with this MSDN knowledgebase article: http://msdn.microsoft.com/en-us/library/cc221408(VS.95).aspx.

Data Binding with Dependency Properties

Silverlight exposes a full data binding framework that is evolutionarilyy better than manual or explicit data binding in code. In the past, .NET or ASP.NET developers exposed public properties and explicitly bound that property to a collection or ADO.NET data interface. This worked well, however it was not reliable and prone to runtime defects. Silverlight improves on the data binding concept by creating an automated bridge between the UI controls and the data context that is exposed to the control or application page. This allows for a natural and holistic flow of data that is less prone to bugs. Furthermore, it provides many pieces of additional settings that enhance data binding without having to write additional code.

The Silverlight data binding framework has its roots in traditional data binding. However, for this automated bridge to work with additional features, the .NET artifacts needed to evolve to support this. The Silverlight/WPF team could have scrapped traditional CLR properties with their get and set accesors and created special Silverlight CLR properties, but they would have broken backwards compatibility and cross-compilation with regular .NET objects. Instead, the team created dependency properties that back up CLR properties and expose additional functionality.

This implementation works really well because the Silverlight framework is smart enough to figure out if there is a dependency property backing it up to expose the additional data binding functionality. Figure B-18 illustrates this concept visually. In this figure, you can see two properties defined. On the left is a traditional CLR property with a get and set accessor functions. On the right is the same property backed up by additional dependency property syntax. What is interesting is that Silverlight is smart enough to understand this and enables data binding. You can see this below each property from the Expression Blend 4 syntax. The traditional CLR property cannot leverage data binding or element binding. Both options are grayed out. However, because the CLR property on the right is backed up by a dependency property, these options automatically become available.

I am dramatically oversimplifying what is going on behind the scenes. However, before proceeding you should understand that dependency property syntax added to traditional CLR properties will enable using the Silverlight data binding framework with all its features.

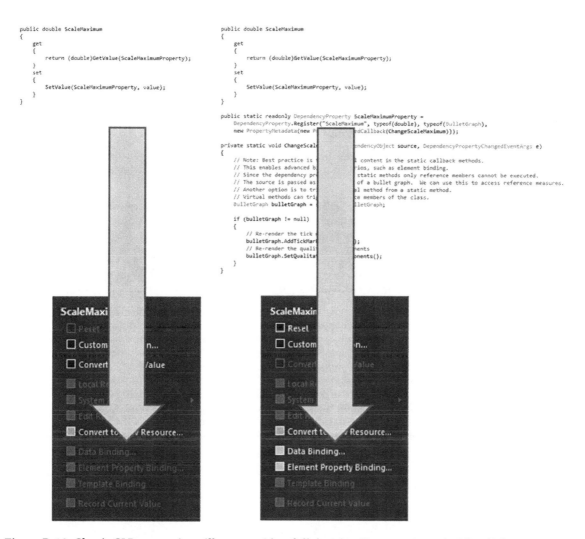

Figure B-18. *Classic CLR properties will not provide a full data binding experience in Silverlight. Enhancing a CLR property with dependency property syntax will enable the full data binding options in Silverlight. In addition, Expression Blend 4 tools can be used to automate data binding with dependency properties. Dependency properties support element property binding in addition to data binding.*

Expression Blend 4 Best Practices and Design-Time Experience

There are varying strategies to implement dependency properties, data binding, and CLR properties that dramatically impact the design experience of a designer. In this implementation, you want to make it very simple for a designer to drag and drop your bullet graph control and immediately start configuring properties and data binding them to a data context.

The main goal is to ensure that the dependency properties you expose automatically flow right into the Expression Blend 4 and Visual Studio 2010 tools that enhance the design experience. This will be achieved by adding five key pieces of syntax to your CLR and dependency property declarations:

- *Category attribute*: Setting the Category attribute on the CLR property declaration will place the property in that property toolbox group. For the bullet graph control, you will group all 17 properties under the Bullet Graph group (see Figure B-19 for an example) This will group all the properties under the Bullet Graph category in both Expression Blend 4 and Visual Studio 2010.

- *Description attribute*: The Description attribute on the CLR property provides a design-time explanation of what each property does and how the setting affects the control.

- *Explicit data types*: Explicit data types will be used for the 17 properties that you want the bullet graph control to bind to. This may seem like a no brainer. However, a lot of control designs focus on taking short cuts or abstracting logic into UI components such as Silverlight ValueConverters. You see a lot of these examples in controls that depend on full control frameworks. Using the explicit data types will allow the particular properties to get design-time dialog boxes in Expression Blend 4 and Visual Studio 2010.

- *Design-Time Feedback*: One of the key aspects of providing a great Silverlight design experience is to provide a WYSIWYG design-time rendering. You want to make sure each time the designer changes a bullet graph component, the design-time rendering reflects this. For example, if the designer changes the satisfactory qualitative range to a color of yellow, this should be immediately reflected in the design-time of the bullet graph control. More importantly, some properties of the bullet graph can impact how the control renders. For example, changing the quantitative scale or hiding certain components should be reflected immediately in the design-time rendering of the control. In the implementation of the bullet graph, you will see certain pieces that require some small syntax tweaks in order for this to work.

- *Element Property Binding*: Silverlight 3 introduced element property binding as an alternative to having to bind dependency properties to a data context. This type of binding requires additional syntax and proper controls in order to function properly. You will want to ensure that your bullet graph can take advantage of element property binding.

Figure B-19 illustrates the property section for the Bullet Graph control grouped into a single category. The picture on the left is from Expression Blend 4 properties window. The property section on the right is from the Visual Studio 2010 properties window. Both Bullet Graph property sections house the complete list of 17 bullet graph measures implemented properly with dependency properties. You can clearly see that the properties expose different configuration settings based on their underlying data type.

Note that both Expression Blend 4 and Visual Studio 2010 highlight properties that have value changed from the default or that are leveraging data binding. For example, the ComparativeMeasure property is leveraging binding syntax. In the left-hand picture you can determine this because the value of the property is highlighted in yellow (you may not see this in the black and white print of the book). This means that the value is coming from data binding. From the Expression Blend 4 (left-hand side) you can tell the value is using binding, but you do not know what it is bound to. The Visual Studio 2010 property settings (right-hand picture) give more information: you can see that the ComparativeMeasure is using element binding, it is bound to a control named slider_Copy, and the property bound is called Value.

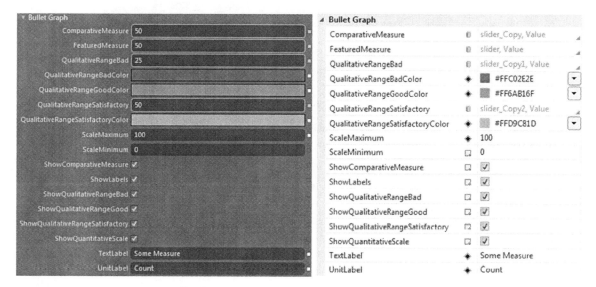

Figure B-19. *Both Expression Blend 4 (left) and Visual Studio 2010 (right), property windows provide a great deal of information when the control properties are designed and exposed using design best practices.*

In addition to grouping and exposing valuable information about your properties for the bullet graph, both Expression Blend 4 and Visual Studio 2010 provide a rich design-time experience for the designer. Figure B-20 illustrates the configuration dialogs for a property that exposes Brush data type in Expression Blend 4. The design tool is smart enough to surface a Brush selector and a color picker.

Figure B-20. Clicking on the color of a property that exposes a Brush data type brings up a rich color editor for setting additional properties, resources or data binding. Leveraging functionality like this makes the design experience for a custom control much more friendly to a developer or designer.

Visual Studio 2010 includes design-time enhancements for properties as well. Figure B-21 shows the data binding dialog for a dependency property. In this dialog, numerous properties can be declaratively set with simple options without having to write XAML or manually binding the UI controls to data.

There are more examples out there on how the Expression Blend 4 and Visual Studio 2010 IDEs help out designers with configuring and data binding controls. The most important takeaway is that you understand that implementing best practices for dependency properties will enable you to leverage this functionality in the bullet graph control.

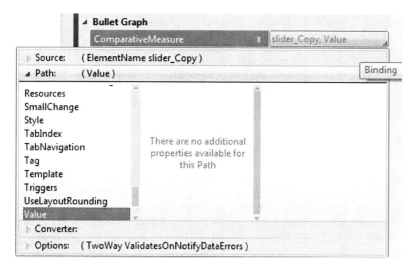

Figure B-21. The rich data binding experience in Visual Studio 2010 allows for complex scenarios to be created without having to write XAML or manual programatic code.

Dependency Property Syntax

After learning about the benefits for dependency properties for custom control development, it is time to understand how the syntax works. I will not cover the full syntax of dependency properties and all the options available. The focus on the dependency property syntax will be on implementing your bullet graph control properties. I will cover the dependency property syntax by highlighting how a simple CLR property is backed up by a dependency property.

Listing B-1 shows a simple CLR property that uses a string data type. The property also has default get and set accessor. There is nothing special about the property—you have probably seen it hundreds of times before.

Listing B-1. A simple public string property

```
public string TextLabel
{
        get;
        set;
}
```

Changing the property in Listing B-1 to property that is backed up by a dependency property involves three steps:

1. *Register the dependency property.* The dependency property will be registered with the control using the Register method of the static DependencyProperty class. The Register method has additional parameters that will be explained later in this section.

511

2. *Create a static property changed callback.* The static PropertyChangedCallback method is a parameter for the PropertyMetadata class. If implemented, this callback is triggered each time the property changes. Strictly speaking, this call back method is optional. However, since your bullet graph control rendering can be affected by any property changing, you will implement this on all of your 17 properties. For example, if the quantitative scale maximum value is changed, this will obviously affect the layout and positioning of the qualitative components (featured measure, comparative measure, qualitative ranges).

3. *Modify the CLR property get and set accessors.* The CLR property has to communicate with the dependency property. The CLR property will still be the main entry point for your code. In order to communicate with the dependency property, you will use the GetValue and SetValue methods on the get and set accessors to retrieve and set the value of the dependency property. This would be equivalent to having a private field that you use in your get and set accessors. However, instead of using a private field you will use the two methods on the dependency property directly.

Following the three steps outlined, a simple CLR property becomes backed up by a dependency property with the syntax shown in Listing B-2.

Listing B-2. A TextLabel property enhanced with a dependency property object

```
public string TextLabel
{
    get
    {
        return (string) GetValue(TextLabelProperty);
    }
    set
    {
        SetValue(TextLabelProperty, value);
    }
}

public static readonly DependencyProperty TextLabelProperty =
    DependencyProperty.Register("TextLabel", typeof(string), typeof(BulletGraph),
    new PropertyMetadata(new PropertyChangedCallback(ChangeTextLabel)));

private static void ChangeTextLabel(DependencyObject source,
DependencyPropertyChangedEventArgs e)
{}
```

The DependencyProperty is a static class that exposes a static Register method. This Register method returns a DependencyProperty object. In Listing B-2 the object is named TextLabelProperty. Essentially, the naming convention for the dependency property is the name of the CLR property appended by the word "Property". This naming convention is recommended by Microsoft for dependency properties. So in your example, this would be "TextLabel" plus "Property".

The Register method includes several parameters that help identify how the control behaves. The first parameter is the name of the dependency property. As you can see, the naming convention is to use the same name as the CLR property. The second parameter is the Type property, which is the underlying data type of the dependency property. The Type property should match the type used in the CLR property. The third parameter is the ownerType, which is usually the name of the class of the custom control. In Listing B-2, the owner type is the BulletGraph. This type is important because it gets passed back as a reference to the PropertyChangedCallback method.

The fourth parameter is the PropertyMetadata object, which can be null. The PropertyMetadata parameter includes a parameter that determines the callback method that will be triggered when the property is changed. It also includes an optional parameter that will set the initial default value for the property. This parameter has minimal use since the default value will probably be overridden by an explicit configuration setting or data binding.

In Listing B-2 the PropertyChangedCallback method was implemented in a static method called ChangedTextLabel. Inside this static method, you can place code you want to execute when the property changes. For example, if the TextLabel changes, you could trigger a story board animation to trigger to let the user know the text was changed.

After the dependency property was registered with the call back method declared, a communication bridge between the CLR property and the corresponding dependency property needs to be added. Listing B-2 shows how this is done by expanding the get and set accessors to utilize the SetValue and GetValue methods. The GetValue and SetValue methods have a single parameter that is a DependencyProperty. If you want to retrieve a value from a dependency property, you would call the GetValue method and pass in the name of the DependencyProperty. GetValue returns an object type. Therefore, the return value needs to be cast to the appropriate property type. The SetValue method simply takes a DependencyProperty parameter and has no return value.

Dependency Property Best Practices

Dependency property implementation includes some simple best practices that should always be followed. Following these best practices will eliminate strange behaviors or hard to find bugs in a custom control.

- *No additional code in the CLR get and set accessors*: There should be no additional code in the CLR property get or set accessors if there is a dependency property associated with that control. If you place any additional code in this section, there is a potential that this code will not be executed in certain data binding scenarios (i.e., element binding). In absolutely no scenario should you change the value of the CLR property before passing it into or returning it from the dependency property. This can cause very strange behavior in your code. The best practice in a case when you need additional processing on the value is to use a ValueConverter.

- *PropertyChanged callback method should include additional processing*: If you need any additional processing or if a dependency property changes, it should be placed in the PropertyChanged callback method. This is a static method; therefore the code cannot reference the main control reference. This would be pretty limiting; however, the method passes in a source parameter that passes in the reference of the dependency property owner (which is usually the control). The source parameter allows developers to overcome the inability to call non-static members in a static method. Listing B-3 shows how to use this functionality.

Listing B-3. Example of Setting Reference Property on the Owner of the Dependency Property

```
private static void ChangeTextLabel(DependencyObject source,
DependencyPropertyChangedEventArgs e)
{
    BulletGraph bulletGraph = source as BulletGraph;

    if (bulletGraph != null)
    {
        TextBlock textBlock = bulletGraph.FindName("textLabel") as TextBlock;

        if (textBlock != null)
        {
            textBlock.Text = e.NewValue as string;
        }
    }
}
```

You are armed with enough knowledge on dependency properties to start using them in your bullet graph implementation. The 17 bullet graph properties will implement using the three dependency property parts shown in Listing B-2. The only variance between the properties will be the additional logic contained in the PropertyChanged callback methods.

Implementing the Bullet Graph in Silverlight

After familiarizing yourself with the bullet graph control and understanding the implementation specification, you are ready to start implementing the bullet graph control in Silverlight.

This section will read somewhere between a coding scenario and technical text. You can think of it as a hybrid coding scenario. The bullet graph implementation has many components and it would be too much to implement the full control step by step. However, I will cover the main key pieces and challenging pieces of code. The full source code for the bullet graph control is available in version 3.0 of the source code on the companion web site.

The implementation section of this chapter is broken down into smaller subsections that will focus on implementing particular pieces of functionality. Each subsection's Visual Studio 2010 solution will be available for download in addition to the full source code. This will allow you to jump in and start coding from the part that interests you. For example, you may be interested in implementing dependency properties rather than creating the layout of the control (which you have done many times in previous chapters).

Bullet Graph Layout and Adding Main Components

This implementation section will cover the creation of the bullet graph project, creating the layout controls, and adding the main control components to the layout.

Starting the Project

The first step in this part is to create a new solution that will contain our bullet graph control as well as a project to test the bullet graph control. Let's create a new Silverlight 4 project in Visual Studio 2010 and name it SilverlightBulletGraphApp.

After creating the new project, we need to add a Silverlight 4 assembly that will host the bullet graph control. Add a new Silverlight Class Library project that targets the Silverlight 4 version. Name the project SilverlightBulletGraph. Next add the SilverlightBulletGraph project reference to the SilverlightBulletGraphApp project.

In the SilverlightBulletGraph project add a new Silverlight User Control item and name it BulletGraph. Your project should look like Figure B-22.

Figure B-22. *The bullet graph shown in the Visual Studio 2010 design window.*

Building the Layout

After the project structure has been created, you can start adding content to the BulletGraph user control XAML file. First, change the DesignHeight to 50 and DesignWidth to 450. These dimensions provide a more realistic rendering of a bullet graph control.

Open the file up in either Visual Studio 2010 or Expression Blend 4 and add the main layout for the bullet graph shown in Listing B-4 below. This will act as the high level layout I covered in the "Creating a Fluid Layout" specification section in this chapter and shown in Figures B-14 through B-17.

Add a Grid called qualitativeComponentsGrid that will host the qualitative components (progress bar scales, comparative measure, and featured measure) for the bullet graph. This grid will be added to Quadrant 1 of the layout (Figure B-14).

Finally, add a Grid called quantiativeScaleGrid. This will host the quantitative scale for the bullet graph. Add this to the bottom right two Grid parts by placing it in Grid.Row=1 and Grid.Column=1 and spanning the layout for two sections.

Listing B-4. The High Level Layout of the BulletGraph.xaml Control

```xml
<UserControl x:Class="SilverlightBulletGraph.BulletGraph"
    xmlns="http://schemas.microsoft.com/winfx/2006/xaml/presentation"
    xmlns:x="http://schemas.microsoft.com/winfx/2006/xaml"
    xmlns:d="http://schemas.microsoft.com/expression/blend/2008"
    xmlns:mc="http://schemas.openxmlformats.org/markup-compatibility/2006"
    mc:Ignorable="d"
    d:DesignHeight="50" d:DesignWidth="450">

    <Grid x:Name="LayoutRoot">

        <!-- Row Definitions -->
        <Grid.RowDefinitions>
            <RowDefinition Height="3*"/>
            <RowDefinition Height="2*"/>
        </Grid.RowDefinitions>

        <!-- Column Deifintions -->
        <Grid.ColumnDefinitions>
            <ColumnDefinition Width="4*"/>
            <ColumnDefinition Width="15*"/>
            <ColumnDefinition Width="1*"/>
        </Grid.ColumnDefinitions>

        <!-- Grid that will host the qualitative components -->
        <Grid x:Name="qualitativeComponentsGrid" Grid.Row="0" HorizontalAlignment="Stretch"
            VerticalAlignment="Stretch" Grid.Column="1">

        <!-- Grid that will host the quantitative scale -->
        <Grid x:Name="quantitaitveScaleGrid" Margin="0,0,0,0" Grid.Row="1" Grid.Column="1"
            Background="{x:Null}" Grid.ColumnSpan="2">
        </Grid>

        </Grid>
<!-- End of LayoutRoot -->
    </Grid>
</UserControl>
```

Adding the Bullet Graph Components

In this section you will add the bullet graph components that make up the bullet graph control. The following controls will be added in this section:

- *Text Label*: A TextBlock control named textLabel will be added to Quadrant 2 (Figure B-14). The control should be vertically aligned in the center and horizontally aligned towards the right. Additional properties like the Font and Margin can be tweaked to enhance the appearance.

- *Unit Label*: A TextBlock control named unitLabel will be added to Quadrant 3 (Figure B-14). The control should be vertically aligned to the top and horizontally aligned towards the right. Additional properties like the Font and Margin can be tweaked to enhance the appearance.

- *Three Qualitative Ranges*: Three Progress Bars will be added to the qualitativeComponentsGrid to represent the qualitative ranges. Name the three progress bars qualitativeRangeGood, qualitativeRangeSatisfactory and qualitativeRangeBad. The qualitativeRangeGood progress bar has a value of 100 and a ForeGround of LightGray. The qualitativeRangeSatisfactory has a default value of 75 and a ForeGround of Gray. The qualitativeRangeBad has a default value of 25 and a ForeGround of DarkGray. These values will obviously be dynamically set by data binding, but the default values provide a great visualization initially to a designer or a developer.

- *Featured Measure*: A single progress bar will be added to the qualitativeComponentsGrid to symbolize the featured measure. According to Stephen Few's design spec, the featured measure should be black. Note that in Figures B-1 through B-5, the featured measure does not take up the full height of the container canvas. Therefore, you will apply a default RenderTransform that will scale the Y-axis to 40 percent of the height to make the qualitative ranges more visible. This is an example of a fluid layout component as it does not depend on an explicit height.

- *Comparative Measure*: A rectangle will be added to the qualitativeComponentsGrid to symbolize the comparative measure. Again, according to Stephen Few's design spec, the comparative measure should be black. Similarly to the featured measure, the comparative measure will have a render transform that will reduce the X and Y axis scales. From the bullet graph figures you can see the comparative measure takes up more space vertically than the featured measure, but less than a full qualitative range scale. I set the value as 60 percent (0.6). The X-axis is much smaller on the horizontal scale, about 1 percent of the total width of the qualitativeComponentsGrid. This is another example of the fluid layout system you want to implement that does not rely on explicit dimensions.

Listing B-5 features the code for the bullet graph components inside the main Grid layout.

Listing B-5. The Bullet Graph Components Added to the Main LayoutRoot and qualitativeComponentsGrid

```
...

<!-- Text Label -->
<TextBlock x:Name="textLabel" Margin="0,0,5,0" TextWrapping="Wrap" Text="Label for BG"
    d:LayoutOverrides="Width, Height"
    VerticalAlignment="Center" FontSize="12.5" HorizontalAlignment="Right"/>

<!-- Unit Label -->
<TextBlock x:Name="unitLabel" HorizontalAlignment="Right" TextWrapping="Wrap" Text="Unit
Label"
    VerticalAlignment="Top" Grid.Row="1" FontSize="10.667" Margin="0,0,5,0"/>

<!-- Grid that will host the qualitative components -->
<Grid x:Name="qualitativeComponentsGrid" Grid.Row="0" HorizontalAlignment="Stretch"
    VerticalAlignment="Stretch" Grid.Column="1">

  <!-- Qualitative Good Range -->
  <!-- Value will always be 100% -->
  <ProgressBar x:Name="qualitativeRangeGood" Value="100" Foreground="WhiteSmoke" />

  <!-- Qualitative Satisfactory Range -->
  <ProgressBar x:Name="qualitativeRangeSatisfactory" Foreground="LightGray" Value="50" />

  <!-- Qualitative Bad Range -->
  <ProgressBar x:Name="qualitativeRangeBad" Foreground="Gray" Value="25"/>

  <!-- Featured Measure -->
  <ProgressBar x:Name="featuredMeasure" HorizontalAlignment="Stretch" Foreground="Black"
  RenderTransformOrigin="0.5,0.5" Value="65">
    <!-- The RenderTransform scales the Y-axis dynamically,
    based on the container dimensions -->
    <ProgressBar.RenderTransform>
      <CompositeTransform ScaleY="0.4"/>
    </ProgressBar.RenderTransform>
  </ProgressBar>

  <!-- Comparative Measure -->
  <Rectangle x:Name="comparativeMeasure" Fill="Black" RenderTransformOrigin="0,0.5"
StrokeThickness="0">
      <!-- The RenderTransform scales the Y and X axes dynamically,
      based on the container dimensions -->
      <Rectangle.RenderTransform>
        <CompositeTransform ScaleY="0.6" ScaleX="0.01" TranslateX="50"/>
      </Rectangle.RenderTransform>
    </Rectangle>
  <!-- End of qualitativeComponentsGrid Grid -->
```

```
</Grid>
```
...

The bullet graph control is starting to take shape. If you are in Visual Studio 2010 or Expression Blend 4, you should see the control resemble a bullet graph control. This is shown in Figure B-23; all the quadrants are defined using the spacing you determined in the implementation.

Figure B-23. The bullet graph shown in the Visual Studio 2010 design window

Before proceeding to the next section, let's add the bullet graph control to the MainPage.xaml to the SilverlightBulletGraphApp project. This will allow you to see how the control would appear to the designer and at runtime. Figure B-24 below shows the bullet graph in debug mode after being added to the SilverlightBulletGraphApp project.

▧ **Note** If you cannot see the BulletGraph control in the Expression Blend 4 asset panel, ensure that you added the SilverlightBulletGraph project reference to the SilverlightBulletGraphApp project.

Figure B-24. The runtime control is already resembling the structure of the bullet graph.

Styling Qualitative Ranges & Adding Dynamic Content

This implementation section will cover the styling of the progress bar controls in the qualitative ranges, math required for rendering the position of the components, and the quantitative scale.

▧ **Note** The SilverlightBulletGraphApp_Part1_ BulletGraphLayout folder of the source code zip file includes the implementation thus far.

Styling the Qualitative Ranges

Looking at Figure B-23, you can see that the qualitative ranges are overlapping each other. Furthermore, they have rounded corners, borders, and a gradient fill. Stephen Few's design specification is explicit: these components should not have a border and should be a single color. While the specification does not directly mention that rounded corners are bad, you can clearly tell that 90 degree edges are the preferred rendering to make qualitative analysis easier.

Since you are leveraging the ProgressBar control for the qualitative ranges, you simply need to change the underlying style of the control and tweak the settings that make the most sense for your bullet graph control.

This part is done much easier in the Expression Blend 4 product. Open up the SilverlightBulletGraph project in Expression Blend 4. Highlight any of the qualitative range progress bars. Right click on it and select Edit Template and then Edit a Copy… (shown in Figure B-25). Name the style QualitativeRangeProgressBar. Then create a new resource dictionary called BulletGraphResourceDictionary.xaml. This will add a new resource dictionary for the bullet graph control project.

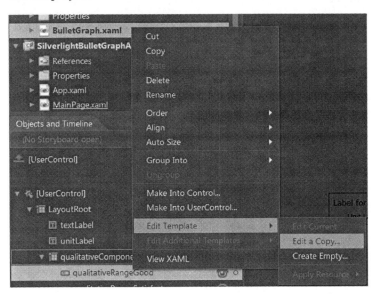

Figure B-25. *Editing the current template for a qualitative range progres bar.*

Exit out of the template and go through the three qualitative ranges and the featured measure to apply the QualitativeRangeProgressBar style to all of them. This will allow you to quickly see the effects of your changes in the bullet graph control. This step is shown in Figure B-26. The first qualitative range progress bar you created the style for will already have the style applied.

■ **Note** Do not apply the style to the Comparative Measure because it is a Rectangle control and not a ProgressBar control.

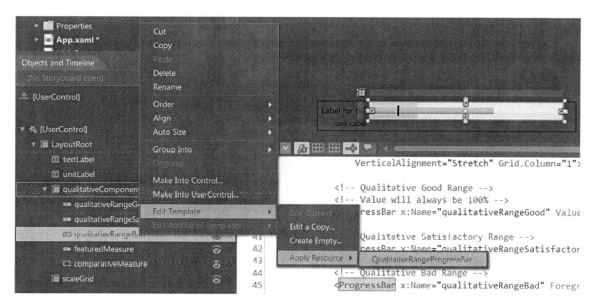

Figure B-26. Applying the newly created QualitativeRangeProgressBar style to your four progress bar controls

Open up the BulletGraphResourceDictionary.xaml file in Expression Blend 4. The first thing to do is to change the BorderThickness on line 7 in the BulletGraphResourceDictionary.xaml file from 1 to 0. This will remove the border of the progress bar. Running the project, you will notice that the border of the progress bars has been removed.

Now, navigate to line 48 and edit the ProgressTrack Border. Remove the Background attribute and set the CornerRadius from 3 to 0. If you build and run the project now, you will now be able to see all three qualitative ranges.

Navigate to line 50. For the ProgressBarRootGradient Rectangle control you will set the RadiusX and RadiusY values to 0 from 1.5. This will render the rectangle controls with sharp 90 degree angles. Also set the StrokeThickness to 0 as this will remove any border offset.

Navigate to line 83. For the ProgressBarIndicator Rectangle control, set the RadiusX and RadiusY values to 0 from 1.5. This will render the rectangle controls with sharp 90 degree angles. Run the application now and you will notice the ranges have sharp clear edges.

Navigate to line 50 and in the ProgressBarRootGradient Rectangle, remove the Rectangle.Fill. You can either manually remove the element or in Expression Blend 4 highlight the ProgressBarRootGradient and the Fill property to No Brush.

The last step is to set the Margin of the DeterminateRoot to 0 on line 69 of the BulletGraphResourceDictionary.xaml file.

▪ **Note** There were a lot of changes made to the ProgressBar style that required a good understanding of how margins, thickness, and border effect the layout of the Silverlight controls. If you had trouble following the instructions, simply copy and paste the `BulletGraphResourceDictionary.xaml` file over your current file.

You have made a lot of changes to the QualitativeRangeProgressBar style. The bullet graph control should now look like the one pictured below in Figure B-27.

Figure B-27. *The changes to the progres bar style dramtically improves the look of the bullet graph control. Notice that the control now resembles the sharp and clean look of the screen shots defined in Stephen Few's design specification.*

Adding the Quantitative Scale

Up to this point you have created static content. The control has a layout, defined control components, and some styles. However, you are missing the quantitative scale (tick marks and labels). The main reason you have not added this scale in the previous section is that it needs to be dynamic because it depends on certain variables like the minimum scale or maximum scale.

This dynamic code will be added programmatically in the codebehind of the bullet graph user control. You need a location to place into the control. If you are not familiar with control development, this is where you may falter. Some places that come to mind are the constructor, Loaded event, and LayoutUpdated event. The constructor is always a poor choice for adding UI controls to a layout container. The LayoutUpdated event is a good choice, but it can be called multiple times as multiple render passes execute. The Loaded is a possibility but it is not the last event in the control lifecycle so there are some properties that might not be set due to the asynchronous nature of Silverlight control rendering. What do you do?

The Silverlight framework includes an event called SizeChanged. According to the MSDN documentation, the SizeChanged event is raised when "either the ActualHeight or the ActualWidth properties change value on a FrameworkElement." This is a really important concept to understand for fluid layouts. You will need these properties to be set with the proper values in order to be able to calculate the dynamic positions of the UI components.

You may ask yourself why you need to worry about this if you're going to drag and drop the bullet graph control and set its width and height explicitly. In that scenario, you would be correct. However, imagine if a designer places the bullet graph control in a list box that is dynamically stretched. The width and height values would not be updated, and the math calculations would either error or cause incorrect values. Therefore, retrieving the ActualWidth and ActualHeight dimensions after the Silverlight rendering process has determined the place of the control is quite important.

Open up the BulletGraph.xaml file. In the UserControl element, add SizeChanged event. This will create a UserControl_SizeChanged event handler in the codebehind. You should now have an event handler as shown in Listing B-6.

Listing B-6. The UserControl_SizeChanged Event that Hosts the Main Layout Content

```
...
public BulletGraph()
{
  InitializeComponent();
}

private void UserControl_SizeChanged(object sender, SizeChangedEventArgs e)
{
}
...
```

Now that you know you will place your dynamic layout code in the SizeChanged event handler, it's time to add the quantitative scale dynamically. This will be done in two steps. First, create a series of private members that will hold the values that are calculated from the layout. Then, create a method called AddTickMarks() that will be responsible for the math and adding the quantitative scale components.

If you look back at any of the sample bullet graphs, you can see the quantitative scale consists of a rectangular tick mark and a label. The implementation is actually quite simple. You will programmatically create a StackPanel control using a vertical orientation. Inside the StackPanel control, a tick mark represented by a rectangle will be added. Directly below the tick mark, a TextBlock will be added that will serve as a label for the tick mark. Figure B-28 illustrates this implementation.

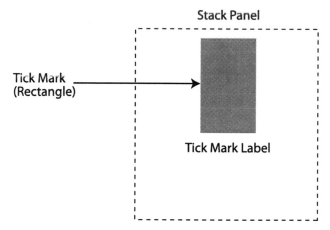

Figure B-28. The quantitative scale components include a series of StackPanel controls that include a rectangular tick mark and a TextBlock label.

The math inside of the AddTickMarks() method is actually pretty simple. First, you calculate the offset between each tick mark. For example, if the bullet graph renders a quantitative scale Grid of a width of 100 and 5 tick marks, then each space between them will be 25 (100/(5-1). Note that you subtract 1 from the number of tick marks; this is because you do not count the first starting tick mark. The center of each tick mark (width divided by two) will be positioned directly under the qualitative range scale. The full code for adding the quantitative scale is shown in Listing B-7.

Listing B-7. The Code Required to Create the Dynamic Quantitative Scale

```
public partial class BulletGraph : UserControl
{
    // private field that will hold the actual width value
    private double actualWidth;
    // private field taht will hold the width of the qualitative components grid
    private double qualitativeComponentsGridWidth;
    private double comparativeMeasureWidth;

    // default values for non-configurable bullet graph components
    // Note: you can factor these values out for extra configuration options
    //   via dependency properties
    private double bottomScalePercentage = 0.8;
    private const double comparativeMeasureScaleX = 0.01;
    private const double tickMarkScaleX = 0.0035;
    private const double tickMarkScaleY = 0.4;
    private int numberOfTickMarks = 5;

    // private field that holds the value of the size changed event was triggered
    private bool hasSizeChangedProcessed = false;

    public BulletGraph()
    {
        InitializeComponent();
    }

    private void UserControl_SizeChanged(object sender, SizeChangedEventArgs e)
    {
        // Note: Use SizeChanged event, because this ensures that
        // ActualWidth and ActualHeight properties are set
        this.actualWidth = this.ActualWidth;

        // Width properties are available after LayoutUpdated event is triggered
        // Bullet Graph canvas takes up 75% of the width of the entire control
        // Note: this event is called multiple times
        this.qualitativeComponentsGridWidth = this.ActualWidth * 0.75;

        // calculate the width of the comparative measure
        this.comparativeMeasureWidth = qualitativeComponentsGridWidth *
comparativeMeasureScaleX;

        this.AddTickMarksAndLabels();
```

```
                // flag that size changed has processed
                // Note: this flag will be used to determine that the ActualWidth and
ActualHeight
                // dimensions were set
                this.hasSizeChangedProcessed = true;
            }

        private void AddTickMarksAndLabels()
        {
            // Retrieve the container of the quantitative scale
            // Clear existing tick marks & labels
            Grid quantitativeScaleGrid = this.FindName("quantitativeScaleGrid") as Grid;
            if (quantitativeScaleGrid != null)
            {
                quantitativeScaleGrid.Children.Clear();
            }

            // Retrieve the minimum and maximum values of the quantitative scale
            double minimumScaleValue = 0;
            double maximumScaleValue = 200;

            // Calculate the scale range
            double tickMarksStep = (maximumScaleValue - minimumScaleValue) /
(this.numberOfTickMarks - 1);

            // Calculate an even area between each tick mark in the quantitative scale
            double tickMarkOffSet = this.qualitativeComponentsGridWidth /
(this.numberOfTickMarks - 1);

            for (int i = 0; i != numberOfTickMarks; i++)
            {
                // Create a stack panel layout container
                StackPanel spContainer = new StackPanel();
                spContainer.Orientation = Orientation.Vertical;
                spContainer.HorizontalAlignment = HorizontalAlignment.Left;
                spContainer.VerticalAlignment = VerticalAlignment.Top;

                // Create a tick mark
                Rectangle tickMark = new Rectangle();
                tickMark.HorizontalAlignment = HorizontalAlignment.Center;
                tickMark.Fill = new SolidColorBrush(Colors.Gray);
                tickMark.StrokeThickness = 0.0;

                // Calculate the tick mark dimensions
                double tickMarkerWidth = this.actualWidth * bottomScalePercentage *
tickMarkScaleX;
                tickMark.Width = tickMarkerWidth;
                tickMark.Height = quantitativeScaleGrid.ActualHeight * tickMarkScaleY;

                // Add the tick mark to the container
                spContainer.Children.Add(tickMark);
```

```
                    // Create a text block label for the tick mark
                    TextBlock tb = new TextBlock();
                    tb.Text = (minimumScaleValue + i * tickMarksStep).ToString();
                    tb.HorizontalAlignment = HorizontalAlignment.Center;
                    tb.TextAlignment = TextAlignment.Center;
                    tb.Width = tickMarkOffSet * 2;

                    // Add the tick mark to the stack panel container
                    spContainer.Children.Add(tb);

                    // Apply a CompositeTransform that will properly set the position of the stack
panel
                    CompositeTransform ct = new CompositeTransform();
                    ct.TranslateX = (i - 1) * tickMarkOffSet;
                    spContainer.RenderTransform = ct;

                    // Add the stack panel container to the quantitative scale grid
                    if (quantitativeScaleGrid != null)
                    {
                        quantitativeScaleGrid.Children.Add(spContainer);
                    }
                }
            }
        }
```

After adding this, you should be able to see the quantitative scale at runtime in your bullet graph control. You can also tweak the number of tick marks or the maximumScaleRange variable (which is hard coded to a value of 100) to confirm your code is truly dynamic. Figure B-29 illustrates a bullet graph rendered with 11 tick marks and the maximum scale range value of 500. This can be done by changing the value of the hardcoded variables. For example, changing the numberOfTickMarks variable (line 30) will affect the number of tick marks shown. In addition, the maximum scale value is changed by setting the maximumScaleValue variable (line 74). Making these changes will render the bullet graph shown in Figure B-29.

Figure B-29. *The bullet graph control can be rendered with varying tick marks. This dynamically alters the UI component dimensions, positions, and layout.*

Implementing Dependency Properties & Design-Time Logic

This implementation section will implement all of the 17 bullet graph properties defined in the specification and the design-time features to enable a great editing experience.

■ **Note** The SilverlightBulletGraphApp_Part2_QualitativeComponents folder of the source code zip file includes the implementation thus far.

Adding Category & Property Descriptions

In Figure B-19, the bullet graph properties are grouped by a category named Bullet Graph. Designers should be able to hover over the property name and it should show a description of what the property affects plus some basic instructions. In order to accomplish this design-time functionality, Category and Description attributes can be applied over the CLR property. Since this process will add a lot of custom text strings, it would be a good idea to place them in a single location.

In Visual Studio 2010 (or Expression Blend 4), add a new static class called BulletGraphTextHelper to the SilverlightBulletGraph Silverlight project. In the class, add two properties shown in Listing B-8.

Listing B-8. The BulletGraphTextHelper Class Hosts the Strings Used for Bullet Graph Descriptions

```
namespace SilverlightBulletGraph
{
    public static class BulletGraphTextHelper
    {
        public const string CategoryName = "Bullet Graph";

        public const string TextLabelDescription = "The text label for the bullet graph
measure.";
    }
}
```

In order to keep this simple, the TextLabel CLR property, the TextLabelProperty dependency property, and the TextLabelChangedProperty will be the first set of properties to be added. As mentioned during the dependency property section, these are the three components that will be added for each of the 17 properties that will be exposed in the bullet graph.

The logic for the TextLabel could not be simpler. When the TextLabel property changes, the UI control that surfaces its value needs to be updated. Therefore, when the TextLabel property changes, the TextBlock control named TextBlock needs to be updated. In the "Implementing Dependency Properties" section, you learned that this type of logic should be implemented in the TextLabelChanged callback.

Look at Listing B-9. Note that the Category and Description attributes were added to the TextLabel CLR property. The TextLabel CLR property get and set accessors utilize the GetValue and SetValue methods to communicate with the TextLabelProperty DependencyProperty. The TextLabelChanged callback method retrieves the source property and converts it to the BulletGraph (since it is the owner of the TextLabelProperty). Using an instance of the bullet graph, a pointer to the textLabel reference can be acquired to set its Text property to the new value of the DependencyProperty object.

Note that in order to utilize the Category and Description properties, the System.ComponentModel namespace needs to be added to the class.

Listing B-9. The Three Main Components of a Bindable User Control Property include a CLR Property, Dependency Propery Object, and a PropertyChanged Callback.

```
...
using System.ComponentModel;
...
[Category(BulletGraphTextHelper.CategoryName)]
[Description(BulletGraphTextHelper.TextLabelDescription)]
public string TextLabel
{
    get
    {
        return (string)GetValue(TextLabelProperty);
    }
    set
    {
        SetValue(TextLabelProperty, value);
    }
}

public static readonly DependencyProperty TextLabelProperty =
    DependencyProperty.Register("TextLabel", typeof(string), typeof(BulletGraph),
    new PropertyMetadata(new PropertyChangedCallback(TextLabelChanged)));

private static void TextLabelChanged(DependencyObject source,
DependencyPropertyChangedEventArgs e)
{
    BulletGraph bulletGraph = source as BulletGraph;

    if (bulletGraph != null)
    {
        TextBlock textBlock = bulletGraph.FindName("textLabel") as TextBlock;

        if (textBlock != null)
        {
            textBlock.Text = e.NewValue as string;
        }
    }
}
...
```

After adding the complete property to the BulletGraph.cs file, the TextLabel property can be altered at design-time. Figure B-30 illustrates the ability to configure the TextLabel property at design-time in Visual Studio 2010. Build the project and try setting the value of the TextLabel of the property at design-time. Notice that the property is updated immediately. Therefore, it is important to note the registered dependency property logic is executed even during design-time. This will come in handy when a designer is setting complex properties. For example, when the comparative measure is set, the design-time canvas will re-render the control and thus give the designer immediate feedback.

Figure B-30. *Adding the TextLabel property with Category and Description attributes places the property in the Bullet Graph group and provides a description when hovering over the property name.*

You should understand how to add all of the remaining 16 properties to the bullet graph control. Hint: the remaining properties are added the exact same way using the same three components: a CLR property, dependency property object, and a property changed callback. Inside the callback method, code needs to be added to perform any additional calculations or UI modifications.

Additional Calculations and Notes

The previous section highlighted how to add a simple string property that is backed by a dependency property. The remaining properties are not as simple as changing the Text property on a TextBlock and require additional calculations. For example, when the ComparativeMeasure property changes, the callback property will need to calculate the position where to render the rectangle symbol. This becomes a little more complex since this property needs to update when other properties change. For example, if the ComparativeMeasure has a value of 50 and the quantitative scale is from 0 to 100, the rectangle will be positioned directly in the center of the qualitative range. What if the designer updates the maximum range property to 200? The control should automatically update the ComparativeMeasure rectangle symbol to about a quarter on the qualitative scale. Therefore, some properties will dependencies on other properties.

■ **Warning** Remember that all calculation and UI logic based off of property values changing belongs in the property callback methods. This applies to properties that depend on each other as well. It might be tempting to place logic in the main event handlers or other locations. However, not following this general design practice could cause bugs or strange behavior.

Listing B-10 illustrates an example of ensuring synchronization of the UI between dependency properties. In the code below, the ScaleMaxiumChanged callback method is shown. When the maximum range changes, you need to re-render the tick marks and the qualitative range components (featured measure, comparative measure, and three qualitative ranges). The same logic will apply to the ScaleMinimumChanged callback method.

Remember the reason why this works is that other property values do not change as a result of this property change. The value of the comparative measure does not change; only the position of the rectangle is affected. For example, if the maximum value of the scale is changed from 100 to 200, the value of the comparative measure value will remain what it was. However, you need to re-render the scale and the tick marks because the rectangle has a different position.

Listing B-10. The ScaleMaximumChanged Callback Property Includes Logic that Requires the Re-rendering of Other UI objects that Depend on its Value.

```
private static void ScaleMaximumChanged (DependencyObject source,
DependencyPropertyChangedEventArgs e)
    {
        // Note: Best practice is to create all calculations in the static callback methods.
        // This enables advanced binding scenarios, such as element binding.
        // Since the dependency properties are static methods only reference members cannot be
executed.
        // The source is passed as a reference of a bullet graph.
        // We can use this to access reference measures.
        // Another option is to trigger a virual method from a static method.
        // Virtual methods can trigger reference members of the class.

        // Retrieve the reference to the bullet graph control
        BulletGraph bulletGraph = source as BulletGraph;

        if (bulletGraph != null)
        {
            // Re-render the tick marks
            bulletGraph.AddTickMarksAndLabels();

            // Re-render the qualitative components
            bulletGraph.SetQualitativeDataComponents();
        }
    }
```

All of the calculations required appear in the full source code of the control. Therefore, the implementation of this control can be what you specified in the implementation—or it could be much more than what was specified.

▨ **Note** The SilverlightBulletGraphApp_Part3_DependencyProperties folder of the source code zip file includes the implementation completed in this section.

Using the Bullet Graph Control

This section will cover how to use the bullet graph implementation and prove that the control can be used to surface various forms business intelligence scenarios.

■ **Note** The SilverlightBulletGraphApp_Part4_BusinessIntelligenceScenarios folder of the source code zip file includes a project with the demos highlighted in this section.

Proving Business Intelligence Scenarios

Now that the bullet graph control is realized, it's time to ensure the implementation provides enough flexibility and configurability for various business intelligence scenarios. Figures B-1 through B-6 illustrated various uses of the bullet graph control with various settings. It is important that this implementation is not too rigid so that it can facilitate various data visualization needs.

Figure B-31 is a screen shot from this section's project that shows the bullet graph control rendered using various configuration options. You can clearly see that the control is highly customizable and can suffice for varying business intelligence implementation.

Figure B-31. *The Silverlight bullet graph control can be used to surface varying business intelligence needs.*

Data Binding & Animations

Up to this point, all the scenarios shown in this chapter are based on explicit setting configuration properties on the bullet graph control. As mentioned, in order to take advantage of the full Silverlight data binding framework, the properties needed to be exposed as dependency properties. Let's make sure the investment in dependency properties paid off for the bullet graph control.

Figure B-32 below shows a bullet graph that has the qualitative ranges, comparative measure, and featured measure bound to four independent sliders using element binding. Moving the sliders around will cause the bullet graph control to update immediately, which proves that this control can leverage Silverlight data binding.

Figure B-32. *The bullet graph dependency properties allow for element binding to sliders.*

Another benefit of using dependency properties is that the properties can take part in animations. The project for this solution includes a sample that shows a story board animation animating qualitative components on the bullet graph. This substantiates that the underlying dependency properties are working in the Silverlight bullet graph implementation.

Alternate Implementations

Please keep in mind that the control you built in this chapter is not 100 percent complete; therefore it's not ready for business intelligence visualizations needs. As mentioned in the beginning of this chapter, I omitted certain functionality for the sake of brevity. Furthermore, as you saw in the bullet graph implementation for SQL Server 2008 R2 Reporting Services, there are hundreds of properties that could be surfaced for developers. Luckily, the bullet graph has had many data visualization vendors include their own implementation in their software. For example, Figure B-33 illustrates a Dundas dashboard that surfaces several bullet graphs on the right pane. Therefore, developers do not necessarily have to invest time in crafting a solution; they can buy ready-to-go bullet graph implementations from vendors such as Dundas. The bullet graph control is part of Dundas's data visualization software for the Silverlight framework.

Figure B-33. *Dundas software provides a bullet graph implementation that is ready to use in your business intelligence dashboards.*

Summary

This Appendix covered the fundamentals and creation of the bullet graph user control using the Silverlight 4 framework and Expression Blend 4. You learned what the bullet graph control component is and how it is used to surface business intelligence insight. More importantly, you learned how you can leverage best practices in the Silverlight framework in order to create your own implementation of the bullet graph or other custom user controls.

The key takeaways from this chapter should be knowledge of how to extend the Silverlight framework to create custom user controls. Silverlight 4 is completely extensible and enables developers to create re-usable controls that can mimic enterprise business intelligence controls. Throughout this chapter I covered important topics like fluid layouts, dependency properties, data binding, and user control testing that apply well beyond just this bullet graph control.

You should be able to take the concepts covered in this chapter and apply them when creating your own user control data visualizations.

Index

A

Access. *See* Microsoft Access
achievements score, 267
ActionScript, 45
"Add Collection Property" option, 478
"Add Complex Property" option, 478
"Add Simple Property" option, 478
AddTickMarks() method, 524
Adobe AIR, 36, 40, 42
Adobe Flash, 36, 39–42, 45, 335
Adobe Flex, 39–40, 42
aggregated data sets, predictive models with, 296
aggregates lists/texts, 266
aggregation, 9
agile development, 18–20
Ajax, 40
    JavaScripts in, 333
    MySpace and, 57
    n-tier architecture and, 57
analysis, with data visualizations, 142
Analysis Services, 10, 48, 194, 240
analytical visualizations, composite visuals for, 227–235
animation framework, in data visualizations, 139–140, 240–249
Apple iPhone OS, 30
application boundary, 56
application manifest file (AppManifest.xaml), 386
application memory, 35
application prototyping with dynamic data, 473–486
    details of, 483–485
    tools for, 473–475
        customizing collections, 479–481
        customizing properties, 479
        customizing sample data sources, 476–478
        defining new sample data, 474–475
applications
    BI 1.0, 14–16, 25
    BI 2.0, 23–25
architecture

64-bit, 66
BI systems, 6–12
    for application integration, 368–372
    BI presentation layer, 11
    data feeds, 7–8
    data warehouses, 10
    for existing BI investments, 375–376
    extract-transform-load process, 8–10
    infrastructure and software, 368–372
    infrastructure, non-Microsoft, 372–373
    integration challenges, 11
    MySpace and, 57
    new BI 2.0 applications, 373–375
    preoptimization by, 59
    Silverlight logic on, 66–70
client distributed, 54–70
client-server, 54–55
distributed
    defined, 54–55
    Microsoft Excel and, 61–64
    MOLAP and, 65
    Pivot and, 64–65
multicore, 321–322
n-tier, 55
    vs. n-layer, 57
    problems with, 56–58
parallel processing, 321
plug-in model, 301, 375–376
scaling BI with client tier, 58–60
SOA (service-oriented architecture), 20, 240, 290, 371
artificial intelligence (AI), 2
ASP.NET, 146, 239
ASP.NET chart, 68
ASP.NET web forms, 35
ASP.NET web parts, 428, 437
assembly caching, 386
asynchronous callback pattern, 333
asynchronous network communication, 333–334

You Need the Companion eBook

Your purchase of this book entitles you to buy the companion PDF-version eBook for only $10. Take the weightless companion with you anywhere.

We believe this Apress title will prove so indispensable that you'll want to carry it with you everywhere, which is why we are offering the companion eBook (in PDF format) for $10 to customers who purchase this book now. Convenient and fully searchable, the PDF version of any content-rich, page-heavy Apress book makes a valuable addition to your programming library. You can easily find and copy code—or perform examples by quickly toggling between instructions and the application. Even simultaneously tackling a donut, diet soda, and complex code becomes simplified with hands-free eBooks!

Once you purchase your book, getting the $10 companion eBook is simple:

❶ Visit **www.apress.com/promo/tendollars/**.

❷ Complete a basic registration form to receive a randomly generated question about this title.

❸ Answer the question correctly in 60 seconds, and you will receive a promotional code to redeem for the $10.00 eBook.

233 Spring Street, New York, NY 10013

LaVergne, TN USA
12 September 2010
196647LV00003B/1/P